VOLUME ONE
Advances in Psychological Assessment

VOLUME ONE

Advances in Psychological Assessment

PAUL McREYNOLDS
EDITOR

SCIENCE AND BEHAVIOR BOOKS, INC.
Palo Alto, California : 1968

Second Printing, April 1970

Contributors

James R. Averill, *Department of Psychology, University of California, Berkeley, California.*

Gerald S. Blum, *Department of Psychology, University of Michigan, Ann Arbor, Michigan.*

Arthur M. Bodin, *Mental Research Institute, Palo Alto, California.*

Thomas J. Bouchard, Jr., *Department of Psychology, University of California, Santa Barbara, California.*

David P. Campbell, *Student Counseling Bureau and Center for Interest Measurement Research, University of Minnesota, Minneapolis, Minnesota.*

Harrison G. Gough, *Department of Psychology and Institute of Personality Assessment and Research, University of California, Berkeley, California.*

C. James Klett, *Central Neuropsychiatric Research Unit, Veterans Administration Hospital, Perry Point, Maryland.*

Walter G. Klopfer, *Department of Psychology, Portland State College, Portland, Oregon.*

Paul McReynolds, *Behavioral Research Laboratory, Veterans Administration Hospital, Palo Alto, California, and Stanford University, Stanford, California.*

George A. Muench, *Department of Psychology, San Jose State College, San Jose, California.*

Edward M. Opton, Jr., *Department of Psychology, University of California, Berkeley, California.*

Kenneth B. Stein, *Department of Psychology, University of California, Berkeley, California.*

H. Edward Tryk, *Department of Psychology, University of Victoria, Victoria, B. C., Canada.*

Robert L. Weiss, *Department of Psychology, University of Oregon, Eugene, Oregon.*

Contents

Preface

I. An introduction to
   psychological assessment   *Paul McReynolds*   1

II. Current conceptions of
   intelligence and their implica-
   tions for assessment   *Thomas J. Bouchard, Jr.*   14

III. Assessment in the study of
   creativity   *H. Edward Tryk*   34

IV. An interpreter's syllabus for the
   California Psychological Inventory   *Harrison G. Gough*   55

V. The TSC Scales: The outcome
   of a cluster analysis of the 550
   MMPI items   *Kenneth B. Stein*   80

VI. The Strong Vocational Interest
   Blank: 1927-1967   *David P. Campbell*   105

VII. Current status of the Rorschach
   test   *Walter G. Klopfer*   131

VIII. Assessment of psychodynamic
   variables by the Blacky Pictures   *Gerald S. Blum*   150

IX. Operant conditioning techniques
   in psychological assessment   *Robert L. Weiss*   169

X. Assessing change in hospitalized
   psychiatric patients   *C. James Klett*   191

XI. The assessment of counseling
   and psychotherapy: Some prob-
   lems and trends   *George A. Muench*   205

XII. Conjoint family assessment:
   An evolving field   *Arthur M. Bodin*   223

XIII. The assessment of anxiety: A
   survey of available techniques   *Paul McReynolds*   244

XIV. Psychophysiological assessment:
   Rationale and problems   *James R. Averill and
   Edward M. Opton, Jr.*   265

Bibliography and Reference Index   289

Subject Index   329

Psychology cannot attain the certainty and exactness of the physical sciences, unless it rests on a foundation of experiment and measurement. A step in this direction could be made by applying a series of mental tests and measurements to a large number of individuals. The results would be of considerable scientific value in discovering the constancy of mental processes, their interdependence, and their variation under different circumstances. Individuals, besides, would find their tests interesting, and, perhaps, useful in regard to training, mode of life or indication of disease. The scientific and practical value of such tests would be much increased should a uniform system be adopted, so that determinations made at different times and places could be compared and combined.

James McKeen Cattell (1890)

Preface

The field of psychological assessment is currently in a state of considerable flux. New techniques are being generated, older ones are being re-evaluated and updated, and fresh conceptual approaches are being developed. This book—the first in a prospective series—presents a group of contributions that, it is hoped, will help the reader to keep abreast of these changes. More specifically, the primary purposes of the series—and of this volume—are first, to describe and evaluate selected new developments in assessment technology; second, to present innovative theoretical and methodological approaches to important issues in assessment; and third, to provide summaries of the current status of important areas in the field. In addition, occasional examinations of the historical backgrounds of important contemporary areas in assessment will be presented, in the belief that such perspectives are helpful in understanding the present scene.

The contributions to this work have been written at a level to be meaningful to advanced students, and the book is intended for use as a supplementary text in courses on assessment, tests and measurements, clinical psychology, counseling psychology, and related fields. Most of the contributions, because of their innovative quality, will also be valuable to specialists in assessment, including both those psychologists emphasizing research and those more interested in practice. A number of the papers—such as those on intelligence and on creativity—may well be of interest to investigators in other areas.

In their range and diversity the chapters that make up this volume reflect the broad scope of contemporary psychological assessment. Psychological tests, including both inventories and projective techniques, are represented by several chapters. Other chapters deal with the assessment of given variables and concepts, such as intelligence, creativity, and anxiety. Still other contributions focus on the objects of assessment—on the individual, on dyadic relationships, on the family, or on personality changes during chemotherapy or psychotherapy. The spectrum of conceptual approaches employed varies from the psychoanalytic to the behavioristic. The inclusion of the latter is especially interesting since until recently behaviorists have generally shown little interest in the problems of assessment. Finally, one chapter is devoted to relevant psychophysiological approaches; this important contribution should help to end the unnatural separation that has existed between psychophysiological technology and psychological assessment.

This first volume, of course, is not intended as a comprehensive survey of the field of assessment. Rather, its aim is to examine a limited number of significant topics in some depth. Because of this restricted coverage, a number of important topics have necessarily been reserved for later volumes. It is believed, however, that the treatments of selected areas included in this book are highly worthwhile in themselves, and that they constitute, in their entirety, a representative picture of the current state of psychological assessment.

All of the papers presented here were prepared especially for this volume, and such merit as the book may possess stems directly from the skill and effort of each of the contributors. I am pleased to have this opportunity to express my appreciation to all of them for their enthusiasm, their dedication, and their promptness during the preparation of this book. I wish especially to thank three of my former colleagues, Drs. Harrison G. Gough, H. Edward Tryk, and Robert L. Weiss, for their wise counsel and warm encouragement. Mrs. Lucy Yoshizawa, Mr. Charles Wilson, Miss Itsuye Sakai, Mr. Richard Gurley, and Miss Harleigh Knott provided invaluable assistance in the preparation of the manuscript. Most of all, I am indebted to my wife, Billie, for her constant support and helpfulness throughout the entire course of this project.

Palo Alto, California
October, 1967

Paul McReynolds

VOLUME ONE
Advances in Psychological Assessment

CHAPTER I

An introduction to
psychological assessment

Paul McReynolds

Progress in psychological assessment is important not only to such applied fields as clinical, counseling, educational and industrial psychology, but is vital also to the continued development of psychology-as-a-whole. Technical advances, both in the development of newer assessment techniques and in the refinement of older ones, are additions not only to the armamentarium of the clinician, but also to the instrumentation of the scientist. Ultimately, both successful practice and fruitful research depend upon adequate under-standing, and this in turn depends in large part upon the availability of satisfactory methods of assessment.

The development and maintenance of an adequate assessment technology are, then, matters of the first importance. Such a technology cannot be static but must reflect innovations growing out of current trends and movements in general theoretical psychology. The chapters that follow will point up some of the more significant and interesting recent developments in psychological assessment, and will review the current situation and the historical back-ground in other selected areas. This first chapter is intended to set the stage for what is to follow, to introduce and put into perspective the various topics that are to be taken up in subsequent chapters.

Specifically, the purposes of this chapter are: first, to examine the nature and scope of assessment in psychology; second, to note briefly some of the major current problems and trends in psychological assessment; and third, to delineate the overall organization of the present volume and to indicate the place of the different contributions in this organization.

THE NATURE AND SCOPE OF PSYCHOLOGICAL ASSESSMENT

What is Psychological Assessment?

By "psychological assessment," in its most general meaning, we mean the *systematic use of a variety of special techniques in order better to understand a given individual, group, or psychological ecology.* The term "special techniques" is used here to refer to those tests and measurement procedures having some degree of consensual acceptance in the professional psychological community, and the word "understanding" implies *knowledge about* rather than *sympathy or empathy with.* The term "psychological assessment" is proposed here as more appropriate for the range of measurement decisions that contemporary psychologists make than several more traditional—but also more restricted—terms such as "mental testing," "tests and measurements," "psychodiagnosis," and "personality assessment." Thus assessment as practiced by psychologists is certainly broader than would be implied by "psychological testing"—as this term is ordinarily used (English & English, 1958)—since it includes interview procedures, behavior-sampling techniques, psychophysiological measurements, and so on. And similarly, current assessment is not limited to diagnostic functions, nor to personality evaluations. There is a need, then, for a more widely embracing term to indicate the varied kinds of assessment that psychologists do. Two terms—"psychological assessment"[1] and "behavioral assessment"—appear to be satisfactory. I have favored the first, without rejecting the second, as being perhaps somewhat more general.

Assessment in psychology is usually considered to deal primarily with the measurement of individual differences. This is true in the sense that psychological assessment is not directed at the development of laws for mankind in general. It is not true in a literal sense, however. Thus, the field of psychological assessment is concerned not only with differences *between* persons, but also with interrelationships among different variables *within* a given person, as well as *changes* within an individual over time. Further, the object of assessment may not be an *individual* at all, but a larger unit. An important object of assessment is the two-person, or "dyadic" group, such as a husband and wife, or a therapist and patient. Another highly meaningful group for which assessment techniques are currently being developed is the

---

[1]The word "assessment"—in the sense of "appraisal" or "evaluation"—has come into increasing use in recent years in describing the analysis of personality, and is sometimes used to refer to the use of an assortment of techniques requiring subjective integration, as contrasted with measurement techniques yielding single, more straightforward values. This distinction, however, is rather superficial, since almost all psychological measurements require some degree of interpretation, and appraisal in terms of several variables is not basically different from appraisal with one. One of the first uses of the word "assessment" in psychology was in the book *The Assessment of Men* (Murray, MacKinnon, Miller, Fiske, and Hanfmann, 1948). In 1949 the word was used in titling the new Institute of Personality Assessment and Research at the University of California. In more recent years courses in personality assessment have become standard in university curricula, and in 1963 the *Journal of Projective Techniques* added the phrase *and Personality Assessment* to its title. The present volume covers a broader area than that usually suggested by "personality assessment," and hence the term "psychological assessment" is the more appropriate here.

family. Still other groups that can be examined in assessment terms are organizations such as Alcoholics Anonymous, sororities, delinquent gangs, and so on. It is also possible to apply assessment techniques to an entire psychological ecology—a school, a psychiatric ward, or a neighborhood— in terms of its implications for behavior. Most of the classical methods of assessment have focused on individuals, and techniques for assessing groups and ecologies are for the most part still in their early stages of development.

Assessment consists, in the main, of either (a) assigning the object of assessment to given categories (e.g., in psychopathology these are sometimes called "diagnoses"; in a school they might be "reading groups"; in vocational guidance, "recommended occupations"), or (b) placing the object of assessment at specific points on given continua (e.g., scores on given test or rating dimensions). It is often conceived that assessment is limited to the collection of a variety of data about a subject, with the information then being turned over to a separate person or agency who uses it to make decisions about the subject. Actually, however, the decision processes themselves are best conceived as an integral part of psychological assessment.

It is important in developing and implementing a conception of assessment to have a general theoretical model of the overall assessment process. In fact, whether aware of it or not, a psychologist does employ an assessment model each time he develops or applies an assessment procedure.

Examination of this interesting topic is beyond the scope of this Introduction, but it is clear that in general an explicit theory is preferable to an implicit one. Briefly, we may note here that the prevailing and now classical assessment model—represented in the works of Kelley (1923), Hull (1928), and Gulliksen (1950)—conceptualizes the assessment device (test, interview, etc.) as a measuring instrument and stresses the importance of accuracy of measurement, with primary emphasis on the concepts of reliability and validity as the major test criteria. As Cronbach and Gleser (1965; original edition, 1957) have pointed out in their important monograph, however, this measurement model is by no means the only possible assessment model and is, in fact, subject to serious limitations.

As an alternate assessment model, Cronbach and Gleser propose a conceptualization based on decision theory. Their approach suggests that the purpose of assessment procedures is to help in making decisions, and that the utility of tests is to be evaluated in terms of this aim, taking into account the particular decisions to be made, the cost of obtaining information, the a priori level of accuracy required, and other factors. It is important to note that the particular assessment model one adopts has important implications for the way he evaluates given instruments. Cronbach and Gleser suggest, for example, that interview and projective techniques, which tend to be ranked as unsatisfactory by the validity criteria of the conventional measurement model, may well show up much better when evaluated in terms of the decision theory model of assessment.

Assessment in Practice and in Research

There is sometimes a tendency to conceive of assessment in narrow and restricted terms. Frequently the field is considered to be concerned solely with practice, with gathering data on which to base real-life decisions—whether a client should go into this or that vocation, whether a patient should be given one or another type of treatment, and so on. This applied domain of assessment is of great social as well as professional importance, but it should be emphasized that decisions are *also* made in *research* (e.g., whether to favor this hypothesis or that one) and that psychological assessment procedures are equally relevant in this domain.

What is being proposed here is a somewhat broadened interpretation of assessment in psychology. Whereas assessment procedures are now generally limited by convention to the techniques employed by clinicians, counselors, and educators in working with patients, clients, or students, it is suggested here that *all* research-oriented measurement devices in which individuals, groups, or ecologies are assigned to classes or given numerical values be considered as part of assessment psychology. The reason for this suggestion is that there is no fundamental methodological difference in assessment techniques as such, whether they are used for practice or for research.

As an example of the broadened usage being proposed, consider the application of the Manifest Anxiety Scale (Taylor, 1953) in the study of complex learning. It is, of course, clear that the MAS is an assessment instrument when it is used in the clinical appraisal of a patient's anxiety; it is also evident, surely, that it is still an assessment device when it is used as a measure of drive in a study relating drive to complex learning. But the present suggestion is that in this instance the measurement of complex learning should *also* be considered within the domain of psychological assessment.

Similarly, problems concerned with the measurement of a wide range of other variables, the appraisal of which is never likely to occur in a clinic, can usefully be considered as part of the field of psychological assessment. These would include constructs such as cognitive complexity, esthetic preference, meaning, and the like, as well as many variables in studies of learning, motivation, and perception. It is doubtful that it is ever very useful to make a rigid distinction between measurement problems encountered in the clinic and those faced in the laboratory. For practical, didactic purposes, such a separation may have some use, but it should be remembered that the dichotomy is to a very large degree arbitrary. Thus, even psychophysical techniques, which traditionally have been concerned with the development of general laws, have been found useful in personality-oriented research (e.g., Riedel, 1965; Tryk, 1966).

As used here, then, "psychological assessment" will refer to the entire range of behavioral evaluation procedures on which individuals, groups, or ecologies may vary; it can be thought of as that branch of psychology particularly concerned with the development and application of such measurement techniques. The advantages of such a broad approach are that it militates against the unfortunate but too frequent *split* between practice and research, and that, in line with the thesis of a recent paper by Anastasi (1967), it can help to prevent the dissociation of psychological testing from the mainstream of contemporary psychology.

THE CURRENT SCENE

It has been noted above, and will be amply demonstrated in the subsequent chapters in this volume, that the field of psychological assessment is currently in a stage of considerable growth and activity. This does not mean, however, that there are no major unsolved problems or that a level of conceptual equilibrium has been achieved. On the contrary, one of the more prominent features of contemporary assessment psychology is its somewhat unsettled state, reflecting the presence not only of a variety of movements and trends, but also of a number of controversial issues. This part of the chapter summarizes some of the more important recent developments in the field and will examine briefly the changing role of assessment in clinical psychology. It is, of course, beyond the scope of an introduction to examine these matters in detail; rather, the intention is to provide, within the limits of the space available, a broad, general picture of the current assessment scene as a background for the chapters to follow.

The Recent Literature

The range and scope of contemporary psychological assessment is perhaps best indicated by a brief survey of the recent literature. The following listing, though not comprehensive, includes most of the more important titles in the areas specified.

Among the general texts in assessment are Anastasi's (1961) *Psychological Testing*; Cronbach's (1960) *Essentials of Psychological Testing*; Freeman's (1955) *Theory and Practice of Psychological Testing*; Goldman's (1961) *Using Tests in Counseling*; Helmstadter's (1964) *Principles of Psychological Measurement*; Horrock's (1964) *Assessment of Behavior*; Kelly's (1967) *Assessment of Human Characteristics*; Kleinmutz's (1967) *Personality Measurement*; Lyman's (1963) *Test Scores and What They Mean*; Nunnally's (1967) *Psychometric Theory*; Super and Crites' (1962) *Appraising Vocational Fitness*: Tyler's (1963) *Tests and Measurements*; and Vernon's (1964) *Personality Assessment; A Critical Survey*. Relevant collections of contributed or reprinted papers include those edited by Anastasi (1967), Barnette (1968), Bass and Berg (1959), Berg (1967), Berg and Pennington (1966), Brozek (1966), Campbell (1960), Hirt (1962), Kornrich (1965), Megargee (1966), Messick and Ross (1962), Murstein (1965), Rickers-Ovsiankina (1960), Semeonoff (1966), and Wolman (1965). Another highly relevant resource is the *Proceedings of the Invitational Conference on Testing Problems*, published annually by Educational Testing Service.

General theoretical contributions in the area of assessment include those by Block (1965), Berg and Adams (1962), Byrne (1964), Cattell (1959), Dunnette (1966), Fiske (1963), Garfield (1963b), Holtzman (1963), Hundleby et al. (1965), Keats (1967), Loevinger (1965), Milholland (1964), Super (1959), Taft (1959), and Torgerson (1961). The historical background of objective testing has been reviewed by Watson (1959). Cattell and Warburton (1967) have organized a highly useful compendium of objective test procedures.

As has been the case for many years, the basic references in assessment are the *Mental Measurements Yearbooks*, the most recent publication of which (Buros, 1965) is the sixth edition. The complementary volume *Tests in Print* (Buros, 1961) is also a highly useful resource. The American Psychological Association (1966) has published an informative and influential booklet on test criteria, the *Standards for Psychological Tests and Manuals*. Readers interested in issues connected with the relation of assessment to the public interest, and with hearings in Congress on this subject, are referred to the *American Psychologist*, 1964, *20*, 857-993 (entire issue for November); and 1966, *21*, 404-423; and to Anastasi (1967) and Messick (1965).

A number of specific topics have been reviewed in recent years. These include the assessment of cognitive complexity (Bieri et al., 1966); ego development (Loevinger 1966); moral values (Pittel & Mendelsohn, 1966); personnel selection (Biesheuvel, 1965; Guion, 1967; Taylor & Nevis, 1961); psychoanalytic variables (Luborsky & Schimek, 1964); psychotherapy (Gottschalk & Auerbach, 1966; Reznikoff & Toomey, 1959; Stieper & Wiener, 1965); and risk-taking (Slovic, 1964). Testing of children has been reviewed by Levine (1966); of the physically handicapped by Wachs (1966); of brain-damaged subjects by Hartlage (1966), Haynes and Sells (1963), and Spreen and Benton (1965); and of neurological patients by Burgemeister (1962). Particular assessment techniques have been the subject of a number of reviews. Among these are: aptitude tests (Ghiselli, 1966); the Bender-Gestalt test (Billingslea, 1963; Tolor & Schulberg, 1963); the Kahn test of symbol arrangement (L'Abate & Craddick, 1965); the MMPI (Tellegen, 1964); projective techniques (Fisher, 1967; Gleser, 1963; Rabin, 1964); psychiatric rating scales (Lyerly & Abbott, 1966); the selection interview (Ulrich & Trumbo, 1965); sentence completion methods (P. A. Goldberg, 1965); and the Wechsler Intelligence Scales (Guertin, 1962; Guertin & Ladd, 1966; Littell, 1960).

As already implied, the above listings are selective rather than comprehensive. Additional relevant references will be found throughout the succeeding chapters.

Some Current Developments

This section will indicate and describe very briefly what appear to be some of the more important current trends and issues in psychological assessment. It is, of course, maintained not that these are the *only* important current developments, but simply that they are representative of the directions characteristic of modern assessment psychology.

1. *A variety of technological advances in other fields are being adapted for use in assessment.* These innovations include the use of modern, high-speed computers; improved transducers and recording apparatus, including telemetry instrumentation, in psychophysiology; and the use of videotape and closed-circuit TV. The full implications of these and other relatively new technical resources is mainly in the future, but it is clear that their influence will be great. Already the availability of computers has brought about notable advances in assessment, not only in the analysis of research data, but also in the automation of diagnostic procedures (Gorham, 1967; Gravitz, 1967; Rome et al., 1962; Sines, 1966).

2. *There is wide interest in the development of new theoretical approaches to assessment.* We have already noted Cronbach and Gleser's (1965) testing model framed in terms of decision theory. Arthur (1966) has proposed an application of operations research to clinical assessment. Wallace (1966, 1967) has outlined an abilities conception of personality that emphasizes the assessment of skills rather than personality dispositions. Gough (1965a) has proposed a three-stage test evaluation process: *primary* evaluation is similar to the concept of validity; *secondary* evaluation seeks to elaborate the meaning of that which is measured; and *tertiary* evaluation concerns the significance of a measure beyond its primary area of relevance. These several contributions are representative of a general receptivity to new theoretical approaches in assessment.

3. *There is a notable concern with the effects of the testing situation, including the examiner, on test results.* Tests are best seen as aspects of a total situation, rather than as fixed instruments independent of the testing environment. This is not a novel point of view, but what is important is the increased tendency in recent years to approach the problem empirically. A considerable body of work has now accumulated showing that test results may be significantly affected by situational and interpersonal factors (Masling, 1960) and, similarly, that experimental results may be significantly influenced by experimenter variables (Rosenthal, 1966). Brim (1965) and Fiske (1967) have investigated the attitudes that the subject brings with him to the test room.

4. *The further development of personality inventories is a particularly active research area.* Pencil-paper tests and questionnaires have long been the most frequently used type of assessment procedure, and there seems little likelihood of a change in the near future. The personality inventory—with regard to questions of reliability, validity, content vs. style, and methods of deriving scales—is probably the most studied topic in all of assessment. In general, inventory scales may be classified, according to derivation, in one of three ways (Messick, 1966; Hase & Goldberg, 1967): rational, factor-analytic, or empirical. An important and illustrative recent study (Hase & Goldberg, 1967) carried out an empirical comparison of these three (and several other) methods of item selection. They were found not to differ significantly in validity, and all were better than chance.

5. *The relative significance of content and style in personality inventories is a major issue.* For several years this has been one of the more controversial questions in assessment. The issue is whether the responses of subjects on Yes-No-type inventory items are primarily a function of the *content* of the items, as a common-sense approach would assume, or of *response sets* within the subject. The two sets most frequently suggested as influential in the subject's response are the tendency to answer items in a socially desirable way (Edwards, 1957) and the tendency to acquiesce or agree (Jackson & Messick, 1958) with the items. A related interpretation, which also assumes that the subject's answers are not primarily influenced by the content or meaning of the items, is Berg's (1955) deviation hypothesis, which asserts that groups can be discriminated solely in terms of atypical item responses, quite independently of item content.

The literature in this area has become quite extensive, and cannot adequately be reviewed here (for selected references see Berg, 1967; Block,

1965; Goldberg & Slovic, 1967; Messick & Jackson, 1961; Rorer, 1965; Rundquist, 1966; Weiss & Moos, 1965). It is the judgment of this reviewer, however, that the accumulated evidence indicates clearly that in most personality inventories item content is the primary determinant of item response. Response sets, however, can undoubtedly be significant determinants of response, and efforts should be made in the design of tests to minimize their effects or to utilize them *systematically* in the assessment of given variables.

6. *Projective tests, though less widely used now than formerly, are still a major focus of research and practice.* In general, projective tests have not shown up well in validity studies, and many psychologists appear ready to reject the approach as inherently unsatisfactory. Such a conclusion, however, would not only be highly premature (the evidence is not that good one way or the other) but also unfortunate in that it would tend to stifle further developments in projective technology. Current developments are taking two main courses: first, the trend toward greater objectivity in scoring (e.g., Holtzman et al, 1961; McReynolds, 1965*b*); second, and more important, the development of new theoretical models of projective psychology. In this regard the systematic proposals of Kenny (1964) on stimulus functions in projective tests, and the conceptualization of Fulkerson (1965)—which, following Cronbach and Gleser, utilizes a decision theory approach—are especially interesting. For other sources on projective devices the reader may consult Fisher (1967), Gleser (1963), Lesser (1961), Murstein (1965), and Rabin (1964).

7. *The issue of clinical vs. actuarial prediction continues to be an active research area.* This interesting problem has been with us for some time, going back to Sarbin's pioneering study in 1941. It is essentially the question of whether a clinical prediction from given data is more accurate when made in a global, judgmental manner by a skilled clinician, or when made on the basis of the best statistical formulae and actuarial data. Most of the comparative studies favor the actuarial over the clinical method, but there is some doubt that the clinical approach has been adequately represented. Gough provides a review of the area up to 1962. Among the better recent papers are those by Lindzey (1965), Meehl (1965), Sines (1966), and Goldberg (1965).

8. *There is a growing tendency to depend less on "tests" and more on other methods of assessment.* I am using "test" here in its conventional and somewhat restricted sense—i.e., to refer to a systematic, standardized procedure administered at one place, typically in one session, and yielding a scorable written protocol (English & English, 1958). The trend appears to be not to give up this approach, which after all has tremendous practical advantages, but to depend upon it less exclusively. Other frequently used methodological approaches include experimental laboratory procedures (e.g. see Weiss in this volume), behavior observations (Fairweather, 1964), and role-playing. Underlying many of these approaches is the view that an assessment datum predicts best when that datum is a realistic sample of the behavior to be predicted.

9. *Another major issue concerns the relative contributions of the individual and the situation to behavioral variation.* The behavior of an individual in a given situation can be conceptualized as in part a function of the stimulus

properties of the situation, and in part a function of the characteristic behavioral tendencies of the individual. Classical assessment procedures have been based very largely on the assumption of the predominance of individual, as opposed to situational, factors in determining behavior. Thus, emphasis has centered on the measurement of traits, dispositions, and capacities, and very little attention has been given to assessing the complementary situational determinants. Another way to state this issue is in terms of generality vs. specificity. The former position holds that the way a person behaves in one situation—e.g., the honesty of his responses—is likely to predict the way he will behave in a different situation, and the latter holds that his behavior is more likely to be influenced by the specific features of the situation.

The empirical research in this area dates back to the classic studies of Hartshorne and May (1928) on honesty-deceit, which tended to support a specificity position. Burton (1963) recently reanalyzed the Hartshorne-May data, however, using modern statistical techniques, and found notable support for generality in moral behavior, though much of the variance remained a function of specific conditions.

The generality-specificity issue is particularly important in psychophysiological studies, as discussed by Averill and Opton in this volume. The relative influence of individual and situational determinants with regard to anxiety, has been studied by Endler and Hunt (1966). It is now clear that both individual and situational factors are important (Moos & Clemes, 1967), and a more fruitful research endeavor than asking which is the *more* influential would be to attempt to specify the conditions contributing to the relative dominance of either kind of determinant. Another vital need here is for a much greater development of concepts and techniques for assessing situations, i.e., the ecology in which behaviors occur. As Anastasi (1966) has noted, little progress has been made in the study of environmental variables. There are, however, at least the beginnings of a significant technology in this area (Barker, 1960; Pace, 1963; Pace & Stern, 1958; Sells, 1963; Wolf, 1966).

The Role of Assessment in Clinical Psychology

The profession of clinical psychology grew out of the work of the early psychometrists, and psychological testing has traditionally been considered the core function, as well as the unique area of competence, of clinical psychologists. At one time testing was essentially the *only* function performed by clinical psychologists, but over the years other tasks—in particular psychotherapeutic and social-psychological functions—have been added. Thus assessment is not as central in clinical psychology as it used to be. In addition, the role of tests in the psychiatric diagnostic process is less straightforward than formerly, perhaps because the entire diagnostic process, in psychiatry as well as in psychology, is less secure and less central than it once was. Furthermore, whereas it was once taken for granted that psychotherapy would benefit from the therapist's knowing as much as possible about the patient, including data from tests, this view is no longer universally held. Indeed, there is a feeling among many humanistically inclined therapists that tests may actually be a hindrance, since they imply that the therapist will take an authoritarian role and use his greater knowledge to direct the client's behavior. Behavior therapy, for quite different reasons, also tends to discourage the use of conventional tests. Specifically, this approach is aimed at the direct modification of behaviors and thus is uninterested in test data concerning internal dynamics. It does, however, have a place for assessment of a different order (Ullmann & Krasner, 1965; Greenspoon & Gersten, 1967; also Weiss, in this volume), e.g., in determining the hierarchy of fear-inducing stimuli (Geer, 1965).

These and other developments have brought about some degree of uncertainty regarding the proper role of assessment in clinical psychology (e.g., see Klopfer, 1962, 1964; Tallent, 1965). The use of tests is, of course, still central and obvious in much—perhaps most—of the clinical psychologist's work—e.g., in his work with the mentally retarded. Also, it should be emphasized that assessment procedures fill important, accepted, and straightforward roles in vocational and educational counseling, in school psychology, and in industrial and personnel psychology. The current ambiguity regarding testing is focused primarily on its role in treatment.

It is clear that certain changes are taking place in the commitment to, and the use of, tests by many treatment-oriented clinical psychologists. It appears upon analysis, however, that the situation is not so much that of giving up assessment as that of seeking—and to a considerable extent using—newer and more appropriate assessment techniques, better suited in many instances to the needs of current treatment practices than many of the more traditional tests. These newer assessment techniques include systematic psychiatric rating scales (Klett, in this volume) and sociometric techniques (Fairweather, 1964).

In any event, any attempt to deemphasize assessment as a major function in clinical psychology in favor of more exclusive attention to techniques of therapy or behavior modification would be extremely unfortunate. On the face of it, any deprecation of the *measurement function* in a science is patently illogical. And so far as the treatment aspect is concerned, it is hard to maintain seriously that a clinician can have too much information about a patient, though in given cases certain classes of information may be irrelevant, insufficiently accurate, or overly costly in one way or another.

ORGANIZATION OF THIS BOOK

There are a number of different ways in which the wide variety of contents in the field of psychological assessment can be organized, and it is instructive to note what some of these are.

One obvious and useful way of subdividing the field is in terms of *techniques of assessment*. According to this conceptualization one could discuss such groupings as psychological tests (used in the limited sense defined earlier, namely, intelligence tests, ability tests, and so on); interview techniques; observer rating procedures; psychophysiological methods; perceptual threshold techniques, and so on.

Another way in which the contents of assessment can be schematized is in terms of the *objects of assessment*. Such a systematization would focus on assessments of individuals, groups, or ecologies, and each of these could be further subdivided—e.g., under individual assessment one could list assessment of infants and children, of the physically handicapped, of the mentally disturbed, and so on.

A third general way in which the psychology of assessment can be broken down is according to the *variables*, or *classes*, in terms of which the assessment is expressed: thus, intelligence, introversion, anxiousness, aggressiveness, reading ability, attitude toward religion, and so on. In addition, many variables can be examined in terms of individual *changes* on pertinent variables, so that the assessment of *change*–e.g., change in knowledge during a course in chemistry, change in maturity level during psychotherapy, and so on–becomes an important subclass of the assessment of variables.

A final principle for the categorization of assessment procedures that we will mention here is to approach the field in terms of *different theoretical models*: e.g., the traditional psychometric model, a decision theory model, a psychoanalytic model, or a behavior theory model.

No single one of the above conceptual frameworks played an exclusive role in determining the topics to be covered in the present volume; at the same time, each of them was influential to some extent, as the examination of the chapter topics to be undertaken below will reveal. The order of chapters is somewhat arbitrary, in that each of them can be read with profit without first having read any of the other chapters. The papers are grouped according to similar topics, but the book is not formally divided into separate parts, and can be best considered as a single unit of fourteen interrelated papers.

After this Introduction, the book continues with two chapters on the assessment of cognitive variables. The first of these, by Thomas J. Bouchard, Jr., is on intelligence, and the second, by H. Edward Tryk, is on creativity. The chapter on intelligence was chosen to lead off the substantive part of the book since intelligence testing, in both a practical and an historical sense, is the nearest thing to a "basic measure" that exists in psychological assessment. Though both of these papers fill important needs in the literature, they are quite different in approach. Bouchard's contribution integrates the various newer conceptions of intelligence—including his own thought-provoking point of view—and shows the implications of these formulations for the assessment of intelligence. It is, I believe, the first work anywhere to bring together the major current theories of intelligence. Tryk's incisive chapter is more measurement-oriented, presenting a critical review of methods for assessing creativity. There have been other papers on this topic, yet this is certainly one of the first to look at the measurement instruments in this significant area with a psychometrically rigorous, yet not unsympathetic eye.

Chapters IV through X are devoted to techniques of assessment, and the first three of these are concerned with psychological inventories. This kind of measure is the most widely used technique in assessment, and it is fitting that it should receive considerable attention here. Harrison G. Gough writes on his widely used California Psychological Inventory; Kenneth B. Stein presents an innovative approach to the Minnesota Multiphasic Personality Inventory; and David P. Campbell surveys the history of the classic Strong Vocational Interest Blank. Gough's authoritative chapter constitutes an important, not to say essential, aid to the clinician or researcher using the CPI; it also presents new research data on that instrument. It inaugurates what is planned as a series of technical papers in this and successive volumes on the improved usage of important psychological tests. Stein's chapter, which presents a host of new research data, describes a set of new scales derived from the MMPI items. Not only do these scales, derived by cluster analysis, appear strikingly plausible, but they represent the first attempt to apply a factor-analytic approach to the entire 550 MMPI items, something which has only recently been made possible by the larger computers. Campbell's chapter on the Strong is an important historical document, and at the same time is altogether fascinating to read. This chapter clearly fulfills the statement in the Preface that an understanding of the historical background of an area helps us better to appreciate recent advances. It can also be seen, in a sense, as a memorial to the late, revered E. K. Strong, Jr.

Chapters VII and VIII are on projective techniques, with Walter G. Klopfer writing on the Rorschach and Gerald S. Blum reporting on the Blacky Pictures. The place of the Rorschach in assessment is unique; it is the oldest of the major assessment instruments still in use in its original form, dating back to 1921. In recent years, however, the Rorschach has come upon a number of detractors and doubters, who join a continuing host of defenders. Klopfer's balanced chapter surveys the recent evaluative work on the test and offers an expert critique of its current status. Blum's contribution can be conceptualized in two ways: first, as a definitive review of studies on, and uses of, the Blacky Pictures; and second, as the delineation of a useful method for the assessment of certain psychoanalytic variables. Particularly interesting in this chapter is the description of special-purpose uses of the Blacky, including the presentation of certain new empirical data. In general, the Blacky Pictures technique has stood up well under research scrutiny, and readers unfamiliar with the instrument will find this chapter, written in Blum's usual appealing style, a helpful introduction.

The breadth of the book is indicated by the fact that Blum's paper, espousing a psychoanalytic point of view, is followed by Robert L. Weiss' chapter utilizing a behavioristic framework. This paper belongs with the preceding five in its concern with techniques of assessment. Rather than dealing with a specific instrument, however, it brings together a variety of procedures, all used in operant conditioning technology, and develops a challenging new theoretical approach to the overall problem of assessment.

Chapter X, by C. James Klett, critically examines the use of behavior-rating scales in the evaluation of change in hospitalized psychiatric patients. Because of its emphasis on assessment techniques, this paper can appropriately be grouped with the preceding six chapters; from another point of view, however, it can meaningfully be grouped with the chapter that follows it, in which George A. Muench discusses the assessment of change during counseling and psychotherapy, since both are concerned with the difficult problem of evaluating personality and behavioral change. Both these chapters can also be grouped with the following one, by Arthur M. Bodin. All three are rather directly concerned with the use of a variety of techniques in important areas of clinical practice. However, Bodin's paper is quite different from the preceding two—and indeed from all other chapters in the book—in that it is concerned with the assessment of a group, the family, rather than with the evaluation of individuals.

During recent years the behavior-rating scale technique has undergone rapid development in psychology, particularly in the assessment of psychiatric variables. This approach has now become the technique of choice in the assessment of the psychological and behavioral effects of chemotherapy, but its potentiality, is of course, much broader than this. Klett's authoritative chapter brings the reader up to date on recent methodological advances. Muench's paper on the assessment of counseling and psychotherapy is conceived as the first, and most general, in a series on this complex and diverse topic. His insightful chapter examines some of the more difficult methodological problems in this area, and in addition—as the opening paper in the prospective series—concisely reviews some of the current trends in assessment-oriented research on counseling and psychotherapy; papers in subsequent volumes will examine the assessment of therapy from more limited conceptual frameworks—e.g., specific measurement techniques, assessment in behavior therapy, assessment in group approaches, and so on. Bodin's chapter on the assessment of families is one of the most innovative contributions in the book. The reader should not expect to find here a definitive statement of how to assess families—the field is not yet sufficiently developed to make that possible. However, the chapter does summarize an exceedingly interesting area that has now progressed far enough to permit a much broader range of family research.

The last two chapters have in common a concern with affective variables, but they are otherwise quite different. Paul McReynolds' paper on the assessment of anxiety is closely related to the preceding three chapters in that it discusses the use of a variety of techniques in an area of direct clinical meaningfulness. It is like Chapters II and III—on intelligence and creativity—in focusing on a variable that is widely used in assessment. The final chapter, by James R. Averill and Edward M. Opton, Jr., is concerned with psychophysiological assessment, in contrast to all other chapters in the book, which deal with behavioral techniques. The psychophysiological approach is ordinarily not represented in works on assessment, and its inclusion here is one result of the broader interpretation of "assessment" delineated earlier in this Introduction. (Another manifestation of this broadened conception is Chapter IX, on operant approaches to assessment.)

The concept of anxiety is one of the more general terms in modern psychology, and it is doubtful that any other variable, except intelligence, has been the subject of measurement by so many different tests. McReynolds' paper brings together and compares these various instruments. Averill and Opton's chapter is devoted primarily to the methodological issues involved in using physiological data to assess psychological variables. Their analysis is at some points quite original, and at all points cogent. It is also written in a style that will be meaningful to the general psychologist, as well as to those trained in psychophysiology.

The reader can look forward, in the following chapters, to an interesting and informative sequence on psychological assessment. Taken in their entirety, the presentations portray the advancing forefront of an important science and profession.

CHAPTER II

Current conceptions of intelligence
and their implications for assessment

Thomas J. Bouchard, Jr.

The measurement of intelligence is fundamental in psychological assessment. The term "intelligence," however, is one that has long carried many different meanings. This chapter will attempt to explicate a number of these meanings in the light of current theory, and to point up their implications for assessment. The focus will be both on those conceptions of intelligence that derive from theoretical considerations and on those that arise from systematic empirical generalizations. The analysis will attempt to point out the commonality among these divergent points of view and the fruitfulness of pursuing research in particular directions. The varied responses to the "puzzle of intelligence" converge on a very general model, a reconceptualization of the problem that carries important implications for both theoretical work and the practical problems of psychological assessment. This model, however, does not answer the question, What is intelligence? Rather, it brings to bear a new perspective and poses even more complex problems.

FACTOR-ANALYTIC THEORIES OF INTELLIGENCE

Factor analysts can be roughly divided into two groups, those who use factorial methods that allow a large general factor to emerge as the first factor and those who prefer methods that yield a number of independent or primary factors and no large general factor. There is some reason to believe that both methods are fundamentally reducible to each other (Bernyer, 1958; Cattell, 1963*b*), but this interpretation has not been generally accepted (Guilford, 1967).

Multiple factors vs *g*

Guilford (1967)[1] is the best representative of multiple-factor analysis in the Thurstone tradition. He argues that current definitions of intelligence are too narrow and too vague, and that preference for a general intellectual factor (*g*) over multiple factors is due to a restricted view of the area of investigation, a view that will hamper progress. He cites the following types of evidence as mitigating against the existence of *g*:

(*a*) The unevenness of ability within persons, not only on traditional types of tests, but also on the more recent tests of creativity.

(*b*) The existence of zero correlations among tests that logically belong in the intellectual realm (cf. Guilford, 1964).

(*c*) The difference in growth curves yielded by various subtests generally included in intelligence batteries.

(*d*) Studies of heredity that suggest differential hereditability for various factors.

(*e*) The failure of most IQ tests to predict achievement adequately.

As an alternative to theories emphasizing *g*, Guilford (1967) has presented a model called the "structure of intellect." The structure-of-intellect model is a "morphological" model that is represented spatially as a three-dimensional cube. The three dimensions are broken into five, four, and six categories, and thereby yield 120 cells, each of which represents a factor.

The first dimension is divided into five operations: cognition, memory, convergent thinking, divergent thinking, and evaluation. The second dimension is divided into four kinds of content: figural, symbolic, semantic, and behavioral. The third dimension is divided into six kinds of products: units, classes, relations, systems, transformations, and implications.

A cross between any three categories yields a factor. An example would be cognition of semantic units, which corresponds to knowing what a word means. As of now, eighty abilities have been demonstrated. Some cells, however, have more than one ability, due to the fact that new factors arise when we distinguish between sense modalities (e.g., visual, auditory, and kinesthetic memory). Guttman (1965) has suggested that each sense modality represents a mode of communication and that each may define a different kind of intelligence. Applying this logic to the Guilford model seriously complicates the theory.

The major alternatives to the multiple-factor model of Guilford are the hierarchical models of Burt (1949) and Vernon (1965). These authors prefer to speak of, and use, factors as "principles of classification" rather than as fundamental or basic units. They prefer factor techniques that yield a large *g* factor. Coan (1964) has suggested that these different theoretical orientations may be simply preferences for different modes of verbal description. Whether this is the case or not, hierarchical models certainly lead to a different kind of research effort.

---

[1] I would like to thank Dr. Guilford for making portions of his manuscript available to me prior to publication.

Vernon's model will be used as the major exemplar of the hierarchical approach. He is very clear about the fact that there is no single hierarchical structure, because the results of any given analysis depend on such variables as technique used, population tested, type and number of tests, etc. The model is represented as an inverted tree. At the top is g, the general intellective factor. This factor is followed at a lower level by two major group factors, verbal-educational ($v:ed$) and spatial-practical-mechanical ($k:m$). Each of these is followed by additional, minor factors such as the creative abilities, verbal fluency, number factors under $v:ed$, and spacial, psychomotor, mechanical information factors under $k:m$. Vernon points out that these factors can all be further subdivided by more detailed testing, but that the resulting factors are highly specific and of trivial importance. It is of interest to note that the group factors under g are located at different distances from g, a fact that suggests various degrees of referent generality (Coan, 1964). This means that factors high on the tree refer to a wide variety of behaviors, and factors low on the tree refer to narrower ranges of behavior. Vernon feels that many of Guilford's and Thurstone's factors are of such a low degree of generalizability that they are of no practical use.

There is no question but that g is there if one chooses the population and procedure necessary to produce it. The question is, Is it of any practical or theoretical value?

In order to answer this question, let us see how Vernon and other adherents of g would counter Guilford's criticism of the concept. To criticism (a), above, adherents of g would argue that there is some unevenness among abilities within persons, but that these differences are secondary to the overall g score; and further that the differential abilities worth measuring are fewer and not nearly so specific as those measured by Guilford. We will discuss an empirical test of these hypotheses below. To criticism (b), Vernon admits that Guilford's originality and creativity factor tests cover some new ground, but holds that the others are simply too specific. McNemar (1964) would second this proposal, and has suggested that creativity factors correlate more highly with intelligence than Guilford supposes. This interpretation has been supported by a considerable amount of research (cf. Yamamoto, 1964c); however, the question is still open (Wallach & Kogan, 1965b). The problem of the different growth curves (c) yielded by various subtests of intelligence or factors does not pose a problem for adherents of g, because most of them do not recognize factors as basic faculties of the mind but rather see them as reflections of the environmental field, which varies as educational and cultural pressures dictate. Thus, differential rates of growth are to be expected. Vernon (1965) makes a distinction between intelligence A (that portion that is due to genetic factors) and intelligence B (that portion due to various environmental determinants). This is a distinction that we will discuss in some detail below. Suffice it to say here that Vernon is far more interested in intelligence B than intelligence A.

The evidence for differential heritability of various abilities defined by factor analysis (d) is quite strong. For example, four of the subtests of the Primary Mental Abilities Test have consistently yielded a significant heritability index (h^2) (Vandenberg, 1966). Nevertheless, it is not clear how this evidence bears on the problem of *g* vs. multiple factors. Multiple factor methods simply spread out the variance normally ascribed to *g* among the various factors. Vandenberg (1966) points out that factors may or may not show increased hereditary components depending upon how close they are to a biologically or environmentally produced mechanism. Since general intelligence tests that load highly on *g* consistently yield higher hereditability coefficients than factor tests, one could argue that *g* is more "biologically real" than primary factors and therefore is more directly controlled by heredity. Burt (1955, 1958) has consistently interpreted the evidence from studies of heredity in terms of a *g* factor. Cattell (1963*b*) takes a similar view but also makes the distinction between intelligence *A* and intelligence *B*, noted above by Vernon.

Criticism (*e*)—that IQ tests fail to predict achievement adequately—is the one most clearly subject to experimental analysis, and consequently has engendered the most controversy. There is fundamental agreement that tests of intelligence, achievement, and aptitude reached a validity plateau in the range of .5 to .6 shortly after World War I and that in spite of extensive increases in sophistication of test construction since then, we are still on that plateau (Guttman, 1965; McNemar, 1964; Vernon, 1965; Michael, 1965). An examination of recent test manuals and the validity studies section of the *Journal of Educational and Psychological Measurement* does not change this appraisal. Ghiselli (1966) has documented a similar argument in the area of prediction of occupational success. He reports a validity ceiling of about .6 for intelligence tests used in the prediction of occupational success.

Can factored tests developed by multiple factors predict achievement better than tests based on *g* (either implicitly or explicitly)? One of the theoretical assumptions underlying multiple-factor tests is that they can be used very efficiently in multiple-regression equations because they combine relatively independent sources of variation, whereas nonfactored tests do not. Guilford, Hoepfner, & Peterson (1965) have subjected the structure-of-intellect theory to just such a test and have claimed moderate success (Guilford, 1966). What are the facts?

Guilford et al. (1965) compared, via multiple correlations, the predictive efficiency of a variety of tests against a final achievement test score in four kinds of mathematics courses. The achievement test was used rather than course grades in order to improve criterion validity; the authors note that course grades were consistently less predictable. The tests used were as follows:[2] two California Test of Mental Maturity scores (CTMM), Language MA and Non-Language MA (.33); three Iowa Test of Basic Skills scores (Iowa), Reading Comprehension, Arithmetic Concepts, Arithmetic Problem Solving (.43); four Differential Aptitude Test scores (DAT), Verbal Reasoning, Numerical Ability, Abstract Reasoning, Clerical Speed and Accuracy

---

[2]The average (via *z* transformation) multiple correlation for all four courses is given in parentheses after each test.

(.53); all nine of the above tests combined (.54); seven factor tests (.45); thirteen factor scores (based on twenty-five tests), (.53); twenty factor predictors (the seven factor tests and thirteen factor scores above), (.55). The four DAT tests and combination of nine standard tests are equivalent to the thirteen factor scores and twenty factor predictors in spite of the fact that there are so many more factor tests and that the factor tests were chosen specifically to predict performance in mathematics. Guilford et al. point out that the factor tests take more time than the nonfactor tests, but suggest that if nonpredictive factor tests were eliminated, the factor battery might be more efficient.

The authors tested this hypothesis by conducting a stepwise multiple regression analysis using only scores that add significantly to the multiple prediction. With the courses collapsed into two groups that used the same criterion-test, the factor test scores and composites (while using only a few more scores) are equivalent to the standard tests (.66 vs. .62). This somewhat substantiates their claim. However, it is of interest to note that the composition of the factor equations changed drastically from one group to the other, while the equation for the standard tests did not. This suggests that the standard tests are more efficient in terms of generalizability. If we look at the validity data for the DAT (Bennett, Seashore, & Wessman, 1952), we find that the median validity coefficients for the Numerical Ability Test *alone* across all types of mathematics courses are .47 for boys and .52 for girls. If we recall that Guilford et al. are using a special criterion that is more stable than grades, these data suggest that many of the factor tests are contributing very little, if anything, more than the standard tests, and may not be nearly as efficient in terms of generality.

One can only conclude that the factor tests have added very little to the predictability of performance in these math courses over and above a simple numerical test. An inspection of all the data indicates that the DAT Numerical and Iowa Reading Comprehension Test can carry the entire load better than any single small group of factor tests. This interpretation is in fundamental agreement with McNemar's (1964) argument that "an intelligence test can serve nearly all, if not all, the purposes for which a multiple aptitude battery is given in the schools [p. 875] ." It also supports Vernon's (1965) admonition that *g* simply cannot be ignored.

Making use of structure-of-intellect concepts, Guilford (1966) has put forth an information-processing model of problem-solving. The model is an elaboration of many earlier suggestions (e.g., Guilford, 1961) and represents problem-solving in terms of the systematic application of five operations to four types of contents and six types of products. Information is stored in memory as contents and products that are continually accessible to all operations. Processing is always subject to evaluation, and there is a search for new information when it is needed. The model is a preliminary step toward describing the dynamic organization underlying the structure-of-intellect. It combines in a conceptual way the fractionated and fragmented abilities of the morphological model and suggests the same principle that *g* has represented for some researchers, namely "that each body has only one brain to do its thinking [Clarke, 1962, p. 412] ."

Fluid and Crystallized Intelligence

Cattell (1963b; Horn & Cattell, 1966) has argued that the general intelligence factor (g) is in fact at least two interrelated and cooperative factors. The first is fluid intelligence G_f, a "general relation-perceiving capacity which operates in all fields" and is biologically determined; the second is crystallized intelligence G_c, a "sum of particular relation-perceiving skills acquired in specific fields" and thereby environmentally determined (Cattell, 1957, p. 877). Cattell explicitly relates this distinction to a number of views that we will mention, as well as a number we will not discuss. Briefly, G_f and G_c have some correspondence with Hebb's (1958) distinction between intelligence A and B, Newland's (1962) *process* and *product*, Guttman's (1965) *analytic* and *achievement* and Ferguson's (1956) *ability* and *learning set*. G_f also corresponds to Spearman's (1932) concept of "eduction of correlates" while G_c corresponds to Hunt's (1961) *information processing strategies*.

In order to test the theory, Cattell (1963b) conducted a factor analysis using four IPAT Culture Free subtests and five Thurstone Primaries as measures of G_f and G_c respectively. He found two second-order factors that corresponded closely to the predicted G_f and G_c factors. The first second-order factor, labeled G_f, consisted of the four Culture Free subtests and the spatial subtest from the Thurstone Primaries. The second second-order factor, labeled G_c, consisted of the verbal, reasoning, and number subtests of the Thurstone Primaries and the series subtest of the Culture Free test. Cattell felt that these data provided strong confirmation of the theory. A factor analysis of the second-order factors caused G_f and G_c to merge. This was interpreted as the result of G_f working on G_c rather than the result of some overriding single influence. A second study, this one by Horn and Cattell (1966), attempted to generalize the theory of fluid and crystallized intelligence. This study, which made use of an older and more varied sample of subjects, was expected to reveal a greater difference between G_c and G_f. Also, it used a considerably different sample of tests, most of which were included to test the additional hypothesis that several other influences, besides G_c and G_f, bore on intelligence test performance. These other influences were predicted to be general visualization, general fluency, and general speediness. The results were very favorable. Almost all of the tests loaded on the various factors as predicted, and a *carefulness* factor was uncovered. As predicted, the correlation between G_f and G_c was lower than in the previous study. This supported the interpretation that as educational opportunities are less closely tied to capacity, G_c will be less closely tied to G_f, and the distinction will be easier to demonstrate.

The theory of fluid and crystallized intelligence, as amended to include general visualization, fluency, speediness, and carefulness, falls somewhere between g and multiple factor analysis. Unlike Burt and Vernon, who view factors as principles of classification, or Guilford, who views them as independent basic units, Cattell views his factors as general functions that are positively related to each other (he makes use of oblique factors) and that work in a cooperative fashion to generate test responses.

These general functions can be seen as the necessary components of a problem-solving model, whose generality falls somewhere between the general model presented by Guilford and the more specific models of Simon and Kotovsky and of Reitman, to be described below. G_f is apparently conceived as some quality of the nervous system upon which the individual, in his encounters with the environment, builds what Cattell calls "general solution instruments" or "aids," and what others call "schemata," "strategies," and "abilities." The sum of these "aids" is the protean factor G_c. These aids are supplemented by the general abilities of visualization, speediness, verbal fluency, and carefulness.

Facet Theory

Guttman (1965) has presented what he calls a "faceted" definition of intelligence:

> An act of a subject is *intelligent* to the (extent) to which it is classified by a (tester) as (demonstrating) a *correct* perception of an unexhibited *logical* (aspect) of a (relation) intended by the tester, on the basis of another (exhibited) *logical* (aspect) of that relation that is correctly perceived by the subject [p. 168].[3]

The most important aspect of the definition is that it generates a relatively clear distinction between analytic ability and achievement. Guttman's analysis of the term "relation" is the basis for this. Relation can be phrased in set-theoretic terms, where a relation is a subset of a Cartesian space. In a Cartesian space with two facets, one facet may be called the domain of the relation, and the other the range. For example, the test item "Who was the first president of Israel?" specifies a Cartesian space with two facets—"first presidents" and "countries." The element "Israel" taken from the domain "countries" is given, and the subject must choose an element from the range of "first presidents" that satisfies the relation. The culling rule is specified and the subject must be able to find the answer. This is an achievement item. The test item "A dog is to a puppy as a cow is to a ___?" is an analytic item. Two elements of a Cartesian space that define a relation are exhibited, and the first element of a similar relation is given. The subject must infer the culling rule in order to satisfy the relation. Guttman (1965; Guttman & Schlesinger, 1966) has presented a number of new types of items that systematically follow from facet design.

It is important to note that facets are logical units, not psychological units or factors. They serve a number of purposes with respect to test construction. First, once a faceted definition of an ability is arrived at, the domain of items is well defined, and content validity becomes a more precise notion. For example, systematic sampling procedures can be applied to the domain. Second, the construction of items is a simple and straightforward procedure. By increasing the number of facets and the relations among them, complex items can be constructed and innumerable abilities defined.

---

[3]Italics and parentheses in original. Italicized words refer to constant features of the definition, words in parentheses refer to sets of ideas.

Both Guttman (1965) and Humphreys (1962) have argued that the three dimensions of Guilford's (1966) structure-of-intellect model can be viewed as facets. Guttman has emphasized that facet theory implies a far greater number of abilities than Guilford's model. Rather than being disturbed by the plethora of possible abilities and tests, he points out that facet analysis supplies us with an a priori rationale for predicting specific statistical relationships among tests. The focus is on the *laws of formation* rather than on idiosyncratic details of elements.

This view generates many problems, however. Facet analysis does not apply at all to some kinds of tests (Guilford, 1967) and applies only partially to others (Guttman & Schlesinger, 1966). The clear distinction between achievement and analytic items, although useful, is to some extent misleading. The discussion of comprehension operators in the next section will make it clear that information retrieval (achievement items) and the ability to discern the relations among elements (analytic items) are often two sides of the same coin. Although they can be separated conceptually, it is likely that they are closely interrelated at the process level. Other difficulties include the fact that subjects do not always pay attention to the dimensions being varied, and may be influenced by perceptual processes rather than by the logical processes that specified the item format (Guttman & Schlesinger, 1966).

A MOTIVATIONAL-EXPERIENTIAL THEORY OF INTELLIGENCE

Hayes (1962) has presented a theory of intelligence with extensive implications for both research and assessment. He argues that intelligence is nothing more than a collection of learned abilities and that individual differences in intelligence are due solely to *experience producing drives* (EPDs), which are inherited tendencies to engage in activities conducive to learning. Hayes differentiates EPDs from primary or biogenetic drives and secondary or derived drives based on primary drives. They are conceptually equivalent to White's (1959) *effectance motivation.* Evidence for this theory is derived from a wide range of fields, and only a portion of it will be presented here. Most of the data relevant to the inheritance of EPDs is drawn from the animal literature and it deals with such things as sex drive, alcohol preferences, exploratory behavior, activity level, aggressiveness, and emotionality. Hayes indicates that the question of how many different EPDs are involved must be answered by behavior genetics. He suggests that intelligence depends not on the average strength of all EPDs but rather on some complex relationship among them. Although no measuring techniques have yet been developed for assessing EPDs, it is likely that EPDs would be found to correspond to preferences for the use of various sense modalities (although it would go beyond this). Guilford's (1966) finding that some abilities have to be differentiated depending on the sense modality used lends support to this interpretation. Guttman (1965) has also suggested that each mode of communication may define a different kind of intelligence.

Hayes spends much time arguing that higher mental functions are pure concepts that have no counterpart in the real world of behaving organisms; he spends less time demonstrating what he means by "learned abilities." His primary examples of learned abilities are Harlow's (1958) *learning sets* and Birch's (1945) observations that young chimpanzees can use sticks as tools when given sufficient experience. This same perspective has been used by Hunt (1961), who has generalized the notion to *information-processing strategies*. Hayes' citations of Hebb (1949) and Lashley (1958) indicate that he believes that simple skills associated with the various sense modalities (primarily perceptual) are, with experience, combined into more complex strategies that can generate solutions to more complex problems.

IQ Constancy

The problem of IQ constancy takes on a quite different meaning from Hayes' perspective. If we view intelligence as a set of learned abilities, then the problem of predicting an individual's future intelligence entails the use of variables that relate to the accumulation of these abilities as well as to a measure of current status. EPDs are just such variables. Predictions in accord with this point of view will be open to empirical testing as soon as adequate methods for assessing and differentiating EPDs are available. This view is also consistent with the *overlap* hypothesis on which Bloom (1964) has elaborated at great length. The overlap hypothesis was originally put forth in a paper by Anderson (1939), which can still be read with great profit. It suggests that the correlation of an IQ measure taken at an earlier date with one taken at a later date is a direct function of the fact that all the ability *assessed* at the earlier date is included in the assessment at the later date. This assumes that the relation between initial scores and gains is zero; that is, gains are a function of something other than present ability. A recent reanalysis of the Harvard Growth Study data by Thorndike (1966) suggests that this is most likely the case. Bloom (1964) has come to the same conclusion, and his reanalysis of the data from a large number of growth studies indicates that the overlap hypothesis does account for the correlations between intelligence at various ages and intelligence at maturity. The main conclusion to be drawn from both Hayes' theory and Bloom's reanalysis of most of the available growth study data is the same. The concept of absolutely constant IQ is inadequate. IQ is more adequately conceptualized as a measure of current status. The increasing stabilitity of IQ is to a large extent a function of the overlap between measures.

Mental Growth

Mental growth curves (Wechsler, 1958; Bayley, 1955) suggest that intellectual growth levels off at between ages 14 and 20. Hayes suggests two possible explanations for this fact: (*a*) After this age individuals have begun to specialize in terms of their learning abilities to such an extent that no test is able to sample properly everyone's abilities and information accumulation. (*b*) EPDs decrease in strength in the maturing individual, and he begins to spend most of his time making use of those skills already acquired. A third possibility is that both (*a*) and (*b*) occur together. Alternative (*a*) is consistent with a sampling view of intelligence (Tuddenham, 1962) and the fact that numerous studies have shown a small but consistent increase in IQ with education (Lorge, 1945) and time (Terman, 1954). Alternative (*b*) is a provocative hypothesis that should be explored. If we assume that increasing stability of interest patterns is an indirect indicator of the waning of EPDs, then this is also evidence for alternative (b) (Tyler, 1965).

A number of other characteristics of growth curves should be examined in light of the EPD theory. Hayes has suggested that the characteristic change in slope of individual growth-curves found at the six-year level may be a function of the interaction of the child's EPDs and the environment. EPDs may be more or less compatible with the home or the school environment, thereby causing this change. We will return to this point later in the chapter.

Language

The relationship of language to intelligence is a major problem in the psychology of cognition. Hayes postulates that the acquisition of language is under the control of EPDs. The acquisition of motor speech skills is under the control of some EPDs, whereas the acquisition of meaning and syntax is under the control of others. He makes it very clear, however, that the cognitive skills necessary to generate and understand language are only a small part of the repertoire of cognitive skills acquired by an individual. This theoretical perspective on language is congruent with much of the data on language and intelligence. The clear separation between motor speech skills and the ability to understand language has been documented by Lenneberg (1964). It also fits in with the findings that suggest that the deaf suffer little intellectual deficit apart from the fact that they find it difficult to learn language. Furth (1964, 1966) has presented a considerable amount of data to support this contention (however, see Blank's [1965] challenge to this interpretation). The theory explains why language learning per se is not due solely to imitative behavior (Lenneberg, 1964) and reinforcement contingencies in the environment (Weir, 1962); and it also takes account of the enormous importance of environment with respect to language content (Bernstein, 1961; Bloom, 1964). The difficulty that individuals have in learning a second language and the extreme importance of motivational factors (Lambert, 1963) support the suggestion that EPDs tend to decrease in strength with age. The theory takes no position on the controversy of how language is learned (Ervin-Tripp & Slobin, 1966), but its total dependence on EPDs and learning is in conflict with the view that there is a biologically based anlage for language acquisition (Lenneberg, 1967).

COMPUTERS AND INTELLIGENCE

Artificial intelligence has been approached from two different directions. One approach focuses on *self-organizing systems* and *random neural nets* that make use of a minimal number of capacities (Yovitts & Cameron, 1960). The other focuses on heuristic programming that incorporates the most powerful systems of problem-solving possible (Feigenbaum & Feldman, 1963). The latter approach is characterized as the information-processing level of explanation, and we will limit our discussion to it.

The information-processing level of explanation assumes that thought processes are built up from elementary symbol-manipulation processes such as "read," "write," "erase," "compare," and "decide on a course of action depending on the results of the comparison." Organized sequences of these elementary processes exemplify both rules and structures. The goal of many information processing theorists is to construct a sequence of these processes (programs) that, when supplied with the appropriate input, will generate output comparable to that generated by humans. Minsky (in Feigenbaum & Feldman, 1963) has reviewed the entire field of artificial intelligence, and Green (1964) has reviewed briefly the narrower area of human intelligence and computer simulation. Most of the broad abilities defined by factor analytic studies have been simulated, but as yet there is nothing even approximating a complete theory of machine intelligence. Here we will limit ourselves to two programs (theories) that attempt to simulate human performance on tasks often included in intelligence tests.

Simon and Kotovsky (1963) have proposed a theory that deals with the ability to extrapolate sequential letter-series. This task (Letter Series Completion Test) represents the reasoning factor in Thurstone's test of Primary Mental Abilities. For example, given the sequence − *aaabbbcccdd* − the subject must predict the next letter. The theory asserts that subjects can generate and fixate a pattern description of the problem and then utilize that pattern to extrapolate the series. The necessary assumptions are that the subjects have in memory the English alphabet, both backwards and forwards, the concepts "same," "equal" and "next on a list" (order). They must also have the abilities to produce a cyclical pattern and to keep track of a small number of symbols. The pattern description of the problem cited above is *[M1 = Alph; a] [M1, M1, M1, N (M1)]*. This means the pattern has a period of three letter lengths beginning with *a* followed by the next *N* letter of a forward alphabet *(Alph)*. After each period the value of *M1* changes to the next letter. The subject must keep his place in the alphabet by always remembering the current value of *M1*. More difficult problems require a more complex iteration sequence and the ability to recall one's place in more than one alphabet. The patterns used in this study can be roughly divided into easy and difficult. The difficult patterns are differentiated from the easy ones by the need to hold more items simultaneously in immediate memory.

A reciprocal relationship holds for constructing the pattern descriptions. The pattern generator constructs pattern descriptions by noting initial conditions *[M1 = Alph; a]*, searching for periodicity (each third letter is the same) or the interruption of a sequence (the relation "same" is interrupted after every third letter), and searching for relations (same, next) within and between letter periods. Changes in the pattern generator, such as a different repertoire of relations it can test, yield changes in the ability of the program. To some extent these changes correspond to differences in ability among subjects.

The most striking finding to emerge from this examination is the dependence of problem solution on immediate memory. Despite the fact that the problem itself is always available, limitations of immediate memory can seriously affect the integration of the information necessary to solve the problem (see Posner, 1965). A second finding of interest is that differences in the repertoire of simple relations such as same or next, and the ability to organize and record simple patterns lead to failures that are similar to those produced by human subjects. This suggests that even simple tests that purport to measure relatively pure factors depend on numerous simpler abilities which interact in complex ways.

The second computer program (theory) to be treated here is called "Argus" (Reitman, 1965). It is conceptually related to Hebb's theory of thinking (Hebb, 1949). Like that theory, Argus attempts to account for the relative distractability of human cognitive behavior. Most computer models make use of strictly sequential, centralized processing mechanisms, which reflect an unnatural single-mindedness (Neisser, 1963). Argus attempts to get around this problem by decentralizing the program to some extent. It does this by using a basic unit called a "semantic element." The semantic element is a purely psychological construct that corresponds to a unit of meaning in human cognition and a cell assembly in Hebb's theory. Semantic elements are active and relatively independent of central processing units. They are characterized conceptually by five parameters: activation, inhibition, threshold, size, and age. Except for the last, these parameters are continuously influenced by experience and use. Cognitive structure is represented as a network of these active semantic elements. Modification of one element can have an effect on remote parts of the system, depending on the state of various parameters within elements. Problem solving is the application of strategies to semantic elements, guided by an executive with a set of rules. The current state of the five parameters, the strategy applied, and the information available all determine the probability of problem solution.

Argus works on analogy problems of the form $A:B: :C:(w,x,y,z)$. The program activates the semantic elements A and B. The question now is "Does this activation propagate sufficient activity to bring a common element to the attention of the executive?" If it doesn't the program fails or applies another strategy. If it does, the program asks, "What is its relation to A?" That piece of information (e) is stored, and elements C and w are activated. If a common element is activated, its relation to C is tested, and the answer compared to (e). If they are identical, the problem is solved. The answer is w. Argus can be programmed to solve both very simple and very difficult analogies, but it solves them in a formally identical way. This presents a problem because Argus does not incorporate any formal notion of difficulty, while for humans, problems are easy, difficult, or impossible. This is true in spite of the fact that we can demonstrate the existence of the relevant information and abilities within the subject. The difficulty seems to be one of organizing information. As Reitman (1965) clearly recognizes, intelligence does not reside so much in the program as such; rather it resides in the fact that "human intelligence is applied beforehand to precode the information into a particular special purpose format [pp. 228-229]."

If this conceptualization is correct, then an analogies test measures to a large extent the efficiency with which an individual structures information. The more efficiently his information is stored, the more easily and rapidly he detects the relevant dimensions required by the problem. Teaching someone how to code efficiently, according to this view, would be equivalent to making him more intelligent. Hayes' theory of EPDs may account for individual differences in ability as a function of a person's having acquired the necessary information by paying attention to different relevant dimensions of the problem, but it does not account for the structure of abilities or the organization of that information. Intelligence is not only a collection of acquired abilities and information; it is also a structure of knowledge (Bruner, 1960). These views are not necessarily incompatible if we recognize that process leads to structure. Reitman (1965) and Simon and Kotovsky (1963), unlike Hayes (1962), suggest what these acquired abilities might look like and how they might yield this structure. The pattern generator in the Simon and Kotovksy model exemplifies a class of mechanisms designated as *comprehension operators*. Comprehension operators transform external data into symbolic representational structures that are subject to decoding into the original input data. Comprehension operators have been constructed in a variety of problem areas, but no major principles have evolved (Reitman, 1965, 1966).

PIAGET'S THEORY

No discussion of intelligence can omit the seminal work of Piaget. Yet this work cannot be treated adequately in a brief chapter such as this one. Here we shall present only a short outline of the theory and attempt to show how it dovetails with other theoretical developments. The synopsis below is drawn from Piaget (1950, 1952), Hunt (1961), and Flavell (1963).

Piaget has shown little concern with measurement and individual differences. His use of the term "intelligence" corresponds more closely to what we would call "cognition" than it does to intelligence in the individual differences sense. Nevertheless the theory has profound implications for the assessment of intelligence.

The theory takes the form of a hierarchical model. There are four major periods of intellectual development, each of which is characterized by a set of stages and substages. These periods and stages represent forms of cognitive organization, each of which is more complex than the preceding. Each stage evolves from the preceding stage, and no stage can be skipped. They are a form of biological adaptation that grows out of organism-environment encounters. Adaptation is conceived of as a process of accommodation and assimilation. Accommodation is the process of modifying an existing schema as a result of repetitively applying the schema to the environment and thereby assimilating it. Accommodation and assimilation are invariant functions; that is, they operate across all levels of cognitive development. For example, at an elementary psychological level their operation would consist of modifying a reflex action system (e.g., sucking schema) with practice. At a more advanced level their operation would consist of studying a new set of complex ideas and incorporating them into a present conceptualization. Assimilation does not refer only to environmental encounters. There is a process called "organizing assimilation," which refers to purely internal restructuring; its purpose is to aid the organism in generalizing and differentiating existing schemata. Clearly, then, the processes of assimilation and accommodation span the terrain generally labeled "learning," "complex problem solving," and "thinking."

The first period is that of *sensorimotor* or *practical* intelligence. This period spans the age range of 0-2 years. During this period the child passes through six stages: The first stage (0-2 months) consists of exercising an already wired-in reflex system. The second stage (2-4 months) consists of the first acquired adaptations. The use of *primary circular reactions* defines this stage. They consist of the repetitive use of various schemata such as sucking, looking, listening, grasping, and making sounds. This leads to the integration and coordination of these schemata (e.g., finger sucking, watching one's hands, etc.). Stage three (4-8 months) consists of the *secondary circular reactions* and procedures for making interesting sights last. The earlier primary circular reactions are more thoroughly integrated and generalized. The child displays intentional behavior and motor recognition by repeating behavior that bears on the external environment as opposed to behavior that bears on his own body. Stage four (8-12 months) consists of the coordination of secondary schemata and their application to new situations. Means-ends relationships and conceptions of object permanence appear. Stage five (12-18 months) consists of the *tertiary circular reactions* and the discovery of new *means* through active experimentation. Tertiary circular reactions are a form of trial-and-error goal-seeking activity in which the response is consistently varied in order to produce novel results. Stage six (18-24 months) consists of the invention of new means through mental combination. This stage is the beginning of systematic intelligence. The child can spontaneously reorganize earlier schemata and apply them to new situations. There is an awareness of relationships apart from receptor inputs, and more rapid internal processing.

These six stages constitute a sequential series of adaptations that follow an orderly course of development from the exercise of simple reflexes to their coordination and internalization in the form of cognitive structures.

The preoperational period spans the ages of from 2 years to about 7 years. During this period a child acquires language and symbolic functions. It is a long transition period during which the child begins to represent internally, in the form of imagery, those behaviors that were earlier external. At first, representation takes the form of motor representation. The mimicking by Piaget's children of the opening and closing of a match box by opening and closing their mouths is a frequently cited example of this form of representation. This representational function develops and is internalized via overt imitation, play, and games. Preoperational thought has some serious limitations. The child does represent reality, but this representation is closer to action than thought. It is thus extremely concrete and egocentric. There is an inability to *decenter* (focus on more than one dimension of a problem at a time), to reverse thought sequences, or to represent simple transformations. It is important to note that although language develops during this period, Piaget does not see language as the vehicle that underlies symbolic functioning.

Continued adaptation via assimilation and accommodation begins to "thaw out" these preoperational structures. Piaget has emphasized the importance of social interaction, which forces the child to justify his thought processes and to take varying perspectives on problems. This helps break down his egocentrism and decenters his thought processes. When this occurs he enters the period of concrete operations (6 years to 11 years).

This period is characterized by a class of abilities suggesting that the concrete operational child has complex, systematic, flexible, and tightly organized systems of operations available to him. Operations correspond to specific actions that can be applied to content. The common mathematical symbols (+, −, ×, ÷, >, =, <, ≠) are examples of such operations. As a child moves through the stages of the concrete operational period, he shows a continual decentering, and his performance on a large variety of experimental tasks reflects thought processes with the following properties: transitivity, associativity, reversibility, identity, tautology, and iteration. Piaget represents these operations as logico-mathematical structures called "groupings." These operations tend to develop separately and sequentially for different properties of objects (e.g., conservation of quantity, weight, and volume) and different materials (number, objects). The limitations of this period are that concrete operations apply only to material objects in the environment and treat different properties of objects separately.

The transformation to the period of formal operations (11 years +) occurs when the adolescent begins to be able to treat problems in a formal manner and to reason with verbal propositions. This is a new orientation toward problem solving. Problems are approached via logical analysis such as hypothetico-deductive and propositional thinking, and operations are performed on operations. Thought processes are highly unified and direct the adolescent's observations rather than his observations directing his thoughts.

TOWARD A GENERAL MODEL OF INTELLIGENCE

Has our review of these varied responses to the puzzle of intelligence succeeded in putting any of the pieces into an array that might suggest an eventual solution?

To answer this question we will have to put both the search for the meaning of intelligence and the conceptions so far examined in this review into the same overall context. As Loevinger (1966) has stated, Binet discovered "that some functions that require intelligence for their exercise still do not provide useful measures of intellectual development [p. 195]." This was a fortunate turn of events for the practical measurement of intelligence, but an unfortunate one for the theory of intelligence. The results of Binet's discovery and of Spearman's (1923) work was a focus on tests and test content that yielded useful measures of intellectual development. Those functions that required intelligence for their exercise but did not provide useful measures were scarcely explored. Consequently Piaget's work, which has uncovered the complexity underlying such fundamental concepts as space, time, and number, has been received with much dismay (Flavell, 1963). That imbalance is now in the process of being redressed, and apart from the work of Piaget and his colleagues, a great deal of research is being focused on basic cognitive processes (Hunt, 1961; Laurendeau & Pinard, 1962; Wright & Kagan, 1963; Smedslund, 1964; Bruner et al., 1966). This research, much of which is not in the tradition of individual differences, is nevertheless generating a reconceptualization of intelligence that will serve as a general background against which to evaluate the theories we have reviewed.

This reconceptualization consists of three interrelated parts: (*a*) a movement away from social and judgmental criteria for tests concerned with assessing theoretical conceptions of intelligence, and a greater emphasis on construct validity; (*b*) the recognition that the problem of intelligence is a sub-problem associated with the more general problem of determining the structure of cognition and thought; (*c*) an emphasis on process. The general model that is emerging as a result of these changes resembles a dynamic information-processing system. It is seen as growing out of a constant environmental-organism interchange in which both heredity and environment are of 100-percent importance (Hebb, 1958) and in which neither is determinate (Hunt, 1961), but whose development is highly dependent on at least an adequate early environment (Bloom, 1964).

Against this background the scientific understanding of intelligence is a matter of describing the structure of cognition and thought, and of specifying the biological and environmental conditions that control its growth and development. The task of assessing intelligence, construed as a scientific endeavor, requires the devising of measures that specify the important parameters of cognitive structure for particular individuals.

Guilford's problem-solving model is a preliminary attempt to develop a theory of this type, and is a major conceptual advance in the theory of intelligence. His structure-of-intellect model attempts to describe the structure of cognition. The problem-solving model introduces a number of new concepts such as attention, feedback, somatic and environmental inputs, etc., which serve to integrate the structure into a dynamic system. His factor tests are devices for specifying parameters of the model for particular individuals. The theory specifically points up a number of problems for future research: How is information processed in terms of specific mechanisms? How is information structured and retrieved?

Information processing theorists have, however, taken up these questions. De Groot (1966) has suggested that the *methods* of problem solving, as revealed by the thinking-aloud technique and modeled by information-processing theorists, may in fact correspond to *factors*. The computer models discussed previously contains examples of such methods (comprehension operators) and others continue to be explored (Paige & Simon, 1966).

The long-range goal of an information-processing theory of intelligence is to simulate the intellectual behavior of human subjects. This formulation requires that the performance of a number of simulated subjects, when subjected to factor analysis, yield the same results as the performance of real subjects. It does not follow, however, that there need be a correspondence between the resultant factors and the mechanisms of the model. The probable relationship of factors to methods, comprehension operators, or processing mechanisms incorporated in information-processing models is difficult to predict; nevertheless, it appears unlikely that factor tests will supply the kind of descriptive parameters we will need to index intelligence conceptualized from an information-processing perspective. A discussion of Guttman's treatment of the problem of intelligence will make clear why this is so.

Guttman's definition of intelligence shares an important characteristic with information-processing models. His distinction between achievement and analytic ability parallels the distinction made in the term "information processing." Both distinctions are based on the fact that a logical separation can be made between a process and the content to which it is applied. In the field of computer simulation the distinction has led to the search for very general heuristics (Reitman, 1965) or rules of thumb that apply across many different types of problems (content). The same distinction underlies the search for culture-free intelligence tests, in which content is held constant by being either totally unfamiliar or totally overlearned. Guttman (1965) has commented on how most existing tests of intelligence violate the distinction between information-retrieval and information-processing, and has suggested that his new type of items, which focus on the distinction, will be superior to existing mixed items. It is more likely that his pure tests, like most factor tests, will also fail to tap the interaction and content present in complex tests and criteria. Our discussion of comprehension operators, earlier in this paper, indicates that process and content are often closely interrelated and that measures of the range and configuration of content will be necessary in order to specify any particular cognitive structure adequately. Facet design may prove to be a very useful technique for studying this relationship.

Advances in computer simulation may illuminate the interactions that occur when a variety of abilities are used simultaneously to solve complex problems. Such interactions clearly violate the assumption of additivity underlying factor analysis (Loevinger, 1951; Taylor, 1966), and hopefully will explain the limitations of factorially pure tests vs. factorially complex tests, when the former are combined into multiple-regression equations and used to predict complex criteria (cf. Michael, 1965; and the discussion of the Guilford et al. study above).

Hayes's theory is compatible with the information-processing view expressed above and focuses on an important drawback of this approach. Simulation theorists have failed to deal adequately with the problem of motivation (cf. Neisser, 1963; Simon, 1967). There is no question that it will be necessary to design models that, when exposed to an informational environment, will select their own information.

The relationship of Piaget's theory to information-processing models is so direct that it has been described as "an attempt to specify this information-processing system at various points in its evolution [Huttenlocher, 1965, p. 114]." Hunt's (1963, 1965) elaboration of Piaget's theory within an information-processing and motivational framework provides us with a basis for discussing this relationship. He argues that there is an epigenesis of what he calls "motivation inherent in information-processing and action [Hunt, 1963, p. 270]." This is a generalization of Piaget's concept of equilibrium, or what Bruner (1959) has called a "trouble theory of motivation." Discrepancies between the child's anticipatory schemata, based on past experience, and the cognition of present experience initiate assimilatory activities that must be equilibrated via the process of accommodation. Discrepancies of this sort initiate goal-completion mechanisms in information-processing models (i.e., they drive the system). There is also a variety of terminating mechanisms that return control to the executive under the following circumstances: when the goal has been achieved, when present achievement is considered "good enough," when time has run out and present achievement is considered "the best so far," or when a set of processes for achieving the goal have been exhausted. Simon (1967) has argued that information-processing theories do contain motivational components, and suggests that the terminating mechanisms mentioned above could be called "aspiration achievement," "satisficing," "impatience," and "discouragement" respectively.

In spite of some severe limitations, information-processing models have evolved to the point where they have the potential for simulating many of the complex cognitive and affective behaviors that we characterize as intelligent. As such, they supply us with a conceptual framework of sufficient complexity and specificity that we can now begin to answer the question, "What is intelligence?" in a far more differentiated way than simply saying, "Intelligence is what intelligence tests measure."

IMPLICATIONS FOR ASSESSMENT

What is the major implication of these theories, and of the information-processing perspective that we have elaborated, for psychological assessment?

The main implication is that we should begin to view intelligence from a broader perspective and should focus on characteristics of intelligent behavior other than problem solution. For example, Hunt (1961) suggests that Piaget's theory outlines a natural ordinal scale of intelligence and that we should view the assessment of intelligence as "sampling behavior for evidence of such organizational structures as schemata, operations, and concepts [p. 344]," rather than as the measurement of dimensions of an individual. The assessment of intelligence from this point of view entails characterizing the individual's cognitive organization rather than simply placing him on a dimension. In order to accomplish this task, Hunt has rejected the compensatory model that underlies current intelligence tests and has constructed an infant test that attempts to sample these structures (Uzgiris & Hunt, 1966). The test, which is still highly provisional, contains six tentative scales representing orderings of behavioral reactions drawn mostly from Piaget's reports. The scales are being developed to study the effects of early environmental experience on the rate and course of cognitive development in young infants. Although they are based on Piaget's sensorimotor stages, they yield a finer grading of steps and should therefore be more sensitive to environmental variation.

This approach to the problem explicitly recognizes that a measure of intelligence is a measure of current status and carries no direct implications about future development. The goal is not to predict the future from the present but rather to formulate laws that "predict the characteristics that organisms with specified genetic constitutions will develop under specific programs of encounters with the environment [Hunt, 1961, p. 310]." This view—that intelligence should be seen as a measure of current status—agrees with our previous interpretation of the data presented by Hayes and Bloom. Tyler (1965) has come to a similar conclusion.

Bloom (1964) has taken the first steps to implement a pattern of research based on this point of view. His focus is primarily on characterizing the ideal environment, which would maximize the development of all individuals; but he does recognize the significance of the heredity-environment interaction, and he emphasizes the importance of taking environment into account when attempting to predict future development. For example, in the Harvard Growth Study the correlation between IQ at ages 7.4 and 16.4 was .58. However, an analogous multiple correlation of .92 was obtained when the educational level of extreme groups of parents was added to the IQ measure at age 7.4 (Bloom, 1964). The lesson for assessment is clear: "introduction of the environment on a variable makes a major difference in our ability to predict the mature status of a human characteristic [Bloom, 1964, p. 184]."

Hayes's theory implies that a description of an individual's cognitive organization is not an adequate assessment of intelligence. A thorough assessment would include measures of important EPDs. As we mentioned earlier, the prediction of future intelligence from this point of view entails the use of a measure of present status *plus* a measure of relevant EPDs. It is of interest to note that Hayes sees EPDs as determinants of certain types of environmental encounters that are significant to the accumulation of specific kinds of abilities. Bloom, on the other hand, sees the environment as impinging itself on the individual and therefore determining which abilities will be acquired. In fact, both states of affairs exist; the individual does chose and the environment does impose itself. For the practical purpose of predicting future IQ, the systematic use of both of these variables would be of value. Bloom (1964) and Barker (1965) have made some excellent suggestions on how to analyze the environment, and the development of these ideals into valid psychometric instruments is highly desirable.

Although there are numerous scales available that purport to measure motivation, none of them incorporates the theoretical and conceptual framework presented by Hayes. The development of instruments adequate to this task would also be highly desirable. In view of the preliminary work reported by Bloom above, and the persistent reports in the literature that highly intelligent and creative individuals have unusual motivational structures, it seems possible that an appropriate combination of an adequate measure of present intellectual status, an estimate of the quality of one's future environment, and measures of relevant EPDs would yield rather precise predictions of future intellectual status.

Hopefully, the information-processing perspective supplied in the previous section will provide test constructors with a pretheoretical model (a model that they have never had before) of sufficient complexity and specificity to enable them to construct tests of intelligence that will reflect that complexity in a more meaningful and significant way. The task will be a long and arduous one, and it seems possible to conclude that it is at the same stage now as Binet's work was when he faced the problem of measuring "the intellectual capacity of a child who is brought to us in order to know whether he is normal or retarded [Binet & Simon, 1905, p. 191]." Like Binet, we know it is there, but we still have only a vague and intuitive notion of how we should measure it.

CHAPTER III

Assessment in the study of creativity

H. Edward Tryk[1]

The purpose of this paper is to present a restricted review and critical evaluation of the standard methods used to assess a variety of variables subsumed under the rubric of *creativity*. Creativity has become a vital issue in the social and physical sciences, in technology, in education, in the arts, and in business and industry, as well as with the public in general. The broad interest in creativity makes it particularly important for psychologists to take a close look at the more widely used methods of assessing creativity. General reviews of theories and research on creativity have been presented by Barron (1965), Golann (1963), Mackler and Shontz (1965a), Stein and Heinze (1960), Torrance (1962), and Yamamoto (1965). This chapter is addressed to three basic aspects of creativity that are relevant to the methodology of assessment: (1) the concept of creativity; (2) the description and evaluation of the more generally used methods of assessing creativity; and (3) a brief discussion of the current problems and issues in creativity assessment.

THE CONCEPT OF CREATIVITY

Before one can properly record or measure an aspect of creativity, one must define what he means by this term. At a very broad level of discourse the word "creativity" conveys a general meaning of the antecedent, concurrent, and/or consequent characteristics of a process by which an individual (or group of individuals) brings into existence a *form* that did not exist

[1] The author wishes to express his gratitude to Paul McReynolds and Allan Sidle whose advice and criticism were of great value in the preparation of this chapter.

before. As a concept describing the general study of this phenomenon, "creativity" is a useful term. When "creativity" is used to denote a *specific* set of phenomena, however, many differences of opinion arise. This lack of a common understanding may be due, in part, to differences in orientation and in interest of the diverse disciplines in which concern for creativity exists. The historian sees creativity essentially as an attribute of great men, evidenced by the cultural monuments produced by these men; creativity is a rare attribute which inspires a sense of awe and mystery. The philosopher and aesthetician see creativity as an attribute of a class of objects and events that produces significant emotional reactions in the observer. The artist sees creativity through his own eyes; it is a process that is usually inexplicable and yet involves a great part of his being. The educator sees creativity as a valuable way of thinking, which can be either nurtured or inhibited during the processes of learning. The industrialist and the businessman see creativity as a climate in which specially selected individuals can produce new products and services that have economic value.

It is not surprising that these different points of view regarding creativity, which had their origins outside of psychology, are now shared by psychologists who have made creativity an object of study. Thus, in recent theoretical expositions and empirical studies on the psychology of creativity, there is considerable lack of agreement as to what is to be included as creative data, and as to how these data are to be described or defined. Although the primary aim of this chapter is to review techniques that have been used for the assessment of creativity, a clear understanding of the rationale underlying these procedures and of the variables being assessed makes it important that we also consider briefly the theories from which methods of assessment have been derived. A selected sample of techniques that have been developed for the assessment of creativity will be reviewed below. For the purposes of exposition, the assessment procedures will be grouped into the following theoretical orientations: creativity as a *product*, creativity as a *capacity*, creativity as a *process*, and creativity as an *aspect of the total person*.

CREATIVITY AS A PRODUCT

The focus of attention upon the product in research on creativity can be seen as an outcome either of an intrinsic interest in the product per se or of a rigorous commitment to operationalism. In the fields of business, industry, and technology, the goal of research is to guide itself towards the manifestation of new products and procedures that have definite utilitarian value (cf., Gamble, 1959; Harmon, 1963). In psychology, product-centered research focuses upon the product because it represents an objective, tangible event upon which one can anchor inferred constructs of direct psychological interest. Proponents of the product approach to creativity include McPherson (1963), C. W. Taylor (1964), and D. W. Taylor (1963).

Although possessing the advantages of objectivity, the product approach to creativity fails to differentiate between creative and noncreative antecedent conditions (e.g., opportunity, availability of materials). When the *quantity* of products is used as an index of creativeness, there is the implicit assumption that productivity is an essential aspect of creativity, an assumption to which many cognitive theorists might object. When *quality* of a product is the measure of creativeness, the methods used to assess quality (i.e., subjective check-lists, rating scales, and ranking methods) are often unreliable and subject to changing fads and other halo-effects of social desirability (cf., Ghiselin, 1963).

The study of creative products in their own right fails to consider variables of psychological interest and thus lies beyond the limits of this paper. The concern with products as indicators of human behavior is, however, relevant and crucial. The assessment of creative products introduces the problem of the establishment of the criteria of creativity. The prevailing point of view, endorsed by the Criterion Committee of the 1959 Utah Research Conference on the Identification of Creative Scientific Talent (Sprecher, 1959), is that the *products* of creative behavior are the basic criteria.

Ghiselin (1963) argues, however, that products provide only approximations to what he calls "ultimate" criteria.

> Among the proximate criteria most often resorted to have been the judgments of experts and the measurement of creative production in terms of published papers, patents, and the like. Estimates of creativity in men and their products have been more or less subjective or objective, ranging in this respect from the simple subjectivity of intuitive appraisal to the still simpler objectivity of numerical counts. The objectivity thus apparently achieved is delusive, for even in those procedures that may seem wholly objective, the count of published papers, for example, the items estimated must be judged to be pertinent—that is, to represent creative work rather than some other sort of performance. Yet in the absence of a sound criterion, the very judgment of their pertinence must rest upon assumption [p. 30].

Ghiselin proposes that the real criteria of creative performance should be established at the cognitive level. He redefines a creative product as

> ... intrinsically a configuration of the mind, a presentation of constellated meaning, which at the time of its appearance in the mind was new in the sense of being unique, without specific precedent. Any such configuration will be new in the totality of its aspect, in the constellation of its component elements of meaning [p. 36].

Unfortunately, Ghiselin places before the investigator the formidable task of translating, into operational terms, concepts like "configuration of the mind," "constellated meaning," and "elements of meaning." It is unlikely that his proposal can serve as anything more than a guidepost until theory and methodology become sophisticated enough that cognitive dimensions of objective creative performance can be stated in ways leading to reliable measurement.

Nevertheless, Ghiselin has pinpointed perhaps the most serious shortcoming in the area of creativity assessment. The critical evaluation of a proposed method of assessing a given aspect of creativity demands that the measure produced by the method be compared with an independent criterion. The assessment of products as criteria continues to be the soundest empirical method of doing this. But as Ghiselin points out, even though the products are tangible, permanent events, their criteriality most often depends upon intuitive judgment. It is unfortunate that the criterion for judging a psychological event should depend upon contemporary standards of taste, especially when wide differences in personal tastes are the rule. Although there does not seem to be an immediate solution at hand to the criterion problem, the recognition of the problem itself is of importance. This is especially true when one attempts to interpret research that evaluates assessment techniques in terms of correlations with objective criteria. As long as the criteria are deficient, it should not be surprising to find low correlations between proposed measures of creativity and their intended criteria.

Three characteristics of products have been generally studied as criteria of creativity: quantity, quality, and significance or "breadth of applicability" (Brogden & Sprecher, 1964). Taylor, Smith, and Ghiselin (1963) report a factor analysis of 47 relevant criterion variables of creativeness and five control variables in a study of 250 physical scientists in two different research centers. Of these variables, 13 were obtained from the assessment of scientific products, 10 from research reports written by the scientists, and 3 from official records. The balance of the criteria were subject variables. The factor analysis produced a total of 15 "relatively independent" factors, of which 5 appear to be descriptive of products. This large investigation exemplifies the complexity inherent in the use of products in the assessment of creativity. Of the five product factors, only two seem to be tapping what is usually considered *creativity*; the other three are descriptive of *productivity*. The variables that show up in the two creative product factors have something in common besides creativity: they are virtually all obtained from experts' *ratings* of specified attributes of the products. One would not be unjustified in concluding that the productivity factors are obtained from *counting* products, and the creativity factors are obtained from having experts *rate* the products.

It appears, then, that the methods that are used to assess the creativeness of products can influence the interpretation of the variables being assessed. In addition, the large number of factors extracted in the study by Taylor et al. (and one would anticipate an even larger array of factors from a more heterogenous population of subjects) emphasizes the danger in assuming that any one product—associated with its method of assessment—will serve as an empirically sound criterion. The investigators who conducted this study admit:

> Initially, we were somewhat puzzled about finding such a great complexity in the total contributions area, as indicated by the many low intercorrelations (low overlap) and thus the high specificity in the measures on contributions. As time has elapsed, however, we are getting indications from other studies (Sprecher, 1959, and Mullins, 1960) that this finding of relatively great complexity is quite sound [Taylor et al., 1963, p. 66].

CREATIVITY AS A PROCESS

A second, more strictly psychological point of view depicts creativity as a process that takes place over time. Since the creative process is considered to be largely subjective and is inferred from observable behavior, this approach tends to be highly theoretical. Different theorists have characterized the process in terms of stages, levels, and types of thinking.

Stages of the Creative Process

The prototypic theory of creativity as a series of *stages* was introduced by Wallas (1926). Wallas described four stages of the creative process: preparation, incubation, illumination, and verification. Harris (1959) expanded Wallas' contribution by adding an antecedent stage, "gathering information," and a terminal stage, "putting ideas to work." The basic assumption of this paradigm is that there is an orderly progression during the creative process from one stage of creation to the next.

Although the literature on creative thinking provides many introspective accounts by eminent thinkers and artists (e.g., see Ghiselin, 1952; Hutchinson, 1949; Vinacke, 1952; Wallas, 1926), the translation of the psychological characteristics unique to each stage into quantifiable behavior has been almost entirely unsuccessful. A further difficulty in attempting an empirical test of the stages hypothesis is the problem of relating behavioral referents of creative thinking to an ordered time-dimension. Crude attempts to validate the hypothesis introduced by Wallas have been reported by Eindhoven and Vinacke with artists (1952), and Patrick with artists (1937), scientists (1938), and poets (1935, 1941). The investigators came to opposing conclusions regarding the progression of stages during creative performance, although their results were not subjected to statistical analysis.

Levels of the Creative Process

The second conceptualization of the creative process, as *levels* of thinking, was suggested early in the writings of Freud. Freud described creative thinking as an interaction between the primary process and the secondary process, wherein the creative act is the result of sublimation (de-sexualization by secondary-process thinking) of the libidinal (primary-process) drive. More recently Kris (1952) and Schafer (1958) have extended the psychoanalytic model to describe creative thinking as a voluntary relaxation of ego-control ("regression in the service of ego") in order that reality-thinking can be expanded by the incorporation and integration of previously repressed material. Kubie (1958) has added a third and intermediate, "preconscious," level of thinking. From a non-psychoanalytic orientation, I. A. Taylor (1962) has distinguished five levels of the creative process: the expressive, productive, inventive, innovative, and emergentive.

Up until 1950, only a handful of studies were published that utilized projective instruments in the investigation of creativity, in spite of the apparent relevance of this technique for theories emphasizing the operation of unconscious thinking in the creative process. During this period of time, only eight such studies could be located by Burchard (1952); and of these, only the Rorschach was represented. Anne Roe (1946a, 1947, 1950) was one of the first to analyze the performance of gifted individuals on the Rorschach. Using standard scoring-categories, Roe was unable to observe any striking differences in the responses to the ink blots among her criterion groups (artists, biologists, physical scientists, and college students). As a check on the reliability of the Rorschach interpretations used in her studies, she sent the protocols of twenty gifted painters to a distinguished expert in Rorschach interpretation for blind analysis. In only seven of the twenty protocols did the expert recognize signs of creative ability; whereas the *absence* of creative potential was judged in eight!

More recently, a new method has been developed by Holt and Havell (1960) for scoring the Rorschach, and by Pine (1960) for scoring the Thematic Apperception Test (TAT) for the subject's ability to indulge in adaptive regression (i.e., "regression in the service of ego"). Holt's scoring procedure yields three scores related to primary-process thinking: quantity of primary process, degree of control of primary thinking exercised, and an operational measure of adaptive regression (a weighted combination of the quantity and control scores). Insufficient data have been reported to evaluate critically Holt's scoring system. The only significant correlations found between Holt's scores and scores from other tests of creativity have been in an extremely small sample (13 male undergraduate students), correlations which were not replicated with samples of 14 female undergraduates and 50 unemployed actors (Pine, 1962; Pine & Holt, 1960). A manual has been prepared by Pine (1960) for scoring the TAT protocols for drive content, but the reliability and validity data are both disappointing and incomplete.

Maddi (1965) has developed a procedure for scoring TAT stories for six classifications of novelty, based upon judgments by trained scorers. He proposes that wanting and seeking novelty are self-activating and motivate creative production. Scoring reliability for Maddi's procedure is only moderately high (median $r = .85$), and the stability of scores over time appears to be lower than desirable (test-retest $r = .55$). The coefficients of equivalence are also of modest magnitude (split-half r's from .63 to .80). In spite of their relative unreliability, novelty-seeking scores on the TAT have been found to be significantly related to other measures of creative behavior. Maddi reports correlations of .57 with the *Unusual Uses* test and .39 with Frank's figure completion task. Correlations of .47 and .45 were obtained between novelty of TAT stories and novelty of endings supplied for similes, and a -.42 with the amount of time spent by subjects in exploring a room during a 15-minute period. The last correlation is in the predicted direction, since theory (Fiske & Maddi, 1961) states that passive (story-telling) and active (overt exploration) novelty-seeking behavior are mutually compensatory.

The use of projective instruments in the assessment of creativity has not been as productive as one might expect. Theories of creativity that emphasize the role of unconscious processes in creative behavior are in need of measures that can assess variables related to primary-process thinking. At the present stage of development, it must be concluded that in spite of the appropriateness of the projective method in assessing cognitive processes theoretically linked to creativity, the empirical basis of these methods has yet to be established.

Types of Creative Processes

A third variety of process theories regards creativity as a *type* of thinking. This point of view is parsimonious and, because of its theoretical simplicity, makes possible direct and concise definitions of creative thinking. An early description of creative thinking as a unitary cognitive process was proposed by Spearman (1930), who labeled the process the "eduction of correlates." Since then other investigators have proposed various unified kinds of thinking as creative: Welch's (1946) "recombination of ideas," McReynolds' (1964) "cognitive innovation," Flanagan's (1963) "ingenuity," and Mednick's (1962) "formation of associative elements into new combinations" are some examples. The definitions of creative thinking that are derived from the type approach to creativity are not necessarily assumed to be all-encompassing. Rather, the intention is most often to describe creative thinking in a way that will generate directly an objective technique for its assessment. The more recent theorists mentioned above have constructed tests that are in essence operational definitions of their respective theories of creative thinking. Thus, we have Welch's Reorganization Test (1946), McReynolds' Obscure Figures Test (Acker & McReynolds, 1965), Flanagan's Ingenuity Test (1963) and Mednick's (1962) Remote Associates Test.

Of the tests of creativity constructed within the formulation of creativity as a type of thinking, the Remote Associates Test (RAT) is the most thoroughly documented and most widely used. Therefore it seems appropriate to describe the RAT and some of the empirical evidence of its usefulness as an instrument for assessing creativity.

The RAT is a verbal paper-and-pencil test that was generated directly from Mednick's associational theory of the creative process. For Mednick the hallmark of creative thinking is the formation of new associational combinations, and the degree of creativeness of the process is a function of the *remoteness* of the associations that enter into these combinations. In this test, the subject is required to produce verbal responses that unify three remotely connected associational systems. The subject is presented with a series of thirty items, each of which is a set of three seemingly unrelated words. The task is to think of a fourth word which is a common associate of the three stimulus-words. The discovery by the subject of the "correct" response thus brings together, within a single associational system, elements that were previously perceived as independent. In a sample item from the test, the three words "poke," "go," and "molasses" are presented as stimulus words. The correct response combining these words in a common associational network is "slow." What makes the RAT a difficult test is both the remoteness of the separate associations required on some of the items and the need to generate associates of a *different form* for the three stimulus-words, so that three identical associations are produced.

The reliability of the RAT appears to be quite satisfactory as compared with other tests of creative thinking. From samples of 215, 288, and 71 undergraduate and graduate university students, corrected odd-even reliability coefficients have been found to be .91, .92, and .86 respectively (Mednick & Mednick, 1967). The alternate-form reliability (Form 1 vs. Form 2) of the RAT (r = .81) was obtained from a sample of 71 undergraduate students (Mednick & Mednick, 1967).

In support of the RAT as a test of verbal creative thinking, the data are encouraging. As already noted in the section above, the selection of a meaningful criterion of creative thinking is exceedingly complex and operationally difficult. Various investigators have obtained positive correlations between the RAT and experts' rating of the creativeness of individuals. Mednick and Halpern (1962) obtained ratings of architecture students by instructors. The correlation between the test scores and the ratings was .70 ($N = 20$). Martha Mednick (1963) had advisors assess the research creativeness of student-advisees by completing a Thurstone-type checklist; the correlation between test scores and the checklist was .55 ($N = 43$). In this study, the correlations of the RAT with GPA and the Miller's Analogies Test were nonsignificant. Gordon (1966) reports a significant relationship between RAT scores and job-grade classifications of scientists in a chemical firm (Kendall's Q coefficient = .84, $p < .01$). Negative results were obtained by Andrews (1962) when RAT scores were compared with supervisors' ratings of the creativity of research personnel in several laboratories ($N = 214$). There appears generally to be a consistent relationship between RAT scores and the quantity and quality of products produced by scientists and engineers according to data summarized by Mednick and Mednick (1967).

Before coming to a conclusion on the validity of the RAT in the assessment of creative thinking, it is necessary to consider the degree to which it might simply be a measure of verbal intelligence. In the RAT manual, Mednick and Mednick (1967) report seven comparisons of this test with a variety of intelligence tests. With the exception of tests of mathematical ability, the RAT correlates with the intelligence measures in the low .40's. Correlations of this magnitude lead one to conclude that to whatever extent the RAT may be a measure of creativity, it is clearly sensitive to individual differences in intelligence.

CREATIVITY AS A CAPACITY

The third conceptualization of creativity emphasizes the *capacity* or *potential* of an individual to perform creatively. Creativity as a capacity is thus assumed to be a trait that is established early in life but that can be modified by later experience. One of the early conceptions of creativity as an ability was presented by Simpson (1922), who defined creative ability as the capacity of an individual to deviate from his stereotyped modes of thinking. Simpson argued that the creative person thinks in a way that is not tapped by traditional tests of intelligence; that tests should assess the searching and combinatorial thinking that leads to synthesis, in addition to the abilities to remember, to analyze, and to deduce. Currently, Guilford (1963, 1966) is the major proponent of the interpretation of creativity as a mental ability. Torrance (1962) is another leading investigator of creative ability, although his theoretical approach is more general than Guilford's and is concerned with creativity as a thinking *process* as well as an *ability*.

The Guilford Tests of Creative Ability

Guilford portrays creativity as a set of quantitatively defined factors (abilities) that are located within his three-dimensional "model of the intellect" (1956). His model is an attempt to represent, within a single system, all of the distinct abilities that comprise the human intellect. In operational terms, the organization of abilities is constructed through the factor analysis of many tests that are hypothesized to represent specific abilities. In these terms, an ability is an independent factor defined by the particular tests that have high loadings on that factor. In Guilford's model, creative abilities are classified largely in terms of divergent thinking applied to semantic contents, although other categories of thinking (convergent and evaluative), contents (symbolic and figural), and products (transformative) are also implicated. (A more detailed description of Guilford's model appears in Chapter II of this book.)

Due to the tremendous volume of research conducted by Guilford and his associates in developing and validating tests of creativity, it is not possible to review their data in any detail here. This discussion will be limited to a small sample of tests that represent four of Guilford's creativity factors. A more complete description of these and other tests has been presented by French, Ekstrom, and Price (1963). The dimension most directly concerned with creative abilities is Guilford's "Originality" factor—"the ability to produce remotely associated, clever, or uncommon responses [French et al., p. 30]." The test that shows the highest loading on this factor is Plot Titles, scored for "cleverness." This test comes in two parts, each part consisting of a story for which the subject must compose as many titles as he can. A second test defining Originality is Consequences, scored for the number of "remote" answers. The test lists a set of hypothetical situations, and the subject is to provide possible consequences for each.

A second creativity factor isolated by Guilford is Semantic Redefinition—"the ability to shift the function of an object and use it in a new way [French et al., 1963, p. 35]." The following three tests yield high loadings on this factor: Gestalt Transformations, Object Synthesis, and Picture Gestalt. Each of the items in Gestalt Transformations lists five common objects, only one of which will solve the problem. A sample problem is "TO START A FIRE—*a*. fountain pen, *b*. onion, *c*. pocket watch, *d*. light bulb, *e*. bowling ball." The correct answer is "*c*. pocket watch" (the glass cover to be used as a magnifying glass). Object Synthesis is a similar test requiring the subject to combine two different objects in a way that yields a third, useful object. For example, a volley ball and a steel spring can be combined to make a punching bag. In Picture Gestalt the subject is to determine which object in a series of photographs will serve a given purpose.

Another of Guilford's creativity factors is Figural Adaptive Flexibility—"the ability to change set in order to meet new requirements imposed by figural problems [French et al., 1963, p. 49]." Two tests that help to define this factor are Match Problems II and Match Problems V. Both tests were developed from the familiar puzzles that require the relocation of one or more matches to alter one rectilinear pattern to another. Match Problems V is slightly more difficult in that it requires the subject to provide more than one solution for each problem.

The last of the Guilford factors to be described here is Semantic Spontaneous Flexibility—"the ability to produce a diversity of verbally expressed ideas in a situation that is relatively unrestricted [French et al., 1963, p. 50]." One of the tests used to measure this factor is Alternate Uses. In this test the subject must list different uses that each of a series of common objects can have. A second test in this factor is Object Naming. The items on the test are class names (e.g., "mineral") for which the subject is to list as many objects as he can that are included in the class.

The Guilford tests function well in defining the structured intellect. The tests are brief (time limits vary from two to ten minutes), can be administered in large groups, and are highly specific in the kinds of abilities required for superior performance—qualities that are ideally suited for factor analysis. Guilford establishes the validity of each test by examining the intercorrelations and factor-loadings of the tests. A valid test is one that has a high loading on the factor predicted for it and that correlates minimally with tests representing other factors. Reliabilities are seldom as high as one would desire for tests designed for predictive purposes. The reliabilities for the tests described above are presented in Table 1. With few exceptions, the reliabilities are split-half correlations corrected by the Spearman-Brown formula, estimates of reliability that fail to indicate how stable test scores are over time.

Table 1

Reliability Coefficients for Selected Guilford Tests.

The entries in the table are alternate-form correlations except where otherwise indicated.

	SIZE OF SAMPLE							
	301[a]	208[b]	212[c]	230[d]	204[e]	229[f]	228[g]	206[h]
Plot Titles (clever)	.57[i]	.79	.80	.74	–	–	–	–
Consequences (remote)	–	.69	–	–	.45	.52	.57	.56
Gestalt Transformations	.51[i]	–	–	–	–	–	–	–
Object Synthesis	.72[i]	.61	–	–	–	–	–	–
Match Problems II	–	.65	–	–	.70	.72	.71	.62
Match Problems V	–	–	–	–	.64	.63	.66	.52
Alternate Uses	–	–	–	–	.62[i]	.85[i]	.76[i]	.78[i]
Object Naming	–	.47	–	–	–	–	–	–

[a]Combined sample of air cadets (Guilford, Wilson & Christensen, 1952).

[b]Sample of air cadets (Guilford, Frick, Christensen, & Merrifield, 1957).

[c]Sample of Coast Guard Academy cadets (Guilford, Christensen, Frick, & Merrifield, 1957).

[d]Sample of naval air cadets (Guilford, Christensen, Frick, & Merrifield, 1957).

[e]Sample of total-range-IQ junior high school students (Guilford, Merrifield, & Cox, 1961).

[f]Sample of middle-range-IQ boys (Guilford, Merrifield, & Cox, 1961).

[g]Sample of middle-range-IQ girls (Guilford, Merrifield, & Cox, 1961).

[h]Sample of high-IQ boys and girls (Guilford, Merrifield, & Cox, 1961).

[i]Odd-even reliabilities, corrected.

The Torrance Tests of Creative Thinking

While Guilford has conceived creative abilities as hypothetical constructs revealed in the form of intercorrelations among test scores, Torrance (1966b) has preferred to describe these abilities as differences in capacity among persons. Although Torrance began his investigation of creativity with some of the Guilford tests, he has recently developed his own battery of tests (including some modified Guilford tests) that are meant to represent miniature models of the total creative act. In addition, Torrance has been primarily concerned with the assessment of creativity in children; Guilford has been primarily interested in adults.

Torrance (1966b) defines creativity as:

a process of becoming sensitive to problems, deficiencies, gaps in knowledge, missing elements, disharmonies, and so on: identifying the difficulty; searching for solutions, making guesses, or formulating hypotheses about the deficiencies, testing and retesting these hypotheses and possibly modifying and retesting them; and finally communicating the results [p. 6].

For Torrance, an ideal test would be one that is sensitive to each of the operations implied in this definition. He has attempted to include in this investigation abilities not only of scientists and engineers, but also of authors, artists, musicians, and dancers.

The Torrance tests are of two types: verbal and figural. Like Guilford, he has constructed alternate forms (A and B) for each of his tests. From a battery of verbal and figural tests, each subject's performance is scored for fluency, flexibility, originality, and elaboration (although the verbal elaboration score is not considered useful). Torrance recommends the use of a total composite score for the assessment of an individual's creative ability.

The Torrance battery (Form A or Form B) comes in two booklets, one containing the verbal tests ("Thinking Creatively with Words"), and the other the figural tests ("Thinking Creatively with Pictures"). Since Forms A and B are parallel, only the tests in Form A will be described here. The first verbal test is called Ask-and-Guess and is presented in three parts: "Asking," "Guessing Causes," and "Guessing Consequences." The stimulus for the Ask-and-Guess test is a free-hand drawing of a pixie-like figure observing his reflection in a pool of water. In Part I ("Asking"), the subject is instructed to write out all of the questions he can think of about the picture. Questions are discouraged that can be answered simply by looking at the picture. In Part II of this test ("Guessing Causes"), the instructions are to list as many causes as possible of the action appearing in the picture. In Part III of the test the subject is asked to list as many consequences as possible of the activity depicted in the picture. Each part of Ask-and-Guess has a five-minute time limit.

The second verbal test is Product Improvement. The stimulus for this test is a sketch of a stuffed toy elephant. The instructions ask the subject to "... list the cleverest, most interesting and unusual ways you can think of for changing this toy elephant so that children will have more fun playing with it [Torrance, 1966*b*, p. 8]." For Product Improvement there is a ten-minute time limit.

Unusual Uses, the third test in the verbal battery, is a modification of Guilford's Brick Uses Test. The Torrance version of this test uses as stimuli cardboard boxes (tin cans in Form B) instead of bricks, since Torrance thinks that his stimuli are more appropriate for use with children. On the Unusual Uses test, the subject is asked to list as many interesting and unusual ways that empty cardboard boxes (or tin cans) can be used. This test also has a ten-minute time limit. Next comes the Unusual Questions test, which uses the same stimulus as Unusual Uses: the boxes. The subject is to write down as many questions as he can regarding the cardboard boxes—questions that will arouse interest and curiosity on the part of someone else. The time limit is five minutes.

The final test in the verbal set is Just Suppose, an adaptation of Guilford's Consequences. The stimulus for this test is a highly improbable situation (i.e., "JUST SUPPOSE clouds had strings attached to them which hang down to earth") for which the subject is to list ideas as to what he supposes would happen. As in all of the Torrance tests, the subject is encouraged to guess and to give unusual, imaginative answers. Just Suppose has a five-minute time limit.

There are only three tests in the Torrance figural booklet, each having a ten-minute time limit. The first figural test, Picture Construction, actually allows the subject to manipulate a stimulus with his hands. The subject is instructed to remove a brightly colored oval piece of paper, stick it on a blank page, and add lines to it to make a picture. The picture drawn is supposed to tell a story, and this is titled by the subject when it is complete. The second figural test, Picture Completion, contains ten boxes, each with a few irregular lines as stimuli. The subject is asked to add lines to the stimuli to make interesting objects or pictures. Again the drawings are titled by the subject. The last of the figural tests is Lines (Circles in Form B). This test contains thirty pairs of vertical parallel lines. The subject is to add lines to each pair so as to make as many different pictures of objects as possible. Testing time to administer both the verbal and figural tests is one hour and fifteen minutes, not including passing out booklets, giving instructions, and so forth.

The manual for the Torrance batteries (Torrance, 1966*b*) is an excellent presentation of relevant psychometric information. In addition to detailed information on the reliability and validity of the batteries, the manual contains an introduction to the theory and rationale lying behind the tests. Since the tests must be scored by hand, they are subject to scoring error. The criterion presented by Torrance for a qualified scorer is that the latter must succeed in producing scores for each of the subtests that correlate at least .90 with scores obtained from highly experienced personnel. Torrance (1966*a*) presents scoring reliabilities of six untrained educators who scored the verbal tests with only the aid of the scoring instructions. Mean scoring-reliability coefficients for these instructors were .96 (Fluency), .94 (Flexibility), .85 (Originality), and .90 (Elaboration). Similar correlations were computed for two educators scoring the figural tests. Mean scorer reliabilities for Fluency, Flexibility, and Originality from these two scorers were .99, .98, and .88 respectively.

A number of studies have been conducted assessing the reliability of the Torrance tests of creativity. In contrast to the data presented by Guilford, who prefers to use the split-half form of reliability, most of the data available on the reliability of the Torrance battery are test-retest stability coefficients. Torrance reports stability coefficients for the various scores on the verbal and figural batteries from two-week to three-year intervals (Table 2); and for three of the scores on three subtests (Unusual Uses, Circles, Product Improvement) and a total score on the Ask-and Guess test (Table 3), over intervals of from two weeks to six months. The reliability information presented in Tables 2 and 3 is incomplete and somewhat inconsistent. However, at the present stage of development of his battery, the data presented by Torrance and other investigators indicates that the scores obtained are moderately reliable for most of the subtests. His verbal tests seem to yield more stable scores than the figural tests, perhaps due to the longer length of the former.

The reliability information contributed by Mackler and Shontz (1967) deserves special note. In order to determine the effects of repeated administration upon scores obtained from some of the Torrance tests, these investigators presented the identical battery to the same subjects three different times, with two weeks between testings. Two verbal tests (Ask-and-Guess and Tin Cans) and two figural tests (Decorations and Circles) were administered to forty undergraduate women. Fluency, Flexibility, and Originality scores were

Table 2

Test-retest Stability Coefficients Obtained on Various Sub-scores on the Torrance Verbal and Figural Tests.

Coefficients are based on correlations between alternate forms (A and B) of the Torrance battery.

| | TEST-RETEST INTERVAL | | | | |
TEST SCORE	2 wks. (N=118)[a]	10 wks. (N=?)[b]	8 mos. (N=28)[c]	8 mos. (N=26)[d]	3 yrs. (N=43)[e]
VERBAL					
Fluency	.93	.82	.79	.59	.82
Flexibility	.84	.78	.84	.61	.35
Originality	.88	.59	.79	.73	.73
FIGURAL					
Fluency	.71	–	.50	.80	–
Flexibility	.73	–	.63	.64	–
Originality	.85	–	.60	.60	–
Elaboration	.83	–	.71	.80	–

[a]Torrance (1962); sample of fourth, fifth, and sixth grade children.

[b]Goralski, as reported by Torrance (1966b); sample of student teachers.

[c,d]Torrance (1962); sample of fifth grade children in creative writing experiment—experimental and controls, respectively.

[e]Dalbec (1966); sample of college students.

Table 3
Test-retest Stability Coefficients Obtained on Specific Torrance Tests.
Coefficients are based on scores obtained from alternate forms of each test.

TESTS	TEST-RETEST INTERVAL				
	2 wks. $(N=40)^a$	4 wks. $(N=40)^a$	10 wks. $(N=22)^b$	10 wks. $(N=22)^b$	6 mos. $(N=31)^c$
UNUSUAL USES					
Fluency	.61	.65	.75	.85	–
Flexibility	.62	.71	.60	.69	–
Originality	.71	.60	.64	.77	–
CIRCLES (Form B)					
Fluency	.72	.47	.76	–	–
Flexibility	.60	.60	.63	–	–
Originality	.63	.57	.79	–	–
PRODUCT IMPROVEMENT					
Fluency	–	–	.69	–	.85
Flexibility	–	–	.64	–	.76
Originality	–	–	.61	–	.68
ASK-AND-GUESS					
TOTAL	.82	.84	.83	–	–

[a]Mackler & Shontz (1967); sample of university students (see text).

[b]Yamamoto (1962); sample of college seniors.

[c]Rouse (1965); sample of mentally retarded children.

determined for each test. The intercorrelations *between* scores on a single test were noticeably higher than intercorrelations *within* scores across the four tests. Apparently the internal consistency of the Torrance tests is higher than the stability of the scores derived from the tests. Nevertheless, the test-retest correlations from time 1 to time 2 to time 3 were consistently high, ranging from coefficients of .47 to .89 (except for the Originality score from Decorations, wherein the correlations were as low as .09 between time 2 and time 3).

There is a growing body of literature that yields information on the validity of the Torrance tests. One recent study by Erikson (1966) was an attempt to predict future behavior from scores obtained from the Torrance battery. Sixty-six high school seniors were given the creativity tests, and five and one-half years later were given a check-list of creative behaviors. The check-list was completed while the students were graduate students. The results were disappointing. Correlations between total Fluency, Flexibility, Originality, and Elaboration scores and the check-list were quite low. Only one of these correlations was significant. When high- and low-creativity groups (determined by creativity test scores) were compared, however, a number of specific activities did differentiate the groups significantly.

A few validity studies have been reported that present correlations of the Torrance tests with various tests and ratings of academic success (Bish, 1964; Cicerelli, 1965; Edwards & Tyler, 1965; Duenk, 1966; Perry, 1966). These investigations are difficult to interpret in support of the Torrance tests as predictors of *creative* academic achievement, since the contribution of intelligence and motivation act as confounding variables.

In other studies, ratings of creativity by peers and teachers have been used as criteria of creativeness. With a sociometric device Yamamoto (1960, 1964*b*) obtained peer-nominations of fluency, flexibility, originality, elaboration, and inventiveness for 459 students in the seventh through the twelfth grades. The obtained correlations were quite low (average *r* approximately .24 for the entire sample). In other studies attempts have been made to predict differences between high- and low-creativity groups defined by teachers' ratings on the basis of scores from the Torrance batteries (Torrance, 1962, 1963; Yamamoto, 1962; Torrance & Myers, 1962; Torrance & Gupta, 1964; Nelson, 1963; Williams, 1965). In general, the results of these studies are positive: the test-scores of high and low groups are significantly different. The most consistently discriminating measures tended to come from verbal subtests and the Fluency, Flexibility, and Originality scores. Though positive, the results of these studies are again difficult to interpret; the correlations with peer nominations account for no more than five percent of the common variance, and the significance of difference between means predicted by the tests tells nothing about the amount of variance accounted for. In addition, the meaning and value of creativity nominations themselves have been strongly criticized (Wallach & Kogan, 1965*a*).

The largest body of data supporting the Torrance tests as valid measures of creativity is the set of studies that shows that these tests predictably differentiate individuals in terms of some of the personality, emotional, and attitudinal characteristics commonly associated with creativity. For a group of thirty-two high IQ fourth graders, Weisberg and Springer (1961) obtained ratings from psychiatric interviews. These ratings suggested that the subjects defined by the Torrance tests as high in creativity had "strength of self-image," "ease of early recall," a sense of humor, availability of "Oedipal anxiety," and uneven ego development. Torrance (1962) observed that the most creative boys and girls (determined on the basis of his tests) in each of twenty-three classes in the primary grades tended to produce "wild and silly ideas," made drawings that were nonconforming, and exhibited humor, playfulness, and a sense of relaxation. Sixty-eight "gifted" elementary school children were given the Torrance tests and the Frenkel-Brunswik Revised California Inventory, a measure of attitudinal rigidity. In this study, the creative children scored lower than noncreatives on the rigidity measure. Long and Henderson (1964) found among a sample of 327 second- through seventh-graders that the pupils scoring high on the Torrance battery were better able than the others to withhold their opinions when information was lacking, to tolerate uncertainty, and to resist preliminary closure.

Dauw (1965) investigated the attitudinal self-descriptions of 712 high school boys and girls separated into high- and low-creativity groups on the basis of the Torrance tests. The statements checked by the creative boys and girls that were not shared by the noncreative students included "adventurous," "willing to take risks," "sense of humor," and planning unconventional, creative careers. In addition, the creative girls described themselves as "desiring to excel," "competitive," "strongly emotional," and "nonconforming." Another group of 115 high school seniors, designated as "highly creative" by Torrance test scores, were given the Runner Studies of Attitudinal Patterns by Torrance and Dauw (1965a, 1965b). The results indicated that the creative students experience intense and prolonged periods of stress, and are concerned over being ridiculed, having restrictions placed on their freedom, and the pressures of time. Weiser (1962) analyzed the adjectives checked as self-descriptive of creative university students ($N = 282$). The creative undergraduates described themselves as adventurous, courageous, determined, energetic, humorous, individualistic, industrious, and versatile. One can conclude from these studies that the personality characteristics differentiating groups defined as creative by the Torrance tests are consistent with what is predicted from theory.

In one of the few validation studies of the Torrance tests using objective criteria of creative behavior, Wallace (1961, 1964) investigated the test performance of 61 saleswomen and 223 salesmen. The subjects were classified according to the sales departments within which they worked and their sales productivity. For the women, the mean test scores of subjects working in departments classified as "creative" (e.g., draperies, ladies' dresses) were significantly higher than subjects working in noncreative departments. Similar results were obtained for the men.

The data presented above on the validity of the Torrance tests of creativity are not exhaustive but do provide a representative picture of the usefulness of the tests for the assessment of creative behavior. In general, the conclusion one draws is in keeping with conclusions drawn in the evaluation of other tests of creativity: the Torrance tests do tap, at statistical levels of significance, a variety of behaviors that can be called creative. On the other hand, the *degree* to which the tests relate to intended criteria is either very low or indeterminant. A good part of the difficulty again is due to the inability to isolate a meaningful and objective criterion of creativity against which to validate the tests.

CREATIVITY AND THE WHOLE PERSON

The fourth general orientation towards creativity is centered on the *person*. Implicit in this approach is the rejection of the idea that creativity can be studied as a variable or set of variables isolated from the totality of an individual's personality. Creativity has been described by some theorists as a manifestation of the basic need of every individual to realize his potential as a complete and efficiently functioning human being. Goldstein (1939), Rogers (1959), and Maslow (1959) have labeled this process "self-actualization." Within the theoretical context of existential psychology, May

(1959) has suggested that the meaningful creative act can occur only when the individual makes a total commitment to some course of action. In general, theories of creativity that are stated in phenomenological terms have not generated active empirical research.

The commitment to the study of creativity as an aspect of the total individual, however, has not prevented empirical research in this area. A notable example is the investigation of creativity that is being conducted at the University of California's Institute of Personality Assessment and Research (IPAR). D. W. MacKinnon (1960), the director of IPAR, has described the institute's goals as follows: " . . . [IPAR's] express purpose was to develop further the assessment method for basic research into problems of personality development and dynamics, with special focus upon the characteristics of the effectively functioning person and the life history determinants of such effectiveness [p. 369]." A brief description of some of the methods used by IPAR in the study of creativity is presented below. (For a more detailed survey, see Barron, 1965.)

Among the first studies of creativity to emerge from IPAR was Barron's investigation of the personality dimension of "complexity-simplicity" (1953). In collaboration with G. S. Welsh, Barron constructed a simple test (the Barron-Welsh Art Scale) that was intended to assess the degree to which individuals have a need to perceive, and deal with, simple as opposed to complex stimuli. The stimuli in the Art Scale are a set of black and white nonrepresentational ink drawings, which the subject is to indicate whether he likes or not. The stimuli fall into two rather discrete classes: drawings that are regular, symmetrical, and precise, and those that are irregular, asymmetrical, and loosely drawn. Greater preference for the complex figures has been found for artists (Rosen, 1955), research scientists (Gough, 1961), architects, writers, and team members of the first American expedition to attempt Mount Everest (Barron, 1963), as compared to samples of subjects assumed to be less creative. Barron (1953) has found that preference for complexity as measured by the Art Scale is positively related to a number of dispositions characteristic of the creative person: verbal fluency, impulsiveness, expansiveness, independence of judgment, originality, and breadth of interest. On the other hand, negative correlations were found between preference for the complex figures and rigidity, control of impulses of repression, social conformity, ethnocentrism, and political-economic conservatism.

Barron (1955) has also studied a second dimension of creative behavior: originality. In this research, the emphasis was transferred from the originality of *responses* to the originality of *persons*. A composite measure of originality was constructed by combining scores from a variety of creativity tests. The composite score was correlated with staff ratings of 100 air force captains, $r = .55$. The composite score was used to form two extreme groups: Originals ($N = 15$) and Unoriginals ($N = 15$), on whom were obtained fourteen additional scores from tests, ratings, and inventories hypothesized to measure originality. In spite of the relative success of this study in developing an empirical measure of originality, the low intercorrelations between the variables contributing to the composite score emphasize the danger of expecting a test to assess even a single dimension of originality. The highest intercorrelation between the originality measures was .46 between two of the Guilford tests (Unusual Uses and Consequences); the median intercorrelation was .17.

Probably the unique contribution of IPAR in the assessment of creativity is the use of the "living-in" method of assessment, originally developed by the Office of Strategic Services in the training and evaluation of espionage agents during World War II. In addition to providing an opportunity to administer large batteries of tests during the days assessees spend at the Institute, the living-in technique makes it possible to obtain ratings of behavior over a period of days by highly trained personnel (MacKinnon, 1960). Three methods have been used to quantify staff observations of creative behavior: ratings of behavioral traits, Q-sort scaling of statements describing an individual's personal functioning, and the completion of an adjective checklist (Gough, 1960). Most of the research to be described below has been based in part upon this method of intensive study of individual subjects.

At IPAR, MacKinnon has attempted to gather information on the general characteristics of individuals varying on objective indices of creativeness. In keeping with the holistic concern with the individual, MacKinnon has drawn from dynamically-oriented personality theorists—in particular, Rank (MacKinnon, 1965). MacKinnon has conducted an intensive investigation of architectural creativity (1962a). Three groups of architects were invited to participate in the living-in program at IPAR. The most creative subjects (Architects I) were nominated by a panel of architectural experts, who chose forty eminent men in this field. A second matched group of subjects (Architects II), who were experienced associates of men in the most creative group, were also selected. A third matched group (Architects III), men inexperienced in the field, completed the total sample of 120 subjects.

The results of the architect study showed, on the basis of performance on a large battery of tests, that there were predicted differences in creativeness between the three samples of architects. A portion of these results will be summarized here. The allocation of subjects to the three groups on the basis of presumed level of creativeness appears to have been successful. Each of the subjects was rated by six groups of architectural experts. The differences between mean ratings among groups were all highly significant, thus ordering the groups in accordance with their designated levels of creativity. Many of the test results differentiated the groups at statistically significant levels of probability. On the other hand, the correlation between rated creativeness and intelligence (estimated from the Terman Concept Mastery Test) was essentially zero ($r = -.08$). The personality characteristics of the creative architects revealed by the performance on psychological inventories (the MMPI, CPI, and the Strong Vocational Interest Blank) present a consistent picture: "The more creative a person is, the more he reveals an openness to his own feelings and emotions, a sensitive intellect and understanding self-awareness, and wide-ranging interests including many which in the American culture are thought of as feminine [MacKinnon, 1962, p. 488]."

The empirical research on creativity conducted at IPAR has been both ambitious and fruitful. The varieties of studies conducted and the assessment procedure used make any kind of overall evaluation prohibitively difficult.

The diversified program of study at IPAR illustrates that deviations from the traditional testing model can contribute valuable assessment procedures in the investigation of creativity.

MAJOR PROBLEMS IN THE ASSESSMENT OF CREATIVITY

Some of the problems existing in the assessment of creativity have already been touched upon. Surely the most difficult and important of these problems is that of the isolation and quantification of meaningful criteria. Another problem is presented by the plethora of theories and definitions of creativity that recently have been proposed. The organization and integration of research that bears upon the assessment of creativity have been inhibited by the absence of a sufficiently general theoretical framework. More work is needed in the critical analysis of existing theoretical viewpoints, such as the analysis presented by Yamamoto (1964a), and in the construction of a more general theory that can integrate the existing theories and the research coming from them. One example of such an integrating theory has been proposed by Jackson and Messick (1965).

The standards by which new measures of creativity are compared are too often similar measures of creativity. It is only when methods that are proposed as measures of creativity are compared with standard tests of intelligence that the inadequacies of the former can be appreciated. Intelligence tests like the Stanford-Binet and the Wechsler scales are the results of years of continuing research. Only in the Torrance tests of creative thinking, and perhaps in the Remote Associates Test, is there even modest evidence of a similar commitment to careful test construction and adequate documentation. Even here, the creativity tests do not compare favorably. The reliabilities of intelligence tests are typically in the high .90's, while those of creativity tests are seldom greater than .70. The intercorrelation between two measures of intelligence are almost as high as their separate reliabilities, whereas the average correlation between tests of creativity is slightly above .30 (Wallach & Kogan, 1965a).

In defense of those who have attempted to construct measures of creativity, one can justifiably argue that the assessment of creativity involves rather different problems than the assessment of intelligence. The relatively poor showing of creativity tests can be attributed to a number of factors. One important difference between the two kinds of tests lies in the rationale underlying the scoring of responses to test items. For most of the items on an intelligence test there is a pre-established, correct response; the scorer's problem is to determine *how close* the testee's answer approximates the correct response. For the majority of items on creativity tests, however, there is no single, correct answer; often the number of correct answers is indeterminate. In practice, the scoring reliability of an intelligence test presents no problem; the best answers are the correct answers. The same is not the case with tests of creativity; the *best* answer has yet to be recorded. It is not surprising that unreliability of scoring contributes a noticeable proportion of error in most creativity tests.

The discussion comparing measures of creativity and intelligence cannot be terminated without considering the problem raised by Thorndike (1963), and Wallach and Kogan (1965*a*): Do creativity and intelligence tests measure, in fact, different domains of cognition? Considering pertinent data on tests constructed by Guilford, Torrance, and others, Wallach and Kogan concluded that the evidence fails to support the claim that standard creativity tests assess a unified domain of cognitive functioning that is different from that assessed by intelligence tests. This conclusion is based primarily upon three kinds of evidence: (*a*) the intercorrelations between intelligence test sub-scales are generally high, (*b*) the intercorrelations between different tests of creativity are generally low, (*c*) and the correlations between intelligence tests and creativity tests are typically of the same magnitude as intercorrelations between creativity tests themselves. This evidence leads Wallach and Kogan to conclude that tests purported to assess creativity do not reflect anything more than what is already assessed by intelligence tests. Wallach and Kogan imply that this state of affairs is due in part to the rigid adoption by the students of creativity of the test-construction model, so successfully used by those who have produced intelligence tests. In particular, these authors object to the use of the single-answer criterion of a correct response, the imposition of time limits, and the competitive atmosphere implied by "taking a test."

Wallach and Kogan attempted to rectify what they perceived as deficiencies in the construction and administration of creativity tests. In a study of 151 fifth-graders, they assessed creative behavior by a procedure that allowed subjects as much time as desired to complete each test item, that was introduced as a game, and that was described to the subjects in a way to minimize peer competition. Under these conditions, which appear to be more representative of the conditions under which creative behavior most often occurs, these authors found that the disturbing covariation between scores from intelligence and creativity tests was essentially zero (average of 100 r's = .09). On the other hand, the intercorrelations between creativity measures (average of 45 r's = .41) and between intelligence measures (average of 45 r's = .51) provided evidence of two independent dimensions of cognition that can be justifiably called "creativity" and "intelligence." Although the criticisms made of standard creativity tests by Wallach and Kogan are not without dispute (cf. Torrance, 1966*a*; p. 24 and p. 42*f*), their penetrating analysis has resulted in the very reasonable admonition that the model that should direct the construction of methods for the assessment of creativity should not be the intelligence-test model but the act of creation itself as it occurs outside of the testing situation.

A final problem to be considered here is the importance of motivation in creative behavior. Introspective accounts of creative activity recorded by great artists, writers, and scientists constantly reiterate the seeming ubiquitousness of an intense drive and dedication involved in creative efforts. Few students of creativity would agree that the creation of socially meaningful products occurs spontaneously and without effort. Those who have constructed tests to assess creative capacity assume that when subjects take the tests, motivation will be constant across subjects. An alternative assumption worthy of consideration is that there are wide individual differences in the capacity to become motivationally involved in creative activity. To be sure, the motivational characteristics of creativity have been studied by many investigators (e.g., Cattell, 1963a; Golann, 1962; MacKinnon, 1965; Maddi, 1965). However, in the validation of creativity tests, motivational factors have been generally neglected. The method of assessing creative potential designed by Wallach and Kogan (1965a), reviewed above, gives testimony to the importance of considering motivational variables as crucial determinants of test-taking behavior in the study of creativity.

CONCLUSION

In spite of the recent upsurge in research, the current status of instruments for assessing creativity is less than satisfactory. Evidence for the validity and reliability of creativity measures fails so far to promote much confidence in their use in assessing specific components of creativity. To end this chapter on a positive note, however, it should be recognized that the empirical study of creativity is a relatively new psychological field, and pessimistic conclusions regarding the present assessment of creativity must be tempered by an optimistic look toward the future.

CHAPTER IV

An interpreter's syllabus for the
California Psychological Inventory

Harrison G. Gough

The California Psychological Inventory (CPI) is intended for diagnosis and evaluation of individuals, with emphasis upon interpersonal behavior and dispositions relevant to social interaction. Although great care was taken in the development of the test and preparation of the manual (Gough, 1957, 1964), so that interpretation of scale scores and profile patterns would not be unduly difficult, the diagnostic implications of the profile are not always self-evident; for this reason it is important that scores on the test be interpreted by a competent psychologist who has become familiar with this particular device. Validity-in-use is not something that resides purely in the inventory itself; it is an outcome that derives from the interpreter's skill and insight in making manifest what is inherent in the instrument.

The CPI contains 480 true-false items, which can be administered either individually or in group testing. The items are printed in an eleven-page booklet, and a special answer sheet is used. The subject reads each item, decides whether he agrees or disagrees with what is said, and then marks *true* or *false* on the answer sheet. If a subject prefers not to answer certain items, he may leave them blank. Testing time, including the reading of instructions, is ordinarily about a class hour in schools and colleges, or about forty-five minutes in individual testing.

No special controls or restrictions are necessary for valid administration of the test. Subjects may begin at one session, and finish at another. Items may be read aloud, or explained if questions are asked. Completion of the test may occur under supervision, or a subject may be allowed to work on his own. The inventory has even been used on a mail-out/mail-in basis (cf. MacKinnon, 1962*b*) with successful results.

Reading ability at the fourth-grade level or higher is required if the questionnaire is to be administered silently. However, with poor readers or in situations where greater control is needed, the items may be read aloud with listeners recording their responses after each item has been heard (cf. Bennett & Rudoff, 1957). Age of the respondent is a factor which should also be mentioned. Although parts of the inventory have been used with grade school children (Reckless, Dinitz, & Kay, 1957), testing with the complete instrument may not be fully valid prior to the seventh grade. From the junior high school level (cf. Keimowitz & Ansbacher, 1960; Lessinger & Martinson, 1961; Pierce, 1961), through high school (Davids, 1966; Snider, 1966) and college (Aiken, 1963b; Holland, 1959; Johnson & Frandson, 1962), across educational levels (Schendel, 1965), and on into adult life (Canter, 1963; Goodstein & Schrader, 1963; Gough, 1966a; Howell, 1966) and even old age (Schaie, 1959), the inventory is capable of yielding valid findings.

At present, the inventory is scaled and profiled for 18 variables. Items in each scale are assigned unit weights (0-1), and raw scores are converted to standard scores (separate norms for males and females) with means of 50 and standard deviations of 10. The purpose of each scale is *to predict what an individual will do in a specified context*, and/or *to identify individuals who will be described in a certain way*. These aims are important both theoretically and practically, and should be distinguished from the more common goal in inventory measurement of trait specification. If a scale is intended to define a unidimensional trait of personality, then it must meet minimal statistical requirements of internal homogeneity, domain reliability, and factorial independence. However, if the purpose of a scale is to forecast what a person will say or do, and/or how he will be described by those who know him well, then these statistical considerations become relevant if, and only if, it can be shown that the predictive utility of the measure is improved by their fulfillment.

Reference to another well-known test, the Strong Vocational Interest Blank (Strong 1943) may help to make clear what is being said. An occupational scale on the Strong, such as minister, is not intended to define a personality trait of ministerialism, but rather to identify individuals whose outlook resembles those in the profession and who might (therefore) feel at home in the indicated environment. Similarly with the CPI, a high score on a scale for social status does not mean that the individual tested has a "trait" of high status, but rather that in viewpoint and outlook he tends to resemble people of high status; presumably, therefore, he may be already of high status, or possessed of those talents and dispositions that will lead him toward such attainment.

The significance of the point that is being emphasized lies principally in the kind of evidence to which one should turn for an evaluation of the worth of the measure. For the scales of the CPI this evidence should come from the context of application: do the scales for achievement motivation forecast scholastic attainment, does the scale for dominance predict ascendant behavior, does the scale for socialization forecast behavior on parole or in other settings where observance of rules and prohibitions is essential, and does the scale for social presence identify people who are at ease, self-assured, and natural in their dealings with others?

CHOICE OF CONCEPTS

A key decision in the development of any measuring instrument is the choice of concepts. Frequently, the appeal of the test developer is to a theory or partial theory of personality, and scales are constructed that relate to traits or dispositions assigned central significance in the theory. For example, an Adlerian might seek to develop a scale for "inferiority," as this constellation of feelings would for him be basic in any diagnosis; or, a student of Durkheim might wish to work with a measure of "anomie," and all that it would imply about alienation and disaffection in the life setting.

Another way to proceed in choosing concepts is, more or less, to let the evidence speak for itself. A factor analysis of a broad range of self-descriptive statements could be conducted, and any internal clusters or themes that emerged could be studied and named so as to illuminate their inferred content. Or, clear and obvious features of the test stimuli could be classified and a score defined as the number of times an individual based his answer on them.

Both of the approaches briefly sketched above are frequently encountered in testing, and the reader should have little difficulty in thinking of many standard tests of each type. As examples, we could cite the Study of Values (Allport, Vernon, & Lindzey, 1960), based on the theoretical position of Spranger (1914), to illustrate the first approach, and the Sixteen Personality Factor Questionnaire (Cattell, 1950) to illustrate the second. Another example of the second approach is the score on preference for asymmetrical designs in the Welsh Figure Preference Test (Welsh, 1959).

A third approach to the choice of concepts is that which draws directly on the context of usage. If an instrument is to be applied in vocational guidance and occupational choice, then a plausible basis for scaling would be found in the jobs that clients would tend to seek. The Strong Vocational Interest Blank illustrates this approach, as it is scaled for the kinds of lifework that college students tend to anticipate—e.g., physician, lawyer, engineer, banker, personnel manager, etc.

Another illustration may be taken from the domain of psychiatric practice. If a test is intended for use in the hospital and psychiatric clinic, then a justifiable rationale would be to develop scales for the diagnostic concepts that are in functional usage in these settings. The Minnesota Multiphasic Personality Inventory (Hathaway & McKinley, 1943), scaled for such syndromes as hysteria, paranoia, and schizophrenia, is based on this principle.

The theoretical basis for the choice of concepts in the CPI is of this third type. Because the instrument is intended for the diagnosis and comprehension of interpersonal behavior, the concepts selected are those that occur in everyday social living and, in fact arise from social interaction. Most simply, such variables may be described as "folk concepts"—aspects and attributes of interpersonal behavior that are to be found in all cultures and societies, and that possess a direct and integral relationship to all forms of social interaction.

Assuming that valid measures of such folk concepts can be developed, important theoretical and practical advantages of an inventory incorporating them would then follow. One of these advantages is an immediate relevance for cross-cultural measurement. If, for example, self-control is a universal variable in interpersonal living, and if in fact all societies and all cultures recognize this variable as well as individual differences in its expression, then a scale developed in any one culture has at least presumptive relevance for the diagnosis of behavior in any other culture.

Many technical problems of measurement immediately come to mind, and of course such relevance must be empirically confirmed and not just assumed. Nonetheless, the wisdom of beginning with folk concepts is that from the very inception of measurement one seeks cross-cultural relevance and validity. A clear and unequivocal goal of the CPI, it may be stated, is to provide measures that retain their validity in cross-cultural application; and the intensive efforts that have been expended in cross-cultural testing follow directly from this theoretical emphasis (cf. Adis Castro, 1957; De Grada, Ercolani, & Terreri, 1966; Gendre, 1964, 1966; Gough, 1964c, 1965b, 1966b; Gough & Sandhu, 1964).

A second advantage in working with folk concepts as a basis for scaling is that the variables are meaningful and readily comprehended by the user. Any scale will carry latent and potential implications, which the skilled interpreter must learn to appreciate, but at the same time no special instruction or insight is required to recognize the main thrust of scales seeking to appraise such interpersonal qualities as dominance, sociability, responsibility, tolerance, social presence, and flexibility.

A third advantage lies in what might be called the power of these folk variables. Deriving from interpersonal living and tied to consistent and characteristic modes of reaction, they can in turn validly forecast future behavior in the same context. Put as a research hypothesis, the assertion is that scales and combinations of scales on the CPI will be of value in forecasting longitudinal and/or remote criteria as well as immediate and current behavior. These theoretical considerations underlie the great emphasis given to longitudinal study of the inventory, as, for example, in the prediction of graduation from high school (Gough, 1966c), success versus failure on parole over a three-year period (Gough, Wenk, & Rozynko, 1965), choice of major field in college (Goldschmid, 1965), choice of medical specialty (Domino, 1967), and adult social adjustment on the basis of personality testing in adolescence (Stewart, 1962).

To summarize the above, we may say that the theoretical basis for scaling in the CPI is found in the ongoing processes of everyday social life, more specifically in what may be called folk concepts. This emphasis insures the relevance of the inventory to problems and issues in interpersonal behavior, and for validation points unmistakably to cross-cultural, longitudinal, and life-centered inquiry. The purpose of each scale is to reflect to a maximum degree some theme or aspect of interpersonal behavior—one that has clear visibility and is conceptually recognized by all people, everywhere. The desideratum for the set of scales is that any social behavior, of whatever variety, can be forecast and comprehended by either a single scale of the inventory or by some simple and meaningful combination of scales.

INDIVIDUAL SCALES

Discussion such as that which has been presented in the preceding section is important background for anyone using a personality inventory, but more central to his needs will be a detailed account of the clinical and other implications inherent in the scales of the instrument. The interpreter, that is to say, must know the theory and background of the inventory, but he must also know what behaviors to expect and what descriptions to invoke when his client scores high or low on a single scale or pattern of scales. An understandable progression in presenting such information is from single scales to combinations, and therefore in this section an attempt will be made to offer information on each of the 18 scales of the inventory that will be of value to the interpreter.

1. *Do* (Dominance)

The dominance scale was developed to identify individuals who would behave in a dominant, ascendant manner, who in interpersonal situations would take the initiative and exercise leadership, and who would be seen as forceful, self-confident, and capable of influencing others. In various groups where individuals knew each other well, nominations of "high dominant" and "low dominant" subjects were obtained, and then responses to individual items of the inventory were correlated with these nominations. In its present form, the scale contains 46 items, each diagnostic of this constellation of attributes and behavioral implications.

To interpret the scale, several points must be kept in mind. First, although the term "dominance" may suggest negative or "domineering" dóminance, the scale is almost entirely free of such connotations. High scorers on *Do* are constructively dominant, and one of the cardinal features of their own introspections is an appeal to socially valid and worthwhile goals as a way of justifying their (occasionally) coercive behavior toward others. Dominance, in other words, is not an end in itself but a means by which one's group can be influenced toward more rational and more moral actions.

In certain settings, one can see, the high scorer may choose to follow rather than lead, and in so doing will dedicate himself to carrying out the wishes and mandates of the leader with the same indefatigable purposiveness that he displays on those occasions when he himself is in command. A very interesting study by Megargee, Bogart, and Anderson (1966) provided evidence on just this point. In task-oriented dyads there was no systematic tendency for high-dominant subjects to assume control; however, when instructions stressed the appraisal of initiative and leadership, 18 of 20 high-dominant subjects took command of the two-person situation.

The descriptions given to high-dominant and low-dominant individuals by peers also afford a basis for conceptualization of the measure.[1] In three fraternities at the University of California, students were tested with the CPI,

---

[1] For a general discussion of the theoretical rationale underlying this method of conceptualizing diagnostic variables see Gough (1965a).

and then each subject was described on the Adjective Check List (Gough & Heilbrun, 1965) by five peers. If an adjective was checked by one observer, a score of 1 was assigned to the subject on that attribute; if three checked the word, the subject's score became 3. If all five observers checked the word, and if in addition three of these observers double-checked the word (to indicate its centrality in characterizing the subject), then the score became eight. There were 101 students in the sample, and in the way indicated each student was given a score on each of the 300 descriptions in the Check List. Similar data were available for 92 females from two University of California sororities, and adjectival totals were likewise computed for them.

By correlating the 300 descriptions with the *Do* scale, for males and females separately, patterns of relationships were specified. The yield of coefficients in each sample significant at or beyond the .05 level of probability for *Do*, and for each of the remaining 17 scales, was typically from 50 to 75 (whereas 15 would be expected by chance). To present all of these words would defeat the purpose of the analysis, which is to bring into focus the major descriptive themes attaching to each scale. For convenience in reporting, and also so as to enhance the diagnostic clarity of each scale, only the 20 most highly correlating descriptions (10 for each sex) will be listed in each discussion.

For the *Do* scale, high-scoring students were differentially characterized by the following words:

Males: ambitious, dominant forceful, optimistic, planful, resourceful, responsible, self-confident, stable, stern.

Females: aggressive, bossy, conceited, confident, demanding, dominant, forceful, quick, strong, talkative.

The high scorer on the *Do* scale, as one would expect, is seen as dominant, forceful, and self-confident, able to define his goals and to move resolutely toward their attainment. Neither the high-scoring man or woman seems particularly conciliatory or the kind of person before whom one would wish to admit weakness or personal shortcomings.

From this adjectival evidence, and from what has been gathered elsewhere, we may attempt a brief summary of the high scorer on dominance: if male, the high scorer will be forceful, resolute, sure of his goals and their philosophical and moral worth, and inexorable in his demands upon self and others. In most settings, his impact on others will be constructive (although not always welcomed), but in certain situations and in instances of self-deception and/or rejection of order, this influence can become disruptive. The high-scoring female is equally strong, but more likely to be coercive. She wears her mantle more aggressively and is more impatient with those who delay or obstruct her progress.

The descriptions of low-scoring subjects were these:

Males: apathetic, indifferent, interests narrow, irresponsible, pessimistic, restless, rigid, reckless, suggestible, submissive.

Females: cautious, gentle, inhibited, peaceable, quiet, reserved, shy, submissive, trusting, unassuming.

The low-scoring male is not just the opposite of the high-scoring. He is, to be sure, less steadfast, less convinced of his own rectitude and destiny, but he is not necessarily any more comfortable with things as they are. The low-scoring female, however, is far more at ease in her status, more acquiescent, and more trusting of what her high-dominant peers will initiate. The low-dominant male is less certain of his role, at times apathetic and indifferent but at others impulsive and erratic. He resists change, but then changes recklessly. Others may gain ascendancy over him, but will seldom win his loyalty; he remains pessimistic, dubious, and uninvolved.

2. Cs (Capacity for Status)

The Capacity for Status scale was also developed empirically, by correlating individual items with an external criterion of status (Gough, 1948, 1949b). The 32-item index attempts to appraise those qualities of ambition and self-assurance that underlie, and lead to, status. Status, it might be interjected, refers to the relative level of income, education, prestige, and power attained in one's sociocultural milieu. Hierarchy is observed in all groups, and status is therefore a concept of universal meaning.

Three themes in the items constituting the Status scale help to illuminate its basis of measurement. One of these deals explicitly with feelings of self-confidence, and a conviction that success can be anticipated both in the present and in the future. A second expresses a somewhat bemused or detached view of the ordinary constraints on behavior that are to be found in any culture; that is, a distinction is made between private and public morality. A third centers on social poise, a feeling of being able to meet stress and unforeseen circumstances without anxiety or self-doubt.

In the samples of 101 college males and 92 college females, the peer descriptions of high scorers on Cs were these:

Males: discreet, forgiving, imaginative, independent, mature, opportunistic, pleasant, praising, progressive, reasonable.

Females: alert, clear-thinking, forceful, individualistic, ingenious, insightful, intelligent, interests wide, logical, versatile.

Both clusters are favorable, although the words opportunistic for males and individualistic for females are not altogether attractive. The picture of the high scorer as a person freely responsive to his environment and able to extract advantage from it is nonetheless clear.

The emphasis of the Cs scale on factors underlying status attainment raises the interesting question of apparent contradictions between potential and achieved status. What might be said, for example, about subjects high on Cs but low on "actual" status? Two studies (Gough, 1949a; Pierce-Jones, 1961) have been devoted to this question, and both revealed upward mobility to be associated with the discrepancy as stated; for subjects above average on current status but below average on Cs, downward mobility may be forecast.

For the low-scoring college students, these descriptions were observed:

Males: bitter, gloomy, greedy, interests narrow, nagging, resentful, restless, tense, touchy, unkind.

Females: absent-minded, cautious, meek, mild, retiring, shy, simple, submissive, timid, weak.

Both clusters are unfavorable, with a kind of petulance and dispiritedness among the males versus resignation and acquiescence among the females.

Tuddenham (1959), indeed, did find a correlation of $-.51$ and $-.33$ between the Cs scale and independence in two samples of females studied in an experiment on pressure to conform to an incorrect consensus.

3. Sy (Sociability)

The criterion for selection of the 36 items in the Sy scale was their correlation with various indices of social participation. Higher scores on the scale identify individuals of outgoing, participative temperament who seek out and enjoy social encounter. Low scores identify individuals who avoid involvement and who tend to fear or dislike social visibility.

High scorers in the college samples were described as follows:

Males: clever, confident, interests wide, logical, mature, outgoing, reasonable, resourceful, self-confident, sociable.

Females: aggressive, confident, dominant, energetic, flirtatious, intelligent, interests wide, outgoing, sociable, talkative.

Both males and females are seen as sociable and expressive, and as having a wide range of interests. Some psychologists would anticipate a factor of shallowness and superficiality in any measure of sociability (or extraversion), but this element does not seem to be present in the Sy scale. Sociability, as assessed by the Sy scale, seems to derive from a healthy, energetic interest in life and from a degree of resourcefulness and confidence sufficient to sustain a high level of interpersonal activity.

These impressions may be contrasted with the descriptions given of low scorers:

Males: awkward, bitter, cold, complaining, confused, hard-hearted, interests narrow, quitting, shallow, unkind.

Females: cautious, inhibited, meek, modest, quiet, retiring, shy, timid, unassuming, withdrawn.

A difference appears in the patterns of reaction for low-scoring males versus low-scoring females. The males seem to be disaffected, even embittered, whereas the females seem simply subdued and even inert.

4. Sp (Social Presence)

The 56-item Sp scale was constructed "rationally"; that is, items were identified that appeared to embody diagnostic implications for social poise, verve, and spontaneity. A total score based on some 85 such items was computed in several samples of males and females, and then each item was correlated with this score. Once the items having highest internal validity had been selected, the 56-item scale was evaluated against external (nontest) criteria.

For example, in a sample of 70 applicants to the University of California School of Medicine, scores on the Sp scale correlated $+.43$ with ratings of "social presence" assigned by a panel of psychologists who had studied the applicants in interviews and other interpersonal situations. In five high schools, principals nominated boys and girls highest and lowest on "social presence." The average score on Sp for 52 boys nominated as "high" was 35.5, versus an average of 30.1 for 52 boys nominated as "low" (the difference between the means is significant well beyond the .01 level of probability); for girls the means for 51 high-nominated versus 51 low-nominated were 34.7 and 30.1.

Support for the inference of spontaneity may be found in a study by Banissoni (1967). She administered the Italian edition of the CPI to 59 students at the University of Rome, and also had these students observe a brief film in which the drawing of a rabbit was altered in a step-by-step manner until it became a duck. Students were asked to record their impressions at seven-second intervals. A correlation of +.47 was obtained between the number of changes of perception and scores on the *Sp* scale.

In the college samples, high-scoring students were described in this way:

Males: adventurous, interests wide, pleasure-seeking, relaxed, self-confident, sharp-witted, unconventional, uninhibited, versatile, witty.

Females: adventurous, daring, flirtatious, mischievous, outgoing, pleasure-seeking, spontaneous, versatile, ingenious, witty.

The aim of the scale—to identify individuals who will manifest verve, spontaneity, wit, and caprice in their social behavior—appears to have been fulfilled.

Low scorers were described in this way:

Males: appreciative, cautious, cooperative, interests narrow, kind, mannerly, patient, prudish, serious, shy.

Females: cautious, conventional, fearful, gentle, reserved, retiring, sensitive, submissive, timid, withdrawn.

The low scorer on *Sp* is more compliant, more conforming, less likely to intrude or force himself upon others, and more hesitant and uncertain in his social actions.

5. *Sa* (Self-acceptance)

The 34-item *Sa* scale was also developed by rational means, with a preliminary pool of diagnostic items first chosen and then reduced to scale length by correlating each with a total score based on the full initial set. The goal of this analysis was to identify individuals who would manifest a comfortable and imperturbable sense of personal worth, and who would be seen as secure and sure of themselves whether active or inactive in social behavior.

However, the adjectival analyses in the college samples introduce a new facet into this picture:

Males: confident, enterprising, egotistical, imaginative, opportunistic, outgoing, polished, self-confident, self-seeking, sophisticated.

Females: adventurous, argumentative, bossy, demanding, determined, dominant, outgoing, sarcastic, talkative, witty.

The new element is one of egocentrism—with high-scorers being viewed as demanding, egotistical, opportunistic, and bossy. Self-confidence and determination are part of the syndrome, but there are also clear manifestations of narcissism and indifference to others.

A possible advantage in this particular constellation is the ability to withstand stress. In a study of the reactions of 35 males and 35 females to an acutely stressful film, it was found that high scorers on *Sa* revealed distinctly less autonomic nervous system turbulence than did low scorers (Lazarus, Speisman, Mordkoff, & Davison, 1962).

This emergent theme in the implications of high scores on *Sa* requires emphasis, as similar phenomena will be encountered in later scales of the inventory (and have also been present, to some extent, in prior scales). The relationship between scores on the scales of the CPI and adequacy or effectiveness of interpersonal behavior is not always rectilinear, or even monotonic. That is, on some scales the optimum score will not be the highest score, and an individual with a very high score might be as out of phase with his culture as a person with a very low score. On the *Sa* scale, for example, a moderate elevation probably points toward a beneficial level of self-satisfaction and internal harmony, but a very high score (standard score of 70 or above) will suggest egotism, manipulative behavior toward others, and even narcissism as a defense against unconscious feelings of self-rejection.

Low scorers on the *Sa* scale in the college samples were described in this manner:

Males: bitter, commonplace, interests narrow, quitting, reckless, submissive, tense, unintelligent, withdrawn, self-denying.

Females: cautious, conventional, gentle, mild, modest, patient, peaceable, shy, trusting, unassuming.

As has occurred before, the patterns of behavior are different for low-scoring males and females. The low-scoring male is ill at ease, discontented with his status, and querulous; the low-scoring female is shy, unobtrusive, and patient.

6. *Wb* (Sense of Well-being)

The 44-item *Wb* scale was constructed empirically, by contrasting the responses of psychiatric patients with experimental subjects attempting to feign anxiety and personal distress. One goal of the scale, therefore, is to identify protocols in which an undue emphasis has been put upon personal problems and negative sentiments. For 354 protocols gathered under conditions of dissimulation, an average score of 11.8 was observed. For a sample of 915 psychiatric patients the average was 34.8, and for a sample of approximately five thousand students and adults, the average of 37.2. Scores of 29 and below, therefore, are suggestive of at least some overemphasis upon worries and personal problems.

However, the *Wb* scale also has diagnostic meaning for normal (i.e., not falsified) protocols. Elevated scores should indicate a sense of good health and a feeling of being equal to the demands for time and energy that are encountered in everyday social living. Low scores, conversely, should betoken a diminished reserve of energy and a feeling of unwillingness or recalcitrance in facing interpersonal demands.

In our samples of college students, high scorers were described in this way:

Males: conservative, dependable, dependent, good-natured, inhibited, logical, pleasant, poised, praising, relaxed, sincere.

Females: calm, capable, clear-thinking, fair-minded, informal, mature, obliging, poised, rational, wise.

High scorers are seen as better-humored and more fair-minded, but there is also a hint of greater conformity and conservatism. The high scorer on *Wb*, it would seem, is comfortable enough with himself and his status, but perhaps too obliging and passive to innovate or take decisive action even where indicated.

The low scorers were described with these terms:

Males: anxious, blustery, distractible, forgetful, hurried, impulsive, mischievous, quitting, shallow, restless.

Females: awkward, defensive, fault-finding, hard-headed, opinionated, sarcastic, self-pitying, tactless, unconventional, unstable.

The low scorer on *Wb* is at odds with himself and with others. He dwells on his problems, commiserates with himself, and resents circumstances more favorable than his.

7. *Re* (Responsibility)

The Responsibility scale was developed empirically, by selecting items revealing significant correlations with ratings of responsibility in several different groups of males and females. The present version of the scale includes 42 items, touching on such issues as civic responsibility, self-discipline, and fiscal integrity. The purpose of the scale is to identify people who are articulate about rule and order, and who believe that life is best if governed by reason.

The high-scoring males and females in the college samples were described as follows:

Males: capable, conscientious, dependable, reasonable, reliable, responsible, serious, stable, steady, thorough.

Females: conscientious, cooperative, discreet, foresighted, insightful, planful, reasonable, reliable, tactful, responsible.

These two portraits may be contrasted with the descriptions given of the low-scoring students:

Males: careless, disorderly, forgetful, irresponsible, lazy, mischievous, pleasure-seeking, reckless, show-off, spendthrift.

Females: arrogant, awkward, bitter, careless, hard-headed, lazy, obnoxious, rebellious, restless, sarcastic.

There is similarity between the two lists, but the characterization of the low-scoring female on *Re* is harsher than that of the low-scoring male. In both instances, the low-scorer is seen as lazy, careless, and likely to behave in an impulsive or improvident way.

8. *So* (Socialization)

The *So* scale is undoubtedly the most thoroughly studied scale in the inventory. Originally developed empirically to identify individuals of asocial, delinquent disposition, and highly valid in this function both in the United States and in extensive cross-cultural application (cf. Gough, 1965*b*), *So* has also been shown to relate significantly to a wide variety of criteria—e.g., academic achievement among college students of unusually high ability (Holland, 1959), the occurrence of career interests among high school girls (Tyler, 1964), performance in mechanical work (Gendre, 1966), graduation from high school (Gough, 1966*c*), unselfish behavior (Turner, 1963), and (but this time with lower scores) creativity in writing, architecture, and mathematics (Barron, 1965).

The scale seeks to classify people along a continuum of socialization, proceeding from highly asocial and criminal dispositions at one end to highly socialized and rule-respecting inclinations at the other. Low scorers tend to be unperceptive concerning the inner needs and feelings of others, little guided by interpersonal nuances, and given to rash and precipitate behavior. High scorers are responsive to what others feel and think, prudent, circumspect, and habitually in accord with the obligations of interpersonal life. Although there are sex differences on the scale (women score higher), the available evidence suggests little relationship with either race (Donald, 1955; Peterson, Quay, & Anderson, 1959) or intelligence (Gough, 1965a).

Cluster analysis of the 54 items in the scale (Stein, Gough, & Sarbin, 1966) revealed three major components: (a) stable home and school adjustment versus waywardness and dissatisfaction with family; (b) optimism and trust in others versus dysphoria, distrust, and alienation; and (c) observance of convention versus asocial dispositions and attitudes.

In the college samples, high-scorers were described as follows: ○

Males: adaptable, efficient, honest, inhibited, kind, organized, reasonable, sincere, thorough, wholesome.

Females: cautious, clear-thinking, conservative, organized, practical, reasonable, reliable, self-controlled, unassuming, wise.

Although only two words appear in both descriptions ("organized" and "reasonable"), the portraits are nonetheless similar. The high scorer on *So* is seen by his peers as reliable, honest, trustworthy, and adaptable.

Descriptions given of low scorers were these:

Males: deceitful, defensive, headstrong, irresponsible, mischievous, outspoken, quarrelsome, rude, sarcastic, unconventional.

Females: defensive, careless, fickle, foolish, impulsive, outspoken, peculiar, pleasure-seeking, reckless, uninhibited.

9. *Sc* (Self-control)

The 50-item *Sc* scale was constructed rationally, by gathering items that appeared to relate to expression of impulse and the management of aggression, and then correlating each with a total score based on the complete initial set. At the high end, the scale was intended to reflect over-control, too much suppression of impulse, and too great an involvement in the dampening and restraint of individuality. At the low end, the scale was intended to reflect under-control, quick and even explosive response to frustration or annoyance, and a tendency to react aggressively to threat or interference.

It is clear that the management of impulse and the control of hostility are problems for both high and low scorers: it is only the strategy of control that differs. Thus, a high scorer may be expected to break through his controls now and then, and to behave in a hostile or vengeful manner; and a low scorer may be expected, at times, to seek suppression of impulse and then to behave in a curiously inert or seemingly inappropriate way. The optimum score, one might think, would be near the midpoint of the distribution (30 to 31). However, the optimum will depend on the values of the interpreter. If social stability, reduction of interpersonal friction, harmony, etc., are esteemed, then an optimum raw score would be about 35; if innovation, spontaneity, and zest in confronting and proposing social change are favored, the optimum would be closer to 25.

In the college samples, high scorers were described in this way:

Males: considerate, dependable, hard-headed, logical, painstaking, precise, reasonable, reliable, self-controlled, self-denying.

Females: calm, conservative, gentle, moderate, modest, patient, peaceable, quiet, reserved, self-controlled.

The mixture of favorable and unfavorable qualities that one would anticipate in the descriptions is in fact observed: high scorers are indeed self-controlled, dependable, and peaceable, but they are also hard-headed and self-denying.

Adjectives correlating negatively with the *Sc* scale, hence characteristic of low scorers, were these:

Males: conceited, fault-finding, hasty, headstrong, impulsive, individualistic, self-seeking, spunky, temperamental, unrealistic.

Females: adventurous, aggressive, arrogant, excitable, impulsive, rebellious, restless, sarcastic, temperamental, uninhibited.

The explosive, willful quality that was sought in constructing the scale seems to be present in these descriptions. The low scorer is seen as headstrong, aggressive, excitable, and temperamental.

10. *To* (Tolerance)

The Tolerance scale was constructed as a subtle or indirect measure of the authoritarian personality syndrome assessed directly by the well-known California F-scale (Adorno, Frenkel-Brunswik, Levinson, & Sanford, 1950). Personality inventory items were correlated with the *E* (ethnocentrism) and *F* (authoritarianism) scales; 32 that revealed significant relationships were chosen for the *To* scale (Gough, 1951).

The *To* scale is intended to reflect benign, progressive, and humanitarian sentiments at one end versus feelings of hostility, estrangement, and disbelief at the other. The typical correlation of *To* with the *F*-scale is −.50.

High scorers in the college samples were described as follows:

Males: forgiving, generous, good-natured, independent, informal, pleasant, reasonable, soft-hearted, thoughtful, unselfish.

Females calm, efficient, insightful, leisurely, logical, mature, responsible, self-controlled, tactful, understanding.

The descriptions of low scorers were these:

Males: affected, cold, egotistical, fussy, hard-hearted, self-centered, shallow, thankless, whiny, fault-finding.

Females: arrogant, autocratic, bitter, defensive, distrustful, hard-headed, infantile, resentful, restless, sarcastic.

11. *Gi* (Good Impression)

The 40-item *Gi* scale has two functions. One of these is to identify protocols in which the respondent has made too strong an attempt to present himself in a favorable light, thus rendering normative data and interpretational lore inapplicable. The empirical development of the scale (Gough, 1952), in which item shifts between normal versus "fake good" instructions were noted, was directed toward this kind of diagnostic usage. Studies of simulation and response bias (Dicken, 1960, 1963) indicate that the *Gi* scale is quite effective in classifying undependable protocols of this type. Raw scores of 32 or above should raise doubts of this kind about the record.

The second function of *Gi* is to assess the "social desirability" factor as it operates under more normal circumstances. The description of self in a more-or less-favorable manner may be viewed as a normally distributed phenomenon in inventory testing. Some people will rank high and, by inference, will be very much concerned about creating a good impression; others will rank low and will insist on an individualized, nonconforming presentation of self. As with the *Sc* scale, the dynamic concern is the same for both the high and low scorer, but the strategy of interpersonal behavior differs. The high scorer seeks acceptance in an overly conventional, too conformist manner; the low scorer seeks acceptance, but only on his own terms and following upon an aggressive and even corrosive assertion of self.

The college students described high scorers in this way:

Males: adaptable, changeable, considerate, kind, self-denying, soft-hearted, tactful, unselfish, warm, friendly.

Females: calm, conservative, mild, moderate, modest, patient, peaceable, trusting, understanding, worrying.

These correlations reflect moderate elevations on *Gi*, rather than scores of 32 and above. Had profiles with very high *Gi* scores been studied, the expectation would be for a somewhat different pattern of characterization. The new themes would include self-centeredness, opportunism, irritability, and a tendency to exploit and manipulate others.

The descriptions of low scorers on *Gi* were these:

Males: complaining, dissatisfied, fault-finding, hasty, headstrong, indifferent, nagging, pessimistic, temperamental, unkind.

Females: changeable, cynical, frank, moody, pessimistic, sarcastic, shrewd, stubborn, temperamental, witty.

12. *Cm* (Communality)

Communality is the third scale (after *Wb* and *Gi*) that serves two functions. The first is to identify protocols in which random or senseless responses have occurred. Each of the 28 items in the scale was verified in many different samples to insure a high frequency of endorsement (95 percent or more of all respondents answering in one direction). The name "communality" is taken from this concentration of agreement.

An attractive feature of these items is that in spite of their modality they do not sound like platitudes or assertions having little differentiating power. Consider the item "I would fight if someone tried to take my rights away." Nearly everyone checks "true" for this item, yet no one in the experience of the writer has ever said, "Why is that question asked? No one would ever disagree with it." In fact, the reaction to items in the *Cm* scale is more often one of "Yes, indeed, here at last is an assertion with which I can wholeheartedly agree (or disagree)." Scores of 18 and below on *Cm* should definitely raise the possibility of random or uninterpretable responding to the inventory.

The second purpose of the *Cm* scale is to differentiate within the normal range of modal vs. idiosyncratic response to the questionnaire. In some ways the *Cm* score, in this function, resembles *P* (popular responses) on the Rorschach Ink Blot test. Subjects scoring high on *Cm* will be in tune with their peers and surroundings, will perceive as their peers perceive, and will form impressions that are sound, stable, and sensible. Subjects scoring low on *Cm* will be more individual, less stereotypic, and more likely to personalize their experiences and to move in new and original directions.

On the profile sheet, the highest standard score that may be achieved is 63 for males and 60 for females. This is understandable if one thinks for a moment of what is connoted by a high score: to score high signifies that one is more like other people than are other people. There is, it is clear, a limit to how unique one can be in an un-unique or modal manner.

The college students described high scorers on *Cm* as follows:

Males: cautious, conscientious, deliberate, efficient, formal, organized, practical, responsible, thorough, thrifty.

Females: clear-thinking, confident, energetic, humorous, practical, rational, rigid, stern, strong, realistic.

Descriptions with largest negative correlations, and hence characteristic of low scorers on *Cm*, were these:

Males: attractive, careless, courageous, daring, distractible, forgetful, leisurely, pleasure-seeking, reckless, spendthrift.

Females: appreciative, artistic, awkward, feminine, forgetful, forgiving, indifferent, irresponsible, unconventional, undependable.

These two clusters are not as internally consistent as has been true of prior clusters. The reason probably lies in the two-fold significance of lower scores: some low scorers have probably answered parts of the inventory carelessly, reflecting impatience with the testing and unwillingness to give full attention to each item. These subjects, one would expect, would draw descriptions such as distractible, undependable, etc. Other subjects would be attentive but idiosyncratic, and for them the descriptions would fall more along the line of artistic, unconventional, etc. This distinction should not be too sharply drawn, but it does highlight an interpretational decision that must be made each time a low *Cm* score is encountered on the profile.

13. *Ac* (Achievement via Conformance)

The *Ac* scale was originally developed in studies of academic achievement at the high school level. Gradually, through working with the scale and through individual acquaintance with high scorers, it became clear that the basic theme of the measure was one of a strong need for achievement coupled with a deeply internalized appreciation of structure and organization. The term "conformance" was chosen to reflect this channeling of the need for achievement, as "conformity" would be too strong and would also connote a kind of unproductive stereotypy that is in fact not strongly embodied in the scale.

The intent of the 38-item index is to identify people for whom achievement is a salient need, and who respond to, and do well in, situations in which performance is structured and the criteria of excellence are clearly specified. One such setting, typically, is in high school, and the *Ac* scale has shown consistent validity (correlations from +.36 to +.44) in forecasting high school grades (cf. Gough, 1964*a*). *Ac* has also revealed significant correlations with performance of stenographers (Gendre, 1964), military officers (Gough, 1958), and students of journalism (Pouncey, 1954), but only modest correlations (r = +.16) with grades in college (Gough, 1964*b*).

High scorers in the college samples were described as follows:

Males: ambitious, capable, conscientious, considerate, intelligent, logical, mature, reasonable, resourceful, responsible.

Females: conservative, efficient, idealistic, enterprising, logical, obliging, planful, reliable, reserved, responsible.

The emphasis in these clusters is on diligent, responsible dedication of effort in pursuit of worthy and meritorious goals.

The low scorers on *Ac* were described in this way:

Males: apathetic, distrustful, hard-hearted, irresponsible, pleasure-seeking, reckless, rude, shallow, shiftless, show-off.

Females: adventurous, careless, easy going, irresponsible, lazy, rebellious, sarcastic, unconventional, uninhibited, zany.

The low scorer on *Ac* is not only an underachiever, but also a rebel. Not surprisingly, delinquents and prison inmates tend to score low on *Ac*, one or more standard deviations below the general mean of 28, and high school disciplinary problems also fall into this low range.

14. *Ai* (Achievement via Independence)

The 32-item *Ai* scale had its origin in studies of scholastic achievement at the college level. In individual application of the measure it gradually became clear that need:achievement, in this variant, was channeled along independent, innovative, and self-actualizing lines. If the psychodynamic forces in *Ac* could be called form-enhancing, those in *Ai* could be termed form-creating.

Scores on *Ai* relate to performance in college (cf. Barnette, 1961; Bendig & Klugh, 1956) and advanced training (cf. Rosenberg, McHenry, Rosenberg, & Nichols, 1962), and also to attitudes toward mathematics (Aiken, 1963*a*), performance as an electronic technician (Gendre, 1966), social insight (Gough, 1965*c*), and creativity among writers (Barron, 1961).

In our college samples, high scorers on *Ai* were described as follows:

Males: foresighted, independent, informal, intelligent, lazy, pleasant, rational, sarcastic, touchy, versatile.

Females: calm, capable, clear-thinking, discreet, intelligent, logical, mature, original, rational, reflective.

The portrait for males puts more emphasis on individuality and independence, but high-scoring females are nonetheless described as original.

Low scorers on *Ai* were described in this manner:

Males: affected, bossy, cautious, cool, egotistical, fearful, frivolous, mannerly, smug, stern.

Females: awkward, excitable, foolish, immature, infantile, rattlebrained, restless, simple, unrealistic, unstable.

In these portraits of the low scorer there is an element of immaturity, and also of a lack of self-insight. The low scorer on *Ai* is likely to do things that are unwise and self-defeating.

15. *Ie* (Intellectual Efficiency)

The 52-item scale for intellectual efficiency was constructed by correlating items with measures of intellectual ability such as the Kuhlmann-Anderson group test (Kuhlmann & Anderson, 1940). The *Ie* scale may therefore be considered a "subtle" measure of intelligence, just as the *To* scale is a subtle index of authoritarianism. Correlations between *Ie* and direct measures of ability have averaged about +.50, including high school, college, graduate school, and adult samples.

The items within the scale fall into four broad categories: (*a*) Self-confidence and self-assurance, freedom from unsubstantiated fears and apprehensions; (*b*) effective social techniques and adjustment, sense of social acceptability without dependence on others; not suspicious, touchy, or overly sensitive; (*c*) good physiological functioning, absence of minor, debilitating symptoms and complaints; and (*d*) liking and respect for intellectual pursuits; wide range of interests.

The word "efficiency" was utilized in the name of the scale so as to emphasize a second aspect of its implications: the ease and efficiency with which an individual is able to direct his effort and apply his abilities. For example, in a sample of 572 high school males who competed in the 1963 Westinghouse Science Talent Search, and who in addition scored above the 80th percentile in a science aptitude examination, scores on *Ie* correlated significantly with ratings made of the science projects each boy had contributed (Parloff & Datta, 1965).

In the college samples, high scorers were described in this way:

Males: capable, confident, efficient, foresighted, independent, intelligent, reasonable, self-controlled, sophisticated, unaffected.

Females: capable, clear-thinking, confident, efficient, informal, intelligent, leisurely, logical, rational, relaxed.

The low scorers obtained these descriptions:

Males: awkward, cold, forgetful, hard-hearted, interests narrow, queer, restless, sensitive, shallow, suggestible.

Females: absent-minded, awkward, interests narrow, nervous, pessimistic, simple, slow, stubborn, tense, withdrawn.

16. *Py* (Psychological-mindedness)

In the late 1940's and early 1950's, a pool of some 300 experimental items was given to a sample of 25 outstanding young psychologists, chosen on the basis of personal acquaintance, and from nominations gathered informally from senior scholars at two universities. The names of these individuals cannot be revealed, but it can be said that as of 1967 three had been elected president of the American Psychological Association, two had won the Association's award for outstanding research, one had won the equivalent award given by the American Personnel and Guidance Association, at least ten had been elected president of different divisions of the American Psychological Association or of regional or state associations, and the combined output of books, papers, reviews, commentaries, and other publications of all 25 would fill a small library.

The responses of this elite group of 25 young psychologists (ages 25 to 35) were contrasted with those of a large sample of subjects in other fields and/or training programs. The items yielded by this procedure were then reproduced and administered to approximately 50 students (male and female) enrolled in graduate seminars in several departments of psychology; the items were correlated with instructors' ratings of the competence and potentiality of these students. Items that correlated with these ratings, and that agreed in direction of response with the first analysis, were retained for the final form of the scale.

This 22-item scale has been designated Psychological-mindedness, as its aim is to identify individuals who are psychologically oriented and insightful concerning others. Because of the strategy of scale construction one would expect a significant correlation with the Psychologist key of the Strong Vocational Interest Blank (Strong, 1943), and in fact the correlation in a sample of 152 males was +.40. In four samples of introductory psychology students (N= 5,103), the mean correlation between Py and course grade was +.24 (Gough, 1964b).

Descriptions of high scorers on Py in the fraternity and sorority samples were these:

Males: aloof, evasive, foresighted, independent, individualistic, persevering, preoccupied, reserved, unfriendly, wary.

Females: capable, cool, independent, ingenious, leisurely, logical, mischievous, self-confident, sharp-witted, undependable.

The expectations of some readers have no doubt been contradicted by these adjectival descriptions: the high scorer on Py is not a patient, kind, sympathetic, nurturant individual. There is, of course, nothing in the theoretical conception of psychological insight that compels its possessor to be warm and indulgent; in fact, some misanthropic souls might insist that the better we understand our fellow men, the less hope we will have for them. Be that as it may, high scorers on Py are incisive and discerning individuals, but not at all forbearing or complaisant.

Low scorers on Py were described in these terms:

Males: active, cheerful, energetic, flirtatious, humorous, kind, opportunistic, outgoing, sociable, talkative.

Females: conventional, generous, honest, kind, praising, tense, trusting, unassuming, warm, worrying.

17. *Fx* (Flexibility)

The 22-item Fx scale was developed rationally, by correlating approximately 50 experimental items with total score based on the full set. Examples of items retained for the final form are these: "I like to have a place for everything and everything in its place" (*false*); "I never make judgments about people until I am sure of the facts" (*false*); and "I often start things I never finish" (*true*).

The purpose of the scale is to identify people of flexible, adaptable, even changeable temperament. Fx, in a sample of 66 males, correlated −.32 with superego strength from Cattell's 16*PF* test (Cattell, 1950), and +.32 with the ergic tension scale from the same instrument. In a sample of 295 males, it correlated +.34 with the *Pt* (psychasthenia) and +.31 with the *Sc* (schizophrenia) scales of the MMPI (Hathaway and McKinley, 1943). In a sample of 180 college students *Fx* correlated −.58 with the *F*-scale for authoritarianism.

High scorers in the two college samples were described as follows:

Males: easy going, fickle, independent, lazy, optimistic, pleasure-seeking, quick, sharp-witted, spendthrift, spontaneous.

Females: careless, clever, daring, imaginative, individualistic, ingenious, mischievous, original, pleasure-seeking, sociable.

The flexibility component is visible enough in these portraits, but there is also an element of instability and inconstancy. A very high score on *Fx* (18-19 and above), in fact, does seem to presage a mercurial, too volatile temperament.

Low scorers were described in this manner:

Males: determined, efficient, hard-headed, organized, planful, practical, stern, stubborn, stolid, thorough.

Females: cautious, conscientious, conservative, defensive, prudish, rigid, slow, simple, sincere, self-punishing.

18. *Fe* (Femininity)

Items for the 38-item *Fe* scale were selected on the basis of two criteria: differentiation between males and females, and between homosexual and heterosexual males matched for age, education, intelligence, and occupation. The scale has three purposes: (*a*) to differentiate males from females, (*b*) to distinguish between deviant and sexually normal persons, and (*c*) to define a personological continuum that could be conceptualized as "feminine" at one pole and "masculine" at the other. In extensive validational study both in the United States and elsewhere (cf. Gough, 1966*b*), *Fe* has yielded encouraging results.

In the college samples, high scorers (more feminine) subjects were described in this way:

Males: appreciative, complaining, feminine, formal, meek, nervous, self-denying, sensitive, weak, worrying.

Females: conscientious, discreet, generous, gentle, helpful, mature, self-controlled, sympathetic, tactful, warm.

The two portraits are not the same; this is to be expected, inasmuch as *Fe* is the one scale on which sex differences are sought and in fact maximized. For males, to score high has principally negative connotations—of nervousness, weakness, and dissatisfaction. For women, to score high is generally favorable—with connotations of maturity, generosity, warmth, and nurturance. This syndrome for the high-scoring woman should be emphasized, as it is in accord with a theory of femininity in women as essentially a conserving, maintaining, and nurturing disposition.

Low scorers on the scale (masculine direction) were described as follows:

Males: adventurous, aggressive, clear-thinking, daring, impulsive, masculine, outgoing, pleasure-seeking, show-off, strong.

Females: coarse, dissatisfied, lazy, masculine, pleasure-seeking, restless, robust, self-centered, touchy, tough.

A contrast also appears in the portraits of low scorers. If a male, the low scorer is described as aggressive, masculine, and strong, whereas if a female, the terms include dissatisfied, coarse, and restless. The masculine man, again in accord with psychodynamic theory, is initiative, aggressive, and a seeker of new experience and adventure. Further, more masculine males appear to excel on tests of motor ability (Merriman, 1960).

Finally, who is more intelligent—the more feminine or the more masculine personality? From evidence now available a rather interesting answer may be given. Among men, *Fe* correlates negatively with ability, whereas among women the correlation is positive.

INTERACTIONS AMONG SCALES

Even though a substantial part of this syllabus on interpretation of the CPI has been devoted to the individual scales, anyone who uses the inventory will soon discover that diagnosis must rest on patterns and combinations just as much as on individual high and low points. A complete treatment of patterns and combinations would require much more space than could possibly be justified here, and in fact it is doubtful if any written presentation could offer all that is needed. Sensitivity to configurations and the ability to translate a complete profile into an individuated analysis are skills that must be developed in practice—not just read about in a book.

Nonetheless, there are a few things that can be said and directions can be suggested that the psychologist interested in a professional level of performance can follow.[2]

A first step is to take note of the interactions between scales (cf. Heilbrun, Daniel, Goodstein, Stephenson, & Crites, 1962). Changes in scores on one scale may alter the interpretive implications of scores on another. Consider, for example, the scales for Dominance and Responsibility. From the preceding section the reader may remind himself of what is to be expected from high or low scores on each. But what about an interaction pattern between these two?

For information on such a pattern we may turn again to the adjectival descriptions gathered from the 101 males and 92 females. In the total sample of 193 subjects, a scatter plot was made of scores on *Do* and *Re*, and axes were introduced so as to define four quadrants: high-high, high-low, low-low, and low-high. Within each quadrant, the 36 students (18 of each sex) most extreme on the bisecting diagonal for the quadrant were selected, and then *t*-tests of the mean scores on the 300 adjectives were made for these 36 versus the remaining 157.

As with the correlational analyses presented earlier, from 45 to 50 differences were significant at the .05 level each time, too many to cite in full. Accordingly, the 10 most significant differences have been selected for each quadrant. For the high-*Do*—high-*Re* students, the 10 most differentiating descriptions were these (listed in descending order): dominant, ambitious,

---

[2]The CPI *Manual* (Gough, 1957, revised 1964) contains a section on profile interpretation, including seven case illustrations and accompanying analyses.

responsible, foresighted, progressive, conscientious, stern, formal, wise, and alert. The "mix" here is about what we would expect for persons high on both measures.

For students high on *Do* but low on *Re*, the most differentiating adjectives were these: touchy, dominant, robust, strong, cynical, tough, hardheaded, aggressive, temperamental, and opinionated. Thus, if a student is high on *Do*, but also low on *Re*, he will be seen as dominant, but dominant in an aggressive, destructive way. This combination will not occur very often (*Do* and *Re* correlate, typically, around +.35), but when it does occur it carries important implications.

The students scoring low on both scales were described in this fashion: irresponsible, suggestible, careless, foolish, unstable, pleasure-seeking, apathetic, changeable, confused, and lazy. This combination (low-low) is not uncommon, and its implications are probably predictable from what is known about the two scales taken alone.

The low-*Do*–high-*Re* quadrant is the one remaining; the most differentiating descriptions of students in this category were: quiet, calm, peaceable, mild, modest, gentle, reserved, thoughtful, cooperative, and honest.

A similar analysis was conducted for the *Ac-Ai* interaction. The major findings are presented below, in an interactional diagram:

	Ac high		
idealistic	mannerly	intelligent	logical
cautious	shy	rational	interests wide
praising	conscientious	realistic	inventive
nervous	inhibited	independent	active
helpful	dull	reasonable	stable

Ai low ———————————————————————— *Ai* high

irresponsible	show-off	spunky	tolerant
careless	touch	reckless	reliable
distrustful	undependable	unexcitable	courageous
disorderly	unstable	foresighted	distractible
indifferent	restless	frank	pleasure-seeking

Ac low

The typical correlation between *Ac* and *Ai* is about +.39, which means that the high-high and low-low categories will occur most frequently. However, among graduate students, researchers, artists, writers, and architects (to name a few), *Ai* tends to exceed *Ac* by 10 to 15 standard score points, so that in many settings where the CPI is used cases will be encountered in the "off" quadrants.

PROFILE ZONES

With respect to another issue in profile reading, i.e., expected covariations and broad zones of related meanings, the profile sheet incorporates an interpretational aid. Those scales that conjointly pertain to *interpersonal* effectiveness, style, and adequacy are grouped together into Cluster I on the profile recording sheet. The appeal in this grouping is to diagnostic convenience, not to factorial consistency, although five of its six scales do constitute such a psychometric unit (Nichols & Schnell, 1963*b*).

The second cluster on the profile sheet includes those six scales whose principal emphasis is upon *intrapersonal* controls, values, styles, and beliefs. Responsibility, for example, stresses the degree to which an individual comprehends and cognizes value and constraint; socialization reflects the degree to which the mandates and constraints of the culture have been effectively internalized; self-control indicates the degree to which the subject espouses or manifestly endorses inhibition and restraint. All three deal with value, but with slightly different emphases, and to be high on *Re*, average on *So*, and low on *Sc* is quite different in personological implications from being low on *Re*, high on *So*, and average on *Sc*.

Cluster III on the profile sheet draws together those three scales that are of basic relevance to academic counseling and guidance (*Ac, Ai,* and *Ie*), so that the counselor may readily observe internal variations among these measures of achievement motivation and achievement potential.

The final grouping of three scales on the profile sheet (*Py, Fx,* and *Fe*) includes measures that ordinarily fall out as residuals in factor analysis, and that, if placed earlier in the series, would interfere with visual recognition of recurrent and diagnostically meaningful configurations. Psychologically these scales reflect broad and far-reaching attitudes toward life.

RESEARCH APPLICATION OF THE INVENTORY

The initial task for the interpreter of the CPI is to comprehend the psychological meanings of higher and lower scores on each of the scales, and the diagnostic implications of scale interactions and profile patterns. Only on the basis of such understanding may valid and perceptive characterizations of individual clients be achieved. The preceding sections of this presentation have, accordingly, dealt almost entirely with data and principles of interpretation pertinent to these issues. However, the Inventory may also be used in nomothetic research where emphasis is upon general trends and relationships and in which one seeks probabilistic laws and forecasting equations. In this concluding section, therefore, three examples of nomothetic analysis will be presented.

The first comes from an unpublished study of airline stewardesses. Sixty females were given the CPI when hired, and after completion of training ratings of in-flight performance were obtained. Because our interest is principally in CPI findings, we will forego any discussion of reliability and validity of the ratings.

Correlations between the 18 scales of the CPI and the criterion ratings ranged from a high of +.25 for Ac to a low of −.18 for Ie. Sc and So had positive coefficients of +.18 and +.14, and Cm had a negative coefficient of −.13. Such a yield of low-magnitude relationships is frequently encountered with criteria not bearing a one-to-one relationship to any single scale of the Inventory. The proper procedure, in these instances, is to search for patterns or combinations of variables that can furnish an acceptable level of predictive validity. A quick and convenient way to identify such combinations is by means of multiple correlation analysis. This technique was applied to the data from the 60 stewardesses, giving rise to a four-variable equation correlating approximately +.40 with the criterion ratings. The equation may be written as follows: $64.293 + .227So -1.903Cm + 1.226Ac -.398Ai$.

Appropriate research methodology, if we wished to apply the equation in any practical way, would call for cross-validation on a new sample of stewardesses. Our purpose, however, is only to illustrate how the CPI may be utilized to help conceptualize a domain of behavior, not to propose an operational index of selection; we shall therefore proceed with our analysis. The first step is to consider the scales included in the equation. So and Ac receive positive weightings, and from the prior discussion of these scales it will be recalled that both stress dependability, dedication to worthwhile goals, and the capacity to organize and structure one's efforts. Cm and Ai receive negative weights, and from the prior discussion we recall that low scorers on these scales tend to be feminine and conscientious. A portrait appears to be emerging, and from further perusal of the scales and their patterns of interactions one could complete the sketch of the equation's implications.

However, there is an equally valid and undoubtedly more rapid way of achieving this formulation: simply to correlate the adjectival descriptions in the sample of 92 young women (described earlier) with scores on the "airline stewardess" equation. To compute such scores, raw values on $So, Cm, Ac,$ and Ai for each subject are entered in the equation, and the indicated computations completed. When this was done, the 92 students attained an average of 49.66, standard deviation 4.65. This array of scores was then correlated with the 300 adjectival descriptions; the adjectives with highest positive and negative correlations are listed below:

(a) Adjectives used most frequently to describe girls with higher scores on the equation: conservative, reserved, idealistic, patient, modest, self-punishing, methodical, planful, feminine, poised, quiet, calm.

(b) Adjectives used most frequently to describe girls with lower scores on the equation: adventurous, zany, curious, frank, sarcastic, witty, pleasure-seeking, uninhibited, impulsive, lazy, humorous, sharp-witted.

The magnitude of the coefficients ranged from +.32 and +.26 for conservative and reserved down to −.34 and −.37 for zany and adventurous.

These descriptive analyses reveal high scorers to be conservative, reserved, and idealistic, and at the same time poised and feminine in manner, whereas low scorers tend to be adventurous, witty, and self-expressive. The diagnostic implications of the equation, it should be noted, run counter to the common stereotype of the ideal stewardess as a buoyant, uninhibited, and adventure-seeking young woman.

A second example of nomothetic application comes from a published study of performance in medical training (Gough & Hall, 1964). The CPI was administered to applicants in the year prior to entry into medical school; five years later, when the senior class was about to graduate, faculty members rated each student on clinical and technical competence. CPI protocols and faculty ratings were available for 34 students.

Regression analysis identified a combination of four scales that would maximize prediction of the ratings: $+.794Sy + .602To + 1.144Cm -.696Cs$. The equation was then cross-validated, in another school of medicine, on 63 students tested as freshmen. The criterion employed was the grade-point average accumulated over four years of medical school. Correlation between scores on the equation and cumulative GPA was +.46. The equation, apparently, is able to predict performance in medical school with reasonable accuracy.

The question may therefore be asked, "On what psychological basis does this forecast rest?" To answer this query, we may again turn to adjectival data. In a sample of 41 undergraduates, of the same age and scholastic achievement as the modal applicant, descriptions of each student were gathered from five peers. Totals on each ACL item were correlated with scores on the equation. The item correlating most highly (+.39) was *unselfish*; i.e., the description most likely to be given of someone scoring high on the equation is "unselfish." The five descriptions with next-highest correlations were these: *considerate, informal, forgiving, reasonable*, and *self-confident*. The most significant negative correlations were with these descriptions: *thankless* (−.38), *cold, cool, prejudiced, fault-finding*, and *restless*.

What the equation favors, in other words, is a configuration of personal resourcefulness coupled with sensitivity to, and respect for, others; and what it disfavors or screens out is a syndrome of petulance, self-centeredness, and intolerance. The equation forecasts performance in medical training, the psychometric analyses have shown, and now in these adjectival explorations it may be seen that its psychological implications are meaningful and in fact reassuring.

A final example of use of the Inventory in nomethetic inquiry comes from a study of academic achievement among high school students (Gough, 1964*a*). An equation to predict grades was developed on a sample of 1,384 students (813 females, 571 males) from five schools. The equation took this form: $20.116 + .317Re + .192So -.309Gi + .227Ac + .280Ai + .244Ie$. The computing weights are for use with raw scores, and the constant of 20.116 is introduced so that the mean of an array of computed scores will approximate 50.00.

The equation was applied to a new sample of 1,371 students (722 females, 649 males) from nine schools, giving rise to a correlation of +.56 with the cumulative high school grade-point averages. Although the equation appears to be statistically valid, the user of the CPI will be perhaps even more interested in its psychodynamic implications than in its psychometric utility. To gain information on these psychodynamic implications, we can again turn to adjectival analyses and to clinical interpretation of the scales included. From such analyses, the high scorer on the equation may be characterized as a responsible, self-disciplined, and socially-insightful person with a strong need for achievement and with superior ability to direct and channel his energy. Academic attainment, as forecast by this equation, springs more from a healthy balance of positive dispositions than from neurotic or self-aggrandizing motives.

To conclude this discussion, perhaps several final comments on test usage may be permitted. Emphasis in personality testing should always be upon psychological meaning—whether one is attending to individual scales, combinations, patterns, or even to predictive equations. Predictive validity is a fundamental requirement, but a test should in addition deepen and expand one's understanding of the criteria forecast and of the bases on which prediction rests. It is hoped that the admonitions and examples set forth above may serve to further both recognition and acceptance of this viewpoint.

CHAPTER V

The TSC Scales: The outcome of a cluster analysis of the 550 MMPI items*

Kenneth B. Stein

The Minnesota Multiphasic Personality Inventory (MMPI) (Hathaway & McKinley, 1951) has had extensive use as a diagnostic and personality instrument in clinical, counseling, and personnel settings. Concurrent with its clinical and assessment uses, it has enjoyed more attention in research than any other psychological test. Many research studies have sought relationships of MMPI scales to other variables, and these have shed a certain amount of light on the meaning of the inventory. Another course of research has been directed toward an understanding of the inventory through the study of its internal structure. In this respect a number of factor analytic studies have been conducted on a variety of samples. Most of these factor analyses were limited to the standard scales, while others included special scales as well. In addition to these studies with scale scores, there have also been a few attempts to factor-analyze the MMPI items. These latter studies, it is important to add, were limited to items within single scales.

It is not the purpose of this chapter to review the factor analytic studies and to discuss their similarities and differences. Rather the focus is upon a methodological problem inherent in these factor-analytic studies—namely, the influence of overlapping items in MMPI scales upon factorial results. Following an exposition and review of studies concerned with the overlap problem, a recent methodological development which allows for the handling of an unrestricted number of variables in cluster- and factor-analysis will be described. The application of this method to the full supply of MMPI items will then be summarized and the results presented. Finally, the development and utilization of the clusters that represent the internal structure of the MMPI as personality and symptom scales will then be set forth.

---

*The 34 MMPI items listed in this chapter are reproduced by permission. Copyright 1943 by the University of Minnesota. Published by the Psychological Corporation, New York, N. Y. All rights reserved.

THE PROBLEM OF OVERLAPPING ITEMS

Criterion Method of Scale Construction

The MMPI scales were developed by means of the criterion approach. In this method various samples defined by certain criteria such as psychiatric diagnosis are selected for study. A criterion sample (for example, patients with the diagnosis of schizophrenia) is administered a large number of questionnaire-type items to which the subjects respond in a specified way, such as *true* or *false* as on the MMPI. Similarly these items are administered to a normal or control group matched on important variables. The items that are responded to in a significantly different manner by the two samples are selected to form a criterion scale—for example, the Schizophrenia Scale. If the scale development has been rigorous, utmost care and attention will have been paid to the criterion definition and cross-validation.

Needless to say, reliability is also important. Since scale construction depends upon the relation of items to the criterion, a test-retest rather than a split-half method of reliability is often used. Dahlstrom and Welsh (1960) present split-half coefficients of four clinical samples. The median coefficients for these scales range from .55 (*MF*) to .91 (*Sc*), with the median of these median reliabilities at the level of .78. Compared with the test-retest data (Dahlstrom & Welsh, 1960) the magnitude of the split-half coefficients is generally higher. There is some question as to the appropriateness of the test-retest method. Especially when the inventory is designed to measure traits and symptoms that are not invariant, repeated administrations of the same instrument over a wide interval of time does not appear indicated as a measure of reliability. Certainly in the MMPI, in which such symptom pictures as depression, somatic concerns, and various other disturbed emotional states are expected to change with time and treatment, stability of scores is not only unlikely but undesirable. The alternate form, though rarely used in the criterion scales, is the more appropriate reliability method.

In the criterion approach to test construction, a large pool of items can be used in unlimited fashion; that is, the pool can be used repeatedly with different criterion groups. The number of scales that can be derived in this manner is therefore limited only by the number of different criterion groups available. The MMPI pool of items is an example of the extent to which a proliferation of scales can occur. Dahlstrom and Welsh (1960) list over 200 scales and subscales in their *MMPI Handbook*, and a large number have been added in the years since its publication.

Methodologically, one problem becomes clear. When different criterion scales are derived from a common pool of items, these scales are likely to have varying amounts of overlapping items. In the MMPI the scale with the largest number of unique—that is, non-overlap—items is *Mf* with 58 percent. This scale is not strictly one of the clinical scales. The proportion of unique items among the more strictly clinical scales runs considerably lower, ranging from 17 to 33 percent. The importance and implications of the overlap problem will be more fully discussed below.

Factor Analysis

Since the MMPI scales are not in fact operationally independent of each other—that is, they contain overlapping items—the relevance of overlap depends upon how the clinician or researcher plans to use the scales. The clinician who wishes to use two- or three-high-point scales or configural analyses in order to arrive at diagnostic conclusions will find a good deal of empirical meaningfulness in various diagnostic patterns, regardless of overlapping items. He may, however, be concerned with whether the efficiency and economy of the inventory or test might better be served with pure scales. The researcher who is interested in using one or more of the scales or patterns as independent variables may also not be too concerned with the overlap problem as long as he feels relatively sure of the validity of the scales and patterns to classify his subjects. When he uses the scales as dependent variables, however, as is more often the case, item overlap does raise a problem. In the use of successive t and F tests there is the assumption that the dependent variables should be at least operationally independent. Therefore, when two samples are being compared on a number of MMPI scales for mean differences, this assumption of independence cannot be met.

To the researcher who wishes to study the internal structure of the MMPI, the presence of scales with overlapping items is likely to present problems. Thurstone (1947) first warned against the use of factor analysis with variables that were not operationally independent. Guilford (1952) more recently has emphasized that one should not factor-analyze if there is a lack of independence. He states:

> There are a number of situations in psychological investigations in which specific and error variances actually contribute to intercorrelations where they should not be permitted to do so. One common situation is in connnection with personality inventories in which the same items are scored with weights for more than one trait variable. . . . For every item that is weighted in two scores, there is a contribution to the obtained correlation between these scores [p. 22].

However, it may very well be that an overlapping item measures a factor common to several scores, and would therefore represent valid variance. But, as Guilford points out, the item's contribution to any total score of necessity encompasses some specific and error variances that contribute to the intercorrelation of items.

Attempts to Deal With the Overlap Problem

A number of studies will now be reviewed that have addressed themselves to the overlap problem in the factor analysis of the MMPI scales. It will be noted that some writers consider the problem unimportant and dismiss it, while others show concern and point to the influence of overlap upon the factorial results.

Wheeler, Little, and Lehner (1951), in one of the early factor-analytic studies, dealt with the overlap problem only up to a point and then dismissed it. Their initial concern with the problem led to the calculation of interscale common-element correlations in order to indicate the amount of communality between scales as a result of item overlap. Rather than making any correction for, or extracting the influence of, these overlapping items, these authors reasoned that "positive item overlap is one way in which the scales are related and should not be interpreted as detracting from empirical relationships based on scores obtained on the scales [p. 136]."

Welsh (1956) attempted to deal with the overlap problem in his factor-analytic studies by developing "pure" or primed scales on the MMPI. This he accomplished by eliminating positive overlapping items from the standard MMPI scales and factoring these scales together with the Gm scale, a scale composed of items that appeared in three or more scales. As a result of a factor analysis and the development of special scales A and R, each representing one of the two main factors, Welsh in a subsequent factoring found that A and R actually possessed the highest factor loadings in their respective factors. His two factors were interpreted as anxiety for the first factor, and repression and denial for the second. Adams and Horn (1965) raised several criticisms that should be considered. First, Welsh did not eliminate the same items when they were scored in opposite directions; hence his "pure" scales were not strictly non-overlapping. Second, he did not use all possible items, and therefore some scales are shorter than they need be, and consequently less reliable.

Adams and Horn (1965) provided a set of operationally independent keys for the clinical scales, for certain frequently used non-clinical scales, and for several new scales of the MMPI. It would be of interest to compare the factorial dimensions resulting from the use of these pure scales with those found by Welsh. Such a study with the Adams and Horn scales has not as yet been done. The problem, however, with such a proposed factorial study lies in the fact that when these overlapping items are removed, they find no representation in the analysis. Also the shortened pure scales suffer from lowered reliability, which in turn affects the intercorrelations of scales.

Shure and Rogers (1965) studied the influence of overlap in a series of factor-analytic studies. First, they factored on the common-elements correlation based on the overlapping items only; second, they factored on the original scales with overlapping items included; and third, they factored on truncated scales in which overlapping items were eliminated. The results showed that the so-called "neurotic" and "psychotic" factors identified in a number of factor-analytic studies appeared similarly for both the full MMPI scales and the common-elements correlation matrix. These factors did not emerge for the truncated scales, however. These findings strongly suggest that the overlapping items contribute to a built-in correlation resulting in a built-in factor structure. Anderson and Bashaw (1966), however, take issue with this conclusion, primarily on the basis of the fairly low magnitude of the overlap coefficients forming the common-elements correlation matrix. They suggest a more conservative interpretation, which emphasizes that the overlapping items are an indication of the similarity between the latent (criterion) variables and therefore represent valid common variance.

Block (1965) also addressed himself to the question of overlapping items but directed his attention to the issue of acquiescent response style, a tendency to respond "true" to inventory items regardless of their content. More specifically, his arguments dealt with the factorial results of Jackson and Messick (1961; 1962), who used a design involving a correlation matrix based on scores derived from separating MMPI scales into those scored *true* and those scored *false*. These authors demonstrated in their factor analyses of several samples that the first factor contained an almost complete separation of *true* and *false* scales, and they concluded that these results reflect the presence of an acquiescence dimension in the MMPI. Block argued that the Jackson and Messick results were confounded by the presence of overlapping items, the extent of overlap being reflected in the fact that 59 percent of the items in the scales under study appeared in more than one scale. As he correctly pointed out, even though a portion of the variance due to overlap is valid in that it reflects a legitimate relationship between latent or criterion variables, the fact remains that item overlap also contributes a built-in error and item-specific variance. Block makes a convincing presentation of data and arguments for a content-relevant, rather than an acquiescence-set, interpretation of the MMPI factors.

It should also be noted that in the same work, Block (1965) suggests a method to handle the overlap problem that would eliminate the influence of overlap from the correlation matrix while recognizing the valid portion of the variance. This method involves the calculation of the correlations between scales with the overlapping items eliminated, and then correcting the correlations by the Spearman-Brown formula. In this manner the coefficient would reflect the scale's original length. Block justified this method on the basis of the assumption of item interchangeability. If one argues that in the criterion approach items correlate with the criterion and not necessarily with each other, the acceptance of the assumption of item interchangeability may be questionable. However, the data on split-half reliability for the MMPI scales cited earlier suggest that Block's assumption is fairly credible. But these reliability coefficients, some of which are very low, vary both with the samples and scales; therefore the method must be used with some caution.

FACTOR ANALYSES OF MMPI ITEMS

The review of the studies and arguments concerning the factor analysis of MMPI scales with overlapping items does not lead to a firm or settled answer to the overlap problem. The various solutions offered for controlling overlap may be circumventing a more central issue, the derivation of the internal structure of the MMPI based upon the full supply of items rather than upon the scale scores. This direct approach to the items themselves would not only render the overlap problem nonexistent, but also has the advantage of drawing upon the full supply of 550 items, the total-item pool from which the criterion scales were derived.

Although this seems to be the more direct approach, the problem of adequate computer programs and the limitations of computers to handle such a large number of variables as 550 have been major obstacles to such an analysis. Yet attempts at factor analysis at the item level have been made. We will refer to several of these: first, the factor analysis of the items of individual scales; and second, a methodological development that can handle large numbers of items, such as the 550 items of the MMPI.

Factor Analysis of Items Within Scales

There have been a number of factor-analytic studies of individual MMPI scales, but the work of Comrey (1957a; 1957b; 1957c; 1958a; 1958b; 1958c; 1958d; 1958e; 1958f; Comrey & Marggraff, 1958; Comrey & Levonian, 1958) has been the most systematic. He factor-analyzed most of the standard MMPI scales individually and attempted to integrate the major factorial findings. His studies included the following scales: *Hs, D, Hy, Pd, Pa, Pt, Sc, Ma, F* and *K*. Because each scale was analyzed separately, the problem of overlapping items was circumvented for each individual analysis—but not necessarily for the factorial dimensions across all the scales. What appeared to be the same or similar factors emerged in a number of scales. A Neuroticism factor appeared in five different scales: *D, Hy, Pd, Pa* and *Pt*. Poor Physical Health as a factor emerged in six different scales: *Hs, D, Hy, Pt, Sc* and *F*. Poor Concentration as a factor was identified in three scales: *Pt, Sc* and *F*. Although a number of other factors emerged in Comrey's series of factorial studies, the above three appeared to be major ones. In an effort to study the meaning of the repetition of the above factors in different scales, Comrey and Levonian (1958) factor-analyzed the 55 items from the various scales representing these three major factors. Fourteen centroid factors in three different analyses of the same data emerged. Four Neuroticism, three Poor Physical Health, two Poor Concentration and five Residual factors represented the internal structure of the 55 items. The results indicated to Comrey that the factors that he thought reflected identical factors in the various MMPI scales appeared to be different ones. Yet a simple count by the present author showed that 13 of the 21 defining items of the first Neuroticism factor appeared in one or more of the other three Neuroticism factors. This suggests that in a second-order factor analysis, these Neuroticism factors would probably reduce to a smaller number. The same findings appeared for the other factors as well. Of 25 defining items of the first Poor Physical Health factor, 16 appeared in one or both of the remaining two Poor Physical Health factors. Six of the eighteen Poor Concentration first-factor items overlapped with the second. Even one-sixth of the Residual definer items appeared in more than one of the five Residual factors.

This series of studies at the item level sheds additional light on the understanding of the internal structure of the MMPI, but it still leaves open the question of the type of structure that would emerge if it were possible to deal with the full supply of items rather than depending upon items limited to the individual scales.

Cluster Analysis of Full Supply of Items

The BC TRY System of Cluster and Factor Analysis (Tryon & Bailey, 1965; 1966) is composed of more than 30 programs, one sequence of which is the BIGNV (Tryon, 1966a). Before summarizing the BIGNV program, a brief description of the BC TRY System is in order. (For a fuller description the reader is referred elsewhere: Tryon & Bailey, 1965, 1966; Tryon, 1966*a*, 1966*b*, 1967*a*, 1967*b*). Although a major focus of the BC TRY System is upon cluster analysis, the System includes the many varieties of orthodox factor analysis and rotational programs in current usage.

The standard cluster analysis programs are of two major sorts. The first group of component programs is directed to variables. It aims to discover the minimal number of clusters or dimensions that can sufficiently reflect the total supply of variables without loss of generality. Tryon and Bailey explain that "without loss of generality" means that "the reduced set will reproduce all the intercorrelations among the full array. The reduced set also reproduces a salient portion of the variance of each variable, usually that portion known as its communality [1966, p. 96]." This first part of the cluster analysis program is called variable or V analysis.

The second major group of component programs has the objective of deriving patterns or types across the V clusters. The aim of this inverse cluster analysis is similar to that of the V analysis except that here a reduced set of entities, persons, or objects is sought that will generally represent the full set. This set of programs is called object or O analysis.

The BIGNV (meaning *BIG Number of Variables*) is designed in principle to fill a troublesome gap in computer programs—that is, a means for managing a large number of variables in cluster or factor analysis. The need for such a solution became patently clear to Tryon, Chu, and the author while working on an MMPI project (Tryon, Stein, & Chu, in preparation) and led Tryon (1966*a*) to the programming of the BIGNV.

The program operates basically on the principle of estimating the internal structure across the full supply of variables from that discovered in smaller, manageable samples. To summarize the procedures, the full supply of items is broken down into random samples of 120 items each until the full supply of items is utilized. (The BC TRY System can handle a maximum of 120 variables at one time.) The communality of each item within samples is calculated and the items ordered by magnitude of their communalities. The 120 items with the largest communalities are then processed for a full-cycle cluster analysis revealing the structure of these items with the largest generality. Pivotal clusters are selected and preset in the remaining samples of items. Thus, all of the items—that is, those items remaining after items with trivial generality have been eliminated—are consistently related to common subsets of definers. These results are then merged into a composite, from which final determinations are made as to the defining items of the pivotal and dependent clusters. The process of final item selection is both a statistical and rational one. The relevance of an item as a definer for a cluster will depend upon the extent of the magnitude of the oblique factor coefficient in the germane cluster and upon low coefficients in the other clusters, as well as upon the content meaning in the cluster. In the MMPI analysis, 317 items were eliminated for reasons of trivial communality and 57 for being rationally ambiguous in relation to the general content meaning of items within a cluster. This process resulted in clusters that are homogeneous both statistically and in content meaning.

From this brief description of the methodology for handling a large number of variables, the results from the application of the BIGNV procedures to the MMPI will be presented. It should be noted that this study was initiated by Tryon and the late Richard Sears with the gathering of the psychiatric samples. Tryon continued as principal investigator of the project, and was joined early in the study by Chu and the author. The sample from which the item clusters were derived consisted of 310 males—70 VA outpatient schizophrenics, 150 VA outpatient neurotics diagnosed as anxiety reaction, and 90 military officers (who were considered the normal group). The officers and the VA patients were matched for age and education. The sample was purposely drawn to be heterogeneous in regard to emotional disturbance (cf. Tryon, 1966a).

THE MMPI ITEM CLUSTERS

Space does not permit either the reproduction of the content of all of the items within each of the clusters or their oblique factor coefficients and communalities. Some of these data are currently available in Tryon's (1966a) publication, but a fuller and more final report of the MMPI project will be published later (Tryon et al., in preparation). For the reader's convenience, however, the full content of the five items with the highest factor coefficients are listed together with the MMPI booklet numbers for the remaining items. Also provided is the keying of the items true (*T*) or false (*F*).

Cluster I (*I*) *Social Introversion versus Interpersonal Poise and Outgoingness* (26 items)

377. At parties I am more likely to sit by myself or with just one other person than join in with the crowd. (*T*)
57. I am a good mixer. (*F*)
321. I am easily embarrassed. (*T*)
201. I wish I were not so shy. (*T*)
180. I find it hard to make talk when I meet new people. (*T*).
371(*T*), 267(*T*), 172(*T*), 86(*T*), 171(*T*), 547(*F*), 521(*F*), 52(*T*), 309(*F*), 479(*F*), 509(*T*), 292(*T*), 79(*F*), 317(*T*), 264(*F*), 138(*T*), 353(*F*), 304(*T*), 449(*F*), 415(*F*), 482(*F*).

Cluster II (*B*) *Body Symptoms versus Lack of Physical Complaints* (33 items)

243. I have few or no pains. (*F*)
189. I feel weak all over much of the time. (*T*)
108. There seems to be a fullness in my head or nose most of the time. (*T*)
190. I have very few headaches. (*F*)
62. Parts of my body often have feelings like burning, tingling, crawling, or like "going to sleep." (*T*).
175(*F*), 230(*F*), 114(*T*), 47(*T*), 44(*T*), 55(*F*), 29(*T*), 125(*T*), 68(*F*), 10(*T*), 23(*T*), 161(*T*), 544(*T*), 72(*T*), 3(*F*), 36(*F*), 163(*F*), 51(*F*), 103(*F*), 160(*F*), 191(*T*), 153(*F*), 263(*T*), 330(*F*), 2(*F*), 18(*F*), 192(*F*), 14(*T*).

Cluster III *(S) Suspicion and Mistrust versus Absence of Suspicion* (25 items)

404. People have often misunderstood my intentions when I was trying to put them right and be helpful. *(T)*
507. I have frequently worked under people who seem to have things arranged so that they get credit for good work but are able to pass off mistakes onto those under them. *(T)*
383. People often disappoint me. *(T)*
390. I have often felt badly over being misunderstood when trying to keep someone from making a mistake. *(T)*
436. People generally demand more respect for their own rights than they are willing to allow for others. *(T)*
    136*(T)*, 244*(T)*, 348*(T)*, 368*(T)*, 280*(T)*, 265*(T)*, 469*(T)*, 447*(T)*, 319*(T)*, 71*(T)*, 558*(T)*, 406*(T)*, 278*(T)*, 284*(T)*, 438*(T)*, 89*(T)*, 112*(T)*, 426*(T)*, 316*(T)*, 455*(T)*.

Cluster IV *(D) Depression and Apathy versus Positive and Optimistic Outlook* (28 items)

76. Most of the time I feel blue. *(T)*
107. I am happy most of the time. *(F)*
236. I brood a great deal. *(T)*
301. Life is a strain for me much of the time. *(T)*
379. I very seldom have spells of the blues. *(F)*
    487*(T)*, 41*(T)*, 259*(T)*, 418*(T)*, 8*(F)*, 549*(T)*, 67*(T)*, 414*(T)*, 396*(T)*, 61*(T)*, 411*(T)*, 142*(T)*, 397*(T)*, 526*(T)*, 361*(T)*, 384*(T)*, 84*(T)*, 357*(T)*, 168*(T)*, 339*(T)*, 88*(F)*, 46*(F)*, 104*(T)*.

Cluster V *(R) Resentment and Aggression versus Lack of Resentment and Aggression* (21 items).

94. I do many things which I regret afterwards (I regret things more often than others seem to). *(T)*
336. I easily become impatient with people. *(T)*
468. I am often sorry because I am so cross and grouchy. *(T)*
375. When I am feeling very happy and active, someone who is blue or low will spoil it all. *(T)*
    39*(T)*, 381*(T)*, 97*(T)*, 536*(T)*, 139*(T)*, 234*(T)*, 129*(T)*, 145*(T)*, 148*(T)*, 28*(T)*, 162*(T)*, 416*(T)*, 382*(T)*, 106*(T)*, 147*(T)*, 443*(T)*.

Cluster VI *(A) Autism and Disruptive Thought versus Absence of Such Disturbance* (23 items)

559. I have often been frightened in the middle of the night. *(T)*
241. I dream frequently about things that are best kept to myself. *(T)*
15. Once in a while I think of things too bad to talk about. *(T)*
349. I have strange and peculiar thoughts. *(T)*.
425. I dream frequently. *(T)*
    511*(T)*, 545*(T)*, 358*(T)*, 560*(T)*, 329*(F)*, 100*(T)* 345*(T)*, 342*(T)*, 374*(T)*, 459*(T)*, 297*(T)*, 33*(T)*, 359*(T)*, 389*(T)*, 356*(T)*, 40*(T)*, 31*(T)*, 134*(T)*.

Cluster VII (*T*) *Tension, Worry, Fears versus Absence of Such Complaints*
(36 items)

555. I sometimes feel that I am about to go to pieces. (*T*)
431. I worry quite a bit over possible misfortunes. (*T*)
337. I feel anxiety about something or someone almost all the time. (*T*)
217. I frequently find myself worrying about something. (*T*)
238. I have periods of such great restlessness that I cannot sit long in a chair. (*T*).

506(*T*), 543(*T*), 442(*T*), 43(*T*), 242(*F*), 340(*T*), 152(*F*), 448(*T*), 186(*T*), 499(*T*), 166(*T*), 338(*T*), 407(*F*), 182(*T*), 32(*T*), 439(*T*), 335(*T*), 102(*T*), 473(*T*), 158(*T*), 303(*T*), 13(*T*), 388(*T*), 322(*T*), 360(*T*), 22(*T*), 351(*T*), 131(*F*), 365(*T*), 494(*T*), 492(*T*).

A metric presentation of the clusters in relation to their intercorrelations, generality, and reliability can be found in Table 1. Shown above the diagonal are intercorrelations based upon the best 17 items in each cluster, with the exception of the Resentment Cluster in which only the best 16 items were used.[1] Incidentally, these most salient items are the first 17 items in each cluster listed above. The intercorrelations based on the total-cluster items are shown below the diagonal. *It will be noted that clusters I, B, and S are the pivots or the most independent clusters.* The intercorrelations of these three are relatively modest with the highest raw *r* occurring between *I* and *B* of .33. The four remaining clusters, called dependents, are highly correlated with all the clusters. By "dependent" is meant that these four clusters can be predicted from the three pivotal clusters with a fair degree of accuracy.

Attention should also be drawn to the magnitude of the reliabilities shown in row *c* in the same table. For the full supply of defining items the reliabilities range from .85 to .94 with a median *r* of .92. The reliabilities of the best 17 items are also remarkably high, ranging from .81 to .91. This latter finding suggests that shortened scales containing the best 17 items can be used quite reliably for those who need to economize on length.

These seven scales contain 192 items, the distillation from the total 550 MMPI items, and these reproduce the generality of the full supply of the MMPI items.

As a matter of convenience the seven clusters will be referred to henceforth as the Tryon, Stein, and Chu (TSC) psychological scales or clusters.

COMPARISONS OF THE SEVEN ITEM-CLUSTERS WITH THE MMPI SCALES

How do these TSC item-cluster scales compare with the MMPI scales? Chu (1966) approached this question in several ways. First, she observed the extent to which the 192 items of the TSC seven clusters were distributed among the MMPI scales. Table 2 contains such a distribution for the total

---

[1] Intercorrelations were limited to the best 17 items from each cluster scale for the practical convenience of statistical analyses, since the BC TRY System can handle only a maximum of 120 variables at one time.

Table 1
Intercorrelations, Generality, and Reliability of the TSC Item-Cluster Scales

	I	B	S	D	R	A	T
a. *Intercorrelations*[a]							
I Introversion		.33	.24	.73	.49	.41	.61
B Body Symptoms	.48	(pivots)	.30	.48	.44	.51	.66
S Suspicion	.28	.32		.32	.54	.54	.41
D Depression	.75	.60	.40		.64	.57	.78
R Resentment	.61	.53	.63	.74	(dependents)	.59	.69
A Autism	.48	.59	.60	.67	.71		.66
T Tension	.68	.76	.48	.85	.79	.75	
b. *Generality*							
Reproducibility of the 13,806 raw *r*'s.	.65	.55	.41	.83	.72	.67	.88
c. *Reliability*							
(*N* items = 17)	.91	.89	.83	.91	.82	.81	.88
(*N* items = >17)	.93	.92	.85	.94	.87	.86	.92

a, Above the diagonal, raw *r*'s based on best 17 items in each cluster; below the diagonal are found the *r*'s based on the total items in the cluster.

Source: Adapted from Tryon (1966*a*).

items from each cluster. The bottom two rows show the total items in each of the MMPI scales and the total-cluster items in the scale. A proportion can easily be calculated from these data. In the standard scales the proportion of overlap ranges from a low of 7 percent for the *Lie* scale to a high of 77 percent for *Pt*. For the special scales, Welsh's *A* scale contains the largest proportion of cluster items. Eighty-seven percent of its items can be found in the item clusters, whereas this is so for only 28 percent of the *R* scale items. The proportions for the two additional special scales are 40 percent for Barron's Ego Strength scale (*Es*) and 59 percent for Edward's Social Desirability scale (*SD*). It is also of interest to note the concentration of special scale items within clusters. The *A* scale, which purports to measure anxiety, is most heavily loaded with items in the Depression cluster and only secondarily with

Table 2

Distribution of Items of the TSC Psychological Scales on
Clinical and Special Scales of the MMPI

Cluster Name & Symbol	N Items	L	F	K	Hs	D	Hy	Pd	Mf	Pa	Pt	Sc	Ma	Si	Es	A	R	EDW Sd
Social Introversion (I)	26	0	0	4	0	4	5	4	2	1	4	2	3	20	0	3	2	5
Body Symptoms (B)	33	0	2	1	23	10	19	0	0	0	4	4	1	0	9	1	2	2
Suspicion & Mistrust (S)	25	0	1	5	0	1	4	2	4	4	0	0	0	6	1	2	3	1
Depression (D)	28	0	1	2	0	10	3	5	0	1	8	8	0	6	2	13	0	3
Resentment (R)	21	0	1	4	0	2	4	2	1	0	3	1	2	2	2	4	3	1
Autism & Disruptive Thoughts (A)	23	1	2	2	0	1	0	2	2	1	7	8	2	3	7	6	0	2
Tension (T)	36	0	0	2	1	8	4	2	1	4	11	7	4	3	6	5	1	9
Total MMPI Scale Items	(15)	(64)	(30)	(33)	(60)	(60)	(50)	(60)	(40)	(48)	(78)	(46)	(70)	(68)	(39)	(39)	(40)	(39)
Total TSC Items in MMPI Scales	1	7	20	24	36	39	17	10	11	37	30	12	40	27	34	11	23	

Source: Adapted from Chu (1966).

those in the Tension cluster. The *SD* scale, on the other hand, is more heavily loaded in the Tension cluster with a secondary concentration in Introversion. These distributions suggest that the *A* scale may be a measure of depression and Edward's *Sd* a measure of tension and anxiety. Since the items of the cluster scales represent the most general items in the MMPI, Table 2 reflects the extent to which each standard and special scale possesses items that are general and not item specific.

Chu then presented a more direct measure of the relation between the MMPI scales and the item-clusters in the form of correlations, which can be found in Table 3. The *Lie* scale, as expected, has the lowest set of correlations with the cluster scales. Welsh's *A* and the *Pt* scales have the largest magnitude of correlations, but Edward's *Sd* scale is also high. The reader may wish to study this table more carefully since space does not allow for further exposition.

Chu finally examined the extent to which the MMPI standard scales could be predicted from a group of the cluster scales. She showed the extent of such prediction, first from a group of four cluster scales (*I, B, S* and *T*), and second from just the three pivotal clusters (*I, B* and *S*). The results showed fairly high-ranging multiple correlations for a number of the scales based upon both the four and three item-clusters as predictors. The poorest prediction, as expected, occurred with the *Lie* scale (.31) while the most accurate was with Hypochondriasis (.97). The median multiple correlation was .85 using the four item-cluster predictors, and .82 for the three item-cluster predictors. Chu's conclusion from these data was that the MMPI scale scores can be predicted with fairly good accuracy from the reduced subsets of the TSC scales.

COMPARISONS OF MALE AND FEMALE SAMPLES[2]

The TSC seven item-clusters described above were derived from a male sample. Therefore the question can be raised as to whether this seven-item-cluster structure is applicable to females as well. A direct solution would be to apply the BIGNV procedures to a fairly comparable group of females and then to compare the cluster structure of the male and female samples. The BC TRY program COMP is designed for this purpose, and yields an index of dimensional similarity in the form of a cosine theta. Unfortunately, time has not yet permitted such a study, though one is planned. However, the TSC seven item-cluster scores were available on four comparable sets of male and female samples, with the females being scored on the male-derived clusters. Through the full-cycle cluster analysis of these cluster scores for each of the sex samples, together with the application of the COMP program to each of these sex-paired samples, an indication of the applicability of the male clusters to the females should be revealed. The comparisons are between male and female public counseling, college counseling, and education-abroad

[2]Data presented in the remainder of this chapter are new, having been collected and analyzed by the author, and have not been published elsewhere.

Table 3
Correlations of the TSC Psychological Scales and 17 Standard and Special MMPI Scales

SCALES	L	F	K	Hs	D	Hy	Pd	Mf	Pa	Pt	Sc	Ma	Si	Es	A	R	Edw. SD
Social Introversion	-.21	.54	-.55	.45	.71	.27	.40	.35	.42	.77	.67	-.06	.92	-.61	.76	.35	-.78
Body Complaints	-.11	.48	-.45	.97	.68	.77	.40	.14	.35	.71	.63	.14	.52	-.79	.63	.15	-.70
Suspicion and Mistrust	-.27	.38	-.73	.33	.15	-.05	.34	.04	.16	.47	.52	.53	.30	-.42	.52	-.34	-.51
Depression	-.22	.68	-.64	.57	.81	.47	.68	.43	.50	.91	.85	.20	.76	-.72	.93	.14	-.89
Resentment	-.38	.60	-.79	.52	.51	.24	.61	.31	.38	.81	.79	.39	.60	-.62	.81	-.14	-.79
Autism	-.31	.58	-.70	.57	.47	.34	.51	.31	.35	.79	.82	.41	.49	-.71	.78	-.09	-.75
Tension	-.21	.63	-.68	.73	.76	.56	.62	.32	.49	.93	.85	.25	.70	-.81	.88	.10	-.90

Source: Chu, 1966.

college students, all of whom were seen at the University of California, Berkeley, Counseling Center.[3] The fourth set is composed of pre-therapy schizophrenic male and female subjects from the Camarillo Schizophrenia Research Project.

In order to determine the degree of similarity of cluster structure among male and female samples, cosine theta values have been computed for each of the sex-paired samples on each of the seven clusters.[4] Although there is some variation among sex-paired samples, the magnitudes of the cosine theta are generally high. The median values range from .83 to .92, with the median of these cosine thetas being .91. Thus, the males and females show very similar patterns of intercorrelations indicating similarity of cluster structure.

Age, Education, Intelligence, Family Size, and GPA

The age variable was correlated with each of the seven clusters on six male and three female samples.[5] The male samples are numbers 15, 16, 17, 18, 19, and 20 in Table 4. The female samples are numbers 10, 11, and 12 in Table 5. There are no consistently significant associations across samples.[4] For the males only 3 of 42 correlations are significant. Two of these, however, occurred for samples on the Body cluster, a finding not inconsistent with the expectation that body symptoms increase with age. For the three female samples, 4 of the 21 correlations are significant. Only one of these, however,

---

[3]The author is grateful to a number of colleagues who made various samples of MMPI protocols available to him so that they could be scored and used in various statistical analyses. First, a deep gratitude is extended to Dr. Jack Block, who furnished the IBM punch cards with MMPI item responses on a number of samples. Barbara Kirk was especially helpful in providing six male (samples 15 through 20 in Table 4) and three female (samples 10 through 12 in Table 5) samples. Dr. Donald MacKinnon granted permission to use the military officers (sample 1), while Dr. Gale Bach provided the three groups of enlisted men (samples 2 through 4). Drs. Christine Miller, William Reiss, and Alexander Nemeth supplied male sample 9, the VA clinic general psychiatric cases. Drs. Rhodes Young and Jerome Fisher provided the male and female Langley Porter psychiatric groups. Dr. Fisher also provided a hospitalized VA medical male sample. Drs. Philip May and Luther Distler provided the pre- and post-therapy schizophrenia male and female samples from the Camarillo Hospital Schizophrenia Research Project. Dr. Jeanne Block was kind enough to make available the samples of fathers and mothers of children being studied for familial factors in childhood disease. The Oakland Growth Study male and female samples came from the late Dr. Harold E. Jones. Finally, thanks is extended to Dr. Curtis Hardyck for providing five female samples from the hypertensive research project.

Thanks are particularly due to Drs. R. C. Tryon, T. R. Sarbin, and the editor P. W. McReynolds for their valuable comments.

[4]Supplementary material for this chapter has been deposited with the American Documentation Institute. This material includes all of the cosine theta values showing the comparisons of the sex-paired samples, as well as the male and female profile sheets showing the raw scores and their standard score equivalents. In addition, there are sets of correlations between the seven cluster scores and the following variables: age, education, intelligence, family size, grade point average, OPI scales, EPPS scales and the SVIB scales. Order Document No. 9850 from ADI Auxiliary Publications Project, Photo Publication Service, Library of Congress, Washington, D. C. 20540. Remit in advance $1.25 for microfilm or $1.25 for photocopies and make checks payable to: Chief, Photo Duplication Service, Library of Congress.

[5]Samples utilized here are further described in the next section.

occurs on the Body cluster, and surprisingly enough, this one is negative. Two significant correlations occur for the Autism cluster and one for Depression; each of these is also negative. The highest magnitude of any of these age x cluster correlations is .34. Thus the age factor for the most part appears to have very little influence upon the TSC cluster scores, except possibly in the Body Symptom cluster.

Among the males most of the correlations of education with the clusters tend to be negative. Five of the 42 correlations reach significance, and these are all negative. One each of these correlations occurs on Suspicion, Resentment, and Tension, and two on Autism. The r with the largest magnitude is .29. Among the three female samples two r's are significant. A positive association of .37 occurred with Resentment in the group of public counseling cases. The other is -.28 with Autism for the student education-abroad sample. Education therefore does not emerge as having a consistently significant association with any particular cluster.

The measure of intellectual level varied for the different samples and included the Concept Mastery Test (CMT), SCAT, and the Otis. The intelligence measures were available on four of the male groups and one of the female samples. One of the male samples, applicants for jobs as campus police, does show consistently significant and negative r's with all seven clusters on the Otis, ranging from -.40 to -.64. The forestry camp sample, using the SCAT, shows five of the seven r's as significant, with none reaching a magnitude of over -.40. An industrial selection sample with the Otis shows significant but low negative r's on Suspicion, Autism, and Tension. Generally the significant relationships occur on Suspicion, Depression, Autism, and Tension, and these are all in the negative direction. For the one female sample, the education-abroad students, none of the correlations are significant—a result not too dissimilar from the male education-abroad students.

Family size as a variable does not show any relationship to the seven clusters, either in the three male or two female samples. The number of older and younger siblings was also available, and each was correlated with the clusters. None of the three male and two female samples shows any significant relationships with either the number of older brothers or number of older sisters. For two of the male samples significant but small positive correlations do occur between number of younger sisters and Depression, Autism, and Tension, these positive associations being on the order of .30.

Grade Point Average (GPA) was available only for the male and female samples of education-abroad students. The correlations with the TSC item-clusters are generally non-significant. For the males a correlation of .30 did occur with the Depression cluster, and surprisingly, all of the seven correlations for males are positive while the females show consistently negative relations between GPA and the seven clusters. Only one of these seven female correlations reaches significance, however—GPA with Autism, -.28

In summary, age, education, family size, and GPA do not show any consistent relationships to the TSC scales. Intelligence, however, does show some evidence of covariation with four of the seven clusters across four male samples representing both college and non-college groups. Further research is clearly indicated to explore these relationships, particularly among abnormal groups. These results, however, tentatively suggest that subjects with higher intelligence tend to score somewhat lower on the seven cluster scales. The magnitudes of the correlations, although significant, on the average are not high and account for only a relatively modest proportion of the variance.

OPI, EPPS, and SVIB

The Omnibus Personality Inventory (OPI) (1962) was developed at the Center for the Study of Higher Education at the University of California, Berkeley. There are nine scales for which our male and female education-abroad groups were scored. An examination of the data indicates that the Introversion item-cluster scale is highly correlated with the OPI Social Introversion (Si) scale (.74 for males and .69 for females). Introversion is also significantly correlated with Schizoid Functioning (SF) in both samples, but much more so in the males (.70). Complexity (Co) and Religious Liberalism (RL) are also significantly and postively related with Introversion, but only in the males. In both samples Body cluster has its highest correlation with schizoid functioning. The males also have this cluster positively and significantly associated with RL, while the females show an association with Impulse Expression (IE), Si, and Co. Suspicion cluster is most highly related to SF in both groups, with relations to IE (.37), Autonomy (Au) (-.29), and Thinking Introversion (-.34) also significant for males. Depression among males is positively related to SF, IE, SI, and RL, while this holds only for SF and IE among the females. Resentment follows about the same pattern as Depression among the males except that Si is also highly significant. For females Depression is related positively to SF and IE and negatively to Thinking Introversion (Ti). For Autism both the male and female samples show significance in SF and IE. On the Tension cluster SF, IE, and Si are significant for males, and only SF and IE for females.

The Edwards Personal Preference Schedule (EPPS) (Edwards, 1969) was administered to 50 male forestry students and correlated with the TSC scales. Introversion on TSC and Dominance on EPPS are negatively correlated, as might be expected. Body symptom cluster is positively related to Abasement. Suspicion is positively related to Aggression and negatively to Deference in the EPPS. Depression has its only significant r with Abasement, and Resentment with Heterosexuality, while Autism is positively associated with Abasement and negatively with Achievement. Tension is also negatively related to Achievement but with a lower magnitude, while positively with Abasement and negatively with Change.

The Strong Vocational Interest Blank (SVIB) (Strong, 1959) scores were correlated with the seven TSC scales for the male public counseling cases from the University Counseling Center. The significant correlations of occupational interests and the item-clusters are reflected in the following patterns. Introversion is positively related to occupational interest in the biological, engineering, and physical sciences, as well as in the verbal or linguistic fields, while being negatively related to those in production management, social service or welfare, business administration, and sales. A fairly similar pattern also exists for the Body cluster. Suspicion relates positively mainly to verbal or linguistic fields, and negatively to business detail and administration. Depression is consistently negatively related to social service occupations and business administration but positively to the biological sciences. Resentment, Autism, and Tension produced patterns somewhat similar to that of Depression.

In summary then, each of the TSC scales appears to show meaningful relationships with various correlates, which contribute to their validity. The Introversion cluster is related to another measure of introversion, as well as to schizoid functioning in the form of social alienation, feelings of isolation, loneliness, and rejection. High scorers on Introversion also score low on the trait of dominance, tend to show interest in occupations that do not require outgoing, social, and aggressive behaviors, and lean more toward the sciences.

The Body cluster shows a positive relation to social withdrawal and disturbed emotional functioning with a tendency to self-depreciation and guilt, as reflected in need abasement. The associations with occupational interests are similar to those of the Introversion scale.

The Suspicion cluster has a positive association with impulse expression, a scale in which high scorers purportedly value sensations, have an active imagination, and whose thinking is often dominated by feelings and fantasies. Suspicion is also negatively associated with traits and qualities described under need deference. Unlike the Introversion and Body scales, Suspicion shows little relationship to occupational interests in science, but is positively associated with verbal or linguistic occupational interests and negatively with business administration. It should be noted that it is also positive in its covariation with the OPI schizoid functioning and the various traits and qualities associated with it.

The Depression cluster reflects the association with social alienation, isolation, and loneliness noted in the other clusters as well as with positive relationships to impulse expression and a tendency toward abasement. Depression and occupational interests in social service or welfare are decidedly negative in their association.

The Resentment cluster is positively related to impulse expression, introversion, and social alienation as well as to aggressive and heterosexual needs. Occupational interests are not clearly patterned in relationship to Resentment except to show a similar negative association to social service or welfare.

Autism is also positive in its association with schizoid functioning, impulse expression, aggressive and abasement needs, but negative with achievement. Occupational interest shows up only in business detail and administration, and this relationship is negative.

Tension similarly reflects the emotional dysfunction reflected in the OPI scales of *Si, SF,* and *IE.* In addition, it is associated positively with abasement and negatively with both the achievement and change needs. As for occupational interest, both social service and business detail and administration have negative relationships.

A COMPARISON OF VARIOUS SAMPLES

Tables 4 and 5 present the means and sigmas of the TSC scales for 20 male and 13 female samples. Seven of the male groups (samples 1, 11, 12, 16,

Table 4

Raw Means and Sigmas on Item-Cluster Scales for 20 Male Samples

MALE SAMPLES	N	Means							Sigmas						
		I Introv.	B Body	S Susp.	D Depres.	R Resent.	A Autism	T Tension	I	B	S	D	R	A	T
1) Military Officers (MacKinnon)	100	4.14	3.02	9.90	3.25	4.55	4.75	5.15	3.87	2.71	5.23	2.77	3.82	3.41	3.81
2) Military Recruits—Homosex. (Bach)	31	15.77	12.48	16.13	17.13	13.32	14.03	20.35	5.87	6.38	5.12	5.68	4.74	5.04	8.02
3) Military Recruits—Inaptitude (Bach)	66	15.97	15.08	15.44	17.32	12.38	13.68	21.83	6.25	6.30	4.98	6.54	5.12	5.60	6.95
4) Military Recruits—Adjusted (Bach)	57	9.02	6.09	14.93	8.47	10.56	9.54	10.84	5.15	4.88	4.67	5.00	4.09	4.24	5.45
5) Hospitalized Med., VA (Fisher)	100	7.28	8.44	8.74	5.12	5.55	4.60	7.78	5.66	5.07	4.68	4.52	3.99	3.34	4.56
6) Anx. Neurosis, VA Clinic (Tryon-Sears)	150	13.48	14.55	11.48	14.62	10.42	9.63	18.42	6.90	7.20	5.55	7.00	4.63	4.99	6.92
7) Par. Schizophrenia, VA Clinic (Tryon-Sears)	32	11.56	9.50	13.63	12.13	9.47	8.72	15.59	6.81	7.06	6.05	7.65	5.02	5.17	7.45
8) Other Schizophrenia, VA Clinic (Tryon-Sears)	38	13.58	10.45	12.08	14.34	9.82	9.08	16.68	7.23	5.96	6.14	7.72	5.55	4.49	7.21
9) Gen'l Psychiatric, VA Clinic (Miller et al.)	100	11.92	12.67	11.94	13.58	8.96	8.04	15.98	7.25	6.72	6.27	7.39	4.99	4.42	7.30
10) Gen'l Psychiatric, LP Hospital (Young-Fisher)	202	11.91	10.01	12.40	14.29	9.29	9.24	16.70	6.26	6.30	5.63	6.96	4.69	4.55	7.05
11) Normal Fathers (Block)	95	6.55	3.97	7.75	3.92	5.09	4.69	6.53	4.28	3.03	5.42	3.48	3.40	3.05	4.11
12) Normal Males – OGS (Jones)	46	8.26	4.85	8.98	4.22	5.59	4.52	8.00	6.11	3.73	4.43	3.71	3.04	2.38	4.85
13) Hosp. Schiz. Pre-therapy (May-Distler)	73	12.03	9.01	13.78	11.75	9.27	9.84	15.22	6.65	6.76	6.48	7.43	5.64	5.71	8.81
14) Hosp. Schiz. Post-therapy (May-Distler)	101	9.30	6.59	10.64	8.19	6.83	7.30	10.98	5.92	5.91	5.98	6.68	4.71	4.92	7.40
15) College Counseling (Kirk)	120	11.74	5.81	8.05	9.29	6.20	7.28	10.63	6.44	4.82	4.49	5.98	4.07	3.96	6.09
16) Education Abroad Students (Kirk)	50	6.42	2.36	6.46	3.82	3.82	5.20	5.62	5.12	2.22	3.87	3.94	3.43	2.90	4.35
17) Industrial Selection (Kirk)	50	3.54	1.94	6.24	2.52	3.58	3.96	5.68	4.15	1.98	5.29	2.83	3.51	3.27	4.23
18) Campus Police Applicants (Kirk)	34	3.82	2.47	9.53	3.41	3.18	4.15	5.44	3.07	3.53	5.64	4.47	3.83	4.34	6.08
19) Forestry Students (Kirk)	50	7.88	3.50	8.36	5.06	5.20	3.98	7.32	5.07	2.81	4.20	4.70	3.36	3.83	4.58
20) Public Counseling (Kirk)	50	10.10	4.78	7.80	7.94	5.48	6.14	9.54	5.70	4.85	4.54	6.88	3.75	3.97	6.18
Normative Samples # 1, 11, 12, 16-19	425	5.62	3.24	7.85	3.71	4.21	4.65	5.86	4.98	2.99	5.78	3.67	3.99	3.41	4.80

Source: Stein, unpublished data.

Table 5

Raw Means and Sigmas on Item-Cluster Scales for 13 Female Samples

FEMALE SAMPLES	N	Means							Sigmas						
		I Introv.	B Body	S Susp.	D Depres.	R Resent.	A Autism	T Tension	I	B	S	D	R	A	T
1) College Student Normals (Hardyck)	39	9.64	4.46	9.03	6.13	6.80	6.77	9.59	5.34	2.86	4.36	4.30	4.16	2.62	4.47
2) Coll. Stud. Pre-hypertensive (Hardyck)	37	10.03	4.30	7.68	6.00	6.08	5.51	9.00	6.04	3.13	4.94	4.58	3.50	3.45	4.93
3) General Medical Patients (Hardyck)	42	12.40	14.14	12.17	11.07	9.00	8.24	16.76	5.49	6.96	4.46	5.36	4.08	4.21	6.49
4) High Blood Pressure Patients (Hardyck)	45	11.78	11.40	11.20	9.51	8.51	7.98	14.09	5.91	7.03	4.87	5.74	3.94	4.84	7.17
5) Gen'l Psychiatric, LP Hospital (Young-Fisher)	226	13.37	11.99	10.95	15.04	9.30	9.59	18.75	5.88	6.81	5.81	6.88	4.68	5.28	7.28
6) Normal Mothers (Block)	110	9.62	6.38	6.60	5.61	6.26	5.35	9.77	5.86	4.94	4.93	4.94	3.95	3.80	5.82
7) Hypertensives (Hardyck)	79	10.48	12.00	9.60	7.60	6.91	6.66	13.28	5.80	5.42	5.46	5.11	4.18	3.62	6.42
8) Hosp. Schiz. Pre-therapy (May-Distler)	69	12.30	10.87	13.09	11.33	8.55	9.28	16.12	5.77	6.85	5.54	6.65	4.46	5.62	8.07
9) Hosp. Schiz. Post-therapy (May-Distler)	91	9.70	6.62	9.46	7.37	6.38	6.84	10.46	5.35	5.72	5.58	5.75	4.34	4.73	6.99
10) College Counseling (Kirk)	120	11.34	6.09	7.43	9.61	6.67	7.16	11.86	6.66	4.88	4.92	6.60	4.29	3.61	6.86
11) Education Abroad Students (Kirk)	50	6.64	3.18	5.48	3.56	4.24	5.78	7.06	3.94	2.67	3.22	3.36	3.03	2.88	4.34
12) Public Counseling (Kirk)	50	9.66	5.28	6.44	8.00	5.98	5.08	10.02	4.96	4.48	3.54	5.36	4.14	2.80	5.37
13) Normal Females – OGS (Jones)	49	10.06	7.61	6.47	5.92	6.80	5.78	10.94	6.59	5.96	4.29	5.20	3.59	3.92	6.56
Normative Samples # 1, 2, 6, 11, 13	285	9.23	5.50	6.92	5.43	6.01	5.71	9.37	5.79	4.53	4.59	4.69	3.88	3.42	5.58

Source: Stein, unpublished data.

100 KENNETH B. STEIN

17, 18, and 19) constituted the normal samples used in establishing standard score norms with a mean of 50 and sigma of 10. Five of the female samples (numbers 1, 2, 6, 11, and 13) were utilized in constructing the female norms. Figures 1 through 5 show the sample profiles based on the standard score norms for males and females. The means and sigmas of the cluster scores for the composited normal groups used to form the norms are found at the bottom of each of Tables 4 and 5. A brief description of the samples follows:

Samples 1 through 4 of the males are from the military services. The military officers were those studied in a live-in assessment at the Institute of Personality Assessment and Research of the University of California at Berkeley. The three enlisted military recruit samples, all in basic training, consisted of a group of men discharged for admitted homosexuality, another group discharged for inaptness, and a third sample of recruits who success-fully completed training. Figure 1 graphically shows the patterns of the four groups. The two maladjusted military samples have similar patterns of very high-ranging scores with high points on *B, D,* and *T.* The two adjusted military groups have patterns similar to each other but different from the maladjusted samples and with profile elevations considerably lower. The profile peaks for the two adjusted groups occur on *S* and *R,* and the general profile level is lower for the officers. Maladjustment in the military samples is characterized then by bodily preoccupation, depression or dysphoric mood, anxiety, and tension. Successful adjustment is reflected in such charac-terological manifestations as suspiciousness and mistrust, resentment, and aggression, together with very little in the way of symptomatic complaints.

Figure 2 shows the pattern scores of five psychiatric clinic and counseling center samples (samples 6, 7, 8, 15, and 20 in Table 4). The three psychiatric groups were those utilized in the study sample from which the TSC scales

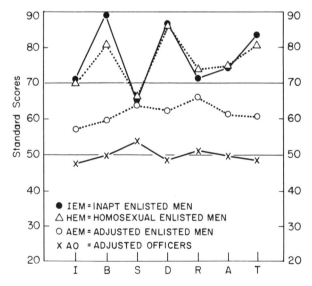

Figure 1. Mean profiles of four male military samples

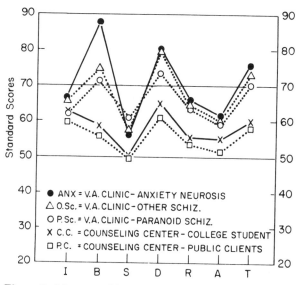

Figure 2. Mean profiles of five Psychiatric Clinic and Counseling Center male samples

were derived. The Counseling Center clients were being seen for vocational and personal counseling. The psychiatric and counseling samples differ both in the magnitude and the pattern of their scores. The distinguishing characteristic of the anxiety sample is the very high peak on B and the low point on S. The paranoids show a generally similar pattern but are lower in elevation than both the anxieties and other schizophrenias on all scores except S. The two counseling groups do not peak on B but rather show a negative slope on the first three clusters—I, B, and S. The college counselees are consistently more elevated than their public counseling counterparts. This finding, however, may be the result of the selection procedure, in which all the public counselees, but only the more disturbed college counselees, were administered the MMPI. Both counseling groups show a D, I high-point pattern.

Figure 3 gives the patterns of four hospitalized samples—one medical and three psychiatric. The medical sample has a generally low-ranging profile except for the B scale. Along with body complaints there is a slight elevation in D, R, T, and I. The Langley Porter new psychiatric admission sample displays the highest-ranging scores of the four samples and reflects the acuteness of the condition of the patients. Although the two schizophrenic samples reveal a similar pattern, the post-therapy patients show a consistently lower score of almost one sigma in magnitude.

The female samples with their means and sigmas are listed in Table 5 and graphically represented in Figures 4 and 5.

Figure 4 contains three hospitalized samples of psychiatric patients and one sample of relatively normal females. The Langley Porter sample has the highest level of scores, reflecting the acute disturbance of these patients. The elevations of the two schizophrenic samples fall between the normal and the

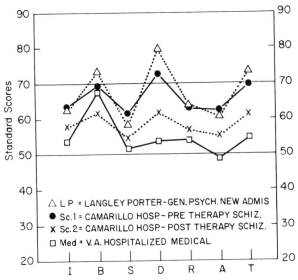

Figure 3. Mean profiles of four hospitalized medical and
psychiatric male samples

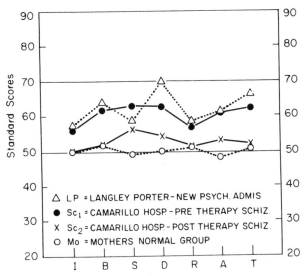

Figure 4. Mean profiles of three hospitalized psychiatric
and one normal female group

Langley Porter samples, with patterns that are also different. Whereas the
Langley Porter sample shows a *D, T, B* pattern the schizophrenics reveal an *S,
D, T* configuration. As with the male counterparts from the Camarillo pro-
ject, the post-therapy schizophrenic sample scores about one sigma below the

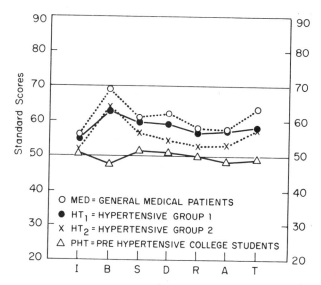

Figure 5. Mean profiles of four female samples from hypertensive study

pre-treatment group, reflecting an apparent decrease in emotional and physical discomfort level.

Samples 1, 2, 3, 4, and 7 were from a project studying hypertensive females. Four of these are shown in Figure 5. The college prehypertensive female sample has the lowest elevation, one that is flat and practically at the mean of each of the cluster scales. In contrast, the general medical patients have the highest-ranging scores with the two hypertensive samples located between the medical and prehypertensive groups.

The patterns of the remaining female samples can be found and compared with above described samples in Table 5.

AN EVALUATION OF THE CLUSTER SCALES

A cluster analysis of items produces a different structure than would emerge from a cluster or factor analysis of MMPI scales. Even so, the question can be raised as to whether the three pivotal item-clusters have any conceptual similarity to the two factors frequently extracted from a cluster analysis of the MMPI scales. The first item-cluster, Social Introversion, shares the same name as the second factor of Kassebaum, Couch, and Slater (1959). The Body cluster as such does not resemble any specific factor found in past factor-analytic studies of MMPI scales. This item-cluster, however, does draw heavily upon items from the neurotic triad of *Hs, D,* and *Hy*–scales that are often heavily loaded on a factor variously called "neuroticism," "repression" and "denial" or "ego control." The Suspicion item-cluster also does not resemble any of the factors of previous studies. It does correlate highly and negatively, however, with the *K* scale and moderately positively with *Sc, Pt, Ma,* and *A*. These are scales that tend to have their highest loadings on the first factor in many studies and have been variously named "psycho-neuroticism," "psychoticism," "ego weakness," "anxiety," and "ego resiliency."

As a set of scales, how can they be evaluated? If we use Gough's (1965a) model for a conceptual analysis of psychological tests, there are questions that can be asked at each of three stages of evaluation. The first stage is the primary evaluation, an assessment of whether the tests or scales measure what they purport to measure, diagnose, or predict. As with the MMPI scales, these item-cluster scales are used to make assessments and diagnoses about emotional and characterological disturbance. In terms of the limited amount of data available at this time, the indications are that the seven item-cluster scales do make diagnostic discriminations between the more and less disturbed groups. Evidence for this conclusion can be seen in Tables 4 and 5 as well as Figures 1 through 5. The use of two- and three-high-point scales and total-scale patterns shows a potential for differential diagnosis among the disturbed groups. A line of research that should prove useful would be to establish pattern types by means of object or inverse analysis (cf. Tryon, 1967a; Chu, 1966), and then to relate these types to various categories of behavior.

The next stage is the secondary evaluation, which relates to the underlying meaning or psychological underpinnings of the scales. Both from an analysis of the item content of each scale and from the correlations with tests such as the OPI, EPPS, and SVIB, the symptomatic and characterological constructs reflected in each of the cluster names do appear to find meaning and validity. However, much more research is needed in order to spell out the fuller conceptual meanings and implications of each scale as well as of their configurations.

The last stage is the tertiary evaluation, which involves the meaningful application of each scale or some pattern of scales to psychological and behavioral areas other than those for which the scale was originally intended. There has been insufficient research thus far to render such an evaluation possible at this time.

As a concluding remark to this chapter, it seems apparent that as more sophisticated computer programs continue to be developed along with more versatile computer hardware, certain methodological problems that have hampered various data analyses should readily find solution. The TSC scales described in this chapter are an example of the outcome of the application of a new and highly effective set of computer programs both to the solution of the methodological problem of factoring a large number of item variables and to the construction of highly reliable and valid personality and clinical symptom scales.

CHAPTER VI

The Strong Vocational Interest Blank: 1927–1967

David P. Campbell

The Strong Vocational Interest Blank (SVIB) has the longest history of any current, widely-used psychological inventory. First published in 1927, the SVIB has been the subject of extensive research for the past forty years. Much has been learned about the meaning of a person's answers to this inventory, and more knowledge is continually coming into existence. Though our areas of ignorance are still great, they are at least becoming better identified, permitting a more efficient concentration of effort; and the coming years should see a substantial expansion of our understanding of what interests are, how they can be measured, and how these measures can be used to make life more pleasant.

This is a brief history of the SVIB; it is not a technical paper in the usual sense, as the development of this inventory is reviewed from an historical rather than psychometric viewpoint. Those who wish more detailed technical information should refer to the Manual (Campbell, 1966a).

The history of a psychological test is not a thrilling saga; there have been no gatherings in dusty squash courts to see if the gadget will really work, no agonizing waits to see if the graft or transplant survives, no tension-ridden countdowns. Like most science, it has been a succession of drab and trivial activities with only an occasionally significant statistic to brighten the day. Even when results look bright and promising, in the social sciences skepticism is so essential until several replications are completed that any thrill of a new breakthrough is dampened by the necessity of oozing under, over, and around the barriers of ignorance until it is certain that the key—and not simply more error variance—has appeared. This means one is never sure just when it was that he learned what he now knows is true.

Lively times have not been entirely absent; any research with people creates its own sparks, whether angry letters from participants, friendly testimonials from the audience, or professional disagreements over the philosophy, techniques, or—not the least—finances of the operations. The recent (1966) revision of the SVIB involved two major investigators, separated by fifty years in age and training; two others, more tangential but with bright, innovative, and occasionally disruptive ideas; a family that justifiably feels possessive about the inventory; a university press publisher that values quality over profit; commercial distributors with somewhat different feelings; four scoring services with a variety of approaches; and a host of professionals who, from years of personal use, feel the Strong Blank is in some sense "their" test. With these diverse outlooks and in the absence of corporation-chart-block-diagram lines of command and communication, the pot boiled occasionally.

However, for the most part, things have been staid, and most of the issues have been no more controversial than "What color paper shall we use?" "Do we need 200 or 400 people to establish a new scale?" "In this form letter to women chemists, what salutation shall we use? Dear Madam . . . Dear Mesdames . . . Dear Dr. . . . , To Whom it May Concern . . . ?" (Eventual solution—Dear Chemist:).

SOME HISTORICAL TRENDS

Those associated with the SVIB—especially its originator, Professor E. K. Strong, Jr.,—have continually insisted on an active research program. They have especially encouraged longitudinal studies so that the place of inventoried interests in long-range career development can be better understood. Even if there were no intrinsic academic reasons for studying this history, the emphasis on long-term projects would make it essential; to comprehend fully the results of studies over time, one must know something about the background of the research.

An appropriate place to begin is with two charts showing trends over time. Figure 1 shows the number of booklets (for the Men's Form only) printed each year since the SVIB was first published. The narrow line is the number actually printed; the broad line is a three-year floating average, a better technique for identifying trends. The line is generally upward with a sizable spurt in 1947, obviously reflecting the counseling of the returning veterans of World War II. Most of the postwar booklets have been reuseable forms so that more recent printing figures are a gross underestimate of the number of men who have filled in the SVIB each year. A rough guess is that each booklet is used approximately two to four times, so perhaps 300,000 to 500,000 men now complete the Strong annually. This corresponds roughly to the collective volume of the commerical scoring services.

The second trend line, in Figure 2, shows the number of technical publications directly related to the SVIB appearing each year since 1926. This figure was built from the list of SVIB references in Buros' *Mental Measurements Yearbook* (Buros, 1965). By 1967, the total number of publications was well over eight hundred, a level of activity that would have amazed and gratified Dr. Strong.

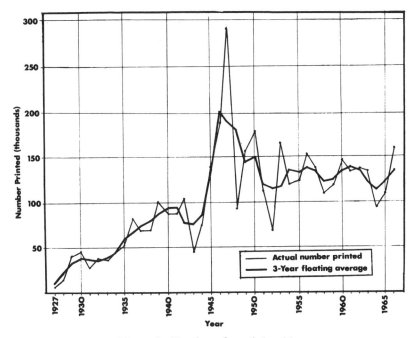

Figure 1. Number of men's booklets

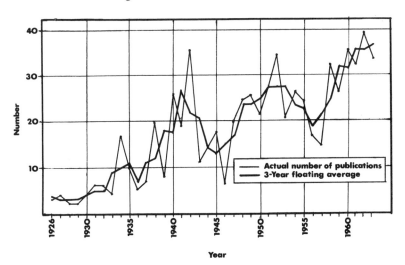

Figure 2. Annual SVIB publications

As a further shorthand for reviewing the history of the SVIB, Table 1 has been prepared. Here historical highlights are listed in three columns: the first deals with the SVIB, the second with Professor Strong's career—for it is meaningless to study the SVIB without reference to his life—and the third with the flavor of the times.

Table 1

Noteworthy Events in the History of the SVIB

Strong Vocational Interest Blank	Edward K. Strong, Jr.	Historical Context
	1884 EKS born in Syracuse, New York.	1884 Grover Cleveland elected President.
	1902 EKS's father takes pastorate in San Francisco.	
	1906 EKS earns B.A. in biology from U.C. (Berkeley); takes job briefly with U.S. Forest Service.	1906 San Francisco earthquake; galleys of U.C. 1906 yearbook destroyed at print shop, so EKS's class had none.
	1909 EKS earns M.A. from Berkeley, leaves for Columbia to study with Cattell and Thorndike.	1909 Peary acclaimed for reaching North Pole.
	1911 EKS marries Margaret Hart, student at Barnard; receives Ph.D. from Columbia; publishes first technical paper, "The Effect of Various Types of Suggestion upon Muscular Activity" (*Psych. Review*); spends next three years doing research on advertising methods.	1911 "Alexander's Rag Time Band" published.
	1912 Daughter, Margaret, born; she later marries Thomas Harrell, currently Professor of Psychology in School of Business at Stanford.	
	1914-1917 EKS joins psychology faculty at George Peabody College, Nashville, Tennessee.	
	1914 Birth of son, Edward—now a physician in San Francisco.	1915 Sinking of Lusitania; America edges toward war.

1917 U.S. enters World War I.

1919 World War I ends; U.S. Senate votes not to enter League of Nations.

1920 Harding elected President; Prohibition comes in; America enters Roaring Twenties.

1921-1923 Chinese Communist party founded.

1927 Lindbergh flies the Atlantic; Stalin takes over Russia.

1916 Birth of daughter, Frances, who is later to marry Ralph Berdie, now Professor of Psychology at Minnesota.

1917-1919 EKS serves with Army Committee on Classification of Personnel.

1919 EKS publishes *Introductory Psychology for Teachers* (Warwick and York).

1919-1923 EKS teaches at Carnegie Institute of Technology, Pittsburgh.

1922 EKS publishes *The Psychology of Selling Life Insurance* (Harper and Brothers).

1923 EKS moves to Stanford as Professor of Psychology in School of Business; publishes (with R. S. Uhrbrock) *Job Analysis and the Curriculum* (Williams and Wilkins).

1925 EKS publishes *The Psychology of Selling Advertising* (McGraw-Hill).

1926 EKS publishes (at age 42) first article on interest measurement, "An Interest Test for Personnel Managers" (*Journal of Personnel Research*).

1919 Yoakum's seminar at Carnegie Tech prepares 1,000-item pool of interest items.

1923 Karl Cowdery builds 263-item inventory for project under Strong.

1927 EKS publishes 420-item SVIB, building from Carnegie Tech work and Cowdery's project (Stanford University Press).

1928 First SVIB Manual published.

Table 1 (Continued)
Noteworthy Events in the History of the SVIB

Strong Vocational Interest Blank	Edward K. Strong, Jr.	Historical Context
		1929 "Black Tuesday" stock-market crash.
	1931 EKS publishes *Change of Interests with Age* (Stanford University Press).	1932 Franklin D. Roosevelt pledges "New Deal" for American public; elected President.
1933 Women's SVIB copyrighted; 410 items, 262 in common with Men's Form.	1933 EKS publishes *Vocational Aptitudes of Second-Generation Japanese in the United States*, and *Japanese in California* (Stanford University Press).	1934 DPC born in Bridgewater, Iowa.
1935 First Manual for Women's Form.		
1938 Major revision of Men's Form—400 items; "modern" profile adopted.	1938 EKS publishes *Psychological Aspects of Business* (McGraw-Hill).	1938 B. F. Skinner publishes *Behavior of Organisms* (D. Appleton Century Co.).
		1939 Germany invades Poland; World War II starts.
1941 John G. Darley, at Minnesota, publishes first monograph on SVIB, *Clinical Aspects and Interpretation of the SVIB* (Psychological Corporation).	1943 EKS publishes *Vocational Interests of Men and Women* (Stanford University Press); awarded Butler Medal from Columbia University for this work.	1941 Japanese bomb Pearl Harbor; U.S. enters war.
		1945 World War II ends.

1948 Truman upsets Dewey for Presidency.

1952 Eisenhower elected, goes to Korea to review war.

1955 Rock 'n roll music comes in: "See You Later, Alligator," and Elvis Presley begin climb to fame; Iron Curtain countries sign Warsaw Pact.

1957 Russia launches Sputnik.

1960 Kennedy elected President; launches New Frontier.

1962 John Glenn orbits the earth.

1948 EKS begins follow-up study of Stanford students tested in 1920's and 1930's.

1949 EKS retires from Stanford.

1955 EKS comes to Minnesota to talk about revision; publishes *Vocational Interests Eighteen Years after College* (University of Minnesota Press).

1958 EKS gives Walter Bingham Lecture at Minnesota, "Satisfactions and Interests" (published in *American Psychologist*).

1962 EKS makes last visit to Minnesota to review revision decisions with Berdie, Campbell, and Clark.

1946 Women's Form revised to parallel Men's Form—400 items; Elmer Hankes, in Minneapolis, invents first automatic scoring machine for SVIB.

1955 U. of Minnesota has symposium on SVIB; results published in *The Strong Vocational Interest Blank: Research and Uses*, edited by W. L. Layton (University of Minnesota Press); John G. Darley and Theda Hagenah publish *Vocational Interest Measurement* (University of Minnesota Press).

1958 All SVIB criterion-group data transferred to Minnesota for computer analysis.

1959 First "modern" SVIB Manual published by Consulting Psychologists Press.

1962 National Computer Systems, Minneapolis, builds first SVIB scoring machine using digital computer.

Table 1 (Continued)
Noteworthy Events in the History of the SVIB

Strong Vocational Interest Blank	Edward K. Strong, Jr.	Historical Context
1963 U. of Minnesota establishes Center for Interest Measurement Research; remainder of EKS files shipped to Minnesota; Measurement Research Center, Iowa City, enters SVIB scoring field.	1963 [December 4] EKS passes away in Palo Alto, California.	1963 Kennedy assassinated.
	1964 EKS's last publication appears: "Proposed Scoring Changes for the SVIB" (with Campbell, Berdie, and Clark, *Journal of Applied Psychology*).	1964 Johnson swamps Goldwater for Presidency.
1966 Major revision of Men's Form published— 399 items.		
1968 [?] Major revision of Women's Form.		

THE EARLY HISTORY

The genesis of psychological tests and inventories in America dates back to about 1900. The first attempt to deal specifically with interests was probably made by E. L. Thorndike and reported in the *Popular Science Monthly* (1912) as "The permanence of interests and their relation to abilities." In this project, 100 college students were asked to rank-order their interests as they remembered them in elementary school, in high school, and at the time of testing. Then they were asked to rank-order their abilities for the same periods. Thorndike computed correlations between the various rank orders and (perhaps going a bit beyond his data) concluded:

> These facts unanimously witness to the importance of early interests. They are shown to be far from fickle and evanescent. . . . Interests are also shown to be symptomatic, to a very great extent, of present and future capacity or ability. Either because one likes what he can do well, or because one gives zeal and effort to what he likes, or because interest and ability are both symptoms of some fundamental feature of the individual's original nature, or because of the combined action of all three factors, interest and ability are bound very closely together. The bond is so close that either may be used as a symptom for the other almost as well as for itself.

We have since learned that the relationship between interests and abilities is much more complex.

A second early attempt was a questionnaire developed by T. L. Kelley (1914), asking questions such as: "If you had the opportunity, which one of the following would you attend, supposing each one of them to be first class of its kind?" (Then follow 14 amusements, such as "Circus" and "Grand Opera.")

Kelley's questionnaire apparently was not noticed by others, and the real beginning of the interest inventory as we know it was at the Carnegie Institute of Technology in Pittsburgh shortly after World War I. An active group of industrial psychologists, headed by Walter Bingham, attacked many applied psychological problems, including the problem of measuring interests. Douglas Fryer, in his 1931 book, *The Measurement of Interests*, summarized the early activities:

> The earliest investigation in this [Carnegie Tech] group undertaking was one by Bruce Moore in which an attempt was made to measure the mechanical and social interests of engineers (Moore, 1921). Other early investigations from this source were studies made by Ream (1924), who endeavored to distinguish by their interests between successful and unsuccessful salesmen, and by Freyd (1924), who continued the research of Moore in a further attempt to distinguish by their interests between mechanical and social groups of people. Miner's work (Miner, 1922) upon the inventorying method was a factor in this undertaking which has made the measurement of interests a feasible enterprise.

... further work has continued in the development of a standardized inventory along the line laid down by its beginnings. Research under the direction of Strong at Stanford University and Paterson at the University of Minnesota has been most fruitful in increasing the scope and standardization of the inventories and the development of scoring keys designating the interests of various social groups [p. 61].

One focus of the work at Carnegie Tech, about 1919, was a seminar conducted by C. S. Yoakum; under his direction a group of graduate students prepared an extensive pool of items for interest inventories. This pool—about 1000 items—has had considerable historical influence as the following inventories are direct descendants from Yoakum's seminar (and most other modern inventories have probably borrowed from them in one way or another):

The Carnegie Interest Inventory, 1921
The Carnegie Interest Analysis, 1923
Occupational Interests, published by Freyd in 1923
The Interest Report Blank, by Cowdery at Stanford in 1924
The General Interest Inventory, by Kornhauser in 1927
The Purdue Interest Report Blank, by Remmers in 1929
Strong's Vocational Interest Blank, 1927, developed mainly from Cowdery's inventory with the addition of several more items
The Minnesota Interest Inventory, Paterson in the early thirties (not to be confused with Clark's Minnesota Vocational Interest Inventory, developed during the fifties)
The InterestAnalysis Blank, by Hubbard at Minnesota in the mid-thirties, using Paterson's blank as a beginning

Some of the early activity at Carnegie Tech was described in a 1927 letter from Professor J. B. Miner of Kentucky to Strong; a condensed version is printed below. Miner's letter mirrors the early thinking, and his sharp comment makes it clear that professional sensitivities over citations and credits have always been with us. (In the collection of old inventories at Minnesota are two from the 1920's. They are identical down to the last comma and period, except that one carries a copyright from Carnegie Tech, the other from the University of Kentucky.)

Lexington, Kentucky
August 22, 1927

[the day before the execution
of Sacco and Vanzetti]

My Dear Strong:

You suggest that I describe the sequence of events starting with my Vocational Analysis Blank. As far as I have been able to trace it, it was like this: the idea of paired interest-contrasts occurred to me as a method of getting records of interests which might later be worked up for discriminating vocational interests. I included it in the first blank "An Analysis of Vocational Interests" which was tried out in the Pittsburgh high schools in 1918. The paper of 1921 summarized the results, but included only the suggestion of using the interest-contrasts for discovering unusual interests of students: Did a student have an interest like 1 in 15, etc.

Bruce Moore apparently paid no attention to my method of recording interests, did not even mention it in his thesis although he must have seen the blank as I think he worked out his plan there at Tech. He seems to have been the first to use the occupational names to discriminate groups. Ream, Freyd, you, and Cowdery have since tried and modified his method. . . . I think my first blank also contained the first attempt to make a functional classification of occupations so that students or adults would consider certain behavior resemblances and interest likenesses rather than the U.S. Census classification. . . .

My method for evaluating the psychograph of interests has, I think, one essentially correct idea. Those in each occupational group should be compared with those in a random group of people of the sort that would make the choices contemplated. . .

J. B. Miner

The last paragraph reports the genesis of "Men-in-General," a central concept in Strong's method of measuring interests.

THE DEVELOPMENT OF THE SVIB AT STANFORD

In 1923 the industrial psychology program at Carnegie Tech was discontinued. At an informal gathering after the farewell banquet, someone asked Bingham what he thought the major contribution of the program had been. He replied, as Strong recollected later, that the measurement of interests would probably prove to be the most important.

This impressed Strong and when he joined the Stanford faculty the next year—recruited in part by Lewis Terman, who was then working on his high-IQ students—one of the first projects carried out under Strong's direction was a thesis by Karl Cowdery on the interests of physicians, engineers, and lawyers. Strong (1927a) later summarized the study:

Cowdery finds that the five groups—(a) freshmen and sophomores planning to be engineers; (b) juniors and seniors in engineering school; (c) engineers in graduate work; (d) engineers with less than 5 years practical experience; and (e) engineers with more than 5 years practical experience—all score approximately the same on the interest test. The same holds true with respect to physicians and lawyers. . . .

If all this is correct, it means that what is measured by this test is present in men prior to technical training and practical experience and presumably leads to their vocational choice and is not a resultant of that vocational choice.

The middle twenties were active years; the landmarks were Strong's first publication in interest measurement in 1926, the copyright of the booklet in 1927, and the distribution of the first Manual—a mimeographed document—in 1928. The state of the art then can perhaps be best understood by quoting extensively from that Manual:

There has been such an insistent demand from many to use this test for one purpose or another that the author feels constrained to issue these instructions although very much remains to be done before the test should be considered as properly standardized. . . .

It is believed that scores on this test are indicative of whether or not a young man would like the work of a given occupation. His score is a measure of how nearly his interests agree with those of the average man successfully engaged in that occupation.

It will be some time before the validity of this test can be exactly determined. The results so far obtained seem to show that the test has genuine merit. Nevertheless, the test should be used only by those who approach the problem of vocational guidance with an experimental point of view and who will use the test results with proper safeguards. [Note: This caution about experimental point of view appeared in the 1928, 1929, 1930, and 1931 manuals, disappearing in 1933 after the first longitudinal data became available.—DPC]

If a man scores low, for example, in the interests of lawyers, it means that he would not like that occupational environment. If he scores high, the score may be interpreted in three ways depending upon how he scores in other interests. First, if he scores higher in law than any other occupation, presumably he should enter law. Second, if he scores higher in some other occupation than in law, he possibly should enter that other occupation. But third, he may better plan his career to utilize his interests in two or more occupations. Thus, if he scores high in both law and engineering, he might prepare for both and become a patent attorney, or a lawyer specializing in engineering problems. . . .

Practical use of the test for vocational guidance purposes must be based for some time to come on several assumptions, which our data suggest are true. Nevertheless, extensive research is necessary before these assumptions can be viewed as established.

The first assumption is that a man will be more effective in his vocational career and also be happier if he is engaged in work that he likes than if he is forced to do many things he dislikes.

Second, men who have continued to work at a given occupation for a considerable period of time, and are considered to be successfully earning a living must like that occupational environment fairly well (or at least like it better than any other they can enter).

Third, it is assumed that interests as measured by this test are fairly permanent from the time one enters college to later life, and that they are not particularly affected by technical training and practical experience. In other words, the interests of a young man of 20 are largely responsible for his choice of career. If such interests are very strong, the man becomes an artist, accountant, or lawyer, almost regardless of present day environmental factors; if these interests are weak, the environmental factors play a very much larger role in determining what he does in life.

The 1928 Manual listed these scales:

Now Available: Advertising, Architect, Certified Public Accountant, Chemist, Engineer, Journalist, Lawyer, Minister, Psychologist, School Teacher and Administrator.

Under Development: Author, Artist (painter), Farmer, Life Insurance Salesman, District Manager (specialty), Civil Engineer, Electrical Engineer, Mechanical Engineer, Mining Engineer, Purchasing Agent, YMCA General Secretary.

Expected Soon: Banker, Credit Manager, Office Worker, Personnel Manager, Physician, Real Estate Salesman.

In the 1929 Manual under the heading "To Whom the Test Should Be Given" are the following paragraphs:

The scales and norms are based upon *adult men.* Our results indicate that in the case of *college men* (20 to 30 years of age) that the test can be used with success.

There are no data upon *high school boys.* Their scores probably average lower than what these same boys will obtain ten years later. Allowance should be made for this constant error in the test.

There are no data on *women.* It is very questionable whether women should be scored upon this test. They should not be given their ratings unless an emphatic statement is made that no one knows the significance of their ratings.

Validity and reliability concerned Strong from the beginning. Though he felt concurrent validity—the ability of the test to separate adult occupations—had been established early, he was concerned with predictive validity to the end of his career. In his first publication on this specific topic, "The Diagnostic Value of the Vocational Interest Test" (Strong, 1929), he reported:

One hundred and fifty-six seniors of the class of 1927 at Stanford filled out the Vocational Interest Blank two weeks before graduation. In January, 1928, they reported their occupational choice. Comparison of these two sets of data show:

1. 46 percent have entered the occupation on which they scored highest on the test.

2. 20 percent have entered the occupation on which they scored second highest.

3. 11 percent have entered the occupation on which they scored third highest.

. . . only 18 percent have entered an occupation for which, according to the test, they have no interest.

His early concern for reliability was stated clearly in "Permanence of Interests of Adult Men" (Strong & McKenzie, 1930):

If interests are constantly changing, either back and forth or in some progressive manner, their determination may be of use in diagnosing an individual's present condition, but they will be of little significance in guidance for the future. It is extremely important, then, that the permanence of interests be ascertained.

The present study reports the permanence of interests of adult men over a period of a year and a half. Records were obtained from 100 ministers and 100 certified accountants upon the Cowdery Interest Blank in April and May, 1925. In December of 1926, these men were asked to fill out the Strong Interest Blank. Complete records were obtained from 61 ministers and 32 certified public accountants. . . . A marked degree of permanence (correlations between .74 and .90) was found for interests over a period of a year and a half.

During the early years, Strong was continually collecting information from other occupations and adding new scales to the profile. As the number of scales increased, he began to search for meaningful ways to group them. He asked L. L. Thurstone, who was then working on his factor analysis methods, for help, and from that resulted a profile with five occupational groups. Thurstone's letter transmitting the findings, dated the week before the stock-market crash, will interest many psychometricans:

Chicago, Illinois
October 23, 1927

Dear Strong:

The table of intercorrelations that you sent me shows five constellations of varying strength. I found it rather interesting to apply my new method of constellational analysis to your table, especially as I do not know what most of your symbols are. Now that I have the symbols arranged in several constellations, I think I can make a fairly good guess as to the meanings. . . .

The first two constellations are very strong. They are conspicuous clusters. I venture the guess that since the symbols E and F are associated with Chemistry, they probably refer to engineering and farming but, of course, this might be entirely wrong. I have been wondering whether the notation Ad may refer to administration or advertising but, at any rate, it forms a very strong cluster with L and J which may possibly be law and journalism.

The third constellation is a fairly strong one but not so strong as the first two.

The fourth and fifth constellations are not so conspicuous as the others but they nevertheless form definite clusters.

I had the idea for this scheme for analyzing constellations when we were in Pittsburgh but, for some reason, I had never tried it out on any data until I did so on your table of correlations.

I believe we are on the track of a method of analyzing constellations of traits, which lends itself to a very refined mathematical development and which I believe may turn out to be much more powerful and flexible than the Spearman two factor analysis for which I have, however, very great respect. I am not yet sure that my method is novel but it seems that I would have heard about it if it had been used before. . . .

Cordially,

L. L. Thurstone

P.S. [in handwriting]: It would be a joke on us as psychologists if by any chance *R* should represent Real Estate and *PS* Psychology but here I am only guessing.

THE ADVENT OF SCORING MACHINES

By 1930, then, a useful though limited system for measuring interests had evolved. Materials had been prepared, printed, and made available for distribution; scoring techniques had been developed; and some basic psychometric information had been accumulated. The remaining hurdle was the problem of data processing. Interest inventories are nothing more than questionnaires that can be empirically keyed; to make them practically useful, techniques to score them in bulk have to be devised, and the history of the SVIB has been greatly influenced by the availability of data-processing systems.

The first information on scoring machines for the SVIB appeared in the 1930 Manual. Scanning these comments makes one appreciate how far we have come:

At the present time, [scoring] arrangements can be made with Dr. Ben Wood, Columbia University, Mr. P. H. Rulon, University of Minnesota, or the author. The author charges $2.00 for scoring a blank on all twenty-two scales. . . . [Note: 1967 prices range from about 25¢ to 65¢, depending on volume scored, for about 60 scales.—DPC]

The procedure for scoring on the Hollerith machine, as developed by Mr. Rulon, is as follows: A Hollerith card is provided for liking, another for indifference, and another for disliking each of the 420 items, making 1,260 cards in all. Each of these cards has punched on it the appropriate scores for the twenty-two occupational scales. When a blank is scored, cards are taken from the file corresponding to the circlings on the blank. (Cards can be "pulled" for approximately five blanks an hour.) The cards are then run through the tabulator and totals for ten scales recorded. They must be run through twice more to obtain the totals for the remaining scales. When this has been accomplished, the cards are run through the sorter and finally returned to the files to be used again.

At Stanford we have found twenty-five duplicates sufficient, thus employing 31,500 cards in all. The cards are kept in open files 15" x 10 3/4" with two partitions 15" x 4" that run longitudinally. Heavy cardboard dividers keep the cards separated. These are deeply notched so as to fit over the two partitions. The assistant pulls out with his right hand the like, indifferent, or dislike card, according as the blank is marked opposite item one, and places it on the table, while with his left hand he pulls the first divider forward, exposing the cards for item two. This is repeated for the 420 items.

Then, as now, data-processing systems depended on people, and people are wondrously ingenious in mastering these systems for their own ends; one such episode was reported in a reminiscing letter from Mrs. Thomas Harrell (Strong's daughter and office manager during the thirties):

> We had some problems that didn't seem funny at the time. . . . Using the scoring device for the tabulator as demonstrated by IBM, one could score about 6 blanks an hour. One of the scorers, probably someone with a musical bent, discovered you could get the same results by maintaining a speed in rhythm with the machine—there would be no incessant clanking as one card at a time finished a cycle—and you could go twice as fast. But you had to maintain the beat or you would be selecting the response for item #48 on the card for #47, or some such confusion. . . .

> It was a messy deal—the students felt, with some justification, that they were giving a fair day's work for their time so long as they were doing the quota. We couldn't just raise the quota to 12 since there were some people who couldn't manage to stay on the beat, and we needed every scorer we had because the machines were going 24 hours a day.

> How we solved this problem, I don't remember, but we did.

THE 1930'S: CONTINUING RESEARCH

With the system in operation, Strong turned his energies to expanding the framework of knowledge surrounding his inventory. In 1932 he contacted the Stanford seniors tested in 1927 and reported in the 1935 Manual:

On the basis of a 5 year follow-up of these Stanford seniors, it may be concluded that:
1) Men continuing in an occupation obtain a higher interest score in it than in any other occupation.
2) Men continuing in an occupation obtain a higher interest score in it than men entering some other occupation.
3) Men continuing in an occupation obtain higher scores in it than men who change from that occupation to some other (based on relatively few data).
4) Men changing from some other occupation to occupation *A* score higher in *A* prior to the change than they did in other occupations.

In 1934, Strong published on the relationship between interests and sales ability. (He had done some earlier work but was too cautious to publish.) He reported, "The data in the first table show such surprising correlation between life insurance interest scores and production that at the time (1927), the writer did not feel warranted in publishing them until they could be substantiated by further evidence." That article includes the table reproduced here as Table 2, showing an impressive relationship between scores on the Life Insurance Salesman scale, reported as letter ratings with *C* low and *A* high, and annual production.

During the early thirties, Strong worked on many more mundane technical issues, such as comparing various methods of deriving item weights, studying the effect of sample size, and exploring the influence of age and sex on the scoring scales.

While involved in these practical questions, Strong paused in his presidential address to the Western Psychological Association in 1933 (at a convention where a demonstration of television was one of the notable features) to ponder the schism between basic and applied science:

It has been my observation that when students read Hull's statement that 30 percent efficiency is about the upper limit to aptitude testing, they tend to throw up their hands and say, "What's the use?" Is this a fair and appropriate reaction?

Pure and applied scientists approach a question of this sort from two different points of view. The former seeks perfection; he longs for correlations of unity. Moreover, to a very large degree, he selects the problems he would solve and he very nimbly dodges those that do

Table 2
Life Insurance Interest Ratings of Certain Groups of Life Insurance Men

Group	Number	Years of Experience	Average Annual Paid-for Production	Percent Having Various Life Insurance Interest Ratings				
				C	B-	B	B+	A
Criterion group of agents	288	At least 3 years	$100,000 up	1	2	6	16	75
L. I. general agents	204			3	1	8	15	73
Company W	108	At least 3 years	225,648	2	2	4	15	77
Company W	102	At least 4 years	207,980	2	2	4	15	77
Agency X, all given a contract	20	Complete record	205,000	10	0	15	35	40
Agency X, all writing $100,000 a year for at least a year	15	Complete record	285,000	7	0	13	40	40
Agency Y	37	At least 3 years	106,000	11	5	19	33	32
Group Z, rated as "failures," "unhappy," "not doing as well as they should," etc.	73	3.5 years	66,000	32	5	23	18	22
Group Z, rated as "failures" (included in above)	46	2.6 years	41,000	35	7	30	17	11
1927 Stanford Seniors, 5 years after graduation	222			73	8	12	4	3

not look promising. The applied scientist, on the other hand, must attempt the solution of problems which are thrust upon him and, moreover, he must solve them some way or other and usually within a short period of time. Is it any wonder then that any contribution that bears upon the problem is highly prized by him? Is it any wonder that the pure scientist frequently views the solutions of the applied scientist with sarcasm and that the latter feels hurt that his contribution is not appreciated?

He expressed the same feelings years later, after retirement, and always felt mild chagrin that his work had not been more influential on the main stream of psychology, especially psychological theory. His perception was certainly accurate; when interest measurement is covered in introductory psychology textbooks, for example, it is usually presented only as a useful technique in vocational guidance; in the text currently used for the introductory course at, of all places, Minnesota, there is no mention of E. K. Strong, the SVIB, or vocational interests.

THE 1938 REVISION

During the decade 1927-1937, Strong continually made changes to improve the system. The Manual—an eight-page "throw-away" booklet—was rewritten almost every year; the scoring weights were lowered from an initial range of ± 30 in 1927, to ± 15 in 1930, to ± 4 in 1938 (and to ± 1 in 1966); items in the booklet were changed; the arrangement of scores on the profile varied from year to year; and none of this was very disruptive as the operation was still small and under Strong's day-to-day control. (The situation in 1967 is very different. We have evolved from a one-man, hip-pocket operation into a bureaucracy, with all that that implies: on the one hand, organizational inertia, vested interests, and committee decisions; on the other, a capacity for amassing a wide range of talent, sufficient funds to free the researcher from clerical drudgery, and enough power to have some influence on what is happening "out there.")

Then, in 1938, a major revision of the Men's Form was published, incorporating all of the changes that had been accumulating. The major ones were:

(1) The men-in-general reference group was changed from what was essentially a collection of all the blanks Strong had in his files to a group representing a sampling of occupations, based on the U.S. Census, with incomes over $2500—usually professional and higher-level business groups.

(2) The occupational criterion groups were increased in size, where possible, to a minimum of 250.

(3) The derivation of item weights was changed slightly.

(4) Raw scores were converted to standard scores using means and standard deviations instead of percentiles, and the letter ratings (A, B+, B, . . .) were based on standard deviation units instead of quartiles.

(5) Occupations were clustered on the profile into eleven groups—essentially the same profile that is used today.

The 1938 booklet and profile achieved widespread use in the next twenty-eight years, and are the forms familiar today to most psychologists.

Five years later, in 1943, Strong published his massive book, *Vocational Interests of Men and Women*, A work crammed with solid data that had been accumulating for twenty years. Though it is not a book for easy reading, it was well received and even now continues to sell. For this, Columbia University presented Strong with the Butler Medal, an award presented to their alumni for high achievement.

With the exception of this book, the level of activity in the early forties was low. World War II siphoned off manpower and energy, as well as funds, and only projects promising immediate military payoff were started. Nothing came of them.

SCORING BECOMES AUTOMATED

After the war the tempo picked up again, and in 1946 came a breakthrough with an immediate and lasting impact. Elmer Hankes, an engineer in Minneapolis, built the first automatic scoring and profiling machine for the SVIB. An article in the Minneapolis *Star-Journal*, July 8, 1946, described it:

The exterior appearance of the machine is deceptive. What looks like a crude wooden desk, with some mysterious dials on a 10-inch panel, actually contains three miles of fine wiring, 40,000 separate parts—including 37,000 resistors—and 80,000 hand-soldered connections.

When in operation, this collection of gadgets scores electronically the vocational interest test perfected by Dr. E. K. Strong of Stanford University.

The device is in use today in the very place that Hankes built it—the living room of his small apartment.

This machine, with its later modifications, was the only source of automatic scoring and profiling for the next several years. Although several offices, including Strong's, continued to score the SVIB using the IBM tabulator or IBM 805 scoring machine, these operations were inefficient and accounted for a progressively smaller portion of the scoring volume.

In 1962-63, several new SVIB scoring services were established, reflecting the *Zeitgeist* of the digital computer. National Computer Systems in Minneapolis built a flexible system around an optical scanner hooked into a Control Data Computer; Measurement Research Center in Iowa City offered scoring services on the electronic scanners developed by E. F. Lindquist for scoring his and other achievement tests; and Dela Data, working closely with Consulting Psychologists Press in Palo Alto, designed a service around IBM Mark Sense cards. TestScor, Elmer Hankes' company, also switched in 1962 from an analog to digital scoring machine. The new technology and fresh competition reduced scoring costs by a factor of three or four, and also encouraged vast improvements in tangential services, such as provisions for item response tabulations and descriptive statistics. Such trends will undoubtedly continue.

STRONG'S RETIREMENT

In 1949, Strong retired from Stanford University but not from his research. The 1951 Manual reflects his activity; for the first time appeared the mean score on the relevant occupational scale for each occupation and for men-in-general. It seems inconceivable now that the SVIB could have existed for over twenty years before this basic information was published; the data had been available earlier, but it apparently had not seemed important to include them in the Manual. (The American Psychological Association's *Technical Recommendations for Psychological Tests and Diagnostic Techniques* did not appear until 1954.) The more extensive information of mean scores for all samples on all SVIB scales was not published until 1959, and even then the table had many gaps. One's first thought—that this information became available then because of the advent of large computers in the late fifties—is inaccurate; to the end, Strong did these calculations by hand, usually using computational shortcuts derived in the thirties or a small desk calculator.

The 1951 Manual also included Strong's first report on his longitudinal follow-up of Stanford students. Because these data provide the most important foundation for the use of the SVIB, I am quoting him at length:

Since the Vocational Interest Test is mainly used to aid in vocational counseling, it is not sufficient for the test to have high validity in differentiating adults; it must be demonstrated that interests do not change appreciably over a considerable period of time and that there is a reasonable degree of agreement between interest test scores and vocational choice. . . .

A twenty year follow-up of 670 Stanford freshmen, seniors, and graduate students shows a high degree of agreement between interest scores in 1927-30 and occupations engaged in in 1949. For example, 137 of these students became physicians. The distribution of their physician interest scores, expressed in percentages, is given in Table 3, in comparison with the scores of the criterion group of physicians. The students scored nearly as high as the criterion group.

Among the 670 students, 132 had A ratings and 67 had B+ ratings in physician interest. How many of these 199 students became physicians? Of the 132 men with A ratings, 53 percent became physicians. Assuming that the students could have entered one hundred different occupations, then on this basis the chance that anyone would go into medicine is 1 percent. If, however, they have an A rating on the physician scale, there is a 53 percent chance they will become physicians.

Table 3

Distribution of Physician Interest Scores of Criterion Group
and of 137 Students Who Became Physicians

Rating	Criterion Group	Students
A	70	64
B+	12	13
B	8	10
B–	5	8
C	5	5
Mean	50	47.8
Sigma	10	10.3

The remaining 47 percent did not go into every imaginable pursuit. Five percent became dentists or biologists, occupations which correlate .80 to .90 with physician interests. Eight percent became architects, psychologists, and chemists (correlation .70-.75) and 14 percent became engineers, writers, geologists (correlation .52-.62). Altogether, 80 percent of those with A ratings became physicians or entered an occupation whose interests correlate .50 or higher with that of a physician.

Of the 67 students with B+ ratings in physician interest, 21 percent became physicians; 3 percent, biologists; 10 percent, architects, psychologists, or chemists; and 28 percent, engineers, writers, or geologists—a total of 62 percent.

THE 1950'S AND 60'S: REGROUPING

In the 1950's, Strong again became concerned with the revision of the booklet. Many of the items had become outdated, and a few other changes seemed necessary. From his correspondence files and notes, it is clear that he spent many hours pondering how to proceed. There were two types of questions, technical and administrative. The first included issues such as: Which items are obsolete? Which are useless? Should the test be shortened? Lengthened? Should the scoring system be changed? Should the profile be rearranged?

The second group, the administrative questions, filtered down to: Who should do the work?

The first questions had to be largely ignored until the second was answered, and not much progress was made for several years. Probably Strong felt unable, because of his advancing years and lack of knowledge about modern data processing equipment, to undertake it himself; whatever the reason, he did seek advice from many people as to the best way to proceed. During his several visits to Minnesota in these years, several groups assembled, talked about the problem, and disassembled. Finally, through the mysterious way of group processes, three people emerged as the guiding force for the

SVIB revision: Strong, Kenneth Clark, then Chairman of the Psychology Department at Minnesota, and Ralph Berdie, Strong's son-in-law, and then Director of the Student Counseling Bureau at Minnesota.

The technical work began. All of the criterion group inventories were shipped to Minnesota, and the task of preparing them for computer analysis began. Strong tackled the question of which items to change; Clark and Berdie began the data analysis. I became involved as a graduate student who was supposed to know something of computers. During the next few years, due to Strong's illness, Clark's leaving Minnesota to become a Dean, and Berdie's extensive administrative responsibilities, I was swept to the center of the vacuum and there have remained.

During this unsettled time, Berdie, while on leave in India, wrote to Strong with some suggestions for future arrangements. Strong's reflective answer is relevant here:

Palo Alto, California
December 15, 1962

Dr. Ralph Berdie
Ford Foundation
Calcutta, India

Dear Ralph:

Your letter of October 16 raises the question as to the best way to keep the vocational interest measurement research both centralized and active. If there is a central person or agency, this will provide a focus for communication and will facilitate reporting of research underway and completed. This stimulates conducting research and makes it easier to obtain support, particularly financial support, for research.

The Vocational Interest Research has been supported almost entirely by profit from scoring blanks. In early days funds were received from the Carneigie Corporation and the Laura Spellman Fund. But no such funds have been received since some time before the last war.

The University [Stanford] has supplied space for my research and accounting of funds but has made no contributions or received any money from the Research Bureau. It did take over the obligation to supply pensions to my employees at the time I retired.

I shall not be able to continue direction of the Research Bureau very much longer. Mrs. Nicholson, my assistant for many years, retired this year but does give some time to it. The other two employees can handle the scoring but not research. Income from scoring just about maintains the present office activities.

What is the Vocational Interest Research? It is the name I gave to my research. It is associated by many people with Stanford University and recognized by the University. For many years it has been financed by profit from scoring blanks. It has been a place to which people have turned for advice in their research. It has helped many in their research by supplying blanks and varying amounts of statistical service. When I am gone, there will be nothing left except the name and some records. Profits from scoring have decreased in recent years and presumably will be too slight to keep the office going.

Has the University acquired 'squatter's rights' in the name and the records? Will the University insist on keeping both or permit those assets to be transferred elsewhere?

As far as I know, there is no one at Stanford that is interested in my research or would be willing to take charge of the Bureau. My daughter and her husband, Thomas Harrell, are more interested than anyone but have their own commitments and say they would not want this added responsibility. There is no one at the University Press who is competent to direct research: there is no reason why there should be. . . .

The two places that occur to me where a bureau of vocational research might be established are at the University of Colorado and of Minnesota because of the presence there of Ken Clark and yourself, respectively. There is no reason why such research should not be carried out in both places and, in fact, in other places as well. For various reasons I believe it would be best at the present time to centralize activities at one place. Later on, similar research might be established at other locations.

I don't believe it makes much difference how the unit is set up—as an institute, or what. The important thing is that there is a man really interested in such a project, and facilities by which he can carry on his research. Dave Campbell appeals to me as such a man, but I don't know whether he would want to devote his time to such an enterprise. It is not necessary for him to devote full time. I carried on a full teaching program in the Graduate School of Business until I retired in 1949 and directed research in my spare time.

I think your suggestion is excellent that the advisory committee formulate what should be done to transfer the research bureau from Stanford to Minnesota, or elsewhere. This constitutes an organization that is respected and can deal with the necessary negotiations.

I have not talked this matter over with anyone at Stanford and will not do so until I hear from you. There may be complications I have not thought of; many become exercised when they think they are going to lose something even though they have not concerned themselves previously.

Sincerely,

E. K. Strong, Jr.

In the fall of 1963, the University of Minnesota formally established the Center for Interest Measurement Research, and located it administratively within the Student Counseling Bureau, which is under the direction of the Office of the Dean of Students. Shortly after that, the remaining files from Stanford were shipped to Minneosta, and a general announcement over the signature of F. E. Terman, Stanford Vice-President and Provost (and son of the man who helped bring Strong to Stanford 40 years earlier) was released:

After serving customers for more than a quarter of a century, Dr. Edward K. Strong has announced the closing of the Strong Vocational Research Bureau, effective September 1, 1963. Dr. Strong has not been well for several months, and his illness has prevented him from participating as fully as he would prefer in the activities of the Bureau. I am certain you will understand the reluctance with which he has made the decision.

Professor Strong is one of our most distinguished emeritus professors, and soon he will complete his fortieth year at Stanford. During his tenure he has been a tireless and thorough researcher, continuing to improve his tests and the criteria for their evaluation. He designed his service particularly for the guidance of counselors and administrators in education and business, and more recently he extended the applicability of his techniques for us in the professions. In addition to his research, Professor Strong won admiration among colleagues and students as a skillful and understanding teacher.

Dr. Strong passed away the following December in Palo Alto.

THE 1966 REVISION

In 1966, the revision of the Men's Form finally was published, accompanied by an extensive expansion of the Manual. Following is a listing of some of the more important changes:

(1) Obsolete items and those that did not distinguish well between occupations were replaced by items in areas not well covered in the earlier item pool, such as art, philosophy, and modern technology.

(2) Scoring was simplified by reducing the item weights from ±4 to ±1.

(3) Several new scales were added to the profile, including Computer Programmer, Community Recreation Administrator, and Credit Manager.

(4) A new scale related to scholastic performance was added: Academic Achievement.

(5) A new men-in-general group was assembled, including men from a variety of occupations, tested between 1927 and 1964.

(6) Group III on the profile, formerly limited to Production Manager, was expanded to include Army Officer and Air Force Officer scales; this cluster now reflects interests in "Technical Supervision." Group VI, formerly limited to Musician, now includes Music Teacher, Artist, and Librarian scales, and suggests cultural-aesthetic interests.

With the revision finally completed, much of the research during the 1960's at Minnesota has capitalized on the presence of Strong's extensive files. Studies of change within occupations over time have been done by comparing current samples with those tested by Strong in the 1930's (Campbell, 1966b); profiles of outstanding people have been sifted out of Strong's groups for special treatment—one example is the publication, with their permission, of the SVIB profiles for 50 past presidents of the American Psychological Association (Campbell, 1965b); another study involves the locating and retesting of 2000 15- and 16-year-old boys originally tested by Strong in 1930. Over 80 percent of them, now about 52 years old, have been located and about 60 percent have been retested.

Some of the more interesting projects planned for the immediate future include testing identical and fraternal twins to explore the genetic components of interests, the study of husbands and their wives to learn something about assortive mating, and the collection of interest inventories from specific occupations in other countries to study the cross-cultural value of the SVIB.

More research on women's occupations is currently underway, and a complete revision of the Women's Form—analogous to the Men's—is scheduled for publication in 1968.

This, then, has been a brief history of one of the country's best known psychological inventories. It has not been a critical review; some biases have crept—or more accurately—marched in boldly. I have been greatly impressed by E. K. Strong's methodicalness and persistence in pursuing this research, and believe he made a substantial contribution to our understanding of human nature. He immersed himself so completely in this work and studied each problem with such absorption that one is hesitant to critcize any of his techniques without overwhelming justification.

Of course, a critical perspective is still essential, especially in psychological testing; I have observed that psychological instruments exert almost charismatic control over their authors, and most of them treat their tests as objectively as they treat their children. Professor Strong managed better than anyone else I know to maintain, over forty years, a strictly empirical orientation toward his inventory—almost all decisions were based on data, not emotion—and that is surely one of the reasons that the SVIB has withstood the test of time. I hope his successors can do as well.

CHAPTER VII

Current status of the
Rorschach test

Walter G. Klopfer

In this chapter an attempt will be made to assess the current status of the Rorschach test, primarily on the basis of the literature of the past decade. The survey will begin with a discussion of the general works that have been published on the test, with emphasis on novel methods of interpretation. Studies on the nature of the instrument will be reviewed, especially those dealing with the stimulus value of the cards and those in which predictions are made directly from theoretically-based test variables. A discussion of new research techniques, such as the semantic differential, the "body image" system, and developmental scores, will follow. Then, after a discussion of the transient and situational variables as they influence Rorschach test performance, a critique of the "sign" approach will be presented. This will be illustrated by a review of studies concerning the prediction of special behavior, psychiatric categories, success in therapy, and personnel selection.

VIEWPOINTS AND STUDIES ON THE TEST ITSELF

A comprehensive survey by Jackson and Wohl (1966) indicated that the major universities still emphasize the Rorschach test in the teaching of psycho-diagnostic methods. Instruction is regrettably often at a very elementary level, with nothing much more than scoring being taught. The student is likely to be left either to his own devices or at the mercy of his practicum supervisors when it comes to learning to use the instrument for any significant clinical or research purpose. The instructors are likely to be young and poorly trained, with a minimum of clinical experience. The two major scoring systems being used are those of Beck and Klopfer.

General Viewpoints

The viewpoints published during recent years run the whole gamut from highly speculative intuitive ones to those closely tied to empirical data. A book by Phillips and Smith (1953) provided various "norms" for a variety of interpretative predictions. The authors offered a conceptual schema that was empirical in form, though purely intuitive in its source. A German textbook by Bohm (1957) systematically presented Rorschach's original ideas with very little reference to research findings of the last three decades. A recent paper by Schafer (1960) once again presented his own method of analyzing the test. His main suggestions were (a) to pursue a compelling hypothesis exhaustively, (b) to seek convergence between approaches such as scoring and analysis of content, and (c) to interpret the data at more than one level of organization of functioning. Schafer's approach is a very thorough and systematic one, in contrast to some of the loose methods used by others.

Another approach was published by Rothschild (1964), who defined a Rorschach situation as a power relationship in which the subject could move away from, move toward, or move against the examiner. On the basis of this framework, he obtained a large number of interlocking theoretical equations. It seems somewhat difficult, however, to ascertain how such a system would permit prediction of the kind usually demanded from the clinician.

Piotrowski (1965) has published a chapter on the Rorschach in a rather comprehensive handbook of clinical psychology. In it he claims that the test "reveals the individual's inner attitudes much more directly and fully than it does his specific overt actions." He goes on to say, "Specific behavior can be inferred from the test findings only with difficulty, if at all [p. 523]." Piotrowski maintains that because the Rorschach is a fantasy-level instrument, behavioral criteria for evaluating validity are irrelevant. He describes four means of diagnosis: the use of pathognomonic signs, the use of crude statistical devices, the use of systematic or complex statistics, and the comprehensive (idiographic) approach. His own *alpha* formula for distinguishing schizophrenics from neurotics is given a stellar role in the review. The alpha formula is based on $F\%$ and its relationship to other test factors. In general, Piotrowski focuses on the old literature and the traditional hypotheses.

Another important position paper is presented by Eron in the recent *Progress in Clinical Psychology*, Vol. VII (Abt & Ries, 1966). As part of the chapter on psychological tests and clinical practice, Eron has a small section on the Rorschach. He expresses astonishment that the test continues to be used in spite of all the alleged evidence of lack of reliability and validity. He feels that the reason the test is still being utilized is that when content instead of formal scoring is used, certain valid results can be obtained.

The most recent volume on the test is the one by Schachtel (1966). He introduces his book as one that will provide the long overdue theoretical rationale for the empirical findings concerning the test. This seems to overlook all the other authors who have been attempting to do the same thing over the years. Schachtel's book is entitled *Experiential Findings of Rorschach's Test*. In this title, "experiential" refers to the experiences of the trainee in attempting to give interpretations of the blots. Schachtel provides a searching discussion of the stimulus-subject interaction and demonstrates a thorough familiarity with the theoretical literature. He considers structure, subject reaction to ambiguity, conceptual physiology, perceptual and cognitive style, meaning of experiences, symbolization by determinants, and other variables. The major difficulty with his discussion is that although the analysis is tied to phenomenal, logical, and psychoanalytic concepts, it is not tied to empirical data, even at times when it easily could be. Its major value lies in its keen appraisal of what the blot-subject interaction really consists of, even at the risk of deflating some notions that clinicians are particularly fond of (such as the father-mother card hypothesis reviewed below).

Administration of the Test

In the opinion of the present writer, the typical instructions in the Rorschach test result in a very interesting "double bind." The subject is told that there are no right or wrong answers and is expected to believe it. Thus, it would seem that the explicit instructions call for a complete disregard of blot stimulus and a complete dependence on one's fantasy or imaginary capacities. The game calls for the patient to pretend that he believes these instructions but, at the same time, to act upon the paranoid assumption that there really are right or wrong answers, which he had best think of lest the examiner make some decision about him against his perceived best interests. The same point is made by Haan (1964), who describes the Rorschach situation as "a partial moratorium on reality."

Some examples of studies in the area of test administration are as follows: Voigt (1966) had 23 trainees score a standard list of 150 Rorschach responses and also take the Edwards Personal Preference Scale. Systematic errors made by the trainees were found to be related to scores on the EPPS. This seems to imply that to the extent that scores are based on too little data (poor inquiry), the examiner would be forced to rely upon his own imagination and thus to exercise projection in arriving at a scoring decision. One particularly interesting variation upon the usual administrative procedure was published by Roman and Bauman (1960). In this variation two people who have a significant emotional relationship to one another negotiate final decisions about responses to each card, having first taken the individually administered Rorschach test. The method is illustrated in a paper by Kaldegg (1966). A logical extension of this technique is the family Rorschach (Loveland, Wynne, & Singer, 1963): family members, after taking an individual Rorschach, come together to negotiate, transact, and generally utilize the Rorschach materials in a novel and direct way. In an excellent study by Sanders and Cleveland (1953), a group of graduate students received training in Rorschach administration after taking the test themselves. Each examiner then gave Rorschachs to 20 undergraduate subjects. The subjects rated the examiners on hostility and anxiety. Holding the number of responses constant, it was found that the examiners rated high in anxiety by their subjects elicited more responses, more white space responses, and more color responses. Those rated high in hostility had more $Y\%$ and $A\%$, as well as less hostile and human content. It appears from this study that a considerable portion of Rorschach variance may be accounted for by examiner characteristics and examiner-subject interaction. Thus, information about the public characteristics of the examiner and the kind of responses he is likely to evoke in his subjects must certainly be considered in interpreting responses. An article by Rosner (1960) deals with the inquiry. The author notes the recent emphasis on content and deplores the reliance on universal symbols. He holds that even statistical support for a content interpretation is a travesty on the interpretation of content based on idiographic association. He therefore feels that it is important to get each subject's own association to a particular kind of content, instead of relying upon a stereotyped one.

An article by Huberman (1965) deals with the testing-of-the-limits procedure and discovers an acquiescence dimension. There appears to be an acceptance–non-acceptance dimension that cuts across such areas as popularity and use of color. Huberman used four cards in his study and compared his derived acquiescence score with scores on a dogmatism scale. He discovered that the attitude of the subject toward authority is a better predictor of whether the subject will accept the concept than is its popularity. The above studies certainly indicate that the administration of the Rorschach test is not the precise laboratory procedure that we might hope it to be.

Studies of Card Stimulus Value

A valuable contribution has been made by those investigators who have tried to determine something about the stimulus value of the cards themselves. The main work in this area has been carried on by Baughman (1959). In a series of articles, Baughman reported having varied the plates with regard to shading, color, and figure background. He reported that the "paired comparison" method of scoring increased the reliability of scoring and clarified the degree to which card stimulus-value contributed to the responses given. Schleifer and Hire (1960) studied the association of adjectives with cards and described card pull on this basis. This was suggested as an aid in interpretation. Although it appears to help when norms regarding card pull are provided, it should be kept in mind that individual associations may differ and that the empirical approach to predicting individual associations has its limitations. By the use of a structured inquiry following the administration of the test proper, Hafner (1961), in one of his normative studies, demonstrated that card pull for children is different from that for adults.

Kuntz (1964) tested the effect of card pull upon conceptions of masculinity and femininity. He gave 50 college students the five achromatic blots in three sets, varying the darkness, lightness, and size dimensions. The masculinity-femininity dimension was evaluated by means of the semantic differential and a dichotomous masculinity-femininity sorting. This study determined that mass has little influence when compared to shading.

Marsh (1961), in another study on card pull, focused upon the "mother-father" dimension. This study demonstrated that subjects who rated cards 4 and 7 high along the predicted dimension were those who felt their parents were hostile. Thus, it can be concluded that parental figures (or other things) are likely to be projected into ambiguous stimulus situations if there is residual conflict causing such projection to take place. Another study on card pull regarding cards 4 and 7 was carried on by Zelin and Sechrest (1963). They conducted one experiment in which the therapists' judgments regarding parental roles were compared to parental role predictions by four judges based on cards 4 and 7 protocols. The results were inconclusive. In a second experiment (Zelin & Sechrest, 1963) self-report data from college students on parental relationships were compared with predictions from cards 4 and 7. The results were insignificant. The above studies seem to be reasonable approaches to the question of whether stereotypes concerning card pull could be assumed in a large sample of subjects, regardless of their personal associations.

The remaining studies concerning card pull are primarily normative ones, such as the papers by Cass and McReynolds (1951), Rossi and Neuman (1961), and Bloom (1962). The Cass and McReynolds norms are used in many other studies, sometimes appropriately; Rossi and Neuman studied a group of medical students and found them to be comparable on the Rorschach with previously published norms for medical students. Subgroup norming of this sort seems to be a great improvement over the rather bland assumption made by some investigators that every mature person, irrespective of occupation or socioeconomic background, will have the same kind of Rorschach protocol. Bloom studied popular responses among Hawaiian schizophrenics and, in comparing them to mainland norms, found some evidence for cross-cultural popularity of responses. He suggested a continuum of popularity rather than a dichotomy of popular-nonpopular.

Reliability

In the past decade little work has been done on the reliability of the Rorschach. Stein (1960) studied the odd-even (split-half) reliability of scores, calculating separately those responses in the regular position and those when the card was turned. In order to get sufficient data, he increased the response by encouraging card-turning. If one were to grant that psychometric reliability is important, then it would follow that having few responses is a problem. However, the relevance of split-half reliability, in view of the differences in card stimuli, is rather questionable.

In a study by Voigt and Dana (1964), ten graduate students in clinical psychology were given 150 responses representing a wide gamut of determinants. Criterion scoring was assigned by majority agreement; interscore reliability was .69, and intra-score reliability or consistency was .73. The authors conclude that scoring was rather subjective. It might be pointed out that sign approaches based on scores are no more valid than the scoring is reliable. A complete review of reliability studies on the Rorschach is to be found in the book by Zubin, Eron, and Schumer (1965).

Predicting from the Test

Relatively few attempts have been made to predict directly from test theory, as opposed to using a completely empirical approach. The nature of Rorschach prediction in general is evaluated in a rather devastating study by Turner (1966). Turner used four groups of judges: fellows of the Society for Projective Techniques, new Ph.D.'s in clinical psychology, graduate students, and undergraduate students. They made predictions on the basis of free associations alone, free associations plus locations, free associations plus locations and inquiry, and the entire protocol. The result was that neither greater experience nor increasing data helped in making more accurate predictions. Generally the predictors were most successful in such areas as intelligence, ambition, and degree of illness. They were least successful in areas like hostility, sex, and temperament. Thus, it might be concluded that predictions of overt phenomena are safest, whereas predictions of an intrapsychic nature can be made with equal accuracy by relying upon one's own imagination and ability to project.

Color on the Rorschach has been a subject of several recent studies. In a review by Cerbus and Nichols (1963), Rorschach is quoted as positing a relationship between color and affect. This has been interpreted to mean that color perception involves less delay and less rational control. In their review, "color percent" (percent of responses to cards 8, 9, and 10) turned out to be independent of the presence of color in the cards. Two studies on color vs. impulsivity (Gardner, 1951; Holtzman, 1950) yielded contradictory results. Neither was assaultiveness (Finney, 1955) clearly related to color. A group of studies on psychotics, epileptics, and delinquents was reviewed; these indicated that color responses in these groups were low or not significantly different from normal controls. Reviewing their own study of 1962, Cerbus and Nichols noted that they had found a number of criteria derived from the Rorschach to be correlated with preference for colored over achromatic pictures; to the present writer this seems to be a rather tangential way of testing color hypotheses.

Richards and Murray (1958) hypothesized that in sum of color women would differ from men, on the grounds that both femaleness and color indicate "passivity." However, no such result could be obtained. Other studies (Singer & Spohn, 1954; Clark, 1948) tested the hypothesis that color is related to a mild hypomanic tendency, and discovered this not to be the case. Color scores were also found to be unrelated to anxiety measures and negatively related to depression (Fisher, 1964; Kobler & Steil, 1953; Cass & McReynolds, 1951). To derive subhypotheses from generalizations such as the assumption that color is equivalent to impulsivity, independence, and passivity, and then to assume that psychotics, men, or other criterion groups should differ along these dimensions, seems dubious.

Exner (1962) investigated the "cards 8, 9, and 10 percent" hypothesis (namely, that unusual responsiveness to these cards predict emotional reactivity). He used two matched groups of college students, who were given cards 8, 9, and 10 and achromatic facsimiles. The number of responses derived was significantly greater (beyond the .01 level) on cards 8 and 9 for colored cards; the opposite was true (at the .05 level) for card 10. The author attributes his success in teasing out color as an influence to careful matching of his two groups. However, there was no cross-validation, in spite of the fact that only 20 subjects were in each group. Another approach was that of Lytton (1966), who found that his sample of 24 children liked the colored cards and color in the abstract, but gave few color-determined responses. The assumption that color responses and color attitudes need to be equivalent seems rather gratuitous.

Rosenthal (1962) studied the behavioral correlates of the Rorschach experience balance. Response style seems to pay off as a common denominator for the Rorschach and behavior. The group of subjects showing more M than sum C generally showed more delay in behavior and less physical activity. Singer and Spohn (1954) found a regular increase in sum C in conjunction with increased activity among schizophrenic patients observed in a waiting room. This indicates that the experience balance can undergo transient changes.

Movement responses were used as a basis of prediction by Reisman (1960), who used operational definitions attributed to Piotrowski, suggesting that m responses represent blocked tendencies, and that M and FM responses represent tendencies pressing for outward manifestation. Thus, he predicted that the type of m response (flexor, extensor, or block) would be opposite in any given individual's protocol to his M and FM responses. In his sample of disturbed children, however, it was found that this was not the case. In an ingenious study by Wagner (1965) it was found that seven striptease artists, compared to three control groups of women matched for relevant factors, showed more "exhibitionistic" M than the other subjects. The kind of movement (exhibitionistic) was satisfactorily defined, so as to allow reliability of scoring. In this study M refers to an actual behavioral potential. Perhaps other M's do also; thus, it might be safe to assume that more of the movement responses are related to behavior than has been previously supposed.

In another study Wagner (1961) stated the hypothesis that subjects who give both aggressive and anatomical responses show anxiety. He found that a group of college students who were given the Rorschach and the I.P.A.T. Anxiety Scale did show predictable I.P.A.T. anxiety on the basis of the bi-serial r (.561) with both Rorschach measures, although chi squares between aggression and anatomical responses computed separately were not significant. However, there was no cross-validation, which makes it difficult to generalize from the study.

Ray (1963) studied the meaning of the white space response. His criterion was response to prestige suggestion on the autokinetic phenomenon. He found that extratensive individuals with high S showed negativism, in the sense that they tended not to change their judgments. This result tends to give some credence to the general hypothesis that S is related to negativism. Exner (1961), using color versions of cards 4 and 6, found no differences from the ordinary cards. The conclusion was drawn that since "achromatic color" is of no significance in determining the usual "skin" responses, this scoring should be given up.

In a paper by Haan (1964), ten coping mechanisms and ten defense mechanisms were culled from many hours of interview material. It was discovered that global Rorschach scores related better than "formal" scores to coping mechanisms. This finding suggests that these formal scores may not be the most valuable way of analyzing Rorschach material for purposes of prediction.

NEW METHODOLOGICAL APPROACHES

Studies Using the Semantic Differential

A number of studies have employed the semantic differential developed by Osgood, Suci, and Tannenbaum (1957). Zax and Loiselle (1960) varied the order of the cards and demonstrated that their semantic ratings were greatly altered by this method. This suggests that such factors as card pull and sequence are ignored at the peril of accuracy of prediction. Sines (1960) studied the connotive meaning of cards 4 and 7 for parental symbolism. In a sample of 20 college sophomores he got essentially negative results. Zax and Loiselle (1960) in another study found semantic differences in card pull between schizophrenic and normal subjects. This suggests that just as constellations from psychometric tests must be interpreted differently for various clinical groups, so card reaction might best be considered within the subgroup norm. Zax and Benham (1961) extended the semantic differential study of the Rorschach cards to a child population. Ratings for each card on 21 semantic dimensions were made separately and card descriptions were derived. Children, as compared to college students, tend to have a generally more favorable attitude toward the cards.

Goldfried (1963) used the semantic differential to unearth common associations to animal concepts. He used mean scale scores and considered that the deviation of one scale score from the normal was directionally significant. His empirical findings confirmed some hypotheses and failed to confirm others.

Loiselle and Kleinschmidt (1963) obtained semantic ratings both of cards projected on a screen and of percepts given to the cards. Of the 94 significant directional differences for cards and the 70 for percepts, 56 were joint. This suggests that card pull is so significant that it can be assumed to tone the percept. It raises considerable question as to whether the Rorschach is as unstructured a projective test as has been assumed.

Hafner and Rosen (1964) compared semantic ratings of Rorschach cards themselves with the semantic ratings of nine common responses representing various determinants, as well as the ratings of two disembodied determinants. They found that connotive meaning can be determined for age and sex subgroups, but that it is not justified to speak of connotive meaning in general.

Crumpton and Groot (1966) compared colored and noncolored cards by means of semantic differential ratings. In this study apparently all colored cards were connotively different from those that were not colored. They were high in activity and evaluation, and low in potency. When cards 2, 3, 8, 9, and 10 were presented in noncolor form, they did not have the same connotive stimulus-value. The details of this study are rather confusing, and color reactions appear to be at least partly the result of card pull. In general, one might say that the use of the semantic differential for studying the connotive meaning of the Rorschach cards is a popular method of investigation and seems to have added something to our understanding of what the card stimulus adds to the response apart from the perceiver's mentation.

Studies Using "Body-Image" Scores

There have been a number of studies using the Penetration and Barrier scores developed by Fisher and Cleveland (1956, 1958, 1960). Boundary responses are those protected by a surface that would make penetration difficult (*skin, shell, armor*). Penetration responses are those suggesting vulnerability (*X-rays, broken, torn*). It was found that in cancer pathology, patients with surface cancers have a greater Barrier score; those with internal cancers have a greater Penetration score. High-barrier persons tend to be more adjusted and independent; high-penetration persons show ego-weakness and pathology.

A study by Eigenbrode and Shipman (1960), attacking the body-image concept, compared patients with internal diseases with those with skin diseases and found no difference. McConnell and Daston (1961) studied 28 pregnant women during the last two months of pregnancy and again three days after delivery. They discovered that after delivery Penetration decreases although Barrier does not change. The authors suggest that changes in a complex content score like Penetration run parallel to a real life situation, but they fail to explain why the Barrier score shows no change.

In a study by Jaskar and Reed (1963) hospitalized and nonhospitalized subjects were compared on the body-image dimension, with minimal differences being discovered. Fisher (1964) found that the more definite the boundaries were on the Rorschach, the more able the patient was in an interview situation to communicate, demonstrate identity, and have insight. He suggests that the Barrier score is a general measure of mental health. Fisher (1966) also was able to relate the Barrier score to the achievement motive in boys and, to some extent, in girls. It might be said that the Barrier score in any event seems to have some general adjustive meaning, and that some investigators seem to have more success with it than others.

Developmental Level

A number of scores of developmental level have been suggested, and a good deal has been published along this line. For example, Kaden and Lipton (1960) related a developmental score to functional integration and to post-hospital adjustment. Eisdorfer (1960) did a study of 48 elderly volunteers of average intelligence without brain damage. They were divided into three groups according to vision, and into two according to audition. A Rorschach developmental score showed decrement associated with hearing but not with vision. Thus, it would appear that generalizations about the aged can be refined by taking specific deficits into account.

Goldfried (1962) showed that a developmental score on the Rorschach bears no relation to measured pathology on the MMPI. He arrived at this conclusion on an actuarial basis. The author was disappointed, and concluded that the two scores measure different things. The present writer would agree that they measure different things but would not share the disappointment, since he sees no compelling reason for positing such a relationship in the first place. Friedman and Orgel (1964) examined the protocols of five groups of adults with a wide IQ range and found that the relationships of "genetic" score to IQ was generally insignificant. From these illustrations it will be clear that the use of developmental scores, while increasing in popularity, has not given very clear-cut or consistent results.

Singer and Wynne (1963) used a genetic score to distinguish the parents of four groups of children (autistic, withdrawn, acting out, and young adult schizophrenic). Singer's own measures of thinking disorder were found to be correlated with the genetic level score.

Studies Using the Concept of "Levels"

There have been many suggestions on how "levels of awareness" may be measured, including that of Leary (1957), who distinguished between the level of public communication (operationally defined by sociometric rankings), the level of conscious perception (operationally defined as self-ratings on the Interpersonal Check List), and the level of private symbolization (operationally defined as projective test performance). Stone and Dellis (1960) attacked the question of why projective techniques do not intercorrelate if, as alleged, they all tap the same level. They studied 50 "pseudoneurotic" schizophrenic subjects and found evidence that the Rorschach and Draw-A-Person correlate with one another, but not with other projective measures such as the Thematic Apperception Test (TAT) and Sentence Completion Test, nor with nonprojective measures such as the Wechsler-Bellevue and case histories. The authors concluded that the Rorschach measures a different or "deeper" level, although another possible interpretation of this study is that the subjects may take seriously the "moratorium on reality" mentioned above.

King (1960), who reported that paranoid patients with interpersonal delusions give more M than those with somatic delusions, suggests that human movement responses may lead not only to hypotheses concerning internal phenomena, but also to legitimate behavioral predictions. A paper by McCully (1962) suggests that thinking disorders revealed on the Rorschach and on a psychiatric examination are quite different from one another, and that on the Rorschach the range of stimulation is extended. Borderline schizophrenics show exterior facade, but there is welter within. Thus, McCully suggests that there is no "correct" diagnosis, regardless of the frame of reference.

A study by Orlinski (1966) demonstrates intralevel (private symbolization) consistency between dreaming and Rorschach fantasy, and also interlevel (public versus private) consistency, showing that behavior and fantasy are correlated. It may well be that in certain instances behavioral ratings made by judges can be correlated with interpretations of projective data, although neither affects conscious perception, which can be the victim of ego-defense.

Miscellaneous Approaches

Levine and Spivack (1962) have published a series of papers concerning the "Index of Repression," based upon details of language use. In this particular study (1962), the index was found to be correlated with M and with spontaneous verbs, suggesting that it may be a stylistic variable cutting across media. McReynolds (1966b), in his Concept Evaluation Technique, presents an objective method for testing the limits. It yields nine scores, measuring the dimensions of conformity, conceptual deviance, and response style. Piotrowski and Rock (1963) have developed a scale for the selection of top managers. It consists of a number of interesting Rorschach signs and indicates that there is no reason why straightforward empiricism, if thoroughly cross-validated, cannot be used on the Rorschach for a purpose of this kind. Pruitt and Spilka (1964) have constructed a Rorschach empathy-object relationship scale, which was developed on the basis of quality and quantity of M and H. It was demonstrated that this scale distinguished between two groups of job-seekers—one vocationally adjusted, the other maladjusted. The authors concluded that group therapy promoted empathy (or perhaps increased interest in, and attention to, other persons); however, cross-validation of this scale is still awaited.

Meyer and Caruth (1965) have published a Rorschach index of ego process. They present a manual, but one without standardization or measures of reliability or validity. McCully (1965) has proposed another manual for clinical use—this one presenting a procedure called "process analysis." McCully's ideas are very interesting, but again there are no norms, no reliability, and no validity measures.

FACTORS INFLUENCING TEST PERFORMANCE

One of the most important of recent publications on the Rorschach was a review by Masling (1960) of the influence of situational and interpersonal variables on projective testing. Masling concluded that studies on attempts to fake (Fosberg, 1943; Carp & Shavzin, 1950) cancelled each other out, since the results did not fall in any particular direction. In a study by Abramson (1951), two groups were equated and then given inconsistent instructions about locations. When they were told that W or D was more typical of successful people, they emphasized the appropriate one. Fabrikant (1954) was able to increase movement, color, and shading in groups with an experimental set significantly more than in control groups. Henry and Rotter (1956) were able to change a number of factors on the Rorschach by instructing subjects that the test was given for the purpose of discovering emotional disturbance. Drugs and alcohol have been found to influence Rorschach performance in various ways. For example, Rabin, Papnia, and McMichael (1954) found that alcohol increases accuracy of perception, attention to detail, self-critical attitudes, and self-controlling attitudes. Hypnosis seems to affect test performance, but not in a consistent direction. Sex of the examiner seems to influence some measured traits. In a study by Rabin, Nelson, and Clark (1954), it was found that males in a room with nude pictures gave more sex responses to male examiners than did either subjects in a room with anatomical charts or control subjects. Warmth of administration produced more positive attitudes toward the blots (Luft, 1953), more responses, and more ease in interpersonal relationships (Lord, 1950). Wickes (1956) demonstrated that operant-conditioning techniques increase the number of responses in successive cards. Examiner differences were identified in a study by Gibby, Miller, and Walker (1953) when their well-controlled experiment elicited systematic differences in determinants obtained by different examiners. This suggests that almost any Rorschach variable could be conditioned, either with or without the examiner's conscious control. Berger (1954) found a relationship between Rorschach traits of trainees and traits derived from protocols they administered. Masling thus seems to be quite justified in concluding that the Rorschach procedure, instead of being an X-ray, serves more as a mirror reflecting impartially the subject, the examiner, the situation, and their interaction with one another.

A study by Phares (1960) involved telling subjects that the Rorschach was a test of whether they could see things as well as others. Their performance did not differ from a control group. This suggests that the usual instructions do not fool people, and that subjects simply do not believe that there are no right or wrong answers. Rosenberg and Starer (1960) presented their subjects with multiple choices. In addition to the usual administration, they used photos of common details, with specific stimulus properties varied. This worked well with chronic psychiatric patients and increased the data that could be gathered. Entirely missing from the study, however, are any data suggesting what these results mean—i.e., whether the authors' logically derived hypotheses have any validity.

Zax, Stricker, and Weiss (1960) provided another review similar to Masling's and concluded that sets, both overt and covert, as well as situational factors, influence test performance. Though their coverage of the literature was not as extensive as Masling's, their conclusions were parallel to his. In discussing Rorschach research, these authors note that the methods of administration of the test are rarely specified, that the choice of subjects is often quite esoteric, and that the scoring systems are often inconsistent.

In a study by Lucas (1961), children were given the Rorschach after being put in impossible problem-solving situations. Lucas discovered to her chagrin that upon re-testing the control subjects showed more hostility than the experimental group. Although the author tried to rationalize this result, it seems rather damaging to the validity of either the frustration-aggression hypothesis or the Rorschach test. Goldmann and Hermann (1961) did a study on the effect of immobilization on the Rorschach movement responses, similar to the one by Bendick and Klopfer (1964). Both studies showed that movement responses could be influenced by such transient situational sets as sensory deprivation and motor inhibition. This is rather damaging to the X-ray hypothesis, and suggests that movement responses can be manipulated through external stimulation.

Horivichi (1961) presented the cards both normally and tachistoscopically. She discovered that temporal factors, such as exposure time, affect perception. Although she tried to generalize from these results, it seems most parsimonious simply to assume that the longer one looks at the cards, the more he can pick out. McCully (1961) discovered that human movement responses in pre-adolescent boys suffering from progressive muscular loss do not differ from those in a control group. Palmer (1963) tested subjects under experimental conditions of sleep-, food- and water-deprivation, and obtained a variety of different and contradictory results.

It seems safe to conclude on the basis of the above review that transient and situational variables are always extremely influential, and can never be overlooked as sources of influence upon test performance.

Diagnostic Prediction

General critique of the sign approach: In spite of the obvious difficulties with the sign approach, it continues to be used in research. However, it is heartening to note that a number of investigators have clearly expressed their reservations. For example, Masling (1960) points out that since the Rorschach is an empirical rather than a theoretical instrument, investigators finding "signs" that distinguish experimental and control groups have been unable to interpret them. Fulkerson and Barry (1961) show that "signs" used to predict termination of therapy consistently wash out with cross-validation. Tizard (1962) points out that epileptic "signs" identified in institutions do not apply to epileptics in the community. This suggests that such "signs" are neither universal nor even common.

Kinslinger (1966) also found that signs, in this case among occupational groups, do not survive cross-validation. Finney (1955) found that Rorschach scores did not distinguish such gross behavioral differences as assaultiveness-nonassaultiveness (perhaps because, as it seems to this writer, these scores are not behaviorally based, but phenomonological). Reed (Reed, M.R., personal communication) suggests that signs are ineffective because of the heterogeneity of the criterion groups. Ainsworth (1954) suggests that scores do not correlate with any criteria because they have no single interpretative meaning. And finally Voigt and Dana (1964) show that scores are unreliable, thereby invalidating combinations of scores. In spite of all these criticisms, the sign approach is still being used, as shown below.

Prediction of special behavior: Richards and Murray (1958) compared the global evaluation of Rorschach performance with the use of scores. They found no sex differences in color scores. Neuringer (1962) reviewed the manifestations of anxiety on the Rorschach and emphasized the confusion resulting from the general lack of cross-validation, the use of differing subject populations, and the presence of varying operational measures of anxiety. Suicide has been the subject of considerable empirical investigation with the Rorschach. For example, Hertz (1948) presented a massive amount of empirical data, based on a large number of suicidal and nonsuicidal subjects. Her attempt at actuarial prediction was painstaking, and therefore has been somewhat successful. Sakheim (1955) found five or more of Hertz's configurations in 88 percent of suicidal, and only 28 percent of nonsuicidal, subjects. This represents a rare phenomenon in Rorschach research—namely, cross-validation. Again, Daston and Sakheim (1960) used a group of signs developed by another investigator and cross-validated them on two groups of suicidals, both successful and unsuccessful, as well as on control subjects. A sophisticated discussion of base rates is included in Daston and Sakheim's paper.

The base-rate problem manifested itself in a dialogue between Appelbaum and Holzman (1962) and Pauker (1962). Appelbaum and Holzman pursued a hunch that using shading in a colored area was a predictor of suicide, and attempted to demonstrate this by studying a number of different groups. However, Pauker pointed out that consideration of total base rate in the criterion group should lead to the more modest conclusion that the use of test signs correctly identifies 10 percent more suicidal subjects than does the use of the base rate. Cooper, Bernstein, and Hart (1965) took a single sign of suicide (use of d at the bottom of Card 7) and disconfirmed it by cross-validation. Neuringer (1965) reviewed the literature on suicide and found vague criteria for suicide, a general lack of cross-validation on signs, a tendency toward unreliable scoring of configurational cues, and frequent meaninglessness of hypotheses. The situation concerning the prediction of suicide is rather typical of other areas of Rorschach prediction.

Storment and Finney (1953; Finney, 1955) found very few scores that distinguished assaultive from nonassaultive patients. Gardner (1951) had somewhat better luck with impulsivity. However, Holtzman (1950), using interfraternity ratings of impulsivity, found no consistent Rorschach score relationships. Hammer (1966) found that he could distinguish college students from clinic patients by how they identified the sex of the figures on Card 3. However, there was no cross-validation, and the significance of this study is somewhat questionable.

Tahka (1966), studying Finnish alcoholics, found no Rorschach differences between alcoholics and a control group. Tarlan and Smalheiser (1951) studied patients with malignant tumors of the breast and cervix and, on the basis of data on only 33 subjects, concluded that breast cancer patients were psychologically more impoverished. Kobler and Steil (1953) reviewed nine publications that indicate pure color is reduced in depression. They also found this to be true in their own study. Moylan, Shaw, and Appleman (1960) demonstrated that passive-aggressiveness visible to others appears on the Rorschach, whereas passivity hidden in the passive-dependent type of personality is not measured at the Rorschach level. These results raise the question as to whether the alleged passivity is there at all, or whether perhaps the Rorschach does not focus as deeply as it has previously been assumed to do.

Prediction of psychiatric categories: Epileptics were studied by Loveland (1961) and Tizard (1962). Even though the conventional signs turned out to be useless, Loveland was reluctant to give them up. Tizard, on the other hand, concluded that when really comparable groups are studied, results cannot be replicated, and that perhaps researchers working in institutions and those working in the community have difficulty in communicating with one another. Schizophrenics too are still being studied. For example, McReynolds (1966a) has derived a new score for his concept-formation technique that distinguishes schizophrenics from his two criterion groups. Neiger, Slemon, and Quirk (1962) point out that often poor controls and lack of cross-validation characterize studies on schizophrenia with the Rorschach. This study casts some doubt on whether the instrument is capable of distinguishing between deteriorated schizophrenics and organics. Klinger and Roth (1965) have demonstrated that a combination of clinical and actuarial indicators show the most promise in diagnosing schizophrenia from the Rorschach. Finally, Murstein (1960), in reviewing factor-analytic studies on the Rorschach, concluded that conventional scores have failed to reveal any consistent distinctions between the patients adjudged mentally ill and normal controls.

A new trend is to emphasize content scores in diagnostic distinctions. For example, Silverman and Silverman (1960) developed a theory-related hypothesis defined in an operational manner and obtained empirical verification of "intrauterine fantasies" among heroin users. Rychlak and Guinouard (1960) found the results of a high school personality questionnaire and sociometrically determined popularity to be correlated with Rorschach content. Silverman (1963) studied stylistic consistency between social unacceptability of thinking, as measured by the Rorschach, and behavior. Rychlak and O'Leary (1965) measured unhealthy content in the responses of children and discovered that adultomorphism is not a safe frame of reference in predicting behavior from the Rorschachs of children. They concluded that unhealthy contents in a child's Rorschach do not have any particular predictive meaning. Murray and Rychlak (1966) found that schizophrenics give more neutral content than normals, the content of the normals being both more "healthy" and more "unhealthy." This seems to imply that schizophrenics respond to the "double-bind" instructions by being cautious, whereas normals are more trusting of the examiner and his instructions. The above studies on the use of content in prediction seem quite encouraging.

OTHER MEASURES OF VALIDITY

Concurrent Validity

Concurrent validity studies seem to fall into two groups—those that relate intellectual predictions from the Rorschach to the results of intelligence tests, and those that compare Rorschach personality variables with the results of inventories.

In a study by Tolor, Glass, and Mermelstein (1960) the number of rejections in children's Rorschachs were found to be insignificantly correlated with intelligence test scores. Davis (1961) predicted IQ's from the Rorschach without vocabulary, from the vocabulary alone, and from the entire Rorschach, using three judges. All predictions exceeded chance. Partial correlations showed that vocabulary contributed more to the accuracy of prediction than did the profiles alone. This suggests that a variable like vocabulary, which does not depend on formal scoring, is more easily translated into other behavior.

Pauker (1963) repeated a study by this writer (Klopfer, Allen, & Etter, 1960) in determining the correlation between intelligence and content diversity. His results were the same as in the previous study—no significant findings. Blatt and Allison (1963; Allison & Blatt, 1964) did two studies on the W response and its predictive meaning. They pointed out earlier that most research tends to lump all W together and that this is unjustified. They chose to present a qualitative continuum of W, from very vague to highly organized, and used several other tasks of an integrative sort as criteria. They found that problem-solving ability is correlated with articulated and organized W responses, but not with vague ones. This finding suggests that scores are useful insofar as their predictive meaning is closely tied to behavior. Studies such as this one, which fill in new ways of categorizing data and make it more meaningful, are very desirable. The second study of Allison and Blatt used children as subjects and again found only the cognitively complex and accurately perceived *W*'s to be related to IQ's.

The Strong interest test and the Rorschach were compared in studies by Kates (1950) and by Klopfer, Allen, and Etter (1960). Kates, using New York City policemen as subjects, found a negative relationship between Rorschach adjustment and level of job satisfaction, as measured by the Strong. Klopfer et al. reported in their study that animal percent on the Rorschach is not related either to interest range on the Strong or to intelligence as measured by the Wechsler. The MMPI and the Rorschach have frequently been compared. For example, Clark (1948) discovered that item analysis of the MMPI responses suggests a possible relation between higher sum *C* on the Rorschach and hypomanic tendency on the MMPI. Taulbee (1961) showed that flexor *M* responses on the Rorschach were related to the *D* and *Pt* scales on the MMPI, and that extensor *M*'s could be used to predict whether or not a patient is likely to continue in psychotherapy. This study showed cleverness in using empirical data to test theory.

By using the Rorschach prognostic rating scale (RPRS), and correlating it with MMPI factors, Adams, Cooper, and Carrera (1963) manage to get away from the procedure of correlating criteria with scores for which there is no single interpretation. They found twice as many significant correlations as might be expected on the basis of chance. As might be expected, the pathological MMPI scales correlated negatively and the healthy ones, like Ego-Strength, correlated positively with the RPRS. This suggests that better results can be expected with a complex instrument like the RPRS than with single Rorschach scores.

The TAT and the Rorschach have been compared by Hafner and Kaplan (1960). Their purpose was to develop comparable Hostility scales for the two tests. Items were submitted to judges to be rated on a hostility continuum, with an attempt being made to distinguish overt and covert hostility. As it turned out, the judges were reliable, but the correlation between the Rorschach and the TAT scales was low. Since no external criterion was used for either TAT or Rorschach indices, there is no way of knowing what their lack of correlation implies.

Palmer and Lustgarten (1962), in an ingenious study, used the prediction of TAT structure as a test of the Rorschach's experience balance. They found that introverts show more productivity on the TAT, meaning that fantasy interest, as a stylistic variable, cuts across test boundaries. This result is more encouraging than a study by Carrigan (1960), the results of which indicated that factorially deduced "extraversion" bears no statistical relationship to "extratension" on the Rorschach. This finding suggests that whatever certain Rorschach variables mean, they must be carefully and operationally defined, since their relationship to like-named factors derived from other sources may be unclear or nonexistent. Kraus (1964) reported no relationship between Cornell Selectee Index measures of anxiety and those of the Rorschach. Waller (1960) failed to find significant relationships between Rorschach shading responses and either anxiety indices from the MMPI or observers' ratings. However, it would be difficult to find anywhere in the literature a statement suggesting that shading in general would be expected to be pathognomonic of anxiety.

Prognosis

One of the tasks frequently demanded of the Rorschach test is the prediction of treatment outcome. An earlier review of this subject by Filmer-Bennett (1952) noted a trend in nine studies for patients who respond to treatment to react more to color on the test. However, his own study contradicted this finding. A study by Lessing (1960) revealed a number of signs that were being used in an effort to predict treatment outcome. The criterion was therapists' post-hoc sorting of cases into improved and unimproved. Only one sign was found to be discriminatory, and it washed out in cross-validation.

Zamansky and Goldman (1960) compared global and sign approaches in assessing therapeutic change. They found the global judgments to be related to the criteria, whereas 10 out of their 11 signs were not. The signs were all based on formal test scores. The most complete review of this area is by Fulkerson and Barry (1961), who focused on the Rorschach Prognostic Rating Scale (RPRS) published by Klopfer et al. (1951). Kirkner, Wisham, and Giedt (1953) found a correlation of .67 between the RPRS and improvement ratings obtained by reading terminal notes on 40 therapy patients. Mindess (1953) also obtained a correlation of .66 between RPRS and the diagnostic criterion, running from normal through neurotic through psychotic, obtained six months after the initiation of therapy. Filmer-Bennett (1952, 1955) found no significant relation between the RPRS and global judgments. The criterion was a dichotomous improvement-unimprovement sorting. Cartwright (1958) showed that the RPRS can predict the outcome of client-centered therapy beyond chance. In another outcome study, Bloom (1962) discovered that high responsivity on the Rorschach correlated with high RPRS.

Fulkerson and Barry (1961) found that studies on the prediction of termination by Rorschach "signs" show familiar patterns. Initially a study shows differences, which then gradually wash out with cross-validation. The only sign other than RPRS which holds up is R, or total number of responses, which is demonstrated as a predictor of termination by Affleck and Mednick (1959) and Taulbee (1958). Davids and Talmadge (1963), using having "moved" in case work as a criterion, postdicted better original adjustment. If we can accept this as a criterion, then the Davidson list of adjustment signs stands validated by this study. Gaylin (1965) demonstrated changes in self-image that occur as a result of therapy. In this case the changes were measured by content rather than scores. Ward (1966) reviewed the different meanings of M in terms of whether they imply observable social behavior or only inner fantasy. On the basis of rather inadequate evidence he concluded that the bulk of opinion favors the overt behavior hypothesis.

Personnel Selection

Another way of evaluating the validity of the test might be to look at its ability to distinguish occupational groups and to predict occupational success.

The greatest amount of work in this area has been done by Roe (1946*b*, 1949, 1950, 1953), who studied occupational groups with great thoroughness, though without many positive results. She concluded this finding might be due to the lack of systematic personality differences between occupational groups, to the possibility that Rorschach scores are not relevant to these differences, or to the possibility that the group Rorschach procedure that she used was not adequate for the measurement of relevant differences.

Kurtz (1948) studied successful versus unsuccessful life insurance salesmen and found 32 signs. However, they washed out on cross-validation. Rieger (1949) compared occupational personalities and found only gross verbal versus manipulative differences. The Rorschach may be of very little value in personnel work from the trait-factor standpoint, except to pick out acutely disturbed individuals.

Miller (1955) at first found differences on the multiple-choice Rorschach among drivers who had a high or low accident rate, but cross-validation eliminated every distinguishing sign. Roe and Mierzwa (1960) found the research in the area of personnel selection on the Rorschach to be quite discouraging, and concluded that the Rorschach does not give specific information relevant to this problem. Super and Crites (1962) attacked the position that personnel maladjustment is necessarily damaging to work efficiency. In a review by Kinslinger (1966), it was pointed out that the Rorschach might be of value in the evaluation of maladjustment, stress tolerance, flexibility, and capacity utilization.

In the same review, Kinslinger (1966) pointed out that most positive results wash out with cross-validation. The results with the multiple-choice Rorschach he writes off as being inconsequential. He concludes that the Rorschach is better for distinguishing normals from abnormals than for distinguishing normals from one another. Such variables as job performance, job satisfaction, and occupational preference show little relation to Rorschach variables.

CONCLUSION

The present status of the Rorschach test is quite different from what it was thirty years ago when the test was first introduced to the American scene. It is no longer considered a magical instrument with a mysterious capacity for probing beyond the immediate and mystically revealing the inner essence of the individual. This change in attitudes toward the Rorschach is due partly to the fact that most personality assessors these days refuse to recognize the presence of any such inner essence. Rather, they are interested in predicting behavior under various specified conditions. Thus, the fact that the Rorschach can be so easily influenced by transient and situational variables can be considered hopeful rather than discouraging if specific sampling of behavior under specified conditions is of interest.

Special methods, such as the semantic differential, seem to offer the hope of establishing a level of information about the Rorschach cards and their contributions to the responses elicited that has heretofore been lacking. In predicting psychiatric categories and special group membership, the studies that have focused upon content have been more encouraging than those in which formal scores have been employed. It may well be that even the discouraging results in the personnel area would be changed if vocabulary were used as a stylistic variable to be focused upon as a means of judging vocational interests, rather than relying upon far-fetched hypotheses derived by rather gratuitous inferences from Rorschach scores. Thus, it would appear that the Rorschach, rather than having been made obsolete as a result of the evidence indicating its inability to reveal the mystical, has risen like a phoenix from its ashes. It has been brought back into the fold as a fascinating set of stimuli about which there is an accumulating range of information, and which can be varied, both with regard to content and method of presentation, as a means of obtaining useful information concerning many areas of human behavior.

CHAPTER VIII

Assessment of psychodynamic variables by the Blacky Pictures

Gerald S. Blum

This is the tale of a dog wagging his theory. It will concern some of the research adventures of the Blacky Pictures, a modified projective technique designed to investigate psychosexual dimensions of personality (Blum, 1950). By virtue of its construction, the method has proven especially suited to empirical study of psychoanalytic theory and the dynamics of clinical syndromes. In addition, an attempt will be made to illustrate the versatility of a theory-based assessment device in exploring a variety of other domains, such as the systematic measurement of psychological defense preferences and problem-solving ability with emotionally loaded material.

Dogs rarely live to be twenty years old. Blacky, born in 1946, is clearly an exception. He has been unleashed upon the mainland of Asia and allowed to roam freely in darkest Africa, Europe, and Australia. Despite infrequent bouts with would-be dog catchers like Vance Packard in his native land, it might be said that he feels the world is his kennel. Blacky's ubiquity in clinical settings is matched by a steadily growing volume of research (more than one hundred and fifty references) and by having been singled out as one of the few projective devices to have increased in research usage during recent years (Mills, 1965).

To what can we attribute the sturdy constitution of this peripatetic little fellow? Certainly not to a penchant for clean living. Nor can we credit him with a particularly pleasant disposition conducive to a life without stress. Perhaps the secret lies in his nose for the Unconscious. No creature with a psychological bent can go hungry in that nether world of choice tidbits and tantalizing scraps. All of which is a roundabout way of saying that the Blacky technique is geared directly to a set of psychodynamic variables that have long since come of age. Psychoanalysis, not without controversy in either its

150

·theoretical or its applied senses, has nevertheless pointed to personality dimensions whose recognition is widespread. These dimensions of psychosexual development—including stages of conflict, types of defense mechanisms, and forms of interpersonal relationship—constitute Blacky's skeleton.

The pictures are a series of cartoons with the cast of characters including the hero, Blacky (described to female subjects as a girl dog); his parents, Mama and Papa; and a sibling of unspecified sex and age, Tippy, Successively, Blacky is seen nursing from Mama (I); chewing aggressively on Mama's collar (II); relieving himself between the parents' doghouses (III); observing Mama and Papa make love (IV); exploring his own sex organs (V); watching a knife about to fall on the tail of Tippy (VI); admonishing a wooden toy fashioned in his own image (VII); watching the parents pet Tippy (VIII); cowering before a scolding superego figure (IX); dreaming of an ideal self (X); and dreaming of a love object (XI). The subject is asked to make up a vivid, imaginative story for each of the cartoons. After every story there are a number of multiple-choice and short-answer inquiry items relating to the specific psychosexual dimension. Finally, the cartoons are sorted according to the subject's likes and dislikes. When used with children, the inquiry items are presented in a simplified version. The canine medium was originally chosen to facilitate freedom of personal expression in situations where human figures might provoke too much resistance. Owing to the prevalence of animated cartoons and comic strips, the dog cartoons preserved sufficient reality so that subjects can identify fully with the characters and project their own innermost feelings.

Traditionally, responses have been scored for research purposes in terms of a combined analysis of the four sources of information: spontaneous stories, answers to inquiry questions, cartoon preferences, and related comments appearing on other cartoons. Subjects end up with a conflict score of Very Strong (++), Fairly Strong (+), or Weak or Absent (0) on each of the following thirteen psychosexual dimensions: *Oral Eroticism, Oral Sadism, Anal Expulsiveness, Anal Retentiveness, Oedipal Intensity, Masturbation Guilt, Castration Anxiety (males) or Penis Envy (Females), Identification Process, Sibling Rivalry, Guilt Feelings, Ego Ideal, Narcissistic Love Object, Anaclitic Love Object.* Issues pertaining to the reliability and validity of this scoring approach have been discussed in detail previously (e.g., Blum & Hunt, 1952; Granick & Scheflen, 1958; Berger & Everstine, 1962). In the most recent comprehensive review Sappenfield (1965) concludes that "almost all of the research studies having some bearing on validity have provided some indications in favor of the Blacky technique's validity."

In 1962 an alternative method was presented for scoring male protocols (Blum, 1962). All themes, inquiry answers, and cartoon preferences of 210 male undergraduates were recorded, intercorrelated, and factor-analyzed separately on each of the eleven pictures. Two or three orthogonal factors emerged per picture, making a total of thirty. (See Table 1.) Next the factors were related to a host of criterion variables in order to ascertain their construct validity. Available measures provided information on siblings, defense preferences, interests and values, demographic family characteristics, perceived child-rearing practices of parents, past and present physical complaints,

Table 1

List of Blacky Factors by Cartoon

Cartoon I (Oral Eroticism)

I-A   Oral Craving
I-B   Oral Rejection
I-C   Sugar Coating

Cartoon II (Oral Sadism)

II-A   Playfulness
II-B   Supply-Seeking
II-C   Resentment over Oral Deprivation

Cartoon III (Anal Sadism)

III-A   Exploitation
III-B   Choosing Obvious Neutral Responses
III-C   Attempted Denial of Anal Preoccupation

Cartoon IV (Oedipal Intensity)

IV-A   Undisguised Oedipal Involvement
IV-B   Disguised Oedipal Involvement

Cartoon V (Masturbation Guilt)

V-A   Fear of Punishment for Masturbation
V-B   Concern over Sexual Maturation
V-C   Denial of Masturbation Guilt

Cartoon VI (Castration Anxiety)

VI-A   Overwhelming Castration Conflict
VI-B   Minimizing Castration Anxiety

Cartoon VII (Identification Process)

VII-A   Father as Preferred Identification Object
VII-B   Mother as Preferred Identification Object
VII-C   Evasion of Identification Issue

Cartoon VIII (Sibling Rivalry)

VIII-A   Overt Hostility toward Sibling and
         Mother
VIII-B   Reaction Formation to Sibling
         Rivalry
VIII-C   Rejection in Favor of Sibling

Cartoon IX (Guilt Feelings)

IX-A   Partial Denial of Guilt
IX-B   Guilt-Ridden Hostility toward
       Sibling
IX-C   Qualification of Pervasive Guilt

Cartoon X (Ego Ideal)

X-A   Overtly Positive Perception of Self
      and Father
X-B   Negative Perception of Self and Father

Cartoon XI (Love Object)

XI-A   Mother-Surrogate as Love Object
XI-B   Heterosexual Fantasy
XI-C   Narcissism

field of specialization in college, grade-point average, social perception, interpersonal mechanisms, and others.

RESEARCH BEARING DIRECTLY ON PSYCHOANALYTIC THEORY

The first study done with the Blacky Pictures sought to test psychoanalytic hypotheses about dimensional interrelationships and sex differences (Blum, 1949). Comparisons of responses of male and female undergraduates revealed a number of statistically significant differences between them; intercorrelating scores on all the dimensions also produced a number of significant relationships. These significant test data, which fell into 31 areas, were then analyzed in terms of their correspondence to theory. Agreement between test and theory was noted in 14 of the 15 test areas in which the viewpoint of the theory was found to be stated specifically, and in all eight in which a theoretical viewpoint could be inferred. In the remaining eight areas, the theory provided neither postulates nor material suitable for inference, so that no comparisons were possible.

Besides providing an opportunity to check psychoanalytic hypotheses empirically, the test responses lent themselves to the following formulations of psychosexual development in males and females:

> . . . In both sexes the early stages of development appear to be interrelated to the extent that disturbances at one level are associated with disturbances at the others. In the case of males, castration anxiety, originating in the phallic period, is also accompanied by earlier oral and anal conflicts. The male typically resolves the Oedipus situation by identifying predominantly with a father figure and by introjecting that figure as his superego. Those who depart from the normal sequence by later seeking narcissistic love objects are found to have strong, unresolved oedipal conflicts accompanied by the lack of a positive father identification. The growing influence of the mother in American families is reflected in the proportion of males (almost one-third) whose superegos do appear to contain more maternal than paternal features. Generally the superego in males, according to the test data, represents more a threat of external punishment than an internalized fear of losing love. The setting up of a positive ego ideal seems to vary inversely with early oral and anal fixations, and directly with an anaclitic (motherly) type of object choice.

> The psychosexual development of the female, as portrayed by the Blacky test findings, is more involved. The early preoedipal ambivalence of the girl toward her mother seems to have a pronounced effect on the entire development process. Strong oral-sadistic tendencies persist along with repressed anal sadism. The oedipal involvement is less complete than in the case of males, since fear of losing the love of the frustrating mother continues as a dominant motif. The subsequent identification process is less clear-cut and it appears that largely through the mechanism of "identification with the aggressor" the girl is able to pattern herself after the mother toward whom she still harbors strong undercurrents of hostility. Once the mother has been

introjected as the superego, the aggressions formerly directed toward her are turned inward and result in strong guilt feelings. The disturbed sequence culminates in the greater incidence of a narcissistic type of object choice in females. Penis envy also seems to play a prominent role in the latter connection [Blum 1949, pp. 72-3].

In 1958 Neuman and Salvatore performed a centroid-oblique factor analysis on these original dimensional intercorrelations and concluded that the resulting factor structure for males was consistent with psychoanalytic theory but that the female factors contained contradictions. Recently Robinson and Hendrix (1966), making use of more advanced computer techniques, reanalyzed the same data by the principal component method with varimax rotation. For the male sample the 13 Blacky dimensions yielded six orthogonal factors (*oral, anal, phallic, latent, genital,* and *guilt*), which were construed to account for the levels of psychosexual development. For the female sample, unlike the earlier study, a consistent picture also emerged— five factors labeled *oral, anal, phallic, genital,* and *guilt.*

The lack of congruence between female factors and psychoanalytic theory in the Neuman and Salvatore study raised two possibilities—that the theory of female psychosexual development might be faulty and that a dog named Blacky might provide an inappropriate identification figure for female subjects. Several investigators (Wolfson & Wolff, 1956; Dean, 1959; Rossi & Solomon, 1961) suggested or demonstrated that females tend to consider Blacky masculine, at least in the absence of prior instruction to the contrary. However, King and King (1964) subsequently found that females do not seem to identify with "Whitey the cat" more than with "Blacky the dog." They point to the prevalent use in this culture of the masculine form of the pronoun for the third person singular whenever sex ambiguity exists. Robinson and Hendrix also note that the mere substitution of a cat for a dog would not necessarily facilitate feminine identification. Their positive findings in the female factor structure lead them to suggest instead that it may be sufficient to indicate initially to the female subject, as the test manual directs, that Blacky is a female character.

A recent study of the psychoanalytic concept of *ambivalence* (Minkowich, Weingarten, & Blum, 1966) made use of the latest Blacky scoring system. Ambivalence toward mother and father was assessed in 62 male college students by means of two paper-and-pencil tests. In the first, S was presented with a booklet of 10 pages, each headed by one of these figure names: Parent, Mother, Father, Brother, Sister, God, Judge, Male Teacher, Female Teacher, and Matronly Woman. He was instructed to write as quickly and frankly as possible the first 10 descriptive adjectives that he associated with each figure. The number and duration of response latencies was recorded. After completing his associations to all 10 figures, S was asked to mark each of his responses in one of three ways: to assign a + if the adjective connoted a positive quality in the figure rated; a − if it seemed a negative characteristic; or a 0 if neutral in connotation.

In the second session one week later, S evaluated the same 10 figures on a series of antonym pairs presented in the form of seven-point scales, as in

Osgood's semantic differential. Some equivalent pairs of antonyms were included. The following six variables were then used to score ambivalence:

(1) Assignment of both positive and negative ratings to a figure on the first administration of the Adjective Booklet.

(2) Rating changes of the same adjective between first and second administrations.

(3) Response latencies (blocking) in the writing of adjectives for a figure.

(4) Inappropriate ratings of adjectives.

(5) Discrepancies in rating a figure on equivalent scales in the Semantic Differential.

(6) Restriction of Semantic Differential ratings to neutral midpoints of the scales.

Correlates of ambivalence toward parents were sought in sociocultural data and perceived family relationships as well as psychosexual conflicts. Among the latter, ambivalence toward the mother covaried with Oral Craving, a factor describing Blacky's voracious craving for oral supplies and concern over potential deprivation. Elevated ambivalence scores toward both parents were manifested by male Ss high on the factor Exploitation, which deals primarily with Blacky's selfish expression of aggressive impulses, especially anal exploitation of parental figures. Also, Undisguised Oedipal Involvement, a factor saturated with various sexual references toward Mama, comments about Blacky's jealousy toward Papa and expected retaliation, was significantly related to heightened ambivalence toward both parents.

From a series of similar investigations employing the Ambivalence Assessment Technique with schizophrenics and schoolboys, in addition to male and female undergraduates, it was possible to formulate a psychodynamic account of high ambivalence:

Evidence of actual identification disturbances is suggested by the more ambivalent schoolboys' tendency to perceive themselves as different from their fathers on evaluative dimensions. Later in life these trends continue to appear as personality correlates, for ambivalent college students report patterns in church attendance and strength of religious feeling which are discrepant from those of their parents.

A relationship between ambivalence and moral behavior, suggested by psychoanalytic theory, is demonstrated in the present data. Ambivalent individuals display defects in the internalization of moral standards, in fantasied violations of sexual and aggressive norms, and in minimizing feelings of remorse over deviant behavior. Moral decisions and feelings appear to be based on external factors or impulsive tendencies rather than on introjected values. Accompanying this rebellious attitude, however, is an undifferentiated general guilt reaction. The rebellion is reflected further in ambivalent Ss' emphasis on freedom as a childrearing objective rather than on love, guidance, or the inculcation of moral standards. Resentment of parents and revolt against their value systems are symptomatic of underlying conflict.

The dynamic picture suggested by personality correlates of high ambivalence is one of unresolved oedipal conflict and exploitative impulses directed toward parental figures. Not only do ambivalent children fail to incorporate parental models, but early patterns of psychosexual conflict remain dominant aspects of their personality functioning. Oral conflict, particularly unmet dependency needs, is typical of Ss whose opposed emotional attitudes center around the mother. Further support for analytic propositions is obtained from the generality study which demonstrates the subsequent extension or transfer of coexisting opposed feelings to persons outside the immediate family. Emerging factors seem to follow well-defined patterns centering around male authority figures, female authority figures, and peers. The use of particular defenses, especially projection, is also typical for ambivalent Ss when dealing with psychosexual conflict, but further investigation seems necessary to establish the significance of ambivalence in this and other areas relating to psychopathology [Minkowich, Weingarten, & Blum, 1966, pp. 39-40].

Though interpreted as supporting some very general psychoanalytic notions about ambivalence, the findings are viewed mainly as a promising first step in the pursuit of a much-needed detailed, well-articulated theoretical account of this crucial personality characteristic.

RESEARCH ON THE PSYCHODYNAMICS OF SYNDROMES

In addition to providing a vehicle for the investigation of psychoanalytic theory itself, the Blacky Pictures permit empirical research into applications of the theory to various clinical syndromes. Psychodynamic formulations thus become eligible for independent check. Several illustrations will be offered next.

Among the earliest studies in this category were those by Aronson (1953) on the dynamics of paranoia and Lindner (1953) on sexual offenders. The former administered the Blacky Pictures to 30 paranoid schizophrenics, 30 nonparanoid schizophrenic controls (absence of delusions), and 30 normal controls. The paranoid group yielded evidence of strong underlying oral deprivation, oral sadistic conflict, and especially strong anal retentive fixations, in agreement with the psychoanalytic viewpoint that anal disturbance is central to paranoia. Other evidences of disturbance were masturbation guilt, conscious attempts at denial of intense underlying castration anxiety, a consistent tendency toward feminine identification, severe superego conflict, and a preference for narcissistic types of love-object choice.

Lindner used the technique with 67 male sexual offenders in prison and a matched group of nonsexual offender inmates. The experimental group was comprised (in decreasing order of frequency) of cases of homosexuality, sodomy, rape, pedophilia, exhibitionism, carnal knowledge, and contributing to the delinquency of minors. These sexual offenders turned out to be significantly more disturbed on 9 of the 13 Blacky dimensions: Oral Eroticism, Oral Sadism, Oedipal Intensity, Masturbation Guilt, Castration Anxiety, Sibling Rivalry, Guilt Feelings, Narcissistic Love Object, and Anaclitic Love Object. The author interpreted the data as supporting psychoanalytic formulations of sexual deviation.

Psychosomatic disorders—for example, peptic ulcer and bronchial asthma—have been the subject of a number of investigations. The initial Blacky exploration of the dynamics of peptic ulcer was carried out by Blum and Kaufman (1952), who studied 14 adult male patients. Though all showed strong conflict in their stories on Cartoon I (Oral Eroticism), half the group picked disturbed choices on the inquiry items for that dimension whereas the other half picked the neutral choices. The former, labeled the "primary" subgroup, seemed to be openly accepting of their dependency needs in contrast to the "reactive" subgroup, which consciously rejected such tendencies. Analysis of data from other tests given in the same battery appeared to confirm these observations (Marquis, Sinnett, & Winter, 1952). Streitfeld (1954), concerning himself with the hypotheses of oral dependency and aggression, found a group of 20 male and female ulcer patients to score higher than a nonulcer psychosomatic control group on Oral Sadism (Cartoon II) but not on Oral Eroticism (Cartoon I). Bernstein and Chase (1955), also investigating 20 ulcer patients and controls, did not find more widespread disturbance in the stories of the ulcer group for Cartoon I, but the inquiry responses did follow the pattern described earlier by Blum and Kaufman.

The most systematic follow-up was done by Winter (1955), working with the records of 68 male ulcer patients in a Veterans Administration facility. He elaborated the theory of primary versus reactive ulcer types, consistent with formulations of Franz Alexander, and also expanded the Blacky criteria for distinguishing between them. A high scorer on the primary scale was described as a person who is very demanding and immature. Because of strong passivity needs, he continually seeks to establish dependent relationships with others. His desires for love and protection are insatiable, and he often feels—and actually is—rejected. He reacts to frustrations with resentment against the environment. A high scorer on the reactive Blacky scale is also basically passive, but he is unable to accept and express his dependency needs. He overcompensates by playing the role of a responsible, productive, striving citizen. Aggressive impulses are channeled into high aspirations for success and conscientious efforts to achieve. His feelings of inadequacy lead to attempts to raise his self-esteem.

Predictions concerning life-history data were then made for the two subgroups of ulcer patients. Of 32 predictions, 15 were confirmed statistically. Examples are positive relationships between the reactive type and high occupational level, high educational level, keeping appointments in the clinic, food rejection, and anal symptoms; between the primary type and low rank in military service. Winter concluded that clearly no single description of personality dynamics fits the ulcer syndrome and that the primary versus reactive distinction appears to be meaningful.

Berger (1959) applied Winter's Blacky system for assessing primary and reactive types to a nonulcer control group of 30 male VA patients recovering from minor surgery. He found the two patterns occurring in this group as well and emphasized the logical conclusion that, while relevant to an understanding of the dynamics of ulcer formation, the patterns cannot be considered sufficient in a causal sense.

With reference to bronchial asthma, Margolis (1961) utilized the Blacky

Pictures to check the French and Alexander notion of early maternal rejection—accompanied by excessive dependence on, and longing for, the mother—as central to the genesis of childhood asthma. Rejecting mothers, often carrying their own unresolved conflicts into relationships with their children, are considered to have an unconscious need to keep their asthmatic offspring in a helpless and dependent state. The groups tested were 25 mothers of asthmatic children along with 25 mothers of children with rheumatic heart conditions and 25 whose children were relatively healthy. Results showed the asthma mothers to be more disturbed on the oral and oedipal dimensions, a trend that held up for both white and Negro subgroups in the sample. Evasiveness characterized their responses—for example, either ignoring or minimizing the fact that Mama is nursing Blacky on Cartoon I.

Seiden (1966) studied the psychoanalytic significance of onset age in 45 children with bronchial asthma. He divided the sample, which ranged in age from 9 to 16 years, into three matched groups according to whether the onset of disease was in the first year of life (oral phase), 2 to 3 years (anal phase), or 4 to 7 years (phallic phase). Two hypotheses were tested from the Blacky data: (a) age of onset is related to overall amount of psychosexual conflict; and (b) age of onset is related to type of psychosexual conflict; that is, the strongest conflict will occur in the psychosexual area coincident with onset of asthma. With respect to the first hypothesis, the mean amount of conflict differed significantly in the three onset-age groups, the anal group being the most disturbed overall and the phallic group the least. The second hypothesis was confirmed in that children tended to obtain their highest conflict scores in those psychosexual areas associated with the particular age of onset.

Some illustrative research applications outside the psychosomatic category involve groups of stutterers, amputees, and heavy smokers. Carp (1962) administered the Blacky Pictures to 20 undergraduate stutterers and 20 controls, and found statistical confirmation for the theoretical predictions of stronger oral eroticism, oral sadism, and phallic disturbance in the experimental group, but not for the prediction of stronger anal sadism. Block and Ventur (1963) checked the assumption of symbolic castration in a group of 20 adult male amputees. The results agreed with the specific prediction of greater castration anxiety in the amputees than in normals and also supported a series of postulates derived syntactically from psychoanalytic theory. Kimeldorf and Geiwitz (1966), using the latest factor scoring system, tested the prediction of oral disturbance among heavy smokers. Compared to 15 nonsmokers, the group of 7 heavy smokers scored significantly higher on Oral Craving (Cartoon I) and the defensive factor Playfulness on Cartoon II. Consequently, the authors describe the heavy smoker as "an individual with relatively intense oral desires who tends to avoid overt exhibition of animosity in interpersonal relations, perhaps to avoid offending a possible source of oral supplies."

EXPLORATION OF THEORETICAL HUNCHES

Thus far we have described some of Blacky's forays in the realm of theory-testing as he sought to track down psychoanalytic concepts and their application to various syndromes. But dogs like to explore as well as hunt, and in this respect Blacky has lived up to canine expectations. There are many areas where psychodynamic theory, though seemingly relevant, does not point as clearly to specific predictions. Investigators typically follow their hunches in such instances, hoping to emerge eventually with a well-formulated account of the behavior in question. Blacky's role in some of these more devious enterprises will be summarized next.

An early study by Swanson (1951) analyzed the relationship between patterns of Blacky scores and observed behavior in discussion groups. A series of criterion variables concerning participation and attitudes was available for two groups of men and women attending a summer session of the National Training Laboratory in Bethel, Maine. Some of these variables were total volume of participation, direction and extent of influence, desire to lead, desire to conform, and satisfaction with own performance in group. From his knowledge of psychoanalytic theory, Swanson made predictions as to patterns of Blacky dimensional scores that should be associated with these various tendencies. For example, he reasoned that high scores on Oral Sadism, Anal Expulsiveness, Oedipal Intensity, Sibling Rivalry, and Guilt Feelings should raise the total amount of an individual's actual participation in a permissive group, whereas Oral Eroticism, Anal Retentiveness, and Anaclitic Love Object choice should lower it. The resulting rank-order correlations (.63 for the example cited) generally were in line with his intuitive pattern analyses.

Rabin (1958) used the Blacky Pictures in another social psychological setting as a means of checking the influence of family structure upon personality development. With a Hebrew translation he tested 27 fourth-grade Israeli boys reared in a kibbutz and a control group of 27 raised within a traditional family structure. His theoretical reasoning led to the hypotheses of less oedipal intensity in the kibbutz group; stronger identification with the father in the traditional family; and more sibling rivalry in the latter. All three hypotheses received some measure of statistical support, leading Rabin to conclude that "the type of family structure has considerable influence on the nature of the identification process, relationship to parents, and attitude to siblings."

Christiansen (1959), employing a Norwegian translation and modification of the Blacky technique, tested students of the military and naval academies at Oslo and also ascertained their attitudes toward foreign affairs. Among other conclusions, he notes that (a) lack of psychodynamic conflicts is positively correlated with tendencies toward assigning responsibility to one's own nation for solving international conflicts, and negatively correlated with preferences for aggressive national reaction patterns; and (b) tendencies toward aggressive international reactions are correlated more highly with conflicts in connection with oral aggression than with conflicts in connection with other basic impulse patterns.

A very different kind of investigation combined operant-conditioning techniques and derivations from psychosexual theory. Timmons and Noblin (1963) hypothesized that oral characters, presumed to be more susceptible to suggestion, should respond more to verbal conditioning than anal characters, who tend to be obstinate and resistant. Having selected 15 "oral" and 15 "anal" subjects by means of the Blacky Pictures, they carried out a Taffel-type verbal conditioning experiment. Their prediction was confirmed in that the oral group did condition markedly better than the anal group when mild, affirmatory words from an authority figure were used as reinforcing stimuli.

An area of exploration that has received attention in several studies is the college student's choice of field of specialization. Teevan (1954), administering the Blacky Pictures to 85 male undergraduates, found significant differences among three broad groupings of college majors: the literature division (English, art, languages) had higher disturbance scores on Oral Eroticism than the other divisions; the social science division (economics, government, and history) had higher scores on Oral Sadism, Oedipal Intensity, Guilt Feelings, and Anaclitic Love Object choice; and the science division (geology, astronomy, biology, physics, and chemistry) had the lowest scores on nearly all dimensions. Magnussen (1959) attempted to replicate Teevan's findings in 60 male undergraduates divided into the same categories of major field. The literature group again turned out to be higher on Oral Eroticism, and the science majors again showed the least disturbance across practically all dimensions. The social science results were repeated only with respect to higher Oral Sadism. Magnussen reiterates Teevan's conclusion that, in the early stages of academic specialization, individuals tend to migrate to specific college majors because of personality characteristics.

Information on undergraduate field of specialization was also collected as part of the large-scale revision of the Blacky scoring system (Blum, 1962). Since the new Blacky factors do not correspond to the dimensional scores and the categories of college major are different, it is not possible to relate the findings to those of Teevan or Magnussen. Nor does the small number of subjects for whom such information was available (N of 71 divided among six categories) permit, in the absence of cross-validation, much confidence in those scattered correlations that attained statistical significance. Briefly, the results were as follows: engineering majors scored high on Playfulness, a defensive factor serving to avoid expression of hostility toward the mother; premedical students were high on Concern over Sexual Maturation and Qualification of Pervasive Guilt; physical or natural science majors showed evidence of Resentment over Oral Deprivation and Overwhelming Castration Conflict; business or prelaw correlated positively with Oral Rejection and Negative Perception of Self and Father; liberal arts majors were high on Partial Denial of Guilt; and social science students had elevated scores on Qualification of Pervasive Guilt and Mother-Surrogate as Love Object.

SPECIAL-PURPOSE USES OF THE BLACKY PICTURES

This last section will deal with special uses for which the pictures themselves have proven highly adaptable. For example, the Blacky cartoons were pressed into service early as experimental stimuli in a series of studies on perceptual vigilance and defense (Blum, 1954, 1955; Nelson, 1955; Perloe, 1960). Prior exposure to the pictures facilitated personal involvement and permitted assessment of psychosexual conflicts and defenses, whose operation was subsequently traced in perception experiments by means of tachistoscopic presentations of the pictures. They have also served as stimuli in studies of visual imagery under different conditions of arousal and in a series of explorations of memory where subjects were asked to recall all eleven pictures as rapidly as possible (Blum, 1961). Another experimental function has been to pinpoint an individual's past affective experiences—having him tell stories about Blacky while awake, followed by more personal accounts associated and relived under hypnosis—as an aid in training him to undergo precise degrees of anxiety or pleasure upon instruction (Blum, 1961, 1967).

Adaptations of the technique have been employed in a variety of assessment contexts as well. In the ambivalence research mentioned earlier, superego functioning was assessed from a specially modified set of inquiry items. Information was thus obtained concerning compliance and transgression fantasies about behavior, and four categories of superego affect: (*a*) an *internal orientation*, consisting of satisfaction over self-control and guilt over transgression; (*b*) an *external orientation*, including anticipation of rewards for compliance and fear of punishment for transgression; (*c*) an *impulsive orientation*, consisting of frustration over impulse inhibition and also satisfaction over impulse gratification; and (*d*) an *avoidant orientation*, derived from noncommittal responses to questions about affect resulting from compliance or transgression.

The two adaptations for special assessment purposes that have been researched most extensively are the Defense Preference Inquiry (DPI) and the Blacky Analogies Test (BAT). The purpose of the DPI is to tap defensive reactions to psychosexual stimuli in an indirect but objectively scorable fashion. The subtlety of the approach lies in the fact that the subject is asked to judge a series of alternatives, each an operational definition of a defense mechanism, in terms of "how well they represent the way Blacky seems to be feeling or acting" in a particular picture—in other words, encouraging him to identify with Blacky and thereby reveal his own personal reactions. The five defenses covered on each cartoon are avoidance (repression-denial family), reaction formation, projection, regression, and intellectualization. Spontaneity of response is facilitated by very short time limits, which preclude the possibility of careful deliberation in assigning ranks to the five statements.

The following is an illustrative set of DPI items to be ranked according to "how well they fit" Cartoon II (Oral Sadism). The latter depicts Blacky chewing vigorously on Mama's collar.

(*Rg*) A. When Blacky gets angry, he often throws a temper tantrum like he did in his earlier days.

(*RF*) B. Blacky tries to pretend that he's ferocious, but when Mama is around he is sure to be overly gentle, calm, and well-behaved.

(*Int*) C. Blacky is a firm believer in the idea of releasing one's aggressions, so he feels justified in ripping Mama's collar here.

(*AV*) D. Blacky is so intent on chewing the collar to pieces that he doesn't even realize it belongs to Mama.

(*P*) E. In Blacky's own way of thinking, his family has been treating him so unfairly that he feels entitled to chew up the collar.

The early studies of the DPI have been summarized previously (Blum,

1956). Several explored the consistency of defense preferences across the psychosexual dimensions. The majority of college students tend to choose a variety of defenses, for example, avoidance on Oral Eroticism, reaction formation on Oral Sadism, projection on Oedipal Intensity, and so on. However, a significant minority tend to choose the same defense regardless of the conflict dimension. These people with fixed preferences–labeled "general defenders" in contrast to the more flexible "specific defenders"–turn out to be more disturbed according to genotypic measures of personality, including the Munro Inspection Technique for the Rorschach and spontaneous stories to the Blacky. On the more phenotypic Guilford–Martin GAMIN inventory, general defenders in the avoidance and reaction formation categories show high facade scores; that is, they are defensive in filling out the inventory in an effort to look good even when their responses are anonymous. No differences between the defender types appear on measures of rigidity such as the California F-scale.

A number of the early studies related defense preferences to a variety of behavioral situations. It was found that college girls in the general defender category were less able to express feelings of hostility or dependency toward their mothers during a personal interview. Avoidance preferences in male undergraduates were associated with perceptual defense in a task involving tachistoscopic presentation of the Blacky pictures; forgetting the pictures in a series of recall tasks; picking neutral rather than conflict-relevant solutions in word-completion and anagram experiments; and poor recall of pertinent humorous cartoons. In another experiment subjects were paired in terms of their defense preferences and required to interact in a task designed to arouse a specific psychosexual disturbance that they had in common. Two people who both tended to project the impulse experienced their paired interaction as more negative than pairs of people who utilized other defenses (Cohen, 1956).

The DPI has also been used to explore national differences in choice of defense mechanisms. In two investigations (Blum, 1956, 1964) data were collected from male samples at leading urban universities in eight countries. Both studies revealed the variability of preferences among the individuals of a given country to be as great as the variability between countries. However, some national differences did appear, including an overall preference for avoidance in Dutch and Danish students, and for intellectualization in the French. It was also possible to compute dissimilarity indices among all eight countries. The U.S. is closest to Italy but quite dissimilar to the other six; England has its closest relationships to the Netherlands, Italy, and France; Germany, Italy, and the Netherlands are all grouped fairly close to Israel and France and intermediate to Denmark; Israel and England are especially far apart on the scale, as are the U.S. and Denmark.

The Blacky Analogies Test (BAT) is designed to measure intellectual performance in the presence of emotionally loaded stimuli. The items are analogies of the usual form except that the missing term has to be filled in by choosing one out of four Blacky pictures. For the original version items were constructed according to the following criteria: (*a*) ability to discriminate in a college population; (*b*) solution involving a readily agreed-upon interpretation of the picture; and (c) only one correct alternative among the four pictures presented for an item (eight pictures in all are employed throughout the test). Early forms were administered to various groups of graduate and undergraduate students. Item difficulty and internal consistency scores served as the basis for a series of revisions, which culminated in the current 40-item test.

The items themselves are of several different types. Some are conventional analogies depicting a conceptual relationship existing between pairs of words, e.g., RUSTY: OIL: :PARCHED: *Picture A* (Blacky nursing). Others involve manipulating letters in words, e.g., CHEW:HEW: : *Picture F* (dog's tail about to be chopped off) :HOP. In some cases less common meanings of the words must be thought of in order to solve the analogy, e.g., RE-LIEF: RELIEVE: :CHARITY: *Picture C* (Blacky "relieving himself"). Thus *S* is required to shift sets fairly rapidly throughout the test, with a time limit of 25 minutes. Although time pressure is introduced by this limit, most *S*s are able to attempt all items. On the other hand, no one has yet attained a perfect score. The instructions, in addition to describing the form of the analogies, also direct *S* to study each picture for 20 seconds, thereby familiarizing him with its content and allowing emotional reactions to occur. During the test the eight lettered pictures are all available for easy reference on a separate sheet. The suggestion is made to skip items not easily answerable and to return to them afterward. Guessing is encouraged when in doubt.

Preliminary versions of the test were employed in a series of unpublished studies dealing with measures of intellectual ability, criteria of academic success, and personality variables. Correlations with the Miller Analogies Test in two samples of psychology graduate students were .28 and .34; in two undergraduate samples, .66 and .63. Other undergraduate samples yielded *r*'s of .32 with the ACE Psychological Examination and .58 with the Concepts Mastery Test. An investigation of undergraduate grade-point averages in one sample revealed significantly higher BAT scores in the upper third of the group than in the lower third. Relationships with personality variables derived from the MMPI, California Personality Inventory, Cattell 16 PF, and Edwards Personal Preference Schedule were all insignificant except, on the latter, there was a low positive *r* with *n Ach* and a low negative one with *n Def*. Significant but low positive correlations were obtained with two rigidity tasks, the Einstellung and Muller-Lyer. A tendency was noted for individuals who chose avoidance as a defense to have lower BAT scores and those who chose intellectualization to have higher scores.

Once the final items were assembled, systematic analyses of the test's properties were undertaken. Reliability was assessed by dividing the 40 items into two 20-item forms (A and B), matched item-by-item for difficulty and type of analogy (letter-manipulation, reasoning, homonym, etc.). Next the records of another sample of 86 undergraduates were rescored and the resulting uncorrected, split-half *r* between Forms A and B was .90. An earlier odd-even correlation, computed for a sample with no attempt at matching the halves, had been .63. A factor analysis of the BAT items themselves, using *phi* coefficients between all pairs of items, did not yield evidence suggesting the feasibility of establishing subscales. The major interpretable factor dealt with letter transformations, such as addition or subtraction of single letters, pre-fixes, suffixes, letter-reversals, or letter-substitutions.

An extensive study of the intellectual factors operating in BAT perfor-mance was carried out by Vroom (1959). She administered a battery of tests to 114 male and 187 female students enrolled in their first year at the University of Michigan. The entire female sample and 72 of the males were drawn from introductory psychology courses and Ss participated to fulfill a requirement; the remaining 42 males were volunteers. Included in the battery were the following group tests, selected to tap a wide variety of possibly relevant intellectual areas: Hidden Figures (Parts 1, 2), Word Matrix, Logical Reasoning (Parts 1, 2), Associations III (Parts 1, 2), Camouflaged Words (Parts 1, 2), Brick Uses, Things Round, ACE: Completion, ACE: Same-Opposite, ACE: Verbal Analogies, ACE: Arithmetic, ACE: Figure Analo-gies, ACE: Number Series, ACE Reading Comprehension: Vocabulary, ACE Reading Comprehension: Speed, ACE Reading Comprehension: Accuracy, IPAT Anxiety (Parts 1, 2).

Product-moment correlations were computed and a factor analysis per-formed on the test battery. The program, based upon the Thurstone centroid method, employed the Varimax rotation. Data for each sex were analyzed separately. Where part scores were available for a test, including the odd-even halves of the BAT, they were included separately so that it was possible for the two parts to form a factor of their own. Eight factors were extracted in each sample, with a marked similarity of structure appearing between the sexes.

Table 2 presents the obtained factors for both males and females. Tests loading .30 or higher in either sample are listed, except for the two halves of the BAT, which are always included. Interpretation of the first factor (Table 2) as Verbal Comprehension stems from the linguistic portions of the ACE and the Reading Comprehension scores. It is similar to one previously given the same name by Guilford (1957). The two BAT forms load more highly for men than women. All the tests on the second factor seem to involve reason-ing ability that entails initial structuring before solution. Here the BAT has low loadings in both sexes. The third factor, interpreted as the ability to restructure words both conceptually and structurally, is labeled Verbal Flexi-bility. The BAT halves show their highest loadings on this factor. The next, Eduction of Conceptual Relationships, contains small BAT loadings.

The remaining four factors are mostly specific in that they are formed by two parts of the same test. With the exception of IPAT Anxiety, on which the BAT does not load, the names applied are Guilford's (1957). Small load-ings appear on both Adaptive Flexibility and Logical Evaluation. In Table 3 the percentage of BAT common variance distributed across the eight factors is shown. Those accounting for more than half of the common factor variance for males are Verbal Flexibility and Verbal Comprehension. In the female sample slightly more than half is accounted for by Verbal Flexibility alone.

Vroom used grade-point average (GPA) at the end of the first year of college as a criterion of predictive validity. High school percentile rank (HSPR), BAT, and GPA were intercorrelated for the portions of her samples

Table 2

Factors Extracted in Test
Battery, Including BAT Factor Loadings

Test	Factor Loading	

Factor I: Verbal Comprehension

	Male	Female[a]
ACE Reading Comprehension: Vocabulary	.79	.84
ACE Reading Comprehension: Speed	.81	.74
ACE Reading Comprehension: Accuracy	.68	.65
ACE: Same-Opposite	.78	.75
ACE: Completion	.54	.55
ACE: Verbal Analogies	.35	.37
BAT Odd Items	.42	.21
BAT Even Items	.47	.20
Camouflaged Words 2	.02	.45
Associations III, 1	.36	.37

Factor II: Preparatory Reasoning

	Male[a]	Female[a]
ACE: Number	.69	.66
ACE: Verbal Analogies	.59	.54
ACE: Figure Analogies	.51	.57
ACE: Arithmetic	.48	.66
Hidden Figures 1	.17	.30
BAT Odd Items	.11	.25
BAT Even Items	.23	.28

Factor III: Verbal Flexibility

	Male	Female
Camouflaged Words 1	.77	.46
Camouflaged Words 2	.66	.38
Associations III, 1	.39	.20
Associations III, 2	.51	.28
BAT Odd Items	.48	.59
BAT Even Items	.36	.56

Factor IV: Eduction of Conceptual Relationships

	Male	Female[a]
Word Matrix	.37	.36
Associations III, 1	.45	.60
Associations III, 2	.39	.58
BAT Odd Items	.23	.24
BAT Even Items	.24	.21

[a]Factor has been reflected to make highest loadings positive.

Table 2 (Continued)

Test	Factor Loading

Factor V: IPAT Anxiety

	Male[a]	Female[a]
Cattell IPAT A	.87	.78
Cattell IPAT B	.87	.81
BAT Odd Items	.05	.03
BAT Even Items	.01	.10

Factor VI: Ideational Fluency

	Male	Female[a]
Things Round	.71	.70
Brick Uses	.79	.71
BAT Odd Items	.01	.06
BAT Even Items	.23	.10

Factor VII: Adaptive Flexibility

	Male[a]	Female[a]
Hidden Figures 1	.83	.71
Hidden Figures 2	.78	.66
BAT Odd Items	.19	.11
BAT Even Items	.20	.22

Factor VIII: Logical Evaluation

	Male[a]	Female
Logical Reasoning 1	.74	.69
Logical Reasoning 2	.59	.61
BAT Odd Items	.22	.26
BAT Even Items	.22	.17

[a]Factor has been reflected to make highest loadings positive.

on whom data were available ($N = 121$ females and 61 males). Table 4 contains these r's and also multiple R's combining previous high school academic performance and BAT scores in the prediction of GPA for both sexes. While all intercorrelations are positive, the ones for females are lower than for males. BAT scores for females correlate more highly with GPA than does HSPR, whereas the opposite is true for males. However, the multiple R for males shows a more marked increase in prediction of GPA when HSPR and BAT are combined than does the corresponding R for females. It should be noted that the BAT was administered, not as a selection test, but as a research tool and Ss were assured that their scores would not be made available to instructors.

Table 3

Percentage of BAT Common Factor Variance on Factors

	Percent of Variance			
Factor	BAT:	Male	BAT:	Female
	Odd Items	Even Items	Odd Items	Even Items
I. Verbal Comprehension	.32	.36	.07	.07
II. Preparatory Reasoning	.02	.09	.10	.14
III. Verbal Flexibility	.41	.21	.58	.54
IV. Eduction of Conceptual Relationships	.09	.09	.10	.08
V. IPAT Anxiety	.00	.00	.00	.02
VI. Ideational Fluency	.00	.09	.01	.02
VII. Adaptive Flexibility	.06	.07	.02	.08
VIII. Logical Evaluation	.09	.08	.11	.05

Table 4

Intercorrelations and Multiple R's between High School Percentile Rank, BAT, and GPA

Variable	BAT	GPA
HSPR (Male)	.39**	.55**
HSPR (Female)	.17	.20*
BAT (Male)		.45**
BAT (Female)		.34**

Variable	Sample	Multiple R
HSPR + BAT	Male	.69
HSPR + BAT	Female	.39

$**p < .01$ (one-tailed test)
$*p < .05$ (one-tailed test)

Blum and Winter subsequently related BAT scores to GPA at the end of one year of graduate work in psychology, in order to study the instrument's effectiveness at a more advanced academic level where discrimination is typically difficult. The entering graduate classes at the University of Michigan were tested in two successive years. An attempt was made to heighten and maintain emotional involvement throughout the test by requiring S, immediately before each item, to rank order the four pictures presented for that item's solution according to how he viewed them as problem areas—on half the items as problems for himself and on half for "people in general."

Two important restrictions must be kept in mind concerning these samples. First, Ss represent a very highly selected group, having been chosen from among several hundred qualified applicants across the nation each year. The mean number of BAT items correct out of 40 was 29 and 30 respectively in the two years, compared to undergraduate means of 23-25. Second, the range of graduate school grades used as the criterion was extremely narrow—97 percent literally running the gamut from A to B! The resulting product-moment correlation between BAT and GPA for the first entering class was .20 (N = 20 males and 9 females); for the second class it rose to .34 (N = 27 males and 10 females).

Analysis of the distributions revealed the instrument to be most successful at the low end; that is, Ss who did relatively *poorly* on the test tended to be near the bottom in grades. In the first sample a natural break occurred at a score of 23. None of the three cases below the break exceeded the GPA median, two being in the bottom 30 percent. When the same cutting score (23) was applied to the second sample, all four excluded cases were in the bottom 30 percent on academic performance. Thus, in terms of numbers of Ss, the lowest ninth of the BAT distribution after one year almost invariably winds up in the bottom third of the class, despite the very restricted nature both of the samples and criterion.

The BAT, whose development has been described in some detail, demonstrates the versatility of a theory-based assessment device. If, as psychoanalytic theory would lead us to believe, unconscious sexual and aggressive forces are characteristically at work in cognitive activity, then the BAT provides a more natural setting for evaluation. The use of the Blacky pictures also makes possible direct access to personality research, since the effects upon problem-solving ability of such variables as intensity of psychosexual conflict and type of defense preference can readily be investigated by means of existing Blacky assessment procedures.

CHAPTER IX

Operant conditioning techniques in psychological assessment

Robert L. Weiss[1]

Assessment, broadly conceived, is of immediate concern to psychologists interested in "*O* effects," those real or postulated individual difference variables introduced to account for the slippage between *S* and *R* in the *S–O–R* formulation. By expanding somewhat the denotation of the term "assessment" in this manner, a pivotal issue in assessment theory is high-lighted: the origin and nature of the individual difference variables that we introduce into our conceptions of behavior. This bit of epistemology—that the form of our questions determine in large part the answers we obtain—provides the context for this discussion of operant technology in relation to other assessment procedures. The term "other" is used advisedly since the aim of this presentation is to provide a basis for deciding the extent to which operant technology may be employed as objective tests (Loevinger, 1957).

The reasons for suggesting that operant procedures may serve an assessment function derive from a consideration of the question above—namely, the origin and nature of our individual difference variables or, as they are called here, "*O* effects." The obvious answer to the question would appear to be that these variables are introduced by constructs of comprehensive personality theories. In point of fact, however, this rarely occurs, since we lack a comprehensive theory of personality that gives rise to constructs with

---

[1] The author's research was supported by the Veterans Administration while he was associated with the Behavioral Research Laboratory, Palo Alto Veterans Administration Hospital. The writer wishes to acknowledge the helpfulness of his colleagues, Edward Lichtenstein, Gerald R. Patterson, and Leonard G. Rorer, as *N* = 1 representatives of clinical, reinforcement, and assessment points of view, all of whom read an earlier version of this chapter. Responsibility for the ideas expressed in this chapter, however, is solely that of the writer.

empirical consequences. Rather, what does seem to happen is that O effects enter our conceptions of behavior via three predominately empirical avenues: (*a*) As a result of practical or applied needs of our society, assessment devices are developed, and the classes of individual differences comprehended by such devices are, of course, directly referrable to these applied contexts. (*b*) Psychology has frequently appropriated constructs from other branches of science and technology and then developed assessment devices to comprehend the O effects associated with these constructs. (*c*) Test-inferred behavioral dispositions have been introduced from within assessment technology itself. Many of these empirically-introduced foundling constructs already have been influential in clinical and personality theories. How well have they served our purposes?

The explanatory usefulness of many of our analogical concepts—those typically associated with the "medical model"—has been questioned on a broad front (see, for example, Ferster, 1965; Kanfer & Saslow, 1965; Milton, 1965; Sarbin, 1967). The utility of dispositional constructs *sui generis* has been questioned by Wallace (1966), who argues for constructs reflecting response capability. Levy (1961) has shown, for example, how an assessment device rather than the psychological problem itself tends to control the behavior of psychologists. The practice of using test behaviors to infer O effects also has been roundly criticized in its application to personality questionnaires (see e.g., Hase & Goldberg, 1967; Norman, 1963; Rorer, 1965; Weiss & Moos, 1965; Weiss, 1966b). As Loevinger has noted regarding the selection of test items, "The problem is to find a coherent set of operations permitting utilization of content together with empirical considerations [1957, p. 658]." Apparently we have been able in the ensuing years to develop more and more sophisticated techniques, but not with a commensurate gain in O effects of wide applicability.

If it is true that many of our constructs enter into psychology on a more or less empirical basis, then it may be possible—in the sense Cronbach (1957) suggested some time ago—to combine the efforts of our experimental ($S–R$) and correlational ($R–R$) enterprises with an anticipated gain. Operant technology offers an empirical strategy that embodies both experimental control and provision for studying individual difference effects. Emphasizing as it does the functional relatedness of behavior to reinforcing contingencies, it provides a means of studying adaptive behavior as an ongoing process. It is in this sense that the applicability of operant technology to assessment methodology will be spelled out here.

The present chapter is organized into three major sections: In the introductory section, some general comparisons will be drawn between operant technology and assessment methodology in order to clarify possible applications. In the second section, a series of studies will be reviewed in order to determine some of the assessment capabilities of operant strategies, particularly the option of introducing O effects. In the final section, a selection of results from studies conducted by the writer in the area of the "communication of accord" will be presented in order to illustrate more specifically the utility of an empirically introduced O effect that may be assessed via operant techniques.

The scope of the material to be covered is confined to clinical and personality psychology, but the presentation may have relevance beyond these content areas. The reader is asked to adopt an innovating attitude in pursuing this presentation of operant technology as objective testing.

COMPARISONS BETWEEN OPERANT AND ASSESSMENT METHODS

This section provides a general background to the material presented in the latter two sections. Here we will consider suggestions by others for the utilization of operant technology—particularly in clinical psychological applications—and then consider similarities and differences between operant and assessment methodologies. The reader unfamiliar with the more current aspects of the operant viewpoint may find the following sources helpful: For general readings see Ulrich, Strachnik, and Mabry (1966), and Verhave (1966). For clinical applications see Sidman (1962) and Bachrach and Quigley (1966).

Previously Suggested Applications

Psychologists identified with the operant point of view make the assumption that behavioral processes are "explained" by the specification of the stimulus control of responding. Both Skinner (1963) and Weingarten and Mechner (1966) indicate that the "causes" of behavior are to be found in the contingency control of behavior—i.e., the effects of response contingent events. Skinner points out the importance of operant techniques in defining the behavioral effects of numerous variables, such as physiological dimensions or effects of hereditary differences (1963). In principle at least, operant procedures are said to have wide applicability in defining behavioral effects of varied independent manipulations.

Sidman (1962), in his chapter on "Operant Techniques," introduced his discussion of possible clinical applications of operant technology by suggesting that the latter may allow us to generate behavioral principles that would then permit a regrouping of classes of deviant behaviors. Diagnosis of behavior "pathology" would, according to this suggestion, be based explicitly upon functional behavioral adjustments. Kanfer and Saslow (1965) present a clear statement of this idea in their outline for a "behavioral analysis." Their point is that ". . . an effective diagnostic procedure would be one in which the eventual therapeutic methods can be directly related to the information obtained from a continuing assessment of the patient's current behaviors and their controlling stimuli [1965, p. 533]." Kanfer and Saslow acknowledge the similarity of their position to that offered by Ferster (1965) in his argument for the need to specify the reinforcing schedules that maintain behavior. Ferster's point is also that in simply observing the frequency of a response, one does not learn about its functional relationship to the environment; we must know, in addition, the reinforcing history or the ways in which the contingencies were scheduled.

Still another explicit suggestion for a clinical (in this case diagnostic) application has been made by George Stone (1966). Stone devised an operant learning task (not unlike a temporal maze) that has demonstrable sensitivity to changes in patient adjustment as measured by subsequent ward ratings. At this point Stone's suggestions about the use of operant techniques may be useful in setting the stage for contrasts to be drawn with other assessment methods.

Stone notes that instructions are "trained into" the subject in an operant conditioning task and that motivation is provided at each step of the way (by the response contingent reinforcement). Operant conditioning tasks usually involve testing on more than one occasion and, in addition, provide a measure of behavioral change as a function of the reinforcing contingency. "An operant conditioning situation is one in which there are two or more response classes that promptly produce stimulus changes that are discriminable in terms of their value for the subject [Stone, 1966, p. 2]." The outcomes (response-contingent stimulus changes) may be ordered in terms of subjects' preferences for them; the latter are indicated by the subjects' response choices.

From this sketch of operant applications, we see that the basic notion of the contingency (the "if ... then ..." statement) underlies the functionalism of this approach. Behavior is said to be under the control of the contingency, and response-contingent events may be scheduled in elaborate temporal combinations. Response preference to particular classes of contingent events may be instructive from a diagnostic point of view. Unlike other testing procedures the operant techniques provide immediate "knowledge of results" (reinforcement), which, in turn, is intended to change ongoing behavior. This is, of course, radically different from most objective assessment procedures.

The above background information suggests that operant technology has previously been thought of as a possible means of defining behavior effects for more or less diagnostic purposes. We turn now to a comparison of operant and assessment methodologies, in order to highlight points of similarity between the two that are easily overlooked.

Contrasts between Operant and Assessment Methodologies

With the possible exceptions just noted (the suggested diagnostic applications), the Skinnerian or operant point of view in psychology traditionally has not emphasized the importance of individual differences. On the contrary, as already noted above, this point of view is committed to the assumption that all forms of behavior are understandable in terms of stimulus control. Prediction in the sense utilized in assessment theory is not sanctioned within the empirical functionalism of operant technology. Intervening or postulated O effects, it is said, add nothing to the control of behavior nor to analyses of its functional relationship to the environment.

Yet, because of its empirical stance, operant methodology actually is uniquely well suited to deal with individual differences, as implied, for example, by the statement that "the only way to tell whether or not a given event is reinforcing to a given organism under given conditions is to make a direct test [Skinner, 1953, p. 73]." While it is true that from the operant point of view all that is required for prediction is knowledge of what controls behavior, there is nothing incompatible with this position in taking the next step and predicting stimulus control in other situations. In this sense measured *responsiveness to reinforcement* is an *O* effect that may have predictive significance. The nature of these *O* effects will become clearer as we draw further comparisons with assessment testing.

A distinction is usually made in diagnostic testing between test responses conceived as *signs* and test responses conceived as *samples* of the criterion behavior (see Loevinger, 1957; Cronbach, 1960). The distinction refers to test behaviors that are themselves representative of the criterion behavior (e.g., doing arithmetic problems as a sample of intellectual activity) versus test behaviors that have no intrinsic or necessary relationship to the criterion (e.g., most empirical inventories, such as the Strong Vocational Interest Blank). Test behavior scored for thematic content, for example, is "topographically" dissimilar from the criterion behaviors subsequently predicted. In operant technology the behavior under analysis may provide either sign or sample information for the observer.

In Stone's use of operant conditioning methodology (noted above and described in more detail in the next section) the temporal maze behavior was used diagnostically as a *sign* of some presumed disturbance. Responsiveness to *social reinforcement* (see Krasner & Ullmann, 1965) on the other hand, has been studied widely as both an analogue (sample) of other interpersonal contexts (e.g., Williams, 1964; Krasner, 1965) and as a response-inferred predictor (sign) of other interpersonal behaviors (Patterson, 1965; Weiss, Ullmann, & Krasner, 1960; Sarbin, Allen, & Rutherford, 1965; Johannsen & Campbell, 1964). Clearly, the more remote response-inferred predictors become from the content of behavior (more sign-like), the less likely are we to establish generality and validity. Norman (1963) has shown, for example, how predictability to criterion behaviors increases significantly as item content becomes more similar to situationally observable events (see also Peterson, 1965; Wallace, 1967).

The distinction between signs and samples is, of course, relevant to another issue in assessment methodology—namely, the source of the data. For example, Leary, in designing the Interpersonal Check List, explicitly introduced the concept of "levels of behavior," by which he meant to differentiate among the numerous possible *sources* of data about a person (Leary & Coffey, 1955). Self-ratings (as behavior) were to be distinguished from ratings (of behavior) by others. As the source of data about behavior becomes more remote from the behavior (sample) itself, we introduce more possible sources of error variance. It is more difficult to establish the validity of signs than of samples. In a series of studies of rating methodologies (Norman & Goldberg, 1966; Passini & Norman, 1966), Norman stresses how the rater "generates the data," since it is he who must understand the rating dimensions (e.g., traits), and we must assume that the rater has made observations of the ratee necessary for the ratings. However, raters can show remarkable consistency in their ratings of *unknown* ratees simply on the basis of their "implicit personality theories" or on the basis of "what goes with what" (Norman & Goldberg, 1966). It is also possible to show that self-ratings predict clearly defined social behaviors about as well as do sophisticated personality inventories (Hase & Goldberg, 1967). Behavior derived from operant procedures is always from a single source, the subject himself.

Assessment devices of all types must, of course, be concerned with issues of reliability (Tryon, 1957). Whereas in tests composed of discrete items the familiar conceptions of reliability are straightforward, in operant procedures the data of interest are likely to be in the form of change scores reflecting deviation from a base-line of behavior as a function of reinforcement. The representativeness of the base-line behaviors (their stability or asymptotic ceiling) is a major issue here (see Patterson, 1965; Parton & Ross, 1965). Since the responses in an operant situation may be under the control of some aperiodic reinforcement schedule (something other than a 1:1 payoff for each "correct" response), chunking the behavior for reliability determinations is not a straightfoward matter. As Patterson has noted (1965), the subject may change his strategy of responding, making it even more difficult to tie a response-rate to a particular time sample of controlling stimuli. Although it may be quite difficult to establish reliability coefficients with certain forms of operant behaviors, many investigators are nevertheless becoming increasingly concerned with the methodology involved, and one can anticipate greater statistical sophistication in operant applications where prediction is involved.

Primarily because a subject must adjust to the ever-changing demands created by an operant task, it appears that operant methodology, relative to assessment techniques, more clearly reflects situational variables. This is a further elaboration of the sign-sample distinction drawn above. The point is that we might profitably view behavior in the context of task demands and thus sample a wide range of adjustive behaviors. Wallace (1967), operating from an expectancy social learning model (e.g., Rotter, 1960), comes to very much the same conclusion about operant tasks. For Wallace individual differences in the effectiveness of reinforcing events is indicative of *response capability*, the conceptual unit he wishes to substitute for the more familiar *response dispositional* constructs employed in personality research. Now, it is important to know, before making inferences about personality "structures" based on signs, whether certain behaviors are actually in a person's repertoire; operant analyses would be particularly useful in this regard. Wallace elaborates a list of possibilities for operant assessment, noting individual differences in delay of gratification, differences in response to extinction schedules, and differences in response to "nonreward embedded in a series of punishments [1967, p. 59]."

Last to be mentioned in this comparison of operant to other assessment techniques is the format of each. Operant procedures are typically novel, custom-made fabrications, usually housed in laboratories. Are we to give serious consideration to their widespread use in favor of the relative simplicity of paper-and-pencil devices? This is obviously a practical problem based on factors of cost and availability of resources. The gains of operant technology over traditional forms of objective testing will become more apparent, it is hoped, in the following sections, which review the studies germane to operant assessment.

In summarizing this section, it may be said that operant technology actually is quite consistent with an individual differences approach. The typical operant conditioning situation is concerned only with immediate stimulus control; but, as we have seen, responsiveness to reinforcing contingencies may have important predictive significance. We noted the distinction between signs and samples of test behavior and concluded that in view of the unusually great situational dependency of behavior on test conditions in operant methodology, samples are more likely to be involved than signs. Then, we observed that a sampling of capabilities may be provided by operant technology, and indicated the need for giving further attention to reliability issues in this kind of assessment.

In the next section, studies will be presented that illustrate the kinds of *O* effects introduced by operant procedures and that have relevance for issues in personology research.

STUDIES WITHIN AN OPERANT ASSESSMENT PARADIGM

The paradigm for an operant assessment device involves emitted or voluntary behaviors that are measured in terms of rate or frequency of response, on continuing trials, associated with some program of response-contingent events (reinforcing schedule). Change in response rate or response preference over basal response rate (or preference) provides a sample of behavior that may be predictive to other situations or may allow for the differential classification of subjects into groups.

Since the literature has reported a very large number of studies involving operant conditioning applications of one sort or another, rules for excluding studies are needed here. A distinction can be made between studies that purport to show the effects of independent variables on operantly conditioned forms of behavior, and studies in which conditionability or responsiveness to reinforcement per se is predictive of some extra task behaviors. In the first instance response to reinforcement is the dependent variable, while in the second instance response to reinforcement is the predictor (or classificatory) variable.

When response to reinforcement is the *dependent variable*, the aim of the studies is to demonstrate that a particular response class can be conditioned, and/or that some technique or class of reinforcing stimuli is effective in producing change. Summarily, these studies represent the body of technical lore on the conditioning of human behavior, a comprehensive catalogue of which is beyond the scope of this chapter. Systematic partial reviews of this literature may be found in: Bijou and Baer (1966), Kanfer (1966), Krasner (1965, 1966), Greenspoon (1962), and Williams (1964). In some cases this kind of research undertaking has implications for explicating behavioral processes either controlled by, or reflected in, the independent variables. (Illustrative studies will be cited below.)

Those studies in which responsiveness to reinforcing contingencies is not the dependent variable but is *predictive of some other class of behaviors* (or of the same class in other situations) are likely to have more immediate relevance to the assessment enterprise. However, many of these studies are in the form of a *generalization* or *transfer of effects* paradigm. All of the numerous therapeutic or behavior change studies recently reported necessarily fit this category, since the changed behavior (as a function of responsiveness to scheduled reinforcement) is presumed to generalize to subsequent situations. Again, these studies are numerous, and have been surveyed in: Bachrach and Quigley (1966); Eysenck and Rachman (1965); Kalish (1965); Ulrich et al. (1966); Ullmann and Krasner (1965). While certainly fitting the logical form of a predictive assessment model, it should be noted for the record that proponents of an operant technology approach to behavior change *do not* make a distinction between assessment and "treatment"; Kanfer and Saslow (1965) represent a moderate viewpoint in this regard, yet they state quite clearly that an assessment—behavior-change cycle is an ongoing effort, so that prediction (as used here) may be quite limited and encompass only the next step in the therapeutic manipulation.

There is still another sense in which prediction from responsiveness to reinforcing contingencies may be represented in the literature; there are studies, usually of groups, that purport to show a generalization or transfer effect in the usual sense of these terms. Do the effects on behavior of a given conditioning procedure generalize to situation (or task) X? Here too we encounter an expanding and most complex literature, involving the gamut of procedural and population variations, making direct comparisons between studies difficult and probably of little immediate usefulness. A comprehensive listing of the studies in this area can be found in papers by: D'Zurilla (1966); Neuringer, Meyers, and Nordmark (1966); Lanyon (1967); Kanfer (1966); Greenspoon (1962); Stollak (1966). Most of the studies in this transfer paradigm employ verbal operant conditioning procedures. Yet in a number of them specific conditionability scores are not presented, so that it is difficult to know whether reported failures to find generalization are due to failures in obtaining conditioning—i.e., failures in the predictor task itself.

The presentation of studies here will utilize these two broad divisions for viewing responsiveness to reinforcing contingencies—i.e., as *dependent variable* and as *predictor variable*. A third section will present research on responsiveness involving dyadic relationships; the presentation will be somewhat easier to follow by devoting a separate section to the relevant dyadic studies.

Responsiveness to Reinforcement: Dependent Variable

This section will consider illustrative studies that show how responsiveness to reinforcing contingencies provides information about the particular independent variable, information having relevance to the introduction and assessment of O effects.

Dispositional constructs. Responsiveness to social reinforcement may depend upon particular organismic variables. Three studies illustrate this point: Cairns (1959), Goldman (1965), and Noblin, Timmons, and Kael (1966). In both the Cairns and the Goldman studies "dependency anxiety" was used to predict the differential effectiveness of positive or negative reinforcement on conditioning performance. Cairns employed juvenile delinquents in a verbal operant conditioning task and showed that examiner reinforcement was effective for the low dependency-anxious group of subjects, but that it had a deleterious effect on the performance of the high dependency-anxious subjects. Goldman, with schizophrenic patients, also found this type of interaction between quality of reinforcing stimuli and learning. He used praise and punishment (separately), paired-associate learning tasks, and found that dependency-anxious patients performed *better* under punishment than reward.

Noblin et al. used as their independent variable the psychoanalytic constructs of "oral" and "anal" character types (as defined by the Blacky Test). A Taffel conditioning paradigm was used, with the important modification (to control for potential awareness of the contingency) that subjects during conditioning were reinforced on a 75 percent schedule rather than a 100 percent schedule. (Seven of 48 subjects reported awareness and were replaced by subjects of similar character type.) Under positive examiner reinforcement ("mm-hmm," "that's fine") "orals" conditioned whereas "anals" showed the predicted decrement in the response class being observed. Under punishment ("you can do better," "um, not quite") the "orals" did poorly while the "anals" showed a significant increase in the selected response class. (Parenthetically, it may be noted that predictions for "oral" and "anal" types were quite similar to Goldman's low- and high-dependency anxious patients, respectively.)

That responsiveness to social reinforcement may be indicative of O effects has also been propounded by those influenced by Rotter's social learning theory (see Getter, 1966; Baron, 1966). Getter has shown that subjects who conditioned were significantly higher in External Control on Rotter's *I-E* scale (see Rotter, 1966) than other combinations of conditioners-nonconditioners. The implication is that conditioners are persons whose "generalized expectancy [is] that their reinforcements [are] largely caused by forces external to their own control, such as fate, luck or chance [Getter, 1966, p. 397] ."

These illustrative studies indicate that if responsiveness to reinforcement is to be useful as an assessment technique, it will be important to understand more clearly the subject's reinforcing history. Dependency anxiety, psychoanalytic character type, and now locus of control, may be O effects introduced from quite different theoretical models, yet the results just reported with social reinforcement indicate that we must find the common denominator in terms of prior reinforcement experiences.

Personality Traits. Prior reinforcement experience may be directly assessed by simply asking whether particular classes of reinforcing consequences do in fact maintain some given behavior. The previous reinforcing experience of a person can be sampled by the nature of the material selected as the reinforcing stimuli in an operant task.

Brown (1964, 1965) made a rather direct clinical application of operant methods by determining the relative effectiveness of three classes of stimuli as reinforcers with a patient who was presumed to have homoerotic sexual interests. Heterosexual, homosexual, and neutral pictures (of scenes) were presented in an exposure device similar to an ergograph. The patient was required to pull a weighted cord as many times as he could in order to open a shutter while looking at each picture thereby exposed to view. The number of times the shutter was opened for each picture of each stimulus class was used to measure the direction of his sexual interest. Brown found that picture type had a highly significant effect on response rate, with homoerotic pictures being most reinforcing. Brown's procedure could have been improved (see Brown, 1965) by use of a reinforcement schedule, such as variable interval or variable ratio schedule, to provide a more sensitive measure of reinforcing effect unconfounded by length of observations.

Patterson has developed an assessment procedure that he describes as "an operant MMPI" (Patterson, 1967a); starting with the assumption that individual differences in responsiveness to reinforcing stimuli reflect differences in reinforcement histories, Patterson used cartoons depicting aggressive behaviors as response contingent stimuli. Nursery school children pressed a key on a fixed-interval schedule in order to make the cartoons appear in view. The aim of the study was to show a (negative) relationship between "frequency of victimization" and rate of key pressing when the instrumental response was reinforced by aggressively toned pictures. The criterion variable—frequency of victimization—was obtained during a five-week observation period in the classroom. The total number of times each child was attacked during the five week period was used as an estimate of victimization.

As predicted, significant partial r's were obtained between rate of responding on "reinforced" trials and victimization scores (.52 and .70 for two schools; partial r's were used to control statistically for differences in operant key-pressing rates). Children with higher victimization scores showed greater *disruption* of key pressing when aggressive pictures were the reinforcing stimuli. The aggressive pictures were positively reinforcing for the children who were the *aggressors*; aggressive children showed an upward change in key pressing when the aggressive pictures were made response-contingent (Patterson, personal communication to the writer).

In a second study in this series (Patterson, 1967b), the Hypomania (*Ma*) scale of the MMPI was used as the basis for an operant MMPI. As in the previously cited study with aggressive stimulus pictures, items from the *Ma* scale were predicted to be reinforcing stimuli for subjects who described themselves as high *Ma* people. In Patterson's conception of the reinforcing effect, the *Ma* items serve as discriminative stimuli associated with (rewarding) hypomanic-type activities—i.e., activities suggested by the items themselves ("I like to stir up some excitement"). Presentation of the items to the subjects, contingent upon rate of key tapping, would be secondarily reinforcing and would thereby increase the rate of the instrumental response (key tapping). Since Munsinger's (1964) work showed that meaningful words are intrinsically reinforcing stimuli, it was necessary first to estimate the reinforcing effect of words used in *Ma* items. Pilot subjects were reinforced for the key-tapping response by viewing slides of words in random word orders—i.e., the *Ma* items in scrambled word order. The reinforcing effect of the *Ma* item would be demonstrated if the motor response rate for the correct word order exceeded the pilot subjects' average response rate. (Patterson noted that the relationship between *Ma* score and rate of key tapping was not significant for the pilot subjects; high scores on the *Ma* scale *did not* predict faster operant tapping rates.)

With two samples of university and high school female students the correlation coefficients between *Ma* score and increased rate of responding to *Ma* items (presented in the correct word order) were .67 ($p < .05$) and .40 ($p < .10$), for university and high school subjects respectively.

Taken together, the above two provocative studies support the hypothesis that individual differences in responsiveness to classes of reinforcing stimuli reflect differences in reinforcing histories, which may be related to the kinds of individual differences that are of interest to personality theorists. Responsiveness to reinforcing stimuli may provide the transition between self-report statements and overt behaviors.

Whether selecting need-related pictures, aggressive content, or hypomanic items from the MMPI, the nature of the socially reinforcing stimuli must be considered if associative links are to be drawn to the events of everyday life. Using parents and peers as reinforcing agents, Patterson (1965a, 1965b; Patterson, Littman, & Hinsey, 1964) has shown that responsiveness to social reinforcement is related to personality "trait" behaviors. He states that "we are forced to assume that to some extent the culture—in this case parents, teachers, and peer group—are programmed to respond consistently with approval to certain child behaviors and consistently to punish other behaviors [Patterson, 1965a, p. 175]." The specific traits were defined in these studies by a factor rating scale developed from Cattell's items (sample factors included Hostile-Withdrawn, Relaxed Disposition, and Aggression). It was reasoned that a child's responsiveness to social reinforcing agents (parents and peers) would facilitate his acquiring the kinds of personality trait behaviors valued by those agents. Thus, one strategy in Patterson's studies was to determine the relationship between responsiveness to social reinforcement on the one hand and to teacher ratings of personality traits on the other. The pattern of correlations between responsiveness to an agent and trait behaviors would thereby reflect the kinds of behaviors valued by the agents (parents vs. peers).

Responsiveness to social reinforcement was determined by a score reflecting the change in preference for the least preferred of two holes chosen by the child in a marble dropping game (Patterson, 1965a). The reinforcing agents were programmed by the examiner to emit "good," "great," "yes," etc., as social reinforcements contingent upon the child's performance.

Only some of the general findings are mentioned here by way of illustrating the utility of this approach. Correlations between personality traits and responsiveness to social reinforcers were determined for boys and girls and separately for parents and peers. In general, a far greater number of these r's were significant for female children with *parents* as reinforcers. For males responsiveness to *peer* reinforcement in the laboratory was more often related to teacher ratings on the trait scales. Those girls responsive to parental reinforcement were described by their teachers as "almost [fitting] the adult stereotype of the well-adjusted girl [Patterson, 1965a, p. 169]." In terms of the factor scales girls responsive to parental reinforcement were low on Hostile-Withdrawn (Warm, Happy, Loving, etc.), high on the Relaxed Disposition factor (Relaxed, Stable, Not Fearful, etc.), and low on the Aggression factor (Not Demanding, Self Critical, Not Prone to Tantrums, etc.). Those boys who were responsive to peer reinforcement were described by their teachers as being high on Aggression and Dominance factors.

These data, and others relating to parental practices in the home, support the view that responsiveness to social reinforcement provides an operant assessment of the kinds of interpersonal situations a person has been exposed to and reinforced by. The agents of social reinforcement (parents and peers) shape the classes of behavior valued by them, which is what we mean by the term "socialization process." Failures in this process are manifested in reduced or minimal responsiveness to social reinforcement, so that reduced responsiveness may well predict behavioral disturbance.

Sarbin et al. (1965) found that Gough's Socialization (*So*) measure was related to conditionability among adolescent delinquents and nondelinquent controls. Although Sarbin et al. were initially interested in showing that these two subject groups differed in response to social reinforcement (in a verbal operant conditioning task), an inadvertent sampling bias made this impossible to demonstrate. Their findings did indicate, however, that regardless of subject group (delinquent or control) the high socialization subjects showed a significant conditioning effect, whereas the low socialization subjects actually decreased in their use of the selected response class. As with Patterson's work mentioned above, the bridge between reinforcement history and personality "traits" is thus established.

Classification. Can operant technology be employed to differentiate groups of persons into the more familiar diagnostic categories now employed? In light of the stated dissatisfaction with nosological systems (see Kanfer and Saslow, 1965), the success of operant methods in doing so would be only a tactical gain. The studies mentioned here serve to illustrate what has been attempted in this area. (In the next section attempts to illuminate psychological *processes* involved in deviant behavior will be noted.)

One of the characteristics inferred from accounts of the psychopathic personality is lack of responsiveness to social reinforcement (Johns & Quay, 1962). Studies have been reported that use an operant learning technique to establish the differential responsiveness of subjects labeled psychopaths (or sociopaths) and "normals" to social reinforcement. Johns and Quay (1962) and Quay and Hunt (1965) used a factorially derived questionnaire to define samples of psychopaths and neurotics from a group of confined military prisoners. Using a Taffel procedure, the selection of *I* and *we* pronouns was reinforced by *E*'s saying "good" for the experimental groups. Control subjects for both the neurotic and psychopathic groups were given nonreinforced trials. Like the control groups, psychopaths failed to condition, whereas the neurotic group did show evidence of conditioning. In a subsequent study Quay and Hunt (1965) replicated these results by showing that, compared to the psychopathic group, the neurotic subjects showed a significant conditioning effect. In the replication study a small negative, yet significant relationship was found between the Maudsley measure of Extraversion and *I-we* conditionability for all subjects ($r = -.25$); the relationship to Maudsley Neuroticism was not significant. Using basically the same procedures as Quay and Hunt for subject selection and conditioning task, Bryan and Kapche (1967) reported success in conditioning psychopaths; more correctly, the results indicated a significant trials effect for all subjects as one group. Since the trial block means were comparable for psychopaths and nonpsychopaths, Bryan and Kapche concluded that the former group conditioned, although no test of means was performed.

It would be difficult to state unequivocally that psychiatric patients diagnosed as schizophrenic either do or do not show responsiveness to social reinforcement (see Weiss, Krasner & Ullmann, 1963). Comparative studies have been reported by Beech and Adler (1963), Ebner (1965), Slechta, Gwynn and Peoples (1963), all involving verbal operant conditioning paradigms. (Other studies involving a test for the generalization of conditioning in schizophrenic groups will be noted below.) As in the case of differentiating psychopathic groups from controls, the findings with schizophrenic patients are not likely to contribute to the classification issue. Studies that investigate the behavioral processes involved in deviant behavior, however, may be enlightening.

Responsiveness to Reinforcement: Predictor Variable

In this section evidence for the *predictive* value of responsiveness to reinforcement will be presented. In some instances the inclusion of a given study under this heading rather than under the previous one, which dealt with the dependent variable type of study, may seem somewhat arbitrary, since in correlational studies it is possible to "predict" from an assessment test variable to the conditioning variable. The aim is to group studies to highlight most clearly the kinds of approaches now available.

Procedures having diagnostic implications. A number of studies have been reported in which operant methodology has been employed to assess the functioning of hospitalized psychiatric patients. Studies by Ogden Lindsley (1960; Mednick & Lindsley, 1958; Nathan, Schneller, & Lindsley, 1964), have dealt with rate of responding (usually a simple motor response) as a means of indicating day-to-day changes in the patient's psychotic state. Rate of reinforced bar pressing, for example, was seen to decrease as verbal hallucinatory behavior increased (Lindsley, 1960), and testability on conventional psychometric measures was found to be related to operant responding rates in "chronic psychotic" patients (Mednick & Lindsley, 1958). However, King, Merrill, Loevinger, and Denny (1957) found a curvilinear relationship between severity of psychosis and operant response rate; the highest operant rate was observed for moderate values of the severity scale. (Recent papers on the use of "free operants" to explicate psychological functions can be found in Honig [1966] ; drug reactions in humans are discussed by Bullock [1960] .)

Operant techniques are often useful to assess whether a subject (usually a psychiatric patient) has the ability to make necessary discriminations so that reinforcing contingencies could in fact control his behavior. At issue in many tasks is whether an individual can make rudimentary adaptive responses to novel stimuli. Sidman (1962) cites work with acute psychotics that required learning when to make a "switching" response to the plungers in a Lindsley apparatus (Stoddard, Sidman, & Brady 1962). By use of multiple schedules of reinforcement within the same setting, it was possible to create a task that had a differential cost-per-reponse function, depending upon when the switching response (which changed the cost-per-response factor) was made. This meant that subjects could, by their selection of plunger, increase their number of token reinforcements. Nonpatients generally, and some patients rarely, were able to learn the sequentially integrated schedule; i.e., they were able to adjust their performance to maximize reinforcements. Most patients, on the other hand, were unable to adjust their switching behavior, a fact taken by the authors as evidence that a basic variable (reinforcement schedule) was not controlling the behavior of the patient group.

Another approach to the diagnosis of deviant behavior, also involving failure to respond in accord with the reinforcing feedback in operant task, has recently been developed by George Stone (1966) and his associates at the Langley Porter Neuropsychiatric Institute. Using the 10-unit temporal maze of left-right plunger responses (in a Lindsley apparatus), to which we have already referred, Stone provided both positive reinforcement (the lighting of a red-jewelled light above the plunger) for a "correct" choice and aversive feedback (a "raucous sound of a resetting stepping relay") for "incorrect" choices. Each response to a plunger thus resulted in either an immediate light flash associated with *correct*, or a distinctive sound of the stepping switch associated with *incorrect*. (It will be recalled that in a temporal maze the serial organization of choice responses corresponds to turns in a spatial maze.) Initial results for selected cases using error rate indicate that the greatest potential of this procedure is with possible organic cases, including those behaviors in which drug effects may be involved (Stone, 1966).

Generalization and prediction studies. The most interesting assessment devices are those that predict behavior not yet observed. If operant techniques could be shown to yield response measures that make such prediction possible, they would be highly valued. As one looks at the generalization and transfer studies (cited earlier), there appears to be some confusion between the distinction drawn earlier between signs and samples. A study by Wimsatt and Vestre (1963) is often cited in the literature as evidence that verbal conditioning fails to influence "basic personality" variables, or at least fails to obtain transfer effects. This study, because of its similarity to others, will serve to illustrate aspects of methodology relevant to this form of assessment.

Subjects in these generalization studies typically are presented with items from a personality inventory scale, and their endorsement of the item is followed by examiner approval. Wimsatt and Vestre employed psychiatric patients and reinforced response to items from the Social Introversion (Si) scale of the MMPI. For one group "introverted" responses were reinforced, while for the other group "extraverted" choices were reinforced; a control group received no reinforcement for its choices. Generalization to scales from the Guilford-Zimmerman Temperament Survey, known to be significantly associated with Si in a normal sample, was then tested. Si scores were available for the majority of subjects and provided a preconditioning or "operant" measure of Si for group comparisons.

The conditioning effect, measured as mean differences between groups, was quite small. The experimental groups did not differ significantly from the control group, although the experimental groups differed from one another; "introversive" or "extraversive" choices, when reinforced, increased. The authors report that the correlation between the *Si* scores obtained during the experimental sessions and the generalization task, Guilford-Zimmerman Sociability scale, was -.83, so that a high Introversion score during conditioning was associated with a low Sociability score after conditioning. The negative *r* was for the total sample though "extraversive" choices were reinforced for half the subjects. Subjects who continued to choose introversive alternatives during conditioning trials scored low in Sociability after the conditioning task. In the absence of operant-level or preconditioning *Si* scores, we do not know whether *conditionable* subjects were high or low on the generalization measure, i.e., the Sociability scale. Wimsatt and Vestre failed to report the relationship between conditionability or responsiveness to reinforcement and the post-Sociability score. In light of the generally small overall conditioning effect this result is not surprising: introversive patients do not score high on a sociability measure.

If we compare this type of procedure with that described above for Patterson's use of an operant MMPI, some interesting differences appear. It will be recalled that in Patterson's approach item content itself was used to reinforce a motor response; item content was presumed to be reinforcing for particular subjects, those high in the trait reflected by the item content. In the Wimsatt et al. study—and any that employ this paradigm of reinforcing *item choice*—responsiveness was not to item content but to the examiner's social approval. It would be more parsimonious to speak of the transfer effect to a subsequent task of examiner approval (a sample) rather than item content (a sign). Had Wimsatt and Vestre obtained more straightforward evidence of conditioning, we would still be left with an instance of the content of conditioning, *qua* sign, being predictive of other behaviors. As noted above, validation of sign predictions has been traditionally most difficult.

In an earlier study Vestre (1962) demonstrated the utility of the sample approach for operant assessment. Responsiveness to examiner approval (a conditioning measure) was used to predict to subjects' scores on the EPPS (Edwards, 1954) scales. Vestre employed a modified version of the Taffel procedure with hospitalized schizophrenic patients. During the operant trials a record was kept of the rank order of pronoun usage, and during reinforcement trials ("good") pronouns in rank positions three and four (out of six) were now reinforced. (This deviates from the usual notion of reinforcing members of a homogeneous verbal response class.) Two groups were formed, depending upon whether subjects were conditionable or nonconditionable. Vestre predicted and found lower scores for the conditionable group, relative to the nonconditionable subjects, on *n ach*, *n aut*, and *n dom* and higher scores on *n def*, *n aff*, and *n aba*. Higher scores on *n nur* and lower on *n agg* were predicted for the conditionables but were not found.

Vestre points out that "compliancy" and "dependency" describe the conditionable patient in this study. Thus, responsiveness to examiner approval and self-reported compliancy (in hospitalized psychiatric patients) seem to be aspects of the same behavioral domain. (Weiss, Ullmann, and Krasner [1960] showed a significant relationship between conditionability and a questionnaire measure of hypnotizability. See also Getter [1966] above, for results with the *I-E* scale.)

The same point is also illustrated in a study reported by Johannsen and Campbell (1964) with female "chronic schizophrenic" patients. The purpose of the study was to see whether patients who remained in social contact were also more responsive to examiner approval in a Taffel-like conditioning task. Ward ratings of overt social behaviors were made on all patients; these included observations of "friendliness," "isolation," etc. After operant trials *I* and *we* pronouns were either reinforced ("good") or punished ("not so good") in a responsiveness-by-type-of-reinforcement factorial design. The main finding was that conditioning occurred for the high responsive group performing under positive reinforcement. A difference was found for *I* versus *we* pronouns, in that whenever conditioning occurred it was for the *I* component of the *I-we* pair. The point to be noted here is the relative similarity between the behaviors: social responsiveness among patients and their responsiveness to examiner approval, a similarity in samples of behavior.

Finally, a report by Salzinger and Portnoy (1964) has direct bearing on the matter of predicting future behavior from responsiveness-to-examiner reinforcement. Salzinger and his associates (Salzinger & Portnoy, 1964; Salzinger, Portnoy, & Feldman, 1966) have investigated various applications of operant conditioning procedures to the verbal behavior of hospitalized schizophrenics. Their approach has been to reinforce self-referred affect statements in the context of an interview. Both operant rate of emitting self-referred affect statements and change in rate as a function of examiner reinforcement were used as variables for predicting hospitalized status six months later. Neither operant rate nor conditionability differentiated between the two groups who were still hospitalized (In) or out of the hospital (Out) at the six-month follow-up. When the various phases of the interview (operant, conditioning, extinction) were compared *within* the In and Out groups separately, a significant conditioning effect was found only in the Out group. Further analyses indicated that significantly more patients who increased self-referred affect statements under reinforcement *and* whose statements then decreased under extinction were found in the Out group. If one's responsiveness to social reinforcement persists through the personal turmoil of hospitalization, one is likely to engage in behaviors that lead to discharge.

Operant Assessment of Dyadic Behaviors

In this section a form of operant technology involving *conjugate* reinforcement is reviewed as a means of assessing responsiveness in dyadic relationships. With conjugate reinforcement the subject's rate of responding determines the intensity, clarity, or fidelity of a continuously available source of stimulation. A reduction in response rate produces an immediate denegation of the stimulus input; an increase in response rate produces an immediate reinstatement of the stimulus input. Lindsley (1962) first reported on the use of closed-circuit TV for independently measuring looking, listening, and talking behaviors in psychotherapeutic sessions. In this early application, as well as in subsequent reports (Nathan et al., 1964; Nathan, 1965, 1966), two members of a dyad (e.g. patient/therapist, nurse/supervisor) interact with one another by means of a closed circuit audio-video system. However, the reception of both the video and audio signal of one member are made contingent upon the other member's maintaining a fixed rate of responding. Failure to maintain the prescribed response rate on one or both of the manipulanda results in a variable loss of clarity (image or sound) ranging to a complete absence of signal.

By separately measuring looking, listening, and talking (to the partner), it is possible to assess continuously one person's reinforcing effect on another. By gradually increasing the response rate necessary to maintain the audio and video input from the other person, the response cost can be determined. In the Nathan et al. study (1964) 16 new admissions to a state hospital were interviewed by means of the closed-circuit TV system, and an initial response rate of 30 responses per minute was set; some of the better-adjusted patients reached a rate in excess of 120 responses per minute. The authors point out that in this and other studies from Lindsley's laboratory with psychiatric patients there appears to be a negative relationship between severity of behavioral disorder and rate of operant response; the more severely disturbed a patient, the lower his rate of responding (see Matarazzo's [1965a] inverse function between speech duration and severity of "illness"; also Patterson's [1965a] discussion of responsiveness to reinforcement).

In addition to being sensitive to severity of disorder, the Lindsley-Nathan clinical application of conjugate reinforcement is sensitive to thematic content. When discussing clearly affective content about the antecedent events of their hospitalization, the patients decreased their response rates and therefore their looking or listening capabilities.

Nathan has reported additional studies involving nursing-student/ supervisor sessions (Nathan, 1965, 1966; Nathan et al., 1965). Weekly sessions ranging over a 6- to 13-week period were recorded by the TRACCOM (Televised Reciprocal Analysis of Conjugate Communication). The findings of one study will be considered here.

Nathan (1965) measured both the *transmitting* and *receiving* aspects of the dyadic interaction between three student nurses and their supervisor. In the *receiving* aspect subjects maintained a rate of responding on manipulanda that controlled seeing and hearing the partner. *Transmission* refers to sending one's voice ("projecting") and/or picture ("displaying") to the partner. To do this, the sender was required to maintain a specified response rate on one or both of the manipulanda. Using the supervisor's written report about her relationship with the students as a criterion, it was possible for Nathan to relate changes—in (a) the rate of transmitting, (b) the rate of receiving, and (c) the composite rate score—to the "process change" [p. 942] of the interviews. The composite score of operant communication indicated that persons generally communicate at higher rates with others with whom they share "meaningful relationships." Whereas the (trained) supervisor maintained a fairly even rate of responding—both sending and receiving—across sessions, students varied in either direction. If the supervisor judged substantial "growth" to have occurred in the student, then the student's composite rate was found to have increased over 13 sessions; the opposite was true—i.e., the rate decreased—when the experience was judged to be less beneficial to the student.

If this approach is to be more generally useful for defining important aspects of interpersonal interaction, greater statistical treatment of the data will be required. A mutually reinforcing cycle is involved in the transmission-reception functions of these operant communicative behaviors; yet fine-grain sequential analyses to test this hypothesis are lacking. Nathan's applications are much too important and ingenious to remain at the qualitative stage of case presentations.

TOWARD THE ASSESSMENT OF INTERPERSONAL ACCORD

In this section the implications for assessment of a series of studies by the writer concerned with the communication of accord will be presented. By "communication of accord" is meant those instances of voluntary behavior that communicate understanding, interest, agreement, or rapport in inter-personal contexts. From the review of studies of social reinforcement in the previous section (e.g., Patterson and Nathan) it is clear that the motivational effectiveness of social reinforcement in the laboratory derives from its significance in everyday life (Weiss, 1965b). The relationship between labora-tory responsiveness to social reinforcement and various assessment measures of sociability further attests to the ecological validity of the former. A methodology for obtaining samples of reinforcing behaviors in the laboratory that are predictive of individual differences in extralaboratory contexts will be presented here.

Rationale of the Approach

The communication of accord refers to *emitted reinforcing behaviors*, although reinforcing responses treated as emitted (operant) behavior is an unusual but necessary juxtaposition in the study of those everyday life behaviors that communicate interest, understanding, etc. Surprisingly little empirical data have been offered showing how individuals maintain the behavior of one another. (Jones [1964] considers a related kind of behavior called "ingratiation".)

In treating interpersonal accord as emitted reinforcing behavior, we have made the following assumptions: (a) Reinforcing behavior is a nontrivial form of emitted behavior. Individual differences in reinforcing others are the result of "shaping experiences"; i.e., one is reinforced for emitting behaviors that in turn reinforce others. (b) There are reliable individual differences in the frequency and "skillfulness" with which persons emit reinforcing behaviors. (c) Intraindividual consistencies in reinforcing behaviors allow persons to utilize reinforcing output as a basis for making discriminative judgments about the behavior of others. Evaluative judgments—whether A understands B, or is interested in B, etc.—are based upon individual differ-ences in emitted reinforcing behaviors.

Emitted reinforcing behavior is intimately related to socialization since in addition to the frequency of such behavior we are also concerned with its "appropriateness." The "grammar of reinforcement" (Weiss, 1964) encom-passes the occasions for emitting reinforcing responses that are largely under social stimulus control, and may be identified by sampling the reinforcing behavior of the "verbal community" when given appropriate instructional sets. For example, within the context of a speaker/listener relationship, the listening community can be instructed to "maintain rapport" with a speaking person. Instructions, together with the speaker stimuli, will combine to control the "rapport" responses of the listeners—i.e., control the *occasions* when reinforcing responses are emitted, not just their frequency; the latter is assumed to be an individual difference variable.

The assumptive structure underlying emitted reinforcing behavior has been tested in a number of studies conducted by the author (Weiss, 1964, 1965a, 1966a). In the remainder of this section, we will present the technique for assessing interpersonal accord as an illustration of an operantly-conceived procedure for assessing individuals in interpersonal accord.

Sampling Emitted Reinforcing Behavior

The basic technique developed for sampling both frequency and "skill" of emitted reinforcing behavior may be summarized as follows: Subjects are requested to role-play a situation in which a speaker is talking to each listener, and the listener is to maintain rapport with the speaker. The listener is asked to emit those responses he normally would make whenever he strives to make it easy for another person to speak to him. (Reinforcement is not mentioned in the instructions to listeners.) All responses, vocal and gestural , that are consistent with the instructional set to "maintain rapport" are translated into a simple motor response—namely, a button press. A silent button held by each listener, concealed from his neighbor's view, is pressed momentarily whenever the listener emits a response designed to help maintain rapport. Listeners emit these reinforcing responses *during* the speaker's presentation, not retrospectively.

The "speakers" are, in each instance, prerecorded monologues of the candid thoughts, feelings, interests, and future plans of students and psychiatric patients (see Weiss, 1966a).

The basic response measures consist of the number of button presses emitted by each subject and the occurrence of each response relative to what the speaker was saying. The recording apparatus has been described elsewhere (e.g., Weiss, 1966a), and will be mentioned only briefly here.

A multi-pen event recorder graphically records for each listener his button presses on a moving chart. A train of time-marking signals is synchronized with the speaker tape and automatically recorded on the chart. Both the frequency and the point of occurrence of each subject's responses are recorded as the speaker talks, so that by relating the time marks to an accurate typescript of the speech monologue, it is possible to determine which speech events the listener had responded to. If the number of listeners who responded during a fixed interval (e.g., 2 seconds) exceeds chance expectations, an "appropriate" or popular place to reinforce the speaker is thus defined. The probability of finding at least j listeners responding within an interval i can be readily approximated (Weiss & Reichard, 1967) from knowledge of the mean number of responses emitted, length of the speaker tape, and number of listeners in the sample.

A reinforcing "skill" score is defined for each listener by statistically adjusting "hits" at popular points for individual differences in number of reinforcing responses. A listener's *expected* number of hits is derived from the regression of hits on responses; the difference between *observed* and *expected* hits defines skill in reinforcing others. A skillful listener exceeds the number of hits expected for his level of responding, whereas a nonskillful listener's observed scores fall below expectation.

Individual Differences in Reinforcing Frequency and Skillfulness

Results from a number of studies conducted by the writer will be mentioned only briefly here to illustrate further the application of this methodology to assessment of interpersonal accord.

Intraindividual consistency in emitted reinforcing behavior was investigated (Weiss, 1964, 1965a, 1966a; Weiss & Bodin, 1967) and found to be high for a wide variety of listening conditions, audiences, and speaker voices. Product-moment r's between number of responses emitted to each of two speakers ranged from .82 to .95. Among the variations employed in these studies were the following: individual versus group listening context; clear versus filtered (garbled) speech; student, psychiatric patient, and experienced psychotherapist listeners. Amount of reinforcing behavior emitted is a basis for characterizing individual differences.

Correlates of reinforcing output were established for self-report and sociometric ratings of personality (e.g., Weiss, 1967) and an organismic variable of affiliation (e.g., Weiss, 1966a). In these studies responsiveness, in contrast with general motor activity, was shown to be related to peer ratings of overt social behaviors ("fun at a party") and CPI factor scores reflecting Dominance and Ascendance. A birth-order effect was also found indicating greater responsiveness on the part of first-born and only children in contrast to those born later. So-called "response style" measures were unrelated to reinforcing responsiveness (e.g., Social Desirability), but measures of situational anxiety were negatively related to reinforcing output; the more anxious listeners responded less to speakers.

The measure of reinforcing skill derived in these studies intentionally reflects a distinction between responsiveness (frequency of output) and appropriateness (communality of output). At this stage of development it seemed wiser to maintain the distinction so as to clarify the nature of statistical operations; i.e., correlations involving skill scores are not confounded by base rate differences in frequency of responding. To be sure, an adequate conceptualization of the grammar of reinforcement must include responsiveness, since one can only signal one's understanding or interest by behaving at some operant rate greater than zero.

The *reliability* of reinforcing skill means the extent to which a person's "skill" in reinforcing one speaker is consonant with his skill in reinforcing another speaker. Data from nine listening groups (total N = 322) indicated significant r's for two samples of the same speaker (median r = .69, $p < .01$), two different speakers (median r = .50, $p < .01$), and three different speakers, including a psychiatric patient as speaker (median r = .54, $p < .01$; see Weiss [1967]). It would appear from these findings that this behavioral measure of reinforcing skill qualifies reasonably well as a "trait" variable.

In two studies (Weiss, 1967; Weiss & Bodin, 1967) reinforcing skill was found to be related to sociometric ratings. Whereas reinforcing output was related to ratings of *overt* social behavior (e.g., "fun at a party"), the skill measures were related only to ratings of inferred psychological mindedness. For example, listeners rated by their peers as persons "understanding the motives and conflicts of others" also scored high in reinforcing skill (Weiss, 1967), but there was not a significant relationship between these ratings and reinforcing output. In a study of experienced psychotherapists who were in training as family therapists, significant relationships between ratings of therapeutic competence and reinforcing skill were obtained (Weiss & Bodin, 1967). Also of interest from that study was the finding that therapists who were high in reinforcing skill—as here defined—were also more likely to use social-psychological rather than intrapsychic concepts in describing case material, and more likely to be explicit in stating their goals and therapeutic actions in planning a therapeutic regime.

Reinforcing skill has also been found to be related to various self-report measures including the CPI and the Edwards Personal Preference Schedule (EPPS). The factor scores of Person and Value Orientation (Nichols & Schnell, 1963a) were both related to reinforcing skill in two different listening populations (Weiss, 1967). The skillful reinforcer describes himself as psychologically mature, dominant, and concerned with societal values. From the EPPS (Edwards, 1954) we learn that skillful listeners are low in abasement ($r = -.53$, $p \leqslant .05$) yet high in heterosexuality ($r = .50$, $p \leqslant .05$).

A somewhat different approach to defining reinforcing skill may be helpful in illustrating this technique for assessing individual differences in the communication of accord. In other studies we have defined *lack of skill* as the relative frequency of response to speech events not responded to by other listeners; a measure of uniqueness of response. Here too the results are very much as one would expect if the button pressing task does in fact measure an important aspect of social behavior. A significant negative relationship between unique scores and an affection commodity score was found for a large group of college listeners ($r = -.40$, $N = 89$). "Affection commodity" was defined by FIRO-B scores (Schutz, 1958) summed for *expressed* and *wanted* affection scales. Listeners who on the FIRO-B indicate disdain for expressing affection to others and not wanting to be responded to affectionately by others tended to respond more to unique aspects of speech. A similar result was obtained in the Weiss and Bodin study on psychotherapists mentioned above: higher average unique scores were associated with lower overall peer popularity ratings.

The above survey of results illustrates how the construct of reinforcing skill has been related to various aspects of interpersonal behaviors, ranging from overt behavior (presumably in the same behavioral domain) to behaviors more dissimilar from reinforcing skill itself. If we consider how meager these behavior samples are in terms of usual notions about the subtle ways in which accord or interest is communicated, the results are indeed encouraging. From button pressing to sociometric judgments and therapist's ratings of therapeutic skill is a long way around. Or is it that we are simply asking our subjects to emit the kinds of behavior they normally emit in their everyday lives?

In this chapter we have considered various applications of operant technology to the assessment of individual differences. It was noted that the constructs employed in personology research derive in the main from empirical sources rather than from unified theories of behavior. Operant procedures are based on a behavioral functionalism quite consistent with the aims of an individual difference approach to psychology. The studies reported on here reflect the situational-behavioral-sample emphasis of the operant approach, an emphasis which has particular significance for assessment of individual differences.

CHAPTER X

Assessing change in
hospitalized psychiatric patients

C. James Klett

The need for objective assessment of change in psychiatric patients seems so obvious from a research point of view that it is easy to overlook the fact that most clinical decisions are based upon observations of current status, and that nearly all measures of change are simply the difference between two status estimates. It is possible, even today, to find examples of published research in which clinicians have been asked to make direct judgments of change, and ten years ago it was almost the rule to report results of a therapeutic trial in terms of the percentage of patients who in the clinicians' judgment had achieved various stages of improvement. In compiling a long list of these criteria for the Transactions of the Second Research Conference on Chemotherapy in Psychiatry (Lindley, 1958), it was concluded that little could be gained from them that would be of help in setting up standardized terms. Since then, of course, there has been a pronounced tendency to rely more on quantified techniques than on such global clinical impressions. The use of objective measures has made it possible to compare results from one study to the next, to combine results from different hospitals, and to make other uses of the data that were simply not defensible previously.

In the abstract, there is an endless number of ways to assess change in hospitalized psychiatric patients. Half of the devices listed in Buros' *Mental Measurements Yearbook* (1965) could conceivably be used for this purpose, and there seems to be no limit to the ingenuity of investigators in inventing new ones. In practice, however, the number is reduced by a variety of considerations. This chapter deals with objective techniques suitable for fairly large-scale research, which restricts the applicability of many instruments appropriately used in the intensive study of individual patients. Other criteria such as community adjustment after discharge or performance in special situations (e.g., occupational therapy) are not included. Particularly with schizophrenic subjects, most psychological tests and especially the self-inventory variety are of limited value in large-scale research because of the difficulty of separating the motivational aspects from any deficit that may exist. For this reason such otherwise valuable techniques are not discussed in this chapter.

The choice of measuring instrument, like all other aspects of an investigation, should be guided by the nature of the research question. Unless interest is directed chiefly toward charting the natural course of a psychiatric disorder, assessment of change implies some kind of therapeutic intervention. For purposes of this discussion, chemotherapy will be used as the model of a treatment that can be evaluated on a large scale; most of what follows would be equally applicable to evaluation of other treatment modalities or general clinical usage. In psychiatric drug studies the research question has taken many forms, but in one way or another it has usually been concerned with an alteration of the symptomatic status of functionally psychotic patients. Psychotherapy research might also emphasize character changes or shifts in the amount or quality of interpersonal relationships. Except for certain special applications, the choice of measuring devices in psychiatric drug research has been confined to judgments of the patient's condition using rating scales and behavior checklists.

In 1954 Lorr was able to describe all of the rating scales and checklists for evaluating psychopathology introduced during the ten years prior to his review by discussing slightly over a dozen instruments. In a later review (1960) he had extended his list but no longer attempted to provide exhaustive coverage. In a more recent review (Lyerly & Abbott, 1966) discussion is limited to 19 scales. To do a comprehensive review of these devices today would be a major undertaking and probably would not serve a useful purpose in any case. Many have had limited application, and others are only of historical interest. Instead, it is proposed here to discuss some of the characteristics of rating scales, examine several in detail, briefly describe some other scales in common use, and conclude with a discussion of some of the issues involved in the methodology and application of rating scales to hospitalized psychiatric patients.

CHARACTERISTICS OF PSYCHIATRIC RATING SCALES

Rating scales are deceptively simple, and perhaps this accounts for their proliferation in recent years. Actually, there are a number of issues involved in the construction of rating scales that ought to be examined more critically. To begin with, most rating scales used for evaluating psychopathology are not rating scales at all in the traditional sense. Normally, a set of stimuli (statements, objects) are arranged by a number of judges along some relevant continuum (social desirability, attractiveness), and a scale value for each stimulus is derived by one of a variety of techniques. The stimuli can then be positioned on the underlying psychological continuum that has been generated. In the case of attitude measurement, the average of the scale values of the statements endorsed by an individual can be used to position him on the attitude continuum. With only a few exceptions (e.g., Aumach, 1962) psychiatric rating scales do not follow this model. Rather, they are simply a means of obtaining a quantitative description of the patient through the observation and judgments of a second person or rater. In this definition no formal distinction is made between behavior inventories, symptom checklists, and trait ratings. As long as some descriptive statement about a patient is quantified by an observer, the instrument can be considered a rating scale. The four elements of a psychiatric rating scale are (a) the series of descriptive statements or *items* that are to be put in (b) a number of quantitative *categories*, together with (c) the *instructions* for doing so; items falling in various categories are then given (d) numeric values according to some *scoring system*. The first two of these elements can be thought of as "what is being rated" and "how it is rated." Since they are so closely interrelated, they will be discussed together.

Descriptive statements in a rating scale can and do range from the most atomistic aspects of behavior ("shaves himself") to the most global kinds of judgments ("compared to all patients you have known, how severely ill is this patient?"). However, in one way or another, the majority of rating scales in current use are tied to observable behavior. In some scales this is achieved entirely at the item level, in other scales it is accomplished by providing behavioral rating cues and definitions, and in still others by using graded categories in the form of behavioral statements. The rating categories are usually degrees of intensity-severity or frequency, although other dimensions, such as the extent to which the behavior manifests itself in different situations (universality), might also be used. The use of graded categories often combines both a frequency and an intensity continuum. The number of categories provided can vary from two (e.g., Present-Absent), which can be thought of as a truncated frequency continuum, to as many as seven or nine. To illustrate these differences in format, the Nurses Observation Scale for Inpatient Evaluation (NOSIE) (Honigfeld & Klett, 1965) contains 80 ward behavior items, which are rated on a five-point frequency continuum ranging from "Never" to "Always." The Inpatient Multidimensional Psychiatric Scale (IMPS) (Lorr, Klett, McNair & Lasky, 1962) contains 45 nine-point intensity items ranging from "Not at All" to "Extremely," 13 five-point frequency items ranging from "Not at All" to "Very Often," and 17 "Yes-No" items. The Brief Psychiatric Rating Scale (BPRS) (Overall & Gorham, 1962) contains 16 concepts for which brief definitions and rating cues based on a seven-point severity continuum are provided. The Wittenborn Psychiatric Rating Scales (PRS) (Wittenborn, 1964a) rate 72 symptom areas (e.g., sleep difficulty) by means of three or four graded statements indicating the degree of difficulty.

Turning now to the remaining two elements, the instructions define the period of observation, the appropriate rater, the patient to which the scale is applicable, and may include cautions in respect to making inferences, dynamic interpretations, and the like. Scoring systems can vary from simple summations of all items rated in the pathological direction to more complicated weightings and subscale scores. For example, the Ward Behavior Rating Scale (Burdock, Hakerem, Hardesty, & Zubin, 1960) yields a total score consisting of the number of items rated in the pathological direction, and the IMPS yields ten syndrome scores derived from weighted summations of the items, and second-order factors that are composites of the syndromes. These aspects of rating scales can be further illustrated by considering several representative scales, to which we turn next.

MAJOR PSYCHIATRIC RATING SCALES

The Wittenborn Psychiatric Rating Scale (PRS)

This scale is among the oldest of the rating scales still in widespread use. In its original form (Wittenborn, 1955) it consisted of 52 unlabeled symptom areas, each of which was rated by choosing the one of three or four graded response categories that best described the patient during the period of observation. The length of observation and qualifications of the rater were not specified. There were nine scoring categories that had been established by factor analyses of data from a Veterans Administration Hospital (Wittenborn, 1951) and a more acute sample from a Connecticut State Hospital (Wittenborn & Holzberg, 1951). These categories were named: Acute Anxiety, Conversion Hysteria, Manic State, Depressed State, Schizophrenic Excitement , Paranoid Condition, Paranoid Schizophrenic, Hebephrenic Schizophrenic, and Phobic Compulsive. Split-half reliability coefficients for these factors ranged from .67 for Depressed State to .92 for Manic State. In addition to being used as a criterion of change in many studies, the PRS was used by Wittenborn in several interesting attempts to delineate the symptom correlates of psychiatric diagnoses (Wittenborn & Bailey, 1952; Wittenborn & Weiss, 1952; Wittenborn, Holzberg, & Simon, 1953).

The current version of the PRS (Wittenborn, 1964a) has been extended to 72 symptom areas to make it more applicable to chronic patients and to reflect additional dimensions of psychosis (Wittenborn, 1962; 1963). The format is essentially the same with the exception that the rater is directed to select the statement representing the most extreme manifestation of the symptom area during the recommended three- to five-day observation period. In the course of factoring 98 new or revised items rated in this manner, Wittenborn identified 12 major factors, some of which were further broken down into minor components. The following scores can now be obtained: Anxiety; Hysterical Conversion; Manic State; Depressive Total with Obstructive, Apathy, Withdrawal, and Affective Flatness components; Schizophrenic Excitement Total with Attention Demanding and Assaultive components; Paranoia; Hebephrenia with Incontinence, Silliness, and Resistance components; Compulsive-Obessive; Intellectual Impairment; Homosexual Dominance; and Ideas of Grandeur. In nearly every factor analysis it is possible to quarrel about the appropriateness of the factor naming. Although such a criticism of the PRS seems trivial, it might have been desirable to avoid the use of diagnostic terms that have acquired so much surplus meaning. This would also have reduced the natural expectation that the factors measure given clinical entities; e.g., the four items defining the Manic State factor, though clearly related to mania as seen clinically, nevertheless provide a very incomplete description of that disorder.

The Inpatient Multidimensional Psychiatric Scale(IMPS)

This scale (Lorr et al., 1962) represents a complete revision of the Multi-dimensional Scale for Rating Psychiatric Patients (MSRPP) (Lorr, 1953), which, in turn, was a revision of the Northport Record (Lorr, Singer, & Zobel, 1951). The MSRPP was a 62-item scale, 40 items of which were completed on the basis of a psychiatric interview, with the remaining 22 items completed on the basis of ward observation by nursing personnel. The format consisted of questions pertaining to selected symptom areas, and rating categories (3, 4, or 5 plus an unratable category) of the frequency, intensity, and graded type. Each item had a normal value. The item "Does he ever talk to himself or to no one in particular? 1. Never, 2. Only occasionally, 3. Rather frequently, 4. Almost continually" is a unipolar frequency item with a normal value of 1. "How well does he usually eat? 1. Must be tube fed, 2. Requires spoon feeding, 3. Eats poorly—leaves food, 4. Eats adequately, 5. Eats unusual amounts" is a bipolar graded category item with a normal value of 4. Scores on the eleven syndromes were obtained by summing the raw scores and subtracting a correction factor for the normal values. A Total Morbidity Score (the sum of the absolute values of the syndrome scores) was usually calculated. Items judged to be unratable presented some scoring problems, but several methods of dealing with them were recommended. The eleven subscores or syndromes had been derived by factor analysis: Retarded Depression versus Manic Excitement; Compliance versus Resistiveness; Paranoid Projection; Activity Level; Melancholy Agitation; Perceptual Distortion; Motor Disturbances; Submissiveness versus Belligerence; Withdrawal; Self-Depreciation versus Grandiose Expansiveness; and Conceptual Disorganization.

The MSRPP was a very popular scale and was successfully used in many large-scale treatment evaluations, such as the Veterans Administration Study of Prefrontal Lobotomy (Ball, Klett, & Gresock, 1959) and the early VA Cooperative Studies in Psychiatry (Casey, Bennett, Lindley, Hollister, Gordon, & Springer, 1960; Casey, Lasky, Klett, & Hollister, 1960).

In revising the MSRPP, a number of fundamental changes were made. The ward behavior section was eliminated, and all ratings were based upon observations of patient behavior and patient verbal reports of beliefs, attitudes, and feelings made during a psychiatric interview. Nearly all of the items were rewritten so they could be rated on a standard unipolar intensity or frequency continuum, and an attempt was made to make them applicable to all patients so that the "Unratable" category could be eliminated. Additional items were written, and cues to aid the rater were provided in many instances. Two sets of adverbs were chosen for rating the intensity or frequency of the individual items. These adverbs, selected from a larger number that had been scaled by the method of successive intervals, were roughly the same distance apart on the underlying continuum. For all of the intensity items, ratings are made in reference to a normal person.

The initial form of the IMPS went through a succession of applications and revisions. In the first of these a sample of 296 patients, stratified into nine patient types, were rated on a 90-item version of the scale. Some unreliable or otherwise unsatisfactory items were eliminated, and the remainder were factor-analyzed by a multiple group procedure. Ten syndromes, posited by Lorr on the basis of earlier work with the MSRPP and other scales, were extracted (Lorr, McNair, Klett, & Lasky, 1962): Excitement, Hostile Bellig-erence, Paranoid Projection, Grandiose Expansiveness, Perceptual Distortions, Anxious Intropunitiveness, Retardation and Apathy, Disorientation, Motor Disturbances, and Conceptual Disorganization. Three second-order factors were tentatively identified. Subsequent application in two large cooperative studies of chemotherapy (Casey, Hollister, Klett, Lasky, & Caffey, 1961; Overall, Hollister, Pokorny, Casey, & Katz, 1962) led to further revision and refinement before a final form of the scale was achieved. The final form was used in rating a second stratified sample of 207 patients, which, together with ratings from still another chemotherapy study (Lasky, Klett, Caffey, Bennett, Rosenblum, & Hollister, 1962), provided the data for the score norms. A multiple group factor analysis of these data yielded the same ten factors as the original sample.

The IMPS has been widely adopted as a criterion of change in psychiatric drug trials. It has been used in the NIMH collaborative drug studies conducted by the Psychopharmacology Service Center (Cole, Klerman, & Goldberg, 1964) and has continued to be the primary rating instrument in the VA Cooperative Studies in Psychiatry. It has been found to be sensitive to changes over time and to differential change among psychopharmacologic agents in both acute and chronic patients (Honigfeld, Rosenblum, Blumenthal, Lambert, & Roberts, 1965). It has been useful in describing the emergence of psychotic symptoms when tranquilizing drugs were discon-tinued or reduced in amount (Caffey, Diamond, Frank, Grasberger, Herman, Klett, & Rothstein, 1964), in predicting response to drugs (Goldberg, Mattsson, Cole, & Klerman, 1967), and in finding "the right drug for the right patient" (Klett & Moseley, 1965). In addition to these applications in psychi-atric drug research, Lorr and his associates have continued their efforts to establish the dimensions of psychosis (Lorr & Klett, 1965; Lorr, Klett, & Cave, 1967) and to identify empirical profile types (Lorr, Klett, & McNair, 1963; Lorr, 1966).

A slightly revised version of the IMPS has recently been released (Lorr & Klett, 1966). Although the manual has been extensively rewritten and the norms expanded by incorporating data from some of the larger drug trials, the only important changes in the scale itself are the rekeying of two items affecting three syndrome scores, a more definitive description of five second-order factors, and the addition of 14 new items defining three experimental syndromes: Depressive Mood; Impaired Functioning; and Obsessive-Compul-siveness.

Although these changes have improved the IMPS, its use still involves certain problems, some of which are shared by other scales. One of these problems is that the score distributions of all syndromes are positively skewed to the extent that they resemble half of a normal distribution. This can present certain statistical problems, particularly if the scale is used uncriti-cally. In the application of multidimensional scales in treatment evaluations, there is a tendency to sample a symptomatically heterogeneous population and evaluate changes over the entire spectrum of psychopathology rather than to select a target symptom area for evaluation and sample only those patients manifesting the symptom. Using the scale in this manner is more likely to produce positively skewed score distributions and is also somewhat illogical for the evaluation of treatment effectiveness (Lasky et al., 1962).

A second problem for the IMPS, and also for all other scales based on a psychiatric interview, lies in the difficulty of evaluating patients who are mute or who do not verbalize freely. It is not unusual for a patient to become more talkative in the second or third interview than he was during the initial evaluation. To the extent that he produces more pathological material to be rated, the patient may paradoxically appear more symptomatic than he was initially. In the evaluation of individual patients this would be recognized and properly interpreted, but in large-scale research studies the resulting syndrome scores are likely to be uncritically thrown into the statistical pot with some inevitable distortion of the treatment evaluation. The instructions of the IMPS deal with this problem to some extent by restricting its application to patients who can be interviewed, thereby excluding the very inaccessible or mute patient.

Finally, it would seem to be desirable to take into account the differences in clinical significance of the items by the development of some differential weighting system. The solution to this problem is straightforward, and would undoubtedly result in a more sensitive and clinically meaningful scale. However, the author of a rating scale always runs a risk that improvements in a scale, if they make it more difficult to use, may make it less acceptable to the user. Thus, a comprehensive scale that adequately samples the full domain of psychopathology is likely to be judged too long; a scale with a scoring system of too much complexity is also likely to be rejected.

The Brief Psychiatric Rating Scale (BPRS)

Another scale that had its origin in the MSRPP, but which represents quite a different approach to evaluating psychopathology than the PRS or the IMPS, is the 16-item symptom concept scale developed by Overall and Gorham (1962). Their goal was to develop a brief scale that would be sensitive to change during drug treatment. They began (Gorham & Overall, 1960) by cluster-analyzing the change in pre-drug to post-drug ratings of 40 items taken from the interview portion of the MSRPP, as it was used in a double-blind evaluation of six phenothiazine compounds with hospitalized schizophrenics (Casey et al., 1960). The notion was not only that this approach might identify items sensitive to, or reflecting change with, drug treatment, but that the factors of change might be different from the factors of pre-drug status. Although it seems logical enough to have factors of change distinct from factors of status, the results of this analysis yielded nine factors quite similar to those previously identified by Lorr. In a second analysis (Overall, Gorham, & Shawver, 1961) the agreement with Lorr's status factors was not as close, but the peculiarities of the sample used in this study (chronic schizophrenic patients maintained on chlorpromazine), and indeed of the study itself (patients continued on chlorpromazine versus groups shifted to reserpine or placebo), make it questionable whether the results can be generalized.

For the initial version of their abbreviated scale, Gorham and Overall (1960) selected two of the MSRPP items to represent each of the nine factors yielded by the first analysis. When the results using this scale were compared with the results of the parent study, the short scale was apparently more effective in discriminating between drugs than the complete MSRPP. On the strength of this and the application of the 18-item scale to a second, independent sample of chronic schizophrenics, Gorham and Overall suggested that "a nine- or ten-item scale is feasible which would be especially useful in the rapid screening of new drugs [p. 535]." The next step in the evolution of the BPRS (Gorham & Overall, 1961) was to abandon the item form of the MSRPP entirely and, instead, to rate the symptom concept revealed by the factor-analytic studies on a seven-point severity continuum. Their argument was that a trained observer could more effectively synthesize all of the information pertaining to the symptom concept than could rating scales containing molecular bits of information. The symptom concepts included were: Somatic Concern; Anxiety; Emotional Withdrawal; Conceptual Disorganization; Guilt Feelings; Tension; Mannerisms and Posturing; Grandiosity; Depressive Mood; Hostility; Suspiciousness; Hallucinatory Behavior; Motor Retardation; Uncooperativeness; Unusual Thought Content; Blunted Affect. As might be expected, the reliability of the ratings of these concepts is somewhat lower than those reported for the factors of the PRS or the IMPS. In part this may be because reliability is a function of the length of the scale, but it may also be because the variables on this scale are quite abstract. It is to be expected that the more abstract the material to be rated, the more difficult the judgment becomes, the more likely that unique interpretations or inferences are to enter into the rating, and the greater the role that theoretical bias can play; all of these factors could reduce the agreement among raters.

It is chiefly the abstract level of the rated material that makes the BPRS unique among rating scales in current and widespread use. The use of broad concepts has the advantage of approaching the problem with fewer items than is required by behavioral scales; to sample a syndrome adequately at the behavioral level requires a certain amount of redundancy. The concept approach may also seem more direct. The clinician is probably more interested in the general indication of anxiety or tension than he is in the discrete behavior that contributes to its definition. On the other hand, the possibilities of unreliability mushroom as the level of abstraction escalates and the degree of training of the rater becomes a more critical factor. The definitions of the concepts for the guidance of the rater need to be written with exceptional care as, even within one profession, the stereotype of Anxiety or any other concept may be surprisingly diverse. Some of these issues are discussed in a recent paper by Overall, Hollister, and Pichot (1967).

The demand for short scales is understandable. The time of professional people and their tolerance for paper work both seem to be limited. But the consequences of brevity in a rating scale should be taken into account. If the scale is based upon a psychiatric interview, most of the total time spent in the rating procedure is used in the interview. The actual time in making the ratings is trivial in comparison. A 30- to 45-minute interview is ordinarily expected to be adequate to complete the IMPS. Overall and Gorham have suggested a semistructured interview of 18 minutes duration, which they believe is possible because the interviewer can keep in mind the 16 symptom concepts and focus the interview around these areas. The fallacy, however, is that the interview is a behavior sample, and just as in any other kind of sampling, the larger the behavior sample, the more stable or reliable the judgments and the ratings should be. Particularly for some aspects of psychopathology, adequate time must be allowed in the interview for the behavior to occur. A highly skilled interviewer may be able to elicit enough information in these areas in 18 minutes to make good judgments, but the inescapable implication is that the scale may only be valid or reliable for particularly skilled interviewers. If the interview is extended so that it is comparable to that recommended for the IMPS, the expected time advantage of the brief scale is likely to disappear.

These criticisms of the BPRS have been directed toward the choice of abstract symptom concepts to be rated and the questionable effort to achieve brevity. In spite of these criticisms, the BPRS has been both popular and useful. It has been used in dozens of large-scale drug studies (e.g., Gorham & Pokorny, 1964; Overall, Hollister, Meyer, Kimbell, & Shelton, 1964) as well as in attempts to define a classification system for psychiatric patients (Overall & Gorham, 1963; Overall & Hollister, 1964; Overall et al., 1967).

The Psychotic Reaction Profile

The PRP (Lorr, O'Connor, & Stafford, 1960, 1961) is an 85-item ward behavior scale intended for use by psychiatric nurses or aides in describing functional psychotics. Each of the items is rated as *true* or *not true* on the basis of a three-day observation period. Using a method of homogeneous keying rather than factor analysis, four clusters of items were obtained for scoring purposes: Thinking Disorganization; Withdrawal; Paranoid Belligerence; and Agitated Depression. These four clusters seem to correspond to second-order factors hypothesized from earlier studies (Lorr, O'Connor, & Stafford, 1957). In a subsequent factor analysis (Lorr & O'Connor, 1962) seven out of ten hypothesized ward factors were confirmed, and this was later extended to eleven (Lorr, Klett, & McNair, 1964): Paranoid Projection, Hostile Belligerence, Resistiveness, Dominance, Anxious Depression, Seclusiveness, Retardation, Apathy, Conceptual Disorganization, Perceptual Distortion, and Motor Disturbances. Because of the obvious similarities between these factors and those of the IMPS, Lorr undertook to establish the equivalence of the syndromes across both scales (Lorr & Cave, 1966) and concluded that the IMPS and the PRP "do measure eight equivalent dimensions of psychotic behavior." Two additional syndromes were unique to the interview setting. The relationship between the two scales was also studied in a "multitrait-multimethod" analysis (Lorr et al., 1963), and Lorr has shown (1966) a correspondence between a number of profile types generated independently from IMPS and PRP data.

The PRP has provided the criteria of change in ward behavior for nearly all of the VA Cooperative Studies in Psychiatry that have previously been cited, as well as for other large-scale drug studies. In general, the results on the PRP have paralleled those found with the IMPS although on the whole the IMPS has seemed somewhat more sensitive to differential drug effects. Greater sensitivity may be achieved in a new version of this scale called the Psychotic Inpatient Profile by Lorr and Vestre (personal communication), which contains additional items to augment some of the shorter factors and uses a four-point frequency continuum for rating.

The four instruments that have been discussed were selected from the many available because they represent distinct types, and because they illustrate the kinds of research that naturally develop from carefully constructed rating scales. Lorr, Overall, Wittenborn, and their colleagues have all been interested in establishing the primary dimensions of psychosis and the relationship of these dimensions to conventional psychiatric diagnosis. This has led to studies of whether the same kinds and amounts of the dimensions are present in distinct groups—e.g., patients from different cultures or men versus women patients (Lorr & Klett, 1965; Wittenborn, 1964b; Wittenborn & Smith, 1964). The syndromes or dimensions have also provided the parameters to evolve new classification systems for the functional psychoses. In spite of the differences that still exist, the scales are already beginning to provide a common language for the description of psychotic patients. This is less true of some of the following scales which have, however, been used extensively as criteria of change.

Other Scales

The Hospital Adjustment Scale (HAS) (Ferguson, McReynolds, & Ballachey, 1953) is a 90-item behavioral observation scale designed for use by psychiatric nurses and aides. The scale yields a total score and subscores for: Communication and Interpersonal Relations; Self Care and Social Responsibility; and Work, Activities, and Recreation. It is a model of careful scale development and, like the PRS and the MSRPP, is the ancestor of many subsequent scales. Beginning with over 600 behavioral statements obtained by interviewing psychiatric aides, the authors reduced the item pool by discarding duplications and obscure items to 328 statements, which were then rated by 16 professional judges on a nine-point scale of degree of hospital adjustment. After eliminating items with high standard deviations (indicating rater disagreement), the remaining 250 items were used by pairs of raters to describe 63 psychiatric patients. Ninety additional items were eliminated at this stage because of low reliability. The final form of the scale was achieved by an item analysis of the remaining 160 items. Originally the scale was scored by taking the average of the scaled weights for those items marked *true*. However, as this proved to be somewhat cumbersome in practice, a simpler, but apparently equivalent, scoring system was developed. McReynolds (1968) has recently completed a review of the many research applications of the HAS.

The Albany Behavior Rating Scale (Shatin & Freed, 1955) is composed of 100 items adapted from early versions of the HAS, chosen to represent six content areas: self care, orientation, communication and socialization, psychotic behavior, cooperation, and reaction to the environment. Each item is marked *yes* or *no* and the score is the total of items marked in the non-pathological direction. Essentially the same items and format were adopted for a scale used by Burdock, Elliot, Hardesty, O'Neill, and Sklar (1960) in evaluating intensive treatment on a geriatrics ward of a state mental hospital. This scale in turn was an early version of the Ward Behavior Rating Scale (Burdock et al., 1960), which is a 150-item behavior inventory similar in format to the PRP. Although the items are said to represent three observational categories (Appearance and Deportment, Behavior in Verbal Contexts, and Adaptation to Ward Routine), the authors have suggested only the use of a total score consisting of the number of items marked in an a priori deviant direction.

Another scale of the same general type is the Nurses' Observation Scale for Inpatient Evaluation (NOSIE) (Honigfeld et al., 1965). Developed specifically for an evaluation of drugs in older chronic schizophrenics (Honigfeld et al., 1965), it consists of 80 items rated by psychiatric nurses and aides on a five-point frequency continuum. Perhaps the most inbred of all rating scales to date, it is composed of items taken from the PRP, the HAS, the Ward Behavior Rating Scale, the Albany Behavior Rating Scale, and the Social Adjustment Behavior Rating Scale (Aumach, 1962). Items were selected in an attempt to reflect assets as well as liabilities and when necessary were modified to make them suitable for the frequency rating. The NOSIE was later applied in several large-scale drug evaluations in younger, but still chronic, schizophrenic patients; finally, yielding to the pressure for abbreviated scales, it was shortened to a 30-item form called the NOSIE-30 (Honigfeld, Gillis, & Klett, 1966). Made up of "treatment-sensitive" items selected in the manner of the early form of BPRS (Gorham & Overall, 1960), it yields a total score and subscores on Social Competence, Social Interest, Personal Neatness, Irritability, Manifest Psychosis, and Retardation. As this scale is just coming into general use, it is difficult to evaluate how useful it will be, but it does seem to be promising in reflecting changes in the very chronic schizophrenic samples on which it was standardized.

The MACC Behavioral Adjustment Scale is close in lineage to both the MSRPP and the HAS. In its original form (Ellsworth, 1957), it yielded scores for Motility, Affect, Cooperation, Communication, and Total Adjustment from ratings of 14 items of the MSRPP type. All items are unipolar and most of them are of the frequency variety. Form II (Ellsworth, 1962) contains 16 statements contributing to scores on Mood, Cooperation, Communication, and Social Contact.

Other scales that are worth considering for large-scale research with hospitalized patients or are interesting from an historical point of view are the Symptom Rating Scale (Jenkins, Stauffacher, & Hestor, 1959), the Activity Rating Scale (Guertin & Krugman, 1959), the L-M Fergus Falls Behavior Rating Scale (Lucero & Myers, 1951), the Psychiatric Rating Scale (Malamud & Sands, 1947), the Weyburn Assessment Scale (Blewett & Stefaniuk, 1958), and the Mental Status Scale (Bostian, Smith, Lasky, Hover, & Ging, 1959). Still other scales are mentioned in reviews by Lorr (1954, 1960), Jenkins and Lorr (1959), and Lyerly and Abbott (1966).

SPECIAL DEPRESSION SCALES

A small group of scales has been held for separate discussion because of the particular difficulties encountered in evaluating depressive symptomatology. Some of the scales discussed above are applicable in studies of antidepressant drugs—e.g, the PRS has been used in a long series of such studies—but many others do not adequately serve this purpose. Consequently, there has been a number of attempts to focus on this area of psychopathology and often to supplement ratings with self-report inventories.

During the planning of one of the VA Cooperative Studies in Psychiatry that dealt with antidepressant drugs, all of the currently available criteria of depressive symptomatology were surveyed, but none of the standard techniques was felt to be adequate. The solution arrived at for this study was: (*a*) to judge depression in a psychiatric interview, using a special form of the IMPS containing 15 additional items specifically written to cover some of the classic symptoms of depression not included in the standard form; (*b*) to rate depression in the ward situation, using a similarly modified PRP; and (*c*) to obtain a self report from the patient using 166 selected items from the Minnesota Multiphasic Personality Inventory (MMPI) (Hathaway & McKinely, 1951). Twenty psychiatrists and psychologists were asked to select from each of these instruments those items most highly related to clinical depression. In this manner a 31-item depression key was developed for the IMPS, a 26-item key for the PRP, and a 38-item key for the MMPI. Only the scale derived from the IMPS was sensitive to differences between drugs in this study (Overall et al., 1962). Later referred to as the Psychiatric Judgment Depression Scale, or the Manifest Depression Scale, it has been used in a number of evaluations of antidepressant drugs. Overall (1962) found the following factors to be represented in the 31 items: Depression in Mood, Guilt, Psychomotor Retardation, Anxiety, Subjective Experience of Impairment in Functioning, Abnormal Preoccupation with Physical Health, and Physical Response to Stress.

Hamilton's rating scale for depression (1960) consists of 17 fairly global traits such as Guilt, Retardation, and Hypochondriasis, which are rated on a severity continuum from "Absent" to "Clearly Present." Four factors were identified, but it has been stated that "these factors do not portray the classical syndromes of depression [Grinker, Miller, Sabshin, Nunn, & Nunnally, 1961]." For their study Grinker et al. constructed a 47-item Feelings and Concerns Check List and a 139-item Current Behavior Check List. When these were factor-analyzed separately and compared, five feelings and concerns factors, ten current behavior factors, and (combining the two sets) four factor patterns were found, which are now available for further investigation. Depression scales have also been developed by Beck, Ward, Mendelson, Mock, and Erbaugh (1961), Cutler and Kurland (1961) and others (e.g., Greenblatt, Grosser, & Wechsler, 1962), but so far no one scale has achieved preeminence in this area; and current opinion would suggest that a satisfactory scale of depression has yet to be developed. Probably because of the important subjective components of depression, self-inventories are often used with these patients. In spite of Cutler and Kurland's (1961) caution that "it is usually safe to assume that patients sick enough to require hospitalization cannot be objective enough to do their own ratings," it would seem that mood scales such as those developed by Clyde (1963), McNair and Lorr (1964), Nowlis and Nowlis (1956), adjective check lists (Zuckerman and Lubin, 1965) and self-ratings (Zung, 1965) would be useful supplements to the rating scales.

METHODOLOGICAL PROBLEMS

In current discussions of problems involved in the assessment of change produced by psychopharmacologic agents in hospitalized psychiatric patients, there has been a growing awareness that the prevailing methodology, which was satisfactory in screening active agents from placebos or from relatively inert substances, is not adequate for making the more subtle discriminations between active agents that are required by the research questions now being asked.

Some investigators have sought a solution for this problem in statistical terms by recommending the presumably more powerful multivariate techniques of analysis or by requiring considerably larger sample sizes than have generally been used in the past. Although multivariate methods are certainly more likely to detect group differences, when they exist, than the tests of significance that are usually applied, they nearly always pose difficult problems in interpretation. For many of the rating scales that have been discussed, considerable effort has been expended in developing subscales for scoring purposes that are homogeneous in content and meaningful to the clinician. Lorr, Overall, and Wittenborn have all been concerned with establishing something akin to primary dimensions of psychopathology. Multivariate results are expressed in terms of artificial variates that are linear combinations of the scale variables; and often when groups are found to be different, it is difficult to communicate to the clinician *how* they are different. The other recommendation concerning larger sample sizes is based upon the formula for the power of a statistical test (e.g., Overall, Hollister, & Dalal, 1967). Using estimates of the normal variability associated with a particular scale, the number of cases needed to yield a significant difference of some specified size can be solved for quite simply. It is instructive to perform this exercise and to discover the surprisingly large sample sizes that are required to detect even large mean differences when using most rating scales. However, if some reasonable sample size is selected, the same formula can be used to solve for the within-treatments error variance that would still yield a significant finding for a specified mean difference. Since this variance will usually be less than that normally observed, it follows that to do small-sample research some means must be found to reduce this variability. Some workers (e.g., Klett & Moseley, 1965) have tried to achieve this goal by reducing the heterogeneity of sampling by classifying patients into more homogeneous subsets. It seems equally likely that what is needed is a new generation of rating scales, which would capitalize on the work of the last decade but also incorporate some of the more sophisticated psychometric techniques that have been developed during the same period. Lyerly and Abbott (1966), in what is perhaps the most thorough and comprehensive source of information on psychiatric rating scales currently available, point out that these procedures "have had little influence upon makers or users of psychiatric rating scales, and there is little or no evidence that the usefulness of these scales would be significantly increased by such refinements." However, it may be necessary to try them even at the expense of brevity or simplicity of scoring.

More attention may also have to be devoted to the selection and training of raters. The research on this aspect of the rating procedure still seems somewhat scanty (Jensen & Morris, 1960; Gertz, Stilson, & Gynther, 1959; Stilson, Mason, Gynther, & Gertz, 1958; Wittenborn, Plante, & Burgess, 1961). It has become fairly standard practice to have two or more raters observe the patient on the same occasion and independently rate his behavior in an effort to achieve greater reliability, and it has been suggested that repeating this procedure several times at a particular rating interval might have methodological advantages.

SUMMARY

Large-scale studies of change in hospitalized psychiatric patients, best exemplified by the multi-hospital evaluations of psychopharmacologic agents conducted by the Veterans Administration and the NIMH Psychopharmacology Service Center, have with few exceptions limited their choice of criteria to rating scales based upon observations in a psychiatric interview or behavior inventories based upon ward observation. Although these methods have a long history, the publication of three prototype scales coincided with the beginning of the current era of psychiatric drug treatment. The Wittenborn Psychiatric Rating Scales, Lorr's Multidimensional Scale for Rating Psychiatric Patients and the Hospital Adjustment Scale by Ferguson, McReynolds, and Ballachey not only were extensively used during the early years of this era but have served as the source for a host of new scales that have since been constructed. In a sense, the availability of these scales as a way of quantifying patient behavior and change must be credited as one of the primary factors that have transformed this area of investigation from the level of subjective clinical impression to the more objective controlled experiments of recent times.

CHAPTER XI

The assessment of counseling and psychotherapy: Some problems and trends

George A. Muench

The abyss that lies between the scientist and the practitioner has a long history in psychology. This gulf is particularly evident in the breach between the laboratory scientist and the practicing psychotherapist. Although events within the profession in recent years have led to the development of splinter groups representing both extremes of the scientist-versus-artist continuum, there have also been efforts to bridge the gap through continuous attempts at better communication, on the one hand, and through the utilization of traditional laboratory procedures within the context of the clinic, on the other.

It is the purpose of this chapter to survey the current status of attempts to apply acceptable research techniques to the assessment of counseling and psychotherapy. This field of research is extremely broad and diverse, and cannot be encompassed within the bounds of a single chapter. (Readers interested in more extended coverage are referred to Berenson & Carkhuff, 1967; Campbell, 1965a; Dittmann, 1966; Ford & Urban, 1967; Gottschalk & Auerbach, 1966; Goldstein & Dean, 1966; Goldstein, Heller, & Sechrest, 1966; Krasner & Ullmann, 1965; Matarazzo, 1965b; Stollak, Guerney, & Rothberg, 1966; and Stieper & Wiener, 1965.) This paper, therefore, does not purport to be comprehensive; rather, it will point up some of the major methodological problems in the assessment of counseling and psychotherapy and will review some of the more prominent research trends, in order to provide a general overview of the field. In particular, this chapter will not attempt to cover assessment from the viewpoint of specific theories of therapy, such as psychoanalysis, behavior therapy, client-centered therapy, and so on (readers interested in systematic presentations of specific therapeutic approaches are referred to Arbuckle, 1967; Ford & Urban, 1963; Patterson, 1966; Stefflre, 1965; Stein, 1961; and Wolman, 1965), and it is further delimited in that it excludes consideration of group therapy. In general, the focus will be on the kind of individual therapeutic procedures carried on in clinics and university counseling centers.

METHODOLOGICAL PROBLEMS

Unlike the data on normal subjects, as investigated by the experimental psychologist, the data utilized by the research psychotherapist are provided by subjects desperately seeking help in alleviating their distress. The variables to be confronted in psychotherapeutic assessment are exceedingly personal, complex, and difficult to define and measure. The problem of assessing counseling and psychotherapy centers in large part on the fact that important aspects of the therapeutic interaction are covert rather than overt, nonverbal rather than verbal, internal rather than external, and subtle rather than obvious. Many of the data believed to be significant in therapy involve private nuances of phenomenological experience that tend to defy normal modes of communication and investigation. The focal issue, so aptly described by Reznikoff and Toomey (1959), is to specify what is being studied in such a way that it is "both precise enough to be communicable and inclusive enough to be meaningful [p. 5]."

There are, of course, a number of different systematic approaches to counseling and psychotherapy. Regardless, however, of differences in the specific goals and techniques of the various therapeutic models, the ultimate objective is a fundamental change in the client toward increasing mental health. The evaluation of psychotherapy related to this objective involves both the measurement of change occurring in clients during psychotherapy and a precise demonstration that the therapy, in fact, produced the change. Volsky et al. (1965) indicate that there is a need in therapy research "(1) to define goals or outcomes of counseling operationally, and to determine to what extent such goals or outcomes are realized; (2) to develop, as measures of these goals, criterion instruments which will accurately assess clients' extra-clinical behavior; and (3) to define as clearly as possible the nature of the counseling process employed to achieve the defined objectives [p. 5]."

Discussions of the methodological problems involved in research on psychotherapy are extensive and numerous (Berenson & Carkhuff, 1967; Goldstein, Heller, & Sechrest, 1966; Gottschalk & Auerbach, 1966; Reznikoff & Toomey, 1959; Stieper & Wiener, 1965; Stollack et al., 1966; Volsky et al., 1965), and it is not the purpose of this section to recapitulate them. The following discussion, however, will crystallize briefly some of the more important and persistent methodological problems related to the assessment of psychotherapy.

1. *The problem of defining outcome criteria.* If psychotherapy is to be assessed effectively, the nature, direction, and degree of therapeutic change should be stated in terms that are universally understandable and acceptable. Currently there is no such professional agreement, and in fact—as Reznikoff and Toomey (1959) have put it—there is not even an "entirely adequate terminology for discussing criteria [p. 25]." Thus, words such as "cure," "success," and "recovery" are recognized as lacking the precision necessary

for effective use. Travers (1949), in a review of techniques for evaluating guidance, indicated that "until the objectives of guidance have been clearly defined . . . little can be done to evaluate outcomes [p. 214]." Other workers who some time ago emphasized the need for careful specification of outcome criteria include Williamson and Bordin (1941) and Wrenn and Darley (1942). More recently, Cartwright, Kirtner, and Fiske (1963), on the basis of an excellent factor-analytic study, indicate that no conceptually adequate variables for assessing therapy change have been confirmed and that no single score can satisfactorily reflect the changes in psychotherapy. The experimental imperative, which as yet has not been met satisfactorily, is to define therapeutic objectives in terms that are universally comprehensible and experimentally testable.

2. *The problem of obtaining adequate criterion measures.* After the criteria to be measured have been agreed upon and adequately defined, the next step is to select and to develop adequate methods of assessment. The principal problem here lies in the fact that so many of the data of psychotherapy do not lend themselves to the usual methods of measurement. The more obvious behaviors in therapy, which can easily be identified and measured, may be less significant than other factors that are more subtly defined and more resistant to measurement (Dressel, 1953).

The assessment procedures normally used and readily available include (*a*) client and therapist testimonials, which, however, lack necessary objectivity; (*b*) external criteria such as grades, indications of symptom reduction, and improved human relationships, all of which may or may not relate to therapeutic behaviors; (*c*) physiological measures, which at best provide inferential data regarding therapy; (*d*) content analyses of therapy interviews, which—ingenious as some systems may be—provide primarily molecular rather than molar data; and (*e*) psychological tests, the most frequently used mode of assessment.

Unfortunately, there is little evidence, in the case of most psychological tests, that they are sensitive to therapy-induced change; and in research assessing the efficacy of psychotherapy, it becomes difficult to determine whether—to paraphrase Berg (1952)—it is the psychotherapy or the tests that are being evaluated. Obviously, it is inappropriate to utilize measuring instruments whose proficiency in accomplishing the designated task is questionable. The most popular types of psychological test instruments used in the assessment of psychotherapy are the self-report, the projective test, and the behavioral rating scale. Tests such as the Minnesota Multiphasic Personality Inventory, California Psychological Inventory, Security-Insecurity Inventory, and the Mooney Problem Checklist, all of which have been used to assess psychotherapy, are easy to administer and do not require trained test examiners. The items checked or the statements made in such inventories attempt to disclose the subject's feelings and attitudes. The disadvantage of self-report measures is that the subject may consciously or unconsciously present a distorted picture of himself or may attempt to slant his responses according to his interpretation of the purpose of the test. Although some tests, such as the MMPI, have attempted to provide ways of detecting such behaviors, the disadvantages of all self-report scales are very real ones in the assessment of psychotherapy.

Projective tests have the advantage of minimizing the subject's deliberate distortion of responses, since ordinarily he cannot predict what personality traits are being assessed through the less structured instruments. The Rorschach, Thematic Apperception Test, House-Tree-Person Test, the Sentence Completion technique, the Blacky Pictures, and the Szondi Test all have been used in attempts to evaluate psychotherapy. These tests provide impressionistic assessments of personality, supplying information regarding a broad range of personality features, including intimate psychodynamic relationships and unconscious conflicts and motivations. Unfortunately, projective instruments tend to be poorly adapted to quantitative measurements, and tests of their validity have only infrequently met the requirements of research precision.

Behavioral rating scales provide data related to the subject's overt behavior. The observation of the patterns and sequences of overt behavior may, at times, leave little doubt about what a person is experiencing in therapy and how he will probably behave outside of therapy. However, rating scales may not be sensitive enough to provide accurate data about subtle and complex psychological experiences, to give valid indications of whether the behavior observed is typical or atypical, or to permit the equation of ratings by different investigators in different research centers. (For further information on behavior rating scales, the reader is referred to Lyerly & Abbott, 1966; and Klett, this volume.)

Many traditional psychological tests provide data attesting to the degree of the client's psychological deficits. To measure therapeutic change adequately, however, instruments are needed that not only can assess a decreased manifestation of undesirable characteristics but also can reflect increased evidence of positive attributes. It is generally acknowledged (Jahoda, 1958) that psychology has traditionally emphasized "deviations, illness, and malfunctioning" rather than "knowledge of healthy functioning [p. 6]"; nevertheless, measuring instruments tapping the latter have become research necessities. Certain recently developed instruments attempt to do this, such as Dymond's (1954) Q-sort instrument, in which subjects Q-sort "good" and "poor" adjustment items according to the categories "more like me" or "less like me." Spitzer (1966) has developed the Mental Status Schedule, an interviewer checklist that focuses on observable behaviors. The Personal Orientation Inventory (POI) (Shostrom, 1963), based in part upon humanistic and existential theoretical formulations, attempts to assess the patient's positive mental health. Shostrom and Knapp (1966) show generally low intercorrelations in a study comparing the POI and MMPI; they suggest that these instruments are measuring different phenomena, rather than varying degrees of similar or identical psychological dimensions. Lorr and McNair (1965) have developed the Interpersonal Behavior Inventory and the Interview Relationship Inventory (1964), which show promise as methods for predicting therapy behavior, for understanding the patient, and for assessing changes resulting from therapy.

Although the efficacy of these new instruments is as yet merely suggestive, the trend is encouraging. To assess therapeutic changes adequately, it is necessary to solve the measurement problem, in order that the instruments used accurately reflect both the obvious and the subtle changes occurring during therapy.

3. *The problem of controls.* The necessity of controlling pertinent variables is universal in psychological research, but it creates a particular configuration of problems in the evaluation of counseling and psychotherapy. In assessing psychotherapy, the ultimate question, as crystallized by Frank (1959), is directed toward understanding "what kinds of therapist activity produce what kinds of change in what kinds of patient? That is, the independent variables lie in the patient's state before the therapist's intervention and in the therapist's activity, the dependent variables in changes in the patient's feelings and behavior [p. 10]." As Frank points out, few of these variables are adequately defined; further, the researcher can manipulate directly only a few of the more important ones.

Attempts to control important variables in the assessment of psychotherapy have tended toward one of the following: "own" control (in which the client himself acts as the control), client controls, or non-client controls. Although control through matched groups is the most usual approach in experimental design, this method produces problems in therapeutic research. To equate subjects undergoing psychotherapy with subjects not in therapy (either client or non-client controls) on all variables related to personality change is currently impossible. First, the variables are neither known nor clearly defined; and second, the practical conditions of most agencies preclude such ideal matching procedures.

As Reznikoff and Toomey (1959) have observed, the "own" control method circumvents many of the problems of matched groups. With each client serving as his own control, even unknown or ill-defined client variables create no problem. However, situational factors remain uncontrolled; the order of treatment (control-experimental or vice-versa) cannot be varied; and when treatment is withheld, the effects of such withholding remain uncertain.

The problem of providing adequate control groups within the limitations of the clinical setting is an especially difficult one. In this context Goldstein, Heller, and Sechrest (1966) argue that less-than-conclusive research findings are better than none and that the accumulation of data from less-than-adequately-controlled studies will in time produce useful results. Hyman and Breger (1965), on the other hand, recognizing that psychotherapy deals with the unique problems of the individual client, believe that the very nature of the therapy situation makes it inappropriate for controlled experimentation.

The need for establishing effective controls in assessing psychotherapy is universally acknowledged; the difficulty of establishing such controls is just as universally recognized. As Ford and Urban (1967) indicate in reviewing the literature regarding the control problem, "It would appear that one encounters an impasse [p. 360]." It seems clear that either we must be satisfied with limited results in attempting to apply the experimental method under essentially nonexperimental (clinical) conditions, or else we must become more creative within the traditional experimental paradigm and develop new models that provide adequate controls.

4. *The problem of the therapist's interview behavior.* Colby (1964) describes the current state of psychotherapy as one of confusion. He writes, "Chaos prevails. . . . Everyone seems to be going his own way, both within and between [therapeutic] paradigms, regardless of the ensuing disorder [p. 347]." Colby argues that for years therapists have gained a semblance of professional security by identifying with a particular therapeutic paradigm. As such identifications were established, an aura of "sameness" developed, leading to the assumption that therapists within a particular paradigm agree regarding concepts, theories, and techniques.

While recognizing the still-current existence of the traditional paradigms of psychotherapy, Colby suggests that signs of crises have become visible both within and between paradigms. The cause of the chaos, the author suggests, is progress—progress that has provided the profession with tape recordings, motion pictures, and a variety of new training methods. What heretofore was a private experience behind closed therapeutic doors has become a comparatively public exhibition. Discussion and debate about various therapeutic procedures are no longer sufficient; now the raw data of the therapeutic hour are open to direct professional scrutiny. The results, though unexpected to some, have disclosed that therapists, even within the same therapeutic paradigm, use methods and techniques of considerable diversity. Significant differences within and between paradigms have become publicly reflective of the normal reactions to the crumbling of exposed reifications.

If such disclosures have caused chaos—as Colby claims—they should not have. Though researchers have not always taken the data seriously, it has been known for years that therapy is, in large part, an art directly dependent upon the talent, and particularly upon the personality, of the artist.

If such recognition is new to some observers of the therapeutic scene, the advice of certain earlier investigators has gone unheeded. Groves (1947) expressed the idea some twenty years ago: "We have enjoyed looking with microscopic eye at the reactions of others (in therapy), but now it might be well if we turned our psychologically slanted inquisitiveness upon ourselves [p. 57]." Eissler, back in 1943, pointed out that psychotherapy with schizophrenics is dependent upon the therapist's personality—in his ability to develop a therapeutic situation in which the patient feels free to respond—as well as in the disorder itself. Although a current trend has placed renewed emphasis upon therapeutic techniques, especially among therapists utilizing behavior modification techniques, most practicing therapists now accept the central importance of the personality of the therapist, with concomitantly lessened emphasis upon therapeutic technique per se. Little wonder, then, that in the view of some observers chaos reigns, since each therapist applies his unique artistry, even though he may work within the general framework of a particular therapeutic technique. No longer may our assessment procedures assume a priori that we can easily define a particular therapist's mode of therapeutic intervention. The therapist, like all therapeutic variables, must himself undergo research scrutiny.

5. *The problem of the client's unique individuality.* Traditionally, clinical psychology has been preoccupied with placing people into various nosological classifications. Although we understand in principle that the person is a unique individual, not simply a "neurotic" or a "normal," in some of our assessment research with psychotherapy we act otherwise. As Ford and Urban (1967) have emphasized, each client differs from others in the nature of his problems, in his motivations, on demographic variables—in fact, on "most conceivable dimensions [p. 364]." Careful definition of these differences and of their relevance to treatment outcome is a research imperative. In an appraisal of a well-designed study by Volsky et al. (1965), in which the investigators found psychotherapy to yield minimal positive results, Ford and Urban observe that the disappointing results developed "because the assumption was implicit that all patients were essentially the same, that they were undergoing an homogeneous set of treatment conditions, and that the treatment would produce the same changes on the same variables in the same direction for all patients [p. 364]."

CURRENT TRENDS IN THE ASSESSMENT OF COUNSELING AND PSYCHOTHERAPY[1]

Most investigators recognize the special problems that are involved in conducting research on the assessment of counseling and psychotherapy. The large number of studies that are nevertheless reported in this area each year testifies to the urgent need to understand better both process and product in therapy. Rather than focusing on particular techniques of assessment, the remainder of this chapter will briefly examine some of the overall trends in these studies. This review will serve to point up (*a*) some of the major dimensions in terms of which psychotherapy can be assessed (e.g., outcome, treatability of clients, duration of therapy, etc.); (*b*) the current status of research in these areas; and (*c*) some of the outstanding questions on which further assessment research is needed.

1. *Assessing the outcome of counseling and psychotherapy.* Individual practitioners are convinced that psychotherapy "works." If asked to produce sound scientific research evidence to support this conviction, however, they must confess that they cannot. Knight (1941), a psychoanalyst, more than twenty-five years ago proposed criteria for the evaluation of psychotherapy (e.g., symptomatic improvement, improved interpersonal relationships, increased productivity, more adequate sexual adjustment, more effective handling of psychological conflicts and stress). Although universal agreement on such criteria has never been achieved, Knight's suggestions have been generally acceptable to most researchers. When one asks how extensively they have been utilized in research, however, he must conclude, with Berenson and Carkhuff (1967), that "after more than a quarter of a century of continuing and expanding forms of traditional counseling and psychotherapy, *we have not met the challenge of these* [Knight's] *indices* [p. 22]."

---

[1]Portions of this section represent an extension and elaboration of a previous review by the writer (Muench, 1960)

In what Rogers (1951) describes as the first objective study assessing the effectiveness of psychotherapy, Muench (1947) examined the success of client-centered therapy, as measured by the Rorschach and other indices. The study was acclaimed by some investigators as defining a research design that might elicit the data needed to gauge the efficacy of psychotherapy. If it were replicated with numerous cases from various therapeutic orientations, they reasoned, then the results of psychotherapy could be scientifically documented. However, Carr's (1949) attempt to replicate the Muench study yielded results different from the original research. Further, Mosak (1950) and Haimowitz and Haimowitz (1952) obtained results different from both of the earlier studies.

The controversy over the effectiveness of psychotherapy approached a crisis when Eysenck (1952), on the basis of his survey of research on the outcome of therapeutic practices, concluded: "The figures fail to support the hypothesis that psychotherapy facilitates recovery from neurotic disorder [p. 323]." Eysenck's report brought immediate, extensive, and emotion-laden reaction. Sanford (1953), reflecting the attitude of many therapists, replied to Eysenck's challenge by saying ". . . the only wise course with respect to such a challenge is to ignore it [p. 335]." Rosenzweig (1954), Luborsky (1954), and others criticized the various uncontrolled factors in the studies included in Eysenck's review and took the position that the available data did not justify any broad generalizations as to the efficacy of psychotherapy. On the other hand, Berenson and Carkhuff (1967), reflecting on the same data Eysenck reviewed, concluded:

> ". . . at the minimum there were *no average differences in the outcome indices of persons who were treated and persons who were not treated.* At the maximum there is cause for even greater alarm: *There may be justification for leaving some patients alone and relying upon the phenomenon of spontaneous remission rather than treating them in the most traditional psychoanalytic mode of practice.* At the minimum, *therapeutic practices have failed to establish their efficacy.* At the maximum, *they may be very questionable modes of intervention with highly dubious outcomes* [p. 22]."

The controversy aroused by Eysenck's study is with us still, though it has abated considerably. Levitt, in 1957, summarized results of psychotherapy with children that bore a striking similarity to Eysenck's findings on adults. Levitt reported that approximately two-thirds of the patients at the termination of therapy and three-quarters at follow-up showed improvement—about the same proportions as for untreated controls. He concluded that "the results of the present study fail to support the view that psychotherapy with 'neurotic' children is effective [p. 195]." Goldberg and Rubin (1964) recently reported on six chronic patients whose recovery occurred only when the hospital personnel "neglected" them.

Muench (1960) surveyed more than fifty studies related to the results of counseling and psychotherapy, and found little consistency in reported results. Outcomes varied in reported recovery rates from recovery in

70 percent of the cases to recovery approximately that of a control group. Cross (1964), in a review of outcome research in psychotherapy, concluded that "while psychotherapy is probably the most popular single area of specialization within psychology (not to mention psychiatry), its efficacy has not been scientifically demonstrated beyond some reasonable doubt [p. 416]." Kellner (1967) suggests that the results of outcome studies are dependent on the heterogeneity of the group studied.

In his review of studies assessing the outcome of psychotherapy, Bergin (1963) stressed, not the lack of proof that psychotherapy works, but rather the fact that in both treatment and control groups changes do occur. He argues that in the majority of the studies what are called "control groups" do not in fact provide genuine controls in that persons undergoing stress, whether they have formal therapy or not, tend to seek help from other professional or nonprofessional persons. The need is to identify and explicate those variables within a helping relationship that produce positive changes. Bergin also notes, in his analysis of outcome studies by Barron and Leary (1955) and Cartwright and Vogel (1960), that experimental subjects "manifested significantly greater variability in criterion scores at the conclusion of psychotherapy than did the controls [pp. 245-46]," and in addition, that in the latter study clients of experienced therapists showed greater improvement than clients of inexperienced therapists. Such evidence leads Truax and Carkhuff (1964) to conclude that "this generic experience of 'psychotherapy' must have been different for the inexperienced therapists than for the experienced therapists since the outcomes were different [p. 125]." Such a correlational result, however, hardly justifies the conclusion of causation, especially in view of evidence such as that of Strupp (1958b), who found that a therapeutic atmosphere conducive to a helping relationship was more frequently created by inexperienced than by experienced therapists.

Findings presented by Truax and Carkhuff (1963) and by May and Tuma (1963) indicate that most clients in psychotherapy, rather than manifesting consistent unitary gains, evidence a mixture of positive and negative changes. Truax and Carkhuff (1964) conclude: "The major finding growing from all research is that psychotherapy as currently practiced can be both helpful and harmful. That is perhaps a profoundly distressing finding [p. 146]."

In a digest of research findings with implications for research and practice in psychotherapy, Bergin's (1966) first conclusion is: "Psychotherapy may cause people to become better or worse adjusted than comparable people who do not receive such treatment [p. 235]." Further, other papers (Bergin, 1963; Cartwright & Vogel, 1960; Rogers, 1962; Truax & Carkhuff, 1964) have indicated that clients vary in outcome measures according to the quality of the therapeutic situation established by the therapist. The more positive the helping relationship, the greater the therapeutic gain. The assessment task, then, becomes one of discovering—in the words of Truax and Carkhuff— "*what* ingredients of psychotherapy produce positive personality and behavioral change [p. 126]?"

Consequently, some investigators (Seeman & Raskin, 1953; Berman, 1955; Reznikoff & Toomey, 1959; Wallerstein, 1965) have concluded that the most meaningful results will be obtained by studying the process and outcome together. If it were possible adequately to understand the process of therapy, they argue, this would tend to increase one's confidence in the overall results. Not all investigators agree on this point, however. Dressel (1953) and Winder (1957) both have argued that we must prove psychotherapy works before undertaking study of its course and process. Paul (1966, 1967), who has presented significant original data and reviewed the current status of psychotherapeutic research, argues that the greatest need is for outcome studies. Sanford (1953), on the other hand, believes that outcome studies are irrelevant and that our research efforts should concentrate on studies of process.

Since some persons change under each of various kinds of therapeutic intervention and other persons change in similar ways with no intervention at all, Sanford argues that these diverse results cannot be understood without a complete comprehension of the therapeutic process. Strupp (1960), reflecting on the results of a series of studies, states:

> ". . . it is of little avail to investigate whether psychotherapy 'works,' or even whether one technique is more 'effective' than another. Rather, one must ask: Is this particular therapist, by virtue of being a particular person, capable of creating the kinds of conditions in which a given technique or techniques can attain their maximum usefulness? The question of the relative effectiveness of techniques still has to be answered, but the primary focus is on the *person* of the therapist by whom a particular technique is used [pp. 322-23]."

Irrespective of theoretical arguments, many researchers investigating the effectiveness of psychotherapy have changed their emphasis to studies of process rather than of outcome. The rationale for this change may be clinically sound, but it should be noted that little more is known today than twenty years ago as to whether psychotherapy "works", or whether one technique is consistently more "successful" than others.

2. *Assessing the treatability of clients.* The public need for professional help with emotional problems has traditionally far exceeded the available supply of mental health facilities or personnel. Some investigators, therefore, have attempted to determine whether psychotherapy is more effective with certain types of individuals than with others, and whether it is possible to develop criteria to predict success with psychotherapy. These questions reflect another important area in which psychotherapy can be assessed.

Numerous prediction studies have used the Rorschach as the independent variable and improvement ratings as the dependent variable, with varying success. Employing the Koret-Rubin (1957) approach, Davids and Talmadge (1964), found that in 84 percent of their cases psychologists' ratings, based on the Rorschach, corresponded to social workers' evaluations of patient movement. Endicott and Endicott (1964), utilizing the Rorschach Prognostic Rating Scale (Klopfer et al., 1951), found that patient change—whether or not it was due to therapy—appeared to be predictable with the RPRS. Fiske, Cartwright, and Kirtner (1964), on the basis of a well-designed study employing numerous test variables, including the RPRS, report that the predictions of therapy changes were only slightly better than chance.

McNair et al. (1964), using patients in Veterans Administration outpatient clinics, found such pretreatment variables as anxiety, hostility, ego strength, and dependency to be the best predictors of change. This indicates that patients who were healthiest at the beginning of therapy made the greatest improvement. Rosenbaum et al. (1956) found with 210 individual cases that those patients who had a better childhood environment, the ability to develop better interpersonal relationships, a higher social station, better sexual adjustment, and a more favorable financial status showed the greatest improvement in psychotherapy. Heilbrun (1963), reporting on 241 patients with a wide variety of diagnoses, concluded that psychotic patients benefit little from psychoanalytic psychotherapy, but that cases of neurosis and adjustment reactions of adolescence may improve under this type of treatment.

Russell and Snyder (1963) report a study in which two actors were interviewed by each of 20 student counselors, who were unaware that the actors were not real clients. The results indicated that more anxiety developed in the counselors from hostile than from friendly behavior in the clients. In a study using 34 graduate student interviewers and four actors playing the role of clients, Heller, Myers, and Kline (1963) found that friendly client behavior elicited friendly behavior from interviewers, and hostile client behavior elicited hostile behavior from interviewers. Presumably clients who arouse more anxiety and hostility in the therapist have less likelihood of being helped.

Data indicate that the more likeable the client is to the therapist, the greater the probability of therapeutic success. Stoler (1963) reports that clients who were more successful in psychotherapy were rated as more likeable than those who were less successful. Strupp and his associates (Strupp, 1963) have found the therapist's attitude toward the patient to be significantly related to his expectation for the patient, a favorable prognosis being associated with a positive attitude and an unfavorable prognosis with a negative attitude. Raskin (1961), in a study utilizing 100 Veterans Administration mental hygiene patients, found therapist ratings of patients' motivation to enter therapy to be significantly correlated with education, occupational level, and awareness of psychological difficulties; with the type of treatment the patients expected; and with the therapists' liking for the patients. Garfield and Affleck (1961) showed that therapists' ratings of patient prognosis "were highly correlated with positive feelings of the judges toward the patient [p. 507]." Wallach and Strupp (1960) found that patients who are more highly motivated for therapy tend to engender more positive attitudes in the therapist, which in turn are positively correlated with more favorable clinical evaluations and a more favorable therapeutic atmosphere. In a later study (1965), Strupp and Wallach reconfirmed their earlier results that—as Ford and Urban (1967) put it—"therapists prefer to do what they are trained to do," and work best with clients "who readily fit into their practiced habits of procedure [p. 347]."

These studies indicate that, as Strupp (1962) has noted, therapists tend to agree on what constitutes a promising patient (young, no seriously disabling symptoms, social and vocational skills, attractive, upper-middle class, intelligent, capacity for insight, motivated for help, ability to communicate, etc.), and that the more mentally healthy the patient is at the initiation of therapy, the greater the probability of therapeutic success. There is, however, a clear need for more definitive methods for assessing client treatability.

3. *Assessing the personality of the therapist.* The assessment of the client during and after psychotherapy has been a traditional interest of investigators appraising the efficacy of the process. Currently there is a trend to assess not only the client but also the therapist. Since psychotherapy tends to be an intimate personal relationship, investigators have centered their inquisitiveness upon the personality of the therapist, and in recent years a consistent effort has been made by therapists themselves to make an objective analysis of their own attitudes, feelings, and actions as they affect the therapy process.

In a study utilizing the MMPI, Kuder Interest Inventory, and Heston Personality Inventory with 70 counselor trainees as subjects, Arbuckle (1956) found that the trainees most preferred by their fellows had high literary, persuasive, social service, and scientific interests (Kuder), and appeared to be more self-confident (Heston) and normal (MMPI). Bandura (1956) obtained evidence indicating that nonanxious therapists were more successful than anxious therapists. In a much quoted study, Fiedler (1953) indicated that the experience of the therapist was a greater predictor of success than any given theoretical orientation, and that successful therapists tended to be more empathic toward the clients' feelings, to have a greater sensitivity to their clients' attitudes, and to have a warmer regard for their clients, while at the same time not becoming excessively involved emotionally.

In a series of studies by Whitehorn and Betz (1954), and more recently by Betz (1963), the factors that most significantly differentiated successful therapists from the unsuccessful were found to be the following: successful therapists worked toward patient-oriented, rather than symptom-oriented goals; they tended to see the patient as a person rather than as a case history; they developed an active interpersonal relationship with the client; they tended not to use advice, to interpret, or to emphasize practical care; and they were able to develop and maintain the confidence of the patient. In a paper summarizing the evidence, Rogers (1958) concluded that effective therapists are able (*a*) to be genuine, i.e., are free to be themselves, to experience their true feelings, and to express themselves in therapy; (*b*) to be accepting and to develop warmth in the relationship; and (*c*) to have the desire to understand the client and to possess empathy for, and interest in, the client.

Segal (1954), in a study using the Q-sort method, found that the most significant factor differentiating well- and poorly-integrated therapists was the greater degree of self-understanding and self-acceptance possessed by the better integrated group. Danskin and Robinson (1954) indicated that therapists tend to develop a consistent, personal style in counseling. Grater (1964) found that clients whose primary interest in counseling was for help on educational-vocational problems preferred counselors with cognitive characteristics (e.g., "knowledgeable"), whereas clients with personal-social problems preferred counselors with desirable affective characteristics (e.g., "warm").

In a study reported by Kamin and Caughlan (1963), clients who were interviewed from one to two years after therapy rated as most helpful those therapists whom they described as "warm" and "real." Fox and Goldin (1963), on the basis of their review, consider empathy to be an important capacity in the therapist; and further, they conclude that clients learn to empathize during the course of therapy. Truax (1963), in a series of studies with hospitalized schizophrenics, reported that therapist empathy is a characteristic of crucial importance. Schizophrenic patients treated by psychotherapists high in empathy improved with psychotherapy, while patients treated by therapists low in empathy actually showed a loss in psychological functioning. Psychotherapy, in the hands of some therapists, apparently allows some clients to become less, rather than more, mentally healthy. The data that crystallize the importance of personality variables as contrasted with professional qualifications of the therapist gain support from studies like that of Feifel and Eells (1963), which reported that with psychoanalytically-oriented therapy it made little difference whether the therapist was a psychiatrist, psychologist, or social worker; male or female; or a regular staff member, advanced psychology trainee, or psychiatric resident.

One additional approach to the assessment of therapists should be mentioned. This is the subjective or introspective approach, as illustrated in the work of Wolff (1956), who interviewed 50 therapists of varying orientations concerning the theory and technique of their therapeutic practices; and of Rogers (1956), who has used this approach in attempting to understand the characteristics that are most important in developing a maximally helpful therapeutic relationship. Although data yielded by reports of this kind may be secondary rather than primary, nevertheless they emphasize the interest that contemporary psychotherapists have in examining themselves both in and out of the therapeutic relationship.

4. *Assessing the relationship of therapist and client.* Currently there is a significant emphasis on the assessment of the *relationship* between client and therapist. If research makes it possible to understand the unique human relationship involved in psychotherapy, then it also may be possible to crystallize those variables that are most significant in the therapeutic process. Earlier studies emphasized variables differentiating methods or techniques; current studies tend to concentrate on the personality factors of client and therapist in dynamic interaction.

In a study utilizing a 20-minute psychiatric interview, Raines and Rohrer (1955) found that the personality characteristics that the psychiatrists consciously or unconsciously valued highly were the same characteristics that they tended to see in their patients. Strupp, in a series of studies (1957, 1958a, 1958b), divided his therapist subjects into two groups according to their responses to the same client stimuli. One group, characterized as more tolerant, permissive, democratic, and humane, tended to be less judgmental and "warmer" to the patients. The second group, characterized as more directive, harsh, moralistic, and disciplinarian, tended to be rejecting, "cold," and evaluative of the patient. Contrary to the results of some earlier studies (Fiedler, 1953), the first group were, on the average, less experienced than the second. This finding led the investigator to speculate that a higher percentage of success in therapy or a more precise understanding of factors conducive to therapeutic success do not come from experience. Although Strupp concluded that effective therapists need technical competence as well as warm and empathic personalities, he implied that for successful therapy the latter is of the greater import.

Cartwright and Lerner (1963), utilizing a sophisticated research design with 28 cases, indicated that improvement during therapy was related to the patient's initial need to change, the therapist's empathy for the patient, and the joint effects of these two variables. Feifel and Eells (1963) report that clients, following therapy, considered the most helpful factors during therapy to have been the opportunity to talk things over with the therapist and the effects of therapist's "human" characteristics. Kanfer and Marston (1964), in a therapy analogue study, found that subjects who had only "reflecting" interviewers had a more positive attitude toward their interviewers than did those who had "interpreting" interviewers; but that in the group that had a choice of interviewer, about twice as many chose the "interpreting" interviewer; and further that whichever type the subjects chose, they had a more positive attitude toward that type than toward the other. Frank (1964) compared the effects of directive and non-directive statements by the therapist; he found directive statements to be followed by more client talk of symptoms, and non-directive statements to be followed by client attempts to attain understanding. Caracena (1965) obtained evidence to indicate that therapist behaviors are effective in eliciting given kinds of client responses, but not in reinforcing client responses.

Heine (1950), in a much quoted study, obtained testimony from clients who had completed therapy with psychoanalytic, Adlerian, or client-centered therapists. Irrespective of the therapist orientation, the clients tended to agree that the most helpful factors in their therapy were a feeling of being understood by the therapist, a feeling of trust in the therapist, a feeling of being free to make independent choices, and—of greatest importance—the feeling that the therapist openly stated and clarified feelings that the client approached reluctantly. The clients also agreed that the least helpful elements in their therapy included the therapist's apparent lack of interest, a distance or remoteness, an overemphasis on sympathy, the stating of specific advice, and an emphasis on past rather than present problems. Guided suggestions mildly given by the therapist were neither particularly helpful nor hindering to the process.

Lorr (1965), in a carefully conducted study, found significant correlations between client improvement and the extent to which the therapists were seen by the clients as understanding and accepting. Gendlin (1966), with schizophrenics, and Kiesler, Klein, and Mathieu (1965), with neurotics, indicated that clients with a greater capacity for "experiencing" have a higher probability for therapeutic success, especially if their therapist is high on "empathy" and "genuineness." In a study using actual therapy sessions experimentally, Parloff (1956) found that the therapists who were more able to establish good social relationships outside of therapy also developed more successful relationships within therapy.

Present evidence regarding the psychotherapy relationship emphasizes the importance of the personal and human variables of the therapist and his ability to express these variables in the authentic psychotherapeutic encounter, rather than his mode of training, his theoretical orientation, or his length of experience. A therapist who is warm, natural, accepting, and empathic, and who can communicate these personal traits in a significant interpersonal relationship with his client, develops the kind of atmosphere most conducive to therapeutic success. In simple sum, the available data indicate what we should already have known—that the more psychologically healthy the client and particularly the more psychologically healthy the therapist, the more psychologically healthy the relationship and the greater the probability of therapeutic success.

5. *Assessing the duration of treatment.* The final aspect of the assessment of psychotherapy that we will consider here is the variable of therapy duration. This dimension is particularly important in that most mental health agencies dedicated to treating emotionally disturbed individuals by traditional therapeutic methods discover, sooner or later, that they are plagued with the universal problem of increasingly long waiting lists. Counseling centers and mental health clinics associated with colleges and universities have experienced the problem even more sharply because of rapidly increasing student populations. While these agencies have been struggling to provide psychotherapy—for up to 10 percent of the student population (Farnsworth, 1957)—additional evidence has indicated the growing magnitude of the problem. Srole et al. (1962), in their Midtown Manhattan Study, found 23.4 percent of their urban sample to show definite psychiatric impairment, and over 80 percent to manifest some psychiatric symptomatology. The extensiveness of the problem is further substantiated by results from Leighton et al. (1963), whose study on a rural sample in Canada indicated 31 percent to show "clear psychiatric disorder," and only 17 percent to show no psychiatric symptomatology. Whether the extent of the need for psychotherapeutic help is 10 percent, 20 percent, or 80 percent, all data indicate that our clinic facilities are hopelessly inadequate to meet the need. Consequently, numerous clinics and counseling centers throughout the country have been experimenting with various nontraditional approaches to psychotherapy; the attempt is to discover a therapeutic procedure that is realistic and economical in relating available staff time to the current and projected public demand for psychotherapeutic services.

Since most clinics are aware of the need to increase the economy and efficacy of therapy, the recent literature includes a number of novel approaches to the psychotherapeutic enterprise. Thus, Abse and Ewing (1960) use "reverse interpretation," Frankl (1960) "paradoxical intention," Garner (1960) a confrontation technique, Glasser (1965) "reality therapy," LeBaron (1962) an idiometer signalling technique, Phillips and Mattoon (1961) interference therapy, Stampfl (referred to in London, 1964) "implosive therapy," Zirkle (1961) five-minute therapy, and so on. These and other fresh attempts to cope with society's ever-increasing therapeutic demands reflect the rumblings of disenchantment with traditional psychotherapeutic approaches to the human condition.

One study employing an innovative approach to shortening treatment time was carried out under the direction of the writer (Muench, 1965) at the

San Jose State College Counseling Center. In 1959, the staff of the center became interested in possible methods of reducing their increasingly long clinic waiting list. They visited other clinics, interviewed clinic directors and staff members, and in particular, surveyed the literature on economical use of available professional staff time. They were aware that attempts to relate success of psychotherapy to duration of treatment had been inconclusive, although the weight of evidence leaned toward higher success ratings for the longer cases. Ford and Urban (1967), after surveying the mounting evidence, concluded that the majority of therapy cases are terminated in no more than 10 to 20 sessions.

In view of conflicting research results on time-in-therapy, the San Jose staff hypothesized that factors other than duration were primarily responsible for therapeutic success. Consequently, they set an arbitrary limit of ten sessions for a random selection of clients and designed a study to test the effectiveness of ten-session, time-limited therapy compared to traditional short-term and long-term therapy.

The results of the study (Muench, 1965) indicated that on the experimental measures used in the study significant positive changes occurred for both the short-term and the time-limited groups, but that no significant changes were found in the long-term therapy group. Since other evidence indicated that the results could not be accounted for by differences in the effectiveness of the therapists or of the degree of illness of the clients, it was concluded that under the conditions of this study time-limited therapy was as effective as short-term therapy and more effective than long-term therapy.

Numerous studies have attempted to analyze why some clients tend to remain in therapy while others terminate. The prevailing assumption has been that the remainers were better therapeutic risks than the terminators, and efforts have been made to keep clients in therapy. As stated by Seeman (1961), "One of the difficult problems raised in clinical practice concerns the clients who terminate before they have become really involved in the therapeutic process [p. 176]." Some recent evidence, however, seems seriously to question whether the remainers are selectively better therapeutic risks or whether they make more progress during psychotherapy. Bailey et al. (1959) found only two variables to be of any predictive value in determining the length of stay in therapy; these were years of education and amount of previous experience in therapy. Matarazzo (1965b) noting that the majority of clients seen in college clinics typically return for less than ten sessions, hypothesized that the longer-term clients (remainers) are those who start therapy in September and tend to terminate in June, and that those who initiate therapy at a later date also tend to terminate in June. Diener and Young (1961) concluded that the greater the patients' psychiatric disability and the closer their homes to the clinic, the more likely they are to seek treatment. Garfield (1963) reported that those patients who allegedly terminated therapy prematurely, often giving as their reason some external difficulty such as no transportation, were making as adequate an adjustment as those who remained in therapy.

Although the evidence is not completely consistent (Strickland & Crowne, 1963), the results from the studies just surveyed not only question the validity of the assumption that remainers tend generally to be better therapeutic risks than terminators, but further suggest that even the contrary may be true. The remainers may be those clients who choose the secure dependency of psychotherapy rather than utilize the process as a means toward self-actualization. If this is true, then the imposition of time limits may act as a necessary motivation for the client to accept more responsibility for progress in therapy and, therefore, may accelerate the process of growth. At least it would eliminate those clients who cannot maximally profit from the experience.

Some recent evidence indicates that there may be a distinct discrepancy between the attitudes and expectations of individuals who come for psychotherapeutic help and those of the professional therapists who administer the help. Garfield and Wolpin (1963) report that 73 percent of the patients in their clinic indicated, prior to psychotherapy, that they expected some improvement in five sessions, and that 70 percent expected the entire treatment not to last more than ten sessions. Such attitudes hardly reflect those of the typical, traditional clinic staff. Tuckman and Lavell (1959) found that in eleven child clinics over 40 percent of the cases terminated therapy before treatment was judged by clinic staffs to be completed. Apparently this discrepancy in expectations exists not only at the initiation of treatment, but also at termination. Although the professional's judgment might be assumed to be more accurate than the patient's, some research evidence seems to question this assumption. Stieper and Wiener (1959) reported that the majority of long-term cases were being treated by therapists who possessed what the investigators described as "dependency nurturing." Wood et al. (1962) reported that hospital patients undergoing psychotherapy tended to stay longer than those not in therapy, in part because of the involvement of the residents in the treatment.

Although such studies are at best merely suggestive, they do prompt the speculation that, along with the client's dependency needs to stay in therapy longer than may be therapeutically essential, various needs of the therapist may cause him to retain clients longer than necessary. In time-limited therapy, where both therapist and client are aware of termination dates, therapeutic hours are less likely to be used to satisfy the dependency, nurturance, or related needs of either client or therapist. Clearly, the dimension of therapy duration is one in which further assessment research is needed.

SUMMARY AND CONCLUSIONS

This chapter has examined five of the most crucial methodological problems involved in the assessment of psychotherapy and has surveyed research trends in five of the most frequently studied topics in this area. Continuing progress toward effective assessment will depend in large part upon how willing therapists are to expose both their therapeutic techniques and themselves to experimental scrutiny; how effectively they are able to utilize current research tools, while seeking more productive methods of investigation; and how inclined they are to revise established therapeutic positions as new research evidence reveals the need.

Utilizing both experiential and empirical means, we must continue to experiment broadly, both with the principles of the art and the settings in which the artistry proceeds. It has been the thesis of this chapter that the progress of psychotherapy will be determined largely by the fruitfulness of bold, extraordinary experimentation. To that end we have surveyed the current research scene related to assessment in this area.

CHAPTER XII

Conjoint family assessment:
An evolving field

Arthur M. Bodin

Most of our current assessment techniques are designed for use with individuals. These techniques sample individuals' behavior repertoires under various stimulus conditions in an attempt to arrive at an understanding and description of the patterns of the individuals' response propensities. These data may then be used as a basis for predicting or evaluating the future or past effects of various types of therapeutic intervention, or of the absence of such intervention. The majority of our present techniques focus, either explicitly or implicitly, on *traits* as inherent characteristics of and *in* individuals. A new view is emerging, however, that gives increased emphasis to the social learning contexts in which maladaptive behaviors are instigated and maintained as inappropriate response patterns. Family therapy is only one of several historic influences contributing to this sociotherapeutic shift, which Hobbs (1964) has termed "mental health's third revolution." The advent of community mental health centers bespeaks growing appreciation of the importance of the patient's whole social context in the treatment, as well as the etiology of his problems in living. This paper describes and evaluates some of the family assessment techniques that have been evolving as approaches to the proliferating problems now being recognized in family research and therapy.

As will become evident in this chapter, most standard existing assessment techniques are unsuitable for family assessment. An attempt will be made here to define a new category of assessment techniques appropriate to the concepts and methods of conjoint family therapy. This category is distinguished by evaluation of interaction patterns of whole and partial families as *systems*, requiring simultaneous focus on two or more family members in terms of their transactions. Designed to parallel what goes on in conjoint family therapy, this new concept of the test situation emphasizes interpersonal factors even more than intrapsychic factors—though in relation to these. The aim is to find out, not only how the individuals characteristically respond to certain kinds of stimuli, but also what types of stimuli these family members characteristically present to one another, and in response to what. Thus, the family members are viewed as participants in interaction sequences that cannot be understood in purely individual terms, because such event chains cannot occur in isolated individuals, except perhaps at an imaginary level. Though the fantasied relationships of family members may be interesting and important, their actual relationships are at least as important, and cannot be investigated merely by attempts to integrate individual family members' fantasies into a coordinated picture of the crucial family facts.

One reason why this extrapolation is impossible is that a salient feature of many families is the range and intensity of disparities that bar any integrated picture based on simple summation or comparison of individual points of view. Another factor making such extrapolation a futile exercise is the emergent quality of unpredictable uniqueness in family interaction or, for that matter, in any interpersonal interaction. Indeed, this quality constitutes the defining characteristic of conjoint family therapy, the advent of which necessitates the development of a new kind of assessment analogous to the situation existing in conjoint family therapy. It is extremely difficult to predict family interaction from results of individual testing, because the subject's responses are so largely determined by his relationship with the tester. The test results may therefore reflect the tester-subject relationship to an indeterminate degree, thus actually obscuring analysis of family interaction. It is better to obtain family interaction data in the first place.

Since the investigation of family interaction is still in the experimental stage there is no widely accepted conceptual scheme suitable for family diagnosis in a formal sense. Normative data on family interaction are still woefully unavailable. Consequently most family assessment is based on clinical experience and is descriptive of individual cases.

APPROACHES TO FAMILY ASSESSMENT

This section will describe briefly the different approaches that have been employed in the assessment of families. These may be referred to as individual, conjoint, and combined approaches.

Individual Approaches

The traditional approach to family assessment has been to test each member of the family with conventional assessment techniques. A review of the literature on marital and family testing within this framework is not within the scope of this paper. Suffice it to say that the overwhelming majority of marital and family studies have been of this kind. Some of the salient literature summarizing this work is listed in the categories below.

(1) *Reviews of family research* include those by Cottrell (1948), Dager (1956), Ehrmann (1957, 1958), Framo (1965), Handel (1965), Heer (1963), Hill (1951a, 1951b, 1955, 1958), Rabkin (1965), and Walters (1962, 1963).

(2) *Marital prediction testing* has been reviewed by Adams (1950) and Ellis (1948), who took an evaluative approach. A more methodical and theoretical approach was taken by Karlsson (1963), who focused on marital satisfaction; by Levinger (1965), who focused on marital cohesiveness and dissolution from a theoretical viewpoint; and by Locke and Wallace (1959), who focused on the methodology of shortening marital tests while retaining reliability and validity. A substantial bibliography on this topic has been compiled by Kirkpatrick (1963).

(3) *The sociology of marriage and family behavior*, though not developed only on the basis of formal tests or questionnaires, has evolved largely on the basis of conventional individual data. This literature has been extensively reviewed by Christensen (1964), Hill (1958), and Kirkpatrick (1963).

Perhaps the most promising of the individual approaches to family assessment are the Interpersonal Check-List (ICL) (La Forge & Suczek, 1955), the FIRO-B (Schutz, 1958), the Self-Disclosure Questionnaire (Jourard, 1964; Bodin, 1966*a*), and the Interpersonal Method (IPM) (Laing, Phillipson, & Lee, 1966). Each of these instruments yields individual scores, which can be compared with those of the other individual to produce a picture of interpersonal patterns that, though not actually interactional, are nonetheless meaningful.

Conjoint Approaches

The literature in the area that will now be referred to as "conjoint family testing" is of two kinds. The first and larger category is subjective in its methodology in that reliance is placed on the ratings of judges. The second category uses data that are derived from objective measures and are rigorously quantifiable. The importance of this distinction, particularly in conjoint family testing, lies in the fact that an observer is severely limited in his attempt to judge a system that has a shared history, shared traditions, subtle "shorthand" ways of communicating, and shared expectations of continued mutual dependence. The multiple levels of meaning so prevalent in the interaction of "traditioned" groups tend to be so subtle that their full significance is easily undetected, misconstrued, or at best only superficially comprehended by "outsiders."

The whole spectrum of family research is covered by the *International Bibliography of Research in Marriage and the Family: 1900-1964* (Aldous & Hill, 1967). In addition, Haley and Glick (1965) published an excellent annotated bibliography of articles on psychiatry and the family from 1960 through 1964. Both of these works confirm the impressions that only a small proportion of the work on families has dealt with family groups as interacting systems, and that a still smaller proportion of the work has been objective and quantitative.

Combined Approaches

Combined approaches are those that utilize both individual and interactional data. The basic paradigm is that of the "revealed differences" technique (Strodtbeck, 1951), which gets its name from the fact that the spouses first respond separately, as individuals, to situations calling for a *yes* or *no*, and then are asked to respond again, this time together as a couple, but only to those items on which their individual answers conflicted. Thus, the couple cannot present a completely united front since they now have to deal with their revealed differences. This has been modified to an "unrevealed differences" technique (Bodin, 1966a; Ferreira, 1963; Ferreira & Winter, 1965, 1966), in which the individuals are *not* informed of the differences in their individual protocols when embarking on the conjoint procedure. Three classes of data emerge from this two-stage procedure: (a) individual scores, (b) conjoint or interactional scores, and (c) individual-conjoint comparison or "change" scores. With appropriate modifications in administration, scoring, and interpretation, such traditional test materials as the Rorschach (Levy & Epstein, 1964) and the Wechsler-Bellevue Intelligence Scale (Bauman & Roman, 1966) have been used in the unrevealed difference paradigm.

The remainder of this chapter will focus on conjoint and combined approaches to family assessment.

SUBJECTIVE TECHNIQUES

Family Tasks

"Rigged" conflicts. Family tasks may be viewed as standard work samples. They may be novel or familiar. Novel tasks probably afford a more valid basis for assessing family response to new situations, whereas familiar tasks probably tap more habitual modes of interaction, though interaction may sometimes prove similar with both types of tasks. Experimental assessment of modes of conflict resolution is the topic of an extremely clever study by Goodrich and Boomer (1963). Their procedure, taking 10 to 20 minutes, was to present specially prepared color panels to married couples seated on opposite sides of an easel blocking their vision of each other. Each participant's panel displayed thirty colored squares of paper. These were arranged in five vertical columns, within each of which were six squares of varying shades of a single basic color. The task was presented as a test of ability to discriminate fine gradations of color. The experimenter hung a colored square for both mates to compare to their own panels so as to arrive at an agreement as to which of their own cards best matched the comparison card. Of 20 such matches, 10 were designed to be impossible, in that the couples' panels were "rigged" to be contradictory. Among the 50 couples tested a variety of reactions ensued. Some couples engaged in mutual verbal assault. Some agreed to disagree. Some took turns deciding whose answer to use. Some discussed the nature of color and attempted to reformulate their standards against visible parts of the room. And some considered the possibility that discrepancies had been built into their panels. The manner in which a couple coped with their disagreements was taken as an indication of the maturity of their relationship. This work has been extended by Ryder and Goodrich (1966), and replicated twice by Ryder (1966).

Ratings of instrumentality and emotionality. One of the few studies bridging traditional small-group research and family investigation is by Leik

(1963) on "Instrumentality and Emotionality in Family Interaction." He studied these two aspects of interaction in terms of sex-role differentiation and effects of consensus and satisfaction. Nine triadic "family" groups participated in 27 experimental discussions. One-third of the groups were homogeneous with regard to age and sex, one-third were "structured" families by virtue of having family-like age-sex composition while being composed of strangers, and one-third were actual families. Each of the 27 participants experienced the three foregoing types of groups in this order: *ad hoc*, structured, and actual families. Results showed diminution of sex-role stereotypy in family interaction and differential effects of instrumentality and emotionality in stranger groups compared with family groups. Although this experiment is exciting because of its ingenious approach to integrating the work on authentic families, artificial families, and other *ad hoc* groups, the methodology depends on subjective ratings by judges using simplified categories derived from the Bales system. The disadvantages of outsiders' subjective judgments in family research have already been discussed, and the Bales system forces into a single category each unit of behavior, though its very ambiguity may be maddening to some family members.

Another intriguing study using an abridged version of the Bales system is that of O'Rourke (1963) on "Field and Laboratory: The Decision-Making Behavior of Family Groups in Two Experimental Conditions." He investigated the premise that family interaction would vary as a function of social context. Twelve families from each of two churches participated as volunteers: half of each of these groups included a male child, the other half a female child, in the experimental triad. The children ranged from 15 to 17 years of age, and all had at least one nonparticipating sibling. Each of the 24 family triads was observed in both laboratory and home sessions. Results showed significant differences in the balance between instrumental and social-emotional behavior as a function of situational context and sex of the included child. O'Rourke concluded that families seen at home are likely to experience less disagreement among members, perform less actively but more efficiently at decision-making, and display more emotionality than they would in the laboratory. Though this experiment is important because of its start in attacking the variable of situational context for a "traditioned" group, it appears to lack a counter-balanced order needed to control for sequence effects. Thus, the effects of practice or boredom might be offered as alternative explanations. The latter, in fact, seems a reasonable basis for all three major findings cited.

Pictorial apperception tests. Although conventional TAT cards have been used in conjoint family research by Winter, Ferreira, and Olson (1965), there have been few attempts to use special TAT-type stimuli showing family scenes. One such attempt, by Howells and Lickorish (1963), is fundamentally an individual use of family stimuli inasmuch as only the disturbed child in question participates in the testing with the examiner. A genuinely conjoint application of family-type TAT stimuli was developed at the Wiltwyck School for Boys (Esopus, N.Y.) and reported by Elbert, Rosman, Minuchin, and Guerney (1964). They presented a method for the clinical study of family interaction based on a specially prepared Family Interaction Apperception Test (FIAT). The ten cards in this TAT-style test all portray family scenes that are clearly recognizable, familiar, interesting, and sufficiently concrete not to require great imagination or verbal ability on the part of the participants. Moreover, the features are drawn with ambiguous racial characteristics so as to permit members of any ethnic group to identify with the figures. This excellent feature was built into the test because the Wiltwyck sample was drawn from a population having many Negro and Puerto Rican as well as Caucasian families. The substantive findings reported for this instrument will not be presented here; it is mentioned because it is a particularly interesting instrument designed to explore the feelings of family members regarding the important topics of guidance, control, aggression, and nurturance.

Structural family interviews. The FIAT was developed for use in conjunction with the "Wiltwyck Family Task." This is a structured family interview developed by the Family Research Unit of the Wiltwyck School for Boys. It consists of eight subtasks, the last three of which are especially imaginative and meaningful in their design. The first five subtasks are as follows: (*a*) agreeing on a meal everyone would enjoy; (*b*) discussing "who's the most bossy, the biggest troublemaker, the one who gets away with murder, the one who gets away with most, the biggest cry baby"; (*c*) discussing the origin, process, and outcome of a remembered argument at home; (*d*) agreeing on a mutually satisfactory way to spend a hypothetical ten-dollar gift; and (*e*) having each member tell what things every other member does that please him most and make him feel good, and also what things each one does that make him unhappy or mad. The remaining three tasks are notable for their realism. The first of these is: (*f*) building something together—Creative Playthings asymmetric construction A812—which the family reassembles after each member starts with an equal number of pieces. (Up until this point the family has been receiving its instructions from a tape recorder set up by the psychologist before he retired to the other side of the one-way mirror.) At this point the psychologist rejoins the family, makes a few general comments about the last subtask and then initiates the remaining subtasks, as follows: (*g*) He leaves the room again after offering three gifts to the family, from which they can select only one. The choice of gifts offered to the family includes a group game, an individual game, and an age- or sex-specific game tailored to the structure of the family at hand. The gifts range in price from $1.00 to $1.50. (*h*) Interaction regarding nurturance is assessed by offering refreshments to the family in such a way as to provide one cupcake more and one coke and cup less than the number of family members present. The last two subtasks have the additional virtue of creating situations with authentic rather than hypothetical outcomes, so that the family must live with its choices. The potential importance of this innovation is suggested by an experiment by Gallo, reported by Gallo and McClintock (1965). In his experiment a two-person, mixed-motive game resembling "prisoner's dilemma" was played for real and imaginary payoffs of $16.00 per participant. Players for imaginary money *lost* an average of $38.80 per pair over the 20 trials, whereas players for real money *won* an average of $9.92 per pair. Only 2 of the 16 pairs playing for imaginary money showed a profit, while 14 of the 16 pairs playing for real money came out ahead. One implication of this work is that game behavior cannot be generalized to the players' actual life situations unless they are intensely motivated in the game by the announced availability of some award having authentic value for them. The incorporation of this feature to the final parts of the Wiltwyck Family Task is an impressive and promising innovation.

The structured family interview format developed at the Wiltwyck School is one of several in use at this time. Another is being developed at the U.C.L.A. Department of Psychology by Love, Rodnick, and Kaswan (Lenore Love, 1966: personal communication). Their interview is designed to be studied with the aid of video-tape equipment. These interviews have the potential for objective quantification.

Another structured family interview, probably the one in widest use today, was conceived by Bateson, Haley, and Weakland in 1957 at the Palo Alto Veterans Administration Hospital. Its present form was evolved under the direction of Watzlawick, at the Mental Research Institute (MRI) in Palo Alto, with the collaboration of Jackson.

Unlike the Wiltwyck Family Test, the MRI Structured Family Interview is administered, not by a tape recorder, but by an interviewer who observes parts of the proceedings from another room. The interview is designed to give the interviewer and any observers a wealth of clinically valuable impressions in a space of about an hour. Furthermore, it is designed to interest the family participants in the kinds of mutual exploration it demands, so as to begin engaging them in the tasks of therapy from the outset. Thus, this assessment procedure serves also as a catalyst in the initial stage of therapy and, in fact, is itself often felt to be therapeutic by all concerned. Clinicians who have both given and observed this interview find they can get more out of it when they are freed from the requirements of participation. For this reason, at least within the context of the training of family therapists at MRI, another clinician generally gives the Structured Family Interview while the therapist observes through the one-way mirror. The procedure ends with the interviewer introducing the therapist, who then has a brief discussion with the family about the interview. All five parts of the MRI Structured Family Interview have been vividly presented by Watzlawick (1966).

Numerous variations of the MRI Structured Family Interview have been tried over the past six years in the family therapy training courses at the Mental Research Institute. Some of these variations—introduced by Virginia Satir (1966)—are mentioned briefly below.

In the decision-making part of the interview ("Plan something together"), a series of overlapping stages has been used, with the following family members present at each of these junctures: (a) all, (b) all except father, (c) all except mother, (d) children only, (e) mother and daughter(s), (f) mother and son(s), (g) father and son(s), (h) father and daughter(s), and finally (i) husband and wife. This step-wise sequence permits comparison of all the foregoing combinations, a process akin to the disentangling of relationships that Virginia Satir alludes to as having the complexity of a "can of worms." At the cost of considerably lengthening the interview, this variation sometimes reveals striking contrasts as a function of (sub)group composition. For example, one family's members showed great animation and enthusiastic interaction at all steps except the final one, involving only the marital pair. Their sudden switch to a diametrically opposite emotional climate of interaction could scarcely be attributed to sheer fatigue, particularly in the light of their earlier discussion of how they got together; father described it as, "Just chance, it took months to recognize it; it just evolved," to which mother replied, "It was a *blind* [italics mine] date; it never would have happened except that I was . . . . ready to get married." With these bits of information it is reasonable to surmise that the parents rely on their children to infuse an otherwise missing bit of *joie de vivre*.

Another variation is the addition of a final section on Similarity and Differentness. With the whole family together, father and mother are asked, in turn, "Which one of your children do you think is most like you?" and also, "Which one do you think is most like your wife (husband)?" Each child is then asked, "Which one of your parents do you think you are most like?" Next, each child is asked these stereotype-disrupting questions: "You said you were most like your mother (father). How are you like your father (mother)? How are you *unlike* your mother (father)?" Finally each mate is asked, "How are you like your spouse? How are you different from your spouse?" Even without detailed presentation, it is obvious that such questions provide a basis for summarizing data in an "identification matrix" with potential utility for both research and clinical application.

In one instance a delinquent daughter, whose younger sister had the same first name as her mother, made clear dis-identification with her mother by stating first that she was most like her father, and then that the way she was like her mother was that their little fingers were similar.

As with other conjoint testing procedures, a post-test period of mutual feedback is helpful. The interviewer can often extend his own understanding of the family—as well as theirs—by commenting on some of the interactions, telling them some of his impressions or inferences, and trying to fit these together with any different explanations offered by members of the family.

Family Strengths Inventory

The history of research on individual dynamics is already repeating itself in work with families; there is far more attention to family problems and pathology than to family strengths or factors favoring what might be termed "eufunctioning" (good functioning). Only a few books focusing on approaches to this area have been published, such as *Family Worlds* by Hess and Handel (1959), and *Success in Family Living* by Mudd, Mitchell, and Taubin (1965). The family strength literature has been reviewed by Gabler (1963) and reported by Gabler and Otto (1964). Otto developed family strength categories and incorporated these in the "Otto Family Strength Survey" (1962), a pencil-and-paper form to facilitate taking inventory in the following 15 areas: (1) "strength" through family physical and other resources"; (2) "family traditions"; (3) "family participation in community, local, and national issues"; (4) "fostering curiosity and interest"; (5) "family recreation and leisure time"; (6) "meeting family emotional needs"; (7) "building friendships and relationships"; (8) "providing an environment of honesty and integrity"; (9) "child-rearing practices and discipline"; (10) "spiritual life"; (11) "developing creativity"; (12) "relationships with relatives"; (13) "giving encouragement"; (14) "family management"; and (15) "other family strengths." For each of these areas about half a dozen subcategories are specified. These are presented in a format permitting the family to indicate their consensual claim regarding the extent to which they perceive each strength within their own family. The four categories—none, little, some, and much—are provided, not only beside the standard items, but also beside each of several lines left blank for writing in additional strengths in every area covered.

Despite the unclear measurement properties of the Otto Family Strength Survey, it may prove useful as an assessment instrument in research and therapeutic work with families. An interesting aspect of this instrument is suggested by its prefatory statement: "The Survey is designed to help you assess the range of strengths to be found in your family with the recognition that *the process of gaining a better understanding of these strengths can contribute to family strength*" (Otto, 1962).

One implication for the utilization of the Otto Family Strength Survey lies in Otto's observation that "the average healthy individual has considerable difficulty listing his personal strengths" (1964). Therapeutic benefits may be derived from overcoming, not only the ordinary rationalization that listing one's strengths is immodest, but also the resistance to claiming strengths that would thenceforth be standards to be met.

Family Art

Marbles test. One of the cleverest and most intriguing developments in conjoint family testing was originated in Argentina and reported by Usandivaras, Grimson, Hammond, Issaharoff, and Romanos (1967). It is called simply the Marbles Test, since it requires a set of marbles and a board on which to set them.

Though the test can be given by one person, it is easier to have two people conducting it: one to administer the test and one to record the details of its results. The test begins with the family members standing around a table on which there are opaque bags, each containing 20 marbles of one color. No two bags contain the same color, and there are just enough bags for each family member to choose one, which they do without knowing the identifying color of the set of marbles within it.

The board is square and has an arbitrary number of holes in which to place the marbles. The number of holes suggested for a family of three is 225 (15 rows × 15 columns); for a couple, 144 (12 × 12); and for a family of four or five members, 400 (20 × 20). The participants are asked only to put the marbles in the holes to make something, working together with the others. These vague instructions permit myriad possibilities for forming different patterns, either all together (simultaneously), or with some rotation of turns. Yet the resulting complexities can be quantified and expressed in rigorously defined terms such as the following: (*a*) *indices of contact* of each color with the same color, with each other color, with the conjunctions of other colors, and with vacant spaces; (*b*) distance from each color's *center of gravity* to the over-all center of gravity and to the center of gravity of every other color; (*c*) each color's *area and perimeter*; (*d*) each color's *permeability*—i.e., the *number* of unfilled holes within its perimeter; and (*e*) each color's *porosity*—i.e., the *proportion* of vacant holes within a given color's perimeter (porosity = permeability/area).

Results can be recorded by an observer who colors (or codes) the circles on a pre-printed chart representing the board. Giving three successive trials per family provides a basis for sequential comparisons and allows changes to be described. The analyses fall into three main categories, the first of which is the most promising so far: (1) "disposition"—i.e., whether the marbles are arranged so as to be contacting, noncontacting, or "segmented"; (2) "manner"—i.e., whether the marbles are distributed in lines, in compact units, or in a scattered manner; and (3) "form"—i.e., regularity or irregularity of the "manners" (Wilbur Grimson, 1966: personal communication). In addition, observations may be made regarding family communication and rule-making. Finally, the charts made by the observer may be explained to the family members, who can be asked to describe what they were thinking and feeling during the test and what the various charts suggest to them.

Additional aspects of the analysis of the Marbles Test include the following: (*a*) classifying the configuration as a geometric figure or as non-representational, (*b*) describing the macro-sequence across the series of three trials, and (*c*) describing the micro-sequence within each trial—a demanding task, which the Argentinian team has planned to render practical by developing an automated electronic recording device.

Using a square of composition pegboard, the author tried the Marbles Test with several families and couples. Even without the formal mathematical treatment of results, some interesting aspects of interaction became apparent. For example, one couple consisted of a husband still pursuing studies and a wife who had recently completed some grueling overseas service and was embarking on a new long-term professional training commitment likely to entail many difficulties. In the Marbles Test she started by placing her first marble in one corner and working her way hole-by-hole straight up the diagonal to the opposite corner. Since her goal was obvious almost as soon as they began the test, it would have been easy for her husband to block her steady progress had he wished to do so. Instead, he staked his claims around her projected "moves," always keeping out of her way. This sequence suggested an agreement to cooperate mainly by not interfering with each other's going his separate way. This pattern was interesting, to say the least, particularly in the light of earlier hints of the wife's single-mindedness, as well as her husband's subsequent compliance with her request to have him do his last year of study alone while she moved to another city to begin her own professional studies. Though each spouse had been in individual therapy with a different therapist, they had never tried conjoint marital therapy. Their pattern of separateness was fully manifested a year later by an uncontested divorce action.

The Marbles Test seems to offer a clinically meaningful way of obtaining information about family interaction. The method has the virtues of being a highly palatable test, since it seems almost like a game; of being rapid; and of combining the rigor of mathematical conceptualization and formal quantitative treatment with the clinical "feel" of new projective techniques, such as conjoint painting.

Drawing. A particularly interesting development is the use of drawing to aid in family assessment while engaging the family members in the tasks of family therapy on a nonintellectualized plane. Kwiatkowska (1967) described a promising six-step procedure as follows: (1) individual free drawings ("Draw whatever comes to mind"), (2) individual drawings of the whole family, (3) abstract drawings of the whole family (like step 2 above, but without human figures), (4) individual free scribbles, (5) a joint scribble, and (6) another set of individual free drawings. The abstract family picture often taps deeper emotional meanings than the family picture, which immediately precedes it, since the nonrepresentational "set" helps break free from sheer literal portrayal. The free scribbles often reveal individual differences in spontaneity, as well as attitudes about where others in the family stand in this respect. Freer members may comment about the hesitation of stiffer members to let their hair down. The joint scribble often elicits comments revealing awkwardness or uncertainty about how to coordinate a joint effort. Some couples discuss whether to use one pen or two, whether to scribble independently or to make a single integrated scribble, whether to take turns or work simultaneously. The comments and how they are made provide material for assessment and therapy just as valuable as, if not more valuable than, the joint scribble itself.

OBJECTIVE TECHNIQUES

Communication

Two investigations relevant to the concept of family homeostasis were conducted by Haley (1962, 1964). His first work in this area concerned coalition flexibility in family triads deprived of ordinary verbal communication. He used a device permitting any pair of family members to form an alliance by simultaneously pressing their coalition buttons. In one part of his experiment he permitted the families to make their own plan of coalition control. Fifteen of 30 schizophrenic families (families with a schizophrenic member) failed to carry out their own plan to have a certain member win by accumulating the greatest time spent in coalition, whereas only 2 of 30 normal families failed. This difference is significant at the .001 level. Thus, coalition flexibility may be a sensitive indicator of strained family homeostasis.

In his other research related to family homeostasis, Haley (1964) studied speech sequences (who follows whom) in family triads. To facilitate accurate data collection, he used an automatic counting machine activated by throat microphones worn by each of the three participating family members. The instrument kept a running tally of all six dyadic speech sequence possibilities: (1) father followed by mother, (2) mother followed by father, (3) father followed by child, (4) child followed by father, (5) mother followed by child, and (6) child followed by mother. Haley found the speech sequences in 40 normal family triads were more random than those in

40 abnormal families ($p < .001$). In the normal group the mother-child interchange was most frequent; in the abnormal group the mother-father interchange was most frequent. Furthermore, the percentage of speeches contributed by each individual in the normal group differed significantly ($p < .001$) from corresponding percentages in the abnormal group, and a more detailed breakdown of the data demonstrated that the difference could not be attributed to the "identified patient." These lines of evidence provide confirmation for one of Haley's hypotheses, which he stated as follows:

> Organization means limitation, and the more pathological the more limited. Therefore on this frequency count the more normal families will use more of the possible sequences more often, and the disturbed families use fewer of the possibilities and use some of them more often than others. Therefore, on a scale of deviation from random behavior, the normals will tend toward randomness and the disturbed will tend away from randomness [p. 51].

Such constriction may be viewed as endogenous constraint on family spontaneity. Mutually engendered rigidity of this sort may be a symptomatic expression of a last-ditch struggle to preserve a marginally stable family equilibrium in the face of stresses already taxing available group-maintenance resources to the limit of homeostatic tolerance.

A subsequent study by Haley (in press) compared speech sequences of normal and abnormal families with two children present and found no evidence of greater flexibility in the normal families. The discrepant findings pose questions concerning the differences in group processes operating in tetrads in contrast to triads. Implications for the study of subgroups within the family and for interaction in one-child versus two-child families need exploration.

Game Applications

Game theory approaches to family assessment have received relatively little attention, despite the extensive work in this area using *ad hoc* pairs or groups. Coalition formation and flexibility in problem, normal, and "synthetic" family triads were studied by Bodin (1966*a*), using a modified parchesi board similar to that employed by Vinacke and Arkoff (1957). A three-person negotiable game yielded a record of bargaining and coalition behavior under three patterns of relative power allocation: all-equal (1-1-1), one stronger (3-2-2), and one all-powerful (3-1-1). Players rotated power positions in each of three eight-game rounds, the last one designed to test family flexibility under instructions to shift from previous outcome tendencies. Details of game play were combined to form indices of *accommodative* versus *exploitative* strategy, which, however, did not prove consistently sensitive to these three types of triad distinctions, though there were significant differences among family types with regard to some details of game-playing. Each family's cumulative scoring hierarchy on the game was compared with that family's overall influence hierarchy on the family questionnaire, taken jointly after individual administration. The parents in each type of family allowed their son more power in the situation defined as a game. This finding calls into question the assumption that games can be used to assess the *whole* spectrum of family interaction, but the marital dyad might well be studied in game situations with far less chance of being influenced by the artificiality of the situation. Findings are briefly discussed later in this chapter.

An experimental study of marital discord and decision-making utilizing a game involving road choices in a simulated driving situation was reported by Ravich, Deutsch, and Brown (1966). Each of 38 marital pairs with at least one member in therapy was tested conjointly but at separate consoles. Each console displayed information on the relative position of two toy trucks, each controlled only from its own console. A map given to each player showed different starting points and destinations, and various routes, the shortest of which entailed a common stretch of one-way road passable by only one truck at a time. Couples played for imaginary monetary rewards, determined individually by each player's elapsed driving time. Players were told by taped instructions that they could take as much time as they wanted for discussions between trips. An unseen experimenter monitored the details of play over the course of each couple's 20 trials, noting how decisions were arrived at and communicated, how losses and rewards were shared, which routes were chosen, how many head-on confrontations developed and who backed out first, and how many times each player shut his partner out of the one-lane section by utilizing a special remote-controlled roadblock.

Cooperative, competitive, and individualistic styles of play were further classified into five distinct categories. The results were stated as follows:

(1) *Sharing.* Sixteen of the 38 couples (42%) used a strategy whereby they alternately went through the one-lane section of the main route first while the other partner waited. This required effective communication, essential agreement, and resulted in a maximization of profits and equal sharing in earnings.

(2) *Dominating and submitting.* Five couples (13%) played the game in such a way that one partner consistently came out at least 20 cents ahead of the other. This strategy may or may not involve communication.

(3) *Inconsistent.* Ten couples (26%) inconsistently utilized a combination of the first two strategies described above. At times these couples took the one-lane road alternately and shared the profits, while during other sequences they did not do so. These couples had intermittent difficulty in communication, and could not reach a stable agreement that they could carry out in a consistent fashion.

(4) *Intensely competitive.* Three couples (7%) played the game in an intensely competitive way, refusing to communicate information to each other, unwilling to back down when in the head-on position on the one-lane section, and using the gates to block one another while taking the alternate route in order to reach the destination before the other partner. These couples were willing to sustain

very substantial losses, individually and as a pair, in order to come out ahead.

(5) *Dysjunctive.* Four couples (10%) played the game in an entirely asymmetrical manner, in the sense that they perceived and played two entirely different games having no apparent relationship to each other [Ravich, Deutsch, and Brown, 1966, pp. 93-94].

The investigators were encouraged by their impression that the game elicited interaction styles that paralleled those inferred from clinical interviews with the families.

Conflict Resolution

One of the most important recent developments in family theory is the concept of family homeostasis (Jackson, 1959). Though there is a wealth of clinical observation that makes sense when interpreted in this framework, there is a dearth of relevant research. One of the few exceptions is Verwey's (1962) investigation of the relationship of adaptability to interactional contingency and interpersonal prediction. She presented two marital problems for discussion by each of 27 married couples and 27 cross-sex pairs of strangers. These participating pairs were divided into control groups with free interaction, and experimental groups with "rigged" interaction. In order to introduce the experimental variable of "asymmetrical contingency," one member of each experimental pair was privately instructed to be disagreeable during the ensuing discussion, which was observed and tape-recorded. The ratio of adaptive acts to total acts was taken as the measure of adaptability used in the comparisons: (*a*) married vs. stranger pairs, (*b*) experimental vs. free-interaction control groups, (*c*) males vs. females, and (*d*) problem one vs. problem two.

Results showed the married pairs were less adaptable in the face of disagreeableness than were the pairs of strangers. Moreover, regardless of sex or marital status, disagreeableness on the part of either member was generally reciprocated by the other, a finding in line with Jackson's suggestion that families commonly operate as though guided by a rule of *quid pro quo* (1965). Verwey concluded that interaction is less adaptable among married pairs than among paired strangers and that adaptability is a function of the relationship between individuals—not simply of individuals per se. The greater marital inflexibility may result from the presence of pre-experiment norms regarding the level of agreeableness to be expected from one's mate, so that the failure to conform to such expectations is met with attempts to re-enforce the norms by stubbornly holding out for the anticipated acquiescence.

Revealed differences technique. One of the earliest conjoint approaches to investigating marital interaction was Strodtbeck's "revealed differences" technique, which he defined as follows: "The essence of the revealed differences technique here described consists of: (*a*) requesting subjects who have shared experiences to make individual evaluations of them; and then (*b*) requesting the subjects to reconcile any differences in interpretations which may have occurred" (1951). By presenting problems requiring commitment to one of only two possible alternatives, Strodtbeck maximized personal involvement, precluded any possibility of compromise on any given question, and thus provided a simple way to determine who had "won" a particular decision. He found that the allocation of such influence within the marriage was related both to the degree of participation in the marital situation studied and to the power distribution in the larger cultural context.

The revealed differences technique was extended to the study of coalitions within family triads in a later investigation by Strodtbeck (1954). This work was oriented toward theoretical questions that are less important in this context than the fact that his method involved extending a quantifiable interaction measurement technique to three-person families studied in the home.

Unrevealed differences technique. A modification of Strodtbeck's revealed differences technique was devised by Ferreira (1963), who investigated individual and conjoint decisions of 25 normal and 25 pathologic family triads. The main feature of Ferreira's procedure was that the experimenter did not reveal to the families the specific instances in which they disagreed. This nonintervention permitted the family members to remain blissfully (or painfully) unaware of each other's individual choices if they chose not to come out in the open with clear-cut communication of their personal preferences. An additional feature introduced by Ferreira was the availability of more than two alternatives. This allowed the families to make "chaotic" choices in the conjoint phase of the decision-making task by selecting, as a family, some alternative not chosen by any of them as individuals in their earlier independent choices. More specifically, Ferreira's questionnaire contained 16 relatively "neutral" items with three alternatives apiece, to which the family members assigned preference rankings, first individually and independently, and then all together as a family. Four conjoint decision types were distinguished: (1) *unanimous*, (2) *majority*, (3) *dictatorial*—"strong" dictatorial decisions adopting the choice of one member over the choice agreed on by the other two members, and "forced" dictatorial decisions adopting the choice of one member when no two individuals agreed initially—and (4) *chaotic*.

Results supported the hypothesis that normal families would differ from pathologic families in their decision-making process. More explicitly, the normal families differed significantly from the abnormal families in showing a higher degree of "spontaneous agreement" in initial individual choices and in showing greater parent than child influence in deciding what *not* to do, and a lower incidence of "chaotic" decisions. In addition, the total group of 50 families showed a higher degree of "spontaneous agreement" than the chance expectation, and a lower degree of influence by the child than by either parent. Moreover, a higher rate of successful (decision-winning) coalitions involved child and same-sex parent than child and opposite-sex parent—though this sex-related finding was obtained only in normal families.

In another study using "neutral" items to investigate family interaction in family decision-making, Ferreira and Winter (1965) relied on seven sets of questions, expanding the item format of each by offering 10 alternatives per situation. The two-phase task was similar to the one already presented except in calling for the family members to rank only their first three choices and requiring undifferentiated X marks for their last three choices with the other four choices left blank.

In addition to the variable of "spontaneous agreement" studied in the foregoing investigation, conjoint "decision-time" was analyzed as was "choice-fulfillment"—i.e., the number of instances in which each individual's preferred choices were subsequently chosen in the family's conjoint decisions.

The results fully confirmed 9 of the 18 hypotheses tested and partially confirmed 2 more. Two are singled out for presentation here because of the fact that they received full confirmation in an independent investigation carried out by Bodin (1966b), who used a questionnaire differing in form as well as content. Perhaps there is reason to take encouragement from the fact that the two propositions investigated in both studies were supported. These findings—which now appear well established—are as follows: (1) spontaneous agreement in family triads of parents and child exceeds chance expectation, and (2) spontaneous agreement is higher in normal than in abnormal families. It should be further noted that Ferreira's (1963) original unrevealed differences study produced these same two findings.

Because of its inclusion of both actual and "synthetic" or *ad hoc* family triads, Bodin's (1966a) investigation links clinical and social psychological concepts. This study arose from a recognition that traditional small-group research has rarely dealt with actual families, and that family experimentation has barely begun to capitalize on the techniques of traditional small-group research. To help bridge this gap, a set of samples was selected so as to include both *ad hoc* triads of strangers and actual family triads. Moreover, the methods were drawn both from traditional small-group research and from recent family experimentation.

The 36 families investigated were of three types: (1) father, mother, and delinquent son; (2) father, mother, and nondelinquent son; and (3) father, mother, and nondelinquent son, but each from a different family and all total strangers to one another prior to the experiment. These three triad types were called, respectively, *problem, normal,* and *synthetic,* family triads. In all instances the son was a teenager from an intact family in which neither a parent nor any sibling was a member of any of the mental health professions. The participants were closely matched on a variety of potentially relevant biographical details.

The procedure included two main tasks, the first drawn from traditional small-group research and the second adapted from recent family research. The first task was the coalition game, described above in the section on game applications. The second task is called a Family Agreement Measure (FAM). It is a two-stage paper-and-pencil questionnaire combining elements of an "unrevealed differences" task with the format of a multiple-choice sentence completion test, modified to require ranking all the alternative completions. The content of the family questionnaire was adapted from recent family research and included two questions, with five alternatives apiece, on each of the following six areas of common family concern: (1) *strengths,* (2) *problems,* (3) *authority,* (4) *communication,* (5) *defensiveness,* and

(6) *discipline*. Participants ranked all 60 items (12 paired sentence stems, each with five completions), first individually—in separate rooms—and then as a family group, together. For illustration, 3 of the 12 groups of items are presented below:

WHO IS IN CHARGE IN THIS FAMILY?

_____ a. Whoever cares most about a particular issue or decision.

_____ b. No one person: we have freedom in our family to make individual decisions.

_____ c. Everyone: we all agree on important decisions.

_____ d. There's confusion: everyone tries to take charge, but no one really can.

_____ e. It depends on the situation: we're flexible in some, but follow "set" rules in others.

COMMUNICATION IN OUR FAMILY WOULD BE BETTER IF WE CUT DOWN ON:

_____ a. Changing the subject, indirectness, and evasion.

_____ b. Confusing present disputes by dragging in old issues and switching from one meaning to another.

_____ c. Saying something hostile or hurtful, but denying it was meant that way.

_____ d. Pretending to be joking about serious matters; teasing that isn't funny.

_____ e. Interrupting or rephrasing, to tell others what they "really" mean.

DISCIPLINE WOULD BE BETTER IN OUR FAMILY IF:

_____ a. Mother and Father imposed the same standards, instead of letting child(ren) see they disagree.

_____ b. Child(ren) wouldn't pit Mother and Father against each other by asking for something from one parent after the other has already said "no."

_____ c. Mother and Father wouldn't compete for child(ren)'s love by being "soft" or spoiling him.

_____ d. Mother and Father would give more trust and freedom when it has been earned.

_____ e. Mother and Father would give less trust and freedom when it has been abused.

Following each task, the participants ranked one another on a hierarchy to indicate each one's perceptions of who had won most and least game points or questionnaire decisions.

The major hypotheses were: (*a*) the *authenticity hypothesis*, predicting differences between synthetic families and authentic families, and (*b*) the *normality hypothesis*, predicting differences between problem and normal families.

Though the results showed significant differences among the family types studied with regard to details of play in the coalition game described above, there were no significant overall differences in accommodative versus exploitative strategy. Thus, the game data failed to support the hypotheses, except in certain respects, e.g., that the normal families, in comparison with the problem families, showed: (a) less tendency to "go it alone," (b) more tendency to "share and share alike," and (c) more tendency for fathers to show benevolence by forming coalitions even when all-powerful.

The FAM results, however, conclusively supported both hypotheses. Findings supporting the authenticity hypothesis included: (a) consistently higher overall and parental agreement in real than in artificial families, (b) greater maternal compromise in synthetic than in normal families, and (c) more efficient joint decision-making in actual than in artificial families. Findings supporting the normality hypothesis include: (a) greater father-son agreement in normal than in problem families, (b) greater maternal influence in normal than in problem families, and (c) more perceptual distortion by mothers—overrating their husbands and underrating themselves—in normal than in problem families.

In sum, though the three family types studied differed little in overall game strategy, they produced three distinctive scoring patterns on the FAM. There is evidence, then, that task relevance is important in determining behavioral differences among family types. In this case, the FAM appeared to be superior to the game. Additional distinctions on the FAM among family types rest on differences in individual roles (mothers showing the most distinctive behavior), and also in family rules (synthetic families functioning least efficiently, probably because they lost time developing interaction norms akin to those already evolved by real families).

On the basis of the preceding findings, the FAM appears potentially useful in clinical practice as well as research. It may be used therapeutically by employing the assessment data for further family discussion. Test behavior is particularly revealing in the FAM. For example, one man took the test home to his wife while on weekend hospital pass, having gone through the revised instructions with the investigator, who was taking this man and his wife into an ongoing group for couples therapy. When the test was returned, it showed a total disagreement score of only 8. Since the overall mean in this study was about 80 with a standard deviation of about 13, the obtained score was suspect, to say the least. When asked to reconstruct exactly how he and his wife took the test, the man asserted that his wife had been quite independent, just as he had been, though he "borrowed" her completed answer page because he "had trouble seeing the small print." As expected, he proved very passive in therapy, showing no annoyance at his wife for keeping small secrets that other group members saw as his vital concerns. On the other hand, he knew he and his wife were not supposed to compare answers until their joint decision-making sessions, which fact suggests that his departure from the instructions had an aggressive component. Similarly, he departed from his wife's instructions to take a more active interest in his family. He kept her fuming that his passivity made her do everything. He was extremely angry that the therapist chose to focus on the meaning of their test behavior rather than on the test scores.

Two couples in therapy found it impossible, they said, to agree even about when or whether to sit down together for the joint phase of the FAM. A third couple in therapy with this investigator proved quite willing and even eager to talk about particular items on which they knew they disagreed; but they were reluctant to discuss the fact that the *way* they knew they disagreed was through silent individual comparison of the two papers rather than through free-and-easy joint discussion. A recurrent theme in their therapy was the husband's complaint that there was no activity whatever that he could suggest to his wife and have her agree to do *with* him. He complained with great bitterness that, after refusing to participate with him, she makes clear her dislike for him by doing the same activities alone.

Another couple completed the questionnaire without difficulty and expressed delight to find their agreement score above the average for actual families. They made rapid strides in therapy and reported substantial improvements in their relationship, which seemed mirrored in their therapy behavior, such as having some appropriate laughs at themselves.

The unrevealed differences technique provides bases for operationally defining certain theoretical constructs, such as family "symmetry" and "efficiency," individual dissatisfaction, couple disagreement, absolute and relative compromise behavior, and absolute and relative variability of each person's accommodative behavior. These concepts, along with a computer program for converting FAM raw data into such indices, are further discussed in Bodin (1966*b*).

DIFFICULTIES IN CONJOINT FAMILY ASSESSMENT

The paucity of studies on conjoint family assessment that are both objective and quantitative reflects several impediments to such investigations. Understanding these barriers may help in hurdling them or even lowering them. One such block is the feeling expressed in the following lines from the poem, "On Family Therapy": "Why has family therapy been/avoided/in the past?/Remember it's man's/first institution/ . . . It's too damn close/to home! [Brodey, 1963, p. 287]."

Another obstacle to conjoint family research lies in the irrelevant transitional political struggles as one *Zeitgeist* shades into another. Thus, there is a certain amount of friction between spokesmen advocating adherence to the traditional intrapsychic focus and those promulgating a transition to an interactional focus. As with most such power struggles, much energy is expended in contention with the opposition, regardless of whether this is the best way to illuminate the issues. Thus, enthusiasts for both the intra- and interpersonal points of view sometimes abandon their scientific objectivity and engage in polemics about which of their special vocabularies is the "right" one to reflect "reality" accurately. Those who prefer to focus on the family are still handicapped in such disputes by the fact that there are not yet very many terms that are specifically suited to describing what goes on *between* individuals in a social system as distinct from what goes on *within* individuals in isolation.

Perhaps it would be well if differing theorists and practitioners would bear in mind this thought from Bronowski's Phi Beta Kappa–Sigma Xi lecture, "The Logic of Mind," presented to the American Association for the Advancement of Science: "And finally, Tarski's theorem demonstrates, I think conclusively, that there cannot be a universal description of nature in a single, closed, consistent language [1966]."

In order to discuss the remaining difficulties, it is necessary to distinguish three levels of family research: Level I involves comparisons of authentic families with "*ad hoc* families" composed of strangers (though in some future research *ad hoc* families might more appropriately be synthesized from other families whose members do actually know one another and have shared histories and traditions). Level II research involves comparisons of normal vs. problem families. And Level III involves comparisons of families having different types of problems. We can now appreciate a third difficulty in doing family research. The problem, most relevant at Level I, is inherent in the fact that questionnaire or discussion items with family relevance may have different task significance for actual vs. synthetic families. The traditional sociological significance assigned to the distinction between *instrumental* or *task* orientation on the one hand and *emotional* orientation on the other cannot be accepted with any confidence in family research. The dichotomous boundary is blurred by the coincidence that the mother's emotional orientation occurs within a context defining her *instrumental* role as the maintenance of *emotional* harmony.

A fourth pitfall in family research, mainly at Level II, lurks in the inescapably different demand characteristics of the conjoint family assessment situation for families seeking help and for families singled out to exemplify some kind of "normality" or "pathology." The former have reason to reveal as well as conceal what they conceive to be their difficulties. The latter two may show off their normality or focus on denying blame, respectively, since the test situation for normal families implies approval, whereas for problem families it contains a covert accusation, usually about the parents.

PROSPECTS FOR CONJOINT FAMILY ASSESSMENT

The gap between clinical and social psychology needs more bridges, and conjoint family assessment can help support such spans. Additional support must be provided through such comparisons of established and *ad hoc* nonfamily groups as the one recently reported by Hall and Williams (1966), a comparison of decision-making performances. The eventual value of conjoint family research will depend on its theoretical implications and practical applications. These may include the following: (*a*) the extent to which these studies facilitate a two-way flow of traffic between family research and traditional small-group research; (*b*) the heuristic harvest from the questions of technique and theory that such research answers and raises; and (*c*) its utility in helping set the stage for potentially significant programs, such as constructing an objective and quantifiable family typology with enough generality, validity, depth, and detail to contribute some of the specificity of science to the maturing art of family diagnosis and therapy.

If these benefits are soon to be reaped, then without ignoring the traditional field of personality, with its focus on the individual, psychological techniques must now be developed and applied to investigate the emergent qualities of systems of interacting individuals. To generalize usefully to such functioning systems as those seen in conjoint family therapy, systematic data must be gathered in the closely analogous situation of conjoint family assessment.

CHAPTER XIII

The assessment of anxiety:
A survey of available techniques

Paul McReynolds

Anxiety is one of the central constructs in modern psychology. It appears as an important variable in the areas of learning, motivation, personality, and psychopathology. Further, the concept of anxiety plays a major role in theoretical formulations as otherwise diverse as those of Freud, Goldstein, Spence, Rogers, Wolpe, Horney, and May. If anxiety is to serve adequately as an experimental variable, however, it is necessary that satisfactory techniques be available for its identification and measurement; otherwise, it amounts to little more than a convenient literary expression. The purpose of this chapter is to survey the psychometric and behavioral techniques constructed for the assessment of anxiety, with particular emphasis upon the more recently developed instruments.[1]

The psychological tests and procedures available for measuring anxiety are, we will find, numerous and heterogeneous, with many—perhaps most—of them still in an experimental stage. However, for several of them, such as the Manifest Anxiety Scale (MAS) and the IPAT Anxiety Scale, the literature is enormous. Accordingly, the present review, which emphasizes breadth of coverage, is necessarily highly selective with respect to given tests. (For other treatments of anxiety assessment see Byrne, 1966; Cattell & Scheier, 1961; Krause, 1961; Lazarus, 1966; Levitt, 1967; Martin, 1961; Martin & Sroufe, in press; Sarason, 1960.)

---

[1] Because of space limitations, physiological approaches to anxiety assessment will not be covered here. This area has recently been reviewed elsewhere by the writer (McReynolds, 1967a) and by Martin and Sroufe (in press). It may be noted, however, that physiological techniques appear to be most useful in the assessment of induced anxiety—i.e., increments in anxiety brought about by experimental procedures or environmental events—and least helpful in assaying individuals' characteristic levels of anxiety.

THE CONCEPT OF ANXIETY

Any attempt to assess anxiety presupposes some systematic understanding of what is meant by the term, i.e., of what it is that one is trying to measure. A brief treatment of the concept of anxiety is therefore necessary at the outset. (For other discussions of this topic see Aiken, 1962; Cattell & Scheier, 1961; Lazarus, 1966; Levitt, 1967; May, 1950; McReynolds, 1956, 1960; Ruebush, 1963.) The most common meaning of "anxiety" is that of a felt affect, a dysphoric mental state. Another common usage of "anxiety" is as a motivating condition. This meaning is explicit in certain drive theories (e.g., Brown, 1961). Though this interpretation can be stated in phenomenal terms—as when a person says "I am anxious to see that movie"—it is perhaps most usefully conceptualized as an intervening variable (Lazarus, 1966). Still another meaning of "anxiety" is in terms of overt, public behaviors (McReynolds, 1965a); thus a patient may be said to be anxious when, and only when, he exhibits certain observable movements—tremors, pacing the floor, sighing, and so on. For practical purposes these responses become a *definition* of anxiety. Similarly, anxiety is sometimes identified and, in effect, defined in terms of certain physiological variables—rapid pulse, increased skin conductance, and the like.

Most usages of "anxiety" appear to be derived largely from the phenomenal or mental-state conception of anxiety as an unpleasant felt affect. Even definitions in terms of overt or autonomic responses frequently assume that such responses reflect an inner, unpleasant affect. The mental-state conception of anxiety, however, can hardly be defended in itself as an adequate scientific approach. Simply to say that anxiety is an affect that is unpleasant and therefore to be avoided is, after all, only a naive negative hedonism, and is of little use scientifically. This statement does not deny the reality of the feeling state of mental anguish that is conventionally termed "anxiety," but rather insists that the recognition of the existence of this state is not per se an adequate scientific conception of anxiety (McReynolds, 1960). To be maximally useful as a scientific construct, it would be necessary to formulate the concept of anxiety in terms of broader psychological theory, in order that the relation of anxiety to other variables could be stated explicitly. In principle, this procedure would mean that anxiety could be defined in terms of other, more adequately measurable variables to which its relationship was specified.

This degree of theoretical elegance—which, in a sense, would make the concept of anxiety superfluous—is probably some time away. For the present, anxiety assessment techniques are based largely upon descriptive and consensual, rather than upon theoretical, definitions of anxiety. (E.g., the MAS, though widely used in the study of theoretical issues, is itself based upon clinical descriptions of anxiety.) This does not mean, however, that such techniques cannot be useful. Though anxiety tests are far from having reached the level of sophistication of intelligence tests, an analogy with the latter may be instructive. Intelligence tests are of enormous practical value, not because they are based on detailed theories of intelligence—which, for the most part, they are not—but rather because their use handles a great deal of otherwise unexplained variance in a variety of researches, and because they

have important predictive significance. These same criteria, more than theoretical elegance, will determine the utility of anxiety scales.

Let us examine some of the more specific issues faced in the assessment
of anxiety. It is possible to make a distinction between how anxious a person
is *currently* and how anxious he is *characteristically*. This latter concept is, of
course, an abstraction, in that a person is never anxious "characteristically,"
but only "right now"; nevertheless it is frequently useful to conceive of a
person as having a certain characteristic level of anxiety at a given period in
his life. Only in this sense can we make a statement like "Jones is an anxious
man." Such a statement is a reference to what Cattell and Scheier (1961),
Heath and Korchin (1963), Spielberger (1966), and others have called *trait
anxiety*; it is to be contrasted with what they call *state anxiety*, which refers
to an individual's current level. The distinction between the characteristic and
current levels of anxiety is also implied in McReynolds' (1967a) concepts of
base anxiety and *induced anxiety*: here "base" refers to the level of anxiety
that a subject brings with him to the laboratory, and "induced" designates
the additional anxiety that may be brought about by the experimental procedures. The characteristic/current distinction is implied in Smith and Wenger's
(1965) *chronic* and *phasic* anxiety, and in Brown's (1961) and Lazarus'
(1966) *chronic* and *acute* anxiety, though in somewhat different ways in
each.

The concept of *characteristic anxiety* is quite complex. Essentially, it is
open to two different interpretations. It can be held that the characteristically anxious person is (*a*) one who has in his cognitive structure a mass of
accumulated unsolved problems, which constantly bear upon him and cause
him to be continuously anxious; or (*b*) one who is particularly susceptible to
anxiety, and whose relatively constant anxiety is a function of being vul-
nerable to a variety of stimuli that most people could take in their stride. The
first of these positions posits a trait of *anxiousness*, the second a disposition
toward *anxiety-proneness*. Conclusive evidence is lacking to reject either
interpretation, and probably both are in part correct. It is noteworthy that
even the chronically anxious person does not report feeling anxious *all* of the
time: the *unsolved problems* interpretation attributes his calm periods to
input—such as watching an interesting TV show, which distracts him from his
problems; the *increased susceptibility* interpretation, on the other hand,
could explain these periods as occurring when there are no anxiety-provoking
stimuli.

The range and kinds of stimuli that can induce anxiety vary greatly from
person to person. The intensity of anxiety reported by a person in a given
stimulus situation (Endler, Hunt, & Rosenstein, 1962) can be analyzed into
the variance due to the individual and that attributable to the situation.
Further, since anxiety is often assayed by various means (*feeling uneasy,
pacing floor, perspiring*, etc.), it is possible to identify the mode of response
as a third contributor to the overall variability. Endler and his associates have
studied the trait of *anxiousness* in terms of these three sources of variance.
Their view is: "Anxiety is not a unidimensional trait residing within the
individual, but is a complex behavioral event that is influenced by situational,

personality, and mode of response factors, and their interactions [Endler & Bain, 1966, p. 221]." Endler and Hunt (1966) conclude, however, that "the question of whether individual differences or situations are the major sources of behavioral variance . . . turns out to be a pseudoissue. . . . There is no single major source of behavioral variance, at least so far as the trait of anxiousness is concerned [p. 344]."

There are many "kinds" of anxiety, in the limited sense that anxiety can evidently be derived from, or focused upon, a variety of situations or topics. Thus, in a descriptive sense one can speak of separation anxiety, test-taking anxiety, social anxiety, and so on. But a more basic question is whether the affect of anxiety as such—independent of the particular *content* on which it is focused—is a unitary personality trait. With presently available methodology, this question can best be approached through techniques of multivariate analysis. It is significant that the bulk of relevant factor and cluster analytic studies (Alexander & Husek, 1962; Barratt, 1965; Bendig, 1966; Cattell, 1964, 1966; Cattell & Scheier, 1958, 1961; Fenz & Epstein, 1965; Horn 1963; Lorr, Daston, & Smith, 1967; Martin, 1958, 1959*a*; Nowlis, 1965; Rickels & Cattell, 1965; Stein, this volume), based upon a wide variety of data, have found evidence for a first- or a second-order factor that can most plausibly be termed "anxiety." Several studies (Buss, 1962; Eysenck, 1961; Hamilton, 1959; Wilensky, 1957) have implicated two factors—experiential anxiety and somatic reactivity—but it is most plausible to consider the experiential dimension as closest to what is conventionally meant by "anxiety," with the somatic dimension reflecting autonomic changes associated with anxiety under certain conditions (McReynolds, 1967*a*). Factor analyses of particular anxiety tests (Bendig, 1958, 1962; Dunn, 1964; O'Connor, Lorr, & Stafford, 1956; Sassenrath, 1964; Sassenrath, Kight, & Kaiser, 1965) have indicated considerable factorial heterogeneity, but these results probably apply more to specific tests than to the concept itself.

To sum up, it can be said that the construct of anxiety, though conceptually imprecise, has nevertheless proved generally useful, and seems basically well founded. We turn, then, to a survey of the various techniques that have been developed for its assessment. For most—though not all—of these, validity data are relatively meager. Most of the available data concern concurrent validity, specifically the comparison of given techniques with either psychiatric ratings or other anxiety tests. Such intercorrelations, however, are of somewhat limited usefulness in assessing the validity of given instruments, since there are no criterion anxiety scales of unquestioned high validity. Nevertheless, they are of interest in indicating the extent to which different scales are getting at the same variable and the extent to which one test can be replaced by another. There have also been a large number of studies using anxiety scales to test theoretical predictions, thus yielding construct validity data.

SELF-REPORT TECHNIQUES: SELF-RATINGS

The most straightforward way to find out how anxious a person feels is to ask him. This direct avenue, of course, has always been one of the main resources of the clinician. Among the first to employ it systematically were Mowrer, Light, Luria, and Zeleny (1953), who used self-ratings of tension to evaluate psychotherapy. Davids, in 1955, developed a four-part self-rating anxiety scale that correlated[2] up to .74 with the Manifest Anxiety Scale (MAS) and appeared to be less influenced by motivational factors. Walk (1956) used a thermometer-like figure divided into 10 parts to obtain self-ratings of anxiety in military airborne trainees. This scale has been further used by Lang and Lazovik (1963). McReynolds (1958) devised several different self-rating anxiety scales, including one in which the endpoints are defined in terms of the subject's own experience ("How anxious do you feel now as compared to the *least* and *most* anxious you have ever felt?"). Schachter (1959) utilized a six-point rating scale in which the subjects were asked, "How nervous or uneasy do you feel about taking part in this experiment and being shocked?" In a part of the same overall investigation, Wrightsman had subjects report a number between 0 and 100 to indicate how "at-ease" or "ill-at-ease" they felt about participating in an experiment (Schachter, 1959). Mattson (1960) obtained an internal consistency coefficient of .88 for a self-rating anxiety scale consisting of six subscales. Byrne (1961) had subjects rate their own "feelings of nervousness and uneasiness" and how "nervous or uneasy" they felt other subjects were. Strong presumptive evidence for the construct validity of the self-rating approach is afforded by the fact that in all of these studies the experimental hypotheses were supported, at least in part, by self-rating data. Scheier, Cattell, and Sullivan (1961) have reported the correlations between a number of self-rated anxiety symptoms and a psychometric criterion reflecting Cattell's anxiety factor.

Robbins (1962a) found subjects' self-rated reactions to taped selections of anxiety-evoking material to correlate significantly with the duration of their exposure to the material. Desroches, Kaiman, and Ballard (1966) reported self-ratings of nervousness to correlate .69 with the Zuckerman Affect Adjective Check List measure of anxiety, and .58 with the Bendig short form of the MAS. Acker and McReynolds (1966) developed an anxiety affect self-rating scale that correlated .50 with the IPAT Anxiety Scale and up to .75 with the MAS, and was more successful (McReynolds, 1967b) than the latter in predicting from an experimental hypothesis. The same authors (1966) found a "nervousness" self-rating to correlate .75 with the MAS for a sample of psychiatric patients. Kelly (1966) devised a 10-point anxiety self-rating that significantly separated normals, mixed neurotics, and anxiety state patients. Miller, Fisher, and Ladd (1967), in a highly valuable comparative study, found a 13-point anxiety self-rating to correlate .41 with the MAS, .45 with the MMPI *Pt* scale, and .30 with the IPAT Anxiety Scale.

It seems clear that self-rating anxiety scales, despite their brevity and simplicity, have considerable utility. Their most appropriate uses are in the assessment of current levels of anxiety, and of changes in anxiety under given experimental treatment.

---

[2]The correlation coefficients listed in this paper, unless otherwise noted, are significant at the .05 level or better, and in almost all instances represent Pearsonian values.

SELF-REPORT TECHNIQUES: ADJECTIVE CHECKLISTS

In the adjective checklist procedure the subject indicates, either by checks or ratings, which of a number of adjectives characterize his mood. Assuming that certain of the words have been predetermined to constitute what the experimenter or clinician *means* by anxiety, we can then determine an anxiety score. The use of adjective checklists of mood was pioneered by Nowlis (1953; Nowlis & Nowlis, 1956). Kerle and Bialek (described in Berkun, Timiras, & Pace, 1958) developed a Subjective Stress Scale (SSS), in which the subject chooses the *one* adjective most descriptive of his mood (see also Berkun et al., 1962). Davitz (1959) used an adjective checklist measure of anxiety in obtaining support for a hypothesis concerning social perception, and Martin (1959b) reported evidence for the validity of the Feeling Inventory, a forced-choice adjective checklist test for anxiety.

Currently the most widely-used adjective checklist measures of anxiety are the Mood Adjective Check List (MACL) (Nowlis, 1965), the Multiple Affect Adjective Check List (MAACL) (Zuckerman & Lubin, 1965), and a checklist developed by Lorr and his associates (Lorr & McNair, 1966; Lorr, Daston, & Smith, 1967). All of these include scales other than anxiety. Of the three, the one presently most fully developed, and also the only one having a detailed manual, is the MAACL. The anxiety scale of the MAACL is identical to the Affect Adjective Check List (AACL), a device developed by Zuckerman in 1960 and later incorporated in the longer instrument. The Nowlis and Lorr anxiety scales are based on extensive factor-analytic research, whereas the Zuckerman scale was determined on the basis of item analyses against empirical criteria. Another newly developed checklist that promises to be useful in anxiety assessment—though very little has been published on it as yet—is the Brentwood Mood Scale (Crumpton, Grayson, & Keith-Lee, 1967).

Most of the work on the MACL appears to have been done on 130- or 145-word lists, but a short, 33-word form is available (Nowlis, 1965). Anxiety words include *clutched up, jittery,* and *fearful.* Handlon (1962) reported daily mood ratings to correspond with certain biochemical changes, and Lazarus et al. (1962) found the MACL anxiety factor to be highly sensitive to presumed mood changes induced by films.

The MAACL anxiety scale includes 11 "anxiety-plus" words (e.g., *afraid, desperate, fearful*), and 10 "anxiety-minus" words (e.g., *calm, cheerful, happy*). Alternate instructions focus on how the subject feels "Generally" or how he feels "Today." Internal consistency estimates range from .72 to .85, being higher for Today-anxiety than for General-anxiety; test-retest reliability, however, is higher for General-anxiety than for Today-anxiety. Some of the reported correlations with other instruments are: for General-anxiety, .65 with the Welsh A Scale, .56 with the IPAT Anxiety Scale, and .57 with the MAS; and for Today-anxiety, .53 with the Welsh Anxiety Index, .55 with the IPAT, and .52 with the MAS (Zuckerman & Lubin, 1965; see also Zuckerman et al., 1967). A number of experimental studies (e.g., Winter, Ferreira, & Ransom, 1963) have shown the MAACL anxiety scale to be sensitive to examination-induced anxiety, and Levitt, Persky, and Brady (1964) found the AACL to reflect hypnotically-induced anxiety.

The work by Lorr and his associates was first concerned primarily with psychiatric patients (Lorr & McNair, 1966; McNair & Lorr, 1964), but recently their work has been extended to samples of college students (Lorr, Daston, & Smith, 1967). Approximately sixty adjectives are included in these studies, and anxiety words include *nervous, anxious,* and *shaky.*

Though the adjective checklist technique has only recently come to be widely used as a means of assessing anxiety, the results that have been obtained are, on the whole, quite impressive. An obvious limitation of the method is that it can utilize only those kinds of cues that can be put into adjectival form; the inventory, which we will next consider, permits a broader and more flexible approach.

SELF-REPORT TECHNIQUES: INVENTORIES

An almost bewildering number of inventory scales have been developed for the assessment of anxiety. Unlike self-rating scales and adjective checklists, which are used most frequently for the assessment of a person's *current* level of anxiety, inventory scales are typically used to measure his *characteristic* anxiety level. Within this framework, there are several further ways in which the different inventory approaches can be classified.

First, inventory scales can be subdivided in terms of whether they are intended to assess (*a*) characteristic level of *existent anxiety*, or (*b*) the *proneness to become anxious* under given conditions.

Second, scales can be subdivided—assuming that anxiety is conceptualized as an intervening variable—in terms of whether they focus primarily on (*a*) the *antecedent*, or (*b*) the *consequent* aspects, that is, on the *stimulus* or on the *response* aspects of anxiety (Aiken, 1962). Items focusing on antecedent conditions of anxiety (referred to as "anxors" by Aiken) can specify either (1) personal problems that the subject "has" and that presumably contribute to his anxiety (e.g., "Difficulties with my family") or (2) immediate stimulus situations that provoke anxiety (e.g., "Seeing a snake"). Items focusing on consequent aspects of anxiety can be referred to as "anxiety reactions" (Aiken, 1962) or, more conventionally as "symptoms."

Third, anxiety scales can be classified according to whether they attempt to measure a subject's (*a*) *overall* (sometimes called "general") anxiety, or (*b*) his anxiety *in given specific respects*. If one is dealing with antecedent or stimulus-oriented scales, then these "specific respects" refer to particular problems or stimuli associated with anxiety (e.g., one might say that a person has a high level of dependency anxiety, or that he is fearful of animals); if one is dealing with symptom-oriented scales, then the "specific respects" refer to the mode of reaction (e.g., worry, gastrointestinal symptoms, etc.).

Stimulus-oriented Measures of Existent Anxiety

We will consider first a number of inventories designed to survey the particular problems about which a person is worried or concerned and from which inferences can be drawn regarding both the specific areas and the characteristic overall level of his anxiety. The Mooney Problem Check List

(R. L. Mooney & L. V. Gordon, 1950), which is available in several forms and has a detailed manual, is the most comprehensive instrument of this kind, containing up to 330 items that the subject can underline to indicate his problem areas (e.g., "Not really having any friends"). May (1950), in a similar approach, had women report their frequency of "worry" about each of a number of topics (e.g., "What my men friends think of me"). Neither the Mooney nor the May techniques emphasize overall scores; however, evidence obtained by Hammes (1959), Aiken (1962), and Nicolay, Walker, and Riedle (1966) indicates that such scores can meaningfully be interpreted as indices of anxiety.

E. M. Gordon and S. B. Sarason (1955) were apparently the first to develop a formal measure of overall anxiety utilizing the problem-oriented approach. Their 29-item test (sample item: "Worry about sexual adjustment"), described as the Generalized Anxiety Scale and also referred to as the General Anxiety Questionnaire (GAQ) (I. G. Sarason, 1958), yielded a test-retest (3-1/2 months) reliability of .81. I. G. Sarason (1958) developed a somewhat similar measure of anxiety, a 24-item true-false test termed the General Anxiety Scale. The same investigator also devised a 42-item Lack of Protection Scale, based on the Freudian interpretation of anxiety as a situation of helplessness (sample: "When I was a child, I often wondered about how much my father loved me"). This test is particularly interesting in that it is derived from a major theory of anxiety.

McReynolds and Acker (1966) have constructed a 45-item Assimilation Scale (AS) for the assessment of anxiety in male psychiatric patients. The subject responds to each item (sample: "some problems with my family") by rating how "unsettled" he feels about that topic. The AS is based upon McReynolds' (1956, 1960) theory of anxiety, which conceptualizes anxiety as a function of the magnitude of unassimilated percepts. An internal consistency coefficient of .95 and a correlation of .38 with clinical ratings of anxiety have been reported. AS scores on schizophrenics decreased significantly after therapy (Gorham & Pokorny, 1964).

Several inventories have been developed in the context of the behavior therapy movement. The items in these inventories tend to refer to specific anxiety-inducing stimuli (e.g., "Dentists," "Cats," "Darkness"). There are currently three major scales of this type, all similar and all termed the Fear Survey Schedule (FSS) or, sometimes, the Fear Inventory, with sublabels I, II, and III. Instructions for FSS-III, which are typical, request the subject to rate each stimulus to indicate "how much you are disturbed by it nowadays" (Wolpe & Lazarus, 1966). FSS-I was used by Lang and Lazovik (1963) in a study of phobias. FSS-II, developed by Geer (1965) and consisting of 51 items, is the most carefully constructed of the three. Geer reports it to have a consistency reliability of .93 and to correlate significantly (r's from .39 to .57) with the MAS and the Welsh A-Scale. Fear Survey Schedules are used primarily for the assessment of anxiety hierarchies; it is clear, however, that total scores, at least on FSS-II, reflect overall anxiety. FSS responses can also be considered as measures of anxiety-proneness in that they gauge the extent to which a person reacts to given stimuli with anxiety.

Symptom-oriented Measures of Existent Anxiety

These scales infer the level of an individual's anxiety from his reports of feelings and behaviors assumed to be symptomatic of anxiety. This is currently the most widely-used class of anxiety assessment instruments.

MMPI anxiety scales. A number of MMPI scales have been developed for the measurement of anxiety. The most prominent of these—indeed, the most popular of all anxiety tests—is the Manifest Anxiety Scale (MAS),[3] developed by Janet Taylor, later, Janet Taylor Spence (1953, 1956; for reviews see Byrne, 1966; Lazarus, 1966). The MAS consists of 50 MMPI items (samples: "I cry easily"; "I am a high-strung person"); the main criterion of item selection was that the items should conform—in the opinion of expert judges—with Cameron's (1947) definition of chronic anxiety.

Taylor (1953) reported an MAS test-retest reliability of .89 over a three-week period, and Rankin (1963) obtained an internal consistency reliability (K-R 21) of .81. A number of validity studies have shown the MAS to correlate substantially with clinical estimates of anxiety (e.g., Buss, Wiener, Durkee, & Baer, 1955; Gleser & Ulett, 1952; Hoyt & Magoon, 1954; Zuckerman et al., 1967). Rubin et al. (1956) found psychiatric adjustment, as evaluated by the McReynolds-Ferguson Hospital Adjustment Scale, to be negatively ($r = -.49$) related to the MAS. Kelly (1966) reported the scale to differentiate significantly normals, mixed neurotics, and anxiety patients. Kausler et al. (1959) found MAS responses to be significantly related to decision time variability, presumably an indicant of anxiety. However, there have also been several validity studies yielding predominantly negative results (Kendall, 1954; Miller, Fisher, & Ladd, 1967; Rubin & Townsend, 1958). Finally, though the literature is too extensive to review here, it should be noted that the MAS has been used with considerable success in studies testing theoretical predictions and requiring assessments of anxiety (see Spence & Spence, 1966a).

The MAS has 13 items in common with the Psychasthenia (*Pt*) scale of the MMPI, with which it typically correlates in the .80's or low .90's (e.g., Brackbill & Little, 1954; Miller et al., 1967); this is in the same range as MAS reliability. The MAS also correlates in the .80's with the Edwards Social Desirability Scale, but this is hardly a fair test of its social desirability bias, since the two scales have 22 items in common; the corresponding correlation between the MAS and the Marlowe-Crowne *SD* Scale has been reported as -.32 (not significant) (McReynolds, 1967b). O'Connor, Lorr, and Stafford (1956) identified five factors in the MAS items; a multifactor structure was also indicated for the scale by Fenz and Epstein (1965).

Taylor's purpose in constructing the MAS was to obtain an index of drive (*D*), in the Hull-Spence sense. (She assumed that *D* would be reflected by

---

[3]The popularity of the MAS can be attributed not only to its psychometric characteristics but also to the prestige it has gained through its association with a highly respected field of experimental psychology (learning theory). It may also be noted that the term "manifest" in the MAS (and several other scales) is something of a misnomer, since it gives the impression that the MAS assesses overt, public cues of anxiety, whereas in fact the majority of the items refer to private *experiencings*; and even those behaviors that are in principle public are assayed by the subject himself.

level of anxiety.) It should be emphasized, however, that this historical fact neither detracts from, nor adds to, the scale's utility as a measure of anxiety. Nor is there any good evidence that the MAS measures D any better than other anxiety scales; indeed one recent study (Crumpton et al., 1967) raises considerable doubt of the adequacy of the MAS itself as a measure of drive.

A number of authors (e.g., Taylor, 1956; Desiderato, 1964) have suggested that MAS scores may reflect "different potentialities for anxiety arousal" (Taylor, p. 306). The issue here is whether the MAS measures existent anxiety—as ordinarily supposed—or proneness (disposition) to become anxious. Among recent studies, that of Desiderato (1964) favors the "proneness" interpretation, whereas those of Hammes (1959, 1961) support the "existent level" interpretation. In view of the obvious heterogeneity of the items and the scale's multifactorial structure, it seems probable that both hypotheses are in part valid.

Several alterations of the MAS have been put forth: Heineman (1953) constructed a multiple-choice version in order to minimize social desirability set, and Bendig (1956) offered a 20-item short form that correlated .93 with the full scale. Christie and Budnitzky (1957) then proposed the use of the Heineman forced-choice technique with the Bendig list of 20 items.

Other than the MAS, the most prominent MMPI anxiety scales are those developed by Welsh. In 1952 Welsh proposed an Anxiety Index (AI) that could be computed from a combination of the Hs, D, Hy, and Pt scales. A reliability of .84 has been reported for the AI, and a correlation of .89 with the MAS (.39 when overlapping items are eliminated) (Alpert & Haber, 1960). In 1956 Welsh (see also Welsh, 1965) published two new MMPI scales—A (Anxiety) and R (Repression)—both developed on the basis of extensive item analyses and factor analyses of MMPI scales. The A scale includes 39 items, all but one keyed *true*. Branca and Podolnick (1961) found scores on this scale to increase in hypnotized subjects under anxiety suggestions. Miller et al. (1967) reported A to correlate .75 with the AI, .31 with the patients' self-rated anxiety, .83 with Pt, and .88 with the MAS, though not significantly (.13) with the therapists' ratings of patients' anxiety.

We will briefly note two other MMPI anxiety scales. Tuthill, Overall, and Hollister (1967) have reported the 20 MMPI items, from a selected list of 166, that correlated highest with clinical ratings of anxiety. Though not proposed as a special MMPI scale, these 20 items obviously could form the basis for developing an anxiety measure. And finally, Tryon, Stein, and Chu (Stein, this volume) have recently cluster-analyzed the entire 550 MMPI items. One of the clusters they derived is described as "Tension, Worry, and Fears."

The IPAT Anxiety Scale. This instrument was developed by Cattell and Scheier (1961; Cattell, 1964, 1966) at the Institute for Personality and Ability Testing (IPAT), primarily on the basis of factor-analytic techniques. It is a 40-item questionnaire divided into two 20-item subscales, one designed to measure *overt* anxiety (e.g., "I sometimes feel compelled to do things for no particular purpose. True   Uncertain   False"), and the other *covert* anxiety (e.g., "Often I get angry with people too quickly. True   In between   False").

The scale is intended also to measure five first-order factors, but its adequacy in this regard has been questioned by Bendig (1962). Cattell and Scheier (1963) have reported a test-retest reliability (one-week interval) of .93 and an internal consistency reliability of .91 for the test. Bendig (1962) reported an internal consistency reliability (K-R formula 20) of .83, with the "overt" items being more reliable (.79) than the "covert" (.63). Levitt and Persky (1962) reported that the IPAT, but not the MAS, reflected hypnotically-induced anxiety; the two instruments intercorrelated .55. Correlations in the .70–.80 range between these two scales have also been obtained (Cattell and Scheier, 1961). Zuckerman et al. (1967) reported the IPAT Anxiety Scale to show up the best of several test measures against anxiety-rating criteria, and Paul (1966) found the IPAT to reflect changes under psychotherapy also evident by other criteria. A test manual (Cattell & Scheier, 1963) is available, and recent research has been surveyed by Scheier (1967).

Other symptom-oriented anxiety scales. Dibner (1958; Clemes & D'Andrea, 1965) devised a series of "anxiety cards" (e.g., "I felt restless most of the time"), which the subject sorts into three degrees of descriptiveness in order to indicate how anxious he felt during a given procedure. Haywood (1962) has developed a 75-item Anxiety Questionnaire; he reports it to have an internal consistency reliability of .96, and to correlate .47 with clinical ratings of anxiety. The Nicolay-Walker (Walker & Nicolay, 1963; Nicolay, Walker, & Riedle, 1966) Personal Reaction Schedule is a 117-item anxiety scale yielding separate scores for motor-tension anxiety, object anxiety, personal inadequacy anxiety, and total. Volsky, Magoon, Norman, and Hoyt (1965) on the basis of considerable pretesting and extensive item analyses, have recently developed the Minnesota Manifest Anxiety Scale (MMAS). This scale consists of 52 items, many from the MMPI; it correlated .81 with the MAS, with which it has eight items in common. Spielberger and Gorsuch have constructed a State-Trait Anxiety Inventory (STAI) (described in Levitt, 1967), consisting of 20 self-descriptive statements (e.g., "I am calm"), to which the subject responds on a five-point rating scale. Clearly, the STAI, though formally an inventory, is somewhat similar to adjective checklists. It can be filled out as the subject feels "generally" or as he feels "right now," thus providing measures of either trait or state anxiety. Leventhal (1966) has recently developed a 22-item anxiety scale for the California Psychological Inventory.

Measures of General Anxiety-Proneness

As noted above, it is possible to interpret the MAS as reflecting both anxiety-proneness and anxiety level. The FSS can also be interpreted in this way. We note now two other inventories, each of which appears to be a rather direct measure of general anxiety-proneness, even though it is difficult in practice to separate level from susceptibility, since presumably the subjects with highest susceptibility in most instances also have the highest levels.

The Saslow Screening Test (SST) (Saslow, Counts, & DuBois, 1951) requires the subject to imagine himself in typical anxiety-provoking situations and then to check from a list of 24 symptoms those that apply to him under such circumstances. Gleser and Ulett (1952), suggesting that the SST could be considered a measure of anxiety-proneness, obtained correlations in the .50's between the SST and anxiety-proneness ratings. The Activity Preference Questionnaire (APQ), developed by Lykken (1957), represents a highly novel approach and is one of the most promising of the newer anxiety assessment procedures. Each test item lists two activities, both of which are unpleasant—one because it is presumably anxiety-arousing (e.g., "Making a parachute jump"), and the other because it is onerous (e.g., "Digging a big rubbish pit"). For each item the subject is asked to choose his preferred activity; the degree to which he rejects the "frightening" responses is taken as an index of the degree to which he is prone to anxiety. The latest form of the APQ (Lykken, private communication, 1967) consists of 100 items and is available in two forms that correlate in the high .80's. The test's purpose is not apparent to the subject. Obtained reliability coefficients vary from the high .70's to the low .90's. Sociopaths score as less anxiety-prone than other subjects on the APQ (Lykken, 1957), as some theories would predict. Rose (1964) found that APQ scores correlate .41 with the MMPI *Pt* scale and .43 with ratings of anxiety-proneness based on MMPI profiles.

Measures of Specific Anxiety-Proneness

We turn now to a group of inventories sometimes considered as measures of "situational" anxiety, in that they are intended to reflect a person's current anxiety in given situations, such as when taking a test. These scales can also be categorized as measures of specific anxiety-proneness, however, in that they follow the paradigm of asking the subject how anxious he would be under given conditions.

Measures of proneness to anxiety when taking tests. The pioneering scale in this area, the Test Anxiety Questionnaire (TAQ), was developed by Mandler and S. B. Sarason (1952; Sarason & Mandler, 1952; Mandler & Cowen, 1958), and includes 39 rating-type items (e.g., "While taking a group intelligence test to what extent do you perspire?"). Both test-retest and split-half reliabilities have been reported (Mandler & Cowen, 1958) as .91. The TAQ was found to correlate .47 with the General Anxiety Questionnaire (GAQ) (Gordon & Sarason, 1955) and .59 with the MAS (Mandler & Cowen, 1958). These moderately low *r*'s are in accord with the assumption that test anxiety is a more restricted concept than general (overall) anxiety. Kissel and Littig (1962) have provided experimental support for the validity of the TAQ as a measure of test anxiety. Cowen (1957) constructed a high school form of the test. Another modification of the TAQ, this one for college students, is that by Harleston (1962). In 1958 I. G. Sarason published a 21-item true-false Test Anxiety Scale (TAS). As compared with low TAQ subjects, high subjects tend to describe themselves in more negative terms (Sarason & Ganzer, 1963).

The test-anxiety instruments just described all focus on the debilitating effects of anxiety. The Alpert-Haber (1960) Achievement Anxiety Test (AAT) is a definite advance in that it includes two scales, one (AAT+) to assess the *facilitating* effects of anxiety (sample: "Nervousness while taking a test helps me do better"), and one (AAT-) to assess the *debilitating* effects of anxiety (sample: "Nervousness while taking a test hinders me from doing well"). The AAT+ scale includes 9 items, the AAT- scale 10. Test-retest reliabilities (10-week interval) for the two scales respectively have been reported as .83 and .87, and the intercorrelation between the two as high as -.48. The AAT- scale was found to correlate .64 with the Mandler-Sarason TAQ (Alpert & Haber, 1960).

Other measures of proneness to specific anxieties. One of the more interesting recent inventories is the S-R Inventory of Anxiousness (SRIA) Endler, Hunt, & Rosenstein, 1962; Endler & Bain, 1966; Endler & Hunt, 1966). This test assays the subject's self-reported tendency to become anxious under each of 11 different imaginary situations (e.g., "You are alone in the woods at night," "You are getting up to give a speech before a large group"). These situations appear to have been chosen as ones likely to induce anxiety. For each situation the subject rates the extent to which each of 14 modes of response (e.g., "Heart beats faster," "Experience nausea") would characterize him. The test thus emphasizes both anxiety stimuli and anxiety responses, making it possible, as noted earlier in this chapter, to break overall variance down into that due to individuals, to situations, and to typical modes of response. The internal consistency reliability of the SRIA total score is reported as .97, with subscale reliabilities varying from .62 to .93. The total score correlated .40, .34, and .44 with the GAQ, the MAS, and the TAQ respectively. Paul (1966) found the SRIA score for the speech-giving situation (see sample above) to decrease significantly under therapy judged, on other criteria, to reduce public speaking fears.

Other instruments which can be interpreted as measures of proneness to specific anxieties are Robbin's (1962*b*) 114-item Medical Attitude Survey, which concerns anxiety relating to illness, and Paul's (1966) revision of Gilkenson's Personal Report of Confidence as a Speaker, concerned with fear of public speaking.

General Comments

Because of their objectivity, convenience, and face validity, anxiety inventories are used very widely. This is particularly true of symptom-oriented scales, of which the most popular is the MAS. This pioneering scale clearly deserves great credit for having opened up a whole new field of research. There is no convincing evidence, however, that its psychometric properties are superior to those of a number of other currently available scales; indeed, its reliabilty is evidently less than that of several other standard inventories. Further, the overall methodology of scale construction has clearly been more elaborate and sophisticated in a number of the newer scales—the IPAT Anxiety Scale, the Activity Preference Questionnaire, and the Achievement Anxiety Test, to mention only three.

At present there are insufficient grounds for concluding that any one inventory is better than the others. Because of the problem of response sets, the possibilities of faking, and uncertain validities, great caution should be exercised in using any inventory scale as a measure of anxiety in individuals. For use in group research or in broad comparative studies, however, anxiety inventories have demonstrated considerable usefulness.

PROJECTIVE TECHNIQUES

Inkblot Tests

Both the Rorschach and the Holtzman Inkblot Technique have been utilized in the assessment of anxiety, though much more work has been done on the older, more established Rorschach test. Goldfried (1966) and Neuringer (1962) have provided careful reviews of the rather extensive literature in this area. Assessment of anxiety by means of Rorschach responses takes two forms: first, assessment in terms of certain postulated Rorschach "signs" of anxiety, such as shading responses; and second, assessment in terms of a systematic scale of anxiety based on Rorschach content. The literature on specific cues, which remains controversial, has been reviewed by Neuringer (1962), who concludes that a distinction must be made between determinants associated with laboratory-induced stress and those associated with long-term characteristic anxiety. Levitt and Grosz (1960) identified several Rorschach changes (e.g., decreases in $F+$) under hypnotically-induced anxiety.

The primary Rorschach anxiety scale is the Rorschach Content Test (RCT), developed by Elizur in 1949. (Another, similar scale is that used by Holt [1966].) The RCT scoring system assumes that anxiety can be inferred from responses such as "A man hiding in fear," "A frightened animal," and the like. Reported inter-scorer reliabilities of the RCT are in the .80's and .90's. Elizur obtained a correlation of .71 between the RCT and interviewer ratings of anxiety, and Stewart (1950) obtained an analogous coefficient of .39. In general, correlations between the RCT and inventory measures of anxiety have been low (Goldfried, 1966; Mogar, 1962), with construct validity data somewhat more favorable; e.g., Vernallis (1955) confirmed his prediction that tooth-grinding students would obtain higher RCT scores than non-toothgrinders.

The Elizur content approach has been adapted to the Holtzman Inkblot Test (HIT) (Holtzman, Thorpe, Swartz, & Herron, 1961). Data summarized by Holtzman et al., (1961) fail to indicate any significant relationship between HIT anxiety scores and inventory anxiety measures; and Zuckerman et al. (1967), in the excellent study referred to earlier, obtained little evidence of correlation between HIT scores and ratings of anxiety.

Figure-drawing Tests

Figure-drawing procedures, such as the Draw-a-Person (DAP) and House-Tree-Person (HTP) tests, have frequently been employed by clinicians for the assessment of anxiety (e.g., Buck, 1948; Machover, 1949), primarily through the use of specific signs or impressionistic cues. The literature in this area has recently been reviewed by Handler and Reyher (1965). In general, findings have indicated little relationship (Hoyt & Baron, 1959; Mogar, 1962) between figure-drawing signs and inventory (MAS) measures of anxiety; relations between figure-drawing signs and RCT scores appear to be low but positive (Mogar, 1962). Some evidence of the construct validity of the figure-drawing approach has recently been presented by Handler and Reyher (1966). Research utilizing the figure-drawing approach will probably be greatly increased by the recent publication of a detailed manual (Handler, 1967) for scoring anxiety on the DAP.

Other Projective Approaches

A number of possible TAT (Thematic Apperception Test) signs of anxiety were suggested by Lindzey and Newburg (1954). However, in the Zuckerman et al. (1967) study, TAT anxiety scores based on judges' ratings failed to correlate with other indices of anxiety. The Freeman (1953) Manifest Anxiety Scale (FMAS) may also be mentioned here, since—though an inventory—it is based on a projective rationale. The test consists of 141 items presented to the subject as a measure of his ability to judge other people, and it is assumed that his own level of anxiety is reflected via projective mechanisms. Alpert and Haber (1960) reported a reliability of .73 for the FMAS, and correlations of .32 and .34 with the MAS and Welsh's AI, respectively. Ends and Page (1957) and Volsky et al. (1965) found little support for the validity of the test, but Goldstein (1965) has used it with some apparent success.

General Comments

The status of projective measures of anxiety remains somewhat unclear. Though they are generally found to be unrelated to inventory assays of anxiety, this in itself does not mean that projective devices do not reflect some other meaningful aspect of anxiety, as Holtzman et al. (1961) have noted. It is clear that there is a need for further clarifying research in this area. Part of the problem is the question of just what anxiety variable projective tests are best suited to assess. Goldfried (1966) suggests that the RCT has primary applicability to an individual's characteristic anxiety level; a good case could be made, however, that projective measures are more reflective of current anxiety.

MEASURES OF ANXIETY IN CHILDREN

The anxiety tests now to be considered could have been included at appropriate places in the above presentation; they are brought together here, however, for convenience to the reader. The extensive literature on anxiety assessment in children has been afforded excellent reviews by Ruebush (1963) and S. B. Sarason (1966).

Anxiety Inventories

The Children's Manifest Anxiety Scale (CMAS) was published by Castaneda, McCandless, and Palermo in 1956, and includes 42 MAS items modified to be meaningful to fourth-, fifth-, and sixth-grade children. Test-retest reliability coefficients (Horowitz, 1962) are in the .80's. Iscoe and Cochran (1959) and Horowitz (1962) found the CMAS to be related, respectively, to personal adjustment and adequacy of self-concept. However, negative validity findings have been reported by Wirt and Broen (1956), Kaplan and Hafner (1959), and Stone, Rowley, and Keller (1965); in all of these studies the CMAS failed, in general, to separate subject groups assumed to differ on anxiety level; and in the first study it failed to correlate with clinical ratings of anxiety. Levy (1958) has offered a short form of the CMAS.

The Test Anxiety Scale for Children (TASC) (S. B. Sarason, Davidson, Lighthall, & Waite, 1958; Sarason, Davidson, Lighthall, Waite, & Ruebush, 1960) consists of 30 yes-no questions (e.g., "Do you worry when the teacher says that she is going to ask you questions to find out how much you know?"). The General Anxiety Scale for Children (GASC) (Sarason et al., 1960) is similar in format; it deals, however, with a wide variety of situations (e.g., "Are you afraid of things like snakes?") that might provoke anxiety. The two scales are frequently given together. Both are administered orally and can be given as low as the first grade. The TASC is the more widely used, and has generated an extensive literature (see Sarason et al., 1960; Ruebush, 1963; Hill & Sarason, 1966). Both scales have adequate reliability, and the TASC has yielded low but significant correlations with teacher ratings of anxiety (Sarason et al., 1958). The factor structure of the TASC has been studied by Dunn (1964). Hafner, Quast, Speer, and Grams (1964) found the CMAS and the GASC to intercorrelate .67 and .71 in two groups of children. In addition to these formal anxiety inventories, a number of "worry inventories" have been used with children. These have been reviewed by Sarason et al. (1960).

Projective Techniques

Temple and Amen (1944; Amen & Renison, 1954) developed a projective anxiety test for use with children. It consists of a series of pictures (e.g., a child eating) in which the face is blank and the subject chooses for it either a happy or an unhappy face. The test does not appear to have generated much empirical support, but the idea is clever. More recently, Rosenblum and Callahan (1958) have put forth the Children's Anxiety Pictures test; this correlated negatively with the CMAS, however, and its status is in doubt.

OTHER PSYCHOMETRIC TECHNIQUES

Cattell and Scheier have developed two objective measures of anxiety that are not obviously related to this variable and hence not likely to be answered in terms of a set to appear nonanxious. One of these instruments is the Objective-analytic Anxiety Battery (Cattell & Scheier, 1966; Rickels & Cattell, 1965), which consists of 10 subtests (e.g., Susceptibility to Common Annoyances, Number of Good Friends). The other is the 8-Parallel Form Anxiety Battery (Scheier & Cattell, 1960). Interform reliabilities range from .41 to .85. Miller et al. (1967) found this test, with forms assigned randomly, to correlate significantly with Welsh's A (.44), the MAS (.39), and Pt (.44), but not with observer ratings of anxiety. Manuals are available for both tests, and recent research has been surveyed by Scheier (1967).

Perhaps the oldest systematic approach to the assessment of anxiety is the word-association technique; Jung used it as early as 1906 for the detection of areas of emotional disturbance (complexes). The most recent and promising instrument of this kind is the Phrase Association Test (PT), devised by Heath (1960, 1965) for the purpose of determining an individual's anxiety thresholds for given interpersonal areas. Test Stimuli are 48 five-word phrases (e.g., "He suddenly struck his father") representing six interpersonal threat areas (e.g., Rejection by mother) as well as neutral content. The subject responds by giving the first word or sentence that comes to his mind, and responses are scored in terms of specific criteria (e.g., reaction time, repetition of a stimulus word). Scoring reliabilities and split-half reliabilities are both in the .90's. The study of Mandler, Mandler, Kremen, and Sholiton (1961) provides some evidence of construct validity for the PT.

A refreshingly new approach to the assessment of anxiety is provided by the Anxiety Differential (AD) of Alexander and Husek (1962). This technique is intended to measure current anxiety in given areas—e.g., the anxiety present just prior to an examination. It is based on the assumption that "the person who is anxious for a short period . . . perceives things differently from when he is not anxious [p. 326]." The test is modeled after the semantic differential technique and consists of a series of pairings—some quite novel—of scales and concepts (e.g., FINGERS: stiff—relaxed). The anxiety side is determined empirically (*stiff* in the example just given). Preliminary reliability and validity data (Alexander & Husek, 1962; Husek & Alexander, 1963) are impressive, although in Paul's (1966) study the AD failed to reflect anxiety reduction as indicated by several other measures.

Still another unusual approach to the assessment of anxiety is the *incongruency technique* of McReynolds (1958). This procedure is based on McReynolds' (1956, 1960) theory of anxiety, which holds anxiety to be a function of unassimilated affecto-cognitive material. Percepts are assumed to be unassimilable when there are significant incongruencies in the region of the cognitive structure into which they would be incorporated. The technique attempts to identify such areas of incongruency, and hence of particular anxiety-proneness. Though the procedure has not yet been fully developed, preliminary findings (McReynolds, 1958; Byrne, Terrill, & McReynolds, 1961) are quite encouraging.

It has often been suggested that low digit span on tests such as the Wechsler series is indicative of anxiety. The research evidence (reviewed by Walker & Spence, 1964), however, gives the relationship only very meager support. Other possible Wechsler signs of anxiety (reviewed by Jurjevich, 1963) also have only a weak empirical basis.

VERBAL ANALYSIS TECHNIQUES

It has been observed that evidences of current emotional disturbance show up in one's speech and, presumably, in one's written output as well. Dollard and Mowrers' (1947) Discomfort-Relief Quotient (DRQ) appears to have been the first systematic attempt to measure "tension" through this channel. The DRQ is the ratio of the number of *discomfort* words to the number of *discomfort plus relief* words in given verbal samples. Meadow, Greenblatt, Levine, and Solomon (1952), however, reported that the DRQ did not correlate significantly with ratings of tension, though it was related to measures of adjustment. Work by Mowrer et al. (1953) indicated the DRQ to be an accurate measure of improvement in psychotherapy, but this conclusion was questioned by Murray, Auld, and White (1954). A second and more elaborate approach to the assessment of current anxiety through content analysis of verbal samples is that developed by Gleser, Gottschalk, and Springer (1961). This highly promising scale is based on the coding of verbal output—typically the subject is asked to speak for five minutes on some personal experience—in terms of six anxiety subtypes (e.g., death anxiety, separation anxiety). Scoring reliability is reported as .86, and the content score was found to correlate .66 with clinical ratings of anxiety and .51 with the *Pt* scale. A third verbal content measure of anxiety that appears to have some promise is that of Dollard and Auld (1959).

The above techniques involve verbal *content*; other approaches concern the *expressive characteristics* of verbal output. Dibner (1956) used a number of such cues (for example, unfinished sentences, blocking, stuttering), for assessing current anxiety, with some apparent success. Mahl (1956) devised a Speech Disturbance Ratio, reflecting the number of speech disturbances (e.g., "ah," repetition, stutter) per unit number of words. This ratio was found to increase (Mahl, 1959) during an anxiety-inducing interview; however, an attempt by Boomer and Goodrich (1961) to substantiate Mahl's approach was inconclusive.

OBSERVER-RATING TECHNIQUES

Perhaps the most common method of assessing anxiety, aside from the self-report, is that of observer ratings. A number of instances of the use of observer ratings as criterion measures for anxiety tests have already been referred to in this chapter. Most attempts to rate anxiety appear to be based on unstated and perhaps unknown criteria. There have, however, been several attempts to develop systematic rating procedures.

Elizur (1949) defined anxiety in a fairly detailed way and used a nine-point rating scale; he obtained an inter-rater reliability of .70. Buss, Wiener, Durkee, and Baer (1955), utilizing detailed categories of anxious behavior, obtained a mean inter-judge reliability of .83. Hamburg et al. (1958) obtained mean inter-rater reliabilities of .78 and .82 for two groups of judges rating anxiety. Raskin (1962) used 15 observable signs to assess anxiety in initial interviews. Buss (1962) factor-analyzed patients' reported and observed symptoms, and obtained two factors, one indicative of somatic signs and the other of motor and ideational cues. Hamilton (1959) devised a detailed schedule for rating the anxiety of neurotics. Its mean inter-rater reliability was .89. McReynolds (1965a) has developed an Anxiety Behavior Checklist (ABC) consisting of 25 behaviors (e.g., "Hands tremble," "Paces floor") selected from a larger list by empirical criteria. Inter-rater reliability was reported as .84 for two raters combined. The Brief Psychiatric Rating Scale (BPRS), constructed by Overall and Gorham (1962), includes a seven-point anxiety scale. This has a reliability of .86 for two combined raters and is perhaps the most widely used anxiety rating scale (e.g., Tuthill et al., 1967). Dildy and Liberty (1967) have utilized peer ratings of anxiety. Airmen differentiated by such ratings (extreme groups) differed significantly on a number of MMPI scales including Depression, the MAS, and the Welsh *A*-score.

As already noted, observer ratings of anxiety have often been found to correlate substantially with psychometric measures of anxiety. This appears, however, to be due primarily to the fact that *observer ratings typically are based substantially upon self-report data*, as are most psychometric indices. When behavioral ratings are based solely on *non-self-report* cues, their correlations with anxiety inventories drop markedly (Buss et al., 1955; Raskin, 1962; McReynolds & Acker, 1966; McReynolds, Acker, & Brackbill, 1966), frequently becoming insignificant. The better clinical ratings of anxiety presumably represent a kind of global, intuitive combination of self-report and observational data. It has never been convincingly demonstrated, however, that such global ratings are more accurate than the better psychometric or self-report procedures.

DISCUSSION AND CONCLUSIONS

Perhaps the most striking impression to be gained from the preceding survey is the large number of techniques that psychologists have developed for the assessment of anxiety. A total of 88 formal anxiety measurement procedures—not counting parallel forms and including only instruments put forth for general use—have been reviewed. This productivity testifies not only to the centrality of the anxiety concept and the vitality of this area of research, but also to the fact that the current status of anxiety assessment technology is something less than satisfactory.

Despite the seeming superabundance of anxiety measurement techniques, there is a conspicuous sameness about many of them, particularly about the symptom-oriented inventories, which have tended to dominate the field. With regard to such inventories, it is doubtful—despite the present availability of more sophisticated test development techniques—that a great deal of further improvement in validity can be expected. Accordingly, it is particularly important to note those instruments that represent promising new departures in methodology. In this category, certainly, should be listed the Anxiety Differential (Alexander & Husek, 1962), the Activity Preference Questionnaire (Lykken, 1957), the Objective-analytic Anxiety Battery (Cattell & Scheier, 1966), and the verbal content anxiety scale of Gleser et al. (1961). New ideas have also appeared in the design of anxiety inventories, particularly in the Achievement Anxiety Test (Alpert & Haber, 1960) and the S-R Inventory of Anxiousness (Endler et al., 1962). In the list of dramatically new approaches, too, could be placed the less developed but promising incongruency technique of McReynolds (1958) and the procedure of Riedel (1965) relating to doubtful judgments in a psychophysical paradigm.

This reviewer has been very favorably impressed with the demonstrated utility of self-rating and adjective checklist measures of anxiety, and wishes to counsel against acceptance of the idea that such measures, merely because they are relatively simple and straightforward, are necessarily inferior to the more complex inventories. On the contrary, they may often represent the technique of choice, particularly in the measurement of current anxiety.

It is important to emphasize that the assessment of anxiety does not involve merely a single variable, but is concerned rather with several quite distinct dimensions. This is a fact that many test users, as well as test designers, have not taken sufficiently into account. While there have been a number of attempts—*after* given tests are in use—to determine just what aspect(s) of anxiety they actually measure, it is obviously preferable to construct tests for a specific, manageable purpose in the first place. In a measurement sense there is no such simple variable as "anxiety," but only such specific variables as "characteristic overall anxiety," "current proneness to test anxiety," and so on. There appear to be, in principle, at least eight potential types of anxiety scores[4] (though not all would necessarily be useful). These can be conceptualized (Figure 1) by thinking of a cube, the dimensions of which are the dichotomies "characteristic vs. current," "overall vs. specific," and "existent vs. proneness." For example, the IPAT Anxiety Scale is a measure of characteristic, overall, existent anxiety; the TAQ is a measure of characteristic proneness to a specific (test-taking) anxiety; and so on. Further, any of the eight scores can, in principle, be assessed in terms of either stimulus or response concomitants.

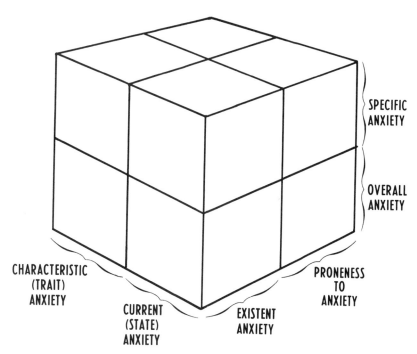

Figure 1. Representation of interrelations among different anxiety variables that can, in principle, be measured.

---

[4] This of course does not mean that there are eight different "kinds" of anxiety, any more than, say, "current temperature" and "average temperature" imply different "kinds" of temperature.

There are a number of opportunities for important additional research on anxiety assessment. More needs to be known about the lability of current levels of anxiety. It is possible that the variability of such levels over time would itself be a useful test variable. With regard to the development of new instruments for assessing anxiety, the most obvious opportunity is in the development of a test that systematically utilizes *both* the stimulus and response approaches, in separate parts, in order to gain greater validity. The S-R Inventory of Anxiousness is, of course, representative of this approach, but it makes no pretense to surveying systematically either anxiety-producing antecedents or anxiety symptoms. A paper by Aiken (1962) in which both stimulus and response items are rigorously derived is a step in the direction suggested, though that author has not proposed the construction of a test using both kinds of items.

The best counsel to give the user of anxiety tests is that he take care to select instruments that will yield measures of the particular anxiety variables in which he is interested. For example, if his real concern is with current anxiety, there is little point in his utilizing a measure of characteristic anxiety. It can be expected that as anxiety assessment instruments become more sophisticated, they will increasingly focus on specific, identifiable variables. Concomitant with this development and in a sense underlying it, a further growth in the theoretical bases of the construct of anxiety can be anticipated.

CHAPTER XIV

Psychophysiological assessment: Rationale and problems[1]

James R. Averill and Edward M. Opton, Jr.

By "psychophysiological assessment" we mean the process of making inferences about psychological phenomena on the basis of physiological data. In terms of formal procedures this is a relatively new method of assessment; however, the rationale behind it is very old. There is, for example, an anecdote concerning the Roman physician Galen in which he diagnosed the malady of a female patient as one of love, the basis of the diagnosis being a quickening of the pulse to the name of a certain dancer, but not to that of any other (Watson, 1963). But Galen did not limit himself to the assessment of emotions. He is perhaps best known to psychologists for his classification of the temperaments (which through the years were reduced to four: sanguine, melancholic, choleric, and phlegmatic) based upon the four bodily humors (blood, black bile, yellow bile, and phlegm). This is an instance of the psychophysiological assessment of personality, albeit a very speculative one.

With the advent of modern recording devices, the use of psychophysiological techniques has been extended into almost every area of psychology. It would be impossible in a short chapter to review exhaustively the resulting literature. Certain limitations must be placed, therefore, on the topics that will be covered in the following pages. We will not discuss the many technical factors involved in the sensing and recording of psychophysiological data.

[1]Preparation of this chapter was supported in part by the Rehabilitation Services Administration, Department of Health, Education, and Welfare, Washington, D.C.; grant No. RH-4.

Two manuals have recently appeared on this topic (Brown, 1967; Venables & Martin, 1967). Neither shall we examine in detail the physiological mechanisms that underlie the various response measures; there are an ample number of excellent physiological textbooks (e.g., Ruch & Patton, 1965) that should be consulted on such matters.

Even with the above exclusions it would be impossible to cover thoroughly the many research uses to which psychophysiological assessment has been put. Reflecting this fact, the first part of this chapter will be relatively "content free." That is, the emphasis will be on methodological issues that are of general importance for psychophysiological assessment. In order to add structure to such a discussion, a logical distinction will be drawn between two types of variables, episodic and dispositional, and the problems related to the assessment of each will be examined. The last part of the chapter will be devoted to a more substantive discussion of emotional reactions and personality traits—examples of episodic and dispositional variables, respectively. These remain today, nearly two millenia after Galen, the areas where psychophysiological assessment finds its widest application.

Before proceeding to a discussion of the problems associated with psychophysiological assessment, it might be helpful to outline some of the advantages offered by physiological variables. Perhaps the major reason for using psychophysiological techniques is to avoid certain sources of error characteristic of other assessment procedures. An individual's overt behavior—be it assessed by self-reports, clinical observation, or behavioral performance—is readily subject to distortion. This may stem from his conscious or unconscious need to present himself or the situation other than it is, or from his conformity to the mores and standards of conduct specific to a particular culture. It is generally assumed that physiological responses are less influenced by such factors and, hence, are more "objective." This assumption cannot be accepted uncritically. Nevertheless, it is true that a person's voluntary control over his physiological reactions is generally meager and indirect, although by no means absent. Similarly, physiological processes (urination and defecation excluded) are not typically subject to reinforcement during socialization and, therefore, are less likely to reflect institutionalized cultural patterns.

For reasons such as the above, psychophysiological assessment procedures are especially advantageous in situations where verbal and behavioral reports are difficult to interpret—e.g., with infants, the severely disturbed, and subjects in cross-cultural studies. This does not mean, of course, that physiological measures are free from all distortion. On the contrary, we will have occasion to note how physiological reactions are affected by defense mechanisms and coping behavior, and may even be used as indices of the success of such psychological processes. Moreover, the prevalence of psychosomatic illness is testimony to the extent to which the soma may be subject to its own kinds of distortion. Psychophysiological techniques should therefore be considered not a substitute for, but a valuable adjunct to, more standard assessment procedures.

In addition to their empirical usefulness, psychophysiological techniques may help provide a sounder theoretical foundation for traditional areas of assessment. In the not too distant past it was commonly asserted that psychology should eschew physiology, both in theory and in practice. It was argued that the concern of psychology should be the elucidation of behavioral laws based upon stimulus-response contingencies, and that events inside the organism are irrelevant to such a program. We do not agree. Although as a practical matter one cannot place electrodes in the brain of a recalcitrant student, or record the skin conductance of a diplomat during negotiations, many situations do allow physiological recordings, and the resulting data may afford opportunities for better theoretical understanding, prediction, and control. We shall return to this point and provide concrete illustrations in the latter part of the chapter.

Many other advantages of psychophysiological techniques could be cited, but our purpose is not to proselytize. We must assume that the reader already has an interest in this area and that we may therefore proceed directly to an examination of some of the conceptual and methodological problems involved in psychophysiological assessment.

THE DISTINCTION BETWEEN DISPOSITIONAL AND EPISODIC VARIABLES: SOME METHODOLOGICAL CONSIDERATIONS

The purpose of this section is to make explicit a logical distinction that is of considerable importance for psychophysiological assessment, namely that between dispositional and episodic variables. Briefly, *dispositions* refer to properties and traits, while *episodes* refer to particular incidents or events. For example, solubility and hostility are dispositional properties; dissolving and aggressing are episodes. This distinction may seem rather obvious; nevertheless, it has often been confused in the psychological literature or recognized only on an intuitive level. It is important to avoid such confusion because the problems and techniques involved in the measurement of the two types of variables are different, although by no means independent.

It should be emphasized that the distinction that we are considering is a logical one common to all branches of science, not just to psychology (Feigl, 1951; Hampshire, 1953; Pap, 1962; Ryle, 1949). At the risk of oversimplification it may be said that episodic variables refer to palpable states of affairs—e.g., events or reactions. They may therefore be defined ostensively, at least in principle; that is, one may figuratively point to and name them. The definition of dispositional variables is conceptually much more difficult. The most favored solution is currently in terms of "reduction sentences" (Carnap, 1936; Hempel, 1960). These are statements that follow the paradigm: If an object x is subjected to specified test conditions or stimuli, then the attribute 0 may be assigned to x if, and only if, x shows a characteristic mode of response. For example, *hostility* might be defined as follows: If individual x is subjected to mild provocation in the absence of internal or external restraints, then x is hostile if, and only if, x aggresses.

The reduction sentence indicates that dispositional variables do not refer to particular events but rather are manifested in such events. It is perhaps this feature that meets the most resistance, or is the least understood, since it seems to provide no concrete locus or referent for this type of concept. The question is naturally raised, if dispositional variables do not refer to episodes or events, what is their function? In physical theory they serve as characteristic constants and parameters—e.g., Young's modulus of elasticity; in psychology they are exemplified by intervening variables in the sense of MacCorquodale and Meehl (1948). More informally, dispositions may be viewed as shorthand statements for laws (Feigl, 1951) or as "inference tickets" (Ryle, 1949), because they tell us what results to expect under appropriate conditions.

Before proceeding to a discussion of the assessment of dispositional and episodic variables, a few words should be said concerning their temporality. Dispositions may be short-term or long-term—e.g., moods and motives as opposed to abilities and personality traits. Similarly, episodes may be acute or chronic (in the sense of long-enduring, continuous reactions)—e.g., a sudden fright as opposed to a prolonged anxiety reaction. One of the most common and serious confusions in psychophysiological assessment is the interpretation of short-term dispositions as chronic episodes. This, for example, appears to have been the rationale behind many of the attempts to relate dispositional anxiety, as measured by such scales as the Taylor (1953) Manifest Anxiety Scale (MAS),[2] to physiological activity in the resting or nonstimulated subject. Such studies have been rather uniformly unsuccessful (McReynolds, unpublished manuscript). As will be discussed subsequently, there is a sense in which dispositional variables are amenable to investigation and interpretation on a more molecular—e.g., physiological—level. But there is no reason to expect that a disposition such as anxiety will be characterized by the same physiological variables that are indicative of episodic anxiety. To repeat, psychological dispositions are not palpable states of affairs or events—behavioral, mental, or physiological—no matter how subtle or prolonged. This is a matter of logic, not of psychology or physiology.

The Assessment of Episodic Variables

Most techniques of psychophysiological assessment involve the measurement of some reaction—e.g., a change in electrodermal activity or heart rate. These are episodic variables that may be of interest in their own right, or that may be used to infer the presence of some dispositional property. The latter application will be discussed subsequently; in this section we will be concerned with four issues of importance for the measurement and interpretation of psychophysiological reactions per se. These include the generality, patterning, intensity, and temporal characteristics of the response.

Response generality. Conceptually, the measurement of psychophysiological episodes presents little difficulty, although the technical problems may be great. Their interpretation is another matter. Physiological reactions do not come with psychological labels attached, such as "fear" or

---

[2]It might be objected that "manifest" anxiety is not a dispositional variable. The complexity of the MAS unfortunately allows for a variety of interpretations. We believe, however, that there are sufficient grounds, both logical and empirical (see Cattell & Scheier, 1961; Spielberger, 1966), to consider the MAS primarily a measure of dispositional anxiety.

"anger." This is a matter of inference, the accuracy of which depends to a certain extent on the generality of the response measure. Whenever a single physiological variable is measured, valid inferences to a psychological state can be made only if the measure is specific to that state, or if the eliciting conditions are such that if any reaction occurs, it can be indicative of only one form of response. Instances of the first type are rare, although the use of penile plethysmography as a measure of sexual arousal is a good example (Freund, Sedlacek, & Knob, 1965). More typically, a response measure is chosen, not because it is specific to a particular psychological state, but because it is easily recorded and is sensitive to nearly any form of stimulation.

The galvanic skin response (GSR), by far the most commonly used psychophysiological measure, is a good illustration of a very general response variable. The extreme sensitivity of the GSR and the ease with which it can be recorded mean that it may be used in a wide variety of contexts. Extreme caution must be exercised, however, if its usefulness is not to be illusory. By itself the GSR can only indicate that a subject has responded. It affords no information concerning whether the response is one of anger, anxiety, elation, or even emotional arousal. This difficulty can be overcome in part by recording additional variables. In general, however, the investigator must rely on stringent experimental controls in order to rule out alternative explanations whenever the GSR, or any other nondiscriminatory measure, is used as a basis to infer specific psychological reactions.

Some investigators have attempted to assure the soundness of their psychological interpretation by measuring reactions in real-life situations. The development of miniature recorders and telemetry systems (see Caceres, 1965) will undoubtedly make this approach much more popular in the near future. There are obvious limitations to naturalistic observations, however, both from the standpoint of technical feasibility and experimental control. On the other hand, when one brings well-motivated and semi-sophisticated subjects into the laboratory, hardly a thing can be taken for granted concerning their reactions to the experimental manipulations.

In brief, when assessing psychophysiological episodes the investigator must be as concerned about the validity of his psychological independent variable as he is about his physiological dependent variable. In the absence of stringent experimental controls, the psychological phenomenon about which inferences are to be made can be no more specific than the physiological variable upon which the inference is based.

Response patterning. It was suggested above that the assessment of psychophysiological episodes may be made with greater precision if more than one variable is recorded. If the additional variables are not completely redundant, their pattern of activity will carry more information than will any single measure. Physiological response patterns, however, are a function of many factors, three of which are of particular importance for psychophysiological assessment. These include the tendency for a pattern to be specific (*a*) to the individual, (*b*) to the objective parameters of the stimulus, and (*c*) to the subjective appraisal of the stimulus.

(*a*) The principle of *individual response specificity* refers to the tendency of individuals to respond to different stimuli with idiosyncratic patterns of physiological activity (Engel, 1960; Lacey & Lacey, 1958a). It corresponds rather closely to the concept of "response set" in traditional areas of assessment. There are marked individual differences in the tendency toward this form of response patterning; in addition, its manifestation depends upon such factors as the similarity and temporal proximity of the eliciting stimuli, and upon the statistical treatment of the data (Oken, Grinker, Heath, Herz, Korchin, Sabshin, & Schwartz, 1962; Wenger, Clemens, Coleman, Cullen, & Engel, 1961).

Individual response specificity is one factor contributing to the low relationships typically observed among physiological variables when correlations are taken across individuals. That is, one subject may show high reactivity in heart rate and low reactivity in skin conductance relative to the group mean, while another subject may show the opposite pattern to the same stimulus. If there is reason to believe that the psychological reaction is the same for both individuals, the problem arises as to which variable or combination of variables is most indicative of that reaction. When individual response specificity is present (a test for this will be described below), it may be most efficient to use the measure that shows the greatest reactivity for each subject.

(b) The principle of stimulus response specificity refers to the tendency for a response pattern to be specific to the physical parameters or other objective criteria of the eliciting stimulus. This form of response specificity has been most thoroughly investigated by R. C. Davis and his colleagues. Davis (1957) has described, for example, four patterns of autonomic activity: one related to mild exercise; another, to simple visual and sound stimuli; a third, to more complex pictures; and a fourth, to various types of cutaneous stimuli.

The fact that simple stimuli elicit specific physiological response patterns may seem of little interest to psychologists. Unfortunately, what is of little interest is often ignored, even at the expense of clarity. For instance, none of the many studies designed to differentiate emotional states on the basis of physiological reactivity has explicitly controlled for stimulus response specificity. The typical research design has been to elicit each emotion by a different stimulus and then compare reactions. But different reactions should be expected regardless of the emotions if the eliciting stimuli differ markedly, as they usually do.

There are a variety of ways to control for stimulus response specificity. For example, two or more stimuli might be used to elicit the same psychological state. Alternatively, the same stimulus could be used to induce different states, either artificially—e.g., through the use of hypnosis—or naturally, by capitalizing on individual differences in reaction to the stimulus. Neither of these methods is completely satisfactory by itself, but in combination with standard experimental controls they would go a long way toward allowing an evaluation of the extent to which a response pattern is a function of the particular stimulus used.

(c) The precise definition of a stimulus has been a traditional area of disagreement in psychology. Some define a stimulus in terms of objective parameters; others prefer to classify stimuli by relevance to some motivational system. This distinction has its counterpart in the analysis of response patterning. As described above, a response pattern may be specific to an objectively defined stimulus; we will now consider the tendency for a pattern to be specific to the subjective appraisal of a stimulus. The concept of *motivational response specificity*, originally introduced by Ax (1964) in a slightly different context, may be used to describe this tendency.

The distinction between stimulus and motivational response specificity is clearly illustrated in a study by Zimny and Miller (1966). Two groups of *Ss* received a series of either 28 hot or 28 cold stimuli to the arm, with three auditory stimuli interspersed after every eight thermal stimuli. The typical thermoregulatory response is vasodilation to a hot stimulus and vasoconstriction to a cold stimulus. It was found, however, that the initial response to both the hot and cold stimuli, as well as to the interposed sound stimuli, was vasoconstriction. After a number of trials this response habituated out and was replaced by the normal thermoregulatory responses.

In this experiment the vasoconstrictive and vasodilatory thermoregulatory responses to the cold and hot stimuli are clear examples of stimulus response specificity. On the other hand, the vasoconstrictive response that occurred upon the initial presentation of all the stimuli is a good illustration of motivational response specificity. It is one aspect of a more general reaction called the "orienting response," which is characterized by a unique pattern of physiological activity and is relatively independent of the physical parameters of the stimulus. It was first described by Pavlov (1927) as a "reflex which brings about the immediate response in man and animals to the slightest changes in the world around them, so that they immediately orient their appropriate receptor organ in accordance with the perceptible quality of the agent bringing about the change, making full investigation of it [p. 12]." (For a more detailed account of the orienting response and its use in psychological assessment, see Lynn, 1966.)

Other examples of motivational response specificity will be described in a subsequent section on emotional reactions. At present it is sufficient to note that different stimuli may elicit similar response patterns to the extent that they are interpreted alike by the subject. The converse of this proposition may also be true. That is, the same stimulus may produce different response patterns, depending upon differences in its subjective evaluation. This is well illustrated in an experiment by Graham, Kabler, and Graham (1962). These investigators had observed that patients with hives often felt they were being unjustly treated and were helpless to do anything about it. Hypertensive patients, on the other hand, typically felt threatened with harm against which they had to be constantly on guard. Normal subjects were consequently hypnotized and given suggestions related to the attitudes characteristic of these patient groups. Under the threat of a suggested burn it was found, as predicted, that skin temperature rose more when subjects had attitudes similar to those of patients with hives than it did when the subjects had attitudes characteristic of hypertension. The reverse relationship held true for diastolic blood pressure.

The above experiment illustrates that the analysis of response patterning into individual, stimulus, and motivational response specificity does not represent a true trichotomy. It has already been indicated that there is no sharp distinction between stimulus and motivational response specificity; both are related to some aspect of the stimulus situation. We now see that there is no clear dividing line between motivational and individual response specificity; both are a function of the individual. That is, to the extent that a person adopts the same or similar attitudes to diverse stimuli, individual response specificity will be evidenced with respect to those stimuli. Nevertheless, the distinction of these three classes of response patterning is of considerable practical importance for psychophysiological assessment.

Unfortunately, the statistical treatment of response patterns—e.g., their identification and comparison—is a problem for which there is no readily available solution. The response specificities can be considered as two-way interactions within the framework of analysis of variance. This requires a repeated measures design in which a variety of physiological variables are recorded from each individual under diverse situations. The interaction of individuals with response variables indicates individual differences in response patterning, whatever the situation. This is individual response specificity. The interaction between situations and response variables reflects the extent to which different situations tend to elicit unique response patterns, regardless of persons. We have broken this source of variance into stimulus and motivational response specificity. (For a more detailed discussion of the sources of variance in this type of design and their implications for psychological assessment, see Endler and Hunt, 1966.)

Cattell (1965; Cattell & Scheier, 1961) has used to great advantage factor-analytic models for the identification of psychophysiological episodes, which he calls "state" variables. But these, like the analysis of variance, are useful primarily for the identification of response patterns, and not for their comparison. For the latter, the D index described by Osgood and Suci (1958), Cattell's r_p (Cattell, Coulter, & Tsujioka, 1966), and the Kendall coefficient of concordance W (Siegel, 1956) have proven to be of value.

Response intensity. The evaluation of psychophysiological episodes would be greatly simplified if it could be assumed that as the intensity of a psychological reaction increased, the corresponding physiological response pattern would also increase quantitatively, without there being any qualitative change. There are two reasons why this assumption cannot be made, however. In the first place, diverse physiological mechanisms may be triggered as the intensity of the reaction exceeds the thresholds for different variables. Secondly, the size of a reaction may vary as a function of prior physiological activity. Thus, if prestimulus levels are already near their maxima, further stimulation may produce only minor increases or "paradoxical" decreases in activity. This is known as the *law of initial values* (LIV), and it deserves special comment.

The LIV has stimulated a great deal of discussion and research among psychophysiologists (Benjamin, 1963; Hord, Johnson, & Lubin, 1964; Lacey, 1956). The resulting technical and statistical literature presents a formidable barrier to the newcomer—a more formidable barrier than we think is justified. For persons better acquainted with psychological than with physiological measures, a first approximation to the LIV may be had from the familiar "ceiling effect" often observed in the use of rating scales. Suppose that two groups rate themselves on a 10-point scale of anxiety before and during a threatening experience. If the groups differ in mean prestimulus ratings, the poststimulus scores cannot be compared directly. Therefore, we commonly use change scores rather than absolute values. But if one group in our hypothetical example happened to be anxiety neurotics, they might have had initial ratings in the area of 8 and 9, allowing little room for upward change.

There are several ways to deal with this ceiling effect—e.g., by statistical transformation of the raw data and by analysis of covariance. These same methods are used to control for the LIV in psychophysiological data. On a strictly empirical level, therefore, there is little difference between the LIV and similar problems in other areas of assessment. However, the ceiling effect is only one aspect of the LIV. The most important factors underlying the LIV, and the ones that make it an especially vexing problem in psychophysiology, are the homeostatic mechanisms by which the body maintains an internal environment appropriate to the conditions at hand. Whenever a reaction begins to exceed certain limitations, which may vary according to the individual, and the situation, regulatory mechanisms act to return the variable to its usual range.

The LIV is thus one illustration of a more general principle that cannot be overemphasized: psychophysiological assessment deals with systems whose reactions to stimulation take place in a context of continuous regulation by complex feedback mechanisms. Alterations in one part of a system—i.e., a physiological response—can be interpreted only in light of changes occurring elsewhere in the system. The LIV may therefore be generalized to include the dependence of a reaction on prior and concomitant activity in a set of related variables. Thus, a change in heart rate may be a function, not only of prior cardiac activity, but also of blood pressure and peripheral vascular resistance, and even of events occurring outside the cardiovascular system—e.g., respiration. This indicates the importance of recording sufficient variables to allow a physiological as well as a psychological interpretation of any psychophysiological episode.

Temporal characteristics of the response. In psychophysiological assessment the physiological response should be appropriate to the units of time in which the psychological phenomenon occurs. Some variables—e.g., the GSR, heart rate, and peripheral vasoconstriction—respond quickly to stimulation. Others, such as skin temperature and intestinal peristalsis, respond less rapidly but have a longer duration. Still other variables—for example, the secretion of hormones into the blood and their subsequent assay from urinary excretion—can be measured only over periods of hours or days.

In general, short-term psychological reactions should be assessed by physiological measures that respond with like speed. This is not to say that a sudden fright might not produce significant changes in endocrine secretion, but only that momentary endocrine responses cannot be measured reliably under most conditions. On the other hand, endocrine changes hold great promise for the assessment of chronic psychological processes. This is well illustrated in a study by Friedman, Mason, and Hamburg (1963). These investigators related urinary excretion of 17-OHCS, which is a function of adrenal cortical hormone secretion, to the psychological reactions of parents whose children were suffering from leukemia. When the parents' defense mechanisms and coping strategies were taken into account, the hormonal assays proved to be reliable indices of stress.

The temporal characteristics of a response are important in yet another respect. As a physiological reaction is prolonged in time, homeostatic and other mechanisms may be initiated that greatly alter the pattern of activity. Mahl (1953), for instance, has reported increased gastric secretion during chronic fear, but decreased secretion during acute fear. Selye's (1956) general adaption syndrome is another example of a physiological pattern varying over time, even though the initiating conditions remain constant. Obviously, one must control for the chronicity as well as the intensity of a response in the psychophysiological assessment of episodic variables.

The Assessment of Dispositional Variables

There are three general methods for the assessment of dispositional variables. The first is by reduction to some identifiable microproperty; the second, by correlation with some other mensurable attribute; and the third, by the elicitation of appropriate episodes or reactions. The rationale for and problems involved in each of these methods will be discussed below.

The reductive method of dispositional assessment. Dispositional concepts may function as a kind of shorthand for the qualitative or quantitative relationships between variables within a (macro)theory. As such, they cannot be explained within the theory, although they may be reduced to, or explained by, concepts from another (micro)theory. The identification of the appropriate microproperty may thus allow an assessment of the corresponding dispositional variable. For example, an indication of a substance's solubility may be had from a knowledge of its molecular structure.

For reasons that will become apparent below, this method of dispositional assessment is rare within psychology. Nevertheless, it is implicit in the writings of many psychologists. Consider the following quotation from Hebb (1955), p. 249): "And I now propose to you that, whatever you wish to call it, arousal in this sense [mediated by the reticular activating system] is synonymous with a general state, and the conception of drive therefore assumes anatomical and physiological identity." If such an identification proved acceptable, "drive" could be assessed by measuring activity within the reticular formation—e.g., by electroencephalography. Most drive theorists, however, do not consider such a formulation adequate, at least in its present form (see Spence & Spence, 1966b).

The above approach to the assessment of dispositions entails the much-debated issue of reductionism—i.e., the explanation of one theory or set of laws in terms of a theory established in some other area of inquiry (Feigl, 1951; Jessor, 1958; Nagel, 1961). Strictly speaking, only one theory can be reduced to another theory.[3] The feasibility of the reductive method in

---

[3] Some philosophers (e.g., Feigl, 1958; Smart, 1963) have suggested that psychological processes can be conceived as physiological events, just as "lightning" is conceived as an electrical phenomenon. This type of reductionism, known as the "identity thesis," is perhaps of greater relevance to present-day psychology in that it does not require the psychological concept to be embedded within a theory. This fact does not alter the import of the present argument, however.

psychophysiological assessment depends, therefore, upon the stage of development of psychological and physiological theory at any given time. At present, neither of these disciplines possesses the necessary theoretical sophistication for this method to be of much practical importance. It may be a satisfying intellectual task, and is undoubtedly of some heuristic value, to postulate "conceptual nervous systems" to help explain psychological phenomena, but too often such schemes are more akin to translation exercises than to reductionism in the logical sense. That is, physiological jargon is simply substituted for psychological jargon without any increase in explanatory power.

The correlative method of dispositional assessment. This method capitalizes on an empirical correlation between two variables, using the more readily measured variable to estimate the value of the other. Both variables may be dispositional in nature, and they may (but need not) be from different areas of inquiry. When they are from different areas, such as psychology and physiology, this method differs from the reductive technique in that the macroproperty is not identified with, or explained by, the corresponding microproperty. Rather, both are assumed to reflect some other phenomenon which may or may not be understood. The correlative method, therefore, does not require the theoretical sophistication necessary for reduction.

The correlative method has been used quite frequently in psychophysiological assessment, albeit with limited success. Perhaps the best known examples concern the various constitutional taxonomies or somatotypes—e.g., by Kretschmer (1955) and Sheldon (Sheldon & Stevens, 1942). The physique is easily measured, and to the extent that it is correlated with personality traits, it allows a convenient means of assessment. Although somatotypes have received little attention in recent years, psychologists have not completely lost interest in them (see Domey, Duckworth, & Morandi, 1964; Kagan, 1966).

The utility of correlative procedures may be markedly increased through the analysis of internal physiological structures and functions, especially as related to the endocrine and autonomic nervous systems. Some steps have already been taken in this direction—e.g., relating autonomic balance (Wenger, 1966) and lability (Doctor & Friedman, 1966; Lacey & Lacey, 1958b) to personality, diagnostic, and performance variables. The inclusion of physiological variables in factor-analytic studies of psychological traits (e.g., Cattell, 1965) can also be considered a use of the correlative method of dispositional assessment.

The distinction between the correlative and reductive methods of psychophysiological assessment does not, of course, represent a strict dichotomy. Logical reduction constitutes one extreme; the use of a strictly empirical correlation represents another. In between lie the vast majority of cases, in which psychological and physiological variables are linked both for theoretical reasons and on the basis of some empirical correlation. In a sense one might consider any correlative relationship as potentially reductive; the transition, however, must typically await marked advances in conceptualization.

The elicitation method of dispositional assessment. This method takes into account the probability and/or intensity of a reaction elicited under appropriate test conditions. For example, the elasticity of a substance may be measured by subjecting it to a certain stress and recording the resulting deformation or strain. Similarly, a psychological disposition may be assessed by measuring physiological reactions under appropriate circumstances. This method is undoubtedly the most commonly used technique in the psychophysiological assessment of dispositions.

The test conditions used to elicit a reaction may be real-life situations. But such situations are seldom sufficiently defined, either in terms of the effective stimulus or of the response contingencies open to the individual, for the reaction to be considered a clear indication of the disposition being assessed. The elicitation of reactions under controlled laboratory conditions, therefore, promises to be the most fruitful approach to the psychophysiological assessment of dispositional variables. Indeed, it has already proven its worth for the assessment of a wide variety of psychological dispositions—e.g., prejudices (Westie & DeFleur, 1959; Porier & Lott, 1967), defense mechanisms and coping styles (Goldstein, Jones, Clemens, Flagg, & Alexander, 1965), connotative meaning (Feather, 1965), cognitive styles (Israel, 1966), and personality traits (which will be discussed subsequently), to name but a few. Unfortunately, numerous instances of the failure of the elicitation method could also be cited. In the remainder of this section we will discuss three factors that often contribute to negative results when psychological dispositions are related to physiological reactions. They are: (a) the generality of the disposition, (b) the nature of the physiological reaction, and (c) obscuration by confounding variables that covary with the disposition being assessed. A fourth factor, the failure to distinguish ipsative from normative sources of variance, will be discussed in a subsequent section.

(a) One reason for the low relationship often found between psychological dispositions and physiological reactivity is that the dispositional variables are too broadly defined. In order to assess the influence of a general disposition on reactivity, it is necessary to control for any lower-order dispositions that might influence the person's evaluation of the test conditions. This is well illustrated in a study by Hodges and Spielberger (1966) in which they found cardiac acceleration upon threat of shock to be unrelated to scores on the MAS, although it was related to fear of shock as assessed two months prior to the experiment. Fear of shock is, in this sense, a dispositional variable, but of a much more specific nature than that measured by the MAS.

(b) Since the elicitation method requires the measurement of a physiological reaction, most of the considerations previously discussed with reference to episodic variables are of relevance here also. The question of response specificity is of special importance. Stimulus and motivational specificity must obviously be taken into account if one wishes to assess dispositional variables that imply different modes of response. Thus, in order to assess dispositional anxiety, physiological variables indicative of a fear reaction or of episodic anxiety should be measured. Different sets of variables might be appropriate for the assessment of hostility or depression. On the other hand, the presence of individual response specificity might require the assignment of different weights to different variables depending upon the subject.

The response specificities are important for still another reason. As previously noted, they can be considered as two-way interactions in an analysis of variance design. No competent investigator would consciously lessen the power of his statistical analysis by incorporating a significant interaction into his error variance. But it is not uncommon to find studies in which an attempt is made to relate individual differences along some dimension (e.g., a personality trait) to physiological reactivity as measured by a single variable (e.g., skin conductance) elicited under one stimulus condition (e.g., threat of shock). No two-way interactions can be calculated under such conditions, and hence there is no way to assess independently the extent to which any of the response specificities might be operating. But these sources of potential variance have not been eliminated, only ignored. Their effects may appear as increased error variance and insignificant results.

(*c*) A third factor contributing to negative findings with the elicitation method is the failure to control for confounding variables that may covary with the disposition being assessed. For example, to measure which of two substances is more soluble, they could be placed in a solvent and the speed of dissolving measured. Such a test assumes that the only relevant difference between the two substances is a difference in solubility. Unfortunately, a similar assumption can seldom be made with reference to psychological dispositions. The individual with high dispositional anxiety, for instance, is likely to differ from the low anxious person on many relevant variables. Thus, if the high anxious subject has well-developed defense mechanisms, he may show no greater reactivity than a low anxious individual when in a stressful situation of insufficient intensity to break down his defenses. There is, in fact, a growing body of empirical evidence to support the proposition that the presence of successful defenses and coping processes is inversely related to physiological stress reactions (see Lazarus, 1966, pp. 277 *ff.*).

THE PSYCHOPHYSIOLOGICAL ASSESSMENT OF
EMOTIONAL REACTIONS

In this section emotional reactions will be used to illustrate the psychophysiological assessment of episodic variables. Many everyday words with emotional connotations—e.g., "anxious"—may be used in both an episodic and dispositional sense (see Pitcher, 1965); however, this discussion will be concerned only with emotional episodes. We will consider first the physiological differentiation of the so-called "basic" emotions as exemplified by fear and anger. This will be followed by a brief discussion of possible affective dimensions—e.g., pleasantness and activation. Finally, we will examine a recent formulation concerning the interaction between cognitive and physiological factors in the determination of emotional behavior.

Basic Emotions

William James (1890) was not very impressed with the mere cataloging and description of emotional reactions. It was his opinion that "as far as 'scientific psychology' of the emotions goes, I may have been surfeited by too much reading of classic works on the subject, but I should as lief read verbal descriptions of the shapes of the rocks on a New Hampshire farm as toil through them again [p. 448] ." As much as one might sympathize with James on this matter, his well-known suggestion concerning the genesis of affective experience implied that different emotions could be characterized by different patterns of physiological activity. The failure of early investigators to observe such differential patterning formed a crucial aspect of Cannon's (1929) widely accepted attack on the James-Lange theory of emotion. Cannon held that all emotional reactions, if sufficiently intense, are characterized by mass discharge of the sympathetic nervous system.

This "mass action" concept of sympathetic activity has had important consequences for psychophysiological experimentation. For the past thirty or more years psychologists have tended to deemphasize physiological patterns corresponding to specific emotions, and instead have concentrated on measuring the one aspect of emotion that can be assessed under a "mass action" concept, namely intensity. Assessment of the quality of emotional reactions has been left primarily to psychological assessment techniques or has been controlled, more or less successfully, by manipulation of stimulus conditions.

The idea that intensity is the only physiologically important dimension of emotion still has its advocates (e.g., Duffy, 1962) but recent evidence indicates that the mass action hypothesis is a gross oversimplification. The new evidence, plus technical advances in physiologcal transducers and hormonal assay methods, has rekindled interest in assessment of the *quality* of emotion by measurement of physiological response patterns. Patterns have been described for such emotions as fear, anxiety, anger, pain, sadness, mirth, sexual excitement, and startle (Averill, 1966; Ax, 1953; Cattell & Sheier, 1961; Funkenstein, King, & Drolette, 1957; Masters & Johnson, 1966; J. Schachter, 1957; Smith & Wenger, 1965; Sternbach, 1960; 1962; and many others cited by Arnold, 1960). With few exceptions strong sympathetic involvement has been observed regardless of the emotion. The patterns of sympathetic activation differ among emotions, however, as does the involvement of other physiological systems—e.g., the parasympathetic and endocrine systems. Perhaps this research can best be summarized with the observation that the physiological differentiation of emotional states does seem possible, but it depends to a large extent on the number and type of variables measured and the adequacy of the subsequent data analysis. There is not space to review the evidence upon which this conclusion is based. We shall therefore limit our remarks to the physiological differentiation of fear and anger, the most thoroughly investigated emotions.

It has been suggested that during fear and anger there is a preferential secretion of epinephrine (adrenaline) and norepinephrine (noradrenaline), respectively. These hormones are intimately related to the activity of the sympathetic nervous system; both are secreted by the adrenal medulla, and norepinephrine appears to be the chemical mediator released at sympathetic nerve endings (Burn, 1963).

The evidence linking epinephrine and norepinephrine to fear and anger comes from a variety of sources. Ax (1953) and J. Schachter (1957) reached this conclusion on the basis of polygraph data from subjects placed in fear-

and anger-inducing situations.[4] Funkenstein et al. (1957) found that subjects who were either frightened or depressed (interpreted as anger directed toward the self) tended to show a blood pressure response to mecholyl, a parasympathetic stimulant, similar to that observed after a preinjection of epinephrine. On the other hand, subjects who directed their anger outward tended to give a norepinephrine-like response. On the phylogenetic side, Goodall (1951) has reported that aggressive, attacking animals such as the lion have a predominance of norepinephrine in the adrenal glands, whereas epinephrine is predominant in the adrenals of animals that depend primarily on flight for survival.

Direct measurement of epinephrine and norepinephrine during fear and anger has also been attempted. In general, the results have been in favor of differential secretion during these states (Schildkraut & Kety, 1967; Von Euler, 1964), but there have been many exceptions (e.g., Nelson, Minoru, & Holms, 1966). Moreover, in an investigation of conditioned emotional reactions in monkeys, Mason, Mangan, Brady, Conrad, and Rioch (1961) found evidence indicating that ephinephrine-fear and norepinephrine-anger relationships may be the result of a more general characteristic of these emotions. They suggest that uncertainty or unpredictability, in combination with such factors as threat of noxious stimulation and the anticipation of coping behavior, may be the critical factors determining the release of epinephrine and norepinephrine during emotion.

There is also evidence for parasympathetic involvement in angry or aggressive behavior, especially as evidenced by increased gastrointestinal activity (Arnold, 1960; Wolf, 1965). This is consistent with the above-mentioned report that animals that are aggressors in the predator-prey relationship tend to show a relatively higher secretion of norepinephrine. These findings might indicate that some forms of human aggression have their biological roots in predation, a fact that would help explain the prevalence of this behavior. In this respect it is worth quoting a statement by Freeman (1964) that "in the light of recent paleo-anthropological discoveries, the hypothesis has now been advanced that certain aspects of human nature (including possibly aggressivity and cruelty) may well be connected with the special predatory and carnivorous adaptation which were so basic to hominid evolution during the Pleistocene period [p. 124]."

---

[4]One might suppose that the physiological response patterns described by Ax (1953) and J. Schachter (1957) could be used as a practical and objective means of assessing fear and anger. Several precautionary comments are in order, however. (a) The reliability of the patterns has not been adequately demonstrated. The experiment by Schachter used some of the same data previously reported by Ax and hence does not represent a true replication. (b) In both studies there was a confounding of motivational response specificity (the emotional reactions) with stimulus response specificity. That is, one stimulus was used to elicit fear and another to elicit anger, and these stimuli differed along a number of dimensions—e.g., the amount of physical contact and social interaction, which could possibly account for the observed differences in response patterns. (c) Even if the *mean* patterns are reliable and indicative of the emotions as specified, individual differences are so great as to preclude their use in assessing whether a particular subject is expressing fear or anger in a given situation (see Kahn, 1960). In short, the value of these studies is primarily theoretical.

The above evidence on the physiological differentiation of fear and anger, although by no means conclusive, may serve to illustrate several factors of importance for psychophysiological assessment. First, one way in which psychophysiological data may aid theoretical advancement is by providing insights into the biological origins and significance of behavioral reactions. Second, the mere recording and comparison of variables does not guarantee the recognition of differential response patterns; this depends upon an understanding of the physiological principles that underlie those patterns. Before the late 1940's when norepinephrine was recognized as a sympathetic neurohumor and medullary hormone with properties distinct from those of epinephrine, the sympathetic activation observed during fear and anger was generally interpreted in terms of the mass action hypothesis and as evidence against the physiological differentiation of emotional states. That is, similarities were emphasized and differences ignored, in conformity with the theoretical conceptions prevalent at the time. Finally, the fact that epinephrine and norepinephrine may not be related to fear and anger per se but rather to some more general dimension such as uncertainty or unpredictability, indicates the possibility of investigating the physiological correlates of affective dimensions, as opposed to specific emotions. But more of that shortly; first a few words should be said concerning the physiological significance of emotional labels.

There is no reason to expect a unique pattern of physiological activity to correspond to each emotional state that is distinguished linguistically. Emotion-words do not simply describe behavior, either overt or covert. They also place the actions of an individual within the context of the rest of his behavior and within a particular social setting (see Bedford, 1957). Many of the nuances between emotional concepts are therefore of little consequence for physiological functioning. Only a great deal of further research will reveal the extent to which different emotional concepts are based on linguistic discriminations that refer primarily to social and cognitive factors, rather than on more basic biological phenomena. But it does seem likely that physiological differentiation of emotions will be found mainly among those aspects of emotional life that are basic in an evolutionary sense (see McDougall, 1936; Plutchick, 1962).

Affective Dimensions

Wundt (1902) attempted to bring order to the field of emotion with his famous tridimensional theory of feeling. This was the proposal that affective experiences be described in terms of three fundamental dimensions: *pleasantness-unpleasantness, excitement-quiet,* and *tension-relaxation.* Wundt also postulated specific physiological patterns for each dimension; but these received little experimental support, and after an initial flurry of research, interest in them was soon lost. Research into the multidimensional scaling of affect, however, has recently enjoyed a revival. This is due in part to the finding that a reliable scaling of affect can be made on the basis of facial expression, although the labeling of specific emotions is difficult under such circumstances (Osgood, 1966; Schlosberg, 1954; but see Ekman & Friesen, 1967).

No attempt will be made to review the many suggestions concerning the number and nature of possible affective dimensions or their physiological correlates; a few examples will suffice to illustrate their potential usefulness for psychophysiological assessment. Some variant of the pleasantness dimension, often couched in more behavioristic terms such as "approach-withdrawal," has appeared in practically all emotional classifications. Nevertheless, there has been little modern research into the possible physiological correlates of this dimension. Schneirla (1965) has analyzed the approach-withdrawal aspect of behavior in terms of its phylogenetic and ontogenetic development. He postulates that *approach* is typically an energy-conserving process mediated predominantly by the parasympathetic nervous system. *Withdrawal* processes, on the other hand, are conceived to be energy-expending and to involve sympathetic activation.

Some form of activation, the modern equivalent of Wundt's excitement-quiet dimension, has also been widely recognized as a factor of importance in the description of emotional reactions. In contrast to pleasantness, this dimension has been the subject of much psychophysiological research and speculation. This stems in part from the tradition of research on emotional intensity under the mass action concept previously discussed. It received great impetus, however, with the discovery of the brain stem reticular activating system, which seemed to provide a concrete anatomical locus for this dimension (see Duffy, 1962; Lindsley, 1951, 1960; Malmo, 1959).

Schlosberg (1954) has described an affective dimension that he tentatively labeled "attention-rejection." There has been no direct investigation into the possible physiological correlates of this dimension, but of possible relevance is the work of Lacey (Lacey, Kagan, Lacey, & Moss, 1963), which indicates differential autonomic patterning depending upon whether the subject is oriented toward environmental receptivity or rejection. Sokolov's (1963) pioneering studies on the orienting reflex (to novel or "interesting" stimuli) as opposed to the defensive reflex (to high-intensity, painful stimuli) might also be interpreted as a form of "attention-rejection."

Other affective dimensions have been proposed by various investigators, but with little agreement or empirical verification. They will therefore not be discussed here. Two further points need to be emphasized, however. The first is that affective dimensions such as pleasantness and activation are convenient abstractions introduced to simplify a complex area of inquiry. In such a process there is always the danger of oversimplification, especially with respect to physiological mechanisms. There is no a priori reason to expect a single physiological response pattern to correspond to each emotional dimension indentifiable on psychological grounds. To take an obvious example, the profound physiological reactions accompanying the pleasure of sexual orgasm (Bartlett, 1956; Masters & Johnson, 1966) are quite different from those which characterize the pleasure of postprandial relaxation. The second point to note is that there is no basic conflict between the investigation of "basic" emotions, such as fear and anger, and that of affective dimensions. The former may be considered to represent particularly significant points within a multidimensional affective space (see Osgood, 1966).

The Interaction Between Cognitive and Physiological Factors

Stanley Schachter (1966; Schachter & Singer, 1962) has suggested that emotional states be considered a joint function of physiological arousal and of a cognition appropriate to the arousal. That is, the internal cues arising from the increased physiological activity are interpreted on the basis of the immediate situation. "To the extent cognitive factors are potent determiners of emotional states, it should be anticipated that precisely the same state of physiological arousal could be labeled 'joy' or 'fury' or 'jealousy' or any of a great diversity of emotional labels depending on the cognitive aspects of the situation [Schachter & Singer, 1962, p. 398]." Schachter does not deny that different physiological states may accompany different emotions, but he assigns little significance to this possibility—any physiological reaction of sufficient intensity may be interpreted as any emotion depending upon the cognitive interpretation of the situation.

Similar interpretations of emotional behavior have been made in the past (e.g., Duffy, 1941; Harlow & Stagner, 1933), but Schachter is the first to present a body of evidence in its support. There is not space to deal with this evidence in detail, but a few comments are in order because of the wide acceptance that this formulation has enjoyed and because of its obvious relevance for the psychophysiological assessment of emotion. We do not disagree with Schachter on the importance of cognitive factors in the ascription of emotional labels, but we do disagree with the role he assigns to differential physiological response patterns. It is our opinion that such patterns do exist in certain instances, that they provide a potentially important source of information for psychophysiological assessment, and that the afferent feedback from these patterns is an important determinant of the *quality* of different affective experiences.

The primary evidence supporting Schachter's position has come from studies in which subjects report emotional experiences after injection of epinephrine, providing appropriate cognitions are available either from their own past experience or by experimental design. If peripheral physiological arousal is the major factor responsible for these findings, as Schachter assumes, then similar results should be observed after injection of norepinephrine, which is also strongly sympathomimetic. Although norepinephrine has not been tested in situations like those used by Schachter, where specific affective cognitions were provided, it has been administered in many of the same contexts as epinephrine, but without similar effect on affective experience (Frankenhaeuser, Järpe, & Mattell, 1961; Hawkins, Monroe, Sandifer, & Vernon, 1960; King, Sokoloff, & Wechsler, 1952; Swan, 1952; Wenger, Clemens, Darsie, Engel, Estess, & Sonnenschein, 1960). In the absence of evidence to the contrary, it seems likely that the different effects of epinephrine and norepinephrine on affective experience are due to differences in action on the central nervous system, and not to the peripheral effects of these drugs. This does not mean that the data presented by Schachter are without interest, only that they are irrelevant to the thesis that he wishes to defend.

The above discussion of the psychophysiological assessment of emotional episodes can be summarized briefly as follows: (*a*) emotional concepts as expressed in ordinary language depend heavily for their meaning on cognitive and situational factors that are of little relevance to physiological functioning; (b) it appears likely, however, that certain emotions and/or affective dimensions that are basic in an evolutionary sense are characterized by different physiological response patterns; (c) these patterns are important sources of information concerning the quality of emotion, both subjectively and objectively; and (d) an adequate description of emotional episodes will depend not only upon technical advances in the recording and analysis of psychophysiological variables, but also upon conceptual advances concerning the psychological nature of emotions and the principles of organization governing physiological reactivity. These observations obviously are not so much a summary of past achievement as they are prolegomena for future research.

PSYCHOPHYSIOLOGICAL ASSESSMENT OF PERSONALITY TRAITS

We have divided the psychophysiological assessment of dispositional variables into three categories: namely, the reductive, correlative, and elicitation methods. Because the distinction between the first two is somewhat arbitrary, we will combine them in the present discussion; the elicitation method will be discussed separately.

Reductive and Correlative Methods of Personality Assessment

Behavioral and physiological activities are products of a single biological organism; hence, it is to be expected that correlations will exist between these two classes of variables. The correlative method relies on the fact that it is not always necessary to understand the underlying biological mechanisms in order to find and use such correlations for the purpose of assessment.

Some intriguing correspondences have been reported between single personality and physiological measures—for example, Fisher's (1960) finding of differential electrodermal activity in the left and right hands as a function of body-image and sex-role variables. But the many studies relating one or a few pairs of variables have not had as much impact as the few large-scale programs of research using many variables and situations. One of the most important of these programs has been conducted for many years by R. B. Cattell (1965) and his colleagues. Cattell has used a great variety of measuring instruments, including psychophysiological ones, to test a large number of individuals and groups in many situations. Using correlations among measures across individuals (R-technique), Cattell has extracted by factor analysis a considerable number of factors that he believes represent fundamental dimensions of personality.

The usefulness of the factors or personality dimensions described by Cattell is a matter of controversy (Dean, 1963; Gordon, 1966; Jones, 1964), which need not concern us here. A few comments are in order, however, concerning the magnitude of correlations and factor loadings typically obtained. For example, Cattell and Scheier (1960) reported the following loadings for physiological variables on their anxiety factor, "U.I. 24 (+)":

+ .30 higher systolic blood pressure
+ .27 greater volume of saliva secreted

    − .26 lower absolute level of skin resistance

    − .22 small pupil diameter during stress

The modest magnitude of these factor loadings suggests that the usefulness of psychophysiological measures for assessment of individual differences may be quite limited within the context of the correlative method.

The use of purely correlative techniques means that psychological and physiological variables do not mutually anchor each other; for example, no causal network is implied by Cattell's factor-analytic taxonomy of personality. This "fishing expedition" approach (one casts his net upon the waters and pulls in as many correlations as possible) has the advantage of requiring no preconceptions or assumptions about the structure and function of the nervous system. On the other hand, a purely descriptive approach to the use of psychophysiological variables leaves unsatisfied those psychologists who feel a need for more theoretical explanations.

One type of theoretical explanation that has a great appeal for many psychologists involves the reduction of psychological phenomena to physiological processes. The goal is in certain respects similar to the explanation of disease symptoms in terms of underlying physiological mechanisms, or of chemical reactions in terms of molecular structure. Such explanations are among the most powerful and satisfying in science. This accounts, perhaps, for the great perseverance of psychologists in pursuing reductive explanations, in spite of a general lack of success. In this section we will discuss only one theory of personality that is reductive—at least in spirit, if not in actuality: the theory developed by Hans J. Eysenck.

Eysenck's (1960) theory shares much with Cattell's: it depends heavily on factor analysis; it has been developed through use of questionnaire, behavioral, and psychophysiological assessment methods; anxiety and extraversion-introversion are important concepts in its taxonomy of personality; and it claims to be a comprehensive theory of personality—a substitute for, not merely an adjunct to, alternate theories.

But in Eysenck's system, unlike Cattell's, physiological processes play a central explanatory role. Eysenck follows Pavlov in positing that the neural processes of excitation and inhibition are of different strengths or potencies in different individuals. This difference, Eysenck believes, accounts for one of the two primary factorial dimensions of personality, introversion-extraversion. In this theory there is an implicit assumption that the inhibitory and excitatory processes that take place at the level of individual nerve cells also occur as some sort of mass effect over the entire nervous system. Eysenck has had nothing to say about how inhibition and excitation of the whole nervous system occur, or how they might be measured directly; but he does assume that some variables are more closely linked to the neural processes than others, and foremost among these is the conditioning of autonomic variables such as the GSR. Thus, Eysenck is able to make predictions about relationships between relatively less indirect measures of excitation-inhibition, such as acquisition and extinction of the conditioned GSR, and relatively more indirect measures, such as the personality trait of extraversion-introversion.

The validity of the considerable part of Eysenck's system that depends on explanation in terms of presumed neural processes is a subject of considerable controversy—as is, indeed, Eysenck's entire theory. Generally, the experimental papers from Eysenck's own laboratory have been favorable to the theory; reports from his followers elsewhere have mostly been favorable; but there are a considerable number of reports, especially from American researchers, that claim to have obtained results counter to prediction from Eysenck's theory (see Klein, Barr, & Wolitzky, 1967, pp. 499 *ff.*).

In general, we are pessimistic about the possibility of successfully "reducing" personality traits to underlying physiological mechanisms, at least for the foreseeable future. It appears unlikely that normal variations in personality are greatly dependent upon gross constitutional differences in physiological functioning; yet such differences represent the primary source of data currently available for use within the correlative-reductive framework. The normal human nervous system, however, has the capacity and the plasticity to accommodate quite diverse personality developments. Constitutional differences may serve as predisposing factors toward, or set biological limits on, the development of certain personality characteristics; but the normal personality is much less an expression of such physiological factors than it is the result of prior experience. It may, of course, be assumed that all experience is somehow encoded within the nervous system and thus has its physiological substrate. But until such engrams can be identified on a physiological level, and until a far better understanding of the integrative and functional activity of the nervous system is available, such an assumption is of no practical value for personality assessment.

If the above analysis is correct, then two areas of research can be suggested in which the correlative-reductive methods are most likely to yield fruitful results within the near future. One is the area of phylogenetic comparison, where the behavioral effects of cross-species differences in biological endowment are sufficiently great not to be obscured by normal within-species variation. Another area involves situations where physiological functioning is abnormal—e.g., endocrine and neural disorders, inborn errors of metabolism, etc. Both of these areas represent potentially valuable sources of information concerning the biological basis of behavioral traits; nevertheless, they have been relatively neglected by personality theorists.

The Elicitation Method of Personality Assessment

As previously discussed, the most common psychophysiological method of assessing dispositional variables such as personality traits is to elicit a reaction under controlled test conditions. Since psychophysiology has often been too closely associated with emotional expression, we will illustrate the elicitation method with a study by Israel (1966) on cognitive style.

Israel's design was quite simple: she measured the GSR's of 53 subjects— about equally divided among normals and chronic schizophrenics—while she showed them a series of squares in a tachistoscope. Since the novelty or interest-value of this procedure soon wore off for most subjects, their orienting responses, of which the GSR is a measure, habituated (extinguished) quickly for some subjects, less quickly for others. She then showed the same stimulus squares to the subjects, but this time under the instructions for the Schematizing Test (Gardner, Holzman, Klein, Linton, & Spence, 1959). This test evaluates the subject's propensity to use a cognitive "leveling" or "sharpening" style—to assimilate new perceptions to the categories of former experience (leveling) or vigilantly to detect slight changes (sharpening). She then selected the scores of 18 schizophrenics and 13 normals who scored at the extremes of leveling and sharpening, and compared the habituation rates of their orienting response. The results showed that the schizophrenic sharpeners had by far the most slowly habituating orienting responses (i.e., greater GSR resistance to extinction); then, in order, came the schizophrenic levelers, the normal sharpeners, and the normal levelers. Thus, for both chronic schizophrenics and normals, those who failed to make fine perceptual discriminations also had more rapidly extinguishing orienting responses, a result that fits in with Sokolov's (1963) theory that the biological function of the orienting response is to sharpen sensory acuity at all levels of the perceptual system from the receptor organ to the cerebral cortex. Studies of this type are especially important for they open up new possibilities for the psychophysiological assessment of personality; emotional behavior is not the only kind of behavior that has its physiological concomitants.

It would be possible to cite a great many more studies using the elicitation method; but since our purpose is to discuss psychophysiological assessment as a technique, a list of substantive findings would serve little purpose. However, if we were to make such a list, two aspects of this literature would soon become apparent: (a) most correlations between psychophysiological reactions and personality measures are very low, and (b) there is little overlap among the studies; that is, only rarely is it possible to say that the results of any two experiments reinforce or contradict each other; each experimenter has used a unique combination of eliciting stimuli, psychophysiological measures, and personality measures. Consequently, the melange of situations and variables that have been employed do not permit any brief summary of this type of research. This unsatisfactory state of affairs flows in large part from the first aspect of the literature noted above; i.e., most correlations between personality and physiological reactions are quite low. No one tries to replicate a low correlation; one tries instead other variables and stimuli, hoping to hit on the right combination.

Three reasons for the poor results often obtained with the elicitation method have already been discussed and will be summarized again shortly. We now wish to consider one further issue of considerable importance for the psychophysiological assessment of personality. This concerns the distinction between ipsative (within-individual) experimental designs, on the one hand, and normative (between-individual) designs, on the other.

Psychological investigations of personality traits have too often employed a strictly normative approach. That is, subjects who supposedly differ along some dimension are subjected to a stimulus and their reactions compared. The previously cited study by Israel is a good example of this design. Note, however, that Israel's findings can be explained in either of two ways: it is possible that a constitutional weakness of the orienting response prevented the levelers from maintaining continued alertness to the fine changes in the stimuli; but it is equally plausible that levelers—because they cognitively lump the stimuli together in an undifferentiated, more-or-less-the-same-thing style—found less novelty and interest in the stimuli and therefore habituated more quickly. This illustrates a problem that in certain contexts is a major weakness of the normative approach: it does not control for constitutional differences in responsivity. Yet constitutional differences in physiological functioning must be accounted for before inferences can be made to psychological processes.

This is not to say that constitutional differences may not have their own relationships with personality. But as previously noted, such relationships have generally proven rather tenuous. In any case, unless they happen to be under investigation in the particular experiment, constitutional differences are a source of error variance. For those unfamiliar with physiological data, it might be helpful if we draw an analogy with purely psychological assessment. Suppose one were administering Rorschach tests in a country so under-developed that no one wore eyeglasses and so superstitious that no one would come closer than 10 feet to the Rorschach cards. Under such conditions, individual differences in Rorschach responses would be as much a function of individual differences in visual acuity as of individual differences in personality. Visual acuity would be a source of so much error variance that personality differences would be difficult or impossible to assess. A comparable problem exists with psychophysiological assessment, except that the uncontrolled constitutional differences are in the effector rather than the receptor organs. Thus, if one person has a skin conductance of 30 micromhos, another 60 micromhos, the second is not necessarily in a different emotional state than the first; he may well have been born with many more sweat glands on his palms (Kuno, 1956; for a further discussion of individual differences in physiological variables, from the biochemical to the gross anatomical, see Williams, 1956).

Opton and Lazarus (1967) have presented evidence that the most promising solution for this problem is to use a partially intra-individual (ipsative) approach. If Tom's physiological response to a single situation is twice as much as Jerry's, we do not know whether we have learned something about the two men's physiological constitutions or about their different psychological interpretations of the situation. But if we expose both men to several situations and find that Tom's reponse to situation *a* is greater than his own response to situations *b, c, d,* and *e* while Jerry reacts no more to *a* than to *b, c, d,* or *e* then we are in a position to say that situation *a* has elicited a strong reaction from Tom, but not from Jerry. It is this sort of relationship—particular sensitivity to some situations as opposed to others within the same individual—that is implicit in most experimental hypotheses about personality. And until it is made explicit in experimental designs, correlations of marginal significance between physiological reactions and personality variables will continue to be the rule.

This section on the psychophysiological assessment of personality traits may be summarized with the following observations: To the extent that the correlative-reductive techniques depend upon gross constitutional differences in physiological functioning, their range of potential usefulness is rather limited; to the extent that they depend upon subtle differences in neural functioning that are the result of prior experience, they form a program largely for the future.

It therefore appears that for the present the third method of dispostional assessment, the elicitation method, will be the most fruitful for the psychophysiological assessment of personality. Before the potential of this method can be fully realized, however, four factors must be considered. The first factor concerns the generality of the trait being assessed—the more specific a disposition is to the eliciting stimuli, the greater is the relationship to reactivity measures. The second factor has to do with the nature of the physiological reactions—the response specificities represent important sources of variance that cannot be ignored. The intrusion of confounding variables— e.g., defense mechanisms—which may be a function of the trait being assessed, is a third factor to be considered. Finally, ipsative and normative sources of variance must be distinguished; personality traits generally imply differential sensitivity within the same individual.

CONCLUSION

Psychophysiological techniques possess certain unique advantages and liabilities, which can be, and often are, overemphasized. It sometimes seems that a physiological variable is recorded primarily because it lends an air of objectivity, or because it is considered to be somehow more "fundamental" than strictly behavioral measures. Hopefully this chapter has lent no credence to such views. On the other hand, where physiological measures are appropriate, one should not be deterred by technical problems, which are seldom as difficult as they at first appear. One does not need elaborate recorders and massive computers to do meaningful research. Many important findings are amazingly simple, both conceptually and technically—once the appropriate question has been asked. And psychophysiological assessment is still a young discipline; many important questions remain to be asked.

Bibliography

and Reference Index

(The numbers in brackets indicate the pages on which the reference appears in the text.)

Abramson, L. S. The influence of set for area on the Rorschach test results. *J. consult. Psychol.*, 1951, *15*, 337-342. [141]

Abse, D. W., & Ewing, J. A. Some problems in psychotherapy with schizophrenic patients. *Amer. J. Psychother.*, 1960, *14*, 505-515. [219]

Abt, L. E., & Riess, B. F. *Progress in clinical psychology*. Vol. 7. New York: Grune & Stratton, 1966. [132]

Acker, M., & McReynolds, P. The obscure figures test: An instrument for measuring "cognitive innovation." *Percept. mot. Skills*, 1965, *21*, 815-821. [40]

Acker, M., & McReynolds, P. On the assessment of anxiety: III. By self-ratings. *Psychol. Rep.*, 1966, *19*, 251-254. [248]

Adams, C. R. Evaluating marriage prediction tests. *Marriage fam. Liv.*, 1950, *12*, 55-58. [225]

Adams, D. K., & Horn, J. L. Nonoverlapping keys for the MMPI scales. *J. consult. Psychol.*, 1965, *29*, 284. [83]

Adams, H. B., Cooper, G. D., & Carrera, R. N. The Rorschach and the MMPI: A concurrent validity study. *J. proj. Tech.*, 1963, *27*, 23-35. [146]

Adis-Castro, G. A study of selected personality dimensions by means of the questionnaire method in a Latin American culture. Unpublished doctoral dissertation, University of California, Berkeley, 1957. [58]

Adorno, T. W., Frenkel-Brunswik, E., Levinson, D. J., & Sanford, R. N. *The authoritarian personality*. New York: Harper, 1950. [67]

Affleck, D. C., & Mednick, S. A. The use of the Rorschach test in the prediction of the abrupt terminator in individual psychotherapy. *J. consult. Psychol.*, 1959, *23*, 125-128. [147]

Aiken, L. R. Paper and pencil anxiety. *Psychol. Rep.*, 1962, *10*, 107-112. [245, 250, 251, 264]

Aiken, L. R., Jr. Personality correlates of attitude toward mathematics. *J. educ. Res.*, 1963, *56*, 476-480. (*a*) [70]

Aiken, L. R., Jr. The relationship of dress to selected measures of personality in undergraduate women. *J. soc. Psychol.*, 1963, *59*, 119-128. (*b*) [56]

Ainsworth, M. D. Problems of validation. In Klopfer, A., Ainsworth, M. D., Klopfer, W. G., & Holt, R. R. *Developments in the Rorschach Technique*. Vol. 1. New York: Harcourt, Brace & World, 1954. [143]

Aldous, J., & Hill, R. *International bibliography of research in marriage and the family, 1900-1964*. Minneapolis: Univ. Minn. Press, 1967. [225]

Alexander, S., & Husek, T. R. The anxiety differential: initial steps in the development of a measure of situational anxiety. *Educ. psychol. Measmt.*, 1962, *22*, 325-348. [247, 260, 262]

Alpert, R., & Haber, R. N. Anxiety in academic achievement situations. *J. abnorm. soc. Psychol.*, 1960, *61*, 207-215. [253, 255, 256, 258, 262]

Allison, J., & Blatt, S. J. The relationship of Rorschach W responses to intelligence. *J. proj. Tech. & pers. Assess.*, 1964, *28*, 255-261. [145]

Allport, G. W., Vernon, P. E., & Lindzey, G. *Study of values.* (3rd ed.) Boston: Houghton-Mifflin, 1960. [57]

Amen, E. W., & Renison, N. A study of the relationship between play patterns and anxiety in young children. *Genet. psychol. Monogr.*, 1954, *50*, 3-41. [259]

Anastasi, A. *Psychological testing.* (2nd ed.) New York: Macmillan, 1961. [5]

Anastasi, A. (Ed.) *Testing problems in perspective.* Washington, D.C.: American Council on Education, 1966. [9]

Anastasi, A. Psychology, psychologists, and psychological testing. *Amer. Psychologist,* 1967, *22*, 297-306. [4, 5, 6]

Anderson, H. E., & Bashaw, W. L. Further comments on the internal structure of the MMPI. *Psychol. Bull.*, 1966, *66*, 211-213. [83]

Anderson, J. E. The limitations of infant and preschool tests in the measurement of intelligence. *J. Psychol.*, 1939, *8*, 351-379. [22]

Andrews, F. Creativity and the scientist. Doctoral dissertation, University of Michigan, Ann Arbor, 1962. [41]

Appelbaum, S. A., & Holzman, P. S. The color-shading response and suicide. *J. proj. Tech.*, 1962, *26*, 155-162. [143]

Arbuckle, D. S. Client perception of counselor personality. *J. counsel. Psychol.*, 1956, *3*, 93-96. [216]

Arbuckle, D. S. *Counseling and psychotherapy*: An overview. New York: McGraw-Hill, 1967. [205]

Arnold, M. B. *Emotion and personality.* New York: Columbia Univ. Press, 1960. [278, 279]

Aronson, M. A study of the Freudian theory of paranoia by means of the Blacky pictures. *J. proj. Tech.*, 1953, *17*, 3-19. [156]

Arthur, A. Z. A decision-making approach to psychological assessment in the clinic. *J. consult. Psychol.*, 1966, *30*, 433-438. [7]

Aumach, L. A social adjustment behavior rating scale. *J. clin. Psychol.*, 1962, *18*, 436-441. [193, 201]

Averill, J. R. Autonomic response patterns during sadness and mirth. Unpublished doctoral dissertation, University of California, Los Angeles, 1966. [278]

Ax, A. F. The physiological differentiation between fear and anger in humans. *Psychosom. Med.*, 1953, *15*, 433-442. [278, 279]

Ax, A. F. Goals and methods of psychophysiology. *Psychophysiology*, 1964, *1*, 8-25. [271]

Bachrach, A. J., Quigley, W. A. Direct methods of treatment. In I. A. Berg & L. A. Pennington (Eds.), *Introduction to clinical psychology.* (3rd ed.) New York: Ronald Press, 1966. Pp. 482-560. [171, 176]

Bailey, M. A., Warsaw, L., & Eichler, R. M. A study of factors related to the length of stay in psychotherapy. *J. clin. Psychol.*, 1959, *15*, 442-444. [220]

Ball, J., Klett, C. J., & Gresock, C. J. The Veterans Administration study of prefrontal lobotomy. *J. clin. exper. Psychopath.*, 1959, *20*, 205-217. [195]

Bandura, A. Psychotherapists' anxiety level, self-insight, and psychotherapeutic competence. *J. abnorm. soc. Psychol.*, 1956, *52*, 333-337. [216]

Banissoni, M. Rigidità percettiva e dogmatismo. *Riv. Psicol.*, 1967, *61*, 226-231. [63]

Barker, R. G. Ecology and motivation. In M. R. Jones (Ed.), *Nebraska symposium on motivation.* Lincoln, Nebr.: Univ. Nebr. Press, 1960. Pp. 1-49. [9]

Barker, R. G. Explorations in ecological psychology. *Amer. Psychologist*, 1965, *20*, 1-14. [32]

Barnette, W. L. A structured and semistructured achievement measure applied to a college sample. *Educ. psychol. Measmt.*, 1961, *21*, 647-656. [70]

Barnette, W. L. *Readings in psychological tests and measurements.* (2nd ed.) Homewood, Ill.: Dorsey, 1968. [5]

Baron, R. M. Social reinforcement effects as a function of social reinforcement history. *Psychol. Rev.*, 1966, *73*, 527-539. [177]

Barratt, E. S. Factor analysis of some psychometric measures of impulsiveness and anxiety. *Psychol. Rep.*, 1965, *16*, 547-554. [247]

Barron, F. Complexity-simplicity as a personality dimension. *J. abnorm. soc. Psychol.*, 1953, *48*, 163-172. [50]

Barron, F. The disposition towards originality. *J. abnorm. soc. Psychol.*, 1955, *51*, 478-485. [50]

Barron, F. Creative vision and expression in writing and painting. In *Proceedings, Conference on "The Creative Person."* Berkeley, California: University of California, University Extension, Liberal Arts Department, 1961. Part II, pp. 1-19. [70]

Barron, F. Discovering the creative personality. In College Entrance Examination Board, *College Admissions 10: The behavioral sciences and education.* Princeton, N.J.: CEEB, 1963. [50]

Barron, F. The psychology of creativity. In *New directions in psychology: II.* Ann Arbor, Mich.: Holt, Rinehart, and Winston, 1965. Pp. 1-134. [34, 50, 65]

Barron, F., & Leary, T. Changes in psychoneurotic patients with and without psychotherapy. *J. consult. Psychol.*, 1955, *19*, 239-245. [213]

Bartlett, R. G., Jr. Physiologic responses during coitus. *J. appl. Physiol.*, 1956, *9*, 468-472. [281]

Bass, B. M., & Berg, I. A. *Objective approaches to personality assessment.* New York: Van Nostrand, 1959. [5]

Baughman, E. E. An experimental analysis of the relationship between stimulus structure and behavior on the Rorschach. *J. proi. Tech.*, 1959, *23*, 134-183. (*b*) [134]

Bauman, G., & Roman, M. Interaction testing in the study of marital dominance. *Fam. Process*, 1966, *5*, 230-242. [226]

Bayley, N. On the growth of intelligence. *Amer. Psychologist*, 1955, *10*, 805-818. [22]

Beck, A. T., Ward. C. H., Mendelson, M., Mock. J., & Erbough, J. An inventory for measuring depression. *Arch. gen. Psychiat.*, 1961, *4*, 561-571. [202]

Bedford, E. Emotions. *Proc. Aristotelian Soc.*, 1957, *57*, 281-304. [280]

Beech, H. R., & Adler, F. Some aspects of verbal conditioning in psychiatric patients. *Behav. Res. Ther.*, 1963, *1*, 273-282. [181]

Bendick, M., & Klopfer, W. G. The effects of sensory deprivation and motor inhibition on Rorschach movement responses. *J. proj. Tech. pers. Assmt.*, 1964, *28*, 261-264. [142]

Bendig, A. W. The development of a short form of the manifest anxiety scale. *J. consult. Psychol.*, 1956, *20*, 384. [253]

Bendig, A. W. Identification of item factor patterns within the manifest anxiety scale. *J. consult. Psychol.*, 1958, *22*, 158. [247]

Bendig, A. W. The reliability and factorial validity of the IPAT anxiety scale. *J. gen. Psychol.*, 1962, *67*, 27-33. [247, 254]

Bendig, A. W. Reliability of and intercorrelations between Cattell's IPAT anxiety and neuroticism scales. *J. gen. Psychol.*, 1966, *75*, 1-7. [247]

Bendig, A. W., & Klugh, H. E. A validation of Gough's Hr scale in predicting academic achievement. *Educ. psychol. Measmt.*, 1956, *16*, 516-523. [70]

Benjamin, L. S. Statistical treatment of the law of initial values (LIV) in autonomic research: A review and recommendation. *Psychosom. Med.*, 1963, *25*, 556-566. [272]

Bennett, G. K., Seashore, H. G., & Wessman, A. G. *Differential aptitude tests, manual.* (2nd ed.) New York: Psychol. Corp., 1952. [18]

Bennett, L. A., & Rudoff, A. Evaluation of modified administration of the California psychological inventory. *J. clin. Psychol.*, 1957, *13*, 303-304. [56]

Berenson, B. G., & Carkhuff, R. R. (Eds.) *Sources of gain in counseling and psychotherapy: Readings and commentary.* New York: Holt, Rinehart and Winston, 1967. [205, 206, 211, 212]

Berg, I. A. Measures before and after therapy. *J. clin. Psychol.*, 1952, *8*, 46-50. [207]

Berg, I. A. Response bias and personality: The deviation hypothesis. *J. Psychol.*, 1955, *40*, 62-72. [7]

Berg, I. A. (Ed.) *Response set in personality assessment.* Chicago: Aldine, 1967. [5, 7]

Berg, I. A., & Adams, H. E. The experimental bases of personality assessment. In A. J. Bachrach (Ed.), *Experimental foundations of clinical psychology.* New York: Basic Books, 1962. Pp. 52-96. [5]

Berg, I. A., & Pennington, L. A. *An introduction to clinical psychology.* New York: Ronald Press, 1966. [5]

Berger, D. Examiner influence on the Rorschach. *J. clin. Psychol.*, 1954, *10*, 245-248. [142]

Berger, L. Cross-validation of "primary" and "reactive" personality patterns with non-ulcer surgical patients. *J. proj. Tech.*, 1959, *23*, 8-11. [157]

Berger, L., & Everstine, L. Test-retest reliability of the Blacky pictures test. *J. proj. Tech.*, 1962, *26*, 225-226. [151]

Bergin, A. E. The effects of psychotherapy: Negative results revisited. *J. counsel. Psychol.*, 1963, *10*, 244-250. [213]

Bergin, A. E. Some implications of psychotherapy research for therapeutic practice. *J. abnorm. Psychol.*, 1966, *71*, 235-246. [213]

Berkun, M. M., Bialek, H. M., Kern, R. P., & Yagi, K. Experimental studies of psychological stress in man. *Psychol. Monogr.*, 1962, *76*, No. 15 (Whole No. 534). [249]

Berkun, M. M., Timiras, P. S., & Pace, N. Psychological and physiological responses in observers of an atomic test shot. *Psychol. Rep.*, 1958, *4*, 679-682. [249]

Berman, L. Some problems in the evaluation of psychoanalysis as a therapeutic procedure. *Psychiatry*, 1955, *18*, 387-390. [213]

Bernstein, B. Aspects of language and learning in the genesis of the social process. *J. Child Psychol. Psychiat.*, 1961, *1*, 313-324. [23]

Bernstein, L., & Chase, P. H. The discriminative ability of the Blacky pictures with peptic ulcer patients. *J. consult. Psychol.*, 1955, *19*, 377-380. [157]

Bernyer, G. Second order factors and the organization of cognitive functions. *Brit. J. statist. Psychol.*, 1958, *11*, 19-29. [14]

Betz, B. J. Bases of therapeutic leadership in psychotherapy with the schizophrenic patient. *Amer. J. Psychother.*, 1963, *17*, 196-212. [216]

Bieri, J., Atkins, A. L., Briar, S., Leaman, R., Miller, H., & Tripodi, T. *Clinical and social judgment*. New York: Wiley, 1966. [6]

Biesheuvel, S. Personnel selection. *Annu. Rev. Psychol.*, 1965, *16*, 295-324. [6]

Bijou, S. W., & Baer, D. M. Operant methods in child behavior and development. In W. K. Honig (Ed.), *Operant behavior: Areas of research and application*. New York: Appleton-Century-Crofts, 1966. Pp. 718-789. [175]

Billingslea, F. Y. The Bender Gestalt: A review and a perspective. *Psychol. Bull.*, 1963, *60*, 233-251. [6]

Binet, A., & Simon, T. New methods for the diagnosis of the intellectual level of subnormals L'Annee Psychologique, 1905, *12*, 191-244, Trans. by E. S. Kite and reprinted in A. Binet, & T. Simon, *The development of intelligence in children*. Baltimore: Williams & Wilkins, 1916. [33]

Birch, H. G. The relation of previous experience to insightful problem-solving. *J. comp. Psychol.*, 1945, *38*, 367-383. [22]

Bish, G. G. A study of the relationships of intelligence, achievement, creativity, anxiety and confidence among intermediate grade pupils in a suburban area elementary school. Doctoral dissertation, George Washington University, Washington, D.C., 1964. [48]

Blank, M. Use of the deaf in language studies: A reply to Furth. *Psychol. Bull.*, 1965, *63*, 442-444. [23]

Blatt, S. J., & Allison, J. Methodological considerations in Rorschach research: The W response as an expression of abstractive and integrative strivings. *J. proj. Tech. pers. Assess.*, 1963, *27*, 269-279. [145]

Blewett, D. B., & Stefaniuk, W. B. Weyburn assessment scale. *J. ment. Sci.*, 1958, *104*, 359-371. [201]

Block, J. *The challenge of response sets*. New York: Appleton-Century-Crofts, 1965. [5, 7, 84]

Block, W. E., & Ventur, P. A. A study of the psychoanalytic concept of castration anxiety in symbolically castrated amputees. *Psychiat. Quart.*, 1963, *37*, 518-526. [158]

Bloom, B. J. *Stability and change in human characteristics*. New York: Wiley, 1964. [22, 23, 29, 32]

Bloom, B. L. The Rorschach popular responses among Hawaiian schizophrenics. *J. Proj. Tech.*, 1962, *26*, 173-182. [135, 147]

Blum, G. S. A study of the psychoanalytic theory of psychosexual development. *Genet. psychol. Monogr.*, 1949, *39*, 3-99. [153, 154]

Blum, G. S., *The Blacky pictures: A tech-*

nique for the exploration of personality dynamics. Ann Arbor, Mich.: Psycho-dynamic Instruments, 1950. [150]

Blum, G. S. An experimental reunion of psychoanalytic theory with perceptual vigilance and defense. *J. abnorm. soc. Psychol.*, 1954, *49*, 94-98. [160]

Blum, G. S. Perceptual defense revisited. *J. abnorm. soc. Psychol.*, 1955, *51*, 24-29. [160]

Blum, G. S. Defense preferences in four countries. *J. proj. Tech.*, 1956, *20*, 33-41. [161, 162]

Blum, G. S. *A model of the mind*. New York: Wiley, 1961. [161]

Blum, G. S. A guide for research use of the Blacky pictures. *J. proj. Tech.*, 1962, *26*, 3-29. [151, 160]

Blum, G. S. Defense preferences among university students in Denmark, France, Germany, and Israel. *J. proj. Tech.*, 1964, *28*, 13-19. [162]

Blum, G. S. Hypnosis in psychodynamic research. In J. E. Gordon (Ed.), *Handbook of clinical and experimental hypnosis*. New York: Macmillan, 1967. Pp. 83-109. [161]

Blum, G. S., & Hunt, H. F. The validity of the Blacky pictures. *Psychol. Bull.*, 1952, *49*, 238-250. [151]

Blum, G. S., & Kaufman, J. B. Two patterns of personality dynamics in male peptic ulcer patients, as suggested by responses to the Blacky pictures. *J. clin. Psychol.*, 1952, *8*, 273-278. [157]

Bodin, A. M. Family interaction, coalition, disagreement, and compromise in problem, normal and synthetic family triads. Unpublished doctoral dissertation, State University of New York at Buffalo, 1966. (a) [225, 226, 234, 238]

Bodin, A. M. Family interaction: A social-clinical study of synthetic, normal, and problem family triads. Paper read at Western Psychological Association, 1966. (b) [238, 241]

Bohm, E. *Lehrbuch der Rorschach-psychodiagnostik fuer psychologen, aertzte und paedogogen*. Bern: Verlag Hans Huber, 1957. [132]

Boomer, D. S., & Goodrich, D. W. Speech disturbance and judged anxiety. *J. consult. Psychol.*, 1961, *25*, 160-164. [261]

Bostian, D. W., Smith, P. A., Lasky, J. J., Hover, G. L., & Ging, R. J. Empirical observations on mental status examination. *A.M.A. Arch. gen. Psychiat.*, 1959, *1*, 253-262. [201]

Brackbill, G., & Little, K. B. MMPI correlates of the Taylor scale of manifest anxiety. *J. consult. Psychol.*, 1954, *18*, 433-436. [252]

Branca, A. A., & Podolnick, E. E. Normal, hypnotically induced, and feigned anxiety as reflected in and detected by the MMPI. *J. consult. Psychol.*, 1961,

25, 165-170. [253]

Brim, O. G. American attitudes toward intelligence tests. *Amer. Psychologist*, 1965, 20, 125-130. [7]

Brodey, W. On family therapy—a poem. *Fam. Process*, 1963, 2, 280-287. [241]

Brogden, H. E., & Sprecher, T. B. Criteria of creativity. In C. W. Taylor (Ed.), *Creativity: Progress and potential*. New York: McGraw-Hill, 1964. Pp. 156-176. [37]

Bronowski, J. The logic of mind. *Amer. Sci.*, 1966, 54, 1-14. [242]

Brown, C. C. (Ed.) *Methods in psychophysiology*. Baltimore: Williams and Wilkins, 1967. [266]

Brown, J. S. *The motivation of behavior*. New York: McGraw-Hill, 1961. [245, 246]

Brown, P. T. On the differentiation of homo- or hetero-erotic interest in the male: An operant technique illustrated in the case of a motorcycle fetishist. *Behav. Res. Ther.*, 1964, 2, 31-35. [177]

Brown, P. T. A reply to Koenig. *Behav. Res. Ther.*, 1965, 2, 309-311. [177, 178]

Brozek, J. (Ed.) *The biology of human variation*. New York: New York Academy of Science, Vol. 134, 1966. [5]

Bruner, J. S. A psychologist's viewpoint. Review of Barbel Inhelder and J. Piaget's The growth of logical thinking. *Brit. J. Psychol.*, 1959, 50, 363-370. [30]

Bruner, J. S. *The process of education*. Cambridge, Mass.: Harvard Univ. Press, 1960. [26]

Bruner, J. S., Olver, R. R., Greenfield, P. M., et al. *Studies in cognitive growth*. New York: Wiley, 1966. [29]

Bryan, J. H., & Kapche, R. Psychopathy and verbal conditioning. *J. abnorm. Psychol.*, 1967, 72, 71-73. [180]

Buck, J. N. The H-T-P technique: A qualitative scoring manual. *J. clin. Psychol.*, 1948, 4, 317-396. [257]

Bullock, D. H. Some aspects of human operant behavior. *Psychol. Rec.*, 1960, 10, 241-258. [181]

Burchard, E. M. L. The use of projective techniques in the analysis of creativity. *J. proj. Tech.*, 1952, 16, 412-427. [38]

Burdock, E. I., Elliott, H. E., Hardesty, A. S., O'Neill, F. J., & Sklar, J. Biometric evaluation of an intensive treatment program in a state mental hospital. *J. nerv. and ment. Dis.*, 1960, 130, 271-277. [201]

Burdock, E. I., Hakerem, G., Hardesty, A. S., & Zubin, J. A ward behavior scale for mental hospital patients. *J. clin. Psychol.*, 1960, 16, 246-247. [193,201]

Burgemeister, B. B. *Psychological techniques in neurological diagnosis*. New York: Hoeber, 1962. [6]

Burn, J. H. *The autonomic nervous system*. Philadelphia: F. A. Davis, 1963. [278]

Buros, O. K. (Ed.) *Tests in print*. Highland Park, N.J.: Gryphon Press, 1961. [6]

Buros, O. K. (Ed.) *The sixth mental measurements yearbook*. Highland Park, N.J.: Gryphon Press, 1965. [6, 106, 191]

Burt, C. L. The structure of the mind: A review of the results of factor analysis. *Brit. J. educ. Psychol.*, 1949, 19, 100-111, 176-199. [15]

Burt, C. L. The evidence for the concept of intelligence. *Brit. J. educ. Psychol.*, 1955, 25, 158-177. [17]

Burt, C. L. The inheritance of mental ability. *Amer. Psychologist*, 1958, 13, 1-15. [17]

Burton, R. V. Generality of honesty reconsidered. *Psychol. Rev.*, 1963, 70, 481-499. [9]

Buss, A. H. Two anxiety factors in psychiatric patients. *J. abnorm. soc. Psychol.*, 1962, 65, 426-427. [247, 261]

Buss, A. H., Wiener, M., Durkee, A., & Baer, M. The measurement of anxiety in clinical situations. *J. consult. Psychol.*, 1955, 19, 125-129. [252, 261, 262]

Byrne, D. Anxiety and the experimental arousal of affiliation need. *J. abnorm. soc. Psychol.*, 1961, 63, 660-662. [248]

Byrne, D. Assessing personality variables and their alteration. In P. Worchel and D. Byrne (Eds.), *Personality change*. New York: Wiley, 1964. [5]

Byrne, D. *An introduction to personality*. Englewood Cliffs, N.J.: Prentice-Hall, 1966. [244, 252]

Byrne, D., Terrill, J., & McReynolds, P. Incongruency as a predictor of response to humor. *J. abnorm. soc. Psychol.*, 1961, 62, 435-438. [260]

Caceres, C. A. (Ed.) *Biomedical telemetry*. New York: Academic Press, 1965. [269]

Caffey, E. M., Jr., Diamond, L. S., Frank, T. V., Grasberger, J. C., Herman, L., Klett, C. J., & Rothstein, C. Discontinuation or reduction of chemotherapy in chronic schizophrenia. *J. chronic Dis.*, 1964, 17, 347-358. [196]

Cairns, R. B. The influence of dependency-anxiety on the effectiveness of social reinforcers. Unpublished doctoral dissertation, Stanford University, 1959. [176]

Cameron, N. *The psychology of behavior disorders*. Boston: Houghton-Mifflin, 1947. [252]

Campbell, D. P. *The results of counseling: Twenty-five years later*. Philadelphia: W. B. Saunders, 1965. (a) [205]

Campbell, D. P. The vocational interests of APA presidents. *Amer. Psychologist*, 1965, 20, 636-644. (b) [130]

Campbell, D. P. *Manual for the Strong vocational interest blanks for men and women.* Stanford: Stanford Univ. Press, 1966. (*a*) [105, 106]

Campbell, D. P. The stability of vocational interests within occupations over long time spans. *Personnel guid. J.*, 1966, *44*, 1012-1019. (*b*) [130]

Campbell, D. T. Recommendations for APA standards regarding construct, trait, or discriminant validity. *Amer. Psychologist*, 1960, *15*, 546-553. [5]

Cannon, W. B. *Bodily changes in pain, hunger, fear, and rage.* (2nd ed.) New York: Appleton-Century, 1929. [278]

Canter, F. M. Simulation on the California psychological inventory and the adjustment of the simulator. *J. consult. Psychol.*, 1963, *27*, 253-256. [56]

Caracena, P. F. Elicitation of dependency expressions in the initial stage of psychotherapy. *J. counsel. Psychol.*, 1965, *12*, 268-274. [218]

Carnap, R. Testability and meaning. *Phil. Sci.*, 1936, *3*, 419-471; 1937, *4*, 1-40. [267]

Carp, A. L., & Shavzin, A. R. The susceptibility to falsification of the Rorschach diagnostic technique. *J. consult. Psychol.*, 1950, *3*, 230-233. [141]

Carp, F. M. Psychosexual development of stutterers. *J. proj. Tech.*, 1962, *26*, 388-391. [158]

Carr, A. C. An evaluation of nine nondirective psychotherapy cases by means of the Rorschach. *J. consult. Psychol.*, 1949, *13*, 196-205. [212]

Carrigan, P. M. Extraversion-introversion as a dimension of personality: A reappraisal. *Psychol. Bull.*, 1960, *57*, 329-361 [146]

Cartwright, D. S., Kirtner, S. L., & Fiske, D. W. Method factors in changes associated with psychotherapy. *J. abnorm. soc. Psychol.*, 1963, *66*, 164-175. [207]

Cartwright, R. D. Predicting response to client-centered therapy with the Rorschach PR scale. *J. counsel. Psychol.*, 1958, *5*, 11-15. [147]

Cartwright, R. D., & Lerner, B. Empathy, need to change, and improvement with psychotherapy. *J. consult. Psychol.*, 1963, *27*, 138-144. [218]

Cartwright, R. D., & Vogel, T. J. A comparison of changes in psychoneurotic patients during matched periods of therapy and no therapy. *J. consult. Psychol.*, 1960, *24*, 121-127. [213]

Casey, J. F., Bennett, I. F., Lindley, C. J., Hollister, L. E., Gordon, M. H., & Springer, N. N. Drug therapy in schizophrenia. *Arch. gen. Psychiat.*, 1960, *2*, 210-220. [195]

Casey, J. F., Lasky, J. J., Klett, C. J., & Hollister, L. E. Treatment of schizo-phrenic reactions with phenothiazine derivatives. *Amer. J. Psychiat.*, 1960, *117*, 97-105. [195, 197]

Casey, J. F., Hollister, L. E., Klett, C. J., Lasky, J. J., & Caffey, E. M., Jr. Combined drug therapy of chronic schizophrenics. *Amer. J. Psychiat.*, 1961, *117*, 997-1003. [196]

Cass, W. A., & McReynolds, P. A. A contribution to Rorschach norms. *J. consult. Psychol.*, 1951, *15*, 178-185. [135, 136]

Castaneda, A., McCandless, B. R., & Palermo, D. C. The children's form of the manifest-anxiety scale. *Child Develpm.*, 1956, *27*, 317-326. [258]

Cattell, J. McK. Mental tests and measurements. *Mind*, 1890, *15*, 373-381.

Cattell, R. B. *The sixteen personality factor questionnaire: Handbook and tabular supplement.* Champaign, Ill.: Inst. Pers. & Abil. Test., 1950. [57, 73]

Cattell, R. B. *Personality and motivation structure and measurement.* New York: Harcourt, Brace & World, 1957. [19]

Cattell, R. B. Foundations of personality measurement theory in multivariate experiment. In B. M. Bass & I. A. Berg (Eds.), *Objective approaches to personality assessment.* New York: Van Nostrand, 1959. Pp. 42-66. [5]

Cattell, R. B. Personality and motivation of the researcher from measurements of contemporaries and from biography. In D. W. Taylor & F. Barron (Eds.), *Scientific creativity: Its recognition and development.* New York: Wiley, 1963. Pp. 119-131. (*a*) [54]

Cattell, R. B. Theory of fluid and crystallized intelligence: A critical experiment. *J. educ. Psychol.*, 1963, *54*, 1-22. (*b*) [14, 17, 19]

Cattell, R. B. Psychological definition and measurement of anxiety. *J. Neuropsychiat.*, 1964, *5*, 396-402. [247, 253]

Cattell, R. B. *The scientific analysis of personality.* Baltimore: Penguin Books, 1965. [272, 275, 283]

Cattell, R. B. Anxiety and motivation: theory and crucial experiments. In C. D. Spielberger (Ed.), *Anxiety and behavior.* New York: Academic Press, 1966. Pp. 23-62. [247, 253]

Cattell, R. B., Coulter, M. A., & Tsujioka, B. The taxonometric recognition of types and functional emergents. In R. B. Cattell (Ed.), *Handbook of multivariate experimental psychology.* Chicago: Rand-McNally, 1966. Pp. 288-329. [272]

Cattell, R. B., & Scheier, I. H. The nature of anxiety: A review of thirteen multivariate analyses comprising 814 variables. *Psychol. Rep.*, 1958, 351-388. [247]

Cattell, R. B., & Scheier, I. H. Stimuli related to stress, neuroticism, excitation, and anxiety response patterns: Illustrating a new multivariate design. *J. abnorm. soc. Psychol.*, 1960, *60*, 195-204. [283]

Cattell, R. B., & Scheier, I. H. *The meaning and measurement of neuroticism and anxiety.* New York: Ronald Press, 1961. [244, 245, 246, 247, 253, 254, 268, 272, 278]

Cattell, R. B., & Scheier, I. H. *Handbook for the IPAT anxiety scale questionnaire.* Champaign, Ill.: Inst. Pers. & Abil. Test., 1963. [254]

Cattell, R. B., & Scheier, I. H. *Handbook and test kit for the objective-analytic (O-A) anxiety battery.* Champaign, Ill.: Inst. Pers. & Abil. Test., 1966. [259, 262]

Cattell, R. B., & Warburton, F. W. *Objective personality and motivation tests.* Chicago: Univ. of Ill. Press, 1967. [5]

Cerbus, G. & Nichols, R. C. Personality variables and response to color. *Psychol. Bull*, 1963, *60*, 566-575. [136]

Christensen, H. T. Development of the family field of study. In H. T. Christensen (Ed.), *Handbook of marriage and the family.* Chicago: Rand-McNally, 1964. [225]

Christiansen, B. *Attitudes toward foreign affairs as a function of personality.* Oslo: Oslo University Press, 1959. [159]

Christie, R., & Budnitzky, S. A short forced-choice anxiety scale. *J. consult. Psychol.*, 1957, *21*, 501. [253]

Chu, Chen-Lin. *Object cluster analysis of the MMPI.* Unpublished Ph.D. dissertation, University of California, Berkeley, 1966. [89, 91, 93, 104]

Cicirelli, V. G. Form of the relationship between creativity, IQ, and academic achievement. *J. educ. Psychol.*, 1965, *56*, 303-308. [48]

Clark, J. H. Some MMPI correlates of color in the group Rorschach. *J. consult. Psychol.*, 1948, *12*, 384-366. [136, 146]

Clarke, P. R. F. Complexities in the concept of intelligence. *Psychol. Rep.*, 1962, *11*, 411-417. [18]

Clemes, S. R., & D'Andrea, V. J. Patients' anxiety as a function of expectation and degree of initial interview ambiguity. *J. consult. Psychol.*, 1965, *29*, 397-404. [254]

Clyde, D. J. *Clyde mood scale manual.* Coral Gables, Fla.: University of Miami, Biometrics Laboratory, 1963. [203]

Coan, R. W. Facts, factors and artifacts: The quest for psychological meaning. *Psychol. Rev.*, 1964, *71*, 123-140. [15, 16]

Cohen, A. R. Experimental effects of ego-defense preference on interpersonal relations. *J. abnorm. soc. Psychol.*, 1956, *52*, 19-27. [162]

Colby, K. M. Psychotherapeutic processes.

Annu. Rev. Psychol., 1964, *15*, 347-370. [210]

Cole, J. O., Klerman, G. L., & Goldberg, S. C. Phenothiazine treatment in acute schizophrenia. *Arch. gen. Psychiat.*, 1964, *10*, 246-261. [196]

Comrey, A. L. A factor analysis of items on the MMPI hypochondriasis scale. *Educ. psychol. Measmt.*, 1957, *17*, 568-577. (*a*) [85]

Comrey, A. L. A factor analysis of items on the MMPI depression scale. *Educ. psychol. Measmt.*, 1957, *17*, 578-585. (*b*) [85]

Comrey, A. L. A factor analysis of items on the MMPI hysteria scale. *Educ. psychol. Measmt.*, 1957, *17*, 586-592. (*c*) [85]

Comrey, A. L. A factor analysis of items on the MMPI psychopathic deviate scale. *Educ. psychol. Measmt.*, 1958, *18*, 91-98. (*a*) [85]

Comrey, A. L. A factor analysis of items on the MMPI paranoia scale. *Educ. psychol. Measmt.*, 1958, *18*, 99-107. (*b*) [85]

Comrey, A. L. A factor analysis of items on the MMPI psychasthenia scale. *Educ. psychol. Measmt.*, 1958, *18*, 293-300. (*c*) [85]

Comrey, A. L. A factor analysis of items on the MMPI hypomania scale. *Educ. psychol. Measmt.*, 1958, *18*, 313-323. (*d*) [85]

Comrey, A. L. A factor analysis of items on F scale of MMPI. *Educ. psychol. Measmt.*, 1958, *18*, 621-632. (*e*) [85]

Comrey, A. L. A factor analysis of items on the K scale of the MMPI. *Educ. psychol. Measmt.*, 1958, *18*, 633-639. (*f*) [85]

Comrey, A. L., & Levonian, E. A comparison of three point coefficients in factor analysis of MMPI items. *Educ. psychol. Measmt.*, 1958, *18*, 739-755. [85]

Comrey, A. L., & Marggraff, W. A factor analysis of items on the MMPI schizophrenia scale. *Educ. psychol. Measmt.*, 1958, *18*, 301-311. [85]

Cooper, G. W., Bernstein, L., & Hart, C. Predicting suicidal ideation from the Rorschach: An attempt to cross-validate. *J. proj. Tech. pers. Assmt.*, 1965, *29*, 168-170. [144]

Cottrell, L. S., Jr. The present status and future orientation of research on the family. *Amer. soc. Rev.*, 1948, *13*, 123-136. [224]

Cowen, J. E. Test anxiety in high school students and its relationship to performance on group tests. Unpublished doctoral dissertation, Harvard University, 1957. [255]

Cronbach, L. J. The two disciplines of psychology. *Amer. Psychologist*, 1957,

12, 671-684. [170]

Cronbach, L. J. *Essentials of psychological testing.* (2nd ed.) New York: Harper, 1960. [5, 173]

Cronbach, L. J., & Gleser, G. C. *Psychological tests and personnel decisions.* (2nd ed.) Urbana, Ill.: Univ. Ill. Press, 1965. [3, 7]

Cross, H. J. The outcome of therapy: A selected analysis of research findings. *J. consult. Psychol.,* 1964, *28*, 311-316. [213]

Crumpton, E., & Groot, H. The "meaning" of Rorschach color cards as a function of color. *J. proj. Tech. pers. Assmt.,* 1966, *30*, 359-364. [138]

Crumpton, E., Grayson, H. M., & Keith-Lee, P. What kinds of anxiety does the Taylor MA measure? *J. consult. Psychol.,* 1967, *31*, 324-326. [249, 253]

Cutler, R. P., & Kurland, H. D. Clinical quantification of depressive reactions. *Arch. gen. Psychiat.,* 1961, *5*, 280-285. [202]

Dager, E. Z. A review of family research in 1955. *Marriage fam. Liv.,* 1956, *18*, 168-176. [224]

Dahlstrom, W. G., & Welsh, G. S. *An MMPI handbook.* Minneapolis: Univ. Minn. Press. 1960. [81]

Dalbec, Sister E. Creative development over a three-year period in a Catholic liberal arts college. Master's research report, University of Minnesota, Minneapolis, 1966. [46]

Danskin, D. G., & Robinson, F. P. Differences in "degree of lead" among experienced counselors. *J. counsel. Psychol.,* 1954, *1*, 78-83. [216]

Daston, P. G., & Sakheim, G. A. Prediction of successful suicide from the Rorschach test using a sign approach. *J. proj. Tech.,* 1960, *24*, 355-362. [143]

Dauw, D. C. Life experiences, vocational needs and choices of original thinkers and good elaborators. Doctoral dissertation, University of Minnesota, Minneapolis, 1965. [49]

Davids, A. Relations among several objective measures of anxiety under different conditions of motivation. *J. consult. Psychol.,* 1955, *19*, 275-279. [248]

Davids, A. Psychological characteristics of high school male and female potential scientists in comparison with academic underachievers. *Psychol. in the Sch.,* 1966, *3*, 79-87. [56]

Davids, A., & Talmadge, M. A study of Rorschach signs of adjustment in mothers of institutionalized emotionally disturbed children. *J. proj. Tech. pers. Assmt.,* 1963, *27*, 292-297. [147]

Davids, A., & Talmadge, M. Utility of the Rorschach in predicting movement in psychiatric casework. *J. consult. Psychol.,* 1964, *28*, 311-316. [214]

Davis, H. S. Judgments of intellectual level from various features of the Rorschach including vocabulary. *J. proj. Tech.,* 1961, *25*, 155-157. [145]

Davis, R. C. Response patterns. *Trans. N.Y. acad. Sci.,* 1957, *19*, 731-739. [270]

Davitz, J. R. Fear, anxiety, and the perception of others. *J. gen. Psychol.,* 1959, *61*, 169-173. [249]

Dean, S. I. A note on female Blacky protocols. *J. proj. Tech.,* 1959, *23*, 417. [154]

Dean, S. J. Anxiety and neurosis: Fact or fiction (review of The meaning and measurement of neuroticism and anxiety by R. B. Cattell). *Contemp. Psychol.,* 1963, *8*, 467-468. [283]

De Grada, E., Ercolani, A. P., & Terreri, L. S. Attrazione interpersonale, similarità di caratteristiche personali e percezione reciproca. *Riv. Psicol.,* 1966, *60*, 121-153. [58]

De Groot, A. D. Perception and memory versus thought: Some old ideas and recent findings. In B. Kleinmuntz (Ed.), *Problem solving: Research, method and theory,* New York: Wiley, 1966. [29]

Desiderato, O. Effect of anxiety and stress on reaction time and temporal generalization. *Psychol. Rep.,* 1964, *14*, 51-58. [253]

Desroches, H. F., Kaiman, B. D., & Ballard, H. T. A note on the use of a simple measure of nervousness. *J. clin. Psychol.,* 1966, *22*, 429-430. [248]

Dibner, A. S. Cue-counting: A measure of anxiety in interviews. *J. consult. Psychol.,* 1956, *20*, 475-477. [261]

Dibner, A. S. Ambiguity and anxiety. *J. abnorm. soc. Psychol.,* 1958, *56*, 165-174. [254]

Dicken, C. F. Simulated patterns on the California psychological inventory. *J. counsel. Psychol.,* 1960, *7*, 24-31. [68]

Dicken, C. F. Good impression, social desirability, and acquiescence as suppressor variables. *Educ. psychol. Measmt.,* 1963, *23*, 699-720. [68]

Diener, R. G., & Young, J. J. Factors contributing to requests for mental hygiene clinic treatment by veterans with psychiatric disorders. *J. clin. Psychol.,* 1961, *17*, 397-399. [220]

Dildy, L. W., & Liberty, P. G. Investigation of peer-rated anxiety. Proc., 75th Annu. Conv. Amer. Psychol. Assn., 1967, 371-372. [261]

Dittman, A. T. Psychotherapeutic processes. *Annu. Rev. Psychol.,* 1966, *17*, 51-78. [205]

Doctor, R. F., & Friedman. L. F. Thirty-day stability of spontaneous galvanic skin responses in man. *Psychophysiology,* 1966, *2*, 311-315. [275]

Dollard, J., & Auld, F., Jr., *Scoring human*

motives: A manual. New Haven: Yale Univ. Press, 1959. [261]

Dollard, J., & Mowrer, O. H. A method of measuring tension in written documents. *J. abnorm. soc. Psychol.*, 1947, *42*, 3-33. [260]

Domey, R. G., Duckworth, J. E., & Morandi, A. J. Taxonomies and correlates of physique. *Psychol. Bull.*, 1964, *62*, 411-426. [275]

Domino, G. Personality patterns and choice of medical specialty. Unpublished doctoral dissertation, University of California, Berkeley, 1967. [58]

Donald, E. P. Personality scale analysis of new admission to a reformatory. Unpublished master's thesis, Ohio State University, Columbus, 1955. [66]

Dressel, P. L. Some approaches to evaluation. *Personnel Guid. J.*, 1953, *31*, 284-287. [207, 214]

Duenk, L. G. A study of concurrent validity of the Minnesota tests of creative thinking, abbreviated Form VII, for eighth grade industrial arts students. Doctoral dissertation, University of Minnesota, Minneapolis, 1966. [48]

Duffy, E. An explanation of "emotional" phenomena without the use of the concept "emotion." *J. gen. Psychol.*, 1941, *25*, 283-293. [282]

Duffy, E. *Activation and behavior.* New York: Wiley, 1962. [278, 281]

Dunn, J. A. Factor structure of the test anxiety scale for children. *J. consult. Psychol.*, 1964, *28*, 92. [247, 259]

Dunnette, M. D. *Personnel selection and placement.* Belmont, Calif.: Wadsworth, 1966. [5]

Dymond, R. F. Adjustment changes over therapy from self-sorts. In C. R. Rogers & R. F. Dymond (Eds.), *Psychotherapy and personality change.* Chicago: Univ. Chicago Press, 1954. Pp. 76-84. [208]

D'Zurilla, T. J. Persuasion and praise as techniques for modifying verbal behavior in a "real life" group setting. *J. abnorm. Psychol.*, 1966, *71*, 369-376. [176]

Ebner, E. Verbal conditioning in schizophrenia as a function of degree of social interaction. *J. pers. soc. Psychol.*, 1965, *1*, 528-532. [181]

Edwards, A. L. *Edwards personal preference schedule.* New York: Psychol. Corp., 1954. [183, 189]

Edwards, A. L. *The social desirability variable in personality assessment and research.* New York: Dryden, 1957. [7]

Edwards, A. L. *Edwards personal preference schedule manual.* New York: Psychol. Corp., 1959. [96]

Edwards, M. P., & Tyler, L. E. Intelligence, creativity, and achievement in a non-selective public junior high school. *J. educ. Psychol.*, 1965, *56*, 96-99. [48]

Ehrmann, W. A review of family research in 1956. *Marriage fam. Liv.*, 1957, *19*, 279-294. [224]

Ehrmann, W. A review of family research in 1957. *Marriage Fam. Liv.*, 1958, *20*, 384-396. [224]

Eigenbrode, C. R., & Shipman, W. G. The body image barrier concept. *J. abnorm. soc. Psychol.*, 1960, *60*, 450-452. [139]

Eindhoven, J. E., & Vinacke, W. E. Creative processes in painting. *J. gen. Psychol.*, 1952, *47*, 139-164. [38]

Eisdorfer, C. Developmental level and sensory impairment in the aged. *J. proj. Tech.*, 1960, *24*, 129-133. [139]

Eissler, K. R. Limitations to the psychotherapy of schizophrenia. *Psychiatry*, 1943, *6*, 381-391. [210]

Ekman, P., & Friesen, W. V. Head and body cues in the judgment of emotion: A reformulation. *Percept. mot. Skills*, 1967, *24*, 711-724. [280]

Elbert, S., Rosman, B., Minuchin, S., & Guerney, B. A method for the clinical study of family interaction. Paper read at American Orthopsychiatric Association, Chicago, March 1964. [227]

Elizur, A. Content analysis of the Rorschach with regard to anxiety and hostility. *Rorschach res. Exc. & J. proj. Tech.*, 1949, *13*, 247-284. [257, 261]

Ellis, A. The value of marriage prediction tests. *Amer. soc. Rev.*, 1948, *1*, 710-718. [225]

Ellsworth, R. B. *Manual for the MACC behavioral adjustment scale.* Los Angeles: Western Psychol. Serv., 1957. [201]

Ellsworth, R. B. *Manual: The MACC behavioral adjustment scale (Form II).* Los Angeles: Western Psychol. Serv., 1962. [201]

Endicott, N. A., & Endicott, J. Prediction of improvement in treated and untreated patients using the Rorschach prognostic rating scale. *J. consult. Psychol.*, 1964, *28*, 342-348. [214]

Endler, N. S., & Bain, J. M. Interpersonal anxiety as a function of social class. *J. soc. Psychol.*, 1966, *70*, 221-227. [247, 256]

Endler, N. S., & Hunt, J. McV. Sources of behavioral variance as measured by the S-R inventory of anxiousness. *Psychol. Bull.*, 1966, *65*, 336-346. [9, 247, 256, 272]

Endler, N. S., Hunt, J. McV., & Rosenstein, A. J. An S-R inventory of anxiousness. *Psychol. Monogr.*, 1962, *76*, No. 17 (Whole No. 536). [246, 256, 262]

Ends, E. J., & Page, C. W. A study of the functional relationships among measures of anxiety, ego strength and adjustment. *J. clin. Psychol.*, 1957, *13*, 148-150. [258]

Engel, B. T. Stimulus-response and individual-response specificity. *Arch. gen. Psychiat.*, 1960, *2*, 305-313. [270]

English, H. B., & English, A. C. *A comprehensive dictionary of psychological and psychoanalytic terms.* New York: David McKay, 1958. [2, 8]

Erikson, G. The predictive validity of a battery of creative thinking tests and peer nominations among University of Minnesota high school seniors seven years later. Master's research paper, University of Minnesota, Minneapolis, 1966. [47]

Ervin-Tripp, S., & Slobin, D. Psycholinguistics. In P. R. Farnsworth (Ed.), *Annual review of psychology, Vol. 17, 1966.* Palo Alto: Annual Reviews, Inc. 1966. [23]

Exner, J. F. Achromatic color in cards IV and VI on the Rorschach. *J. proj. Tech.*, 1961, *25*, 38-41. [137]

Exner, J. F. The effect of color productivity in cards VIII, IX, X of the Rorschach. *J. proj. Tech.*, 1962, *26*, 30-34. [136]

Eysenck, H. J. The effects of psychotherapy: An evaluation. *J. consult. Psychol.*, 1952, *16*, 319-342. [212]

Eysenck, H. J. *The structure of human personality.* (2nd ed.) London: Methuen, 1960. [284]

Eysenck, H. J. Classification and problems of diagnosis. In H. J. Eysenck (Ed.), *Handbook of abnormal psychology.* New York: Basic Books, 1961. [247]

Eysenck, H. J., & Rachman, S. *The causes and cures of neurosis.* San Diego: Robert R. Knapp, 1965. [176]

Fabrikant, B. Rigidity and flexibility on the Rorschach. *J. clin. Psychol.*, 1954, *10*, 255-258. [141]

Fairweather, G. W. (Ed.) *Social psychology in treating mental illness: An experimental approach.* New York: Wiley, 1964. [8, 10]

Farnsworth, D. L. *Mental health in college and university.* Cambridge, Mass.: Harvard Univ. Press, 1957. [219]

Feather, R. W. Semantic generalization of classically conditioned responses: A review. *Psychol. Bull.*, 1965, *63*, 425-441. [276]

Feifel, H., & Eells, J. Patient and therapists assess the same psychotherapy. *J. consult. Psychol.*, 1963, *27*, 310-318. [217, 218]

Feigenbaum, E. A., & Feldman, J. *Computers and thought.* New York: McGraw-Hill, 1963. [23, 24]

Feigl, H. Principles and problems of theory construction in psychology. In *Current trends in psychological theory.* Pittsburgh: University of Pittsburgh Press, 1951. Pp. 178-213. [267, 268, 274]

Feigl, H. The "mental" and the "physical." In H. Feigl, M. Scriven, & G. Maxwell (Eds.), *Minnesota studies in the philosophy of science.* Vol. 2. Concepts, theories, and the mind-body problem. Minneapolis: Univ. Minn. Press, 1958. Pp. 370-497. [274]

Fenz, W. D., & Epstein, S. Manifest anxiety: Unifactorial or multifactorial composition. *Percept. mot. Skills*, 1965, *20*, 773-780. [247, 252]

Ferguson, G. A. On transfer and the abilities of man. *Canad. J. Psychol.*, 1956, *10*, 121-131. [19]

Ferguson, J. T., McReynolds, P., & Ballachey, E. L. *Hospital adjustment scale.* Palo Alto: Consulting Psychologists' Press, 1953. [200]

Ferreira, A. J. Decision-making in normal and pathologic families. *Arch. gen. Psychiat.*, 1963, *8*, 68-73. [226, 237, 238]

Ferreira, A. J., & Winter, W. D. Family interaction and decision-making. *Arch. gen. Psychiat.*, 1965, *13*, 214-223. [226, 237]

Ferreira, A. J., & Winter, W. D. Stability of interactional variables in family decision-making. *Arch. gen. Psychiat.*, 1966, *14*, 352-355. [226]

Ferster, C. B. Classification of behavioral pathology. In L. Krasner & L. P. Ullmann (Eds.), *Research in Behavior Modification.* New York: Holt, Rinehart & Winston, 1965. Pp. 6-26. [170, 171]

Fiedler, F. E. Quantitative studies on the role of therapists' feelings toward their patients. In O. H. Mowrer (Ed.), *Psychotherapy: Theory and research.* New York: Ronald Press, 1953. Pp. 296-315. [216, 217]

Filmer-Bennett, G. Prognostic indices in the Rorschach records of hospitalized patients. *J. abnorm. soc. Psychol.*, 1952, *47*, 502-506. [147]

Filmer-Bennett, G. The Rorschach as a means of predicting treatment outcome. *J. consult. Psychol.*, 1955, *19*, 331-334. [147]

Finney, B. C. Rorschach test correlates of assaultive behavior. *J. proj. Tech.*, 1955, *19*, 6-16. [136, 143, 144]

Fisher, R. L. Body boundary and achievement behavior. *J. proj. Tech. pers. Assmt.*, 1966, *30*, 435-439. [139]

Fisher, S. Right-left gradients in body image, body reactivity, and perception. *Genet. psychol. Monogr.*, 1960, *61*, 197-228. [283]

Fisher, S. The body boundary and judged behavioral patterns in an interview situation. *J. proj. Tech. pers. Assmt.*, 1964, *28*, 181-185. [136, 139]

Fisher, S. Projective methodologies. In Farnsworth, P. (Ed.), *Annual review of psychology.* Palo Alto: Annual Reviews, 1967, *18*, 165-190. [6, 8]

Fisher, S., & Cleveland, S. E. Relationship of body image to site of cancer. *Psychosom. Med.*, 1956, *18*, 304-309. [139]

Fisher, S., & Cleveland, S. E. Body image boundaries and sexual behavior. *J. Psychol.*, 1958, *45*, 207-211. [139]

Fisher, S., & Cleveland, S. E. A comparison of psychological characteristics and physiological reactivity in ulcer and rheumatoid arthritis groups. II. Differences in physiological reactivity. *J. psychosom. Med.*, 1960, *22*, 290-293. [139]

Fiske, D. W. Problems in measuring personality. In J. M. Wepman & R. W. Heine (Eds.), *Concepts of personality.* Chicago: Aldine, 1963. Pp. 449-473. [5]

Fiske, D. W. The subject reacts to tests. *Amer. Psychologist*, 1967, *22*, 287-296. [7]

Fiske, D. W., Cartwright, D. S., & Kirtner, W. L. Are psychotherapeutic changes predictable? *J. abnorm. soc. Psychol.*, 1964, *69*, 418-426. [214]

Fiske, D. W., & Maddi, S. R. *Functions of varied experience.* Homewood, Ill.: Dorsey Press, 1961. [39]

Flanagan, J. C. The definition and measurement of ingenuity. In C. W. Taylor and F. Barron (Eds.), *Scientific creativity: Its recognition and development.* New York: Wiley, 1963. Pp. 89-98. [40]

Flavell, J. H. *The developmental psychology of Jean Piaget.* Princeton: Van Nostrand, 1963. [26, 28]

Ford, D. H., & Urban, H. B. *Systems of psychotherapy.* New York: Wiley, 1963. [205]

Ford, D. H., & Urban, H. B. Psychotherapy. *Annu. Rev. Psychol.*, 1967, *18*, 333-372. [205, 209, 211, 215, 220]

Fosberg, I. A. How do subjects fake results on the Rorschach test? *Rorschach res. Exch.*, 1943, *7*, 119-121. [141]

Fox, R. E., & Goldin, P. C. The empathic process in psychotherapy: A survey of theory and research. Unpublished manuscript, 1963. [217]

Framo, J. L. Systematic research on family dynamics. In Boszormenyi-Nagy, I., & Framo, J. L. (Eds.), *Intensive family therapy.* New York: Harper and Row, 1965. Pp. 407-462. [224]

Frank, G. H. The effect of directive and nondirective statements by therapists on the content of patient verbalizations. *J. gen. Psychol.*, 1964, *71*, 323-328. [218]

Frank, J. D. Problems of controls in psychotherapy as exemplified by the psychotherapy research project of the Phipps Psychiatric Clinic. In E. A. Rubinstein & M. B. Parloff (Eds.), *Research in psychotherapy.* Washington, D. C.: National Publishing Co., 1959. Pp. 10-26. [209]

Frankenhaeuser, M., Jarpe, G., & Mattell, G. Effects of intravenous infusions of adrenaline and noradrenaline on certain psychological and physiological functions. *Acta physiol. Scand.*, 1961, *51*, 175-186. [282]

Frankl, V. E. Paradoxical intention: A logotherapeutic technique. *Amer. J. Psychother.*, 1960, *14*, 520-535. [219]

Freeman, D. Human aggression in anthropological perspective (and chapter discussion). In J. D. Carthy & F. J. Ebling (Eds.), *The natural history of aggression.* New York: Academic Press, 1964. Pp. 109-119, 121-127. [279]

Freeman, F. S. *Theory and practice of psychological testing.* New York: Holt, 1955. [5]

Freeman, M. J. The development of a test for the measurement of anxiety: A study of its reliability and validity. *Psychol. Monogr.*, 1953, Vol. 67, No. 3 (Whole No. 353). [258]

French, J. W., Ekstrom, R. B., & Price, L. A. *Manual for kit of reference tests for cognitive factors.* (Rev. ed.) Princeton, N.J.: Educational Testing Service, 1963. [42, 43]

Freund, K., Sedlacek, F., & Knob, K. A simple transducer for mechanical plethysmography of the male genital. *J. exp. Anal. Behav.*, 1965, *8*, 169-170. [269]

Freyd, Max. The personalities of the socially and the mechanically inclined. *Psych. Monogr.*, 1924, *33*, whole number 151. [113]

Friedman, H., & Orgel, S. A. Rorschach developmental scores and intelligence level. *J. proj. Tech. pers. Assmt.*, 1964, *28*, 425-429. [139]

Friedman, S. B., Mason, J. W., & Hamburg, D. A. Urinary 17-hydroxycorticosteroid levels in parents with neoplastic disease: A study of chronic psychological stress. *Psychosom. Med.*, 1963, *25*, 364-376. [273]

Fryer, D. *The measurement of interests*, 1931. New York: Henry Holt & Co. [113]

Fulkerson, S. C. Some implications of the new cognitive theory for projective tests. *J. consult. Psychol.*, 1965, *29*, 191-197. [8]

Fulkerson, S. C., & Barry, J. R. Methodology and research on the prognostic use of psychological tests. *Psychol. Bull.*, 1961, *58*, 177-205. [143, 147]

Funkenstein, D. H., King, S. H., & Drolette, M. E. *Mastery of stress.* Cambridge: Harvard Univ. Press, 1957. [278, 279]

Furth, H. G. Research with the deaf: Implications for language and cognition. *Psychol. Bull.*, 1964, *62*, 145-164. [23]

Furth, H. G. *Thinking without language:*

Psychological implications of deafness. New York: Free Press, 1966. [23]

Gabler, J. S., & Otto, H. A. Family strengths: Review of social work literature on family strengths, 1963. Unpublished master's thesis, University of Utah, 1963. [230]

Gabler, J. S., & Otto, H. A. Family strengths in family life and other professional literature: A comparative study. *J. Marriage Fam.*, 1964, *26*, 221-222. [230]

Gallo, P. S., & McClintock, C. G. Cooperative and competitive behavior in mixed motive games. *J. confl. Resolut.*, 1965, *9*, 68-78. [228]

Gamble, A. O. Suggestions for future research. In C. W. Taylor (Ed.), *The third (1959) University of Utah research conference on the identification of creative scientific talent.* Salt Lake City: Univ. Utah Press, 1959. Pp. 104-123. [35]

Gardner, R. W. Impulsivity as indicated by Rorschach test factors. *J. consult. Psychol.*, 1951, *15*, 464-468. [136, 144]

Gardner, R. W., Holzman, P. S., Klein, G. S., Linton, H. B., & Spence, D. P. Cognitive control: A study of individual consistencies in cognitive behavior. *Psychol. Issues*, 1959, *1*, No. 4. [286]

Garfield, S. L. A note on patients' reasons for terminating therapy. *Psychol. Rep.*, 1963, *13*, 38. (*a*) [220]

Garfield, S. L. The clinical method in personality assessment. In J. M. Wepman & R. W. Heine (Eds.), *Concepts of personality.* Chicago: Aldine, 1963. Pp. 474-502. (*b*) [5]

Garfield, S. L., & Affleck, D. C. Therapists' judgments concerning patients considered for psychotherapy. *J. consult. Psychol.*, 1961, *25*, 505-509. [215]

Garfield, S. L., & Wolpin, M. Expectations regarding psychotherapy. *J. nerv. ment. Dis.*, 1963, *137*, 353-362. [221]

Garner, H. H. A confrontation technique used in psychotherapy. *Comprehensive Psychiat.*, 1960, *1*, 201-211. [219]

Gaylin, N. Changes in self-concept after therapy as related to Rorschach performance. Unpublished doctoral dissertation, University of Chicago, 1965. [147]

Geer, J. H. The development of a scale to measure fear. *Behav. Res. Ther.* 1965, *3*, 45-53. [10, 251]

Gendlin, E. T. Research in psychotherapy with schizophrenic patients and the nature of that "illness." *Am. J. Psychother.*, 1966, *20*, 4-16. [218]

Gendre, F. Validation d'une "batterie secrétaire." *Bull. Cent. Étud. Rech. Psychotech.*, 1964, *13*, 167-180. [58, 70]

Gendre, F. Évaluation de la personnalité et situation de sélection. *Bull. Cent. Étud. Rech. Psychol.*, 1966, *15*, 259-361. [58, 65, 70]

Gertz, B., Stilson, D. W., & Gynther, M. D. Reliability of the HAS as a function of length of observation and level of adjustment. *J. clin. Psychol.*, 1959, *15*, 36-39. [204]

Getter, H. A personality determinant of verbal conditioning. *J. Pers.*, 1966, *34*, 397-405. [177, 183]

Ghiselin, B. *The creative process.* New York: New American Library, 1952. [38]

Ghiselin, B. Ultimate criteria for two levels of creativity. In C. W. Taylor and F. Barron (Eds.), *Scientific creativity: Its recognition and development.* New York: Wiley, 1963. Pp. 30-43. [36]

Ghiselli, E. *The validity of occupational aptitude tests.* New York: Wiley, 1966. [6, 17]

Gibby, R. G., Miller, D. R., & Walker, E. L. The examiner's influence on the Rorschach protocol. *J. consult. Psychol.*, 1953, *17*, 425-428. [142]

Glasser, W. *Reality Therapy.* New York: Harper & Row, 1965. [219]

Gleser, G. C. Projective methodologies. *Annu. Rev. Psychol.*, 1963, *14*, 391-422. [6, 8]

Gleser, G. C., Gottschalk, L. A., & Springer, K. J. An anxiety scale applicable to verbal samples. *Arch. gen. Psychiat.*, 1961. *5*, 593-604. [261, 262]

Gleser, G., & Ulett, G. The Saslow screening test as a measure of anxiety proneness. *J. clin. Psychol.*, 1952, *8*, 279-283. [252, 254]

Golann, S. E. *The creativity motive. J. Pers.*, 1962, *30*, 588-600. [54]

Golann, S. E. Psychological study of creativity. *Psychol. Bull.*, 1963, *60*, 548-565. [34]

Goldberg, A., & Rubin, B. Recovery of patients during periods of supposed neglect. *Brit. J. Med. Psychol.*, 1964, *37*, 265-272. [212]

Goldberg, L. R. Diagnosticians vs. diagnostic signs. *Psychol. Monogr.*, 1965, *79*, No. 9 (Whole No. 600). [8]

Goldberg, L. R., & Slovic, P. The importance of test item content: An analysis of a corollary of the deviation hypothesis. *J. counsel. Psychol.*, 1967, *14*, 462-472. [8]

Goldberg, P. A. A review of sentence completion methods in personality assessment. *J. proj. tech. pers. Assmt.*, 1965, *29*, 12-45. [6]

Goldberg, S. C., Mattsson, N., Cole, J. O., & Klerman, G. L. Prediction of improvement in schizophrenia under four phenothiazines. *Arch. Gen. Psychiat.*, 1967, *16*, 107-117. [196]

Goldfried, M. R. Rorschach developmental level and the MMPI. *J. proj. Tech.*, 1962, *26*, 187-192. [139]

Goldfried, M. R. The connotive meaning of some animal symbols for college students. *J. proj. Tech.*, 1963, *27*, 60-67. [138]

Goldfried, M. R. The assessment of anxiety by means of the Rorschach. *J. proj. Tech. pers. Assmt.*, 1966, *30*, 364-380. [257, 258]

Goldman, A. R. Differential effects of social reward and punishment of dependent and dependency-anxious schizophrenics. *J. abnorm. Psychol.*, 1965, *70*, 412-418. [176]

Goldman, L. *Using tests in counseling*. New York: Appleton-Century-Crofts, 1961. [5]

Goldmann, A. E., & Hermann, J. L. Studies in vicariousness: The effect of immobilization on Rorschach movement responses. *J. proj. Tech.*, 1961, *25*, 164-166. [142]

Goldschmid, M. L. The prediction of college major in the sciences and the humanities by means of personality tests. Unpublished doctoral dissertation, University of California, Berkeley, 1965. [58]

Goldstein, A. P., & Dean, S. J. *The investigation of psychotherapy*. New York: Wiley, 1966. [205]

Goldstein, A. P., Heller, K., & Sechrest, L. B. *Psychotherapy and the psychology of behavior change*. New York: Wiley, 1966. [205, 206, 209]

Goldstein, I. B. The relationship of muscle tension and autonomic activity to psychiatric disorders. *Psychosom. Med.*, 1965, *27*, 39-52. [258]

Goldstein, K. *The organism*. New York: American Book Co., 1939. [49]

Goldstein, M. J., Jones, R. B., Clemens, T. L., Flagg, G. W., & Alexander, J. E. Coping style as a factor in psychophysiological response to a tension-arousing film. *J. pers. Soc. Psychol.*, 1965, *1*, 290-302. [276]

Goodall, McC. Studies of adrenaline and noradrenaline in mammalian heart and suprarenals. *Acta physiol. Scand.*, 1951, *24* (Suppl. 85). [279]

Goodrich, D. W., & Boomer, D. S. Experimental assessment of modes of conflict resolution. *Fam. Process*, 1963, *2*, 15-24. [226]

Goodstein, L. D., & Schrader, W. J. An empirically-derived managerial key for the California psychological inventory. *J. appl. Psychol.*, 1963, *47*, 42-45. [56]

Goralski, P. S. Creativity: Student teachers' perception of approaches to classroom teaching. Doctoral dissertation, University of Minnesota, Minneapolis, 1964. [46]

Gordon, E. M., & Sarason, S. B. The relationship between "Test Anxiety" and "Other Anxieties." *J. Pers.*, 1955, *23*, 317-323. [251, 255]

Gordon, G. The identification and use of creative abilities in scientific organizations. Paper presented at the Seventh National Research Conference on Creativity, Greensboro, N.C., 1966. [41]

Gordon, J. E. Archetypical, Germanic, factorial, brilliant and contradictory (review of *Personality and social psychology* by R. B. Cattell). *Contemp. Psychol.*, 1966, *11*, 236-238. [283]

Gorham, D. R. Validity and reliability studies of a computer-based scoring system for ink-blot responses. *J. consult. Psychol.*, 1967, *31*, 65-70. [6]

Gorham, D. R., & Overall, J. E. Drug-action profiles based on an abbreviated psychiatric rating scale. *J. nerv. & ment. Dis.*, 1960, *131*, 528-535. [197, 198, 201]

Gorham, D. R., & Overall, J. E. Dimensions of change in psychiatric symptomatology. *Dis. nerv. Syst.*, 1961, *22*, 576-580. [198]

Gorham, D. R., & Pokorny, A. D. Effects of a phenothiazine and/or group psychotherapy with schizophrenics. *Dis. nerv. Syst.*, 1964, *25*, 77-86. [199, 251]

Gottschalk, L. A., & Auerbach, A. H. *Methods of research in psychotherapy.*, New York: Appleton-Century-Crofts, 1966. [6, 205, 206]

Gough, H. G. A new dimension of status: I. Development of a personality scale. *Amer. sociol. Rev.*, 1948, *13*, 401-409. [61]

Gough, H. G. A new dimension of status: III. Discrepancies between the St scale and "objective" status. *Amer. sociol. Rev.*, 1949, *14*, 275-281. (a) [61]

Gough, H. G. A short social status inventory. *J. educ. Psychol.*, 1949, *40*, 52-56. (b) [61]

Gough, H. G. Studies of social intolerance: II. A personality scale for anti-Semitism. *J. soc. Psychol.*, 1951, *33*, 247-255. [67]

Gough, H. G. On making a good impression. *J. educ. Res.*, 1952, *46*, 33-42. [67]

Gough, H. G. *Manual for the California psychological inventory*. Palo Alto, Calif.: Consulting Psychologists' Press, 1957. Revised edition, 1964. [55, 74]

Gough, H. G. An assessment study of Air Force officers. Part IV: Predictability of a composite criterion of officer effectiveness. Lackland Air Force Base, Texas: Wright Air Development Center, Personnel Laboratory, 1958. (Technical Report WADC-TR-58-91(IV), ASTIA Document No. AD 210 219) [70]

Gough, H. G. Techniques for identifying the creative research scientist. In *Conference on the creative person*, Berkeley:

University of California, Institute of Personality Assessment and Research, 1961. [50]

Gough, H. G. The adjective check list as a personality assessment research technique. *Psychol. Rep.*, 1960, *6*, 107-122. [51]

Gough, H. G. Clinical versus statistical prediction in psychology. In L. Postman (Ed.), *Psychology in the making*. New York: Knopf, 1962. Pp. 526-584. [8]

Gough, H. G. Academic achievement in high school as predicted from the California psychological inventory. *J. educ. Psychol.*, 1964, *55*, 174-180. (*a*) [70, 78]

Gough, H. G. Achievement in the first course in psychology as predicted from the California psychological inventory. *J. Psychol.*, 1964, *57*, 419-430. (*b*) [70, 72]

Gough, H. G. A cross-cultural study of achievement motivation. *J. appl. Psychol.*, 1964, *48*, 191-196. (*c*) [58]

Gough, H. G. Conceptual analysis of psychological test scores and other diagnostic variables. *J. abnorm. Psychol.*, 1965, *70*, 294-302. (*a*) [7, 59, 66, 104]

Gough, H. G. Cross-cultural validation of a measure of asocial behavior. *Psychol. Rep.*, 1965, *17*, 379-387. (*b*) [58, 65]

Gough, H. G. A validational study of the Chapin social insight test. *Psychol. Rep.*, 1965, *17*, 355-368. (*c*) [70]

Gough, H. G. Appraisal of social maturity by means of the CPI. *J. abnorm. Psychol.*, 1966, *71*, 189-195. (*a*) [56]

Gough, H. G. A cross-cultural analysis of the CPI femininity scale. *J. consult. Psychol.*, 1966, *30*, 136-141. (*b*) [58, 73]

Gough, H. G. Graduation from high school as predicted from the California psychological inventory. *Psychol. in the Sch.*, 1966, *3*, 208-216. (*c*) [58, 65]

Gough, H. G., & Hall, W. B. Prediction of performance in medical school from the California psychological inventory. *J. appl. Psychol.*, 1964, *48*, 218-226. [78]

Gough, H. G., & Heilbrun, A. B., Jr. *The adjective check list manual*. Palo Alto, Calif.: Consulting Psychologists' Press, 1965. [60]

Gough, H. G., & Sandhu, H. S. Validation of the CPI socialization scale in India. *J. abnorm. soc. Psychol.*, 1964, *68*, 544-547. [58]

Gough, H. G., Wenk, E. A., & Rozynko, V. A. Parole outcome as predicted from the CPI, the MMPI, and a base expectancy index. *J. abnorm. Psychol.*, 1965, *70*, 432-441. [58]

Graham, D. T., Kabler, J. D., & Graham, F. K. Physiological responses to the suggestion of attitudes specific for hives and hypertension. *Psychosom. Med.*, 1962, *24*, 159-169. [271]

Granick, S., & Scheflen, N. A. Approaches to reliability of projective tests with special reference to the Blacky pictures test. *J. consult. Psychol.*, 1958, *22*, 137-141. [151]

Grater, H. A. Client preferences for affective or cognitive counselor characteristics and first interview behavior. *J. counsel. Psychol.*, 1964, *11*, 248-250. [216]

Gravitz, M. A. A new computerized method for the fully automated printout of MMPI graphic profiles. *J. clin. Psychol.*, 1967, *23*, 101-102. [6]

Green, B. F., Jr. Intelligence and computer simulation. *Trans. N. Y. Acad. Sci.*, 1964, *27*, 55-63. [24]

Greenblatt, M., Grosser, G. H., & Wechsler, H. A comparative study of selected antidepressant medication and EST. *Amer. J. Psychiat.*, 1962, *119*, 144-153. [202]

Greenspoon, J. Verbal conditioning and clinical psychology. In A. J. Bachrach (Ed.), *Experimental foundations of clinical psychology*. New York: Basic Books, 1962. Pp. 510-553. [175, 176]

Greenspoon, J., & Gersten, C. D. A new look at psychological testing: Psychological testing from the standpoint of a behaviorist. *Amer. Psychologist*. 1967, *22*, 848-853. [10]

Grinker, R. R., Miller, J., Sabshin, M., Nunn, R., & Nunnally, J. C. *The phenomena of depressions*. New York: Hoeber, 1961. [202]

Groves, C. The counseling process. *Marriage fam. Liv.*, 1947, *9*, 57-58. [210]

Guertin, W. H. Research with the Wechsler intelligence scales for adults: 1955-60. *Psychol. Bull.*, 1962, *59*, 1-26. [6]

Guertin, W. H., & Krugman, A. D. A factor analytically derived scale for rating activities of psychiatric patients. *J. clin. Psychol.*, 1959, *15*, 32-36. [201]

Guertin, W. H., & Ladd, C. E. Research with the Wechler intelligence scales for adults: 1960-1965. *Psychol. Bull.*, 1966, *66*, 385-409. [6]

Guilford, J. P. When not to factor analyze. *Psychol. Bull.*, 1952, *49*, 26-37. [82]

Guilford, J. P. When not to factor analyze. *Psychol. Bull.*, 1952, *49*, 26-37. [82]

Guilford, J. P. A revised structure of intellect. Los Angeles: *University of Southern California Reports from the Psychological Laboratory*, No. 19, 1957. [164]

Guilford, J. P. Factorial angles to psychology. *Psychol. Rev.*, 1961, *68*, 1-20. [18]

Guilford, J. P. Intellectual resources and their values as seen by scientists. In C. W. Taylor & F. Barron (Eds.), *Scientific creativity: Its recognition and development*. New York: Wiley, 1963.

Pp. 101-118. [41]

Guilford, J. P. Zero correlations among tests of intellectual abilities. *Psychol. Bull.*, 1964, *61*, 401-404. [15]

Guilford, J. P. Intelligence: 1965 model. *Amer. Psychologist*, 1966, *21*, 20-26. [17, 18, 21, 41]

Guilford, J. P. *The nature of human intelligence*. New York: McGraw-Hill, 1967. [14, 15, 21]

Guilford, J. P., Christensen, P. R., Frick, J. W., & Merrifield, P. R. The relations of creative thinking aptitudes to non-aptitude personality traits. Los Angeles: *University of Southern California Reports from the Psychological Laboratory*, No. 20, 1957. [43]

Guilford, J. P., Frick, J. W., Christensen, P. R., & Merrifield, P. R. A factor-analytic study of flexibility in thinking. Los Angeles: *University of Southern California Reports from the Psychological Laboratory*, No. 18, 1957. [43]

Guilford, J. P., Hoepfner, R., & Petersen, H. Predicting achievement in ninth-grade mathematics from measures of intellectual-aptitude factors. *Educ. psychol. Measmt.*, 1965, *25*, 659-682. [17]

Guilford, J. P., Merrifield, P. R., & Cox, A. B. Creative thinking in children at the junior high school levels. Los Angeles: *University of Southern California Reports from the Psychological Laboratory*, No. 26, 1961. [43]

Guilford, J. P., Wilson, R. C., & Christensen, P. R. A factor-analytic study of creative thinking. II. Administration of tests and analysis of results. Los Angeles: *University of Southern California Reports from the Psychological Laboratory*, No. 8, 1952. [43]

Guion, R. M. Personnel selection. *Annu. Rev. Psychol.*, 1967, *18*, 191-216. [6]

Gulliksen, H. *Theory of mental tests*. New York: Wiley, 1950. [3]

Guttman, L. A faceted definition of intelligence. *Scripta Hierosolymitana: Studies in psychology*. Jerusalem: The Hebrew University, 1965. [15, 17, 19, 20, 21, 30]

Guttman, L., & Schlesinger, I. M. *Development of diagnostic analytical and mechanical ability tests through facet design and analysis*. Jerusalem: The Israel Institute of Applied Social Research, 1966. [20, 21]

Haan, N. An investigation of the relationship of Rorschach scores, patterns, and behavior to coping and defense mechanisms. *J. proj. Tech. pers. Assmt.*, 1964, *28*, 429-442. [133, 137]

Hafner, A. J. Rorschach card stimulus value for children. *J. proj. Tech.*, 1961, *25*, 166-169. [134]

Hafner, A. J., & Kaplan, A. M. Hostility content analysis of the Rorschach and TAT. *J. proj. Tech.*, 1960, *24*, 137-144. [146]

Hafner, A. J., Quast, W., Speer, D. C., & Grams, A. Children's anxiety scales in relation to self, parental, and psychiatric ratings of anxiety. *J. consult. Psychol.*, 1964, *28*, 555-558. [259]

Hafner, A. J., & Rosen, E. The meaning of Rorschach ink-blot responses and determinants as perceived by children. *J. proj. Tech. pers. Assmt.*, 1964, *28*, 192-200. [138]

Haimowitz, N. R., & Haimowitz, M. L. Personality changes in client-centered therapy. In W. Wolff & J. A. Precker, *Success in psychotherapy*. New York: Grune & Stratton, 1952. [212]

Haley, J. Family experiments: A new type of experimentation. *Fam. Process*, 1962, *1*, 265-293. [233]

Haley, J. Research on family patterns: An instrument measurement. *Fam. Process*, 1964, *3*, 41-65. [233]

Haley, J. Testing parental instructions to schizophrenic and normal children. *J. abnorm. Psychol.*, in press.

Haley, J., & Glick, I. *Psychiatry and the family: An annotated bibliography of articles published 1960-1964*. Palo Alto: Family Process, 1965. [225]

Hall, J., & Williams, M. A comparison of decision-making performances in established and ad hoc groups. *J. pers. soc. Psychol.*, 1966, *3*, 214-222. [242]

Hamburg, D. A., Sabshin, M A., Board, F. A., Grinker, R. R., Korchin, S. J., Basowitz, H., Heath, H., & Persky, H. Classification and rating of emotional experiences. *Arch. Neurol. Psychiat.*, 1958, *79*, 415-426. [261]

Hamilton, M. The assessment of anxiety states by rating. *Brit. J. med. Psychol.*, 1959, *32*, 50-59. [247, 261]

Hamilton, M. A rating scale for depression. *J. Neurol. Neurosurg. Psychiat.*, 1960, *23*, 56-62. [202]

Hammer, M. A comparison of responses by clinic and normal adults to Rorschach card III human figure area. *J. proj. Tech. pers. Assmt.*, 1966, *30*, 161-163. [144]

Hammes, J. A. Relation of manifest anxiety to specific problem areas. *J. clin. Psychol.*, 1959, *15*, 298-300. [251, 253]

Hammes, J. A. Manifest anxiety and perception of environmental threat. *J. clin. Psychol.*, 1961, *17*, 35-36. [253]

Hampshire, S. Dispositions. *Analysis*, 1953, *14*, 5-11. [267]

Handel, G. Psychological study of whole families. *Psychol. Bull.*, 1965, *63*, 19-41. [224]

Handler, L. Anxiety indexes in the draw-a-person test: A scoring manual. *J. proj. Tech. pers. Assmt.*, 1967, *31*, 46-57.

[258]
Handler, L., & Reyher, J. Figure drawing anxiety indexes: A review of the literature. *J. proj. Tech. pers. Assmt.*, 1965, *29*, 305-313. [257]

Handler, L., & Reyher, J. Relationship between GSR and anxiety indexes in projective drawings. *J. consult. Psychol.*, 1966, *30*, 60-67. [257]

Handlon, J. H. Hormonal activity and individual responses to stresses and easements in everyday living. In R. Rilsslert & N. S. Greenfield (Eds.), *Physiological correlates of psychological disorder*. Madison: Univ. Wisc. Press, 1962. [249]

Harleston, B. W. Test anxiety and performance in problem-solving situations. *J. pers.*, 1962, *30*, 557-573. [255]

Harlow, H. F. The evolution of learning. In A. Roe & G. G. Simpson (Eds.), *Behavior and evolution*. New Haven: Yale Univ. Press, 1958. Part II. [22]

Harlow, H. F., & Stagner, R. Psychology of feelings and emotions. II. Theory of emotions. *Psychol. Rev.*, 1933, *40*, 184-195. [282]

Harmon, L. R. The development of a criterion of scientific competence. In C. W. Taylor & F. Barron (Eds.), *Scientific creativity: Its recognition and development*. New York: Wiley, 1963. Pp. 44–52. [35]

Harris, R. A. Creativity in marketing. In P. Smith (Ed.), *Creativity*. New York: Hastings House, 1959. [38]

Hartlage, L. Common psychological tests applied to the assessment of brain damage. *J. project. Tech. pers. Assmt.*, 1966, *30*, 319-338. [6]

Hartshorne, H., & May, M. A. *Studies in deceit*. New York: Macmillan, 1928. [9]

Hase, H. D., & Goldberg, L. R. The comparative validity of different strategies of deriving personality inventory scales. *Psychol. Bull.*, 1967, *67*, 231-248. [7, 170, 173]

Hathaway, S. R., & McKinley, J. C. *Manual for the Minnesota multiphasic personality inventory*. New York: Psychol. Corp., 1943. [57,73]

Hathaway, S. R., & McKinley, J. C. *The Minnesota multiphasic personality inventory manual*. (Rev. ed.) New York: Psychol. Corp., 1951. [80,202]

Hawkins, D.R., Monroe, H. T., Sandifer, M. G., & Vernon, C. R. Psychological and physiological responses to continuous epinephrine infusion — an approach to the study of the affect, anxiety. *Psychiat. res. rep. Amer. Psychiat. Assoc.*, 1960, *12*, 40-50. [282]

Hayes, K. J. Genes, drives, and intellect. *Psychol. Rep.*, 1962, *10*, 299-342. [21, 26]

Haynes, J. R., & Sells, S. B. Assessment of organic brain damage by psychological tests. *Psychol. Bull.*, 1963, *60*, 316-325. [6]

Haywood, H.C. Novelty-seeking behavior as a function of manifest anxiety and physiological arousal. *J. Pers.*, 1962, *30*, 63-74. [254]

Heath, D. H. The phrase association test: A research measure of anxiety thresholds and defense type. *J. gen. Psychol.*, 1960, *62*, 165-176. [259]

Heath, D. H. *Explorations of maturity*. New York: Appleton-Century-Crofts, 1965. [259]

Heath, H. A., & Korchin, S. J. Clinical judgments and self-ratings of traits and states. *Arch. gen. Psychiat.*, 1963, *9*, 390-399. [246]

Hebb, D. O. *The organization of behavior*. New York: Wiley, 1949. [22, 25]

Hebb, D. O. Drives and the C.N.S. (conceptual nervous system). *Psychol. Rev.*, 1955, *62*, 243-254. [274]

Hebb, D. O. *A textbook of psychology*. Philadelphia: W. B. Saunders Co., 1958. [19,29]

Heer, D. M. The measurement and bases of family power: An overview. *Marriage fam. Liv.*, 1963, *25*, 113-139. [224]

Heilbrun, A. B., Jr., Daniel, J. L., Goodstein, L. D., Stephenson, R. R., & Crites, J. O. The validity of two-scale pattern interpretation on the California psychological inventory. *J. appl. Psychol.*, 1962, *46*, 409-416. [74]

Heilbrun, G. Results with psychoanalytic therapy. *Amer. J. Psychother.*, 1963, *17*, 427-435. [215]

Heine, W. A. A comparison of patients' reports on psychotherapeutic experiences with psychoanalytic, nondirective, and Adlerian therapists. Unpublished doctoral dissertation, University of Chicago, 1950. [218]

Heineman, C. E. A forced-choice form of the Taylor anxiety scale. *J. consult. Psychol.*, 1953, *17*, 447-454. [253]

Heller, K., Myers, R. A., & Kline, L. V. Interviewer behavior as a function of standardized client roles. *J. consult. Psychol.*, 1963, *27*, 117-122. [215]

Helmstadter, G. C. *Principles of psychological measurement*. New York: Appleton-Century-Crofts, 1964. [5]

Hempel, C. G. Operationism observation, and theoretical terms. In A. Danto & S. Morgenbesser (Eds.), *Philosophy of science*. New York: Meridian Books, 1960. Pp. 101-120. [267]

Henry, E., & Rotter, J. B. Situational influence on Rorschach responses. *J. consult. Psychol.*, 1956, *6*, 457-462. [141]

Hertz, M. R. Suicidal configurations in Rorschach records. *Rorschach res. Exch.*, 1948, *12*, 3-58. [143]

Hess, R. D., & Handel, G. *Family worlds:*

A psychosocial approach to family life. Chicago: U. of Chicago Press, 1959. [230]

Hill, K. T., & Sarason, S. B. The relation of test anxiety and defensiveness to test and school performance over the elementary school years. *Monogr. soc. Res. Child Develpm.*, Serial No. 104, 1966, *31*. [259]

Hill, R. H. A bibliography of family classics. In W. Waller & R. Hill, *The family: A dynamic interpretation.* New York: Dryden Press, 1951. (a) [224]

Hill, R. H. A review of current research on marriage and the family. *Amer. sociol. Rev.*, 1951, *16*, 694-701. (b) [224]

Hill, R. H. A critique of contemporary marriage and family research. *Sociol. Forces*, 1955, *33*, 268-277. [224]

Hill, R. H. Sociology of marriage and family behavior, 1945-1956: A trend report and bibliography. *Curr. Sociol.*, 1958, 7, l. Pp. iv-98. [224, 225]

Hirt, M. (Ed.) *Rorschach science.* New York: Free Press of Glencoe, 1962. [5]

Hobbs, N. Mental health's third revolution. *Amer. J. Orthopsychiat.*, 1964, *34*, 822-833. [223]

Hodges, W. F., & Spielberger, C. D. The effects of threat of shock on heart rate for subjects who differ in manifest anxiety and fear of shock. *Psychophysiology*, 1966, *2*, 287-294. [276]

Holland, J. G. The prediction of college grades from the California psychological inventory and the scholastic aptitude test. *J. educ. Psychol.*, 1959, *50*, 135-142. [56, 65]

Holt, R. R. Measuring libidinal and aggressive motives and their controls by means of the Rorschach test. In D. Levin (Ed.), *Nebraska symposium on motivation.* Lincoln, Nebr.: University of Nebraska Press, 1966. Pp. 1-47. [257]

Holt, R. R., & Havel, J. A method for assessing primary and secondary process in the Rorschach. In M. A. Rickers-Ovsiankina (Ed.), *Rorschach psychology.* New York: Wiley, 1960. [39]

Holtzman, W. H. Validation studies of the Rorschach test: Impulsiveness in the normal superior adult. *J. clin. Psychol.*, 1950, *6*, 348-351. [136, 144]

Holtzman, W. H. Recurring dilemmas in personality assessment. *J. proj. Tech.*, 1963, *27*, 144-150. [5]

Holtzman, W. H., Thorpe, J. S., Swartz, J. D., & Herron, E. W. *Ink-blot perception and personality.* Austin, Texas: University Texas Press, 1961. [8, 257]

Honig, W. K. (Ed.) *Operant behavior. Areas of research and application.* New York: Appleton-Century-Crofts, 1966. [181]

Honigfeld, G., Gillis, R. D., & Klett, C. J. NOSIE-30: A treatment-sensitive ward behavior scale. *Psychol. Rep.*, 1966, *19*, 180-182. [201]

Honigfeld, G., & Klett, C. J. The nurses' observation scale for inpatient evaluation. *J. clin. Psychol.*, 1965, *21*, 65-71. [193, 201]

Honigfeld, G. H., Rosenblum, M. P., Blumenthal, I. J., Lamberg, H. L., & Roberts, A. J. Behavioral improvement in chronic schizophrenia. *J. Amer. Geriat. Soc.*, 1965, *13*, 57-72. [196, 201]

Hord, D. J., Johnson, L. C., & Lubin, A. Differential effect of the law of initial values (LIV) on autonomic variables. *Psychophysiology*, 1964, *1*, 79-87. [272]

Horivichi, H. A study of perceptual process of Rorschach cards by tachistoscopic method on movement and shading responses. *J. proj. Tech.*, 1961, *25*, 44-54. [142]

Horn, J. L. Second-order factors in questionnaire data. *Educ. psychol. Measmt.*, 1963, *23*, 117-134. [247]

Horn, J. L., & Cattell, R. B. Refinement and test of the theory of fluid and crystallized general intelligence. *J. educ. Psychol.*, 1966, *57*, 253-270. [19]

Horowitz, F. D. The relationship of anxiety, self-concept, and sociometric status among fourth, fifth, and sixth grade children. *J. abnorm. soc. Psychol.*, 1962, *65*, 212-214. [258]

Horrocks, J. E. *Assessment of behavior.* Columbus, Ohio: Chas. Merrill, 1964. [5]

Howell, M. A. Personal effectiveness of physicians in a Federal health organization. *J. appl. Psychol.*, 1966, *50*, 451-459. [56]

Howells, J. G., & Lickorish, J. R. The family relations indicator: A projective technique for investigating intra-familiar relationships designed for use with emotionally disturbed children. *Brit. J. Educ. Psychol.*, 1963, *33*, 286-296. [227]

Hoyt, D. P., & Magoon, T. M. A validation study of the Taylor manifest anxiety scale. *J. clin. Psychol.*, 1954, *10*, 357-361. [252]

Hoyt, T. E., & Baron, M. R. Anxiety indices in same-sex drawings of psychiatric patients with high and low MAS scores. *J. consult. Psychol.*, 1959, *23*, 448-452. [257]

Huberman, J. What do we really measure in "Testing the limits" in the Rorschach. *J. proj. Tech. pers. Assmt.*, 1965, *29*, 171-178. [134]

Hull, C. L. *Aptitude testing.* Yonkers: World Book, 1928. [3]

Humphreys, L. G. The organization of human abilities. *Amer. Psychologist*, 1962, *17*, 475-483. [21]

Hundleby, J. D., Pawlik, K., & Cattell, R.

B. *Personality factors in objective test devices*. San Diego: Knapp, 1965. [5]

Hunt, J. McV. *Intelligence and experience*. New York: Ronald Press, 1961. [19, 22, 26, 29, 31, 32]

Hunt, J. McV. Motivation inherent in information processing and action. In O. J. Harvey (Ed.), *Motivation and social interaction, cognitive determinants*. New York: Ronald Press, 1963. [30]

Hunt, J. McV. Intrinsic motivation and its role in psychological development. In *Nebraska symposium on motivation*; 1965. Lincoln: Univ. Nebr. Press, 1965. [30]

Husek, T. R., & Alexander, S. The effectiveness of the anxiety differential in examination stress situations. *Educ. psychol. Measmt.*, 1963, *23*, 309-318. [260]

Hutchinson, E. D. *How to think creatively*. New York: Abingdon-Cokesbury, 1949. [38]

Huttenlocher, J. Children's intellectual development. *Rev. educ. Res.*, 1965, *35*, 114-121. [30]

Hyman, R., & Breger, L. The effects of psychotherapy: Discussion. *Intern. J. Psychiat.*, 1965, *1*, 317-322. [209]

Iscoe, I., & Cochran, I. Some correlates of manifest anxiety in children. *J. consult. Psychol.*, 1959, *24*, 97. [258]

Israel, N. R. Individual differences in GSR orienting response and cognitive control. *J. exp. res. Pers.*, 1966, *1*, 244-248. [276, 285]

Jackson, C. W., & Wohl, J. A survey of Rorschach teaching in the university. *J. proj. Tech. pers. Assmt.*, 1966, *30*, 115-135. [131]

Jackson, D. D. Family interaction, family homeostasis, and some implications for conjoint family psychotherapy. In J. H. Masserman (Ed.), *Science and psychoanalysis* Vol. 5. Psychoanalytic Education. New York: Grune & Stratton, 1959. [239]

Jackson, D. D. Family rules: The marital quid pro quo. *Arch. gen. Psychiat.*, 1965, *12*, 589-594. [236]

Jackson, D. N., & Messick, S. Content and style in personality assessment. *Psychol. Bull.*, 1958, *55*, 243-252. [7]

Jackson, D. N., & Messick, S. J. Acquiescence and desirability as response determinants on the MMPI. *Educ. psychol. Meas.*, 1961, *21*, 771-792. [84]

Jackson, D. N., & Messick, S. J. Response styles on the MMPI: Comparison of clinical and normal samples. *J. abnorm. soc. Psychol.*, 1962, *65*, 285-299. [84]

Jackson, P. W., & Messick, S. The person, the product, and the response: Conceptual problems in the assessment of creativity. *J. Pers.*, 1965, *33*, 309-329. [52]

Jahoda, M. *Current concepts of positive mental health*. New York: Basic Books, Inc., 1958. [208]

James, W. *The principles of psychology*. Vol. 2. New York: Henry Holt, 1890. [277]

Jaskar, R. O., & Reed, M. R. Assessment of body image organization of hospitalized and non-hospitalized subjects. *J. proj. Tech.*, 1963, 185-190. [139]

Jenkins, R. L., & Lorr, M. Symptom scales and check lists for determining symptomatic improvement in psychotic patients. In Cole, J. O., & Gerard, R. W. (Eds.), *Psychopharmacology: Problems in evaluation.*, Washington: National Academy of Sciences, National Research Council, 1959, 469-477. [201]

Jenkins, R. L., Stauffacher, J., & Hester, R. A symptom rating scale for use with psychotic patients. *A.M.A. Arch. gen. Psychiat.*, 1959, *1*, 197-204. [201]

Jensen, M. B., & Morris, W. E. Reliability-unreliability of ancillary psychiatric evaluations. *J. clin. Psychol.*, 1960, *16*, 248-252. [204]

Jessor, R. The problem of reductionism in psychology. *Psychol. Rev.*, 1958, *65*, 170-178. [274]

Johannsen, W. J., & Campbell, S. Y. Verbal conditioning in chronic schizophrenia: Effects of reinforcement class and social responsiveness. *Psychol. Rep.*, 1964, *14*, 567-572. [173, 184]

Johns, J. J., & Quay, H. C. The effect of social reward on verbal conditioning in psychopathic and neurotic military offenders. *J. consult. Psychol.*, 1962, *26*, 217-220. [180]

Johnson, R. T., & Frandsen, A. N. The California psychological inventory profile of student leaders. *Personnel guid. J.*, 1962, *41*, 343-345. [56]

Jones, E. E. *Ingratiation*. New York: Appleton-Century-Crofts, 1964. [186]

Jones, R. E. Anxiety and neuroticism: Transatlantic semantics. *Contemp. Psychol.*, 1964, *9*, 267-268. [283]

Jourard, S. M. *The transparent self*. Princeton, N. J.: Van Nostrand Co., 1964. [225]

Jurjevich, R. M. Interrelationships of anxiety indices of Wechsler intelligence scales and MMPI scales. *J. gen. Psychol.*, 1963, *69*, 135-142. [260]

Kaden, S. E. & Lipton, H. Rorschach developmental scores and post-hospitalization adjustment of married male schizophrenics. *J. proj. Tech.*, 1960, *24*, 144-148. [139]

Kagan, J. Body build and conceptual impulsivity in children. *J. Pers.*, 1966, *34*, 118-128. [275]

Kahn, M. A polygraph study of the catharsis of aggression. Unpublished doctoral dissertation, Harvard University, 1960. [279]

Kaldegg, A. Interaction testing: An engaged couple of drug addicts tested separately and together. *J. proj. Tech. pers. Assmt.*, 1966, *30*, 77-88. [133]

Kalish, H. I. Behavior therapy. In B. B. Wolman (Ed.), *Handbook of clinical psychology*. New York: McGraw-Hill, 1965. Pp. 1230-1253. [176]

Kamin, E., & Caughlan, J. Patients report the subjective experience of outpatient psychotherapy. *Amer. J. Psychother.*, 1963, *17*, 660-668. [217]

Kanfer, F. H. *Verbal conditioning: A review of its current status.* Kentucky conference on verbal behavior. Lexington, Kentucky, 1966. [175, 176]

Kanfer, F. H., & Marston, A. R. Characteristics of interactional behavior in a psychotherapy analogue. *J. consult. Psychol.*, 1964, *28*, 456-467. [218]

Kanfer, F. H., & Saslow, G. Behavioral analysis. *Arch. gen. Psychiat.*, 1965, *12*, 529-538. [170, 171, 176, 180]

Kaplan, A. M., & Hafner, A. J. Manifest anxiety in hospitalized children. *J. clin. Psychol.*, 1959, *15*, 301-302. [258]

Karlsson, G. *Adaptability and communication in marriage.* (2nd rev. ed.) Totowa, N. J.: Bedminster Press, 1963. [225]

Kassebaum, G. G., Couch, A. S., & Slater, P. E. The factorial dimensions of the MMPI. *J. consult. Psychol.*, 1959, *23*, 226-236. [103]

Kates, S. L. Rorschach responses, Strong blank scales, and job satisfaction among policemen. *J. appl. Psychol.*, 1950, *34*, 249-254. [146]

Kausler, D. H., Trapp, E. P., & Brewer, C. L. Time score as a criterion measure on the Taylor manifest anxiety scale. *J. clin. Psychol.*, 1959, *15*, 51-55. [252]

Keats, J. A. Test theory. *Ann. Rev. of Psychol.*, 1967, *18*, 217-238. [5]

Keimowitz, R. I., & Ansbacher, H. L. Personality and achievement in mathematics. *J. indiv. Psychol.*, 1960, *16*, 84-87. [56]

Kelley, T. L. Educational guidance. An experimental study in the analysis and prediction of ability of high school pupils, T. C. Columbia University *Cont. to Education*, No. 71, 1914. [113]

Kelley, T. L. *Statistical method.* New York: Macmillan, 1923. [3]

Kellner, R. The evidence in favor of psychotherapy. *Brit. J. med. Psychol.*, 1967, *40*, 341-358. [213]

Kelly, D. H. W. Measurement of anxiety by forearm blood flow. *Brit. J. Psychiat.*, 1966, *112*, 789-798. [248, 252]

Kelly, E. L. *Assessment of human characteristics.* Belmont, Calif.: Brooks/Cole, 1967. [5]

Kendall, E. The validity of Taylor's mani-

fest anxiety scale. *J. consult. Psychol.*, 1954, *18*, 429-432. [252]

Kenny, D. T. Stimulus functions in projective techniques. In B. Maher (Ed.), *Progress in experimental personality research.* New York: Academic Press, 1964. Pp. 285-354. [8]

Kiesler, D. J., Klein, M. H., & Mathieu, P. L. Sampling from the recorded therapy interview: The problem of segment location. *J. consult. Psychol.*, 1965, *29*, 337-344. [218]

Kimeldorf, C., & Geiwitz, P. J. Smoking and the Blacky orality factors. *J. proj. Tech.*, 1966, *30*, 167-168. [158]

King, B. D., Sokoloff, L., & Wechsler, R. L. The effects of 1-epinephrine and 1-nor-epinepherine upon cerebral circulation and metabolism in man. *J. clin. Investig.*, 1952, *31*, 273-279. [282]

King, F. W., & King, D. C. The projective assessment of the female's sexual identification. *J. proj. Tech.*, 1964, *28*, 293-299. [154]

King, G. F. An interpersonal conception of Rorschach human movement and delusional content. *J. proj. Tech.*, 1960, *24*, 161-164. [140]

King, G. F., Merrell, D. W., Loevinger, E., & Denny, M. R. Operant motor behavior in acute schizophrenics. *J. Pers.*, 1957, *25*, 317-326. [181]

Kinslinger, H. J. Application of projective techniques in personnel psychology since 1940. *Psychol. Bull.*, 1966, *66*, 134-150. [143, 148]

Kirkner, F. J., Wisham, W. W., & Giedt, F. H. A report on the validity of the Rorschach prognostic rating scale. *J. proj. Tech.*, 1953, *17*, 465-470. [147]

Kirkpatrick, C. *The family as process and institution.* (2nd ed.) New York: Ronald Press, 1963. [225]

Kissel, S., & Littig, L. W. Test anxiety and skin conductance. *J. abnorm. soc. Psychol.*, 1962, *65*, 276-278. [255]

Klein, G. S., Barr, H. L., & Wolitzky, D. L. Personality. *Ann. Rev. Psychol.*, 1967, *18*, 467-560. [285]

Kleinmuntz, B. *Personality measurement.* Homewood, Ill.: Dorsey, 1967. [5]

Klett, C. J., & Moseley, E. C. The right drug for the right patient. *J. consult. Psychol.*, 1965, *29*, 546-551. [196, 203]

Klinger, E., & Roth, I. Diagnosis of schizophrenia by Rorschach patterns. *J. proj. Tech. pers. Assmt.*, 1965, *29*, 323-336. [144]

Klopfer, B., Kirkner, F. J., Wisham, W., & Baker, G. Rorschach prognostic rating scale. *J. proj. Tech.*, 1951, *15*, 425-428. [147, 214]

Klopfer, W. G. The role of diagnostic evaluation in clinical psychology. *J. proj. Tech.*, 1962, *26*, 295-298. [10]

Klopfer, W. G. The blind leading the

blind: Psychotherapy without assessment. *J. proj. Tech. pers. Assmt.*, 1964, *28*, 387-392. [10]

Klopfer, W. G. Allen, B. V., & Etter, D. Content diversity on the Rorschach and "range of interests." *J. proj. Tech.*, 1960. *24*, 290-292. [145, 146]

Knight, R. P. Evaluation of the results of psychoanalytic therapy. *Amer. J. Psychiat.*, 1941, *98*, 434-446. [211]

Kobler, F. J., & Steil, A. The use of the Rorschach in involutional melancholia. *J. consult. Psychol.*, 1953, *17*, 365-370. [136, 144]

Koret, S., & Rubin, E. Z. Utilization of projective tests as a prediction of casework movement. *Amer. J. Orthopsychiat.*, 1957, *27*, 365-374. [214]

Kornrich, M. *Psychological test modifications.* Springfield, Ill.: Chas. C Thomas, 1965. [5]

Krasner, L. Verbal conditioning and psychotherapy. In L. Krasner & L. P. Ullmann (Eds.), *Research in behavior modification.* New York: Holt, Rinehart & Winston, 1965. Pp. 211-228. [173, 175]

Krasner, L. Behavior modification research and the role of the therapist. In L. A. Gottschalk & A. H. Auerbach (Eds.), *Methods of research in psychotherapy.* New York: Appleton-Century-Crofts, 1966. Pp. 292-311. [175]

Krasner, L., & Ullman, L. P. (Eds.) *Research in behavior modification.* New York: Holt, Rinehart, Winston, 1965. [173, 205]

Kraus, J. Clinical utility of Rorschach anxiety signs. *J. proj. Tech. pers. Assmt.*, 1964, *28*, 300-303. [146]

Krause, M. S. The measurement of transitory anxiety. *Psychol. Rev.*, 1961, *68*, 178-189. [244]

Kretschmer, E. *Körperbau und Charakter.* (21/22nd ed.) Berlin: Springer, 1955. [275]

Kris, E. *Psychoanalytic explorations in art.* New York: International Universities Press, 1952. [38]

Kubie, L. S. *Neurotic distortion of the creative process.* Lawrence: Univ. Kans. Press, 1958. [38]

Kuhlmann, F., & Anderson, R. G. *Kuhlmann-Anderson Intelligence Test.* (5th ed.) Minneapolis, Minnesota: Educational Test Bureau, 1940. [71]

Kuno, Y. *Human perspiration.* Springfield, Ill.: Chas. C Thomas, 1956. [287]

Kuntz, K. J. Mass and shading effects on masculine-feminine judgments on the Rorschach. *J. proj. Tech. pers. Assmt.*, 1964, *28*, 201-206. [134]

Kurtz, A. A research test of the Rorschach test. *Personnel Psychol.*, 1948, *1*, 41-51. [148]

Kwiatkowska, H. Family art therapy. *Fam. Process*, 1967, *6*, 37-55. [233]

L'Abate, L., & Craddick, R. A. The Kahn test of symbol arrangement (KTSA): A critical review. *J. clin. Psychol.*, 1965, *XXI*, 115-135. [6]

Lacey, J. I. The evaluation of autonomic responses: Toward a general solution. *Ann. NY Acad. Sci.*, 1956, *67*, 123-164. [272]

Lacey, J. I., Kagan, J., Lacey, B. C., & Moss, H. A. The visceral level: Situational determinants and behavioral correlates of autonomic response patterns. In P. H. Knapp (Ed.), *Expression of the emotions in man.* New York: International Universities Press, 1963. Pp. 161-196. [281]

Lacey, J. I., & Lacey, B. C. Verification and extension of the principle of autonomic response specificity. *Amer. J. Psychol.*, 1958, *71*, 50-73. (*a*) [270]

Lacey, J. I., & Lacey, B. C. The relationship of resting autonomic activity to motor impulsivity. In H. C. Solomon, S. Cobb, & W. Penfield (Eds.), *The brain and human behavior. Association for research in nervous and mental disease.* Vol. 36. Baltimore: Williams & Wilkins, 1958. Pp. 144-209. (*b*) [275]

La Forge, R., & Suczek, R. The interpersonal diagnosis of personality: III. An interpersonal checklist. *J. Pers.*, 1955, *24*, 94-112. [225]

Laing, R. D., Phillipson, H., & Lee, A. R. *Interpersonal perceptions: A theory and a method of research.* New York: Springer Publishing Co., 1966. [225]

Lambert, W. E., Gardner, R. C., Barik, H. C., & Tunstall, K. Attitudinal and cognitive aspects of intensive study of a second language. *J. abnorm. soc. Psychol.*, 1963, *66*, 358-368. [23]

Lang, P. J., & Lazovik, A. D. Experimental desensitization of a phobia. *J. abnorm. soc. Psychol.*, 1963, *66*, 519-526. [248, 251]

Lanyon, R. I. Verbal conditioning: Transfer of training in a therapy-like situation. *J. abnorm Psychol.*, 1967, *72*, 30-34. [176]

Lashley, K. S. Cerebral organization and behavior. *Res. Publ. Assoc. nerv. mentl. Dis.*, 1958, *36*, 1-18. [22]

Lasky, J. J., Klett, C. J., Caffey, E. M., Jr., Bennett, J. L., Rosenblum, M. P., & Hollister, L. E. Drug treatment of schizophrenic patients. *Dis. nerv. Syst.*, 1962, *23*, 698-706. [196, 197]

Laurendeau, M., & Pinard, A., *Causal thinking in the child: A genetic and experimental approach.* New York: International Universities Press, 1962. [29]

Lazarus, R. S. *Psychological stress and the coping process.* New York: McGraw-Hill, 1966. [244, 245, 246, 252, 277]

Lazarus, R. S., Speisman, J. C., Mordkoff, A. M., & Davison, L. A. A laboratory study of psychological stress produced by a motion picture film. *Psychol. Monogr.*, 1962, *76*, No. 34, 1-35 (Whole No. 553). [63, 249]

Leary, T. F. *The interpersonal diagnosis of personality.* New York: Ronald Press, 1957. [140]

Leary, T., & Coffey, H. S. Interpersonal diagnosis: some problems of methodology and validation. *J. abnorm. soc. Psychol.*, 1955, *50*, 110-124. [173]

LeBaron, G. I. Ideomotor signalling in brief psychotherapy. *Amer. J. clin. Hypnosis*, 1962, *5*, 81-91. [219]

Leighton, D. C., Harding, J. S., Macklin, D. B., Hughes, C. C., & Leighton, A. H. Psychiatric findings of the Stirling county study. *Amer. J. Psychiat.*, 1963, *119*, 1021-1026. [219]

Leik, R. Instrumentality and emotionality in family interaction. *Sociometry*, 1963, *26*, 131-145. [226]

Lenneberg, E. H. Speech as a motor skill with special reference to non-aphasic disorders. In U. Bellugi & R. Brown (Eds.), The acquisition of language. *Monogr. Soc. Res. Child Developm.*, 1964, *29*, 115-127. [23]

Lenneberg, E. H. *The biological foundations of language.* New York: Wiley, 1967. [23]

Lesser, G. S. Custom-making projective tests for research. *J. proj. Tech.*, 1961, *25*, 21-31. [8]

Lessing, E. E. Prognostic value of the Rorschach in a child guidance clinic. *J. proj. Tech.*, 1960, *24*, 310-322. [147]

Lessinger, L. M., & Martinson, R. A. The use of the California psychological inventory with gifted pupils. *Personnel guid. J.*, 1961, *39*, 572-575. [56]

Leventhal, A. M. An anxiety scale for the CPI. *J. clin. Psychol.*, 1966, *22*, 459-461. [254]

Levine, M. Psychological testing of children. In L. Hoffman & M. L. Hoffman (Eds.) *Review of child development research.* Vol. 2. New York: Russell Sage Foundation, 1966. [6]

Levine, M., & Spivack, G. Human movement responses and verbal expression on the Rorschach test. *J. proj. Tech.*, 1962, *26*, 299-305. [140]

Levinger, G. Marital cohesiveness and dissolution: An integrative review. *J. Marriage Fam.*, 1965, *27*, 19-28. [225]

Levitt, E. E. The undemonstrated effectiveness of therapeutic process with children. *J. consult. Psychol.*, 1957, *21*, 189-196. [212]

Levitt, E. E. *The psychology of anxiety.* Indianapolis: Bobbs-Merrill, 1967. [244, 245, 254]

Levitt, E. E., & Grosz, H. J. A comparison of quantifiable Rorschach anxiety indicators in hypnotically induced anxiety and normal states. *J. consult.*

Psychol., 1960, *24*, 31-34. [257]

Levitt, E. E., & Persky, H. Experimental evidence for the validity of the IPAT anxiety scale. *J. clin. Psychol.*, 1962, *18*, 458-461. [254]

Levitt, E. E., Persky, H., & Brady, J. P. *Hypnotic induction of anxiety.* Springfield, Ill.: Chas. C. Thomas, 1964. [249]

Levy, J., & Epstein, N. B. An application of the Rorschach test in family investigation. *Fam. Process*, 1964, *3*, 344-376. [226]

Levy, L. H. Anxiety and behavior scientists' behavior. *Amer. Psychologist*, 1961, *16*, 66-68. [170]

Levy, N. A short form of the children's manifest anxiety scale. *Child. Develpm.*, 1958, *29*, 153-154. [259]

Lindley, C. J. (Ed.) Chemotherapy in Psychiatry. Transactions of the Second (1957) Research Conference, Washington D. C., Veterans Administration, 1958. [191]

Lindner, H. The Blacky pictures test: A study of sexual and non-sexual offenders. *J. proj. Tech.*, 1953, *17*, 79-84. [156]

Lindsley, D. B. Emotion. In S. S. Stevens (Ed.), *Handbook of experimental psychology.* New York: Wiley, 1951. Pp. 473-516. [281]

Lindsley, D. B. Attention, consciousness, sleep and wakefulness. In H. W. Magoun (Ed.), *Handbook of Physiology.* Section 1: Neurophysiology, Vol. 3. Washington: American Physiological Society, 1960. Pp. 1553-1593. [281]

Lindsley, O. R. Characteristics of the behavior of chronic psychotics as revealed by free-operant conditioning methods. *Dis. nerv. Sys.*, 1960, *21*, 66-78. [181]

Lindsley, O. R. Direct behavioral analysis of psychotherapy sessions conjugately programmed closed-circuit television. Paper read at American Psychological Association, St. Louis, September, 1962. [184]

Lindzey, G. Seer vs. sign. *J. exp. Res. Pers.*, 1965, *1*, 17-26. [8]

Lindzey, G., & Newburg, A. S. Thematic apperception test: A tentative appraisal of some "signs" of anxiety. *J. consult. Psychol.*, 1954, *18*, 389-395. [258]

Littel, W. M. The Wechsler intelligence scale for children: Review of a decade of research. *Psychol. Bull.*, 1960, *57*, 132-157. [6]

Locke, H. J., & Wallace, K. M. Short marital-adjustment and prediction tests: Their reliability and validity. *Marriage fam. Liv.*, 1959, *21*, 251-255. [225]

Loevinger, J. Intelligence. In H. Helson (Ed.), *Theoretical foundations of psychology.* New York: Van Nostrand, 1951. [30]

Loevinger, J. Objective tests as instruments of psychological theory. *Psychol. Rep.*, 1957, *15*, 635-694. [169, 170, 173]

Loevinger, J. Measurement in clinical research. In B. Wolman (Ed.), *Handbook of clinical psychology*. New York: McGraw-Hill, 1965. Pp. 78-94. [5]

Loevinger, J. The meaning and measurement of ego development. *Amer. Psychologist*, 1966, *21*, 195-206. [6, 28]

Loiselle, R. H., & Kleinschmidt, A. A comparison of the stimulus value of Rorschach ink-blots and their percepts. *J. proj. tech. pers. Assmt.*, 1963, *27*, 191-194. [138]

London, P. *Modes and morals of psychotherapy*. New York: Holt, Rinehart & Winston, 1964. [219]

Long, B. H., & Henderson, E. H. Opinion formation and creativity in elementary children. Unpublished manuscript. University of Delaware, Newark, 1964. [48]

Lord, E. Experimentally induced variation in Rorschach performance. *Psychol. Monogr.*, 1950, *64*, (10, Whole No. 316). [141]

Lorge, I. Schooling makes a difference. *Teach. Coll. Rec.*, 1945, *46*, 483-492. [22]

Lorr, M. Multidimensional scale for rating psychiatric patients. *Veterans Administration Technical Bulletin*, Nov. 16, 1953, TB 10-507. [195]

Lorr, M. Rating scales and check lists for the evaluation of psychopathology. *Psychol. Bull.*, 1954, *51*, 119-127. [201]

Lorr, M. Rating scales, behavior inventories, and drugs. In Uhr, L. & Miller, J. G. (Eds.), *Drugs and behavior*. New York: Wiley, 1960. Pp. 519-539. [201]

Lorr, M. Client perception of therapists: A study of the therapeutic relationship. *J. consult. Psychol.*, 1965, *29*, 146-149. [218]

Lorr, M. (Ed.) *Explorations in typing psychotics*. London: Pergamon, 1966. [196, 199]

Lorr, M., & Cave, R. The equivalence of psychotic syndromes across two media. *Multivariate Behav. Res.*, 1966, *1*, 189-195. [199]

Lorr, M., Daston, P., & Smith, I. R. An analysis of mood states. *Educ. psychol. Meas.*, 1967, *27*, 89-96. [247, 249, 250]

Lorr, M., & Klett, C. J. Constancy of psychotic syndromes in men and women. *J. consult. Psychol.*, 1965, *29*, 309-313. [196, 200]

Lorr, M., & Klett, C. J. *Inpatient multidimensional psychiatric scale: Manual.* (Rev.) Palo Alto: Consulting Psychologists' Press, 1966. [196]

Lorr, M., Klett, C. J., & Cave, R. Higher Level Psychotic syndromes. *J. Abnorm. Psychol.*, 1967, *72*, 74-77. [196]

Lorr, M., Klett, C. J., & McNair, D. M. *Syndromes of psychosis.* Oxford: Pergamon, 1963. [196, 199]

Lorr, M., Klett, C. J., & McNair, D. M. Ward-observable psychotic behavior syndromes. *Educ. Psychol. Meas.*, 1964, *24*, 291-300. [199]

Lorr, M., Klett, C. J., McNair, D. M., & Lasky, J. J. *Inpatient multidimensional psychiatric scale: Manual.* Palo Alto: Consulting Psychologists' Press, 1962. [193, 195]

Lorr, M., & McNair, D. M. The interview relationship in therapy. *J. nerv. ment. Dis.*, 1964, *139*, 328-331. [208]

Lorr, M., & McNair, D. M. Expansion of the interpersonal behavior circle. *J. pers. soc. Psychol.*, 1965, *2*, 823-830. [208]

Lorr, M., & McNair, D. M. Methods relating to evaluation of therapeutic outcome. In Gottschalk, L. A., & Auerbach, A. H. (Eds.), *Methods of research in psychotherapy*. New York: Appleton-Century-Crofts, 1966. Pp. 573-594. [249, 250]

Lorr, M., McNair, D. M., Klett, C. J., & Lasky, J. J. Evidence of ten psychotic syndromes. *J. consult. Psychol.*, 1962, *26*, 185-189. [196]

Lorr, M., & O'Connor, J. P. Psychotic symptom patterns in a behavior inventory. *Educ. Psychol. Meas.*, 1962, *22*, 139-146. [199]

Lorr, M., O'Connor, J. P., & Stafford, J. W. Confirmation of nine psychotic symptom patterns. *J. clin. Psychol.*, 1957, *13*, 252-257. [199]

Lorr, M. O'Connor, J. P., & Stafford, J. W. The psychotic reaction profile. *J. clin. Psychol.*, 1960, *16*, 241-245. [199]

Lorr, M., O'Connor, J. P., & Stafford, J. W. *The psychotic reaction profile (PRP).* Los Angeles: Western Psychol. Serv., 1961. [199]

Lorr, M., Singer, M., & Zobel, H. Development of a record for the description of psychiatric patients. *Psychol. Serv. Cent. J.*, 1951, *3*, No. 3. [195]

Loveland, N. T. Epileptic personality and cognitive functioning. *J. proj. Tech.*, 1961, *25*, 54-69. [144]

Loveland, N. T., Wynne, L. C., and Singer, M. T. The family Rorschach: A new method for studying family interaction. *Family Process*, 1963, *2*, 187-215. [133]

Luborsky, L. A note on Eysenck's article, The effects of psychotherapy: An evaluation. *Brit. J. Psychol.*, 1954, *45*, 129-131. [212]

Luborsky, L., & Schimek, J. Psychoanalytic theories of therapeutic and development change: Implications for assessment. In P. Worchel and D. Byrne (Eds.), *Personality change*. New York: Wiley, 1964. [6]

Lucas, W. B. The effects of frustration on the Rorschach responses of nine-year-old children. *J. proj. Tech.*, 1961, *25*, 199-205. [142]

Lucero, R. J., & Myer, B. T. A behavior rating scale suitable for use in mental hospitals. *J. clin. Psychol.*, 1951, *7*, 250-254. [201]

Luft, J. Interaction and projection. *J. proj. Tech.*, 1953, *17*, 489-492. [141]

Lyerly, S. B., & Abbott, P. S. *Handbook of psychiatric rating scales (1950-1964)*. Washington: Government Printing Office, 1966. [6, 192, 201, 203, 208]

Lykken, D. T. A study of anxiety in the sociopathic personality. *J. abnorm. soc. Psychol.*, 1957, *55*, 6-10. [255, 262]

Lyman, H. B. *Test scores and what they mean*. Englewood Cliffs, N. J.: Prentice-Hall, 1963. [5]

Lynn, R. *Attention, arousal, and the orientation reaction*. Oxford: Pergamon Press, 1966. [271]

Lytton, H. Children's expression of like-dislike and their responses to color in the Rorschach. *J. proj. Tech. pers. Assmt.*, 1966, *30*, 51-54. [136]

MacCorquodale, K., & Meehl, P. E. On a distinction between hypothetical constructs and intervening variables. *Psychol. Rev.*, 1948, *55*, 95-107. [268]

Machover, K. *Personality projection in the drawing of the human figure*. Springfield, Ill.: Chas. C Thomas, 1949. [257]

MacKinnon, D. W. The highly effective individual. *Teachers College Record*, 1960, *61*, 367-378. [50, 51]

MacKinnon, D. W. The nature and nurture of creative talent. *Amer. Psychologist*, 1962, *17*, 484-495. (a) [51]

MacKinnon, D. W. The personality correlates of creativity: A study of American architects. In G. H. Nielsen (Ed.), *Proceedings of the XIV International Congress of Applied Psychology, Copenhagen, 1961*. Vol. II, 11-39. Copenhagen: Munksgaard, 1962. (b) [55]

MacKinnon, D. W. Personality and the realization of creative potential. *Amer. Psychologist*, 1965, *20*, 273-281. [51, 54]

Mackler, B., & Shontz, F. C. Creativity: Theoretical and methodological considerations. *Psychol. Rec.*, 1965, *15*, 217-238. (a) [34]

Mackler, B., & Shontz, F. C. Characteristics of responses to tests of creativity. *J. clin. Psychol.*, 1967, *23*, 73-80. [46, 47]

Maddi S. R. Motivational aspects of creativity. *J. Pers.*, 1965, *33*, 330-347. [39, 54]

Magnussen, M. G. The Blacky pictures as personality measures for undergraduate areas of specialization. *J. proj. Tech.*, 1959, *23*, 351-353. [160]

Mahl, G. F. Physiological changes during chronic fear. *Ann. N. Y. Acad. Sci.*, 1953, *56*, 240-249. [274]

Mahl, G. F. Disturbances and silences in the patient's speech in psychotherapy. *J. abnorm. soc. Psychol.*, 1956, *53*, 1-15. [261]

Mahl, G. F. Measuring the patient's anxiety during interviews from "expressive" aspects of his speech. *Trans. N. Y. Acad. Sci.*, 1959, *21*, 249-257. [261]

Malamud, W., & Sands, S. L. A Revision of the psychiatric rating scale. *Amer. J. Psychiat.*, 1947, *104*, 231-237 [201]

Malmo, R. B. Activation: A neurophysiological dimension. *Psychol. Rev.*, 1959, *66*, 367-386. [281]

Mandler, G., & Cowen, J. E. Test anxiety questionnaires. *J. consult. Psychol.*, 1958, *22*, 228-229. [255]

Mandler, G., Mandler, J. J., Kremen, I., & Sholiton, R. D. The response to threat: Relations among verbal and physiological indices. *Psychol. Monogr.*, 1961, *75*, No. 9 (Whole No. 513). [260]

Mandler, G., & Sarason, S. B. A study of anxiety and learning. *J. abnorm. soc. Psychol.*, 1952, *47*, 166-173. [255]

Margolis, M. The mother-child relationship in bronchial asthma. *J. abnorm. soc. Psychol.*, 1961, *63*, 360-367. [157]

Marquis, D. P., Sinnett, E. R., & Winter, W. D. A psychological study of peptic ulcer patients. *J. clin. Psychol.*, 1952, *8*, 266-272. [157]

Marsh, L. F. Parental attitudes as the basis for attributing meaning to Rorschach cards IV and VII. *J. proj. Tech.*, 1961, *25*, 69-75. [134]

Martin, B., A factor analytic study of anxiety. *J. clin. Psychol.*, 1958, *14*, 133-138. [247]

Martin, B. The measurement of anxiety. *J. gen. Psychol.*, 1959, *61*, 189-203. (a) [247]

Martin, B. The validity of a self-report measure of anxiety as a function of the time interval covered by the instructions. *J. consult. Psychol.*, 1959, *23*, 468. (b) [249]

Martin, B. The assessment of anxiety by physiological behavioral measures. *Psychol. Bull.*, 1961, *58*, 234-255. [244]

Martin, B., & Sroufe, L. A. Anxiety. In Costello, C. G. (Ed.), *Symptoms of psychopathology*. New York: Wiley, in press. [244]

Masling, J. The influence of situational and interpersonal variables in projective testing. *Psychol. Bull.*, 1960, *57*, 65-85. [7, 141, 143]

Maslow, A. H. Creativity in self-actualizing

people. In H. H. Andersen (Ed.), *Creativity and its cultivation.* New York: Harper, 1959. [49]

Mason, J. W., Magan, G., Jr., Brady, J. V., Conrad, D., & Rioch, D. Concurrent plasma epinephrine, norepinephrine and 17-hydroxycorticosteroid levels during conditioned emotional disturbances in monkeys. *Psychosom. Med.,* 1961, *23,* 344-353. [279]

Masters, W. H., & Johnson, V. E. *Human sexual response.* Boston: Little, Brown & Co., 1966. [278, 281]

Matarazzo, J.D. The interview. In B. B. Wolman (Ed.), *Handbook of clinical psychology.* New York: McGraw-Hill, 1965. Pp. 403-450. (*a*) [185]

Matarazzo, J. D. Psychotherapeutic processes. In *Annu. Rev. Psychol.,* 1965, *16,* 181-224. (*b*) [205]

Mattsson, P. O. Communicated anxiety in a two-person situation. *J. consult. Psychol.,* 1960, *24,* 488-495. [248]

May, P. R. A., & Tuma, A. H. Choice of criteria for the assessment of treatment outcome. Paper read at West. Psychol. Assoc., Santa Monica, April 18, 1963. [213]

May, R. *The meaning of anxiety.* New York: Ronald, 1950. [245, 251]

May, R. The nature of creativity. In H. H. Andersen (Ed.), *Creativity and its cultivation.* New York: Harper, 1959. [49]

McConnell, O. L., & Daston, P. G. Body image changes in pregnancy. *J. proj. Tech.,* 1961, *25,* 451, 457. [139]

McCully, R. S. Human movement in the Rorschach materials of a group of preadolescent boys suffering from progressive muscular loss. *J. proj. Tech.,* 1961, *25,* 205-212. [142]

McCully, R. S. Certain theoretical considerations in relation to borderline schizophrenia and the Rorschach. *J. proj. Tech.,* 1962, *26,* 404-418. [140]

McCully, R. S. Process analysis: A tool in understanding ambiguity in diagnostic problems in the Rorschach. *J. proj. Tech. pers. Assmt.,* 1965, *29,* 436-445. [141]

McDougall, W. *An introduction to social psychology.* (23rd ed.) London: Methuen, 1936. [280]

McNair, D. M., & Lorr, M. An analysis of mood in neurotics. *J. abnorm. soc. Psychol.,* 1964, *69,* 620-627. [203, 250]

McNair, D. M., Lorr, M., Young, H. H., Roth, I., & Boyd, R. W. A Three-year follow-up of psychotherapy patients. *J. clin. Psychol.,* 1964, *20,* 258-264. [215]

McNemar, Q. Lost: our intelligence. Why? *Amer. Psychologist,* 1964, *19,* 871-882. [16, 17, 18]

McPherson, J. H. A proposal for establishing ultimate criteria for measuring creative output. In C. W. Taylor and F.

Barron (Eds.), *Scientific creativity: Its recognition and development.* New York: Wiley, 1963. Pp. 24-29. [35]

McReynolds, P. A restricted conceptualization of human anxiety and motivation. *Psychol. Rep., Monogr. Suppl. 6,* 1956, 293-312. [245, 251, 260]

McReynolds, P. Anxiety as related to incongruencies between values and feelings. *Psychol. Rec.,* 1958, *8,* 57-66. [248, 260, 262]

McReynolds, P. Anxiety, perception, and schizophrenia. In D. Jackson (Ed.), *The etiology of schizophrenia.* New York: Basic Books, 1960. Pp. 248-292. [245, 251, 260]

McReynolds, P. Toward a theory of fun. *Amer. Psychologist,* 1964, *19,* 551-552. (Abstract) [40]

McReynolds, P. On the assessment of anxiety: I. By a behavior checklist. *Psychol. Rep.,* 1965, *16,* 805-808. (*a*) [245, 261]

McReynolds, P. *Manual: Rorschach concept evaluation technique.* Los Angeles: Western Psychological Services, 1965. (*b*) [8]

McReynolds, P. A comparison of normals and schizophrenics on a new scale of the Rorschach CET. *J. proj. Tech. pers. Assmt.,* 1966, *30,* 262-264. (*a*) [144]

McReynolds, P. The concept evaluation technique: A survey of research. *J. of Gen. Psych.,* 1966, *74,* 217-230. (*b*) [141]

McReynolds, P. Relations between psychological and physiological indices of anxiety. Paper presented in symposium on "The concept of anxiety," Western Psychol. Assoc. Convention, May 5, 1967. (*a*) [244, 246, 247]

McReynolds, P. The motivation to avoid anxiety as a function of the existent level of anxiety. Submitted for publication, 1967. (*b*) [248, 252]

McReynolds, P. The hospital adjustment scale: A review of research. Unpublished manuscript. [200]

McReynolds, P., & Acker, M. *The obscure figures test, Form I: Manual for administration and scoring.* Palo Alto: VA Hospital (Research Report No. 34), 1965. [40]

McReynolds, P., & Acker, M. On the assessment of anxiety: II. by a self-report inventory. *Psychol. Rep.,* 1966, *19,* 231-237. [251, 262]

McReynolds, P., Acker, M., & Brackbill, G. On the assessment of anxiety: IV. By measures of basal conductance and palmar sweat. *Psychol. Rep.,* 1966, *19,* 347-356. [262]

Meadow, A., Greenblatt, M., Levine, J., & Solomon, H. C. The discomfort-relief quotient as a measure of tension and adjustment. *J. abnorm. soc. Psychol.,*

1952, 47, 658-661. [260]

Mednick, M. T. Research creativity in psychology graduate students. J. consult. Psychol., 1963, 27, 265-266. [41]

Mednick, M., & Lindsley, O. R. Some clinical correlates of operant behavior. J. abnorm. soc. Psychol., 1958, 57, 13-16. [181]

Mednick, S. A. The associative basis of the creative process. Psychol. Rev., 1962, 69, 220-232. [40]

Mednick, S. A., & Halpern, S. Ease of concept attainment as a function of associative rank. J. exp. Psychol., 1962, 6, 628-630. [41]

Mednick, S. A., & Mednick, M. T. Examiner's Manual: Remote associates test—college and adult forms 1 and 2. Boston: Houghton-Mifflin, 1967. [40, 41]

Meehl, P. E. Seer over sign: The first good example, J. exp. Res. Pers., 1965, 1, 27-32. [8]

Megargee, E. I. (Ed.) Research in clinical assessment. New York: Harper & Row, 1966. [5]

Megargee, E. I., Bogart, P., & Anderson, B. J. Prediction of leadership in a simulated industrial task. J. appl. Psychol., 1966, 50, 292-295. [59]

Merriman, J. B. Relationship of personality traits to motor ability. Res. Quart., 1960, 31, 163-173. [74]

Messick, S. Personality measurement and the ethics of assessment. Amer. Psychologist, 1965, 20, 136-142. [6]

Messick, S. Personality measurement and college performance. In Anastasi, A. (Ed.), Testing problems in perspective. Princeton, N. J.: Educ. Testing Service, 1966. Pp. 557-572. [7]

Messick, S., & Jackson, D. N. Acquiescence and the factorial interpretation of the MMPI. Psychol. Bull., 1961, 58, 299-304. [8]

Messick, S., & Ross, J. (Eds.) Measurement in personality and cognition. New York: Wiley, 1962. [5]

Meyer, M. & Caruth, E. Rorschach indices of ego process. J. proj. Tech. pers. Assmt., 1965, 29, 200-219. [141]

Michael, W. B. A short evaluation of the research reviewed in educational and psychological testing. Rev. educ. Res., 1965, 35, 92-99. [17, 30]

Milholland, J. E. Theory and techniques of assessment. Annu. Rev. Psych., 1964, 15, 311-346. [5]

Miller, C. A. A comparison of high-accident and low-accident bus and street car operators. J. proj. Tech., 1955, 19, 146-151. [148]

Miller, N. B., Fisher, W. P., & Ladd, C. E. Psychometric and rated anxiety. Psychol. Rep., 1967, 20, 707-710. [248, 252, 253, 259]

Mills, D. H. The research use of projective techniques: A seventeen year study. J. proj. Tech., 1965, 29, 513-515. [150]

Milton, O. (Ed.) Behavior disorders. New York: Lippincott, 1965. [170]

Mindness, H. Predicting patients' responses to psychotherapy: A preliminary study designed to investigate the validity of the Rorschach prognositc rating scale. J. proj. Tech., 1953, 17, 327-334. [147]

Miner, J. B. An aid to the analysis of vocational interests, J. of educ. Res., 1922, 5, 311-323. [113]

Minkowich, A., Weingarten, L. L., & Blum, G. S. Empirical contributions to a theory of ambivalence. J. abnorm. Psychol., 1966, 71, 30-41. [154, 156]

Mogar, R. E. Anxiety indices in human figure drawings: A replication and extension. J. consult. Psychol., 1962, 26, 108. [257]

Mooney, R. L., & Gordon, L. V. Manual: The Mooney problem check lists. New York: Psychol. Corp., 1950. [251]

Moore, B. V. Personnel selection of graduate engineers, Psych. Monogr., 1921, 30, whole number 138. [113]

Moos, R. M., & Clemes, S. A multivariate study of the patient-therapist system. J. consult. Psychol., 1967, 31, 119-130. [9]

Mosak, H. Evaluation in psychotherapy: a study of some current measures. Doctoral Thesis, University of Chicago, 1950. [212]

Mowrer, O. H., Light, B. H., Luria, Z., and Zeleny, M. Tension changes during psychotherapy, with special reference to resistance. In O. H. Mowrer (Ed.), Psychotherapy: Theory and research. New York: Ronald Press, 1953. [248, 260]

Moylan, J. J., Shaw, J., & Appleman, W. Passive and aggressive responses to the Rorschach by passive-aggressive personalities and paranoid schizophrenics. J. proj. Tech., 1960, 24, 17-21. [144]

Mudd, E. H., Mitchell, H. E., & Taubin, S. B. Success in family living. New York: Association Press, 1965. [230]

Muench, G. A. An evaluation of nondirective psychotherapy with the Rorschach and other indices. Applied Psychol. Monogr., 1947, 13, 168. [212]

Muench, G. A. An evaluation of student mental health services. Amer. J. Orthopsychiat., 1960, 30, 608-617. [211, 212]

Muench, G. A. An investigation of the efficacy of time-limited psychotherapy. J. counsel. Psychol., 1965, 12, 294-298. [219, 220]

Mullins, C. J. The prediction of creativity in a sample of research scientists. In G. Finch (Ed.), Symposium on Air Force human engineering, personnel and train-

ing research. Washington, D.C.: National Academy of Sciences–National Research Council, Publication 783, 1960. Pp. 144-161. [37]

Munsinger, H. L. Meaningful symbols as reinforcing stimuli. *J. abnorm. soc. Psychol.*, 1964, *68*, 689-691. [178]

Murray, E. J., Auld, F., & White, A. M. A psychotherapy case showing progress but no decrease in the discomfort-relief quotient. *J. consult. Psychol.*, 1954, *18*, 349-353. [261]

Murray, H. A., MacKinnon, D. W., Miller, J. G., Fiske, D. W., & Hanfmann, E. *Assessment of men.* New York: Holt, Rinehart & Winston, 1948. [2]

Murray, J. D., & Rychlak, J. F. Healthy, neutral and unhealthy content in the Rorschach responses of schizophrenic and normal adults. *J. proj. Tech. pers. Assmt.*, 1966, *30*, 254-262. [145]

Murstein, B. I. Factor analysis of the Rorschach. *J. consult. Psychol.*, 1960, *24*, 262-275. [144]

Murstein, B. I. (Ed.) *Handbook of projective techniques.* New York: Basic Books, 1965. [5, 8]

Nagel, E. *The structure of science.* New York: Harcourt, Brace & World, 1961. [274]

Nathan, P. E. "Transmitting" and "receiving" in psychotherapy and supervision. *Amer. J. Orthopsychiat.*, 1965, *35*, 937-952. [184, 185]

Nathan, P. E. Influence of stimulus preference and feedback delay on extinction of operant communication behavior. *Behav. Res. Ther.*, 1966, *4*, 53-58. [184, 185]

Nathan, P. E., Marland, J., & Lindsley, O. R. Receptive communication in psychiatric nurse supervision. *J. counsel. Psychol.*, 1965, *12*, 259-261. [185]

Nathan, P. E., Schneller, P., & Lindsley, O. R. Direct measurements of communication during psychiatric admission interviews. *Behav. Res. Ther.*, 1964, *2*, 49-57. [181, 184, 185]

Neiger, S., Slemon, A. G., & Quirk, D. A. The performance of "chronic schizophrenic" patients on Piotrowski's Rorschach sign list for organic CNS pathology. *J. proj. Tech.*, 1962, 419-429. [144]

Neisser, U. The multiplicity of thought. *Brit. J. Psychol.*, 1963, *54*, 1-14. [25, 30]

Nelson, G. N., Minoru, M., & Holmes, T. H. Correlations of behavior and catecholamine metabolite excretion. *Psychosom. Med.*, 1966, *28*, 216-226. [279]

Nelson, J. F. The construction of a scale of teacher judgment of pupil creativity. Master's research paper, University of Minnesota at Duluth, 1963. [48]

Nelson, S. E. Psychosexual conflicts and defenses in visual perception. *J. abnorm. soc. Psychol.*, 1955, *51*, 427-433. [160]

Neuman, G. G., & Salvatore, J. C. The Blacky test and psychoanalytic theory: A factor-analytic approach to validity. *J. proj. Tech.*, 1958, *22*, 427-431. [154]

Neuringer, C. Manifestations of anxiety on the Rorschach test. *J. proj. Tech.*, 1962, *26*, 318-326. [143, 257]

Neuringer, C. The Rorschach test as a research device for the identification, prediction, and understanding of suicidal ideation and behavior. *J. proj. Tech. pers. Assmt.*, 1965, *29*, 71-83. [134]

Neuringer, C., Myers, R. A., & Nordmark, T., Jr. The transfer of a verbally conditioned response class. *J. counsel. Psychol.*, 1966, *13*, 208-213. [176]

Newland, T. E. The assessment of exceptional children. In W. M. Cruickshank (Ed.), *Psychology of exceptional children and youth.* New York: Prentice-Hall, 1962, Ch. 2. [19]

Nichols, R. C., & Schnell, R. R. Factor scales for the California psychological inventory. *J. consult. Psychol.*, 1963, *27*, 228-235. (*a*) [189]

Nichols, R. C., & Schnell, R. R. Factor scores for the California psychological inventory. *J. consult. Psychol.*, 1963, *27*, 236-242. (*b*) [76]

Nicolay, R. C., Walker, R. E., & Riedle, R. G. Anxiety as a correlate of personal problems. *Psychol. Rep.*, 1966, *19*, 53-54. [251, 254]

Noblin, C. D., Timmons, E. O., & Kael, H. C. Differential effects of positive and negative verbal reinforcement on psychoanalytic character types. *J. pers. soc. Psychol.*, 1966, *4*, 224-228. [176]

Norman, W. T. Relative importance of test item content. *J. consult. Psychol.*, 1963, *27*, 166-174. [170, 173]

Norman, W. T., and Goldberg, L. R. Raters, ratees, and randomness in personality structure. *J. pers. soc. Psychol.*, 1966, *4*, 681-691. [173]

Nowlis, V. The development and modification of motivational systems in personality. In *Current theory and research in motivation.* Lincoln, Nebr.: University Nebraska Press, 1953, Pp. 114-138. [249]

Nowlis, V. Research with the mood adjective check list. In S. Tomkins & C. Izard (Eds.), *Affect, cognition and personality.* New York: Springer, 1965. Pp. 352-389. [247, 249]

Nowlis, V., & Nowlis, H. H. The description and analysis of mood. *Ann. N. Y. Acad. Sci.*, 1956, *55*, 345-355. [203, 249]

Nunnally, J. *Psychometric theory.* New York: McGraw-Hill, 1967. [5]

O'Connor, J. P., Lorr, M., & Stafford, J.

W. Some patterns of manifest anxiety. *J. clin. Psychol.*, 1956, *12*, 160-163. [247, 252]

Oken, D., Grinker, R. R., Heath, H. A., Herz, M., Korchin, S. J., Sabshin, M., & Schwartz, N. B. Relation of physiological response to affect expression. *Arch. Gen. Psychiat.*, 1962, *6*, 336-351. [270]

Omnibus personality inventory-research manual. University of California, Berkeley: Center for the Study of Higher Education, 1962. [96]

Opton, E. M., Jr., & Lazarus, R. S. Personality determinants of psychophysiological response to stress: A theoretical analysis and an experiment. *J. pers. Soc. Psychol.*, 1967, *6*, 291-303. [287]

Orlinski, D. E. Rorschach test correlates of dreaming and dream recall. *J. proj. Tech. pers. Assmt.*, 1966, *30*, 250-254. [140]

O'Rourke, J. F. Field and laboratory: The decision-making behavior of family groups in two experimental conditions. *Sociometry*, 1963, *26*, 422-435. [227]

Osgood, C. E. Dimensionality of the semantic space for communication via facial expressions. *Scand. J. Psychol.*, 1966, *7*, 1-30. [280, 281]

Osgood, C. E., & Suci, G. J. A measure of relation determined by both mean difference and profile information. *Psychol. Bull.*, 1958, *49*, 251-262. [272]

Osgood, C. E., Suci, G. J., & Tannenbaum, P. H. *The measurement of meaning.* Urbana: Univ. Ill. Press, 1957. [138]

Otto, H. A. The Otto family strength survey. Graduate School of Social Work, University of Utah, Salt Lake City, Utah: Author, 1962. [230, 231]

Otto, H. A. The personal and family strength research projects: Some implications for the therapist. *Ment. Hyg.*, 1964, *48*, 439-450. [231]

Overall, J. E. Dimensions of manifest depression. *Psychiat. Res.*, 1962, *1*, 239-245. [202]

Overall, J. E., & Gorham, D. R. The brief psychiatric rating scale. *Psychol. Rep.*, 1962, *10*, 799-812. [193, 197, 261]

Overall, J. E., & Gorham, D. R. A pattern probability model for the classification of psychiatric patients. *Behav. Sci.*, 1963, *8*, 108-116. [199]

Overall, J. E., Gorham, D. R., & Shawver, J. R. Basic dimensions of change in the symptomatology of chronic schizophrenics. *J. abn. soc. Psychol.*, 1961, *63*, 597-602. [197]

Overall, J. E., & Hollister, L. E. Computer procedures for psychiatric classification. *J. A. M. A.*, 1964, *187*, 583-588. [199]

Overall, J. E., Hollister, L. E., and Dalal, S. N. Psychiatric drug research. *Arch. Gen. Psychiat.*, 1967, *16*, 152-161. [203]

Overall, J. E., Hollister, L. E., Meyer, F., Kimbell, I., & Shelton, J. Imipramine and Thioridazine in depressed and schizophrenic patients. *J. A. M. A.*, 1964, *189*, 605-608. [199]

Overall, J. E., Hollister, L. E., and Pichot, P. Major psychiatric disorders. *Arch. Gen. Psychiat.*, 1967, *16*, 146-151. [198, 199]

Overall, J. E., Hollister, L. E., Pokorny, A. D., Casey, J. F., & Katz, G. Drug therapy in depressions. *Clin. Pharm. & Therap.*, 1962, *3*, 16-22. [196, 202]

Pace, C. R. *CUES: College and university environment scales.* Princeton, N. J.: Educ. Testing Serv., 1963. [9]

Pace, C. R., & Stern, G. G. *College characteristics index.* Syracuse, N.Y.: Syracuse Univer. Psychol. Res. Center, 1958. [9]

Paige, J. M., & Simon, H. A. Cognitive processes in solving algebra word problems. In B. Kleinzmuntz (Ed.), *Problem solving: Research, method and theory.* New York: Wiley, 1966. [29]

Palmer, J. O. Alteration in Rorschach's experience balance under conditions of food and sleep deprivation: A construct validity study. *J. proj. Tech. pers. Assmt.*, 1963, *27*, 208-213. [142]

Palmer, J. O., & Lustgarten, B. J. The prediction of TAT structure as a test of Rorschach's experience-balance. *J. proj. Tech.*, 1962, *26*, 212-220. [146]

Pap, A. *An introduction to the philosophy of science.* New York: Free Press of Glencoe, 1962. [267]

Parloff, M. B. Some factors affecting the quality of therapeutic relationships. *J. abnorm. soc. Psychol.*, 1956, *52*, 5-10. [218]

Parloff, M. B., & Datta, L. Personality characteristics of the potentially creative scientist. In J. H. Masserman (Ed.), *Science and psychoanalysis, Volume VIII: commuication and community.* New York: Grune and Stratton, 1965. Pp. 91-106. [71]

Parton, D. A., & Ross, A. O. Social reinforcement of children's motor behavior: A review. *Psychol. Bull.*, 1965, *64*, 65-73. [174]

Passini, F. T., & Norman, W. T. A universal conception of personality structure. *J. pers. soc. Psychol.*, 1966, *4*, 44-49. [173]

Patrick, C. Creative thought in poets. *Arch. Psychol.*, 1935, *26*, 1-74. [38]

Patrick, C. Creative though in artists. *J. Psychol.*, 1937, *4*, 35-73. [38]

Patrick, C. Scientific thought. *J. Psychol.*, 1938, *5*, 55-83. [38]

Patrick, C. Whole and part relationships in creative thought. *Amer. J. Psychol.*, 1941, *54*, 128-131. [38]

Patterson, C. H. *Theories of counseling*

and psychotherapy. New York: Harper, 1966. [205]

Patterson, G. R. Responsiveness to social stimuli. In L. Krasner & L. P. Ullman (Eds.), *Research in behavior modification*. New York: Holt, Rinehart & Winston, 1965. Pp. 157-178. (*a*) [173, 174, 179, 185]

Patterson, G. R. Parents as dispensers of aversive stimuli. *J. pers. soc. Psychol.*, 1965, *2*, 844-851. (*b*) [179]

Patterson, G. R. The prediction of victimization from an instrumental conditioning procedure. *J. consult. Psychol.*, 1967, *31*, 147-152. *(a)* [178, 179]

Patterson, G. R. An operant MMPI? Unpublished manuscript, 1967. (*b*) [178, 179]

Patterson, G. R., Littman, R. E., & Hinsey, W. C. Parental effectiveness as reinforcers in the laboratory and its relation to child rearing practices and child adjustment in the classroom. *J. Pers.*, 1964, *32*, 180-199. [179]

Pauker, J. D. Base rates in the prediction of suicide: A note on Appelbaum & Holzman's The color-shading response and suicide. *J. proj. Tech.*, 1962, *26*, 429. [143]

Pauker, J. D. Relationship of Rorschach content categories to intelligence. *J. proj. Tech. pers. Assmt.*, 1963, *27*, 220-221. [145]

Paul, G. L. *Insight vs. desensitization in psychotherapy*. Stanford, Calif.: Stanford Univ. Press, 1966. [254, 256, 260, 267]

Paul, G. L. Strategy of outcome research in psychotherapy. *J. consult. Psychol.*, 1967, *31*, 109-118. [214]

Pavlov, I. P. *Conditioned reflexes*. Translated and edited by G. V. Anrep. London: Oxford Univ. Press, 1927. [271]

Perloe, S. I. Inhibition as a determinant of perceptual defense. *Percept. mot. Skills*, 1960, *11*, 59-66. [160]

Perry, J. M. Correlation of teacher prediction for student success six years beyond the sixth grade. Doctoral dissertation, University of Illinois, Urbana, 1966. [48]

Peterson, D. R. Scope and generality of verbally defined personality factor. *Psychol. Rev.*, 1965, *72*, 48-59. [173]

Peterson, D. R., Quay, H. C., & Anderson, A. C. Extending the construct validity of a socialization scale. *J. consult. Psychol.*, 1959, *23*, 182. [66]

Phares, E. J., Stewart, L. M., & Foster, J. M. Instruction variation and Rorschach performance. *J. proj. Tech.*, 1960, *24*, 28-32. [142]

Phillips, E. L., & Mattoon, C. U. Interference vs. extinction as learning models for psychotherapy. *J. Psychol.*, 1961,

51, 399-403. [219]

Phillips, L. & Smith, J. G. *Rorschach interpretation: Advanced technique*. New York: Grune & Stratton, 1953. [132]

Piaget, J. *The psychology of intelligence*. New York: Harcourt, Brace, 1950. [26]

Piaget, J. *The origins of intelligence in children*. New York: International Universities Press, 1952. [26]

Pierce, J. V. Personality and achievement among able high school boys. *J. indiv. Psychol.*, 1961, *17*, 102-107. [56]

Pierce-Jones, J. Social mobility orientations and interests of adolescents. *J. counsel. Psychol.*, 1961, *8*, 75-78. [61]

Pine, F. A manual for rating drive content in the thematic apperception test. *J. proj. Tech.*, 1960, *24*, 32-45. [39]

Pine, F. Creativity and primary process: Sample variations. *J. nerv. ment. Dis.*, 1962, *134*, 506-511. [39]

Pine, F., & Holt, R. R. Creativity and primary process: A study of adaptive regression. *J. abnorm. soc. Psychol.*, 1960, *61*, 370-379. [39]

Piotrowski, Z. The Rorschach ink-blot method. In B. B. Wolman (Ed.), *Handbook of clinical psychology*. New York: McGraw-Hill, 1965. [132]

Piotrowski, Z., & Rock, M. *The perceptanalytic executive scale: A tool for the selection of top managers*. New York: Grune & Stratton, 1963. [141]

Pitcher, G. Emotion. *Mind*, 1965, *74*, 326-346. [277]

Pittel, S. M., & Mendelsohn, G. A. Measurement of moral values: A review and critique. *Psychol. Bull.*, 1966, *66*, 22-35. [6]

Plutchik, R. *The emotions: Facts, theories, and a new model*. New York: Random House, 1962. [280]

Porier, G. W., & Lott, A. J. Galvanic skin responses and prejudice. *J. pers. Soc. Psychol.*, 1967, *5*, 253-259. [276]

Posner, M. I. Memory and thought in human intellectual performance. *Brit. J. Psychol.*, 1965, *56*, 197-215. [24]

Pouncey, T. Psychological correlates of journalism training completion. Unpublished doctoral dissertation, University of Minnesota, Minneapolis, 1954. [70]

Pruitt, W. A. & Spilka, B. Rorschach empathy-object relationship scale. *J. proj. Tech. pers. Assmt.*, 1964, *28*, 331-337. [141]

Quay, H. C., and Hunt, W. A. Psychopathy, neuroticism, and verbal conditioning: A replication and extension. *J. consult. Psychol.*, 1965, *29*, 283. [180]

Rabin, A. I. Some psychosexual differences between Kibbutz and non-Kibbutz Israeli boys. *J. proj. Tech.*, 1958, *3*, 328-332. [159]

Rabin, A. I. Projective techniques. In Abt, L. E., & Reiss, B. F. (Eds.), *Progress in clinical psychology*. New York: Grune & Stratton, 1964. Pp. 2-29. [6, 8]

Rabin, A., Nelson, W., & Clark, M. Rorschach content as a function of perceptual experience and sex of the examiner. *J. clin. Psychol.*, 1954, *10*, 188-190. [141]

Rabin, A., Papania, N., & McMichael, A. Some effects of alcohol on Rorschach performance. *J. clin. Psychol.*, 1954, *10*, 232-255. [141]

Rabkin, L. The patient's family: Research methods. *Fam. Process*, 1965, *4*, 105-132. [224]

Raines, G. M., & Rohrer, J. H. The operational matrix of psychiatric practice. I. Consistency and variability in interview impressions of different psychiatrists. *Amer. J. Psychiat.*, 1955, *111*, 721-733. [217]

Rankin, R. J. Nonfunctioning Taylor manifest anxiety scale items. *Psychol. Rep.*, 1963, *12*, 912. [252]

Raskin, A. Factors therapists associate with motivation to enter therapy. *J. clin. Psychol.*, 1961, *17*, 62-65. [215]

Raskin, A. Observable signs of anxiety or distress during psychotherapy. *J. consult. Psychol.*, 1962, *26*, 389. [261, 262]

Ravich, R. Ad., Deutsch, M., & Brown, B. An experimental study of marital discord and decision-making. In Irvin M. Cohen (Ed.), *Family structure, dynamics and therapy*. Psychiatric Research Report 20, American Psychiatric Association, Washington, D. C., 1966. Pp. 91-94. [235, 236]

Ray, J. B. The meaning of Rorschach white space responses. *J. proj. Tech. pers. Assmt.*, 1963, *27*, 315-324. [137]

Ream, M. J. *Ability to sell: its relation to certain aspects of personality and experience*. Baltimore, 1924. [113]

Reckless, W. C., Dinitz, S., & Kay, B. The self-component in potential delinquency and use of concepts, percepts and rules. *Amer. sociol. Rev.*, 1957, *22*, 566-570. [56]

Reisman, J. M. Types of movement in children's Rorschachs. *J. proj. Tech.*, 1960, *24*, 46-48. [137]

Reitman, W. R. *Cognition and thought* New York: Wiley, 1965. [25, 26, 30]

Reitman, W. R. Modeling the formation and use of concepts, percepts and rules. Mental Health Research Institute, University of Michigan: Preprint #174, 1966 (mimeo.). [26]

Reznikoff, M., & Toomey, L. C. *Evaluation of changes associated with psychiatric treatment*. Springfield, Ill.: Chas. C. Thomas, 1959. [6, 206, 209, 213]

Richards, T. W., & Murray, D. C. Global evaluation of Rorschach performance versus scores: Sex differences in Rorschach performance. *J. clin.*

Psychol., 1958, *14*, 61-64. [136, 143]

Rickels, K., & Cattell, R. B. The clinical factor validity and trueness of the IPAT verbal and objective batteries for anxiety and regression. *J. clin. Psychol.*, 1965, *21*, 257-264. [247, 259]

Rickers-Ovsiankina, M. (Ed.) *Rorschach psychology*. New York: Wiley, 1960. [5]

Riedel, W. W. Anxiety level and the "doubtful" judgment in a psychophysical experiment. *J. abnorm. Psychol.*, 1965, *70*, 462-464. [4, 262]

Rieger, A. F. The Rorschach test and occupational personalities. *J. appl. Psychol.*, 1949, *33*, 572-577. [148]

Robbins, P. R. An application of the method of successive intervals to the study of fear-arousing information. *Psychol. Rep.*, 1962, *11*, 757-760. (*a*) [248]

Robbins, P. R. Some explorations into the nature of anxieties relating to illness. *Genet. psychol. Monogr.*, 1962, *66*, 91-141. (*b*) [256]

Robinson, S. A., & Hendrix, B. L. The Blacky test and psychoanalytic theory: another factor-analytic approach to validity. *J. proj. Tech.*, 1966, *30*, 597-603. [154]

Roe, A. Artists and their work. *J. Pers.*, 1946, *15*, 1-40. (*a*) [38]

Roe, A. A Rorschach study of a group of scientists and technicians. *J. cons. Psychol.*, 1946, *10*, 317-398. (*b*) [148]

Roe, A. Personality and vocation. *Trans. N.Y. Acad. Sci.*, 1947, *9*, 257-267. [38]

Roe, A. Analysis of the group Rorschachs of biologists. *J. proj. Tech.*, 1949, *13*, 24-43. [148]

Roe, A. Analysis of the group Rorschachs of physical scientists. *J. proj. Tech.*, 1950, *14*, 385-398. [38, 148]

Roe, A. A psychological study of eminent psychologists and anthropologists and a comparison with biological and physical scientists. *Psychol. Monogr.*, 1953, *67* (2, Whole No. 352). [148]

Roe, A., & Mierzwa, J. The use of the Rorschach in the study of personality and occupation, *J. proj. Tech.*, 1960, *24*, 282-290. [148]

Rogers, C. R. *Client-centered therapy*. Boston: Houghton-Mifflin, 1951. [212]

Rogers, C. Client-centered therapy: A current view. In Frieda Fromm-Reichmann & J. L. Moreno (Eds.), *Progress in psychotherapy*, 1956. New York: Grune & Stratton, 1956. Pp. 199-209. [217]

Rogers, C. The characteristics of a helping relationship. Unpublished address delivered to American Personnel and Guidance Assoc., March 31, 1958, St. Louis, Missouri. [216]

Rogers, C. R. Toward a theory of

creativity. In H. H. Anderson (Ed.), *Creativity and its cultivation*. New York: Harper, 1959. [49]

Rogers, C. R. The interpersonal relationship: The core of guidance. *Harvard Educ. Rev.*, 1962. *32*, 416-429. [213]

Roman, M., & Bauman, G. Interaction testing: A technique for the evaluation of small groups. In M. Harrower, *et al.* (Eds.), *Creative variations in the projective techniques*. Springfield, Ill.: Chas. C. Thomas, 1960. [133]

Rome, H. P., Swenson, W. M., Mataya, P., McCarthy, C. E., Pearson, J. S., & Keating, R. F. Symposium on automation techniques in personality assessment. *Proc. Mayo Clin.*, 1962, *37*, 61-82. [6]

Rorer, L. G. The great response-style myth. *Psychol. Bull.*, 1965, *63*, 129-156. [8, 170]

Rose, R. J. Preliminary study of three indicants of arousal: Measurement, interrelationships, and clinical correlates. Unpublished Ph.D. dissertation, University of Minnesota, 1964. [255]

Rosen, J. C. The Barron-Welsh art scale as a predictor of originality and level of ability among artists. *J. appl. Psychol.*, 1955, *39*, 366-367. [50]

Rosenbaum, M., Friedlander, Jane, & Kaplan, S. M. Evaluation of results of psychotherapy. *Psychosom. Med.*, 1956, *18*, 113-132. [215]

Rosenberg, L. A., McHenry, T. B., Rosenberg, A. M., & Nichols, R. C. The prediction of academic achievement with the California psychological inventory. *J. appl. Psychol.*, 1962, *46*, 385-388. [70]

Rosenberg, S., & Starer, E. A multiple choice Rorschach technique for increasing test productivity in chronic schizophrenics. *J. proj. Tech.*, 1960, *24*, 429-433. [142]

Rosenblum, S., & Callahan, R. J. The performance of high-grade retarded, emotionally disturbed children on the children's manifest anxiety scale and children's anxiety pictures. *J. clin. Psychol.*, 1958, *14*, 272-275. [259]

Rosenthal, M. Some behavioral correlates of the Rorschach experience-balance. *J. proj. Tech.*, 1962, *26*, 442-446. [137]

Rosenthal, R. *Experimenter effects in behavioral research*. New York: Appleton-Century-Crofts, 1966. [7]

Rosenzweig, S. A transvaluation of psychotherapy–a reply to Hans Eysenck. *J. abnorm. soc. Psychol.*, 1954, *49*, 298-304. [212]

Rosner, S. Inquiry, partial or total. *J. proj. Tech.*, 1960, *24*, 49-51. [134]

Rossi, A. M., & Neuman, G. G. A comparative study of Rorschach norms: Medical students. *J. proj. Tech.*, 1961, *25*, 334-339. [135]

Rossi, A. M., & Solomon, P. A. A further note on female Blacky protocols. *J. proj. Tech.*, 1961, *25*, 339-340. [154]

Rothschild, B. H. Response style: A basis for Rorschach construct validity. *J. proj. Tech. pers. Assmt.*, 1964, *28*, 474-484. [132]

Rotter, J. B. Some implications of a social learning theory for the prediction of goal directed behavior from testing procedures. *Psychol. Rev.*, 1960, *67*, 301-316. [174]

Rotter, J. B. Generalized expectancies for internal versus external control of reinforcement. *Psychol. Monogr.*, 1966, *80* (Whole No. 609). [177]

Rouse, S. T. Effects of a training program on the production thinking of educable mental retardates, *Amer. J. ment. Defic.*, 1965, *69*, 666-673. [47]

Rubin, H., Schneiderman, L., Hallow, W. C., & Jones, R. J. Manifest anxiety in psychotics. *J. clin. Psychol.*, 1956, *12*, 94-96. [252]

Rubin, H., & Townsend, A. H. The Taylor manifest anxiety scale in differential diagnosis. *J. clin. Psychol.*, 1958, *14*, 81-83. [252]

Ruch, T. C., & Patton, H. D. (Eds.) *Physiology and biophysics*. Philadelphia: Saunders, 1965. [266]

Ruebush, B. K. Anxiety. In H. W. Stevenson (Ed.), *Child psychology*. 62nd Yearb. NSSE. Chicago: University Chicago Press, 1963. Pp. 460-516. [245, 258, 259]

Rundquist, E. A. Item and response characteristics in attitude and personality measurement: A reaction to L. G. Rorer's The great response-style myth. *Psychol. Bull.*, 1966, *66*, 166-177. [8]

Russell, P. D., & Snyder, W. J. Counselor anxiety in relation to amount of clinical experience and quality of affect demonstrated by clients. *J. consult. Psychol.*, 1963, *27*, 358-363. [215]

Rychlak, J. F., & Guinouard, D. Rorschach content, personality, and popularity. *J. proj. Tech.*, 1960, *24*, 322-333. [145]

Rychlak, J. F., & O'Leary, L. R. Unhealthy content in the Rorschach responses of children and adolescents. *J. proj. Tech. pers. Assmt.*, 1965, *29*, 254-260. [145]

Ryder, R. G. Two replications of color matching factors. *Fam. Process*, 1966, *5*, 43-48. [226]

Ryder, R. G., & Goodrich, D. W. Married couples' responses to disagreement. *Fam. Process*, 1966, *5*, 30-42. [226]

Ryle, G. *The concept of mind*. New York: Barnes & Noble, 1949. [267, 268]

Sakheim, G. A. Suicidal responses on the Rorschach test: A validation study. *J.*

nerv. ment. Disorder, 1955, 123, 332-344. [143]

Salzinger, K. & Portnoy, S. Verbal conditioning in interviews: Application to chronic schizophrenics and relationship to prognosis for acute schizophrenics. J. Psychiat. Res., 1964, 2, 1-9. [184]

Salzinger, K., Portnoy, S., and Feldman, R. S. Verbal behavior in schizophrenics and some comments toward a theory of schizophrenia. In Paul H. Hoch and Joseph Zubin (Eds.), Psychopathology of schizophrenia. New York: Grune & Stratton, 1966. Pp. 98-128. [184]

Sanders, R., & Cleveland, S. E. The relationship between certain examiner personality variables and subjects' Rorschach scores. J. proj. Tech., 1953, 17, 34-50. [133]

Sanford, N. Clinical methods: Psychotherapy. Annu. Rev. Psychol., 1953, 4, 317-342. [212, 214]

Sappenfield, B. R. The Blacky pictures. In O. K. Buros (Ed.), The sixth mental measurements yearbook. Highland Park, N. J.: Gryphon Press, 1965. Pp. 416-423. [151]

Sarason, I. G. Interrelationships among individual difference variables, behavior in psychotherapy, and verbal conditioning. J. abnorm. soc. Psychol., 1958, 56, 339-344. [251]

Sarason, I. G. Empirical findings and theoretical problems in the use of anxiety scales. Psychol. Bull., 1960, 57, 403-415. [244]

Sarason, I. G., & Ganzer, V. J. Effects of test anxiety and reinforcement history on verbal behavior. J. abnorm. soc. Psychol., 1963, 67, 513-519. [255]

Sarason, S. B. The measurement of anxiety in children: Some questions and problems. In C. D. Spielberger (Ed.), Anxiety and behavior. New York: Academic Press, 1966. [258]

Sarason, S. B., Davidson, K. S., Lighthall, F. F., & Waite, R. R. A test anxiety scale for children. Child Develpm, 1958, 29, 105-113. [259]

Sarason, S. B., Davidson, K. S., Lighthall, F. F., Waite, R. R., & Ruebush, B. K. Anxiety in elementary school children. New York: Wiley, 1960. [259]

Sarason, S. B., & Mandler, G. Some correlates of test anxiety. J. abnorm soc. Psychol., 1952, 47, 810-817. [255]

Sarbin, T. R. Clinical psychology—art or science? Psychometrika, 1941, 6, 391-400. [8]

Sarbin, T. R. The scientific status of the mental illness metaphor. In S. Plog (Ed.), Determinants of psychological disorder, 1967, in press. [170]

Sarbin, T., Allen, V. L., & Rutherford, E. E. Social reinforcement, socialization, and chronic delinquency. Brit. J. soc.

clin. Psychol., 1965, 4, 179-184. [173, 180]

Saslow, G., Counts, R. M., & DuBois, P. H. Evaluation of a new psychiatric screening test. Psychosom. Med., 1951, XIII, 242-253. [254]

Sassenrath, J. M. A factor analysis of rating-scale items on the test anxiety questionnaire. J. consult. Psychol., 1964, 28, 371-377. [247]

Sassenrath, J. M., Kight, H. R., & Kaiser, H. F. Relating factors from anxiety scales between two samples. Psychol. Rep., 1965, 17, 407-416. [247]

Satir, V. Notes on the structured interview. Palo Alto: Author, 1966. (Mimeo.) [229]

Schachtel, E. G. Experiential foundations of Rorschach's test. New York: Basic Books, 1966. [132]

Schachter, J. Pain, fear, and anger in hypertensives and normotensives. Psychosom. Med., 1957, 19, 17-29. [278, 279]

Schachter, S. The psychology of affiliation. Stanford: Stanford Univ. Press, 1959. [248]

Schachter, S. The interaction of cognitive and physiological determinants of emotional state. In C. D. Spielberger (Ed.), Anxiety and behavior. New York: Academic Press, 1966. Pp. 193-224. [282]

Schachter, S., & Singer, J. E. Cognitive, social, and physiological determinants of emotional state. Psychol. Rev., 1962, 69, 379-399. [282]

Schafer, R. Regression in the service of the ego. In G. Lindzey (Ed.), Assessment of human motives. New York: Rinehart, 1958. [38]

Schafer, R. Bodies in schizophrenic Rorschach responses. J. proj. Tech., 1960, 24, 267-282. [132]

Schaie, K. W. The effect of age on a scale of social responsibility. J. soc. Psychol., 1959, 50, 221-224. [56]

Scheier, I. H. (Ed.) Recent data on IPAT anxiety tests. Champaign, Ill.: Inst. Pers. & Abil. Test., 1967. [254, 259]

Scheier, I. H., & Cattell, R. B. Handbook for the IPAT 8-parallel-form anxiety battery. Champaign, Ill.: Inst. Pers. & Abil. Test., 1960. [259]

Scheier, I. H., Cattell, R. B., & Sullivan, W. P. Predicting anxiety from clinical symptoms of anxiety. Psychiat. quart. Suppl., 1961, 1, 1-13. [248]

Schendel, J. Psychological differences between athletes and nonparticipants in athletics at three educational levels. Res. Quart., 1965, 36, 52-67. [56]

Schildkraut, J. J., & Kety, S. S. Biogenic amines and emotion. Science, 1967, 156, 21-30. [279]

Schleifer, M. J., & Hire, A. W. Stimulus

value of Rorschach ink-blots expressed as trite and affective characteristics. *J. proj. Tech.*, 1960, *24*, 164, 171. [134]

Schlosberg, H. Three dimensions of emotion. *Psychol. Rev.*, 1954, *61*, 81-88. [280]

Schneirla, T. C. Aspects of stimulation and organization in approach/withdrawal processes underlying vertebrate behavioral development. In D. S. Lehrman (Ed.), *Advances in the study of behavior*. Vol. 1. New York: Academic Press, 1965. Pp. 1-74. [281]

Schutz, W. C. *FIRO: A three-dimensional theory of interpersonal behavior*. New York: Rinehart, 1958. [189, 225]

Seeman, J. Psychotherapy. In *Annu. Rev. Psychol.*, 1961, *12*, 157-194. [220]

Seeman, J., & Raskin, N.J. Research perspectives in client-centered therapy. In O. H. Mowrer (Ed.), *Psychotherapy: Theory and research*. New York: Ronald Press, 1953. Pp. 205-234. [213]

Segal, J. The differentiation of well and poorly integrated clinicians by the Q-sort method. *J. clin. Psychol.*, 1954, *10*, 321-325. [216]

Seiden, R. H. The psychoanalytic significance of onset age in bronchial asthma. *J. asthma Res.*, 1966, *3*, 285-289. [158]

Sells, S. B. (Ed.) *Stimulus determinants of behavior*. New York: Ronald Press, 1963. [9]

Selye, H. *The stress of life*. New York: McGraw-Hill, 1956. [274]

Semeonoff, B. (Ed.) *Personality assessment*. Baltimore: Penguin, 1966. [5]

Shatin, L., & Freed, E. X. A behavioral rating scale for mental patients. *J. Ment. Sci.*, 1955, *101*, 644-653. [200]

Sheldon, W. H., & Stevens, S. S. *The varieties of temperament*. New York: Harper, 1942. [275]

Shostrum, E. L. *Personal orientation blank*. San Diego, Calif.: Educ. & Indus. Testing Serv., 1963. [208]

Shostrom, E. L., & Knapp, R. R. The relationship of a measure of self-actualization (POI) to a measure of pathology (MMPI) and to therapeutic growth. *Am. J. Psychother.*, 1966, *20*, 193-202. [208]

Shure, G. H., & Rogers, M. S. Note of caution on the factor analysis of the MMPI. *Psychol. Bull.*, 1965, *63*, 14-18. [83]

Sidman, M. Operant techniques. In A. J. Bachrach (Ed.), *Experimental foundations of clinical psychology*. New York: Basic Books, 1962. Pp. 170-210. [171, 181]

Siegel, S. *Nonparametric statistics*. New York: McGraw-Hill, 1956. [272]

Silverman, L. H. On the relationship between aggressive imagery and thought disturbance in Rorschach responses. *J.*

proj. Tech. pers. Asssmt., 1963, *27*, 336-345. [145]

Silverman, L. H., & Silverman, D. K. Womb fantasies in heroin addiction: A Rorschach study. *J. proj. Tech.*, 1960, *24*, 52-63. [145]

Simon, H. A. Motivational and emotional controls of cognition. *Psychol. Rev.*, 1967, *74*, 29-39. [30, 31]

Simon, H. A., & Kotovsky, K. Human acquisition of concepts for sequential patterns. *Psychol. Rev.*, 1963, *70*, 534-546. [24, 26]

Simpson, R. M. Creative imagination. *Amer. J. Psychol.*, 1922, *33*, 234-243. [41]

Sines, J. O. An approach to the study of the stimulus significance of the Rorschach ink-blots. *J. proj. Tech.*, 1960, *24*, 64-66. [138]

Sines, J. O. Actuarial methods in personality assessment. In B. A. Maher (Ed.), *Progress in experimental personality research*. New York: Academic Press, 1966. [6, 8]

Singer, J. L., & Spohn, H. E. Some behavioral correlates of Rorschach's experience balance. *J. consult. Psychol.*, 1954, *18*, 1-9. [136, 137]

Singer, M. T., & Wynne, L. C. Differentiating characteristics of parents of childhood schizophrenics, childhood neurotics and young adult schizophrenics. *Amer. J. of Psychiatry*, 1963, *120*, 234-243. [140]

Skinner, B. F. *Science and human behavior*. New York: Macmillan, 1953.

Skinner, B. F. Operant behavior. *Amer. Psychologist*, 1963, *18*, 503-515. [171, 172]

Slechta, J., Gwynn, W., & Peoples, C. Verbal conditioning of schizophrenics and normals in a situation resembling psychotherapy. *J. consult. Psychol.*, 1963, *27*, 223-227. [181]

Slovic, P. Assessment of risk taking behavior. *Psychol. Bull.*, 1964, *61*, 220-233. [6]

Smart, J. J. C. *Philosophy and scientific realism*. London: Routledge & Kegan Paul, 1963. [274]

Smedslund, J. Concrete reasoning: A study of intellectual development. *Monogr. Soc. Res. Child Develpm.*, 1964, *29*, 1-39. [29]

Smith, D. B. D., & Wenger, M. A. Changes in autonomic balance during phasic anxiety. *Psychophysiology*, 1965, *1*, 267-271. [246, 278]

Snider, J. G. Academic achievement and underachievement in a Canadian high school as predicted from the California psychological inventory. *Psychol. in the Sch.*, 1966, *3*, 370-372. [56]

Sokolov, E. N. *Perception and the conditioned reflex*. Oxford: Pergamon Press,

1963. [63, 281]

Spearman, C. *The nature of intelligence and the principles of cognition*. London: Macmillan, 1923. [28]

Spearman, C. *Creative mind*. London: Cambridge University Press, 1930. [40]

Spearman, C. *The abilities of man*. London: Macmillan, 1932. [19]

Spence, J. T., & Spence, K. W. The effects of anxiety on behavior. In C. D. Spielberger (Ed.), *Anxiety and behavior*. New York: Academic Press, 1966. (*a*) [252]

Spence, J. T., & Spence, K. W. The motivational components of manifest anxiety: Drive and drive stimuli. In C. D. Spielberger (Ed.), *Anxiety and behavior*. New York: Academic Press, 1966, Pp. 291-326. (*b*) [274]

Spielberger, C. D. Theory and research on anxiety. In C. D. Spielberger (Ed.), *Anxiety and behavior*. New York: Academic Press, 1966. Pp. 3-20. [246, 268]

Spitzer, R. L. Mental status schedule: Potential use as a criterion measure of change in psychotherapy research. *Amer. J. Psychother.*, 1966, *20*, 156-167. [208]

Spranger, E. *Lebensformen. Geisteswissenschaftliche Psychologie und Ethik der Persönlichkeit*. Halle (Saale): M. Niemeyer, 1914. (5th ed., 1925, translated by P. J. W. Pigors as *Types of men: The Psychology and Ethics of Personality*. Halle: M. Niemeyer, 1928.) [57]

Sprecher, T. B. A proposal for identifying the meaning of creativity. In C. W. Taylor (Ed.), *The third (1959) University of Utah research conference on the identification of creative scientific talent*. Salt Lake City: Univ. Utah Press, 1959. Pp. 29-45. [36, 37]

Spreen, O., & Benton, A. L. Comparative studies of some psychological tests for cerebral damage. *J. nerv. ment. Dis.*, 1965, *140*, 323-333. [6]

Srole, L., Langer, T. S., Michael, S. T., Opler, M. K., & Rennie, T. A. C. *Mental health in the metropolis*. (The Midtown Manhattan Study.) New York: McGraw-Hill, 1962. [219]

Stefflre, B. *Theories of counseling*. New York: McGraw-Hill, 1965. [205]

Stein, H. Rotation and reliability of the Rorschach. *J. proj. Tech.*, 1960, *24*, 171-182. [135]

Stein, K. B., Gough, H. G., & Sarbin, T. R. The dimensionality of the CPI socialization scale and an emprically derived typology among delinquent and nondelinquent boys. *Mult. Behav. Res.*, 1966, *1*, 197-208. [66]

Stein, M. I. *Contemporary psychotherapies*. New York: Free Press, 1961. [205]

Stein, M. I., & Heinze, S. J. *Creativity and the individual*. Glencoe, Ill.: Free Press, 1960. [34]

Sternbach, R. A. A comparative analysis of autonomic responses in startle. *Psychosom. Med.*, 1960, *22*, 204-210. [278]

Sternbach, R. A. Assessing differential autonomic patterns in emotions. *J. psychosom. Res.*, 1962, *6*, 87-91. [278]

Stewart, B. M. A study of the relationship between clinical manifestations of neurotic anxiety and Rorschach test performance. Unpublished Ph.D. dissertation, University of Southern Calif., 1950. [257]

Stewart, L. H. Social and emotional adjustment during adolescence as related to the development of psychosomatic illness in adulthood. *Genet. psychol. Monogr.*, 1962, *65*, 175-215. [58]

Stieper, D. R., & Wiener, D. N. The problem of interminability in outpatient psychotherapy. *J. consult. Psychol.*, 1959, *23*, 237-242. [221]

Stieper, D. R., & Wiener, D. N. *Dimensions of psychotherapy: An experimental and clinical approach*. Chicago: Aldine Press, 1965. [6, 205, 206]

Stilson, D. W., Mason, D. J., Gynther, M. D., & Gertz, B. An evaluation of the comparability and reliabilities of two behavior rating scales for mental patients. *J. consult. Psychol.*, 1958, *22*, 213-216. [204]

Stoddard, L. T., Sidman, M., and Brady, J. V. Reinforcement frequency as a factor in the control of normal and psychotic behavior. (Cited by M. Sidman, Operant techniques, In Bachrach, 1962.) [181]

Stoler, N. Client likability: A variable in the study of psychotherapy. *J. consult. Psychol.*, 1963, *27*, 175-178. [215]

Stollak, G. E. Conditioning and transfer effects of verbally reinforcing choices of personality statements. *Psychol. Rep.*, 1966, *19*, 427-437. [176]

Stollack, G. E., Guerney, B. G., & Rothberg, M. (Eds.) *Psychotherapy research: Selected readings*. Chicago: Rand-McNally, 1966. [205, 206]

Stone, F. B., Rowley, V. N., & Keller, E. D. Clinical anxiety and the children's manifest anxiety scale. *J. clin. Psychol.*, 1965, *21*, 409-412. [258]

Stone, G. C. Applications of operant conditioning in individual assessment. Paper delivered at California State Psychological Association meetings, San Francisco, 1966. [171, 172, 182]

Stone, H. K., & Dellis, N. P. An exploratory investigation into the levels hypothesis. *J. proj. Tech.*, 1960, *24*, 333-340. [140]

Storment, C., & Finney, B. C. Projection and behavior: A Rorschach study of assaultive mental patients. *J. proj. Tech.*, 1953, *17*, 345-360. [144]

Streitfeld, H. S. Specificity of peptic ulcer to intense oral conflicts. *Psychosom. Med.*, 1954, *16*, 315-324. [157]

Strickland, B. R., & Crowne, D. P. Need for approval and the premature termination of psychotherapy. *J. consult. Psychol.*, 1963, *27*, 95-101. [220]

Strodtbeck, F. L. Husband-wife interaction over revealed differences. *Amer. sociol. Rev.*, 1951, *16*, 468-473. [225, 236]

Strodtbeck, F. L. The family as a three-person group. *Am. Sociol. Rev.*, 1954, *19*, 23-29. [237]

Strong, E. K., Jr. Vocational interest test, *Educ. Rec.*, 1927, *8*, 107-121. (Appendix, pp. 115-121, includes 1927 Manual) [105, 116, 117]

Strong, E. K., Jr. Differentiation of certified public accountants from other occupational groups. *J. educ. Psychol.*, 1927. *18*, 227-238. [115]

Strong, E. K., Jr. Diagnostic value of the vocational interest test. *Educ. Rec.*, 1929, *10*, 59-68. [117]

Strong, E. K., Jr. Interests and sales ability, *Personnel J.*, 1934, *13*, 204-216. [121]

Strong, E. K., Jr. *Vocational interests of men and women.* Stanford, Calif.: Stanford Univ. Press, 1943. [56, 72, 124]

Strong, E. K., Jr. *Strong vocational interest blanks.* Palo Alto: Consulting Psychologists' Press, 1959. [96, 125]

Strong, E. K., Jr., & McKenzie, H. Permanence of interest of adult men. *J. soc. Psychol.*, 1930, *1*, 152-159. [118]

Strupp, H. H. A multidimensional comparison of therapist activity in analytic and client-centered therapy. *J. consult. Psychol.*, 1957, *21*, 301-308. [217]

Strupp, H. H. The performance of psychiatrists and psychologists in a therapeutic interview. *J. clin. Psychol.*, 1958, *14*, 219-226. (*a*) [217]

Strupp, H. H. The psychotherapist's contribution to the treatment process. *Behav. Sci.*, 1958, *3*, 34-67. (*b*) [213, 217]

Strupp, H. H. *Psychotherapists in action.* New York: Grune & Stratton, 1960. [214]

Strupp, H. H. Psychotherapy. *Annu. Rev. Psychol.*, 1962, *13*, 445-478. [215]

Strupp, H. H. The outcome problem in psychotherapy revisited. *Psychother. Theor. Res. Pract.*, 1963, *1*, 1-13. [215]

Strupp, H. H., & Wallach, M. S. A further study of psychiatrist's responses in quasi-therapy situations. *Behav. Sci.*, 1965, *10*, 113-134. [215]

Super, D. E. Theories and assumptions underlying approaches to personality assessment. In B. M. Bass & I. A. Berg (Eds.), *Objective approaches to personality assessment.* New York: Van Nostrand, 1959. Pp. 24-42. [5]

Super, D. E., & Crites, J. O. *Appraising vocational fitness.* New York: Harper, 1962. [5, 148]

Swan, H. J. C. Noradrenaline, adrenaline, and the human circulation. *Brit. med. J.*, 1952, *4766*, 1003-1006. [282]

Swanson, G. E. Some effects of member object-relationships on small groups. *Hum. Relat.*, 1951, *4*, 355-380. [159]

Taft, R. Multiple methods of personality assessment. *Psychol. Bull.*, 1959, *56*, 333-352. [5]

Tahka, V. *The alcoholic personality.* Helsinki: The Finnish Foundation for Alcohol Studies, 1966. [144]

Tallent, N. Clinical psychological testing: A review of premises, practices and promises. *J. proj. Tech. & pers. Assmt.*, 1965, *29*, 418-435. [10]

Tarlan, M., & Smalheiser, I. Personality patterns in patients with malignant tumors of the breast and cervix. *Psychosom. Med.*, 1951, *13*, 117-121. [144]

Taulbee, E. S. Relationship between certain personality variables and continuation in psychotherapy. *J. consult. Psychol.*, 1958, *22*, 83-89. [147]

Taulbee, E. S. The relationship between Rorschach flexor and extensor M responses and the MMPI and psychotherapy. *J. proj. Tech.*, 1961, *25*, 477-480. [146]

Taylor, C. W. Introduction. In C. W. Taylor (Ed.), *Creativity: Progress and potential.* New York: McGraw-Hill, 1964. Pp. 1-14. [35]

Taylor, C. W., Smith, W. R., & Ghiselin, B. The creative and other contributions of one sample of research scientists. In C. W. Taylor & F. Barron (Eds.), *Scientific creativity: Its recognition and development.* New York: Wiley, 1963. Pp. 53-76. [37]

Taylor, D. W. Variables related to creativity and productivity among men in two research laboratories. In C. W. Taylor & F. Barron (Eds.), *Scientific creativity: Its recognition and development.* New York: Wiley, 1963. Pp. 228-250. [35]

Taylor, D. W. Discussion of papers by Adriaan D. de Groot and by Jeffery M. Paige and Herbert A. Simon. In B. Kleinmuntz (Ed.), *Problem solving: Research, method and theory.* New York: Wiley, 1966. [30]

Taylor, E. K., & Nevis, E. C. Personnel selection. *Annu. Rev. Psychol.*, 1961, *12*, 389-412. [6]

Taylor, I. A. The nature of the creative process. In P. Smith (Ed.), *Creativity.* New York: Charles Scribner's Sons,

1962. [38]

Taylor, J. A., A personality scale of manifest anxiety. *J. abnorm. soc. Psychol.*, 1953, *48*, 285-290. [4, 252, 268]

Taylor, J. A. Drive theory and manifest anxiety. *Psychol. Bull.*, 1956, *53*, 303-321. [252, 253]

Teevan, R. C. Personality correlates of undergraduate field of specialization. *J. consult. Psychol.*, 1954, *18*, 212-214. [160]

Tellegen, A. The Minnesota multiphasic personality inventory. In Abt, L. E., & Riess, B. F. (Eds.), *Progress in clinical psychology.* New York: Grune & Stratton, 1964. Pp. 30-48. [6]

Temple, R., & Amen, E. W. A study of anxiety reactions in young children by means of a projective technique. *Genet. psychol. Monogr.*, 1944, *30*, 59-114. [259]

Terman, L. M. The discovery and encouragement of exceptional talent. *Amer. Psychologist*, 1954, *9*, 221-230. [22]

Thorndike, E. L. The permanence of interests and their relation to abilities. *Pop. sci. Monthly*, 1912, *81*, 449-456. [113]

Thorndike, R. L. Some methodological issues in the study of creativity. In *Proceedings of the 1962 invitational conference on testing problems.* Princeton, N. J.: Educational Testing Service, 1963. [52]

Thorndike, R. L. Intellectual status and intellectual growth. *J. educ. Psychol.* 1966, *57*, 121-127. [22]

Thurstone, L. L. *Multiple factor analysis.* Chicago: Univ. Chicago Press, 1947. [82]

Timmons, E. O., & Novlin, C. D. The differential performance of orals and anals in a verbal conditioning paradigm. *J. consult. Psychol.*, 1963, *27*, 383-386. [159]

Tizard, B. The personality of epileptics: A discussion of the evidence. *Psychol. Bull.*, 1962, *59*, 196-211. [143, 144]

Tolor, A., Glass, H. L., & Mermelstein, M. D. Rorschach card rejection as a correlate of intelligence in children. *J. proj. Tech.*, 1960, *24*, 71-74. [145]

Tolor, A., & Schulberg, H. C. *An evaluation of the Bender-Gestalt test.* Springfield, Ill.: Chas. C Thomas, 1963. [6]

Torgerson, W. S. Scaling and test theory. *Annu. Rev. Psycho.*, 1961, *12*, 51-70. [5]

Torrance, E. P. *Guiding creative talent.* Englewood Cliffs, N. J.: Prentice-Hall, 1962. [34, 41, 46, 48]

Torrance, E. P. *Education and the creative potential.* Minneapolis: Univ. Minnesota Press, 1963. [48]

Torrance, E. P. Exploring the limits on the automation of guided, planned experi-

ence in creative thinking. In J. S. Roucek (Ed.), *Programmed teaching.* New York: Philsophical Library, 1966. (*a*) [53]

Torrance, E. P. *Torrance tests of creative thinking: Norms-technical manual, research edition.* Princeton, N. J.: Personnel Press, 1966. (*b*) [44, 45]

Torrance, E. P., & Dauw, D. C. Aspirations and dreams of three groups of creatively gifted high school seniors and a comparable unselected group. *Gifted Child Quart.*, 1965, *9*, 177-182. (*a*) [49]

Torrance, E. P., & Dauw, D. C. Mental health problems of three groups of highly creative high school seniors. *Gifted Child Quart.*, 1965, *9*, 123-127f. (*b*) [49]

Torrance, E. P., & Gupta, R. *Programmed experiences in creative thinking.* Bureau of Educational Research, University of Minnesota, Minneapolis, 1964. [48]

Torrance, E. P., & Myers, R. E. *Teaching gifted elementary pupils how to do research.* Minneapolis: Perceptive Publishing Co., 1962. [48]

Travers, R. M. W. A critical review of techniques for evaluating guidance. *Educ. psychol. Meas.*, 1949, *9*, 211-225. [207] [207]

Truax, C. B. Effective ingredients in psychotherapy: An approach to unraveling the patient-therapist interaction. *J. counsel. Psychol.*, 1963, *10*, 256-263. [213, 217]

Truax, C. B., & Carkhuff, R. R. For better or for worse: The process of psychotherapeutic personality change. Invited address: Recent advances in study of behavior change; Academic Assembly on Clinical Psychology, McGill University, Montreal, Canada, 1963. [213]

Truax, C. B., & Carkhuff, R. R. New directions in clinical research. In L. Abt & B. Riess (Eds.), *Progress in clinical psychology.* New York: Grune & Stratton, 1964. Pp. 124-155. [213]

Tryk, H. E. Word frequency as a psychological variable. *Dissertation Abstr.*, 1966, *26*, 5543. [4]

Tryon, R. C. Reliability and behavior domain validity: Reformulation and historical critique. *Psychol. Bull.*, 1957, *54*, 229-249. [174]

Tryon, R. C. Unrestricted cluster and factor analysis, with application to the MMPI and Holzinger-Harmon problems. *Mult. behav. Res.*, 1966, *1*, 229-244. (*a*) [85, 86, 87, 90]

Tryon, R. C. Comparative cluster analysis of variables and individuals: Holzinger abilities and the MMPI. Presented at the ONR-VA Conference on Cluster Analyses, New Orleans, La., December 1966. (*b*) [86]

Tryon, R. C. Person-clusters on intellectual abilities and MMPI attributes. *Mult. behav. Res.*, 1967, *2*, 5-34. (*a*) [86, 104]

Tryon, R. C. Predicting individual differences by cluster analysis: Holzinger abilities and MMPI attributes. *Mult. behav. Res.*, 1967, *2*, 325-348. (*b*) [86]

Tryon, R. C., & Bailey, D. (Eds.) *Users' manual of the BC TRY system of cluster and factor analysis.* (Taped version.) Berkeley: Univ. of Calif. Computer Center, 1965. [85, 86]

Tryon, R. C., & Bailey, D. The BC TRY system of cluster and factor analysis. *Mult. behav. Res.*, 1966, *1*, 95-111. [85, 86]

Tryon, R. C., Stein, K. B., & Chu, Chen-Lin. The cluster analysis of the MMPI. (Monograph in preparation.) [86, 87]

Tuckman, J., & Lavell, M. Social status and clinical contact. *J. clin. Psychol.*, 1959, *15*, 345-348. [221]

Tuddenham, R. D. Correlates of yielding to a distorted group norm. *J. Pers.*, 1959, *27*, 272-284. [62]

Tuddenham, R. D. The nature and measurement of intelligence. In L. Postman (Ed.), *Psychology in the making.* New York: Knopf, 1962. [22]

Turner, D. R. Predictive efficiency as a function of amount of information and level of professional experience. *J. proj. Tech. pers. Assmt.*, 1966, *30*, 4-12. [135]

Turner, W. S. Correlations between test scores, life data, and behavior during testing. Unpublished doctoral dissertation, University of California, Berkeley, 1963. [65]

Tuthill, E. W., Overall, J. E., & Hollister, L. E. Subjective correlates of clinically manifested anxiety and depression. *Psychol. Rep.*, 1967, *20*, 535-542. [253, 261]

Tyler, L. E. *Tests and measurements.* Englewood Cliffs, N. J.: Prentice-Hall, 1963. [5]

Tyler, L. E. The antecedents of two varieties of vocational interests. *Genet. Psychol. Monogr.*, 1964, *70*, 177-227. [65]

Tyler, L. E. *The psychology of human differences.* New York: Appleton-Century-Crofts, 1965. [23, 32]

Ullmann, L. P., & Krasner, L. *Case studies in behavior modification.* New York: Holt, Rinehart & Winston, 1965. [10, 176]

Ulrich, L., & Trumbo, D. The selection interview since 1949. *Psychol. Bull.*, 1965, *63*, 100-116. [6]

Ulrich, R., Strachnik, T., and Mabry, J. (Eds.) *Control of human behavior.* Glenview, Ill.: Scott, Foresman, 1966. [171, 176]

Usandivaras, R. J., Grimson, W. R., Hammond, H., Issaharoff, E., & Romanos, D. The Marbles test. *Arch. gen. Psychiat.*, 1967, *17*, 111-118. [231]

Uzgiris, I. C., & Hunt, J. McV. An instrument for assessing infant psychological development. Unpublished manuscript, University of Illinois, 1966. (Mimeo.) [31]

Vandenberg, S. G. Contributions of twin research to psychology. *Psychol. Bull.*, 1966, *66*, 327-352. [16, 17]

Venables, P., & Martin, I. (Eds.) *A manual of psychophysiological methods.* New York: Wiley, 1967. [266]

Verhave, T. (Ed.) *The experimental analysis of behavior.* New York: Appleton-Century-Crofts, 1966. [171]

Vernallis, F. F. Teeth-grinding: Some relationships to anxiety, hostility, and hyperactivity. *J. clin. Psychol.*, 1955, *11*, 389-391. [257]

Vernon, P. E. *Personality assessment: A critical survey.* London: Methuen, 1964. [5]

Vernon, P. E. Ability factors and environmental influences. *Amer. Psychologist*, 1965, *20*, 723-733. [15, 16, 17, 18]

Verwey, N. E. Relationship of adaptability to interactional contingency and interpersonal prediction. Unpublished doctoral dissertation, University of Washington, 1962. [236]

Vestre, N. D. The relationship between verbal conditioning and the Edwards personal preference schedule. *J. clin. Psychol.*, 1962, *18*, 513-515. [183]

Vinacke, W. E. Creative thinking. In W. E. Vinacke (Ed.), *The psychology of thinking.* New York: McGraw-Hill, 1952. [38]

Vinacke, W. E., & Arkoff, A. An experimental study of coalitions in the triad. *Amer. sociol. Rev.*, 1957, *22*, 406-414. [234]

Voigt, W. H. Personality variables in Rorschach scoring. *J. proj. Tech. pers. Assmt.*, 1966, *30*, 153-158. [133]

Voigt, W. H., & Dana, R. H. Inter- and intra-scorer Rorschach reliability. *J. proj. Tech. pers. Assmt.*, 1964, *28*, 92-95. [135, 143]

Volsky, T., Magoon, T. M., Norman, W. T., & Hoyt, D. P. *The outcomes of counseling and psychotherapy: Theory and research.* Minneapolis: Univ. Minn. Press, 1965. [206, 211, 254, 258]

Von Euler, U. S. Quantitation of stress by catecholamine analysis. *Clin. pharm. Therapeut.*, 1964, *5*, 398-404. [279]

Vroom, A. L. A validation study of the Blacky analogies test. Unpublished doctoral dissertation, University of Michigan, 1959. [164]

Wacks, T. D. Personality testing of the handicapped: A review. *J. proj. Tech. &*

pers. Assmt., 1966, *30*, 339-355. [6]

Wagner, E. E. The interaction of aggressive movement responses and anatomy responses on the Rorschach in producing anxiety. *J. proj. Tech*, 1961, *25*, 212-215. [137]

Wagner, E. E. Exhibitionistic human movement responses of strippers: An attempt to validate the Rorschach M. *J. proj. Tech. pers. Assmt.*, 1965, *29*, 522-525. [137]

Walk, R. D. Self-ratings of fear in a fear-invoking situation. *J. abnorm. soc. Psychol.*, 1956, *52*, 171-178. [248]

Walker, R. E., & Nicolay, R. C. A re-examination of anxiety: The Nicolay-Walker personal reaction schedule. Unpublished manuscript, Loyola University, 1963. [254]

Walker, R. E., & Spence, J. T. Relationship between digit span and anxiety. *J. consult. Psychol.*, 1964, *28*, 220-223. [260]

Wallace, H. R. Creativity: A factor in sales productivity. *Voc. Guid. Quart.*, Summer, 1961, 223-226. [49]

Wallace, H. R. Creative thinking: A factor in the performance of industrial salesmen. Doctoral dissertation, University of Minnesota, Minneapolis, 1964. [49]

Wallace, J. An abilities conception of personality: Some implications for personality measurement. *Amer. Psychologist*, 1966, *21*, 132-138. [7, 170]

Wallace, J. What units shall we employ? Allport's question revisited. *J. consult. Psychol.*, 1967, *31*, 56-64. [7, 173, 174]

Wallach, M. A., & Kogan, N. *Modes of thinking in young children.* New York: Holt, Rinehart, and Winston, 1965. (*a*) [48, 52, 53, 54]

Wallach, M. A., & Kogan, N. A new look at the creativity-intelligence distinction. *J. Pers.*, 1965, *33*, 348-369. (*b*) [16]

Wallach, M. S., & Strupp, H. H. Psychotherapists' clinical judgments and attitudes toward patients. *J. consult. Psychol.*, 1960, *24*, 316-323. [215]

Wallas, G. *The art of thought.* New York: Harcourt, Brace, 1926. [38]

Waller, P. The relationship between the Rorschach shading response and other indices of anxiety. *J. proj. Tech.*, 1960, *24*, 211-218. [146]

Wallerstein, R. The goals of psychoanalysis: A survey of analytic viewpoints. *J. Amer. Psychoanaly. Assoc.*, 1965, *13*, 748-770. [213]

Walters, J. A review of family research in 1959, 1960 and 1961. *Marriage fam. Liv.*, 1962, *24*, 158-178. [224]

Walters, J. A review of family research in 1962. *Marriage fam. Liv.*, 1963, *25*, 336-348. [224]

Ward, A. J. The meaning of the movement response and of its changes during

therapy: A review. *J. proj. Tech. pers. Assmt.*, 1966, *30*, 418-429. [147]

Watson, R. I. Historical review of objective personality testing: the search for objectivity. In B. M. Bass & I. A. Berg (Eds.), *Objective approaches to personality assessment.* New York: Van Nostrand, 1959. Pp. 1-23. [5]

Watson, R. I. *The great psychologists.* Philadelphia: Lippincott, 1963. [265]

Watzlawick, P. A structured family interview. *Fam. Process*, 1966, *5*, 256-271. [229]

Wechsler, D. *The measurement and appraisal of adult intelligence.* (4th Ed.) Baltimore: Williams & Wilkins, 1958. [22]

Weingarten, J., and Mechner, F. The contingency as an independent variable of social interaction. In Thom Verhave (Ed.), *The experimental analysis of behavior.* New York: Appleton-Century-Crofts. 1966. Pp. 447-459. [171]

Weir, R. H. *Language in the crib.* The Hague: Mouton, 1962. [23]

Weisberg, P. S., & Springer, K. J. Environmental factors in creative function. *Arch. gen. Psychiat.*, 1961, *5*, 554-564. [48]

Weiser, J. C. A study of college of education students divided according to creative ability. Doctoral dissertation, University of Missouri, Columbia, 1962. [49]

Weiss, R. L. The grammar of reinforcement. Paper read at Western Psychological Association Meetings, Portland, Oregon, April, 1964. [186, 187, 188]

Weiss, R. L. Studies in emitted reinforcing behavior. In Symposium on Newer Trends in Human Reinforcement, Western Psychological Association, Honolulu, Hawaii, 1965. (*a*) [187, 188]

Weiss, R. L. Reinforcement in everyday life. Palo Alto: VA Hospital (Research Report No. 33), 1965. (*b*) [186]

Weiss, R. L. Some determinants of omitted reinforcing behavior: Listener reinforcement and birth order. *J. pers. soc. Psychol.*, 1966, *3*, 489-492. (*a*) [187, 188]

Weiss, R. L. "Acquiescence" response set and birth order. *J. consult. Psychol.*, 1966, *30*, 365. (*b*) [170, 186]

Weiss, R. L. Studies of emitted reinforcing behavior: Personality correlates of "reinforcing skill." Paper presented to Western Psychological Association meetings, San Francisco, 1967. [188, 189]

Weiss, R. L., and Bodin, A. M. Behavioral measures of reinforcing skill in family therapists. Paper presented to Western Psychological Association meetings, San Francisco, 1967. [188, 189]

Weiss, R. L., Krasner, L., & Ullmann, L. P.

Responsivity of psychiatric patients to verbal conditioning: "Success" and "failure" conditions and pattern of reinforced trials. *Psychol. Rep.,* 1963, *12,* 423-426. [181]

Weiss, R. L., & Moos, R. H. Response biases in the MMPI: A sequential analysis. *Psychol. Bull.,* 1965, *63,* 403-409. [8, 170]

Weiss, R. L., and Reichard, D. Some determinants of emitted reinforcing behavior: The grammar of reinforcement. Unpublished paper, 1967. [187]

Weiss, R. L., Ullmann, L. P., & Krasner, L. On the relationship between hypnotizability and response to verbal operant conditioning. *Psychol. Rep.,* 1960, *6,* 59-60. [173, 183]

Welch, L. Recombination of ideas in creative thinking. *J. appl. Psychol.,* 1946, *30,* 638-643. [40]

Welsh, G. S. An anxiety index and an internalization ratio for the MMPI. *J. consult. Psychol.,* 1952, *16,* 65-72. [253]

Welsh, G. S. Factor dimensions A and R. In G. S. Welsh & W. G. Dahlstrom (Eds.), *Basic readings on the MMPI in psychology and medicine.* Minneapolis: Univ. Minn. Press, 1956. Pp. 264-281. [83, 253]

Welsh, G. S. *Preliminary manual for the Welsh figure preference test.* Palo Alto, Calif.: Consulting Psychologists' Press, 1959. [57]

Welsh, G. S. MMPI profiles and factor scales A and R. *J. clin. Psychol.,* 1965, *XXI,* 43-47. [253]

Wenger, M. A. Studies of autonomic balance: A summary. *Psychophysiol.,* 1966, *2,* 173-186. [275]

Wenger, M. A., Clemens, T. L., Coleman, D. R., Cullen, T. D., & Engel, B. T. Autonomic response specificity. *Psychosom. Med.,* 1961, *23,* 185-193. [270]

Wenger, M. A., Clemens, T. L., Darsie, M. L., Enger, B. T., Estess, F. M., & Sonnenschein, R. R. Autonomic response patterns during intravenous infusion of epinephrine and nor-epinephrine. *Psychosom. Med.,* 1960, *22,* 295-307. [282]

Westie, F. R., & DeFleur, M. L. Autonomic responses and their relationship to race attitudes. *J. abnorm. soc. Psychol.,* 1959, *58,* 340-347. [276]

Wheeler, W. M., Little, K. B., & Lehner, G. F. J. The internal structure of the MMPI. *J. consult. Psychol.,* 1951, *15,* 134-141. [82]

White, R. W. Motivation reconsidered: the concept of competence. *Psychol. Rev.,* 1959, *66,* 297-333. [21]

Whitehorn, J. C., & Betz, B. J. A study of psychotherapeutic relationships between physician and schizophrenic patients.

Amer. J. Psychiat., 1954, *111,* 321-331. [216]

Wickes, T. A. Examiner influence in a test situation. *J. consult. Psychol.,* 1956, *20,* 23-26. [141]

Wilensky, H. A factorial study of behavioral and psychological measures of anxiety. *J. consult. Psychol.,* 1957, *21,* 216. [247]

Williams, F. E. Practice and reinforcement as training factors in creative performance. Doctoral dissertation, University of Utah, Salt Lake City, 1965. [48]

Williams, J. H. Conditioning of verbalization: A review. *Psychol. Bull.,* 1964, *62,* 383-393. [173, 175]

Williams, R. J. *Biochemical individuality.* New York: Wiley, 1956. [287]

Williamson, E. G., & Bordin, E. S. The evaluation of vocational and educational counseling: A critique of the methodology of experiments. *Educ. psychol. Meas.,* 1941, *1,* 5-24. [207]

Wimsatt, W. R., & Vestre, N. D. Extra-experimental effects in verbal conditioning. *J. consult. Psychol.,* 1963, *27,* 400-404. [182]

Winder, C. L. Psychotherapy. *Annu. Rev. Psychol.,* 1957, *8,* 309-330. [214]

Winter, W. D. Two personality patterns in peptic ulcer patients. *J. proj. Tech.,* 1955, *19,* 322-344. [157]

Winter, W. D., Ferreira, A. J., & Olson, J. L. Story sequence analysis of family TAT's. *J. proj. tech. Pers. Assmt.,* 1965, *29,* 392-397. [227]

Winter, W. D., Ferreira, A. J., & Ransom, R. Two measures of anxiety. *J. consult. Psychol.,* 1963, *27,* 520-524. [249]

Wirt, R. D., & Broen, W. E. The relation of the children's manifest anxiety scale to the concept of anxiety as used in the clinic. *J. consult. Psychol.,* 1956, *20,* 482. [258]

Wittenborn, J. R. Symptom patterns in a group of mental hospital patients. *J. consult. Psychol.,* 1951, *15,* 290-302. [194]

Wittenborn, J. R. *Psychiatric rating scales.* New York: Psychol. Corp., 1955. [194]

Wittenborn, J. R. The dimensions of psychosis. *J. nerv. & ment. Dis.,* 1962, *134* 117-128. [194]

Wittenborn, J. R. Distinctions within psychotic dimensions: A principal components analysis. *J. nerv. & ment. Dis.,* 1963, *137,* 543-547. [194]

Wittenborn, J. R. *Psychiatric rating scales.* New York: Psychol. Corp., 1964. (a) [193, 194]

Wittenborn, J. R. Psychotic dimensions in male and female hospital patients: Principal components analysis. *J. nerv. & ment. Dis.,* 1964, *138,* 460-467. (b) [200]

Wittenborn, J. R., & Bailey, C. The

symptoms of involutional psychosis. *J. consult. Psychol.*, 1952, *16*, 13-17. [194]

Wittenborn, J. R., & Holzberg, J. D. The generality of psychiatric syndromes. *J. consult. Psychol.*, 1951, *15*, 372-380. [194]

Wittenborn, J. R., Holzberg, J. D., & Simon, B. Symptom correlates for descriptive diagnosis. *Genet. psychol. Monogr.*, 1953, *47*, 237-301. [194]

Wittenborn, J. R., Plante, M., & Burgess, F. A comparison of physicians' and nurses' symptom ratings. *J. nerv. & ment. Dis.*, 1961, *133*, 514-518. [204]

Wittenborn, J. R., & Smith, J. B. K. A comparison of psychotic dimensions in male and female hospital patients. *J. nerv. & ment. Dis.*, 1964, *138*, 375-382. [200]

Wittenborn, J. R., & Weiss, W. Patients diagnosed manic depressive psychosis – manic state. *J. consult. Psychol.*, 1952, *16*, 193-198. [194]

Wolf, R. The measurement of environments. In A. Anastasi (Ed.), *Testing problems in perspective.* Princeton, N. J.: Educ. Testing Serv., 1966. Pp. 491-503. [9]

Wolf, S. *The stomach.* New York: Oxford Univ. Press, 1965. [279]

Wolff, W. *Contemporary psychotherapists examine themselves.* Springfield, Ill: Chas. C Thomas, 1956. [217]

Wolfson, W. & Wolff, F. Sexual connotations of the name Blacky. *J. proj. Tech.*, 1956, *20*, 347. [154]

Wolman, B. B. (Ed.) *Handbook of clinical psychology.* New York: McGraw-Hill, 1965. [5, 205]

Wolpe, J., & Lazarus, A. A. *Behavior therapy techniques.* New York: Pergamon, 1966. [251]

Wood, E. C., Rakusin, J. M., & Morse, E. Interpersonal aspects of psychiatric hospitalization: II. Some correlations between admission circumstances and the treatment experience. *Arch. Gen. Psychiat.*, 1962, *6*, 39-45. [221]

Wrenn, C. G., & Darley, J. G. Counseling. *Rev. educ. Res.*, 1942, *12*, 45-65. [207]

Wright, J. C., & Kagan, J. Basic cognitive processes in children. *Monogr. Soc. Res. Child Develpm.*, 1963, *28*, 1-196. [29]

Wundt, W. *Grundzüge der physiologischen Psychologie.* Vol. 2. (5th ed.) Leipzig: Wilhelm Engelman, 1902. [280]

Yamamoto, K. Creativity and sociometric choice among adolescents. Master's thesis, University of Minnesota, Minneapolis, 1960. [48]

Yamamoto, K. A study of the relationships between creative thinking abilities of fifth-grade teachers and academic achievement. Doctoral dissertation, University of Minnesota, Minneapolis, 1962. [47, 48]

Yamamoto, K. Creative thinking: Some thoughts on research. *Exceptional Children*, 1964, *30*, 403-410. (*a*) [52]

Yamamoto, K. Evaluation of some creativity measures in a high school with peer nominations as criteria. *J. Psychol.*, 1964, *58*, 285-293. (*b*) [48]

Yamamoto, K. Role of creative thinking and intelligence in high school achievement. *Psychol. Rec.*, 1964, *14*, 783-789. (*c*) [16]

Yamamoto, K. Validation of tests of creative thinking: A review of some studies. *Exceptional Children*, 1965. [34]

Yovits, M. C., & Cameron, C. (Eds.) *Interdisciplinary conference of self-organizing systems.* New York: Pergamon Press, 1959. [23]

Zamansky, H. S., & Goldman, A. E. A Comparison of two methods of analyzing Rorschach data in assessing therapeutic change. *J. proj. Tech.*, 1960, *24*, 75-82. [147]

Zax, M., & Benham, F. G. The stimulus value of the Rorschach ink-blots as perceived by children, *J. proj. Tech.*, 1961, *25*, 233-238. [138]

Zax, M., & Loiselle, R. H. The influence of card order on the stimulus value of the Rorschach ink-blots. *J. proj. Tech.*, 1960, *24*, 218-221. [138]

Zax, M., Stricker, G., & Weiss, J. H. Some effects of non-personality factors on Rorschach performance. *J. proj. Tech.*, 1960, *24*, 83-94. [142]

Zelin, M., Sechrest, L. The validity of the "mother" and "father" cards of the Rorschach. *J. proj. Tech.*, 1963, *27*, 114-122. [134, 135]

Zimny, G. H., & Miller, F. L. Orienting and adaptive cardiovascular responses to heat and cold. *Psychophysiology*, 1966, *3*, 81-92. [271]

Zirkle, G. A. Five-minute psychotherapy. *Amer. J. Psychiat.*, 1961, *118*, 544-546. [219]

Zubin, J., Eron, L. D., & Schumer, F. *An experimental approach to projective techniques.* New York: Wiley, 1965. [135]

Zuckerman, M. The development of an affect adjective check list for the measurement of anxiety. *J. consult. Psychol.*, 1960, *24*, 457-462. [249]

Zuckerman, M., & Lubin, B. *Manual for multiple affect adjective check list.* San Diego: Educ. & Indus. Testing Serv., 1965. [203, 249]

Zuckerman, M., & Persky, H., Eckman, K., & Hopkins, T. R. A multitrait multimethod approach to the traits (or states) of anxiety, depression, and hostility. *J. proj. Tech. pers. Assmt.*, 1967, *31*, 39-48. [249, 252, 254, 257, 258]

Zung, W. W. K. A self-rating depression scale. *Arch. Gen. Psychiat.*, 1965, *12*, 63-70. [203]

Subject Index

Accord, operant assessment of, 186–89
Achievement Anxiety Test (AAT), 255–56
Activity Preference Questionnaire (APQ), 255, 256
Activity Rating Scale, 201
Adjective Check List (ACL), 60, 78
Adjective checklists and anxiety, 249–50
Affect Adjective Check List (AACL), 248, 249
Affective variables, psychophysiological measures of, 280-81
Albany Behavior Rating Scale, 200–01
Allport–Vernon Study of Values, 57
Ambivalence Assessment Technique (AAT), 155
Anxiety, assessment of
adjective checklists, 249–50
in children, 258–59
general and specific proneness to anxiety, 254–56
intercorrelations of anxiety measures, 247–62 passim
inventories, 250–56
observer ratings, 261–62
projective techniques and, 257–58
reliabilities and validities, 247-62 passim
response sets and, 256
self-ratings and, 247–48
symptom-oriented inventories, 252–54
unusual techniques, 260
verbal analysis technique, 260–61
Anxiety Behavior Checklist (ABC), 261
Anxiety, concept of, 245–47
base and induced, 246
current and characteristic, 246–47
definition, 245
dimensions, 263

Anxiety, concept of (cont.)
literature on, 244, 245, 246
trait and state, 246
Anxiety Differential (AD), 260, 262
Anxiety Index (AI), 253, 258
Anxiety Questionnaire, 254
Anxiety tests and scales
Achievement Anxiety Test (AAT), 255–56
Activity Preference Questionnaire (APQ), 255, 256
Affect Adjective Check List (AACL), 248, 249
Anxiety Behavior Checklist (ABC), 261
Anxiety Differential (AD), 260, 262
Anxiety Index (AI), 253, 258
Anxiety Questionnaire, 254
Assimilation Scale (AS), 251
Brentwood Mood Scale, 249
Brief Psychiatric Rating Scale (BPRS), 193, 197–99, 261
Children's Manifest Anxiety Scale (CMAS), 258, 259
Discomfort-Relief Quotient (DRQ), 260
Eight-Parallel Form Anxiety Battery, 259
Fear Survey Schedule (FSS), 251, 254
Freeman Manifest Anxiety Scale (FMAS), 258
General Anxiety Questionnaire (GAQ), 251, 256
General Anxiety Scale for Children (GASC), 259
Holtzman Inkblot Technique (HIT), 257
Incongruency Technique, 260
Manifest Anxiety Scale (MAS). See Manifest Anxiety Scale

Anxiety tests and scales (*cont.*)
Minnesota Manifest Anxiety Scale (MMAS), 254
Mood Adjective Check List (MACL), 249
Mooney Problem Check List, 207, 250-51
Multiple Affect Adjective Check List (MAACL), 249
Nicolay–Walker Personal Reaction Schedule, 254
Objective-analytic Anxiety Battery, 259
Personal Report of Confidence as a Speaker, 256
Phrase Association Test (PT), 259-60
Rorschach Content Test (RCT), 257, 258
Saslow Screening Test (SST), 254
Speech Disturbance Ratio, 261
S–R Inventory of Anxiousness (SRIA), 256
State–Trait Anxiety Inventory (STAI), 254
Subjective Stress Scale (SSS), 249
Test Anxiety Questionnaire (TAQ), 255, 256, 263
Test Anxiety Scale (TAS), 255
Test Anxiety Scale for Children (TASC), 259
Welsh A-Scale, 251, 253, 259, 261
Art Scale, Barron–Welsh, 50
A-Scale. *See* Welsh A-Scale
Assessment, concept of
defined, 2–4
literature on, 5–6
methods, 7
models, 3
role in clinical psychology, 10–11
standard test references, 6
summary of current trends in, 6–9
textbooks, 5
Assessment Scale, Weyburn, 201
Assimilation Scale (AS), 251
Attitudes, and Blacky Pictures, 159

Barron–Welsh Art Scale, 50
Base vs. induced anxiety, 246
Blacky Analogies Test (BAT), 161–68
Blacky Pictures
description, 151
factor analysis, 151–52, 154, 164
history, 150
reliability and validity, 151
scoring, 151, 153
special-purpose uses, 160–68
use in theory, 158–60
Blacky Pictures, research applications of
academic field and, 160
ambivalence and, 154–55, 161
asthma, 157–58
attitudes, 159
clinical syndromes, 156–58
cross-cultural, 159, 162
defense mechanisms and, 161–62
discussion group behavior, 159
female identification, 154

Blacky Pictures, research applications of (*cont.*)
intelligence, 162–68
kibbutz social behavior, 159
paranoid schizophrenics, 156
perceptual, 160–61
psychoanalytic theory, 153–56
psychosexual development, 153–54
psychosomatic disorders, 157–58
sexual offenders, 156
ulcers, 157
verbal conditioning, 159–60
Brentwood Mood Scale, 249
Brief Psychiatric Rating Scale (BPRS), 193, 197–99, 261

California F-Scale, 67
California Inventory, Revised, 48
California Psychological Inventory, 51, 55–79, 188, 189, 207
cross-cultural studies, 58, 63, 65
description, 55–56
"folk concepts," 57–58
individual scales, 59–74
interactions among scales, 74–75
longitudinal studies, 58
nomothetic studies, 76–79
profile groupings, 75–76
purpose of test, 55–56
research applications, 76–79
theoretical basis, 57–58
validities, 76–79
California Psychological Inventory, scales
Achievement via Conformance (*Ac*), 69–70
Achievement via Independence (*Ai*), 70–71
Capacity for Status (*Cs*), 61–62
Communality (*Cm*), 68–69
Dominance (*Do*), 59–61
Femininity (*Fe*), 73–74
Flexibility (*Fx*), 72–73
Good Impression (*Gi*), 67–68
Intellectual Efficiency (*Ie*), 71
Psychological Mindedness (*Py*), 71–72
Responsibility (*Re*), 65
Self-Acceptance (*Sa*), 63–64
Self-Control (*Sc*), 66–67
Sense of Well-Being (*Wb*), 64–65
Sociability (*Sy*), 62
Socialization (*So*), 65–66
Social Presence (*Sp*), 62–63
Tolerance (*To*), 67
California Test of Mental Maturity (CTMM), 17
Characteristic vs. current anxiety, 246–47
Chemotherapy, and rating scales, 191–92, 204
Children's anxiety tests, 258–59
Children's Manifest Anxiety Scale (CMAS), 258, 259
Clinical vs. actuarial prediction, 8
Clinical psychology, role of assessment, 10-11
Cluster analysis. *See* Factor analysis; TSC scales

Cluster analysis of MMPI. *See* TSC Scales
Complex stimuli and creativity, 50
"Comprehension operators" and intelligence, 26
Computers
 advances in assessment, 6
 "comprehension operators" and, 26
 and factor analysis, 85–87, 92
 and intelligence, 23–26
 scoring SVIB, 124–25
 "semantic elements" and, 25
 simulation, 29–30
 See also Information processing
Concept Mastery Test (Terman), 51, 95
Conflict resolution and family assessment, 236–41
Conjoint family assessment. *See* Family assessment, conjoint
Conjugate reinforcement, 184–85
Counseling, assessment. *See* Psychotherapy and counseling assessment
Creativity, assessment of
 capacity, 41–49
 criteria of, 52
 individual, 49–52
 intelligence and, 53
 in terms of process, 38–41
 in terms of products, 35–37
 "living-in" method, 51–52
 motivation and, 53–54
 recent literature, 34
 reliability, of Guilford tests, 43
 reliability, of Torrance tests, 45–47
 tests used. *See* Tests and scales
 validity of Torrance tests, 47–48
Creativity, concept of
 complex stimuli and, 50
 complexity of, 37–38, 41
 criteria of, 36
 definitions of, 34–35
 levels of, 38–39
 "model of the intellect" and, 41–42
 originality and, 50
 rigidity and, 48
 stages of, 38
 types of, 40–41
Creativity, Guilford tests. *See* Guilford tests of creativity
Creativity, Torrance tests. *See* Torrance tests of creativity
Cross-cultural assessment research
 Blacky Pictures, 159, 162
 California Psychological Inventory, 58, 63, 65
 Rorschach, 135, 144
Cross-validation, Rorschach, 136, 137, 141, 144, 147, 148
Culture-free subtests (IPAT), 19
Current anxiety, 246–47
Current trends in assessment, 6–9

Defense mechanisms, 161–62
Defense Preference Inquiry (DPI), 161–62
Depression, rating scales for, 202–03
Development
 anxiety and, 258–59

Development (*cont.*)
 Harvard Growth Study, 22
 intelligence and, 26–28
 psychosexual, and Blacky Pictures, 153–54
Diagnosis
 in clinical psychology, 9
 operant, 171–72, 181–82
 using Rorschach, 143–45
Differential Aptitude Test (DAT), 17–18
Discomfort–relief Quotient (DRQ), 260
Dispositional and episodic variables, 267–77
Dispositions, operant assessment of, 176–77
Draw-A-Person (DAP), 140, 257–58
Drives, experience-producing (EPDs), 21–32 *passim*
Dyadic behaviors, operant assessment of, 184–86

Edwards Personal Preference Schedule (EPPS), 96, 104, 183, 189
Eight-Parallel Form Anxiety Battery, 259
Emitted reinforcing behavior, 186–89
Emotion, psychophysiological assessment of, 278–81
Emotional reactivity and the Rorschach, 137
Experience-producing drives (EPDs), 21–32 *passim*

Facet theory of intelligence, 20–21
Factor analysis
 of anxiety tests, 247
 of Blacky Pictures, 151–52
 computer, 85–87, 92
 of dependent variables, 82
 of MMPI. *See* TSC scales
 multiple factor tests, validities, 17–18
 rating scales and, 203
 theories of intelligence, 15–18
Family Agreement Measure (FAM), 238
Family assessment, approaches
 combined, 225–26
 conjoint, 225
 individual, 224–25
Family assessment, conjoint
 definiton of conjoint, 224–25
 difficulties in, 241–42
 family assessment literature, 224–25
 individual assessment devices, 225
 interpersonal vs. intrapersonal, 241–42
 levels of family research, 242
 prospects for, 242–43
 revealed and unrevealed differences technique, 225–26, 236–41
Family assessment, objective conjoint techniques
 communication, 233–34
 conflict resolution, 236
 family agreement measure, 239–41
 family homeostasis, 233–34
 game theory, 234–36
 "revealed differences," 236–37
 "unrevealed differences," 237–41

Family assessment, subjective conjoint techniques
  drawing, 233
  family art, 231–33
  Family Strength Inventory, 230–31
  family tasks, 226–30
  Marbles Test, 231–33
  pictorial apperception tests, 227–28
  "prisoners dilemma," 228–29
  "rigged" conflicts, 226
  structured family interview, 228–30
Family Interaction Apperception Test (FIAT), 228
Family Strength Survey, 230–31
Fear, assessment of, 278–80
Fear Survey Schedule (FSS), 251, 254
Figure Preference Test, 57
FIRO-B, 189
Flanagan's Ingenuity Test, 40
Freeman Manifest Anxiety Scale (FMAS), 258
Frenkel–Brunswik Revised California Inventory, 48

Galvanic skin response (GSR), 269, 284, 285, 286
Game theory and family assessment, 234–36
General Anxiety Questionnaire (GAQ), 251, 256
General Anxiety Scale, 251
General Anxiety Scale for Children (GASC), 259
Generality–specificity and assessment, 8–9
Gough Adjective Check List (ACL), 60
Guilford tests of creativity, 42–43, 51
Guilford–Zimmerman Temperament Survey, 182, 183

Harvard Growth Study, 22
Heston Personality Inventory, 216
Holtzman Inkblot Technique (HIT), 257
Homeostasis, family, 233–34
Hormones, and emotion, 278–80
Hospital Adjustment Scale (HAS), 200
House–Tree–Person (HTP) Test, 208, 257

Identification, female, and Blacky Pictures, 154
Incongruency technique, 260
Induced anxiety, 246
Information processing and intelligence, 26–29, 30. See also Computers
Ingenuity Test (Flanagan), 40
Inpatient Multidimensional Psychiatric Scale (IMPS), 193, 194, 195, 202
  development, 195–96
  improvements, 196
  problems, 196–97
  uses, 196
Institute of Personality Assessment and Research (IPAR), 50–52
Intelligence
  "comprehension operators" and, 26
  concrete, 28

Intelligence (cont.)
  constancy, 22
  creativity and, 53
  development of, 26–28
  emotional stimuli and, 162–64
  overlap hypothesis, 22
  "semantic elements" and, 25
  TSC Scales and, 95
Intelligence, theories of
  and assessment, 31–3
  evaluation of, 28–31
  facet, 20–21
  fluid and crystallized, 19–20
  general factor (g), 15
  hierarchical, 15
  information processing, 23–26, 29, 30
  motivational–experiential, 21–23. See also Experience-producing drives
  multiple factor vs. general factor, 16–18
  Piaget's, 26–28
  structure of intellect, 15, 18
  summary of, 19
Interpersonal Behavior Inventory, 208
Interpersonal Check List, 140
Interview Relationship Inventory, 208
Inventories for anxiety measurement, 250–56
Inventories. 113, 250–56. See also Tests and scales; TSC Scales
Iowa Reading Comprehension Test, 18
IPAR, 50–52
IPAT Anxiety Scale, 19, 137, 244, 248, 249, 256, 263
  development and items, 253
  purpose, 254
  reliability and validity, 254

Kuder Interest Inventory, 216
Kuhlmann–Anderson Intelligence Tests, 71

Language and intelligence, 23
Law of initial values (LIV), 272–73
Learning sets, 22
Letter Series Completion Test, 24
"Living-in" method of creativity assessment, 50–51
L–M Fergus Falls Behavior Rating Scale, 201

MACC Behavioral Adjustment Scale, 201
Manifest Anxiety Scale (MAS), 4, 244
  alterations, 213
  construction, 252–53
  correlations with other measures of anxiety, 248–61 passim
  reliability and validity, 252
  utility, 253
Marbles Test, 231–33
Medical Attitude Survey, 256
Mental growth curves, 22–23
Mental Status Scale, 201
Mental Status Schedule, 208
Minnesota Manifest Anxiety Scale (MMAS), 254

Minnesota Multiphasic Personality Inventory (MMPI), 51, 73, 139, 146, 147, 178, 182, 202, 207, 208, 216
anxiety and, 248–61 *passim*
TSC Scales and, 80–93. *See also* TSC Scales
"Model of the intellect" and creativity, 41–42
Mood Adjective Check List (MACL), 249
Mooney Problem Check List, 207, 250–51
MRI Structured Family Interview, 229-30
Multidimensional Scale for Rating Psychiatric Patients (MSRPP), 195
Multiple Affect Adjective Check List (MAACL), 249
Multivariate techniques. *See* Factor analysis

Nicolay–Walker Personal Reaction Schedule, 254
Nurses Observation Scale for Inpatient Evaluation (NOSIE), 193, 201

Objective–analytic Anxiety Battery, 259
Obscure Figures Test, 40
Observer ratings of anxiety, 261–62
Omnibus Personality Inventory (OPI), 96, 97, 104
"Operant MMPI," 178
Operant techniques of assessment
accord, communication of, 186–89
advantages of, 172–74
clinical diagnosis, 171–72, 181–82
conjugate reinforcement, 184–85
contingency and, 171–72
contrasting methods, 172–75
definition, 175
dependent variables, 176–81
dispositions, 176–77
dyadic behaviors, 184–86
emitted reinforcing behavior, 186–89
generalization, 182–83
0 effects in, 171, 172, 173
operant conditioning methodologies, 171
predictor variables, 181–84
rationale for, 169–70
reinforcing skill, 188–89
reliability, 174, 188
research using, 172–86
Originality and creativity, 50
Otis tests of general ability, 95
Otto Family Strength Survey, 230–31

Perceptual research, and Blacky Pictures, 160–61
Personality inventories, development, 7. *See also* Tests and Scales; TSC Scales
Personal Orientation Inventory (POI), 208
Personal Reaction Schedule, 254
Personal Report of Confidence as a Speaker, 256
Personnel selection, with the Rorschach, 147
Phrase Association Test (PT), 259–60

Physiological assessment. *See* Psychophysiological assessment
Primary Mental Abilities Test (PMA), 19, 24
"Prisoners dilemma" in family assessment, 228–29
Process of creavity, 38–41
Products of creativity, 35–37
Profile interpretation of California Psychological Inventory, 74–75
Prognosis, using Rorschach, 146–47
Projective tests, literature on, 8
Proneness to anxiety, 254–56
Psychiatric patient change, 191. *See also* Rating scales, psychiatric
Psychiatric patient testing. *See* Tests and scales
Psychiatric Rating Scale (PRS), 193–94, 201
Psychiatric rating scales. *See* Rating scales, psychiatric
Psychoanalytic theory, research using Blacky Pictures, 153–56
Psychological inventories, early, 114
Psychopharmacology, rating scales and, 192, 204
Psychophysiological assessment
advantages of, 266–67
of affective dimensions, 280–81
of basic emotions, 278
cognitive factors, 282–83
correlation of psychological and physiological variables, 276
correlative methods, 275–77
definition, 265
of dispositional variables, 267–68, 274–77
elicitation methods, 275–77
of emotions, 277–83
of episodic variables, 267, 268–74
of fear and anger, 278–80
galvanic skin response (GSR), 269, 284, 285, 286
by general responses, 268–69
by hormonal change, 278–80
individual response specificity, 269–70
intensity vs. pattern of emotion, 278
law of initial values (LIV), 272–73
motivational response specificity, 271–72
personality traits, 283–88
reductive methods, 274–75
response intensity and, 272–73
by response patterns, 269–70
stimulus, defined, 270–71
stimulus response specificity, 270
temporal variables, 273–74
Psychosomatic disorders, and Blacky Pictures, 157–58
Psychotherapy and counseling, assessment of
controls, 209–10
criterion measures, 207–09
defining therapy outcome criteria, 206–07
deviation and illness, emphasis upon, 208

Psychotherapy and counseling, assessment
of (*cont.*)
duration of treatment, 219–21
effectiveness of psychotherapy, 211–14
expectations of patients, 221
general methodological problems, 206
individuality of patients, 211
outcome of therapy, 211–214
personality of therapist, 216–17
recent literature on, 205
relationship of therapist and client,
217–19
summary of assessment procedures, 207
therapist as variable, 210
treatability of clients, 214–16
trends and status of research in, 211–21
Psychotic Reaction Profile (PRP), 201–02

Q-sort, 208, 216

Rating scales, psychiatric
Activity Rating Scale, 201
Albany Behavior Rating Scale, 200–01
Brief Psychiatric Rating Scale (BPRS),
193, 197–99, 261
Hospital Adjustment Scale (HAS), 200
Inpatient Multidimensional Psychiatric
Scale, 193, 194–97, 202
L–M Fergus Falls Behavior Rating Scale,
201
MACC Behavioral Adjustment Scale,
201
Mental Status Scale, 201
Multidimensional Scale for Rating
Psychiatric Patients (MSRPP), 195
Nurses Observation Scale for Inpatient
Evaluation (NOSIE), 193, 201
Psychotic Reaction Profile (PRP),
199–202
Rorschach Prognostic Rating Scale,
146,147, 214
Symptom Rating Scale, 201
Ward Behavior Rating Scale, 193–94
Weyburn Assessment Scale, 201
Wittenborn Psychiatric Rating Scale,
193, 194, 201
Rating scales, psychiatric, discussion of
characteristics, 192–94
choice of, 192
defined, 192–93
depression scales, 202–03
drug studies, 192
elements of, 193
major scales, 194–201
methodological problems, 203–04
multivariate techniques, 203
raters and, 204
scoring systems, 193–94
shortened forms, 197–99
statistical techniques used in, 203
Reinforcing skill, 188–89
Reliabilities. See specific tests
Reliability of anxiety measures, 247–62
passim
Remote Associates Test (RAT), 40–41
Reorganization Test, (Welch), 40

Response sets
in anxiety inventories, 256
and individual response specificity,
269–70
literature on, 7–8
and Rorschach, 142
types of, 7
Responses, psychophysiological
general, 268–69
intensity, 272–73
motivational, 270–71
patterns, 269–70
specificity, 269–70
Results of therapy and counseling. See
psychotherapy, assessment of
Revealed differences technique for family
assessment, 225–26
Revised California Inventory (Frenkel-
Brunswik), 48
"Rigged conflicts" in family assessment,
226
Rigidity and creativity, 48
Rorschach Content Test (RCT), 257, 258
Rorschach Prognostic Rating Scale
(RPRS), 146, 147, 214
Rorschach Test, 69, 212, 213, 257
administration of, research, 133–34
aggressive and anatomical responses, 137
body image and, 139
card stimulus value (card pull), 134–35
color responses, 136
concurrent validity, 145–47
cross validation, need or use of, 136,
137,141, 143, 144, 147, 148
derived tests, 138–39, 140–41, 146
developmental score, 139–40
diagnostic uses and validity, 143–45
emotional reactivity and, 136
levels of awareness and, 140
literature on, 132–33
movement responses, 137
personnel selection with, 147–48
predictive validity of specific response
variables, 135–37
present status, 148–49
prognostic rating scale, 146
psychiatric categorization with, 144–45
reliability, 135
semantic differential research, 138–39
sign approach, 143
situational variables, 141–43
special behaviors, 144
suicides, scores of, 143–44
white space response, 137
Runner Studies of Attitudinal Patterns, 49

Saslow Screening Test (SST), 254
School and College Ability Tests (SCAT),
95
Security–Insecurity Inventory, 207
Self-ratings of anxiety, 247–48
Semantic Differential, 138–39, 155
"Semantic elements" and intelligence, 25
Sentence Completion Technique, 140, 208
Sexual offenders and Blacky Pictures, 156
Sign approach in the Rorschach, 143

Sixteen Personality Factor Questionnaire, 57, 73
Social behavior, kibbutz, and Blacky Pictures, 159
Social reinforcement, 179–80, 186
Speech Disturbance Ratio, 261
S–R Inventory of Anxiousness (SRIA), 256
State anxiety, 246
State–Trait Anxiety Inventory (STAI), 254
Stimulus response specificity, 270
Strong Vocational Interest Blank, 51, 56, 72, 96, 104, 146
  automated scoring, 124–25
  development, 115–19
  early history, 113–15
  early purpose of SVIB, 116–17
  historical trends, 106–113
  inventories preceding, 114
  longitudinal work, 121, 122, 125–26
  popularity of the test, 106–07
  recent work with, 126–29, 130
  reliability, 117–18
  revisions, 123–24, 125–26, 129–30
  scoring machines, 119–23
  scoring weights, 123
  validity, 117–18
Structured Family Interview, 229–30
Study of Values, 57
Subjective Stress Scale (SSS), 249
Suicide, and Rorschach score, 143–44
Symptom-oriented anxiety inventories, 252–54
Symptom Rating Scale, 201

Temperament Survey, 182
Terman Concept Mastery Test, 51, 95
Test Anxiety Questionnaire (TAQ), 255, 256, 263
Test Anxiety Scale (TAS), 255, 256
Test Anxiety Scale for Children (TASC), 259
Tests
  evaluation process, 7
  measurement function, 10
  reviews, 6
  standard references, 6
Tests and scales
  Achievement Anxiety Test (AAT), 255–56
  Activity Preference Questionnaire (APQ), 255, 256, 262
  Adjective Check List (ACL), 60, 78
  Affect Adjective Check List (AACL), 248, 249
  Ambivalence Assessment Technique (AAT), 155
  Anxiety Behavior Checklist (ABC), 261
  Anxiety Differential (AD), 260, 262
  Anxiety Index (AI), 253, 258
  Anxiety Questionnaire, 254
  Assimilation Scale (AS), 251
  Barron–Welsh Art Scale, 50
  Blacky Analogies Test (BAT), 162–68
  Blacky Pictures. See Blacky Pictures

Tests and scales (cont.)
  Brentwood Mood Scale, 249
  Brief Psychiatric Rating Scale (BPRS), 193, 197–99, 261
  California F-Scale, 67
  California Psychological Inventory (CPI). See California Psychological Inventory
  California Test of Mental Maturity (CTMM), 17
  Children's Manifest Anxiety Scale (CMAS), 258, 259
  Concept Mastery Test, 95
  Defense Preference Inquiry (DPI), 161–62
  Differential Aptitude Test (DAT), 17–18
  Discomfort–Relief Quotient (DRQ), 260
  Draw-A-Person (DAP), 140, 257–58
  Edwards Personal Preference Schedule (EPPS), 96, 104, 183, 189
  Eight-Parallel Form Anxiety Battery, 259
  Family Agreement Measure (FAM), 238
  Family Interaction Apperception Test (FIAT), 228
  Fear Survey Schedule (FSS), 251, 254
  Figure Preference Test, 57
  FIRO-B, 189
  Flanagan's Ingenuity Test, 40
  Freeman Manifest Anxiety Scale (FMAS), 258
  Frenkel–Brunswik Revised California Inventory, 48
  General Anxiety Questionnaire (GAQ), 251, 256
  General Anxiety Scale for Children (GASC), 259
  Guilford tests of creativity, 42–43, 51
  Guilford–Zimmerman Temperament Survey, 182, 183
  Heston Personality Inventory, 216
  Holtzman Inkblot Technique (HIT), 257
  House–Tree–Person Test (HTP), 208, 257
  Incongruency Technique, 260
  Interpersonal Behavior Inventory, 208
  Interpersonal Check List, 140
  Interview Relationship Inventory, 208
  Iowa Reading Comprehension Test, 18
  IPAT Anxiety Scale (IPAT). See IPAT Anxiety Scale
  Kuder Interest Inventory, 216
  Kuhlmann–Anderson Intelligence Tests, 71
  Letter Series Completion Test, 24
  Manifest Anxiety Scale (MAS). See Manifest Anxiety Scale
  Marbles Test, 231–33
  Medical Attitude Survey, 256
  Mental Status Schedule, 208
  Minnesota Manifest Anxiety Scale (MMAS), 254
  Minnesota Multiphasic Personality Inventory (MMPI). See Minnesota Multiphasic Personality Inventory

Tests and scales (*cont.*)
Mood Adjective Check List (MACL), 249
Mooney Problem Check List, 207, 250–51
Multiple Affect Adjective Check List (MAACL), 249
Nicolay–Walker Personal Reaction Schedule, 254
Objective–analytic Anxiety Battery, 259
Obscure Figures Test, 40
Omnibus Personality Inventory (OPI), 96, 97, 104
Otis Tests of General Ability, 95
Otto Family Strength Survey, 230–31
Personal Orientation Inventory (POI), 208
Personal Report of Confidence as a Speaker, 256
Phrase Association Test (PT), 259–60
Primary Mental Abilities (PMA) test, 24
Q-Sort, 208, 216
Remote Associates Test (RAT), 40–41
Rorschach Content Test (RCT), 257, 258
Rorschach Prognostic Rating Scale (RPRS), 146, 147, 214
Rorschach test. *See* Rorschach
Runner Studies of Attitudinal Patterns, 49
Saslow Screening Test (SST), 254
School and College Ability Tests (SCAT), 95
Security–Insecurity Inventory, 207
Semantic Differential, 138–39, 155
Sentence Completion Technique, 140, 208
Sixteen Personality Factor Questionnaire, 57, 73
Speech Disturbance Ratio, 261
S–R Inventory of Anxiousness (SRIA), 256
State–Trait Anxiety Inventory (STAI), 254
Strong Vocational Inventory Blank (SVIB). *See* Strong Vocational Inventory Blank
Structured Family Interview, 229–30
Study of Values, 57
Subjective Stress Scale (SSS), 249
Terman Concept Mastery Test, 51
Test Anxiety Questionnaire (TAQ), 255, 256, 263
Test Anxiety Scale (TAS), 255, 256
Test Anxiety Scale for Children (TASC), 259
Thematic Apperception Test (TAT), 39, 140, 146, 208, 258

Tests and scales (*cont.*)
Torrance tests of creativity, 44–49, 52
Wechsler–Bellevue Adult Intelligence Scale, 140, 260
Welch's Reorganization Test, 40
Welsh A-Scale, 251, 253, 259, 261
Wiltwyck Family Task, 228
Textbooks on assessment, 5
Thematic Apperception Test (TAT), 39, 140, 146, 208, 258
Theoretical contributions to assessment, 5
Therapy. *See* Psychotherapy, assessment of
Thurstone Primary Mental Abilities tests (PMA), 19, 34
Torrance tests of creativity, 44–49, 52
Trait vs. state anxiety, 246
Traits, psychophysiological assessment of, 283–88
Trends in assessment, current, 6–9
TSC Scales
BIGNV program, 85–87
clusters defined, 97
compared with MMPI, 89–92
computer factor analysis of MMPI, 85–87
correlation with MMPI scales, OPI, EPPS, and SVIB, 89–93, 96–97
evaluation of, 103–04
homosexual scores, 100
intelligence and, 95
intercorrelations, 90
male and female comparisons, 92, 94–96
MMPI items in each cluster, 87–89
norms, 97–100
overlapping items on MMPI and, 81–84
profiles, 100–03
psychiatric patient scores, 100–02
reliabilities, 89–90

Unrevealed differences techniques for family assessment, 236–41

Validities. *See* specific tests
Verbal analysis of anxiety, 260–61
Verbal conditioning, and Blacky Pictures, 159–60

Ward Behavior Rating Scale, 193–94
Wechsler–Bellevue Adult Intelligence Scale (WAIS), 140, 260
Welch's Reorganization Test, 40
Welsh A-Scale, 251. 253, 259, 261
Welsh Figure Preference Test, 57
Weyburn Assessment Scale, 201
Wiltwyck Family Task, 228
Wittenborn Psychiatric Rating Scale (PRS), 193–94, 201